Supply Chain Logistics Management

The McGraw-Hill Series in Operations and Decision Sciences

SUPPLY CHAIN MANAGEMENT

Benton
Purchasing and Supply Chain Management
Third Edition

Bowersox, Closs, Cooper, and Bowersox
Supply Chain Logistics Management
Fifth Edition

Burt, Petcavage, and Pinkerton
Supply Management
Eighth Edition

Johnson
Purchasing and Supply Management
Sixteenth Edition

Simchi-Levi, Kaminsky, and Simchi-Levi
Designing and Managing the Supply Chain: Concepts, Strategies, Case Studies
Third Edition

Stock and Manrodt
Fundamentals of Supply Chain Management

PROJECT MANAGEMENT

Brown and Hyer
Managing Projects: A Team-Based Approach

Larson and Gray
Project Management: The Managerial Process
Seventh Edition

SERVICE OPERATIONS MANAGEMENT

Bordoloi, Fitzsimmons, and Fitzsimmons
Service Management: Operations, Strategy, Information Technology
Ninth Edition

MANAGEMENT SCIENCE

Hillier and Hillier
Introduction to Management Science: A Modeling and Case Studies Approach with Spreadsheets
Sixth Edition

BUSINESS RESEARCH METHODS

Schindler
Business Research Methods
Thirteenth Edition

BUSINESS FORECASTING

Keating and Wilson
Forecasting and Predictive Analytics
Seventh Edition

LINEAR STATISTICS AND REGRESSION

Kutner, Nachtsheim, and Neter
Applied Linear Regression Models
Fourth Edition

BUSINESS SYSTEMS DYNAMICS

Sterman
Business Dynamics: Systems Thinking and Modeling for a Complex World

OPERATIONS MANAGEMENT

Cachon and Terwiesch
Operations Management
Second Edition

Cachon and Terwiesch
Matching Supply with Demand: An Introduction to Operations Management
Fourth Edition

Jacobs and Chase
Operations and Supply Chain Management
Fifteenth Edition

Jacobs and Chase
Operations and Supply Chain Management: The Core
Fifth Edition

Schroeder and Goldstein
Operations Management in the Supply Chain: Decisions and Cases
Seventh Edition

Stevenson
Operations Management
Thirteenth Edition

Swink, Melnyk, and Hartley
Managing Operations Across the Supply Chain
Fourth Edition

BUSINESS MATH

Slater and Wittry
Practical Business Math Procedures
Thirteenth Edition

Slater and Wittry
Math for Business and Finance: An Algebraic Approach
Second Edition

BUSINESS STATISTICS

Bowerman, O'Connell, Drougas, Duckworth, and Froelich
Business Statistics in Practice
Ninth Edition

Doane and Seward
Applied Statistics in Business and Economics
Sixth Edition

Doane and Seward
Essential Statistics in Business and Economics
Third Edition

Lind, Marchal, and Wathen
Basic Statistics for Business and Economics
Ninth Edition

Lind, Marchal, and Wathen
Statistical Techniques in Business and Economics
Seventeenth Edition

Jaggia and Kelly
Business Statistics: Communicating with Numbers
Third Edition

Jaggia and Kelly
Essentials of Business Statistics: Communicating with Numbers
Second Edition

McGuckian
Connect Master: Business Statistics

Supply Chain Logistics Management

Fifth Edition

Donald J. Bowersox
David J. Closs
M. Bixby Cooper
John C. Bowersox
Michigan State University

SUPPLY CHAIN LOGISTICS MANAGEMENT

Published by McGraw-Hill Education, 2 Penn Plaza, New York, NY 10121. Copyright © 2020 by McGraw-Hill Education. All rights reserved. Printed in the United States of America. No part of this publication may be reproduced or distributed in any form or by any means, or stored in a database or retrieval system, without the prior written consent of McGraw-Hill Education, including, but not limited to, in any network or other electronic storage or transmission, or broadcast for distance learning.

Some ancillaries, including electronic and print components, may not be available to customers outside the United States.

This book is printed on acid-free paper.

6 7 8 9 GPC 21

ISBN 978-1-260-54782-5
MHID 1-260-54782-5

Cover Image: *(ship)* ©*Shutterstock/Aun Photographer; (warehouse)* © *Shutterstock/Petinov Sergey Mihilovich; (map)* ©*macrovector/123RF; (truck)* © *Shutterstock/Andrey Pavlo*

mheducation.com/highered

About the Authors

This book is dedicated to the memory of Dr. Donald J. Bowersox, visionary, mentor, and friend and one of the founders of the academic disciplines of logistics and supply chain management. Don passed away as the fourth edition was being completed, but his legacy lives on in this fifth edition. Don's legacy will live on through the many contributions to the theory and practice of logistics and supply chain management that will continue through his family, students, and colleagues.

The authors would also like to recognize their families for their encouragement and patience because they ultimately pay the dearest price.

About the Authors

Donald J. Bowersox (1932–2011) is the former University Professor and Dean Emeritus at Michigan State University. He received his Ph.D. at Michigan State and worked with industry throughout this career. He is the author of numerous articles in publications such as the *Harvard Business Review, Journal of Marketing, Journal of Business Logistics,* and *Supply Chain Management Review.* Bowersox was the co-author of what is widely recognized as the first Supply Chain academic text: *Physical Distribution Management–Logistics Problems of The Firm,* first published in 1961. He is the co-author of *Start Pulling Your Chain: Leading Responsive Supply Chain Transformation,* published in 2008. Throughout this career, Bowersox led a number of industry-supported research studies investigating the best practices of Logisticians in North America and around the world. Bowersox is recognized by many as the "Grandfather of Supply Chain" and was recognized by the Council of Supply Chain Management (CSCMP) receiving both the Distinguished Service Award (1966) and in 2011, after his death, with the renaming of the annual Doctoral Symposium in his honor as the Donald J. Bowersox Doctoral Symposium. Don's memory and many accomplishments are cherished and live on in his family, friends, and industry peers.

David J. Closs is the John H. McConnell Chaired Professor of Business Administration and former Chairperson in the Department of Supply Chain Management at Michigan State University. He received his Ph.D. in marketing and logistics from Michigan State. Dr. Closs is the author and coauthor of many publications in journals, proceedings, and industry reports. He was also a principal researcher for *World Class Logistics: The Challenge of Managing Continuous Change* and *21st Century Logistics: Making Supply Chain Integration a Reality.* Dr. Closs is a frequent speaker at industry and academic conferences and presenter at executive education programs. Dr. Closs formerly served as the editor of the *Journal of Business Logistics.*

M. Bixby Cooper is an Associate Professor emeritus in the Department of Supply Chain Management at Michigan State University. He is coauthor of three texts on distribution and logistics, including *World Class Logistics: The Challenge of Managing Continuous Change* and *Strategic Marketing Channel Management.* He is also coauthor of *Managing Operations Across the Supply Chain* published by McGraw-Hill. He served for four years on the Executive Board of the International Customer Service Association as head of the Research and Education Committee.

John C. Bowersox is the Director–Inbound Transportation for True Value Company. He is a graduate of Michigan State University. John is currently responsible for the Strategic and Operational oversight of True Value's Global Inbound Logistics program. Prior to joining True Value, John worked for the Kohler Co., where he held positions in Operations, Customer Service, Logistics, and Strategic Purchasing within the company's Kitchen and Bath Americas as well as Ann Sacks Tile & Stone operating divisions. Mr. Bowersox, in conjunction with his brother Ed and late father Donald, was the recipient of the DSC Movers and Thinkers Award for Innovation in Supply Chain Management. He is an active member of the Council of Supply Chain Management Professionals (CSCMP), a charter member of the Young Professionals Committee, and prior member of the Board of Directors. A close follower of academic and industry research, he is a frequent contributor at industry conferences.

Preface

Over the last eight decades, the discipline of business logistics has advanced from the warehouse floor and transportation dock to the boardroom of leading global enterprises. We have had the opportunity to be actively involved in this evolution through research, education, and advising. *Supply Chain Logistics Management* encompasses the development and fundamentals of the logistics discipline within a supply chain framework. It also presents our vision of the future for business logistics and supply chain management and their role in enterprise competitiveness.

Although individually and collectively the four authors have written extensively on various aspects of logistics and supply chain management, the decision to initially write and subsequently revise *Supply Chain Logistics Management* represents the synthesis of many years of research, augmenting and, in many ways, supplanting earlier works of the authors published by McGraw-Hill. The union of ideas presented in this text provides an integrated supply chain framework for the study of logistics, serves to expand the treatment of supply chain management by placing it firmly in the context of integrated business strategy, and highlights the increasing importance of logistics in the supply chains supporting a global economy.

Logistics includes all the activities required to move product and information to, from, and between partners in a supply chain. The supply chain provides the framework for businesses and their suppliers to jointly deliver goods, services, and information efficiently, effectively, relevantly, and in a sustainable manner to consumers. *Supply Chain Logistics Management* presents the mission, business processes, and strategies needed to achieve integrated logistical management. We hope the text achieves three fundamental objectives: (1) presents a comprehensive description of existing logistical practices in a global economy, (2) describes ways and means to apply logistics principles to achieve competitive advantage, and (3) provides a conceptual approach for integrating logistics as a core competency within enterprise supply chain strategy.

This edition has benefited greatly from thoughtful suggestions from students, colleagues, and reviewers. We note several changes and additions to this new edition:

- Incorporated a section in Chapter 1 that discusses the broad application of logistics and supply chain management to include other applications beyond movement of goods.
- Incorporated considerations for value chain management in the text.
- Reviewed supply chain information technology in Chapter 2 to provide a broad perspective and then again reviewed the relevant technologies in the application chapters.
- Discussed regarding how consumer and technology disrupters will impact logistics and supply chain management.
- Condensed discussion of procurement and manufacturing into one chapter focusing on strategy and interfaces with logistics.
- Incorporated forecasting and planning into a single chapter focuses on integrated operations planning.
- Included updated materials regarding transportation pricing; negotiation; regulation; and modern trends, challenges, and opportunities.
- Synthesized the discussion of handling and packaging with warehousing.
- Expanded the global strategy and operations chapter to include discussion of compliance.

- Expanded the discussion of supply chain network design to include principles that can be applied in nontraditional settings and the major drivers in supply chain design.
- Discussed the future trends in logistics and supply chain management in the final chapter.

Over the past 53 years, the business executives who have attended the annual Michigan State University Logistics Management Executive Development Seminar have been exposed to the basic concepts presented in the text and have given freely of their time and experience. We also acknowledge the long-standing support to Michigan State Department of Supply Chain Management, through the funding of the endowed chairs, provided by the late John H. McConnell, founder of Worthington Industries, and Rob Thull, who is the primary donor for the Bowersox-Thull Chair in Logistics and Supply Chain Management.

The number of individuals involved in teaching logistics around the world expands daily. To this group in general, and in particular to our colleagues at Michigan State University, whose advice and assistance made it possible to complete and enhance this text, we express our sincere appreciation.

Teachers receive continuous inspiration from students over the years, and in many ways the day of judgment in an academic career comes in the seminar or classroom. We have been fortunate to have the counsel of many outstanding young scholars who currently are making substantial impact on the academic and business worlds. In particular, we appreciate the input of students who have used this text in manuscript form and made suggestions for improvement. We also acknowledge the contributions of Drs. Judith Whipple, Stan Griffis, Yem Bolumole, and Thomas Goldsby, who contributed extensively in case and concept development.

We would like to thank the following instructors for their thoughtful contributions to the previous edition review: Gurkan Akalin, Joe T. Felan, EunSu Lee, Penina Orenstein, Thomas Passero, James L. Patterson, Frank R. Scheer, and George Young.

We wish to acknowledge the contributions of Felicia Kramer and Pamela Kingsbury, for manuscript preparation on several earlier versions of this text, and Cheryl Lundeen, who prepared many drafts of the manuscripts. Without Felicia, Pam, and Cheryl, this long-published text in its many variations would not be a reality.

With so much able assistance, it is difficult to offer excuses for any shortcomings that might appear. Any faults are solely our responsibility.

David J. Closs

M. Bixby Cooper

John C. Bowersox

Supplemental Features

Instructor Library

A wealth of information is available online through McGraw-Hill's *Connect*. In the *Connect* Instructor Library, you will have access to supplementary materials specifically created for this text, such as:
- Instructor Solutions Manual
- PowerPoint Presentations
- Problem Set Solutions
- Case Solutions
- Sample Syllabi
- Sample Tests
- Data Sets for Cases

Assurance of Learning

Many educational institutions today are focused on the notion of assurance of learning, an important element of some accreditation standards. *Supply Chain Logistics Management* is designed specifically to support your assurance of learning initiatives with a simple, yet powerful, solution.

Each test bank and end-of-chapter question for *Supply Chain Logistics Management* maps to a specific chapter learning goal listed in the text. You can use the test bank software to easily query for learning goals that directly relate to the learning objectives for your course. You then can use the reporting features of the software to aggregate student results in similar fashion, making the collection and presentation of assurance of learning data simple and easy.

Mcgraw-Hill Customer Care Contact Information

At McGraw-Hill, we understand that getting the most from new technology can be challenging. That's why our services don't stop after you purchase our products. You can e-mail our Product Specialists 24 hours a day to get product training online. Or you can search our knowledge bank of Frequently Asked Questions on our support website.

For Customer Support, call **800-331-5094** or visit www.mhhe.com/support. One of our Technical Support Analysts will be able to assist you in a timely fashion.

![McGraw Hill Education] **connect®** | Students—study more efficiently, retain more and achieve better outcomes. Instructors—focus on what you love—teaching.

SUCCESSFUL SEMESTERS INCLUDE CONNECT

FOR INSTRUCTORS

You're in the driver's seat.

Want to build your own course? No problem. Prefer to use our turnkey, prebuilt course? Easy. Want to make changes throughout the semester? Sure. And you'll save time with Connect's auto-grading too.

65%
Less Time Grading

They'll thank you for it.

Adaptive study resources like SmartBook® help your students be better prepared in less time. You can transform your class time from dull definitions to dynamic debates. Hear from your peers about the benefits of Connect at **www.mheducation.com/highered/connect**

Make it simple, make it affordable.

Connect makes it easy with seamless integration using any of the major Learning Management Systems—Blackboard®, Canvas, and D2L, among others—to let you organize your course in one convenient location. Give your students access to digital materials at a discount with our inclusive access program. Ask your McGraw-Hill representative for more information.

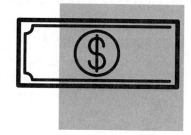

©Hill Street Studios/Tobin Rogers/Blend Images LLC

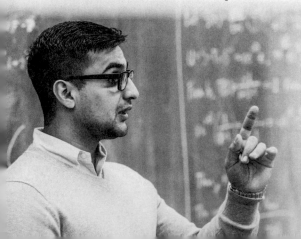

Solutions for your challenges.

A product isn't a solution. Real solutions are affordable, reliable, and come with training and ongoing support when you need it and how you want it. Our Customer Experience Group can also help you troubleshoot tech problems—although Connect's 99% uptime means you might not need to call them. See for yourself at **status.mheducation.com**

FOR STUDENTS

Effective, efficient studying.

Connect helps you be more productive with your study time and get better grades using tools like SmartBook, which highlights key concepts and creates a personalized study plan. Connect sets you up for success, so you walk into class with confidence and walk out with better grades.

©Shutterstock/wavebreakmedia

Study anytime, anywhere.

Download the free ReadAnywhere app and access your online eBook when it's convenient, even if you're offline. And since the app automatically syncs with your eBook in Connect, all of your notes are available every time you open it. Find out more at **www.mheducation.com/readanywhere**

> **"**I really liked this app—it made it easy to study when you don't have your textbook in front of you.**"**
>
> - Jordan Cunningham,
> Eastern Washington University

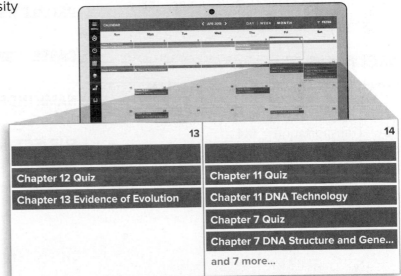

No surprises.

The Connect Calendar and Reports tools keep you on track with the work you need to get done and your assignment scores. Life gets busy; Connect tools help you keep learning through it all.

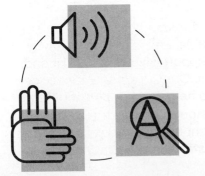

Learning for everyone.

McGraw-Hill works directly with Accessibility Services Departments and faculty to meet the learning needs of all students. Please contact your Accessibility Services office and ask them to email accessibility@mheducation.com, or visit **www.mheducation.com/about/accessibility.html** for more information.

Brief Contents

Contents

PART FIVE
SUPPLY CHAIN LOGISTICS ADMINISTRATION   327

Chapter 12
Relationship Management   328

Chapter 13
Performance Measurement   345

Chapter 14
Supply Chain Trends   370

Supply Chain Logistics Management

PART 1

Supply Chain Logistics Management

Part 1 establishes the strategic importance of logistics to achieving business success by creating value throughout domestic and global supply chains. Chapter 1 describes the current business attention to logistics, supply chain, and value chain management. The supply chain provides the structure within which logistical strategies are developed and executed. Chapter 1 discusses the firm's shift from supply chain to value chain. Chapter 2 introduces a framework for supply chain information systems. The information system framework is introduced early in the text because these applications provide the information storage and data communication that facilitate all logistics and supply chain planning and operations. Logistics, the primary focus of this text, is introduced in Chapter 3. The concept of integrated logistics is developed by discussing how specific work tasks combine to support customer relationship management, purchasing, management, and integrated operations planning. Chapter 4 describes the importance of customer relationship management to successful logistics. The value created by logistics can serve as a facilitator of customer success. One of the key challenges for integrated supply chain management is cross-functional and cross-enterprise collaboration.

CHAPTER 1

21st-Century Supply Chains

Chapter Outline

As recently as the 1990s, the average time required for a firm to process and deliver merchandise to a customer from warehouse inventory ranged from 15 to 30 days, sometimes even longer. The typical order-to-delivery process involved order creation and transfer, which was usually via telephone, fax, electronic data interchange (EDI), or mail; followed by order processing, which involved the use of manual or computer systems, credit authorization, and order assignment to a warehouse for processing; followed by shipment to a customer. When everything went as planned, the average time for a customer to receive items ordered was lengthy.

When something went wrong, as it often did, such as inventory out-of-stock, a lost or misplaced work order, or a misdirected shipment, total time to service customers escalated rapidly.

To support this lengthy and unpredictable time to market, it became common practice to accumulate inventory. For example, duplicate inventories were typically stocked by multiple supply chain channel members. Despite such extensive inventory, out-of-stocks and delayed deliveries were common due, in part, to the large number of product and process variations.

These accepted business practices of the 20th century, as well as the distribution channel structure used to complete delivery, evolved from years of experience dating from the industrial revolution. Such long-standing business practices remained in place and unchallenged because no clearly superior alternative existed. The traditional distribution process was designed to overcome challenges and achieve benefits that long ago ceased to be important. The industrialized world is no longer characterized by scarcity. Consumer affluence and desire for wide choice of products and services continue to grow. Production productivity and capacity have grown substantially due to new digital and processing technologies. In fact, today's consumers want a wide range of product and source options they can configure to their unique specifications. Given the rapid growth of information technology and the accessibility of the Internet, consumer desires have shifted from passive acceptance to active involvement in the design and delivery of specific products and services. Transportation capacity and operational performance have increasingly become more economical and reliable. Today's transportation is supported by sophisticated information systems that facilitate predictable and precise delivery. The capability to continuously track shipments and receive near instant notification of delayed delivery is common practice.

In this initial chapter, the supply chain management business model and value proposition are introduced as a growing strategic commitment of contemporary firms. The chapter reviews the development of the supply chain revolution in business practice that has resulted in a generalized supply chain model. Next, the supply chain concept is presented in a strategic framework. The chapter then examines integrative management, responsiveness, and globalization as forces driving the emergence of supply chain logic. The overall objective of Chapter 1 is to position the logistical challenges of supporting a 21st-century supply chain strategy. The supply chain is positioned as the strategic framework within which logistical requirements are identified and related operations managed.

The Supply Chain Revolution

What managers are experiencing today can be described as the **supply chain revolution** and a related **logistical renaissance**. These two massive shifts in expectation and practice concerning best-practice performance of business operations are highly interrelated. However, supply chain and logistics are significantly different aspects of contemporary management.

The fundamental focus of this text is integrated logistics management. However, to study logistics, a reader must have a basic understanding of supply chain management. Supply chain strategy establishes the operating framework within which logistics is performed. As will be reviewed shortly, dramatic change continues to evolve in supply chain practice. Accordingly, logistics best practice, as described in this text, is presented as a work in progress, subject to continuous change based on the evolving nature of supply chain structure and strategy. Chapter 2, Supply Chain Information Technology, overviews the technology used to support supply chain planning and execution. Chapter 3, Logistics, examines the renaissance taking place in logistics best practice and sets the stage for chapters that follow.

At first glance, supply chain management may appear to be a vague concept. A great deal has been written on the subject without much concern for basic definition, structure, or common vocabulary. Confusion exists concerning the appropriate scope of what constitutes a supply chain, to what extent it involves integration with other companies as contrasted to integrating a firm's internal operations, and how to best implement a strategy concerning competitive practices and legal constraints. For most managers, the supply chain concept has intrinsic appeal because it envisions new business arrangements offering the potential to improve competitiveness. The concept also implies a highly effective network of business relationships that serve to improve efficiency by eliminating duplicate and nonproductive work. Understanding more specifically what constitutes the supply chain revolution starts with a review of traditional distribution channel practice.

To overcome challenges of commercial trading, firms developed business relationships with other product and service firms to jointly perform essential activities. Such acknowledged dependency is necessary to achieve benefits of specialization. Managers, following the early years of the industrial revolution, began to strategically plan core competency, specialization, and economy of scale. The result was realization that working closely with other businesses was essential for continued success. This understanding that no firm could be totally self-sufficient contrasted to some earlier notions of vertical integration.[1] Acknowledged dependence between business firms created the study of what became known as **distribution** or **marketing channels**.

Because of the high visibility of different types of businesses, the early study of channel arrangements was characterized by classification based on specific roles performed during the distribution process. For example, a firm may have been created to perform the value-added services called wholesaling. Firms doing business with a wholesaler had expectations concerning what services they would receive and the compensation they would be expected to pay. In-depth study of specific activities quickly identified the necessity for leadership, a degree of commitment to cooperation among all channel members, and means to resolve conflict. Scholars who conduct research in channel structure and strategy developed typologies to classify observable practice ranging from a single transaction to highly formalized continuous business relationships.

The bonding feature of channel integration was a rather vague concept that all involved would enjoy benefits as a result of collaboration. However, primarily due to a lack of high-quality information, the overall channel structure was postured on an adversarial foundation. When push came to shove, each firm in the channel would first and foremost focus on achieving its individual goals. Thus, in final analysis, channel dynamics were more often than not characterized by a dog-eat-dog competitive environment.

During the last decade of the 20th century, channel strategy and structure began to shift radically. Traditional distribution channel arrangements moved toward more integration and collaboration. Prior to reviewing the generalized supply chain model, it is important to understand why integration creates value.

Why Integration Creates Value

To explain the basic benefits and challenges of integrated management, it is useful to point out that customers have at least three perspectives of value.

The traditional perspective is **economic value**. Economic value builds on economy of scale in operations as the source of efficiency. Economy of scale seeks to fully utilize fixed assets to achieve the lowest, total landed cost. The focus of economic value is efficiency of product/service creation. Economic value is all about doing things as inexpensively as possible. The customer take-away of economic value is **quality at a low price**.

[1] Henry Ford, *Today and Tomorrow* (New York: Doubleday, Page, and Company, 1926). Reprinted by Productivity Press (Portland, OR, 1988).

Economic Value	Market Value	Relevancy Value
• Lowest total cost	• Attractive assortment	• Customization
• Economy-of-scale efficiency	• Economy-of-scope effectiveness	• Segmental diversity
• Product/service creation	• Product/service presentation	• Product/service positioning
Procurement/Manufacturing Strategy	**Market/Distribution Strategy**	**Supply Chain Strategy**

TABLE 1.1
Integrative Management Value Proposition

A second value perspective is **market value**. Market value is about presenting an attractive assortment of products at the right time and place to realize effectiveness. Market value focuses on achieving economy of scope in product/service presentation. The creation of multimerchant shopping malls, large-scale mass-merchandising retail stores, and multivendor Internet fulfillment operations are all initiatives to achieve **market value**. The customer's take-away in terms of market value is **convenient product/service assortment and choice**.

Realization of both economic and market value is important to customers. However, increasingly firms are recognizing that business success also depends upon a third perspective of value, referred to as **relevancy value**. Relevancy value involves customization of value-adding services, over and above basic product characteristics and physical location, that make a real difference to customers. Relevancy value means the right products and services, as reflected by market value, at the right price, as reflected by economic value, modified, sequenced, synchronized, and positioned in a manner that creates customer-specific value. In a consumer context, for example, relevancy means transforming ingredients into ready-to-eat meals. In general merchandise retailing, relevancy means transforming products into fashionable apparel. In manufacturing and assembly, relevancy is achieved by integrating specific components into products to increase functionality desired by a specific customer. The customer's take-away in terms of relevancy is a unique product/service bundle.

The simultaneous achievement of economic value, market value, and relevancy value requires total integration of the overall business process and is known as the integrative management value proposition, as illustrated in Table 1.1.

Generalized Supply Chain Model and Supply Chain Applications

The general concept of an integrated supply chain is often illustrated by a line diagram that links participating firms into a coordinated competitive unit. Figure 1.1 illustrates a generalized model adapted from the supply chain management program at Michigan State University.

The context of an integrated supply chain is multifirm collaboration within a framework of key resource flows and constraints. Within this context, supply chain structure and strategy results from efforts to operationally align an enterprise with customers as well as the supporting distributor and supplier networks to gain competitive advantage. Business operations are ideally integrated from initial material purchase to delivery of finished products and services to customers.[2]

Value results from the synergy among firms constituting a supply chain as a result of five critical flows: information, product, service, financial, and knowledge (see the bidirectional

---

[2] Customers are defined as destination points in a supply chain. Customers either consume a product or use it as an integral part or component of an additional process or product. The essential point is that the original product loses its unique configuration when consumed. Business entities that purchase products from manufacturers for resale, for example, wholesalers and retailers, are referred to as *intermediate customers*.

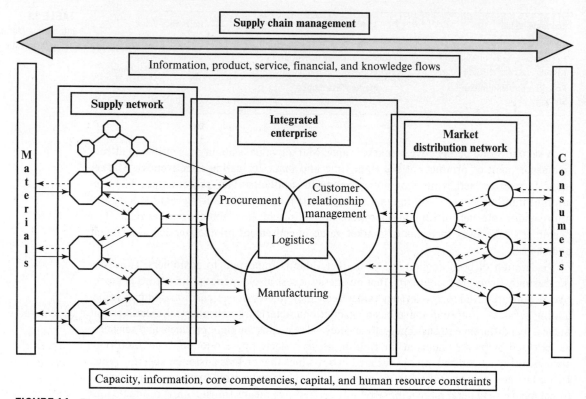

FIGURE 1.1   The Integrated Supply Chain Framework

arrow at the top of the Figure 1.1). Logistics is the primary conduit of product and service flow within a supply chain arrangement. Each firm engaged in a supply chain is involved in performing some aspects of overall logistics. Achievement of logistical integration and efficiency across the supply chain is the focus of this text. The generalized supply chain arrangement illustrated in Figure 1.1 logically and logistically links a firm and its distributor and supplier network to customers. The message conveyed by the figure is that the integrated value-creation process must be aligned and managed from material procurement to end-customer product/service delivery in order to achieve effectiveness, efficiency, relevancy, and sustainability.

The integrated supply chain perspective shifts traditional channel arrangements from loosely linked groups of independent businesses that buy and sell inventory to each other toward a managerially coordinated initiative to increase market impact, overall efficiency, continuous improvement, and competitiveness. In practice, many complexities serve to cloud the simplicity of illustrating supply chains as directional line diagrams. For example, many individual firms simultaneously participate in multiple and competitive supply chains. To the degree that a supply chain becomes the basic unit of competition, firms participating in multiple arrangements may confront loyalty issues related to confidentiality and potential conflict of interest.

Another factor that serves to add complexity to understanding supply chain structure is the high degree of mobility and change observable in typical arrangements. It's interesting to observe the fluidity of supply chains as firms enter and exit without any apparent loss of essential connectivity. For example, a firm and/or service supplier may be actively engaged in a supply chain structure during selected times, such as a peak selling season, and not during the balance of a year. During the 2017 Christmas season, Amazon added 100,000 jobs to accommodate seasonal demand to demonstrate the need for flexibility. Most of these positions are at fulfillment centers (distribution centers) and consolidation points.

Generalized Supply Chain Model

While the typical supply chain is focused on a manufacturer with the support of suppliers, distributors, retailers, and supply chain service providers, there are a number of nontraditional environments where supply chain principles can be effectively applied. Table 1.2 lists and describes some of these nontraditional applications.

Supply Chain Applications	Description
Product supply chain	The product supply chain is the traditional model involving suppliers, manufacturers, distributors, and retailers for consumer products. This is the primary focus of many supply chain classes and texts.
Promotional supply chain	Promotional supply chains are for items that are being heavily promoted such as end-aisle tasting displays in wholesale clubs. The major challenge is that all items related to the promotion (product, utensils, cooking materials, and display materials) must be assembled in the cart and delivered to the store to meet the weekend display schedule.
Bulk material supply chain	Bulk material supply chains are designed to move bulk products such as grains, metals, and chemicals. In many cases, these materials are relatively low value so all movement and handling in the supply chain must take advantage of significant economies of scale and often specialized vehicles.
Talent supply chain	Talent supply chains apply supply chain principles to talent management where individual talent represents the products that are moved through the supply chain with the value-added process being training and education.
Business-to-consumer (B2C) supply chain	Business-to-consumer supply chains represent the increasing volume of product that is sold online from manufacturers or distributors directly to consumers.
Recycling supply chain	Recycling supply chains are responsible for handling product returns for recycling of products, components, reprocessing, and packaging.
Resource supply chain	Resource supply chains are designed to provide facility resources for information-based supply chains such as server farms for cloud or social media applications. This includes the purchasing and sequencing of land, regulatory approvals, utilities, and equipment to provide the technology services.
Construction supply chain	Construction supply chains provide and sequence the equipment and the building supplies for construction.
Recovery supply chain	Recovery supply chains are employed to recover material that has reached its useful life in the field. A recovery supply chain is useful following military, construction, mining, or drilling operations.
Humanitarian supply chain	Humanitarian supply chains provide post-event support for disaster recovery. This includes bringing in equipment for recovery, food and medical care items, and commodities to support reconstruction.
Global supply chain	Global supply chains source and deliver from multiple regions around the world. While most supply chains include global aspects, it is important to consider specific global characteristics such as demand variation, distance, and documentation.
Durables supply chain	Durables supply chains are designed to facilitate the handling and delivery of heavy equipment such as agricultural, construction, or military equipment. The major differentiator for durables supply chains is specialized transportation equipment due to infrastructure restrictions.
Agricultural commodity supply chain	Agricultural commodity supply chains move agricultural product from the farm to the commodity elevator or the processing plant. In most cases, the challenge is to move this bulk product economically and in a way that the farmer can still make money even when the price is set by the buyer. In other words, if the farmer is too far from the buyer, there will be no market for those products.
Innovative supply chain	An innovative supply chain is one that must rapidly introduce new product to the market. This is typically a responsive supply chain that is defined to bring new product variations to market or to have souvenirs such as for movies, athletic events, or customized product introductions available when the event is taking place (e.g., concerts, movies, openings, etc.)
Military supply chain	Military supply chains are designed to support military operations. Specialized requirements include the ability to provide supply chains for a range of products (food, medical, equipment, and ammunitions) in demanding environments (desert, jungle, and supporting combat operations).
Clinical trials supply chain	Clinical trials supply chains are designed to support the very precise demands for completing pharmaceutical clinical trials. Clinical trials are very demanding due to the need for precise controls of dosages, ingredient combinations, and drug combinations.

TABLE 1.2   Supply Chain Applications

Although many believe that supply chain principles and practices are only relevant for major manufacturing firms, Table 1.2 demonstrates that the principles can be applied in many other scenarios and environments. It is important for supply chain professionals to understand the environments that supply chain principles can be applied to.

Supply Chain Definitions and Activities

Due to the many views and perspectives of supply chain, there are varying definitions that include different institutions, processes, and activities. As such, there is no common definition. There is not even a common set of processes or activities that should be included.

However, it is important that this text establish a foundation by providing both a definition and a strategic context. In terms of scope, **supply chain management** is a set of processes to effectively and efficiently integrate suppliers, manufacturers, distribution centers, distributors, and retailers so that products are produced and distributed at the right quantities, to the right locations, and at the right time to minimize system-side costs while achieving the consumer's desired value proposition.

What began during the last decade of the 20th century and will continue to unfold well into the 21st century is what is being increasingly characterized as the **information-based** or **digital supply chain**. In the information or digital age, the reality of connectivity among collaborating business organizations continues to drive a new order of relationships called supply chain management. Managers are increasingly improving and integrating traditional marketing, manufacturing, purchasing, and logistics practices. In light of this information-based evolution, supply chain management's definition is expanded: It is a coordinated, cross-functional strategy, involving both internal and external partners, that utilizes process and information to improve operating efficiency and leverage strategic positioning. Supply chain strategy applies the functions and processes to effectively and efficiently integrate suppliers, manufacturers, distribution networks, and channels as well as final consumers, ensuring the firm's value proposition is achieved while minimizing total system cost.

Logistics management is the process and activities that create value focused on the design and administration of a system to control the timing and geographical positioning of raw material, work-in-process, and finished inventory at the lowest total cost. **Logistics** is the combination of a firm's order management, inventory, transportation, and warehousing management activities as integrated throughout a facility network. **Integrated logistics** serves to link and synchronize the overall supply chain as a continuous process and is essential to achieve the desired outcomes of the firm's value proposition.

While there are other definitions that come from different perspectives (Institute of Supply Management, APICS, and Council of Supply Chain Management Professionals), there are common themes that suggest a common framework. These definitions emphasize key concepts, including effective and efficient flow, cross-functional collaboration, collaborative institutional partners, achieving the consumer's value proposition, and minimizing systemwide cost. Effective and efficient flow emphasizes the need for a firm to work collaboratively with other supply chain partners to deliver the product to the consumer at a minimum cost. The cross-functional collaboration requires that the firm's internal functions, particularly those involved in supply chain, work together to minimize waste and duplication of time and resources. Achieving the consumer's value proposition means that the supply chain can deliver the product or solution in a form that can meet the unique consumer requirements. Finally, deliver at minimum cost means that the firm and its collaborative partners try to deliver the product or solution to the consumer while minimizing the total end-to-end cost for all activities occurring in the supply chain.

Integrative Management and Supply Chain Processes

Across all aspects of business operations, attention is focused on achieving improved integrative management. The challenge to achieving integrated management results from the long-standing tradition of performing and measuring work on a functional basis. Since the industrial revolution, achieving best practice has focused managerial attention on functional specialization.[3] The prevailing belief was the better the performance of a specific function, the greater the efficiency of the overall process. For well over a century, this fundamental commitment to functional efficiency has driven best practice in organization structure, performance measurement, and accountability.

In terms of management, firms have traditionally been structured into departments to facilitate work focus, routinization, standardization, and control. Accounting practices were developed to measure departmental performance. Most performance measurement focused on individual functions. Two examples of common functional measurement are the cost per unit to manufacture and the cost per hundredweight to transport. Cross-functional measurements and allocations were typically limited to costs common to all functional areas of work, such as overhead, labor, utilities, insurance, interest, and so on.

Excellence in supply chain performance requires the simultaneous achievement of eight key processes. Table 1.3 identifies the eight key processes and provides a brief description of each. Although these integrative processes are not the exclusive domain of supply chain logistics, some critical elements of each are integral to a firm achieving high-performance operational success. Therefore, supply chain structure, strategy, and continuous operational execution must be focused on achieving and continuously improving these essential eight processes. Simultaneous operational achievement of these eight processes forms the essence of achieving both operational integration and performance excellence.

[3] Frederick W. Taylor, *Scientific Management* (New York: W. W. Norton, 1967).

Process	Description
Demand planning responsiveness	The assessment of demand and strategic design to achieve maximum responsiveness to customer requirements.
Customer relationship collaboration	The development and administration of relationships with customers to facilitate strategic information sharing, joint planning, and integrated operations.
Order fulfillment/service delivery	The ability to execute superior and sustainable order-to-delivery performance and related essential services.
Product/service development launch	The participation in product service development and lean launch.
Manufacturing customization	The support of manufacturing strategy and facilitation of postponement throughout the supply chain.
Supplier relationship collaboration	The development and administration of relationships with suppliers to facilitate strategic information sharing, joint planning, and integrated operations.
Life cycle support	The repair and support of products during their life cycle, including warranty, maintenance, and repair.
Reverse logistics	The return and disposition of inventories in a cost-effective and secure manner.

TABLE 1.3
Eight Supply Chain Integrative Processes

The fundamental challenge of integrated management is to redirect traditional emphasis on functionality in an effort to focus on process achievement. Over the past few decades, it has become increasingly apparent that functions, individually performed best in class, do not necessarily combine or aggregate to achieve lowest total cost or highly effective processes. Integrative management seeks to identify and achieve lowest total process cost by capturing trade-offs that exist between functions. To illustrate, in terms of logistics, a firm might be able to reduce total cost to serve a customer as a result of spending more for faster, dependable transportation if the overall cost of inventory associated with the process can be reduced by an amount greater than that being spent for premium transportation. The focus of integrated management is **lowest total process cost**, which is not necessarily the achievement of the lowest cost for each function included in the process.

While this text provides detail regarding supply chain processes and activities in later chapters, it is important to offer insight regarding supply chain processes and activities so that the reader can relate to the types of activities involved. Table 1.4 summarizes the processes and activities. The first process is demand planning responsiveness, which balances inventory between supply and demand. The second process includes the activities to develop and maintain customer relationships. The third process includes the activities required to plan order delivery, select product from a warehouse, and deliver product to customers. The fourth process includes the activities to design, manufacture, and promote new products in the supply chain. The fifth process includes tasks related to acquiring raw materials, raw material management, and manufacturing (product conversion). The sixth process includes the activities related to identifying supply sources, minimizing the total cost of acquisition, selecting suppliers, and maintaining a relationship with suppliers. The seventh process includes the activities required for management of spare parts. The final process is the activities related to recycling and product recovery. While not all supply chain organizations include all these activities, the table offers a good overview of the activities that might be included. These activities will be described in more context and detail in later chapters.

Process	Typical Supply Chain Activities				
Demand planning responsiveness	Forecasting	Inventory planning	Cross-functional coordination	Sales and operations planning	Capacity management
Customer relationship collaboration	Relationship management	Order management and processing	Customer service		
Order fulfillment/ service delivery	Logistics planning and control	Transportation	Warehousing	Delivery management	Outsourcing
Product/service development launch	Product design	Launch	Cross-functional coordination		
Manufacturing customization	Materials management	Production and inventory management	Process control	Product conversion	
Supplier relationship collaboration	Sourcing strategies	Sourcing plans	Total cost analysis	Supplier selection	Supplier collaboration
Life-cycle support	Maintain spares inventory	Provide quick response fulfillment			
Reverse logistics	Design recovery system	Operate recovery system	Repair and/or recycle	Sustainability initiatives	

TABLE 1.4   Supply Chain Processes and Activities

The concept of trade-off and the goal of lowest total cost have logical appeal. While deceptively simple, managers continue to find the identification, measurement, and implementation of a process to minimize total cost a difficult task in day-to-day operations. The unavailability of focus on functional goals and the cost measures capable of quantifying cross-functional trade-offs served to stimulate development of such integrative tools as Total Cost Analysis, Process Engineering, and Activity-Based Costing (ABC).

Three important facets of supply chain logic resulted from increased managerial attention to (1) enterprise extension, (2) integrated service providers, and (3) collaboration.

Enterprise Extension

The central thrust of enterprise extension is to expand managerial influence and control beyond the ownership boundaries of a single enterprise to facilitate joint planning and operations with customers and suppliers. The fundamental belief is that collaborative behavior to integrate processes between firms will improve impact, reduce overall risk, and greatly improve efficiency. Enterprise extension builds on two basic paradigms: information sharing and process specialization.

The **information sharing paradigm** is the widespread belief that achieving a high degree of cooperative behavior requires that supply chain participants voluntarily share operating information and jointly plan strategies. The scope of cross-enterprise collaboration should span beyond sales data to include plans detailing promotion, new product introduction, and day-to-day operations. It's important to emphasize that information sharing to support collaboration must not be limited to historical or even accurate current sales data. Of greater importance is a willingness to share information about future strategic initiatives to facilitate joint operations. The guiding principle is that information sharing is essential among supply chain participants to collectively meet customer demand faster and more efficiently.

The **process specialization paradigm** is the commitment to focusing collaborative arrangements on planning joint operations with a goal of eliminating nonproductive or non-value-adding redundancy by firms in a supply chain. The basic idea is to design the overall supply chain processes in a manner that facilitates a specific firm's competencies along with the responsibility and accountability to perform each element of essential work in a manner that maximizes overall results.

Firms participating in a supply chain have specific roles to perform within the context of shared strategic goals. Sharing information and joint planning can reduce risk related to inventory positioning. Collaboration can eliminate duplicative or redundant work, such as repetitive quality inspection, by designating and empowering a specified member of the supply chain to be fully responsible and accountable. Such extended enterprise integration introduces new challenges regarding measurement, benefit and risk sharing, trust, leadership, and conflict resolution. It is clear that the challenges of collaboration and enterprise extension constitute new managerial horizons. A third contributing force to supply chain development is the rapidly changing managerial attitude toward integrated service providers.

Integrated Service Providers

As noted earlier, the origins of contemporary business were grounded in functional specialization. It is not surprising that firms developed the practice of **outsourcing** look to businesses that are specialists in the performance of specific functions. The two traditional logistics service providers are transportation and warehousing specialists.

The for-hire transportation industry consists of thousands of carriers who specialize in product movement between geographic locations. Over the years, a comprehensive carrier network has emerged, providing shippers a broad assortment of services, utilizing all available forms, called **modes**, of transportation and related technology. The value proposition of for-hire transportation is based on specialization, efficiency, and scale economies. Value is generated by a carrier's capability to provide shared transportation services for multiple shippers. The transport alternatives for shippers are either to invest capital in transportation equipment and operations or to engage the services of for-hire carriers. Naturally, a large number of firms develop transportation solutions that combine benefits of these alternatives.

In addition to transportation, a large number of service firms have traditionally provided warehouse services. Traditionally called **public warehouses**, these firms provide product storage supplemented with other specialized services. Two significant benefits are obtained when shippers use public warehouses. First is elimination of capital investment in warehouse buildings. The second is the ability to consolidate small shipments for combined delivery with products of other firms that use the same public warehouse. Such multishipper consolidation achieves transportation efficiency not typically available when firms ship from their own warehouses. Many firms combine private and public warehouses into go-to-market and product supply networks.

In 1980 the landscape of for-hire services in the United States changed dramatically. Within a few short months, the economic and political regulatory infrastructure of transportation in the United States shifted from economic to social regulation as a result of the passage of the Motor Carrier Regulatory Reform and Modernization Act (MCA-80) and the Staggers Rail Act.[4] These regulatory changes, as amended, served to support an open transportation market involving less government economic regulation for all forms of transportation. Over time, this trend extended worldwide to deregulate transportation in most free-market industrialized nations.

In contrast to transportation, firms engaged in public warehousing were not operationally regulated by federal or state governments. In an effort to avoid regulation most warehouse firms did not offer transportation services. However, with the deregulation of transportation, that practice soon changed. Overnight, warehousing firms began to offer transportation services. Likewise, many transport carriers began to offer customers warehouse services.

What occurred in the logistics service industry was a radical shift from single function to multifunctional outsourcing. **Integrated service providers (ISPs)** began to market a range of logistics services that included all work necessary to accommodate customers, ranging from order entry to product delivery. In many situations the foundation of transportation and warehouse services was augmented by the performance of a wide range of special services. These customized services are typically described as **value-added services (VASs)**. For example, United Parcel Service (UPS) stocks Nike shoes and warm-ups at its Louisville warehouse and processes orders hourly. All related communication and financial administration are handled by a UPS call center. Thus, Nike has effectively outsourced basic logistics and related value-added service to UPS.

The common name used throughout industry to describe ISPs is **third-party and fourth-party service providers**. In a general sense, ISPs are commonly classified as being either **asset- or nonasset-based**, the distinction being that asset-based (third-party) firms own and operate transportation equipment and warehousing buildings. In contrast, nonasset service (fourth-party) firms specialize in providing comprehensive information services that facilitate supply chain arrangements. Such fourth-party service providers arrange services, often integrating third-party asset operators on behalf of their customers.

---

[4] Public Laws 96-296 and 96-488, respectively. These laws, as well as others briefly noted here, are discussed in greater detail in Chapter 8.

The 2018 U.S. third-party contract logistics market was estimated to be 55 percent of transportation and 40 percent of warehouse expenses.[5] The growth of integrated service providers makes both the formation and dismantling of supply chain arrangements easier. As an organization's need for speed and operational flexibility change, ISPs can be utilized as needed. Supply chain participants have the opportunity to engage the capabilities of what amounts to a virtual logistics network. Such outsourcing helps facilitate process-focused integrative management.

As discussed, the advent of collaboration, extended enterprise visioning, and the increased availability of integrated service providers combined to drive radically new supply chain solutions. The notion of shared and synergistic benefits served to solidify the importance of relationships between firms collaborating in a supply chain. The extended enterprise logic stimulated visions of increased efficiency, effectiveness, relevancy, and sustainability as a result of sharing information, planning, and operational specialization between supply chain participants. The deregulation of transportation served as a catalyst for the rapid expansion of integrated service providers. This development served to redefine and expand the scope of specialized services available to facilitate supply chain operations. In combination, these drivers helped create integrated supply chain management. They served to identify and solidify the strategic benefits of integrated management. They combined to reinforce the value of core-competence specialization and cast the challenges and opportunity of creating virtual supply chains.

Collaboration

As discussed earlier, the history of business has been dominated by a desire to cooperate but always presented within a competitive framework. Whereas competition remains the dominant model guiding free market economies, the increasing importance of collaboration has positioned the supply chain as a primary unit of competition. In today's global economy, supply chain arrangements compete with each other for customer loyalty. Supply chains dominated by Amazon, Target, and Walmart are direct competitors in many markets. Similar supply chain alignments can be observed in industries ranging from entertainment to food to automobiles to chemicals. The global strategic reach of Mast (Limited Logistics Services) is an example of the complexity of modern supply chain management. Garments manufactured throughout the world are delivered direct to retail stores, and are sold in all fashion seasons to worldwide consumers. Amazon sells millions of products through multiple different channel offerings.

The general impetus to institutionalized collaborative working arrangements was the 1984 enactment of the National Cooperative Research and Development Act, which was expanded in scope by further legislation in 1993 and 2004.[6] This national legislation and its subsequent modification signaled fundamental change in traditional Justice

---

[5] "2018 Third Party Logistics Report," Penske Logistics.

[6] On October 11, 1984, President Reagan signed into law the National Cooperative Research and Development Act of 1984 (Public Law 98-462) in an effort "to promote research and development, encourage innovation, stimulate trade, and make necessary and appropriate modifications in the operation of the antitrust laws." This law enables research and development activities to be jointly performed up to the point where prototypes are developed. The law further determined that antitrust litigation would be based on the rule of reason, taking into account all factors affecting competition. An extension to this act was signed into law by President Clinton on June 10, 1993. The extension, National Cooperative Production Amendments of 1993 (Public Law 103-42), allows joint ventures to go beyond just research to include the production and testing of a product, process, or service. This created a new act called the National Cooperative Research and Production Act of 1993 to replace the 1984 act. Furthermore, this new act established a procedure for businesses to notify the Department of Justice and the Federal Trade Commission of their cooperative arrangement in order to qualify for "single-damages limitation on civil antitrust liability." In 2004 President Bush signed into law the Standards Development Organization Advancement Act (SDOAA, H. R. 1086) which amended the 1993 act to include immunity for standards development organizations and thereby further validated the collaborative doctrine.

Department antitrust philosophy. The basic legislation, as supplemented by administrative rulings, encouraged firms to develop collaborative initiatives in an effort to increase the global competitiveness of U.S.-based firms. Widespread realization that cooperation is both permissible and encouraged served to stimulate formation of supply chain arrangements.

While all forms of price collusion remain illegal, the collaborative legislation served to facilitate cross-organizational sharing of operating information, technology, and risk as ways to increase U.S. competitiveness. The response was a wide variety of new and innovative operating arrangements. One such development was the growing vision of enterprise extension.

Supply Chain Value Proposition

A value proposition refers to the combination of products and services provided to customers and consumers by the supply chain. While the traditional supply chain value proposition focused on providing the desired service objective at a minimum cost, today's value proposition is substantially more complex. It is very important to understand this more comprehensive value proposition to be able to design an appropriate supply chain strategy. Figure 1.2 illustrates this more comprehensive supply chain value strategy, including the four dimensions of effectiveness, efficiency, relevance, and sustainability. This has been termed the EERS model which includes each of the four dimensions (effectiveness, efficiency, relevance, and sustainability). Each dimension is discussed in more detail below.

Effectiveness

Effectiveness refers to the supply chain's ability to deliver products in a timely manner to the consumer's desired location. While this has traditionally implied that the product is delivered to the customer of the manufacturer (i.e., distributor or retailer), the expected delivery point today could be another supply chain partner or even the consumer.

FIGURE 1.2
EERS Value Diamond

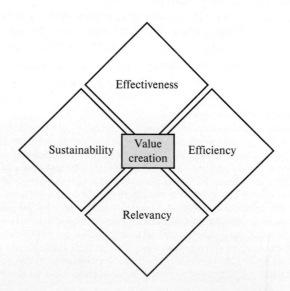

Efficiency

Efficiency refers to the supply chain's ability to deliver products at the minimum total cost, including raw material acquisition, manufacturing, storage, inventory, and transportation. Minimum total cost also includes minimizing the cost across the entire supply chain. The concept of efficiency is to minimize the cost and waste related to product movement while also minimizing the assets required.

Relevancy

Relevancy refers to the supply chain's ability to be able to react to changes in the environment, market place, or consumer requirements. For example, consumer delivery requirements may change based on seasonality, competitive environment, and customization requirements desired by the customer. If the supply chain is flexible enough to meet these changing requirements, it can meet relevancy dimension of the value proposition.

Sustainability

Sustainability refers to the firm's ability to reconfigure the supply chain to enhance both the environment and the firm. While sustainability certainly includes the desire to make supply chains more environmentally friendly such as by reducing fuel consumption and emissions, it also might include supply chain designs that reduce risk, provide access to key talent, and provide a supportive political and regulatory environment.

Value Proposition Conclusion

This discussion illustrates how the traditional value proposition has evolved from the relatively simple effectiveness and efficiency to the more comprehensive dimension defined by the EERS model. While the EERS model illustrates a broader dimension of the value proposition, it is important to realize that not all dimensions should be weighed equally. Specifically, the relative weighting may vary by customer or even by customer situation. For example, in some cases, the customer may place the highest priority on low cost (efficiency), while in others, the customer may place the highest priority on flexibility (relevancy). A high-performance supply chain must be able to deliver to all dimensions and be flexible enough to adapt its offerings to meet the unique situational needs of the customer.

Responsiveness

One could argue that the challenges and benefits of integrative management offers sufficient reason for the supply chain revolution. However, other basic drivers continue to make supply chain arrangements even more appealing. A fundamental paradigm shift in strategic thinking occurred as a direct impact of information technology. Information connectivity creates the potential for developing responsive business models. To elaborate the far-reaching implications of this major development, it is useful to contrast traditional **anticipatory (push)** business practice to the emerging time-based **responsive** (or **pull**) business model. The responsive business model is also referred to as **demand driven**.

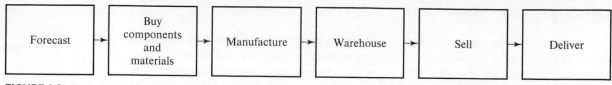

FIGURE 1.3   Anticipatory Business Model

Anticipatory Business Model (Push)

Since the industrial revolution, the dominant business model has required anticipation regarding what customers will demand in the future. Because information concerning purchase behavior was not readily available and firms loosely linked together in a channel of distribution did not feel compelled to share their plans, business operations were driven by forecasts. The typical manufacturer produced products based on market forecast. Likewise, wholesalers, distributors, and retailers purchased inventory based on their unique forecasts and promotional plans. Since the forecast results were typically wrong, considerable differences existed between what firms planned to do and what they in fact ended up doing. Such variation typically resulted in unplanned inventory. Because of high cost and risk associated with conducting business on an anticipatory basis, the prevailing relationship between trading partners was often adversarial; each firm needed to protect its own interest.

Figure 1.3 illustrates the typical stages in a single firm's implementation of the anticipatory business model: forecast, purchase materials, manufacture, warehouse, sell, and then deliver. In retail and wholesale enterprises, operations involved anticipatory purchase of inventory assortments to accommodate expected sales. The key point is that almost all essential work has been traditionally performed in *anticipation* of future requirements. The likelihood of incorrectly anticipating customer requirements rendered the anticipatory business model highly risky. In addition, each firm in the distribution channel duplicated a similar anticipatory process.

Responsive Business Model (Pull)

The fundamental difference between anticipatory and responsive supply chain arrangements is timing. The responsive business model seeks to reduce or eliminate forecast reliance by joint planning and rapid exchange of information between supply chain participants.

The availability of low-cost information has created **time-based competition**. Managers are increasingly sharing information to improve both the speed and accuracy of supply chain logistics. To illustrate, managers may share information to improve forecasting accuracy or even eliminate forecasts in an effort to reduce anticipatory inventory deployment. This transformation from anticipatory toward responsive business is possible because today's managers have sense and response information technology to rapidly obtain and share accurate sales data and exercise improved operational control. When all members of the supply chain synchronize their operations, opportunities exist to reduce overall inventory and eliminate costly duplicate practices. More important, customers can be provided with products they want, fast.

Figure 1.4 illustrates a responsive business model that manufactures or assembles products to customer order. The fundamental difference in responsive models is the sequence of events that drive business practice. Also notable, in comparison to Figure 1.3, are the fewer steps required to complete the responsive process. Fewer steps typically equate to less cost

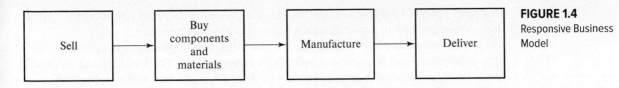

FIGURE 1.4
Responsive Business
Model

and less elapsed time from order commitment to delivery. The responsive sequence is initiated by a sale followed by a sequence of material purchase, custom manufacturing, and direct customer delivery.

In many ways, the responsive business model is similar to traditional build-to-order manufacturing. The primary difference between modern responsive operations and traditional build-to-order are the time to execute and the degree of potential customization. In terms of time to execute the order to delivery, the contemporary responsive system is substantially faster than traditional build-to-order manufacturing. It is becoming common practice to replenish retail store inventories of consumer products on a daily basis. Custom-built automobiles are being promised for delivery within ten working days, with the goal to even further reduce the order-to-delivery cycle. Such compressed order-to-delivery cycles were not even imaginable a few years ago.

Perhaps an even more appealing attribute of responsive supply chains is their potential to uniquely customize products on smaller orders than was typical of traditional build-to-order lot size manufacturing. Direct connectivity with customers via the Internet is accelerating customization. In most traditional anticipatory distribution systems, the customer is a passive participant. About the only power the customer has in the traditional process is the decision to buy or not buy. Direct connectivity of customers in a responsive process has at least three benefits. First, involvement provides comprehensive search capabilities that serve to expand the range of sources and choices a customer can consider when selecting a product or service. Second, customers can be better informed about prices and, in some situations, are able to drive price advantage by virtue of bids and/or auctions. Finally, information-intense responsive systems provide innovation such as a **customer choiceboard** wherein customers design or customize their own product configuration.

Barriers to Implementing Responsive Systems

In reality, today's best supply chain practices do not reflect either extreme anticipatory or responsive design. Most established firms remain, to a significant degree, committed to anticipatory practices. However, responsive strategies are rapidly emerging. Perhaps the greatest barrier to adopting responsive arrangements is the need for publicly held corporations to maintain planned quarterly profits. This accountability creates expectations concerning continued sales and financial results. Such expectations often drive promotional and pricing strategies to "load the channel" with inventory to create timely sales. Conversely, it is never timely to make a major reduction in channel inventory. Efforts to lean or deload inventory to implement a more responsive operating posture require the ability to absorb a one-time sale reduction among supply chain partners. Start-up ventures are ideally positioned to implement responsive fulfillment systems because they do not face the challenge of taking inventory out of an existing channel.

A second barrier to implementing responsive operations is the need to establish and sustain collaborative relationships. Most business managers simply do not have training or experience in how to develop and implement collaborative arrangements designed to share benefits and risks. While managers generally express a high degree of belief in the long-term potential for responsive alliances, they typically confront considerable frustration concerning how to implement such supply chain arrangements.

For the foreseeable future, most firms will continue to implement strategies that combine anticipatory and responsive supply chain arrangements. The trend toward increased involvement in responsive arrangements with specific customers and suppliers will continue to expand as the full advantage of web-based operations materializes.

Globalization

A conservative estimate is that as much as 90 percent of global demand is not fully satisfied by local supply. Current demand coupled with a world population projected to increase by an average of over 200,000 persons per day for the next decade equates to substantial market opportunity. The range of product/service growth potential varies greatly between industrialized and emerging economies. In industrialized sectors of the global economy, opportunities focus on upscale consumer products. These more advanced economies offer substantial opportunities for the sale of products combined with value-added services. While it is true that consumers in developing nations enjoy relatively less purchasing power than those in their industrialized counterparts, demand in such economies for basic products and necessities is huge. Consumers in developing nations are more interested in quality of basic life than in fashion or technology. For example, the growing populations of India and China offer huge market opportunities for basic products like food, clothing, and consumer durables such as refrigerators, washing machines, and automobiles. Firms with aggressive growth goals cannot neglect the commercialization of the global marketplace.

In addition to sales potential, involvement in global business is being driven by significant opportunities to increase operating efficiency. Such operational efficiencies are attainable in at least three areas. First, the global marketplace offers significant opportunity to strategically source raw material and components. Second, significant labor advantages can be gained by locating manufacturing and distribution facilities in developing nations. Third, favorable tax laws can make the performance of value-adding operations in specific countries highly attractive.

The decision to engage in global operations to achieve market growth and enjoy operational efficiency follows a natural path of business expansion. Typically, firms enter the global marketplace by conducting import and export operations. Such import and export transactions constitute a significant portion of global international business. The second stage of internationalization involves a firm's establishment of local presence in foreign nations and trading areas. Such presence can range from franchise and licensing of local businesses to the establishment of manufacturing and distribution facilities. The important distinction between import/export involvement and establishment of local presence is the degree of investment and managerial involvement characteristic of stage two. The third stage of internationalization is the full-fledged conduct of business operations within and across international boundaries. This most advanced phase of international engagement is typically referred to as **globalization**.

The logistics of internationalization involves four significant differences in comparison to national or even regional operations. First, the **distance** of typical order-to-delivery operations is significantly longer in international as contrasted to domestic business. Second, to accommodate the laws and regulations of all governing bodies, the required **documentation** of business transactions is significantly more complex. Third, international logistics operations must be designed to deal with significant **diversity** in work practices and local operating environment. Fourth, accommodation of cultural variations in how consumers **demand** products and services is essential for successful logistical operations.

Finally, 21st-century commerce is conducted within a constant threat of terrorism, which requires increased security. The intensity and severity of terrorist disruption involves both the shipment itself and the exposure to using the logistics infrastructure as a means to deliver explosive and chemical devices. The security aspects of global logistics are further discussed in Chapter 10. It is important to understand that successfully going supply chain global requires mastering the associated logistical challenges.

While logistics principles and the ideals of supply chain integration are essentially the same globally as they are domestically, the above characteristics make operating environments more complex and costly. Such expenditure is required to support internal market expansion and global commerce between both developed and emerging nations. Risk exposure related to capitalizing on international supply chain management and its logistical components requires integrated operating strategies and tactics.

Industry Disruptors

High-performance supply chain and logistics systems must be adaptive to changes in consumer requirements and technology. While these disruptors evolve over time, it is important to identify the current disruptors and how they will drive supply chain and logistics changes. While there are many types of disruptors that can influence supply chain and logistics strategic and operations decisions, the most common represent changes in customer requirements and technology capabilities. Recent research has identified the major consumer and technology disruptors that influence supply chain and logistics.[7] Examples of each are discussed below.

Consumer Requirements

The Gardner research identified five consumer changes that will be disrupting the supply chain: (1) "want it now" mentality, (2) personalization, (3) millennial preferences, (4) omni-channel shopping, and (5) aging consumer needs. Each is briefly discussed below.

The want it now mentality refers to the consumer's desire to have quick access to the desired products at their desired location. In many cases, this implies delivery in a day or less directly to the consumer's home or workplace. This influences supply chain strategy by requiring an increasing number of distribution facilities along with very flexible transportation.

Personalization refers to the increasing trend for consumers to request that the products they demand are customized. The customization may be in the forms of unique monograms or labels, made-to-order sizes, customized durables, or increasingly customized food and drink. The implication is that there are a larger number of products on store shelves and more complex flows from manufacturers to consumers.

Millennial preferences refers to the need for more variation in package sizes. While there have always been multiple package sizes available for many products, millennials desire more variation due to their lifestyle and living arrangements. They typically desire smaller and more sustainable packaging. The implication is that the supply chain is more complex due to increasing variation.

Omni-channel shopping refers to the consumer desire to purchase product from multiple different distribution channels such as retailers, manufacturers, wholesale clubs, or online. While there has been a significant movement toward more online purchasing, it is

[7] Gresham, Tom. "6 Technologies Guaranteed to Disrupt your Supply Chain." Inbound Logistics (July 2016), pp 138–144.

still very common for consumers to buy from brick-and-mortar stores when proximity or price are a major objective. The implication is that firms must manage product movement through multiple channels at the same time.

Aging consumers are also placing increasing demands on supply chain operations. The baby boomer generation represents a significant segment of the population that is demanding more customized products and services, particularly in terms of health care and delivery. The supply chain implication of these aging consumers is that this major segment is requiring more customization and responsiveness from firms desiring their business.

These increasing demands require that today's supply chain become more responsive, flexible, and customized. This results in a significant need for the traditional supply chain, which has been strongly focused on economies of scale, to become more adaptive and complex while still retaining the ability to minimize cost.

Technology Adoption

Research has identified six technology changes that will offer both opportunities and disruption to supply chain and logistics strategy and operations: (1) autonomous vehicles and the Internet of Things (IoT), (2) artificial intelligence, (3) "Uberization," (4) 3D printing, (5) big data, and (6) alternative fuels. Each is discussed below.

Autonomous vehicles offer the opportunity for driverless vehicles for long-haul trucking and delivery, such as by drones. The combination of infrastructure congestion and shortage of drivers make it more difficult to transport product, particularly in times where smaller, more-frequent deliveries are desired. The application of driverless trucks or platooning truck trains offer the opportunity to reduce the number of drivers per ton-mile of freight. The IoT offers opportunities throughout the supply chain to monitor production equipment, transportation equipment, demand, and inventory level without requiring labor time and expertise. In the case of both autonomous vehicles and IoT, the implication is that supply chains will be able to meet increasingly specialized demands with the increasing talent shortage.

Artificial intelligence (AI) is an information-based technology that facilitates the structuring of decision logic so that it can be automated and applied without consuming the time of a subject matter expert. In the supply chain context, AI applications could include forecasting, production scheduling and formulation, inventory management, equipment repair, and vehicle and truck routing. With the increasing complexity involving the interaction between supply chain technology and supply chain talent, AI facilitates the capture and extension of subject matter expertise.

Uberization refers to the application of an Uber-type taxi system for freight. Traditionally, freight has been hauled using private, contract, or common carriage, which means that the carrier provides transportation service on a structured basis in a number of ownership formats. In most cases, transportation formats attempt to consolidate small shipments as much as possible to achieve economies of scale. As in the passenger application, applying the Uber concept to freight allows for more customized delivery of smaller shipments. As an example, both brick-and-mortar retailers and online retailers are using Uber-type applications to provide very quick delivery of small packages. In the supply chain context, the Uber-type service may be provided by the same organizations providing passenger Uber or Lyft services, contract organizations that provide Uber-type services for freight, or even by employees of the retailer on their way home.

Three-dimensional (3D) printing is a technology that can be increasingly applied in supply chain to make customized products and components. A significant supply chain opportunity for 3D printing technology is to manage spare parts for all types of equipment. For example, the automotive companies are required to maintain a range of spare parts in distribution centers around the world so that the parts are both available and relatively close when needed by the customer. The result of such a supply chain strategy is significant inventory, which results in high inventory carrying cost and often obsolescence. The use of 3D printing technology can significantly reduce supply chain inventory as each part can be "printed" when it is needed.

Big data refers to the large amount of data that can be collected regarding supply chain activities. Some specific supply chain types of big data include customer orders, supplier orders, warranty data, shipment data, and manufacturing and handling equipment performance. The collection and analysis of the these data documenting these activities allows supply chain professionals to identify and understand relationships among the activities, the drivers of those activities, and the resulting cost. This insight allows supply chain professionals to better managed their resources.

Supply chains today typically employ petroleum-based fuels such as diesel, gasoline, jet fuel, or bunker fuel for ships. Alternative fuel technologies are being explored today to reduce operating cost and increase sustainable operations. Liquid and compressed natural gas (LNG and CNG) are being applied for truck transportation to increase mileage and reduce emissions. Similarly, battery-powered vehicles are also being tested. While these alternative fuels offer opportunities for more sustainable and less expensive fuels, the support infrastructure is limited, which means that these fuels may not be available where needed in the supply chain. While alternative fuels will offer significant opportunities for the future, it is likely that infrastructure development will take some time.

Conclusion

The combination of the increasing flexibility and responsiveness on the part of consumers places increasing demands on supply chain design and operations. While new technologies open up opportunities to meet these demands, there will still be significant disruption as the technical opportunities must be traded off with the capital investments involved in the existing infrastructure. Decisions regarding these trade-offs are a constant challenge for supply chain professionals.

Summary

The development of integrated management skill is critical to continued productivity improvement. Such integrative management must focus on quality improvement at both functional and process levels. In terms of functions, critical work must be performed to the highest degree of efficiency. Processes that create value occur both within individual firms and between firms linked together in collaborative supply chains. Each type of process must be continuously improved.

The idea that all or even most firms will link together to form highly collaborative end-to-end supply chain initiatives at any time in the foreseeable future is quite unlikely. The dynamics of a free competitive market system will serve to harness such an end state. However, initiatives aimed at cross-enterprise integration along the supply chain are increasingly occurring and, to the extent successfully implemented, offer new and exciting business models for gaining competitive advantage. Once achieved, such supply chain integration is hard to maintain and requires continuous redefinition. What works today may not work tomorrow. Conversely, what won't work today may work tomorrow.

Thus, supply chain collaborations must be viewed as highly dynamic. Such collaborations are attractive because they offer new horizons for achieving market share and operating efficiency. Supply chain opportunities are challenges that 21st-century logistics managers must explore and exploit. However, supply chain integration is a means to increased profitability and growth and not an end in itself.

From the perspective of integrated logistics management, supply chain strategies define the relevant operating framework. What must be logistically accomplished is directly linked to supply chain structure and strategy. When such structure and strategy are internationally positioned, logistics performance must embrace challenges related to globalization. In short, the supply chain strategy or lack of strategy and its related structure serve to shape the framework for logistical requirements. Chapter 3 presents logistics in greater detail.

Study Questions

1. Compare the concept of a modern supply chain with more traditional distribution channels. Be specific regarding similarities and differences.
2. What specific role does logistics play in supply chain operations?
3. Describe and illustrate an integrated service provider. How does the concept of integrated service provider differ from traditional service providers, such as for-hire transportation and warehousing?
4. Compare and contrast anticipatory and responsive business models. Why has responsiveness become popular in supply chain strategy and collaboration?
5. Discuss five non-traditional supply chain applications and describe the similarities and differences between traditional supply chain applications.
6. Describe how one of the consumer disruptors and one of the technology disruptors will impact supply chain design and strategy.

Challenge Questions

1. What are the operating challenges related to a brick-and-mortar retail toy store plan to establish 600 temporary or pop-up seasonal retail outlets? Be specific concerning the supply chain challenges leading into, during, and after the Christmas selling season.
2. Building on your knowledge of the industry, identify and discuss at least one more consumer or industry disruptor that will impact supply chain management.
3. Discuss how reverse logistics can create value.
4. Building on your insight regarding non-traditional supply chain applications, discuss where else supply chain principles could be applied.

CHAPTER 2

Supply Chain Information Technology

Chapter Outline

New advances in information technology have introduced many new opportunities for supply chain and logistics strategy and operations. Since 2000, the world of commerce has been irrevocably affected by computer miniaturization, the Internet, a range of inexpensive information transmission capabilities, and omni-channel supply chain operations. Information characterized by speed, accessibility, accuracy, relevancy, and simplified access are now the norm. The Internet is a common and economical means to complete business-to-business (B2B) and business-to-consumer (B2C) transactions. Internet browsers have become the default standard for exchanging transactions and data between supply chain partners. Three-dimensional (3D) printing has even made it possible for physical products to be transferred across the Internet. Global Internet capability and standardization also facilitates worldwide execution and tracking.

What began during the last decade of the 20th century and will continue to unfold well into the 21st century is what historians are increasingly characterizing as the dawning of the information or digital age. The reality of the digital age is the connectivity among collaborating business organizations, which will continue to drive supply chain management advancement. Managers are increasingly enhancing and integrating traditional marketing, manufacturing, purchasing, and logistics practices. In this new order, products and solutions can be developed to exact specifications and rapidly delivered to customers throughout the globe. Logistical systems exist that have the capability to delivery products/solutions at precise times. Customer order and delivery of product assortments can be performed in hours. The frequent occurrence of service failures that characterized the past are increasingly being replaced by a growing managerial commitment for zero defect or what is commonly called six-sigma performance. Perfect orders—delivering the desired assortment and quantity of products to the right location, on time, damage-free, and correctly invoiced—once the exception, are now becoming the expectation. Perhaps most important is the fact that such high-level performance is being achieved at lower total cost and with the commitment of fewer financial resources that was required in the past. All of this fundamental change in business enterprise structure and strategy is primarily being facilitated by information technology.

While many supply chain and logistics texts segment the discussion of information technology over multiple chapters so that the material is discussed in the chapter to which it applies, this text introduces a supply chain information technology framework so the reader can understand the role of information technology in supply chain design, strategy, and execution. This framework offers the big picture of supply chain information technology while later chapters provide more detail regarding the individual technology modules.

This chapter describes the supply chain information technology framework discussed above. Each framework component is discussed in detail in the following sections.

Information System Functionality

A major enabler of supply chain planning and execution is information technology. Supply chain technology systems initiate activities and track information regarding processes, facilitate information sharing both within the firm and between supply chain partners, and assist in management oversight and decision making. Comprehensive information systems are a combination of transaction, decision support, and communication components.

From its inception, logistics focused on product storage and flow through the supply chain. Information flow and accuracy were often overlooked because they were not viewed as being critical to customers. In addition, information transfer rates were limited to mail or manual processes. There are five reasons timely and accurate information has become more critical in supply chain design and operations. First, customers perceive information regarding order status, product availability, delivery tracking, and invoices as necessary dimensions of day-to-day business operations. Customers demand real-time information. Second, with the goal of managing total supply chain assets, managers realize that information can be used to reduce inventory and human resource requirements. In particular, requirements planning based on timely information can reduce inventory by minimizing demand uncertainty. Third, information increases flexibility with regard to how, when, and where resources may be utilized to achieve competitive advantage. Fourth, enhanced information transfer and exchange utilizing the Internet is facilitating collaboration and redefining supply chain relationships. Finally, with the increasing demand to remove uncertainty and variation from the supply chain, there a corresponding increase in demand to enhance inventory transparency and visibility. A common example of comprehensive information systems driving better supply chain utilization may be found in today's international shipping arena. It is common for a firm to redirect a container mid-transit based on real-time feedback from local markets. This change, enabled by information technology results in higher service levels and simultaneously improved asset utilization.

Supply chain information systems (SCISs) are the thread linking logistical activity into an integrated process. Integration builds on four levels of functionality: (1) transaction systems, (2) management control, (3) decision analysis, and (4) strategic planning. Figure 2.1 illustrates logistics activities and information required at each level. As the pyramid shape suggests, management control, decision analysis, and strategic planning enhancements require a strong transaction system foundation.

A **transaction system** is characterized by formalized rules, procedures, and standardized communications; a large volume of transactions; and an operational, day-to-day focus. The combination of structured processes and large transaction volume places a major emphasis

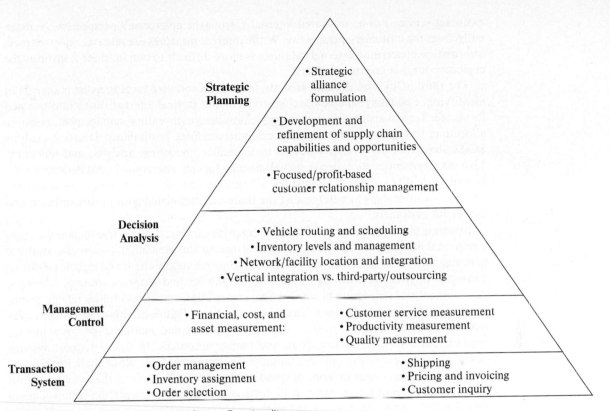

FIGURE 2.1   Supply Chain Information System Functionality

on information system efficiency. At the most basic level, transaction systems initiate and record individual logistics activities and their outcomes. Typical transaction functionality includes order entry, inventory assignment, order selection, shipping, pricing, invoicing, and customer inquiry. For example, customer order entry represents a customer request for products into the information system. Order entry transaction initiates a second transaction as inventory is assigned to the order. A third transaction is then generated to direct warehouse operations to select the order. A fourth transaction initiates order shipment to the customer. A final transaction creates the invoice and a corresponding account receivable. Throughout the process, the firm and customer expect real-time information regarding order status. Thus, the customer order performance cycle is completed through a series of information system transactions.

The second SCIS level, **management control**, focuses on performance measurement and reporting. Performance measurement is necessary to provide feedback regarding supply chain performance and resource utilization. Common performance dimensions include cost, customer service, productivity, quality, and asset management measures. As an example, specific performance measures include transportation and warehousing cost per hundredweight, inventory turnover, case fill rate, cases per labor hour, and customer service level.

While it is necessary that the SCIS report historical system performance, it is also necessary for the system to identify operational exceptions. Exception information is useful to highlight potential customer or operational problems. For example, a proactive SCIS should be capable of avoiding future inventory shortages based on forecast requirements and planned inventory. Exception reporting should also identify potential transportation, warehouse, or labor constraints. While some control measures, such as cost, are well defined, other measures, such as service and quality, may be less specific. For example, customer service can be measured internally, from the enterprise's perspective, or externally, from the customer's perspective. While internal measures are relatively easy to track, information concerning external measures is more difficult to obtain, since it involves the customer or other external partners.

The third SCIS level, **decision analysis**, focuses on software tools to assist managers in identifying, evaluating, and comparing strategic and tactical alternatives to improve performance. Typical analyses include supply chain design, inventory management, resource allocation, transportation routing, and customer segment profitability. Decision analysis SCISs should ideally include database maintenance, modeling, analysis, and reporting. Like management control, decision analysis may include operational considerations such as vehicle routing and warehouse planning. Decision analysis is also being used to manage customer relationships by determining the trade-offs associated with having satisfied and successful customers.

Strategic planning, the final SCIS level, organizes and synthesizes transaction data into a relational database that assists in strategy formation and evaluation. Essentially, strategic planning focuses on information to evaluate and refine supply chain and logistics strategy. Examples of strategic planning include the desirability and scope of strategic alliances, development and refinement of supply chain capabilities, and opportunities related to customer relationship management. The relative shape of Figure 2.2 illustrates SCIS development characteristics and justification. Development and maintenance costs include hardware, software, communications, and human resources. In the past, most systems development focused on improving transaction system efficiency. While these investments originally offered returns in terms of speed and lower operating costs, there are now fewer improvement opportunities. Most SCIS development and implementation is now focused on enhanced supply chain system integration and improved decision making.

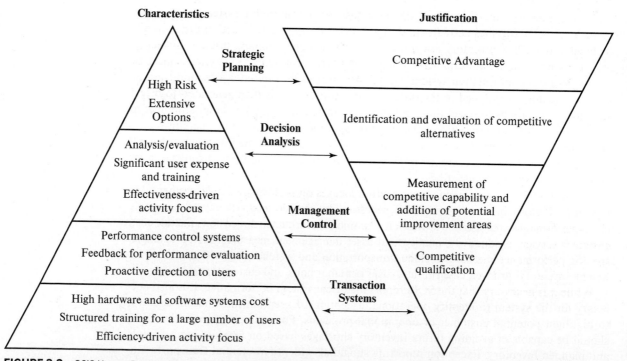

FIGURE 2.2 SCIS Usage, Decision Characteristics, and Justification

Supply Chain Information System Modules

A comprehensive SCIS initiates, monitors, assists in decision making, and reports on activities required for completion of supply chain operations and planning. The major system modules and their interfaces are: (1) **enterprise resource planning (ERP)**, (2) communication systems, (3) execution systems, and (4) planning systems. Figure 2.3 illustrates a more application-oriented perspective. This application perspective is used to discuss each module's specific characteristics and functionality.

The ERP systems in Figure 2.3 are the backbone of most firms' logistics information system. This backbone maintains current and historical data and processes to initiate and monitor performance. During the 1990s, many firms began to replace self-developed functional modules (called "legacy systems") with ERP systems designed as integrated transaction modules and processes with a common and consistent database. The database includes information storage capability for both operations (i.e., product and activity based) and financial (i.e., monetary based) transactions. ERP systems facilitate integrated operations and reporting to initiate, monitor, and track critical activities such as order fulfillment and replenishment. ERP systems also incorporate an integrated corporatewide database, sometimes referred to as a data warehouse, along with appropriate transactions to facilitate logistics and supply chain planning and operations. Supply chain transactions facilitated by ERP systems include order entry and management, inventory assignment, and transportation. Beyond these supply chain applications, ERP systems typically include financial, accounting, and human resource capability. Data mining, knowledge management, and other enterprise integration applications operate using the ERP backbone to develop and organize insight regarding customers, products, and operations.

Enterprise Integration and Administration

Enterprise integration and administration are ERP modules that are not specifically supply chain applications. However, supply chain operations do have substantial interaction with these ERP components. Figure 2.4 illustrates the major enterprise integration and administration components. They are (1) general administration, (2) accounts receivable and payable, (3) financial inventory accounting, (4) general ledger, and (5) human resources.

General administration includes the various transactions to structure the firm and define transaction process flows. Supply chain operations use these modules to define

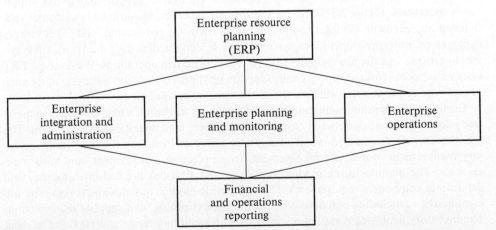

FIGURE 2.3

Application-Oriented SCIS Framework

FIGURE 2.4

Enterprise Integration
and Administration
Components

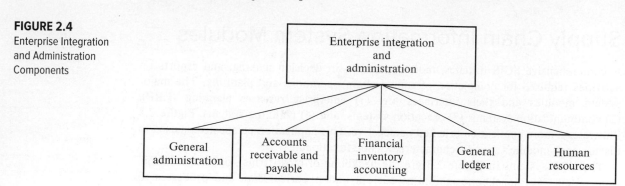

reporting, functional, and organizational structures as well as to define process flows such as customer and replenishment order fulfillment. Accounts receivable and payable represent the functions for invoice collection from customers and invoice payment to suppliers. While these are typically acknowledged as accounting functions, there is a significant interaction with supply chain operations since accounts payable is influenced by materials and services acquisition and accounts receivable is influenced by delivery and invoicing of complete orders. Financial inventory accounting relates to the tracking of value-added processes through the supply chain to facilitate financial and tax reporting. The timing and location of supply chain value-added processes (e.g., production, inventory control, and packaging) can have a significant influence regarding what can be reported to the treasury (for taxation purposes) and the financial markets (for stock valuation purposes). General ledger relates to the structure of the detailed accounts for monitoring and reporting revenues and accounts. Since supply chain involves substantial interaction with firm and external processes, the structure of the general ledger accounts significantly influences the supply chain's ability to measure, monitor, and report cost related to delivering product or serving customers. The human resource module of the ERP systems tracks personnel profiles and their activity levels. Since most firms have a large number of individuals involved in supply chain operations (e.g., manufacturing, logistics, and purchasing) and often in different global environments, the ability to track pay scales and activity levels is critical to make effective supply chain personnel decisions.

Enterprise Supply Chain Operations

Enterprise operations include the SCIS modules required to support day-to-day supply chain operations. Figure 2.5 illustrates the specific modules, including: (1) customer relationship management, (2) logistics, (3) manufacturing, (4) purchasing, and (5) inventory deployment. Enterprise operations systems work in conjunction with the firm's ERP system to provide specific functionality to support supply chain operations. While some ERP systems support required supply chain functionality, others lack some functionality such as that required to support warehouse and transportation operations.

Customer relationship management (CRM) systems, are applications designed to facilitate information sharing between customers, sales force, and operations management. The logistics module directs and monitors logistics activities including finished goods inventory management, warehouse management, transportation management, and yard management. The manufacturing module schedules and allocates production resources and determines component requirements. The purchasing module initiates and tracks procurement activities including purchase order initiation, expediting, and supplier management. The inventory deployment system module schedules and monitors material flows to meet

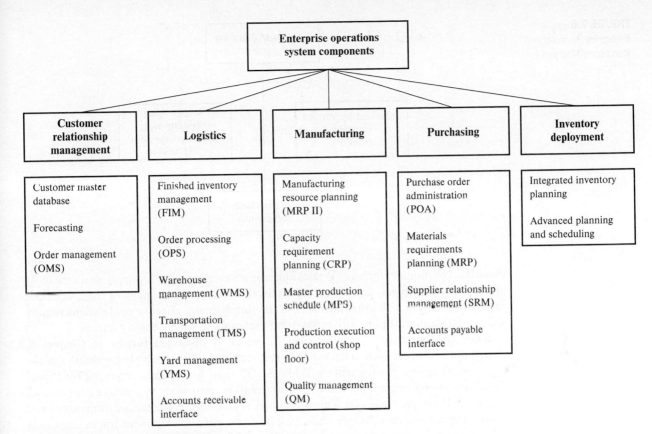

FIGURE 2.5   Enterprise Operations Modules

production and deployment requirements. Typical operational applications included in each module are listed. These applications are discussed throughout the text in conjunction with operational topics.

The traditional information technology delivery method has been for firms to operate and maintain private computer capabilities. Large mainframe computer capacity is essential to operate the varied information technology systems necessary to guide supply chain operations. This commitment to internal computing has rapidly changed in the 21st century. Increasingly firms are purchasing supply chain information technology support in the form of externally hosted systems. These include cloud-based hardware and software. A wide variety of systems, such as **warehouse management (WMS)**, **transportation management (TMS)**, and **yard management (YMS)**, are available from technology application firms that specialize in providing and maintaining state-of-the-art performance systems. These applications are discussed briefly later in the chapter. Typically referred to as **Software as a Service (SaaS)**, these application-specific software packages can be purchased for either internal use or on a hosted basis. When hosted by specialized service firms that provide the application using the capabilities of large computer resources, the application is referred to as **cloud computing**.

Enterprise Planning and Monitoring

Enterprise planning and monitoring are the processes and technologies that facilitate exchange of planning and coordinating information both within the firm and between supply chain partners. Figure 2.6 illustrates the major enterprise planning and monitoring

FIGURE 2.6
Enterprise Planning and
Monitoring Modules

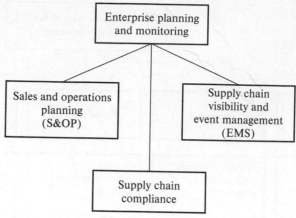

modules. The modules include (1) sales and operations planning, (2) supply chain visibility and event management, and (3) supply chain compliance. Since many of these activities involve interaction with other members of the supply chain, effective applications require substantial standardization with other firm functions and supply chain partners.

Sales and operations planning (S&OP), which is discussed further in Chapter 6, describes the process used to balance demand requirements and supply capabilities of the firm and its supply chain partners. While S&OP itself is a process requiring functional coordination and integration, it requires information technology to evaluate the demand, supply, and resource trade-offs. This technology is generally characterized as planning and scheduling applications. Supply chain visibility and event management tracks shipments while they are in-transit and are increasingly capable of proactively suggesting changes in supply chain flows to minimize the potential of manufacturing shutdowns or service failures. Supply chain compliance systems monitor component and product flow information to make sure they comply with government and regulatory requirements for label, taxation, and security restrictions.

Communication Technology

Communication technology is the hardware and technical software that facilitates information exchange between the systems and physical infrastructure within the firm and between supply chain partners. The real-time information interchange between functions and supply chain partners facilitate coordination of inbound material, production, inventory, customer orders, and customer shipment. From a supply chain perspective, the availability of common and consistent requirements, activity, and performance information between supply chain partners enhances operational effectiveness, efficiency, relevancy, and sustainability.

Consumer Connectivity

The rapid development and deployment of the Internet has added a new dimension to the interface between firms and their customers. Both retailers and manufacturers are increasingly in direct Internet contact with the end consumers. This connectivity has developed along two main dimensions of communication—ordering and after-sale connectivity. Each has supply chain implications.

In terms of ordering, the Internet offers a way for consumers to facilitate and maintain direct contact with retailers and manufacturers. In essence, this form of two-way connectivity is an expansion of traditional mail ordering. Empowered with the speed and flexibility of Internet connectivity, the interactive communications during ordering, determination of inventory status, processing time and location, and product delivery detail can be more diverse and comprehensive. For example, complete order-to-delivery tracking is a common feature. With the ease and speed of Internet connectivity, information concerning the total order to home delivery or retail pickup can be monitored.

With respect to product returns, or what is commonly called **reverse logistics**, the Internet offers a fast and accurate way to facilitate and track the product repair or replacement process. In addition, the existence of direct connectivity between the end consumer and the product manufacturer facilitates the rapid resolution of customer service issues related to product use and warranty.

In addition to information technology, the rapid emergence of supply chain relationships is being driven by four related forces: (1) integrated management and supply chain processes, (2) responsiveness, (3) financial sophistication, and (4) globalization. These forces will continue to drive supply chain structure and strategy initiatives across most industries for the foreseeable future. A brief discussion of each supply chain driver provides a foundation for understanding the challenges supply chain management places on exacting logistical performance.

Blockchain

Blockchain is a communications technology that facilitates secure communication between financial and supply chain institutions. While the traditional mode for information between supply chain partners has been electronic data interchange (EDI), there has been increased concern regarding data accuracy, integrity, and security as information is exchanged between supply chain partners. This has been particularly true for situations involving sources of materials, tracking of production facilities, tracking of products through the distribution system, and global tracking.

While there are numerous industries that are challenged by counterfeiting, raw material falsification, and theft for resale, the firms that face the most significant challenges are those involved in high-value branded goods, repair parts for durable items, health care supplies, alcohol, and pharmaceuticals. In all cases, the combination of high value and the relative ease of counterfeiting in the eye of the consumer provides many opportunities for sale through gray market manufacturers and distributors. Since the packaging and the product often appear similar to the real product, counterfeiters sell the fake product at a premium price, which cheats both the consumer and the owner of the premium product brand.

The pharmaceutical industry is one of those most affected by counterfeiting. The combination of high value, relative ease of falsifying raw material, and use of gray market manufacturers and distributers makes counterfeiting very lucrative for the counterfeiters and very dangerous for consumers. The result is the passage of the Drug Supply Chain Security Act (DSCSA) in the United States and the passage of similar acts in many countries around the world. DSCSA requires that raw materials, finished goods, and packaging be tracked from the initiation of the manufacturing process through to the retailer or institution that transfers the product to the patient.

Blockchain is a distributed database that maintains digital contents regarding transactions or events that makes them tamper-resistant. While many institutions such as suppliers, manufacturers, distributers, retailers, and logistics service providers may access, inspect, or add to the data, they can't change or delete it. The original information is maintained in a permanent and public information trail, or chain of transactions.

Think of it like this: If the entire blockchain were the history of customer or replenishment orders, an individual order would be a single "block" in the chain. Unlike most supply chains, however, there is no single organization (supplier, manufacturer distributor, retailer, or logistics service provider) that controls these transactions. Once the "block" is loaded into the blockchain, it cannot be changed by any party, making it much easier and safer for the supply chain to monitor and track transactions across the Internet.

Blockchain technology allows firms to more securely and transparently track all product movement from manufacture to sale. The results are reduced time delays, added costs, and human error. There are an increasing number of supply chains that are using blockchain technology and it will likely become almost universal for products that are perishable or have expiration dates.

Specifically, blockchain technology can improve supply chain operations by:[1]

- Recording the quantity and transfer of assets—pallets, trailers, containers, etc.—as they move between supply chain nodes.
- Track purchase orders, change orders, receipts, shipment notification, or other trade-related documents.
- Assign or verify certifications or certain properties of physical products.
- Link physical goods to serial number, bar codes, and digital tags like RFID.
- Share information about the manufacturing process, assembly, delivery, and maintenance of products with suppliers and vendors.

Blockchain provides numerous benefits for supply chain operations, including:

- Enhanced transparency. Documenting a product's journey across the supply chain reveals its true origin and touchpoints, which increases trust and helps eliminate the biases found in today's opaque supply chains. Manufacturers making components can also reduce recalls by sharing logs with the assembly manufacturers and regulators.
- Greater scalability. Virtually any number of participants, accessing from any number of touchpoints, is possible.
- Better security. A shared, indelible ledger with codified rules could potentially eliminate the audits required by internal systems and processes.
- Increased innovation. Opportunities abound to create new, specialized uses for the technology resulting from the decentralized architecture.

Logistics Operations Modules

Key elements of the logistics operations system components include (1) a transportation management system (TMS), (2) a warehouse management system (WMS), and (3) a yard management system (YMS). While these systems are discussed in more detail in the relevant functional chapters (Chapter 8 for TMS and Chapter 9 for WMS and YMS), the detail for each application is discussed briefly here to offer a perspective regarding how these components fit into the overall supply chain information system.

The TMS manages the transactions and resources related to the movement, analysis, and performance measurement of goods through the supply chain. The TMS system may be resident on the firm's computers but in most cases today, TMS services are accessible through an external service provider or cloud services to achieve economies of scale by

[1] Cottrill, Ken. "The Benefits of Blockchain: Fact or Wishful Thinking." Supply Chain Management Review (January/February 2018). pp 20–25.

sharing the applications across multiple users. The typical functionality offered by a TMS system includes (1) building loads from multiple orders, (2) identifying possible carriers, (3) maintaining database of shipment rates, (4) determining shipment mode and route, (5) providing documentation to select product to ship and stage it in the warehouse, (6) developing documentation for shipment, (7) tracking the order while it is in-transit between facilities, and (8) transferring shipment information to accounts receivable. The TMS application is discussed in more detail in Chapter 8.

The WMS manages and, in many cases, initiates the transactions that receive, store, retrieve, and ship product from the warehouse. The WMS may drive manual transactions or a sophisticated automated system. Unlike a TMS, which is often in a cloud environment that facilitates the sharing of transportation information between facilities and firms, the WMS is often decentralized with applications in each facility so that a failure in the communication between facilities will not force the warehouse to shut down. The typical functionality offered by a WMS system includes (1) shipment receipt; (2) product storage or put-away; (3) product retrieval from the storage location; (4) product staging for shipment; and (5) initiation of value-added activities such as packaging, labeling, or other forms of customization. The WMS application is discussed in more detail in Chapter 9.

The YMS manages the truck trailer or rail cars in the firm's yard or storage area. A major distribution center may have hundreds or even thousands of trucks in the yard waiting to be loaded or unloaded. In concept, the locations in the yard are similar to the pallet locations in the warehouse. When a distribution center needs an empty trailer to load for a shipment, the YMS directs the yard driver to a location with an empty trailer. In the case when the distribution center needs to access product that is in a trailer in the yard, the YMS indicates to the yard driver where the specific trailer is located and instructs the driver to bring the trailer for unloading. In essence, the YMS maintains the inventory of empty and full trailers in the yard and initiates transactions to move the trailers between the yard and the distribution center. The YMS application is discussed in more detail in Chapter 9.

Summary

Supply chain information systems provide the backbone and nervous system for the modern supply chain. The enterprise resource planning system is the backbone as it includes the data warehouse and the capabilities to complete supply chain transactions such as order entry, inventory receipts, and shipping. Key requirements for the ERP system are data integrity, consistency, and transparency. The requirements for the transaction system are security, flexibility, and speed. While the ERP also provides accounting and human resources support, these are not technically a component of the supply chain information system. The supply chain operations contain the transaction capabilities to support customer relationship management, logistics, manufacturing, purchasing, and inventory deployment.

The enterprise planning and monitoring system provides the ability to complete manufacturing and inventory planning, which often requires trading off forecast accuracy, production cost, and inventory carrying cost. The monitoring system provides the ability to track inventory as it moves through the supply chain and offers visibility to events (weather, congestion, or other types of shipment delays) that may affect supply chain performance. Communication and blockchain capabilities facilitate the exchange and recording of order and inventory information across the entire supply chain.

Study Questions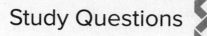

1. Discuss how supply chain information systems can provide a competitive advantage for the firm.
2. Compare and contrast supply chain transaction, management, decision analysis, and strategic planning systems.
3. Describe the benefits provided by blockchain technology.
4. Discuss the role of TMS, WMS, and YMS in supply chain execution.
5. Discuss the role of supply chain event management systems in supply chain competitiveness.

Challenge Questions

1. Discuss how blockchain and tracking systems provide value to a firm's customers.
2. How do the concepts of SaaS and cloud computing differ from the services offered by traditional data processing service centers?
3. Compare and contrast a firm having its own information system, cloud computing, and SaaS.

CHAPTER 3

Logistics

Chapter Outline

No other area of business operations involves the complexity or spans the geography of logistics. Around the globe, 24 hours of every day, 7 days a week, 52 weeks a year, logistics is concerned with getting the right products to the right place at the right time. It is difficult to visualize accomplishing any marketing, manufacturing, or global commerce without logistics. Even though UPS made logistics globally famous to the consumer with their "We Love

Logistics" ad campaign in 2010, most consumers in highly developed insdustrial nations don't truly understand logistics and take a high level of logistical competency for granted. When they purchase goods—at a retail store, over the telephone, or via the Internet—they expect product delivery will be performed as promised. In fact, their expectation is for timely, error-free logistics every time they order, even during the busiest periods. They have little or no tolerance for failure to perform. In fact, over the past decade, the consumer expectation has continued to increase as e-commerce, direct to consumer shipping has become a staple of modern business.

Although logistics has been performed since the beginning of civilization, implementing 21st-century best practices is one of the most exciting and challenging operational areas of supply chain management. Because logistics is both old and new, we choose to characterize the rapid change taking place in best practice as a **renaissance**.

Logistics involves the management of order processing, inventory, transportation, and the combination of warehousing, materials handling, and packaging, all integrated throughout a network of facilities. Supported by robust IT infrastructure, the goal of logistics is to support procurement, manufacturing, and customer accommodation supply chain operational requirements. Within a firm, the challenge is to coordinate functional competency into an integrated supply chain focused on servicing customers. In the broader supply chain context, operational synchronization is essential with customers as well as material and service suppliers to link internal and external operations as one integrated process.

Logistics management is the process and activities that create value focused on the design and administration of a system to control the timing and geographical positioning of raw materials, work-in-process, and finished inventories at the lowest total cost. Logistics is a combination of a firm's order management, inventory, transportation, and warehousing, as integrated throughout a facility network. Integrated logistics services link and synchronize the overall supply chain as a continuous process and are essential to achieve the desired outcome of a given supply chain's value proposition. To achieve lowest total cost means that financial and human assets committed to logistics must be held to an absolute minimum. It is also necessary to hold operational expenditures as low as possible while meeting customer service goals. The combinations of resources, skills, and systems required to achieve superior logistics are challenging to integrate, but once achieved, such integrated competency is difficult for competitors to replicate.

This chapter focuses on the logistics of integrated supply chain management. First, cost and service are emphasized. Next, the logistics value proposition is developed. Then traditional business functions that combine to create the logistical process are reviewed. Next, the objectives of integrated logistics are reviewed. Finally, the importance of logistical synchronization to supply chain integration is highlighted in terms of performance cycle structure and dynamics.

The Logistics of Business Is Big and Important

It is through the logistical process that materials flow into the manufacturing capacity of the nation and finished products are distributed to consumers. The recent growth in global commerce has expanded the size and complexity of logistics operations.

Logistics adds value to the supply chain process when inventory is strategically positioned to achieve sales. Creating logistics value is costly. Although it is difficult to measure, most experts agree that the annual expenditure to perform U.S. business logistics costs (USBLC) in 2016 was approximately 7.5 percent of the $18.57 trillion gross domestic product (GDP), or $1.39 trillion USD.[1] Expenditure for transportation in 2016 was $895 billion,

---

[1] A. T. Kearney, "CSCMP's Annual State of Logistics Report," Council of Supply Chain Management Professionals and Penske Logistics, Oakbrook, Illinois, 2017.

Metric	2007	2008	2009	2010	2011	2012	2013	2014	2015	2016
Nominal GDP ($ billion)	14,478	14,719	14,419	14,964	15,518	16,155	16,692	17,393	18,037	18,566
Total business inventory ($ billion)	2,047	2,195	1,933	2,032	2,271	2,344	2,413	2,514	2,470	2,493
Inventory carrying rate (%)	21	18	19	18	18	17	18	16	17	16
Transportation costs ($ billion)	749	774	623	682	749	786	810	879	901	895
Inventory carrying costs (ICC) ($ billion)	421	397	372	375	400	409	428	407	423	410
Other costs ($ billion)	73	74	68	70	74	79	83	87	90	88
Total USBLC ($ billion)	1,243	1,245	1,063	1,127	1,224	1,274	1,321	1,373	1,414	1,393
Total USBLC (as % of GDP)	8.6	8.5	7.4	7.5	7.9	7.9	7.9	7.9	7.8	7.5
Total business inventory (as % of GDP)	14.1	14.9	13.4	13.6	14.6	14.5	14.5	14.5	13.7	13.4
Transportation (as % of GDP)	5.2	5.3	4.3	4.6	4.8	4.9	4.9	5.1	5.0	4.8

TABLE 3.1   U.S. Business Logistics Costs 2007–2016 in One-Year Intervals

Source: A.T. Kearney analysis.

which represents 64.3 percent of total logistics costs and 4.8 percent of GDP. As detailed in Table 3.1, the logistics of business over the past several years and decades has truly been big business!

Despite the sheer size of logistics expenditure, the excitement about logistics is not limited to cost containment or reduction. The excitement generates from understanding how select firms use logistical competency to help achieve competitive advantage. Firms having world-class logistical competency enjoy competitive advantage as a result of providing their most important customers superior service. Leading performers typically utilize information technology capable of monitoring global logistical activity on a real-time basis. Such technology identifies potential operational breakdowns and facilitates corrective action prior to service failure. In situations where timely corrective action is not possible, customers can be provided advance notification of developing problems, thereby eliminating the surprise of an unavoidable service failure. In many situations, working in collaboration with customers and suppliers, corrective action can be taken to prevent operational shutdowns or costly customer service failures. By performing above industry average with respect to inventory availability, speed, consistency of delivery, and operational efficiencies, logistically sophisticated firms are ideal supply chain partners.

The Logistical Value Proposition

Thus far it has been established that logistics should be managed as an integrated effort to achieve customer satisfaction at the lowest total cost. Logistics performed in this manner creates **value**. In this section, the elements of the logistical value proposition—service and cost minimization—are discussed in greater detail.

Service Benefits

Almost any level of logistical service can be achieved if a firm is willing to commit the required resources. In today's operating environment, the limiting factor is economics, not technology. For example, a dedicated inventory can be maintained in close geographical proximity to a major customer. A fleet of trucks can be held in a constant state of delivery readiness. To facilitate order processing, dedicated communications can be maintained on a real-time basis between a customer and a supplier's logistical operation. Given this high state of logistical readiness, a product or component could be delivered within minutes of identifying a customer requirement.

The key strategic issue is how to outperform competitors in a cost-effective manner. If a specific material is not available when required for manufacturing, it may force a plant shutdown resulting in significant cost, potential lost sales, and even the loss of a major customer's business. The profit impact of such failures can be significant. In contrast, the profit impact of an unexpected one- or two-day delay in delivering products to replenish warehouse inventory could be minimal or even insignificant in terms of impact on overall operational performance. In most situations, the cost/benefit impact of logistical failure is directly related to the importance of service to the end customer. *The more significant the service failure impact upon a customer's business, the greater the priority placed on error-free logistical performance.*

Logistical performance is measured in terms of inventory availability, operational performance, and service reliability. The term **logistics service** describes the level of service a firm provides all established customers.

Availability is the probability of having inventory to consistently meet customer material or product requirements. The traditional paradigm has been the greater the desired availability, the larger the required inventory and associated cost. Information technology that facilitates system flexibility is providing new ways to achieve high availability for customers without correspondingly high capital investment in inventory. Information that facilitates flexibility with respect to inventory availability is critical to achieving high-level logistics performance.

Operational performance deals with the time required to deliver a customer's order. Operational performance involves delivery **speed** and **consistency**. Naturally, most customers want fast delivery. However, fast delivery is of limited value if inconsistent from one order to the next. A customer gains little benefit when a supplier promises next-day delivery but frequently delivers late. Firms typically focus on delivery consistency first and then seek to improve delivery speed. Other aspects of operational performance are also important. A firm's operational performance can also be viewed in terms of its **flexibility** to accommodate unusual and unexpected customer requests. Another aspect of operational performance is frequency of malfunction and, when such malfunction occurs, the typical recovery time. Few firms can perform perfectly all the time. It is important to estimate the likelihood of something going wrong. **Malfunction** is concerned with the probability of logistical performance failure, such as damaged products, incorrect assortment, or inaccurate documentation. When such malfunction occurs, a firm's logistical competency can be measured in terms of **recovery time**. Operational performance is concerned with how a firm handles all aspects of customer requirements, including service failure, on a day-in and day-out basis.

Service reliability involves the **quality** attributes of logistics. The key to quality is accurate measurement of availability and operational performance. Only through comprehensive and consistant performance measurement is it possible to determine if overall logistical operations are achieving desired service goals. To achieve service reliability, it is essential to identify and implement inventory availability and operational performance measurement. For logistics performance to continuously meet customer expectations, it is essential that management be committed to continuous improvement. Logistical quality does not come easy; it's the product of careful planning supported by employee training, operational dedication, comprehensive measurement, and continuous improvement. To improve service performance, goals need to be established on a selective basis. Some products are more critical than others because of their importance to the customer and their relative profit contribution.

The level of logistical service should be realistic in terms of customer expectations and requirement. In most cases, firms confront situations where customers have significantly different service needs and purchase potential. In addition, as outlined in Chapter 1, different supply chain applications such as those of a bulk material supply chain require different processes and specific logistics solutions than those of a humanitarian supply chain, for example. (See Table 1.2.) In general, firms tend to be overly optimistic when committing to basic customer service performance. Inability to consistently meet an unrealistically high basic service target might result in more operating and customer relationship problems than if less ambitious goals had been attempted from the outset. Unrealistic service commitments to all customers can also dilute a firm's capability to satisfy special requirements of high-potential customers.

Cost Minimization

The focus on logistics cost can be traced to relatively recent developments in total cost theory and practice. In 1956, a classic monograph describing potential airfreight economics provided a new perspective concerning logistical total cost.[2] In an effort to explain conditions under which high-cost air transport could be justified, Lewis, Culliton, and Steele conceptualized the **Total Cost Logistics Model**. Total cost was positioned to include all expenditures necessary to perform logistical requirements. The authors illustrated an electronic parts distribution strategy wherein the high variable cost of direct factory-to-customer air transport was more than offset by reductions in inventory and field warehouse costs. They concluded that the least total cost solution to provide the desired customer service was to centralize inventory in one warehouse and make deliveries using air transportation.

This concept of total cost had not previously been applied to logistics operations. Because of the economic climate of the times and the radical departure to traditional practice, the total cost proposition generated a great deal of debate. The prevailing managerial practice, reinforced by accounting and financial control, was to focus attention on achieving the lowest possible cost for each individual aspect of logistics with little or no attention to integrated total cost trade-offs. Managers had traditionally focused on minimizing functional cost, such as transportation, believing that such effort would achieve the lowest combined costs. Understanding total cost opened the door to examining how functional costs interrelate and impact each other. Such impacts are classified as **cost-to-cost trade-offs**. Subsequent refinements provided a more comprehensive understanding of logistical cost components and identified the critical need for developing total cost analysis and **activity-based costing** capabilities. However, the implementation of effective logistical process costing remains a 21st-century challenge. Many long-standing practices of accounting continue to serve as barriers to fully implementing total cost logistical solutions.

[2] Howard T. Lewis, James W. Culliton, and Jack D. Steele, *The Role of Air Freight in Physical Distribution* (Boston: Harvard University Press, 1956).

Logistics Value Generation

The key to achieving logistical leadership is to master the art of matching operating competency and commitment to key customer expectations and requirements. This customer commitment, in an exacting cost framework, is the **logistics value proposition**. It is a unique commitment of a firm to an individual or selected customer groups.

The typical enterprise seeks to develop and implement an overall logistical competency that satisfies customer expectations at a realistic total cost expenditure. Very seldom will either the lowest total cost or the highest attainable customer service constitute the appropriate logistics strategy. Likewise, the desired combination will be different based on the supply chain application and different for unique customers. A well-designed logistics effort must provide high customer impact while controlling operational variance and minimizing inventory commitment. Most of all, it must be relevant to the customer. Remember the EERS model from Chapter 1!

Significant advances have been made in the development of tools to aid management in the measurement of **cost/service trade-offs**. Formulation of a sound strategy requires a capability to estimate operating cost necessary to achieve alternative service levels.

Leading firms realize that a well-designed logistical system can help achieve competitive advantage. In fact, as a general rule, firms that obtain a strategic advantage based on logistical competency establish the standard of performance for their industry. Amazon, in recent years, is the best example of a firm using logistics to create a competitive advantage with its famous Prime service.

The Work of Logistics

In the context of supply chain management, logistics exists to move and position inventory to achieve desired time, place, and possession benefits at the lowest total cost. Inventory has limited value until it is positioned at the right time and at the right location to support ownership transfer or value-added creation. If a firm does not consistently satisfy time and location requirements, it has nothing to sell. For a supply chain to realize the maximum strategic benefit from logistics, the full range of functional work must be integrated. Decisions in one functional area will impact cost of all others. It is this interrelation of functions that challenges the successful implementation of integrated logistical management. Figure 3.1 provides a visual representation of the interrelated nature of the five areas of

FIGURE 3.1
Integrated Logistics

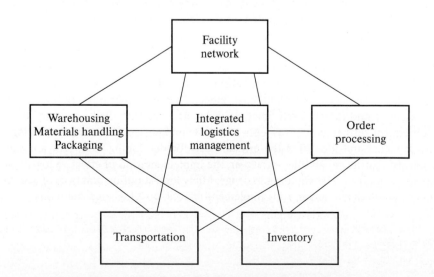

logical work: (1) order processing; (2) inventory; (3) transportation; (4) warehousing, materials handling, and packaging; and (5) facility network. Integrated work related to these functional areas creates the capabilities needed to achieve logistical value.

Order Processing

The importance of accurate information to achieving superior logistical performance has historically been underappreciated. While many aspects of information are critical to logistics operations, the processing of orders is of primary importance. Failure to fully comprehend this importance resulted from not fully understanding how distortion and operational failures in order processing impact logistical operations.[3]

The benefit of fast information exchange is directly related to balancing work. It makes little sense for a firm to accumulate orders at a local sales office for a week, mail them to a regional office, process the orders in a batch, assign them to a distribution warehouse, and then ship them via air to achieve fast delivery. In contrast, Internet transmission of orders direct from the customer, combined with slower, less costly transportation, may achieve even faster and more consistant delivery service at a lower total cost. The key objective is to balance components of the logistics system to achieve the desired service level at the lowest total cost.

Forecasting and communication of customer requirements are the two areas of logistical work driven by information. The relative importance of each facet of operational information is directly related to the degree to which a supply chain is positioned to function on a responsive or anticipatory basis. This balance between responsiveness and anticipatory driven operations, discussed in Chapter 1, constitutes the basic paradigm shift taking place in 21st-century supply chain design. The more responsive the supply chain design, the greater the importance is of accurate and timely information regarding customer purchase behavior.

In most supply chains, customer requirements are transmitted in the form of orders. The processing of these orders involves all aspects of managing customer requirements, including initial order receipt, delivery, invoicing, and collection. The logistics capabilities of a firm can only be as good as its order processing competency.

Inventory

The inventory requirements of a firm are directly linked to the facility network design and the desired level of customer service. Theoretically, a firm could stock every item sold in every facility. Few business operations can afford this strategy because the cost is prohibitive. The objective of an inventory strategy is to achieve desired customer service levels, common referred to as "fill rates" with the minimum inventory commitment. Additional or excessive inventory may compensate for deficiencies in the design of the logistics system but will ultimately result in a higher than necessary total system cost.

Logistics systems should be designed to achieve customer service goals while maintaining the lowest possible financial investment in inventory, the goal is to achieve maximum inventory turnover. A sound inventory strategy considers five aspects of selective deployment:

1. *Core customer segmentation:* Every firm that sells to a variety of customers confronts uneven demand. Some customers are highly profitable or have outstanding demand growth potential; others do not. The profitability of a given customer's business depends on the products purchased, the volume, the accuracy of the forecast, and all supplemental value-added services or activities required to develop and maintain an ongoing relationship.

[3] Benson P. Shapiro, V. Kasturi Rangan, and John J. Sviokla, "Staple Yourself to an Order," *Harvard Business Review,* July–August 1992, pp. 113–121.

Because highly profitable customers should constitute the core market segment of every enterprise, inventory strategies must focus on them. The key to an effective system rests in the discipline to realize all customers are "not created equally" and to prioritize and support core customers.

2. *Product profitability:* Most firms experience a substantial variance in the volume and profitability across product lines. It's not uncommon for a firm to find that less than 20 percent of all available products account for more than 80 percent of total demand and/or profit. While the so called **80/20 rule**, or **Pareto principle**, is common in business, management must attempt to avoid this conundrum by implementing inventory strategies based on product profitability or other classifications. A realistic assessment of the incremental value added by stocking low-profit or low-volume products is essential to avoid excessive inventory. A firm wants to offer high availability (fill rates) and consistent delivery (lead time) for its most profitable products. In some instances, high levels of service on less profitable or lower volume products may be necessary to round out a product line offering and/or to meet a customer need. The trap to avoid is high service performance, in excess of what is truly required of less profitable items typically purchased by fringe or noncore customers. In conclusion, product line profitability analysis is essential in developing an effective inventory stocking strategy.

3. *Transportation integration:* The inventory stocking strategy at a given facility has a direct impact on the efficiency of transportation. Most transportation rates benefit from economy of scale: the larger the shipment, the lower the effective transportation rate per unit. Therefore, it may be a sound strategy to stock a sufficient assortment and/or volume of products at a given facility to achieve consolidated shipments. The cost savings achieved in transportation may more than offset the incremental inventory carrying cost.

4. *Time-based performance:* Also known as transportation lead time, a firms' degree of commitment to deliver products rapidly to meet a customer's requirement is a major competitive factor. Traditionally, whether replenishing a distribution center, or restocking a retail shelf, the shorter and more consistent the delivery time, the less safety stock a customer must maintain to meet desired service levels. The alternative to holding safety stock is to receive exact and timely inventory replenishment. While such time-based programs reduce customer inventory to an absolute minimum, the savings must be balanced against other supply chain costs incurred as a result of the time-sensitive logistical process.

5. *Competitor performance:* Finally, inventory strategies cannot be created in a competitive vacuum. A firm is typically more desirable to partner with if it can promise and perform more rapid and consistent delivery than competitors. Therefore, when evaluating competitive pressure, a firm may choose to position inventory in specific locations or use an expedited transportation service to gain a competitive advantage even if such commitments increase total cost.

Material and component inventories exist in a logistical system for different reasons than finished products. Each type of inventory and the level of commitment must be viewed from a total cost perspective. Chapter 7 will take a deeper look at the types of inventory and different strategies that help further system performance such as manufacturing and geographic postponement among others. Understanding the different components is fundamental to integrated logistics.

Transportation

Transportation is the operational area of logistics that geographically moves and positions inventory. Because of its fundamental importance and visible cost, transportation has traditionally received considerable managerial attention. Almost all enterprises, big and small, have managers responsible for transportation.

Transportation requirements can be satisfied in three basic ways. First, a private fleet of equipment owned by the firm may be operated. Second, contracts may be arranged with dedicated transportation specialists. Third, a firm may engage the services of a wide variety of carriers that provide different transportation services as needed on a per shipment basis. From the logistical system viewpoint, three factors are fundamental to transportation performance: (1) cost, (2) speed, and (3) consistency.

The **cost of transport** is the payment for shipment between two geographical locations and the expenses related to maintaining in-transit inventory. Logistical systems should utilize transportation that minimizes **total system cost**. This may mean that the least expensive method of transportation may not result in the lowest total cost of logistics.

Speed of transportation is the time required to complete a specific movement. Speed and cost of transportation are related in two ways. First, transport firms capable of offering faster delivery typically charge higher rates for their services. Second, the faster the transportation service is, the shorter the time interval during which inventory is in transit and unavailable. Thus, a critical aspect of selecting the most desirable method of transportation is to balance speed and cost of service.

Transportation consistency refers to variations in time required to perform a specific movement over a number of shipments. Consistency reflects the dependability of transportation. For years, logistics managers have identified consistency as the most important attribute of quality transportation. If a shipment between two locations takes three days one time and six the next, the unexpected variance can create serious supply chain operational problems. When transportation lacks consistency, inventory safety stocks are required to protect against service failure, impacting both the seller's and buyer's overall inventory commitment. With the advent of advanced information technology to control and report shipment status, logistics managers have begun to seek faster movement while maintaining consistency. Speed and consistency combine to create the quality aspect of transportation.

In designing a logistical system, a delicate balance must be maintained between transportation cost and service quality. In some circumstances low-cost, slow transportation is satisfactory. In other situations, faster service may be essential to achieving operating goals. Finding and managing the desired transportation mix across the supply chain is a primary responsibility of logistics.

Warehousing, Materials Handling, and Packaging

The first three functional areas of logistics—order processing, inventory, and transportation—can be engineered into a variety of different operational arrangements. Each arrangement has the potential to contribute to a specified level of customer service with an associated total cost. In essence, these functions combine to create a system solution for integrated logistics. The fourth functionality of logistics—warehousing, materials handling, and packaging—also represents an integral part of the logistics operation solution; however, unique to warehousing, materials handling, and packaging is the fact that these are not independent actors, but are an integral part of other the other logistics areas. For example, inventory is usually warehoused, transportation vehicles require materials handling equipment to be loaded and unloaded, and individual products are more efficiently handled when supported with various packaging and conveyance materials.

When distribution facilities are required in a given logistical system, a firm can choose between the services of a warehouse specialist, often referred to as a 3PL (third-party logistics) company, or operate its own facility. This strategic decision must incorporate what value-added services may be required and if the firm has the capabilities to support such services. Examples of such activities are sorting, sequencing, order selection, transportation consolidation, and, in some cases, product modification and assembly related to postponement strategies.

Within the warehouse, materials handling is an important activity. Products must be received, moved, stored, sorted, and assembled to meet customer order requirements. The direct labor and capital invested in materials handling equipment is a significant element of total logistics cost. It stands to reason that the fewer the times a product is handled, the less potential exists for product damage. A variety of mechanized and automated devices exist to assist materials handling. In essence, each warehouse and its materials handling capability represent a minisystem within the overall logistical process.

Finally, an important part of warehousing is the receipt, processing and disposal of returns and damaged inventory. Typically called **reverse logistics**, most firms confront the need to process and dispose overstock, damaged, and/or defective inventory.

When effectively integrated into an enterprise's logistical operations, warehousing, materials handling, and packaging facilitate the speed and overall ease of product flow throughout the logistical system. Chapter 9 will explore warehousing, materials handling, and packaging in much greater detail.

Facility Network Design

Classical economics neglected the importance of facility location and overall network design as it relates to efficient business operations. When economists originally discussed supply-and-demand relationships, facility location and transportation cost differentials were assumed either nonexistent or equal among competitors.[4] In business operations, however, the number, size, and geographical relationship of facilities used to perform logistical operations directly impacts customer service capability and cost. Facility network design is a primary responsibility of logistical management. Typical logistics facilities are manufacturing plants, warehouses, cross-dock operations, and retail stores.

Facility network design is concerned with determining the number, location and ownership arrangement of all types of facilities required to perform the logistics work supporting a given firm's strategy. It is also necessary to determine what inventory and how much to stock at each facility as well as the customer service area of each facility. The facility network creates a structure from which logistical operations are performed. Thus, the network integrates information and transportation capabilities. Specific work tasks related to processing customer orders, warehousing inventory, and materials handling are all performed within the facility network.

The design of a facility network requires careful analysis of geographical variation. The fact that a great deal of difference exists between geographical markets is easy to illustrate. The 50 largest U.S. metropolitan markets in terms of population account for the majority of retail sales. Therefore, an enterprise marketing consumer products on a national scale must establish a logistical network capable of servicing prime markets. A similar geographic disparity exists in typical material and component part source locations. When a firm is involved in global logistics, issues related to network design become increasingly complex.

---

[4] Alfred Weber, *Theory of the Location of Industries,* translated by Carl J. Friedrich (Chicago: University of Chicago Press, 1928); August Lösch, *Die Rümliche Ordnung der Wirtschaft* (Jena: Gustav Fischer Verlag, 1940); Edgar M. Hoover, *The Location of Economic Activity* (New York: McGraw-Hill Book Company, 1938); Melvin L. Greenhut, *Plant Location in Theory and Practice* (Chapel Hill, NC: University of North Carolina Press, 1956); Walter Isard et al., *Methods of Regional Analysis: An Introduction to Regional Science* (New York: John Wiley & Sons, 1960); Walter Isard, *Location and Space Economy* (Cambridge, MA: The MIT Press, 1968); and Michael J. Webber, *Impact of Uncertainty on Location* (Cambridge, MA: The MIT Press, 1972).

The importance of continuously modifying the facility network to accommodate change in demand and supply infrastructures cannot be overemphasized. Product assortments, customers, suppliers, and manufacturing requirements are constantly changing in a dynamic competitive environment. The selection of a superior locational network can provide a significant step toward achieving competitive advantage.

Logistical Operations

The internal operational scope of integrated logistics operations is illustrated by the shaded area of Figure 3.2. Information from and about customers flows through the enterprise as a result of sales activity, supply chain collaborations forecasts, and orders. Vital information is refined into specific manufacturing, merchandising, and purchasing plans. As products and materials are procured, a value-added inventory flow is initiated, which ultimately results in ownership transfer of finished products to customers. Thus, the logistical process is viewed in terms of two interrelated flows: inventory and information. While internal process integration is important to success, a firm must also align and integrate information across the supply chain. To be fully effective in today's competitive environment, firms must extend their enterprise integration to incorporate customers and suppliers. This collaborative extension reflects the position of logistics in the broader perspective of supply chain management. Supply chain integration is discussed later in this chapter (see Supply Chain Synchronization).

Inventory Flow

The operational management of logistics is concerned with movement and storage of inventory in the form of materials, work-in-process, and finished products. Logistical operations start with the initial shipment of materials or component parts from a supplier and are finalized when a manufactured or processed product is delivered to a customer.

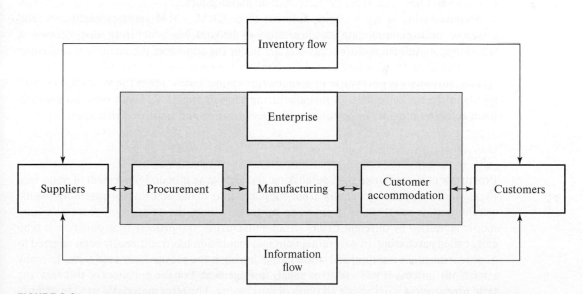

FIGURE 3.2   Logistical Integration

From the initial purchase of a material or components, the logistics process adds value by moving inventory when and where needed. Providing all goes well, materials and components gain value at each step of their transformation into finished inventory.

To support manufacturing, work-in-process inventory must be properly positioned. The cost of material or a component and its movement becomes part of the value-added process. For a more detailed understanding of the inventory flow, it is useful to divide logistical operations into three areas: (1) customer accommodation, (2) manufacturing, and (3) procurement. These components are illustrated in the shaded area of Figure 3.2 as the combined logistics support units of an enterprise.

Customer Accommodation

The movement of finished product to customers is the end objective of logistics. The customer's ship-to location represents the final supply chain destination. The availability of product is a vital part of each channel participant's marketing effort. Unless a proper assortment of products is efficiently delivered when and where needed, a great deal of overall marketing effort may be jeopardized. Dealing with the varied aspects of serving customors is typically called **customer accommodation**. It is through the customer accommodation process that the timing and geographical placement of inventory become an integral part of marketing. To support the wide variety of marketing systems that exist in a highly commercialized nation, many different customer relationship strategies are available. All customer relationship systems have one common feature: They align manufacturers, wholesalers, and retailers into supply chain arrangements to provide customers product availability.

Manufacturing

The area of manufacturing concentrates on managing work-in-process inventory as it flows between stages of manufacturing. The primary logistical responsibility in manufacturing is to participate in formulating a master production schedule and to arrange for its implementation by timely availability of materials, component parts, and work-in-process inventory. Thus, the overall concern of manufacturing support is not how production occurs but rather **what**, **when**, and **where** products will be manufactured.

Manufacturing is significantly different from CRM. CRM services customers, and therefore must accommodate the uncertainty of demand. Manufacturing support involves scheduling movement requirements that are under the control of the manufacturing enterprise. The uncertainties introduced by random ordering and erratic demand related to serving customers is not typical in manufacturing operations. From the viewpoint of overall planning, the separation of manufacturing support from CRM and inbound procurement activities provides opportunities for specialization and improved efficiency.

Procurement

Procurement is concerned with purchasing and arranging inbound movement of materials, parts, and/or finished inventory from suppliers into manufacturing or assembly plants, warehouses, or retail stores. Depending on the situation, the acquisition process is commonly identified by different names. In manufacturing, the process of acquisition is typically called **purchasing**. In government circles, acquisition has traditionally been referred to as **procurement**. In retailing and wholesaling, **buying** is the most widely used term. In many circles, the process is referred to as **supply management**. For the purposes of this text, the term **procurement** will include all types of purchasing. The term **material** is used to identify inventory moving inbound to an enterprise, regardless of its degree of readiness for resale.

Customer Accommodation

Activities related to supporting customer accommodation. Requires performing order receipt and processing, deploying inventories, storage and handling, and outbound transportation within a supply chain. Includes the responsibility to coordinate with marketing planning in such areas as pricing, promotional support, customer service levels, credit delivery standards, reverse logistics, and life cycle support. The primary market distribution objective is to assist in revenue generation by providing strategically desired customer service delivery levels at the lowest total cost.

Manufacturing Production

Activities related to planning, scheduling, and supporting manufacturing operations. Requires master schedule planning and performing work-in-process storage, handling, transportation, and sortation, kilting, sequencing, and time phasing of components. Includes the responsibility for storage of inventory at manufacturing sites and maximum flexibility in the coordination of geographic and assembly postponement between manufacturing and customer relationship management.

Procurement

Activities related to obtaining products and materials from outside suppliers. Requires performing resource planning, supply sourcing, negotiation, order placement, inbound transportation, receiving and inspection, storage and handling, and quality assurance. Includes the responsibility to coordinate with suppliers in such areas as scheduling, supply continuity, hedging, and speculation, as well as research leading to new sources or programs. The primary procurement objective is to support manufacturing or resale organizations by timely purchasing at the lowest total cost.

TABLE 3.2   Specific Logistics Operating Concerns of Customer Accommodation, Manufacturing and Procurement

The term **product** is used to identify value-added inventory that is sold to customers. In other words, materials are involved in the process of adding value through manufacturing whereas products are ready for consumption. The fundamental distinction is that products result from the value added to material during manufacture, sortation, or assembly.

Within a typical enterprise, the three logistics operating areas overlap. Viewing each as an integral part of the overall value-adding process creates an opportunity to specialize performance and capitalize on the unique attributes of each within the overall process. Table 3.2 provides a more exacting definition of the day-to-day work involved in each sub-process of logistics. The overall challenge of a supply chain is to integrate the logistical processes of participating firms in a manner that facilitates overall efficiency.

Information Flow

Information flow identifies the notion that specific locations within a logistics system produce, send, and receive information thus enabling, in an ideal setting, the integration of this information across all operating areas. This information may include size of order, status of a given work process, availability of inventory, or urgency of a given order, for example. The primary objective of information flow management is to reconcile and streamline information connectivity to improve overall supply chain performance. It is important to stress that the information flow is paralleling the actual physical work performed in customer accommodation, manufacturing, and procurement. Whereas these areas contain the actual logistics work, information facilitates real-time status updates—the coordination, planning, and control of day-to-day operations. Without accurate information, the effort involved in the logistical system can be misdirected.

Logistical Integration Objectives

To operationalize logistical integration within a supply chain context, six operational objectives must be simultaneously achieved: (1) responsiveness, (2) variance reduction, (3) inventory reduction, (4) shipment consolidation, (5) quality, and (6) life cycle support. The relative importance of each is directly related to a firm's logistical strategy.

Responsiveness

A firm's ability to satisfy customer requirements in a timely manner is referred to as **responsiveness**. As noted earlier, information technology is facilitating response-based strategies that permit operational commitment to be postponed to the last possible time, followed by accelerated delivery. The implementation of responsive strategies serves to reduce inventories committed or deployed in anticipation of customer requirements. Responsiveness serves to shift operational emphasis from forecasting future requirements toward accommodating customers on a rapid order-to-shipment basis. Ideally, in a responsive system, inventory is not deployed until a customer commits. To support such commitment, a firm must have the logistical attributes of inventory availability and timely delivery once a customer order is received.

Variance Reduction

All operating areas of a logistical system are susceptible to variance. Variance results from failure to perform any facet of logistical operations as anticipated. For example, delay in customer order processing, an unexpected disruption in order selection, goods arriving damaged at a customer's location, and/or failure to deliver at the right location on time all create unplanned variance in the order-to-delivery cycle. A common solution to safeguard against detrimental variance is to use inventory safety stocks to buffer operations. It is also common to use expedited transportation to overcome unexpected variance that delays planned delivery. Such practices, given their associated high cost, can be minimized by using information technology to maintain positive logistics control. To the extent that variance is minimized, logistical productivity will improve. Thus, **variance reduction**, the elimination of operational disruptions, is one basic objective of integrated logistics management.

Inventory Reduction

To achieve the objective of **inventory reduction**, an integrated logistics system must control asset commitment and turn velocity. Asset commitment is the financial value of deployed inventory. Turn velocity reflects the rate at which inventory is replenished over time. High turn rates, coupled with desired inventory availability, mean assets devoted to inventory are being efficiently and effectively utilized; that is, overall assets committed to support an integrated operation are minimized.

It is important to keep in mind that inventory can and does facilitate desirable benefits. Inventories are critical to achieving economies of scale in manufacturing and procurement. The objective is to reduce and manage inventory to the lowest possible level while simultaneously achieving overall supply chain performance objectives.

Shipment Consolidation

One of the most significant logistical costs is transportation. On average, more than 60 cents of each logistics dollar is expended for transportation. Transportation cost is directly related to the type of product, size of shipment, and distance traveled. Many logistical systems that feature direct-to-consumer fulfillment depend on high-speed, small shipments (parcel), which is traditionally the most costly. A system objective is to achieve shipment consolidation in an effort to reduce transportation cost per each individual shipment. As a general rule, the larger the shipment and the longer distance it is transported, the lower the transportation cost per unit. Firms have become increasingly successful in identifying techniques to achieve consolidation. For example, successful e-commerce firms will consolidate final-mile deliveries for a given zip code originating from a single warehouse and "zone skip" the shipment directly for final-mile delivery versus transferring inventory through their warehouse network. This practice achieves shipment consolidation and reduces time, touches, and cost.

Quality

A fundamental operational objective is continuous **quality** improvement. Total quality management **(TQM)** is a major initiative throughout industry. If a product becomes defective or if service promises are not kept, little if any value can be added by the logistics process. Logistical costs, once expended, cannot be reversed or recovered. In fact, when product quality fails after customer delivery and replacement is necessary, logistical costs rapidly accumulate. In addition to the initial logistics cost, products must be returned and replaced. Such unplanned movements typically cost more than original distribution. For this reason, commitment to zero-defect order-to-delivery performance is a major goal of leading edge logistics.

Logistics itself is performed under challenging conditions. The difficulty of achieving zero-defect logistics is magnified by the fact that logistical operations typically are performed across a vast geographical area 24 hours a day without direct supervision.

Life Cycle Support

The final integration design objective is **life cycle support**. Few items are sold without some guarantee that the product will perform as advertised. In some situations, the initial value-added inventory flow to customers must be reversed for various reasons. **Reverse logistics** also results from the increasing number of laws encouraging the recycling of beverage containers and packaging materials. The significant point concerning reverse logistics is the need to maintain maximum control when a potential liability exists, such as potentially contaminated product. A well-designed and coordinated reverse logistical capability is important when firms are required to recall products. During 2010, Johnson & Johnson confronted the need to recall several products. These recalls extended across several months involving a number of different brands. The efficiency and effectiveness of their predetermined reverse logistics capabilities were a major factor in the success of these recalls. The operational requirements for reverse logistics range from lowest total cost, such as returning bottles for recycling, to maximum control in situations involving defective products. Firms that design efficient reverse logistics often are able to reclaim value by reducing the quantity of products that might otherwise be scrapped or sold at a discount. Sound integrative strategy cannot be formulated without careful review of reverse logistical requirements.

For some products, such as copying equipment and printers, primary profit lies in the sale of supplies and aftermarket service. The importance of life cycle support is significantly different in situations wherein a majority of profits are achieved in the aftermarket. For firms marketing consumer durables or industrial equipment, the commitment to life cycle support constitutes a versatile and demanding marketing opportunity as well as one of the largest costs of logistical operations. Life cycle support requires **cradle-to-cradle** logistics. Cradle-to-cradle logistical support goes beyond reverse logistics and recycling to include the possibility of aftermarket service, product recall, and product disposal. The structure and dynamics of logistics operations are discussed next.

Logistical Operating Arrangements

The potential for logistical services to favorably impact customer experience is directly related to operating system design. The many different facets of logistical performance requirements make operational design a complex task. A carefully designed logistics operating structure must offer a balance of performance, cost, and flexibility. When one considers the variety of logistical systems used throughout the world to service widely diverse markets, it is astonishing that any structural similarity exists. But keep in mind that all logistical arrangements have two common characteristics. First, they are designed to manage inventory positioning. Second, the range of logistics alternatives is limited by available technology. These two characteristics tend to create commonly observed logistical operating arrangements. Three widely utilized structures are echelon, direct, and combined.

Echelon

Classification of a logistical system as having an echeloned structure means that the flow of products typically proceeds through an established arrangement of firms as it moves from origin to final destination. The use of echelons usually implies that total cost analysis justifies stocking some level of inventory and/or the performance of specific work at different levels of a supply chain.

Echelon systems utilize warehouses to create inventory assortments and achieve consolidation economies associated with large-volume transportation shipments. Inventories positioned in warehouses are available for rapid deployment to meet customer requirements. Figure 3.3 illustrates the typical echeloned value chain.

Typical echelon systems utilize either break-bulk or consolidation warehouses. A break-bulk facility typically receives large-volume shipments from a variety of suppliers. Inventory is sorted and stored in anticipation of future customer requirements. Food distribution centers operated by major grocery chains and wholesalers are examples of break-bulk warehouses. A consolidation warehouse operates in a reverse profile. Consolidation is typically required by manufacturing firms that have plants at different geographical locations. Products manufactured at different plants are consolidated at a central warehouse facility to allow the firm to ship full-line assortments to customers. Major consumer product manufacturers are prime examples of enterprises using echeloned systems for full-line consolidation. Consolidation warehouses are also common on the inbound side of manufacturing. Component parts and sub-assemblies from suppliers are sequenced and shipped to plants as needed to support manufacturing operations.

Direct

In contrast to inventory echeloning are logistical systems designed to ship products direct to the customer's destination from one or a limited number of centrally located inventories. Direct distribution typically uses the expedited services of premium transport combined

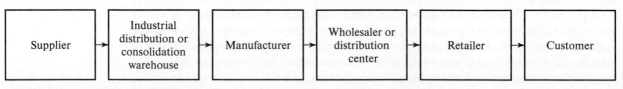

FIGURE 3.3   Echelon-Structured Logistics

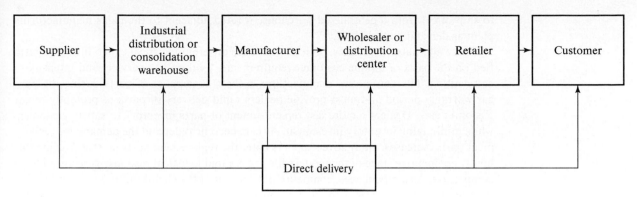

FIGURE 3.4   Combined Echeloned and Direct Delivery

with information technology to rapidly process customer orders and achieve delivery performance. This combination of capabilities, designed into the order delivery cycle, reduces time delays and overcomes geographical separation from customers. Examples of direct shipments are plant-to-customer truckload shipments, direct store delivery, and various forms of direct-to-consumer delivery of products purchased on the Internet. Direct logistical structures are also commonly used for inbound components and materials to manufacturing plants because the average shipment size is typically large.

When the economics permit, logistic planners desire direct shipments because they reduce anticipatory inventories and related product handling. The deployment of direct logistics is limited by high transportation cost. In general, most firms do not operate the number of warehouses today that were common a few years ago and have been able to modify echelon structures to include direct logistics capabilities. Figure 3.4 illustrates direct logistics capability being added to an echeloned logistics structure.

Combined

The ideal logistical arrangement is a situation wherein the inherent benefits of echeloned and direct logistics structures are combined. Inventory strategies often position fast-moving products or materials in forward warehouses, while other, more risky or costly items are stocked at a central location for direct delivery as needed. The basic service commitment and order size economics determine the most desirable and economical structure to service a specific customer.

To illustrate, automobile replacement parts are typically distributed to customers by utilizing a combined logistics strategy. Specific parts are inventoried in warehouses located at various distances from dealers and retail outlets on the basis of pattern and density of demand. As a general rule, the slower the part turnover is, the more erratic the demand is, and therefore the greater the benefits of centralizing inventory. The slowest or least-demanded parts may be stocked at only one location that services customers throughout the world. Fast-moving parts that have more predictable demand are stocked in forward warehouses close to customers to facilitate fast, low-cost delivery.

A contrasting example is an enterprise that sells machine parts to industrial firms. The nature of this business supports a completely opposite distribution design. To offer superior service to customers who experience machine failure and unexpected downtime, the firm stocks slow movers in local warehouses. In contrast to the automotive firm, high-demand, fast-turnover parts in this industry can be more accurately forecasted because of routine preventive maintenance. The least-cost logistical methods for these fast movers are to ship direct from a centralized warehouse located adjacent to the parts manufacturing plant as demand materialized.

These alternative strategies, both of which use different logistical capabilities, are justified on the basis of unique customer requirements, total cost to service, and intensity of competition. The automotive manufacturer is the sole supplier of parts during the new-car warranty period and must provide dealers rapid delivery of parts to promptly repair customer cars. Dealers require fast replenishment of parts inventory to satisfy customers while minimizing inventory investment. As cars become older and the demand for replacement parts increases, alternative suppliers enter the replacement parts market. During this highly competitive stage of the model's life cycle, rapid logistical response is required to be competitive. As a model ages, competition drops out of the shrinking aftermarket, leaving the original manufacturer as the sole supplier.

The industrial component supplier, in contrast to the automotive company, offers standard machine parts having a high degree of competitive substitutability. Whereas products used on a regular basis can be forecasted, slow- or erratic-demand products are impossible to forecast. This enterprise forces a situation wherein customers measure suppliers in terms of how fast unexpected machine breakdowns can be remedied. Failure to perform to the level of customer expectation can open the door for a competitor to prove its capability.

Each enterprise faces a unique customer situation and can be expected to use a different logistics strategy to achieve competitive superiority. The strategy that satisfies customer expectations at lowest attainable total cost typically utilizes a combination of echeloned and direct capabilities.

Beyond the basic channel structure, flexibility can be designed into a logistical system by developing a program to service customers using alternative facilities or different transportation capabilities.

Flexible Structure

Flexible operations are preplanned contingency strategies to prevent logistical failures. A typical emergency occurs when an assigned shipping facility is out of stock or for some other reason cannot complete a customer's order. For example, a warehouse may be out of an item with no replenishment inventory scheduled to arrive until after the customer's specified order delivery date. To prevent back-ordering or delivery cancellation, a contingency operating policy may assign the total order, or at least those items not available, for shipment from an alternative warehouse. The use of flexible operations is typically based on the importance of meeting the needs of a specific customer or the critical nature of the product being ordered.

A flexible logistics capability that has gained popularity as a result of improved communications involves procedures for serving predetermined situations as part of the basic logistical strategy. The flexible logistics rule and decision scenarios specify alternative ways to meet specific service requirements, such as assignment of the order to different shipping facilities or changing methods of delivery. A strategy that utilizes flexible operations is common practice in four different situations.

First, the customer designated delivery facility might be near a point of equal logistics cost or equal delivery time from two different logistics facilities. Customers located at such points offer the supplying firm an opportunity to fully utilize available inventory and logistical capacity. Orders can be serviced from the facility having the best inventory position or the available transportation capacity to achieve timely delivery. This form of flexible logistics offers a way to fully utilize system capacity by balancing workloads between facilities while protecting customer service commitments. The benefit is operating efficiency, which is transparent to the customer, who experiences no service deterioration.

A second situation justifying flexible distribution is when the size of a customer's order creates an opportunity to improve logistical efficiency if serviced through an alternative channel arrangement. For example, when a consumer purchases an individual toilet, he or she will likely do so from a retail or wholesaler. Now compare that to a large builder buying hundreds of toilets for an apartment complex; in this case, it would not be cost efficient for the builder to buy each toilet individually! Provided that alternative methods of shipping meet customer delivery expectations, total logistical cost may be reduced by implementing flexible policies.

A third type of flexible operation may result from a selective inventory stocking strategy. The cost and risk associated with stocking inventory require careful analysis to determine which items and how much to place in each warehouse. With replacement parts, a common strategy mentioned earlier is to stock selected items in specific warehouses with the total line being stocked only at a central facility. In general-merchandise retailing, a store or distribution center located in a small community may stock only a limited or restricted version of a firm's total line. When customers desire nonstocked items, orders must be satisfied from an alternative facility. The term **master facilities** is often used to describe inventory strategies that designate larger facilities for backup support of smaller restricted facilities. Selective inventory stocking by echelon level is a common strategy used to reduce overall inventory risk. The reasons for selective stocking range from low product profit contribution to high per-unit cost of inventory maintenance. One way to operationalize a fine-line inventory classification strategy is to differentiate stocking policy by system echelons. In situations following such classified stocking strategies, it may be necessary to obtain advanced customer approval for split-order delivery. However, in some situations firms that use differentiated inventory stocking strategies are able to consolidate customer orders while intransit for same-time delivery, thereby making the arrangement customer transparent.

The fourth type of flexible operations results from agreements between firms to move selected shipments outside the established echeloned or direct logistics arrangements. Two special arrangements gaining popularity are flow through **cross-docks** and **integrated service provider (ISP)** arrangements. A cross-dock operation involves shipments from multiple suppliers arriving at a designated time at the handling facility. Inventory receipts are sorted by destination across the dock and consolidated into outbound trailers for direct delivery. Cross-dock operations are growing in popularity in the retail industry for building store-specific assortments and are common methods of continuous inventory replenishment for mass merchants. Cross-docking of merchandise direct from manufacture to a customer's retail store eliminates the work and cost associated with utilizing distribution warehouses.

Another form of flexible operations is to use integrated service providers to consolidate products for delivery. This is similar to consolidation for transportation purposes discussed in the previous section of this chapter. However, as a form of flexible logistics, specialists are used to avoid storage and handling of slow-moving products through the mainstream of the echeloned logistics structure. Such service providers can also provide important value-added services. For example, True Value Company partners with 3PL Yusen Logistics for the consolidation of less-than-full-container-load purchase orders at two facilities in China. This consolidation operation results in multiple purchase orders being consolidated to obtain full-container economies that ship directly to True Value's regional distribution centers.

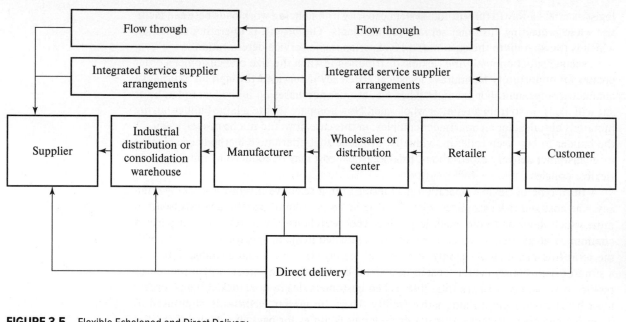

FIGURE 3.5   Flexible Echeloned and Direct Delivery
Arrows reflect information flows facilitating a specific service profile.

Figure 3.5 introduces flexibility to the logistical operating structures previously illus-trated. A prerequisite to effective flexible operations is the use of information technology to monitor inventory status throughout the logistical network and provide the capability to rapidly switch methods for servicing customer orders. The use of flexible operations in emergency situations has a well-established track record. The overall improvement in infor-mation technology is resulting in flexible operations becoming an increasingly important part of basic logistics strategy.

Supply Chain Synchronization

The previous discussion positioned logistics as an integrated management process within an individual firm. A challenge of supply chain management is to integrate operations across multiple firms. In an effort to facilitate logistical operations, supply chain par-ticipants will benefit from jointly planning and implementing logistical operations. Multifirm operational integration across a supply chain is referred to as **supply chain synchronization**.

Supply chain synchronization seeks to coordinate the flow of materials, products, and information between supply chain partners to reduce duplication and redundancy. It also advocates reengineering internal operations of individual firms to leverage overall supply chain capability. Leveraged operations require a joint plan concerning the logistics work that each participating firm in a supply chain will perform and be held accountable for. At the heart of supply chain integration is the goal of leveraging partners' core competencies to achieve overall reduction of **inventory dwell time**.

Dwell time is the ratio of time inventory sits idle in comparison to the amount of time it is being productively moved to a desired location in a supply chain. To illustrate, a product or component stored in a warehouse is dwelling. In contrast, the same part moving in a transportation vehicle on the way to a customer is being productively deployed. Ideally, the shipment will arrive at destination in a timely manner to be immediately used in a value-added process. The desire is to directly integrate inventory into the customer's value-adding process without product being placed in storage or otherwise restricting continuous movement. The benefits of synchronization serve to support the generalization that speed of performing a specific service or product movement is secondary to synchronizing the timing of supply arrival with destination demand requirements.

Performance Cycle Structure

The **performance cycle** represents the elements of work necessary to complete the logistics related to customer accommodation, manufacturing, or procurement. It consists of specific work ranging from identification of requirements to product delivery. Because it integrates various aspects of work, the performance cycle is the primary unit of analysis for logistical design and synchronization. At a basic level, information and transportation must link all firms functioning in a supply chain. The operational locations that are linked by information and transportation are referred to as **nodes**.

In addition to supply chain nodes and links, performance cycles involve inventory assets. Inventory is measured in terms of the asset investment level allocated to support operations at a node or while a product or material is in transit. Inventory committed to supply chain nodes consists of **base stock** and **safety stock**. Inventory is stocked and flows through nodes, necessitating a variety of different types of materials handling and, when necessary, storage.

Performance cycles become dynamic as they accommodate **input/output requirements**. The **input** to a performance cycle is demand, typically an order that specifies requirements for a product or material. A high-volume supply chain will typically require a different and wider variety of performance cycles than a chain having fewer throughputs. When operating requirements are highly predictable or relatively low-volume throughput, the performance cycle structure required to provide supply chain logistical support can be simplified. The performance cycle structures required to support a large retail enterprise like Target or Walmart supply chains are far more complex than the operating structure requirements of a catalog fulfillment company.

Supply chain **output** is the level of performance expected from the combined logistical operations. In Chapter 1, the EERS model (effective, efficient, relevant, and sustainable) was introduced as the framework to achieve the value proposition each given supply chain output is attempting to fulfill. These elements are key components of the performance cycle structure.

Depending on the operational mission of a particular performance cycle in a supply chain structure, the associated work may be under the complete control of a single enterprise or may involve multiple firms. For example, manufacturing support cycles are often under the operational control of a single enterprise. In contrast, performance cycles related to customer accommodation and procurement typically involve multiple firms.

It is important to realize that transaction frequency and intensity will vary between performance cycles. Some performance cycles are established to facilitate a one-time purchase or sale. In such a case, the associated supply chain is designed, implemented, and abolished once the transaction is complete. Other performance cycles represent long-standing operating arrangements. A complicating fact is that any operation or facility in one supply chain may simultaneously be participating in a number of other supply chains. For example, a given ocean carrier or truck load transportation provider may be participating in hundreds of supply chains simultaneously.

When one considers the supply chain of a multinational firm that is involved in marketing a broad product line to numerous customers, with a supply chain spanning raw materials procurement through production, distribution, and delivery on a global basis, the notion of individual performance cycles linking all operations is difficult to comprehend. It is almost mind-boggling to estimate how many performance cycles exist in the supply chain structure of Kellogg or IBM.

Regardless of the number of different performance cycles a specific supply chain deploys to satisfy its logistical requirements, each must be individually designed and operationally managed. The fundamental importance of performance cycle design and operation cannot be overemphasized: **The logistics performance cycle is the basic unit of supply chain design and operational control. In essence, the performance cycle structure is the framework for implementation of integrated logistics across the supply chain.**

Figure 3.6 portrays an echeloned supply chain structure illustrating basic logistics performance cycles. Figure 3.7 illustrates a network of flexible performance cycles integrated in a multiecheloned structure.

Three points are important to understanding the architecture of integrated supply chain logistical systems. First, as noted earlier, the performance cycles are the fundamental unit for integrated logistics across the supply chain. Second, the performance cycle structure of a supply chain, in terms of link and nodal arrangement, is basically the same whether one is concerned with customer relationship management, manufacturing, or procurement. However, considerable differences exist in the degree of control that an individual firm can exercise based on the specific type of performance cycle. Third, regardless of how vast and complex the overall supply chain structure, essential interfaces and control processes must be identified and evaluated in terms of individual performance cycle arrangements and associated managerial accountability.

FIGURE 3.6

Logistical Performance Cycles

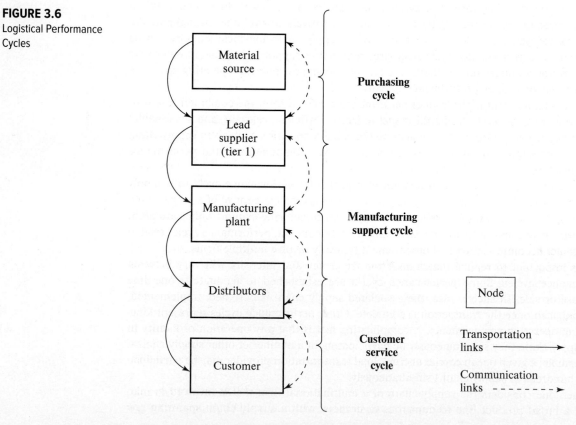

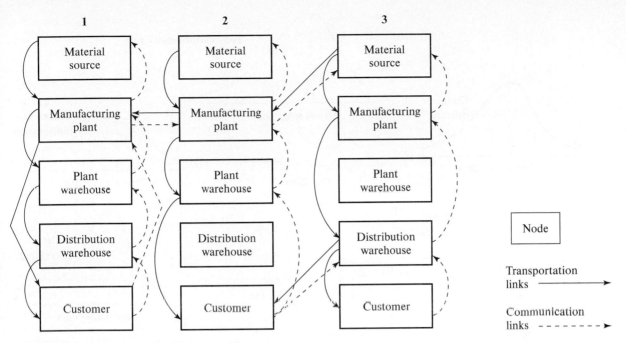

FIGURE 3.7   Multicheloned Flexible Logistical Network

Performance Cycle Uncertainty

A major objective of logistics in all operating areas is to reduce performance cycle uncertainty. The dilemma is that the structure of the performance cycle itself, operating conditions, and the quality of logistical operations all randomly introduce operational variance.

Figure 3.8 illustrates the type and magnitude of variance that can develop in performance cycle operations. The performance cycle illustration is based on finished goods inventory delivery. The time distributions, as illustrated, statistically reflect operational history for each task of the performance cycle. The diagram illustrates the minimum to maximum time historically required to complete each task and the resultant time distribution for the overall performance cycle. The vertical dashed line reflects the average time for performing each task.

In terms of specific tasks, the variance results from the nature of the work involved. Order transmission is highly reliable when electronic transfer **(EDI)** or Internet communications are used and more erratic when telephone or routine mail is used. Regardless of the level of technology deployed, operational variance will occur as a result of daily changes in workload and resolution of unexpected events.

Time and variance related to order processing are a function of workload, degree of automation, and policies related to credit approval. Order selection, speed, and associated delay are directly related to capacity, materials handling sophistication, and human resource availability. When a product is out of stock, the time to complete order selection may include manufacturing scheduling or inventory purchase. The required transportation time is a function of distance, shipment size, type of transport, and operating conditions. Final delivery to customers can vary, depending on authorized receiving times, delivery appointments, workforce availability, traffic congestion and specialized unloading and equipment requirements.

In Figure 3.8, the history of total order-to-delivery time performance ranges from 5 to 40 days. The 5-day cycle reflects the unlikely event that each task will be performed at the minimum possible time. The 40-day cycle represents the equally unlikely opposite extreme

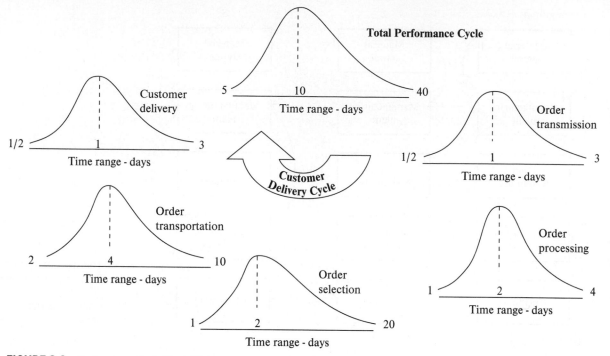

FIGURE 3.8   Performance Cycle Uncertainty

wherein each task requires maximum time. The planned or target order-to-delivery cycle performance is to control combined variance so that actual operations are 10 days as often as possible. Whenever actual performance is anticipated to more or less than 10 days, managerial action may be necessary to inform customers of anticipated variance and planned corrective action.

The goal of performance cycle synchronization is to achieve the planned time performance. Delayed performance at any point along the supply chain results in potential disruption of operations. Such delays require that safety stocks be established to cover variances. When performance occurs faster than expected, unplanned work will be required to handle and store inventory that arrives early. Given the inconvenience and expense of either early or late delivery, it is no wonder that logistics managers place a premium on operational consistency. Once consistent operations are achieved, every effort should be made to reduce the time required to complete the performance cycle to a minimum. In other words, shorter cycles are desirable because they reduce total assets deployed. However, the importance of speed is directly related to performance consistency. Given consistency as the primary goal, faster order cycles reduce inventory risk and improve turn performance.

Summary

Logistics is the process that links supply chain participants into integrated operations. The cost of performing logistics is a major expenditure for most businesses and supply chain arrangements.

Logistical service is measured in terms of availability, operational performance, and service reliability. Each aspect of service is framed in terms of customer expectations and requirements. Logistics is all about providing the essential customer service attributes at the lowest possible total cost. Such customer accommodation, in an exacting cost framework, is the logistics value proposition.

The actual work of logistics is functional in nature. Facility locations must be established to form a network; information must be formulated and shared; transportation must be arranged; inventory must be deployed; and, to the extent required, warehousing, materials handling, and packaging activities must be performed. The traditional orientation was to perform each functional task as well as possible with limited consideration given to how one work area impacted another. Because the work of logistics is extremely detailed and complex, there is a natural tendency to focus on functional performance. While functional excellence is important, it must be supportive of overall logistical competency. Thus, the integrated performance of all logistical functions is of primary importance.

The functions of logistics combine into the three primary operational processes of customer accommodation, manufacturing support, and procurement. To achieve internal integration, the inventory and information flows between these areas must be coordinated.

In supply chain synchronization, the operational focus becomes the logistics performance cycle. The performance cycle is also the primary unit of analysis in logistical design. The performance cycle structure provides the logic for combining the nodes, levels, links, and allocation of assets essential to performing customer accommodation, manufacturing support, and procurement operations. Many similarities and a number of critical differences exist between performance cycles dedicated to these logistics operating areas. Fully understanding these similarities and differences is vital to planning and controlling overall supply chain integration. The basic proposition is that regardless of size and complexity, logistical integration is best understood and evaluated by the structure and dynamics of performance cycles.

The primary goal is to achieve consistant service at the lowest possible total cost. The challenge is to design a supply chain capable of performing the required logistical work as rapidly but, even more important, as consistently as possible. Unexpected delays, as well as faster than expected performance, can combine to increase or decrease the elapsed time required to complete a performance cycle. Both early and late delivery are undesirable and unacceptable from an operational perspective.

Chapter 3 has developed some important foundations of the logistical discipline and how it creates value in a supply chain context. These insights regarding the nature of logistics work, the importance of achieving internal operational integration through managing inventory and information flow, viewing the performance cycle structure as the basic unit of analysis, and the management of operational uncertainty combine to form a logically consistent set of concepts essential to supporting supply chain management. Logistics and supply chain are not one and the same concepts. Supply chain is a strategy that integrates all aspects of satisfying customer requirements. Logistics is the process of positioning and managing inventory throughout the supply chain. Chapter 4 focuses on customer accommodation, which is the primary force driving supply chain performance.

Study Questions

1. Illustrate a common trade-off that occurs between the functional areas of logistics.
2. Discuss and elaborate on the following statement: "The selection of a superior location network can create substantial competitive advantage."
3. Why are customer relationship operations typically more erratic than manufacturing support and procurement operations?

4. Describe the logistics value proposition. Be specific regarding specific customer relationships and cost.

5. Describe the fundamental similarities and differences among procurement, manufacturing, and customer accommodation performance cycles as they relate to logistical control.

6. Discuss uncertainty as it relates to the overall logistical performance cycle. Discuss and illustrate how performance cycle variance can be controlled.

Challenge Questions

1. How has transportation cost as a percentage of total logistics cost tracked since 2007? How do you explain the most recent trend?

2. Why is least total cost performance not always what a customer prefers? Illustrate a situation that supports your answer.

3. What could be gained by "stapling yourself to an order"? Be specific and illustrate your answer.

4. What additional value-added services could True Value consider partnering with Yusen Logistics to implement? What could the benefit or drawbacks of this strategy entail?

CHAPTER 4

Customer Accommodation

Chapter Outline

While in some ways it's an insight into the obvious, it is important to establish initially that logistics contributes to an organization's success by fulfilling customers' delivery and inventory availability requirements. What is not so obvious, however, is what exactly is meant by the term *customer*. The supply chain management concept requires careful consideration of just what is meant by the term and realization that there are many different perspectives.

From the perspective of the total supply chain, the ultimate customer is the end user of the product or service. It has historically been useful to distinguish between two types of end users. The first is a consumer, an individual or a household that purchases products and services to satisfy personal needs. When a family purchases an automobile to be used for personal transportation, that family is the consumer of the supply chain. The second type is an organizational end user. Purchases are made by organizations or institutions to allow an end user to perform a task or job in the organization. When a company buys an automobile for a salesperson or buys tools to be used by an assembly worker in a manufacturing plant, the company is considered to be a customer and the salesperson or assembly worker is the end user of the supply chain's products. A supply chain management perspective demands that all firms in the supply chain focus on meeting the requirements of end users, whether they are consumers or organizational users.

Another perspective of customer exists for a specific firm within the supply chain. This perspective recognizes that intermediate organizations often exist between the firm and end users. Common terminology generally recognizes these organizations as intermediate customers. Thus, in the Procter & Gamble (P&G) supply chain that provides Tide laundry detergent to ultimate consumers, Kroger and Safeway supermarkets are intermediate customers; they purchase Tide from P&G for the purpose of reselling to consumers.

Finally, for a logistician, a customer is any delivery location. Typical destinations range from consumers' homes to retail and wholesale businesses to the receiving docks of manufacturing plants and warehouses. In some cases, the customer is a different organization or individual who is taking ownership of the product or service being delivered. In many other situations the customer is a different facility of the same firm or a business partner at some other location in the supply chain. For example, it is common for the logistics manager of a retail warehouse to think of the individual stores to be served as warehouse customers, even though the stores are part of the same organization.

Regardless of the motivation and delivery purpose, the customer being served is the focal point and driving force in establishing logistical performance requirements. It is critical to fully understand customer needs that must be met in establishing logistical strategy. This chapter details various approaches to accommodating customer requirements. The first section presents the fundamental concepts that underlie customer-focused marketing, with consideration of how logistics supports a firm's overall marketing strategy. The second section describes how supply chain outputs impact end users and how such outputs must be structured to meet their requirements. The sections that follow describe how firms progress through increasing levels of commitment to customers. These levels range from traditional notions of logistics customer service to satisfaction of customers by meeting their expectations to the ultimate goal of helping customers be successful. The chapter concludes with the presentation of a framework for developing customer relationship strategy.

Customer-Focused Marketing

The basic principles of customer-focused marketing have their roots in the **marketing concept**, a business philosophy that suggests that the focal point of a business's strategy must be the customers it intends to serve. It holds that for an organization to achieve its goals, it must be more effective than competitors in identifying specific customer needs and focusing resources and activities on these customer requirements. Clearly, many aspects of a firm's strategy must be integrated, and logistics is only one of these. The marketing concept builds on four fundamental ideas: Customer needs and requirements are more basic than products or services; different customers have different needs and requirements; products and services become meaningful only when available and positioned from the customer's perspective, which is the focus of logistics strategy; and sales volume is secondary to profit.

The belief that customer needs are more basic than products or services places a priority on fully understanding what drives market opportunities. The key is to understand and develop the combination of products and services that will meet those requirements. For example, if customers require a choice of only three different colored appliances, it makes little sense to offer six colors. It also makes little sense to try to market only white appliances if color selection is important from a customer's perspective. The idea is to develop sufficient insight into basic customer needs so that products and services can be matched to these opportunities. Successful marketing begins with in-depth study of customers to identify product and service requirements.

The second fundamental aspect of the marketing concept is that there is no single market for any given product or service. All markets are composed of different segments, each of which has somewhat different requirements. Effective market segmentation requires that firms clearly identify segments and select specific targets. While a comprehensive discussion of market segmentation is beyond the scope of this text, it is important to note that customers' logistical requirements frequently offer an effective basis for classification. For example, a contractor building new homes may place an order for appliances several weeks before needed for installation, while a consumer buying a replacement for a broken appliance may require immediate availability and delivery.

For marketing to be successful, products and services must be available to customers. In other words, the third fundamental aspect of marketing is that customers must be readily able to obtain the products they desire. Four economic utilities add value to customers: **form, possession, time**, and **place**. The product's form is for the most part generated during the manufacturing process. For example, form utility results from the assembly of parts and components for a dishwasher. Marketing creates possession by informing potential customers of product/service availability and enabling ownership exchange. Logistics provides time and place utility. Essentially, this means that logistics must ensure that the product is available when and where desired by customers. The achievement of time and place utility requires significant effort and is expensive. Profitable transactions materialize only when all four utilities are combined in a manner relevant to customers.

The fourth aspect of the marketing concept is the focus on profitability as contrasted to sales volume. An important dimension of success is the degree of profitability resulting from relationships with customers, not the volume sold. Therefore, variations in the basic utilities, form, possession, time, and place, are justified only if a customer or segment of customers values and is willing to pay for the modification. In the appliance example, if a customer requests a unique color option and is willing to pay extra, then the request can and should be accommodated, providing a positive contribution margin can be earned. A final refinement of marketing strategy is based on an acknowledgment that all aspects of a product/service offering are subject to modification when justifiable on the basis of profitability.

Transactional versus Relationship Marketing

Traditional marketing strategies focus on obtaining successful exchanges, or transactions, with customers to drive increases in revenue and profit. In this approach, termed **transactional marketing**, companies are generally oriented toward short-term interaction with their customers. The traditional marketing concept emphasizes accommodating customers' needs and requirements, something few business organizations would argue with. However, as practiced in many firms, the result is a focus on creating successful individual transactions between a supplier and its customers.

Paralleling the development of the supply chain management concept, there has been a shift in philosophy regarding the nature of marketing strategy. This shift has generally been acknowledged as **relationship marketing**. Relationship marketing focuses on the development of long-term relations with key supply chain participants such as consumers, intermediate customers, and suppliers in an effort to develop and retain long-term preference and loyalty. Relationship marketing is based on the realization that in many industries it is as important to retain current customers and gain a larger share of their purchases as it is to attract new customers.[1]

The ultimate in market segmentation and relationship marketing is to focus on the individual customer. This approach, referred to as **micromarketing** or **one-to-one marketing**, recognizes that each individual customer may indeed have unique requirements. For example, although Walmart and Target are both mass merchandisers, their requirements in terms of how they desire to interact logistically with suppliers differ significantly. A manufacturer who wants to do business with both of these major retailers must adapt its logistical operations to the unique needs of each. The best way to ensure long-term organizational success is to intensely research and then meet the requirements of individual customers. While this approach may not be feasible with every customer, one-to-one relationships can significantly reduce transaction costs, better accommodate customer requirements, and make individual transactions routine.

Supply Chain Service Outputs

Imagine a society in which every individual is totally self-sufficient: Each individual would produce and consume all of the products and services necessary for survival so there would be no need for any economic activity related to the exchange of goods and services between individuals. No such society can be found today. In reality, as individuals begin to specialize in the production of specific goods or services, a mechanism must arise for the exchange of those goods and services to satisfy the consumption needs of individuals. To do so efficiently and effectively, firms must overcome three problems known as: discrepancy in **space**, discrepancy in **time**, and discrepancy in **quantity and assortment**.

Discrepancy in space refers to the fact that the location of production activities and the location of consumption are seldom the same. Consider, for example, the household furniture industry. Most household furniture in the United States is manufactured in a small geographic area in North Carolina, and a great deal of office furniture is manufactured in western Michigan. Yet, where is furniture demanded? All over the United States! This difference between the location of production and the location of consumption is a fundamental transportation challenge that must be overcome to accomplish exchange.

Discrepancy in time refers to the difference in timing between production and consumption. Some products, agricultural commodities, for example, are produced during short time periods but are continuously demanded by customers. On the other hand, many products are manufactured in anticipation of future customer demand. Since manufacturing often does not occur at the same time products are demanded, inventory and warehousing are required. It should be noted that much of the discussion in this text is devoted to the challenges firms face in more closely matching the rate of production with market consumption.

Discrepancy in quantity and assortment refers to the fact that manufacturing firms typically specialize in producing large quantities of a limited variety of items. Customers, on the other hand, typically demand small quantities of numerous items. This difference between the production and consumption sectors of the economy must somehow be reconciled to deliver the required product variety and assortment to customers.

To eliminate these discrepancies, Bucklin developed a long-standing theory that specifies four generic service outputs necessary to satisfy customer requirements: (1) spatial convenience, (2) lot size, (3) waiting or delivery time, and (4) product variety and assortment.[2] As discussed above, different customers may have different requirements regarding such services. It follows that different supply chain structures may be required to accommodate such differences.

---

[1] Don Peppers and Martha Rogers, "Return on Customer: A New Metric of Value Creation," *Journal of Direct, Data, and Digital Marketing Practice* (April–June 2006), pp. 318–321.
[2] Louis P. Bucklin, *A Theory of Distribution Channel Structure* (Berkeley, CA: IBER Special Publications, 1966).

Spatial Convenience

Spatial convenience, the first service output, refers to the amount of shopping time and effort that will be required on the part of the customer. Higher levels of spatial convenience can be achieved in a supply chain by providing customers with access to its products in a larger number of places, thus reducing shopping effort. Consider, for example, the household furniture industry. Some manufacturers utilize a structure that includes department stores, mass merchandisers, and numerous chain and independent furniture specialty stores. Ethan Allen, on the other hand, restricts brand availability to a limited number of authorized Ethan Allen retail stores. This difference in the level of spatial convenience has major implications for the overall supply chain structure and for the logistics cost incurred in the supply chain. It is also clear that some customers are willing to expend greater time and effort than others as they search for a desired product or brand.

Lot Size

The second service output is lot size, which refers to the number of units to be purchased in each transaction. When customers are required to purchase in large quantities, they must incur costs of product storage and maintenance. When the supply chain allows them to purchase in small lot sizes, they can more easily match their consumption requirements with their purchasing. In developed economies, alternative supply chains frequently offer customers a choice of lot-size. For example, consumers who are willing to purchase paper towels in a 12- or 24-roll package may buy at Sam's Club or Costco. As an alternative, they may buy single rolls at the local grocery or convenience store. Of course, the supply chain that allows customers to purchase in small quantities normally experiences higher cost and therefore demands higher unit prices from customers.

Waiting Time

Waiting time is the third generic service output. Waiting time is defined as the amount of time the customer must wait between ordering and receiving products: the lower the waiting time, the higher the level of supply chain service. Alternative supply chains offer consumers and end users choices in terms of the amount of waiting time required. In the personal computer industry, a consumer may visit an electronics or computer specialty store, make a purchase, and carry home a computer with literally no waiting time. Alternatively, the customer may order from a catalog or via the Internet and wait for delivery to the home or office. In a general sense, the longer the waiting time required, the more inconvenient for the customer. However, such supply chains generally incur lower costs and customers are rewarded in the form of lower prices for their willingness to wait.

Product Variety and Assortment

Product variety and assortment are the fourth service output. Different supply chains offer differing levels of variety and assortment to consumers and end users. Typical supermarkets are involved in supply chains that provide a broad variety of many different types of products and an assortment of brands, sizes, etc., of each type. In fact, supermarkets may have over 35,000 different items on the shelves. Warehouse stores, on the other hand, offer much less product variety or assortment, generally stocking in the range of 8,000 to 10,000 items, and have a limited number of brands and sizes. Convenience stores may stock only a few hundred items, offering little variety or assortment compared to supermarkets.

Supply chains provide additional service outputs to their customers. In addition to the four generic service outputs discussed above, other researchers have identified services related to information, product customization, and after-sales support as critical to selected customers. The point to keep in mind is that there is no such thing as a homogeneous market where all customers desire the same services presented in the same way. They may differ in terms of which services are most important and in terms of the level of each of the services desired to accommodate their needs. For example, some consumers may require immediate availability of a personal computer while others feel that waiting three days for a computer configured to their exact requirements is preferable. Additionally, customers differ in terms of how much they are willing to pay for services. Since higher levels of service generally involve higher market distribution costs, organizations must carefully assess customer sensitivity to prices relative to their desire for reduced waiting time, convenience, and other service outputs.

Omnichannel Marketing

While many firms have historically utilized multiple distribution channels to reach different market segments, since 2010 there is been a significant increase in what has become known as **omnichannel marketing**. No standard definition of the term *omnichannel* actually exists, but it does seem to be commonly agreed that it is a multichannel approach to sales that seeks to provide the customer with a seamless shopping experience whether the customer is shopping online from a desktop or mobile device, by telephone, or in a bricks-and-mortar facility. It is important to note that omnichannel can be implemented by manufacturers and wholesalers; it is not limited to retail companies.

Omnichannel has significant appeal to customers as it provides them with several alternative combinations of the supply chain service outputs described above. In terms of spatial convenience, for example, customers have no limitations on where and when they can shop, as long as an Internet connection is available. Of course, they still have an option of visiting a store or other facility during normal operating hours. Firms employing an omnichannel approach can typically provide customers with a much broader variety and assortment of products than is typically available in a retail store.

Waiting time is a significant issue in omnichannel marketing, which directly affects a firm's logistical capabilities. Many customers want rapid delivery of orders placed via Internet ordering, which is very challenging to accomplish in a cost-effective manner. Firms have found it very difficult to sort through the alternatives and determine how to accommodate this requirement. Amazon, for example, has opened more than 300 warehouses (and has more in the planning stages) to do so. Traditional retailers have tried to determine whether fulfilling such orders through their retail store inventory, through regular distribution center inventory, or through separate fulfillment facilities is the most efficient way to do so.

There is no question that omnichannel marketing will continue to grow. The interesting questions lie in how order fulfillment will be accomplished. Will it be same day (or even same hour)? Will it be to customer's home, office, or other facility? Will there have to be extra fees to customers who are more demanding in terms of speed and delivery location? If so, how much will those fees be? The logistical challenges raised by omnichannel marketing are likely to be answered differently by different firms. Meeting customer requirements for service outputs has important implications for how supply chains are ultimately configured, what types of participating companies may be included to satisfy service requirements, and the costs that are incurred in the process. Attention is now focused on more specific considerations of customer requirements in a logistical context. Three levels of commitment are discussed: customer service, customer satisfaction, and customer success.

Customer Service

The foundation of logistics commitment is to provide customer service in a cost-effective manner. Although most senior managers agree that customer service is important, they sometimes find it extremely difficult to explain what it is and what it does. While common expressions of customer service include "easy to do business with" and "responsive to customers," to develop a full understanding of customer service, a more thorough framework is required.

Philosophically, customer service represents logistics' role in fulfilling the marketing concept. A customer service program must identify and prioritize all activities required to meet customers' logistical requirements as well as, or better than, competitors. In establishing a customer service program, it is imperative to identify clear standards of performance for each of the activities and measurements relative to those standards. In basic customer service programs, the focus is typically on the operational aspects of logistics and ensuring that the organization is capable of providing the seven "rights" to its customer: the right amount of the right product at the right time at the right place in the right condition at the right price with the right information.

It is clear that outstanding customer service adds value throughout a supply chain. The critical concern in developing a service strategy is: **Does the cost associated with achieving specified service performance represent a sound investment?** Careful analysis of competitive performance and customer sensitivity to service attributes is required to formulate a basic service strategy. In Chapter 3, the fundamental attributes of basic customer service were identified as availability, operational performance, and service reliability. These attributes are now discussed in greater detail.

Availability

Availability is the capacity to have inventory when desired by a customer. As simple as this may seem, it is not at all uncommon for an organization to expend considerable time, money, and effort to generate customer demand and then fail to have product available to fill customer orders. The traditional practice in many organizations is to stock inventory in anticipation of customer orders. Typically an inventory stocking plan is based on forecasted demand for products and may include differential stocking policies for specific items as a result of sales popularity, profitability, or importance of an item to the overall product line.

While the detail of establishing inventory stocking policies is covered in Chapter 7, it should be clear that achieving high levels of inventory availability requires a great deal of planning. In fact, the key is achieving these high levels of availability while minimizing overall investment in inventory and facilities. Programs of inventory availability are not conceived or managed based on averages; availability is based on three performance measures: stockout frequency, fill rate, and perfect orders shipped.

Stockout Frequency

A stockout, as the term suggests, occurs when a firm has no product available to fulfill customer demand. Stockout frequency refers to the probability that a firm will not have inventory available to meet a customer order. For example, studies of retail stores across many industries consistently find that stockouts average about 8 percent. For items that are specifically being promoted, stockouts average about 16 percent![3] It is important to

---

[3] Tom Gruen and Daniel Corsten, "Improve Out-of-Stock Methods at the Shelf," *Chain Store Age* (July 2006), p. 35.

note, however, that a stockout does not have impact until a customer desires a product. The aggregation of all stockouts across all products is an indicator of how well a firm is positioned to provide basic service commitments in product availability. While it does not consider that some products may be more critical in terms of availability than others, it is the starting point in thinking about inventory availability.

Fill Rate

Fill rate measures the magnitude or impact of stockouts over time. Being out of stock does not necessarily affect service performance unless a customer demands a product. Then it is important to determine that the product is not available and how many units the customer wanted. While there are several approaches to measuring fill rates discussed in Chapters 7 and 13, item fill rate is a common approach. For example, if a customer wants 100 units of an item and only 97 are available, the fill rate is 97 percent. To effectively consider fill rate, the typical procedure is to evaluate performance over time to include multiple customer orders. Thus, fill rate performance can be evaluated for a specific customer, product, or any combination of customers, products, or business segments.

Fill rate can be used to differentiate the level of service to be offered on specific products. In the earlier example, if all 100 products ordered were critical to a customer, then a fill rate of 97 percent could result in a stockout at the customer's plant or warehouse and severely disrupt the customer's operations. Imagine an assembly line scheduled to produce 100 automobiles that receives only 97 of its required brake assemblies. In situations where some of the items are not critical to performance, a fill rate of 97 percent may be acceptable. The customer may accept a back order or be willing to reorder the short items at a later time. Fill rate strategies need to consider customer requirements for products.

Orders Shipped Complete

The most exacting measure of performance in product availability and delivery is orders shipped complete. It views having everything that a customer orders as the standard of acceptable performance. Failure to provide even one item on a customer's order results in that order being recorded as zero in terms of complete shipment.

These three measures of availability combine to establish the extent to which a firm's inventory strategy is meeting customer demand. They also form the basis to evaluate the appropriate level of availability to incorporate into a firm's logistical service program. High levels of inventory have typically been viewed as the means to increasing availability; however, new strategies that use information technology to identify customer demand in advance of actual customer orders have allowed some organizations to reach very high levels of availability without corresponding increases in inventory.

Operational Performance

Operational performance deals with the time required to deliver a customer's order. Whether the performance cycle in question is customer service, manufacturing support, or procurement, operational performance is specified in terms of speed of performance, consistency, flexibility, and malfunction recovery.

Speed

Performance cycle speed is the elapsed time from when a customer places an order until the product is delivered and is ready for customer use. The elapsed time required for total performance cycle completion depends on logistical system design and operations strategy. Given today's high level of communication and transportation technology, order cycles can be as short as a few hours or may take several weeks or months.

Naturally, most customers want fast order cycle performance. Speed is an essential ingredient in many just-in-time and quick-response logistical strategies, as fast performance cycles reduce customer inventory requirements. The counterbalance is that speed of service is typically costly: Not all customers need or want maximum speed if it means increased total cost. The justification for speed must be found in the positive trade-offs; the only relevant framework for estimating the value of service speed is the customer's perceived benefits.

Consistency

Order cycle consistency is measured by the number of times that actual cycles meet the time planned for completion. While speed of service is important, most logistical managers place greater value on consistency because it directly impacts a customer's ability to plan and perform its own activities. For example, if order cycles vary, then a customer must carry safety stock to protect against potential late delivery; the degree of variability translates directly into safety stock requirements. Given the numerous activities involved in order cycle execution, there are many potential sources of inconsistency in performance (review Figure 3.8).[4]

The issue of consistency is fundamental to effective logistics operations, as it is becoming increasingly common for customers to actually specify a desired date and even specify a delivery appointment when placing orders. Such a precise specification may be made, taking into consideration a supplier's past performance, but that is not always the case. In fact, customers frequently place orders far in advance of their need for product replenishment. In such situations, it is very difficult for customers to understand why a supplier fails to deliver as specified. Their viewpoint of supplier consistency in operational performance is whether the supplier delivered at the specified date and time. In such situations, the definition of consistency must be modified. It is no longer sufficient to evaluate in terms of planned time, such as 4 days to complete the cycle. It is essential to determine whether the performance cycle was completed according to the customer's specification. Thus, in today's logistical environment, consistency is frequently viewed as a firm's performance in terms of on-time delivery.

Flexibility

Flexibility involves a firm's ability to respond to special situations and unusual or unexpected customer requests. For example, the standard pattern for servicing a customer may be to ship full-trailer quantities to a customer's warehouse. However, from time to time, the customer may desire to have shipments of smaller quantities made direct to individual retail locations. A firm's logistical competency is directly related to how well it is able to accommodate such unexpected circumstances. Typical events requiring flexible operations are: (1) modification to basic service agreements such as a change in ship-to location; (2) support of unique sales promotion programs; (3) new product introduction; (4) product recall; (5) disruption in supply; (6) one-time customization of basic service for specific customers or segments; and (7) product modification or customization performed while in the logistics system, such as price marking, mixing, or packaging. In many ways the essence of logistical excellence rests in the ability to be flexible.

[4] See Figure 3.8, p. 058.

Malfunction Recovery

Regardless of how fine-tuned a firm's logistical operations, malfunctions will occur. The continuous performance of service commitments on a day-in, day-out basis is a difficult task. Ideally, adjustments can be implemented to prevent or accommodate special situations, thereby preventing malfunctions. For example, if a stockout of an essential item occurs at a warehouse that normally services a customer, the item may be obtained from an alternative facility by utilizing some form of expedited transportation. In such situations the malfunction may actually be transparent to the customer. While such transparent recoveries are not always possible, effective customer service programs anticipate that malfunctions and service breakdowns will occur and have in place contingency plans to accomplish recovery and measure compliance.

Service Reliability

Service reliability involves the combined attributes of logistics and concerns a firm's ability to perform all order-related activities, as well as provide customers with critical information regarding logistical operations and status. Beyond availability and operational performance, attributes of reliability may mean that shipments arrive damage-free; invoices are correct and error-free; shipments are made to the correct locations; and the exact amount of product ordered is included in the shipment. While these and numerous other aspects of overall reliability are difficult to enumerate, the point is that customers demand that a wide variety of business details be handled routinely by suppliers. Additionally, service reliability involves a capability and a willingness to provide accurate information to customers regarding operations and order status. Research indicates that the ability of a firm to provide accurate information is one of the most significant attributes of a good service program.[5] Increasingly, customers indicate that advanced notification of problems such as incomplete orders is more critical than the complete order itself. Customers hate surprises! More often than not, customers can adjust to an incomplete or late delivery if they have advanced notification.

The Perfect Order

The ultimate in logistics service is to do everything right and to do it right the first time. It is not sufficient to deliver a complete order but to deliver it late. Nor is it sufficient to deliver a complete order on time but to have an incorrect invoice or to incur product damage during handling and transportation. In the past, most logistics managers evaluated customer service performance in terms of several independent measures: Fill rates were evaluated against a standard for fill; on-time delivery was evaluated in terms of a percentage of deliveries made on time relative to a standard; damage rates were evaluated relative to a standard for damage; etc. When each of these separate measures was acceptable relative to standard, overall service performance was considered acceptable.

Recently, however, logistics and supply chain executives have begun to focus attention on zero-defect or six-sigma performance. As an extension of total quality management (TQM) efforts within organizations, logistics processes have been subjected to the same scrutiny as manufacturing and other processes in the firm. It was realized that if standards are established independently for customer service components, even if performance met standard on each independent measure, a substantial number of customers may have

[5] Donald J. Bowersox, David J. Closs, and Theodore P. Stank, *21st Century Logistics: Making Supply Chain Integration a Reality* (Oak Brook, IL: Council of Logistics Management, 1999).

TABLE 4.1
Typical Perfect Order
Failures

- Wrong quantities (over or short)
- Wrong items
- Late or early delivery
- Missing or incorrect information (e.g., price or promotion codes)
- Wrong transportation mode
- Wrong destination
- Incorrect documentation (e.g., bill of lading, invoice)
- Damaged items
- Incorrect loading/sequencing of shipment
- Incorrect payment processing

order-related failures. For example, if orders shipped complete, average on-time delivery, average damage-free delivery, and average correct documentation are each 97 percent, the probability that any order will be delivered with no defects is approximately 88.5 percent. This is so because the potential occurrence of any one failure combined with any other failure is $.97 \times .97 \times .97 \times .97$. The converse of this, of course, is that some type of problem will exist on as much as 11.5 percent of all orders.

The notion of the perfect order is that an order should be delivered complete, delivered on time, at the right location, in perfect condition, with complete and accurate documentation. Table 4.1 lists some of the most typical failures that arise in the attempt to provide perfect order performance. Each of these individual elements must comply with customer specifications. Thus, complete delivery means all product the customer originally requested, on time means at the customer's specified date and time, etc. In other words, total order cycle performance must be executed with zero defects, availability and operational performance must be perfectly executed, and all support activities must be completed exactly as promised to the customer. While it may not be possible to offer zero defects as a basic service strategy across the board to all customers, such high-level performance may be an option on a selective basis.

It is clear that the resources required to implement a perfect order platform are substantial. Extremely high fill rates require high inventory levels to meet all potential order requirements and variations. However, such complete service cannot be achieved totally on the basis of inventory. One way of elevating logistics performance to at least near zero defects is to utilize a combination of customer alliances, information technology, postponement strategies, inventory stocking strategies, premium transportation, and selectivity programs to match logistical resources to core customer requirements. Each of these topics is the subject of detailed discussion in subsequent chapters. At this time firms achieving superior logistical customer service are well aware of the challenge related to achieving zero defects. By having a low tolerance for errors, coupled with a commitment to resolve whatever problems occur, such firms can achieve strategic advantage over their competitors.

Logistics Service Platforms

To implement a logistics service platform, it is necessary to specify a commitment level to all customers in terms of availability, operational performance, and reliability. The fundamental question, "How much service should the system provide?" is not easy to answer. The fact is that many firms establish their service platforms on the basis of two factors. The first factor is competitor or industry-acceptable practice. In most industries, levels of minimum and average service performance have emerged. These acceptable levels are generally well known by both the suppliers and the customers throughout the industry. It is not uncommon to hear logistics and supply chain executives speak of customer service commitments in terms of doing as well as competition or beating major competitors' performance. The second factor derives from the firm's overall marketing strategy. If a firm desires to differentiate from competitors on the basis of logistics competency, then high levels of basic service are required. If the firm differentiates on price, then it likely will commit to lower levels of logistical service because of the resources required and costs related to high-level commitment.

The fact is that even firms with a high level of basic customer service commitment generally do not take a total zero-defect approach across the board for all customers. The common service commitment is to establish internal performance standards for each service component. These standards typically reflect prevailing industry practice in combination with careful consideration of cost and resource commitments.[6]

Typical service standards such as 97 percent fill rate or delivery within three days may be established, and then performance would be monitored relative to these internal standards. While it is generally assumed that this strategic approach results in servicing customers as well as or better than competitors, it does not assure that customers are, in fact, satisfied with either the overall industry performance or even the performance of an organization that performs above industry standard. In fact, there is only one way to be sure customers are satisfied: ask them.

Customer Satisfaction

Customer satisfaction has long been a fundamental concept in marketing and business strategy. In building a customer satisfaction program, however, the first question that must be answered is, "What does it mean to say that a customer is satisfied?" The simplest and most widely accepted method of defining customer satisfaction is based on customer expectations. Simply stated, if a customer's expectations of a supplier's performance are met or exceeded, the customer will be satisfied. Conversely, if perceived performance is less than what the customer expected, then the customer is dissatisfied. A number of companies have adopted this framework for customer satisfaction and follow a commitment to meet or exceed customers' expectations. In fact, many organizations have gone further by speaking in terms of delighting their customers through performance that exceeds expectations.

While this framework for customer satisfaction is relatively straightforward, the implications for building a customer accommodation platform in logistics are not. To build this platform it is necessary to explore more fully the nature of customer expectations. What do customers expect? How do customers form these expectations? What is the relationship between customer satisfaction and customer perceptions of overall logistics service quality? Why do many companies fail to satisfy customers, and why are so many companies perceived as providing poor logistics quality? If a company satisfies its customers, is that sufficient? The following sections provide some insights to these critical questions.

Customer Expectations

It is clear that when customers conduct business with a supplier they have numerous expectations, many of which revolve around the supplier's logistical service platform; that is, they have expectations regarding availability, operational performance, and service reliability. Frequently, firms have formal programs to monitor supplier performance with respect to each of these dimensions of logistical performance. In a pioneering study

---

[6] For an excellent discussion of cost and service, see Mariah M. Jeffery, Renee J. Butler, and Linda C. Malone, "Determining a Cost-Effective Customer Service Level," *Supply Chain Management* (March 2008), p. 225.

Reliability: Reliability is one of the aspects of the firm's basic service platform. In this context, however, reliability refers to performance of all activities as promised by the supplier. If the supplier promises next-day delivery and delivery takes 2 days, it is perceived as unreliable. If the supplier accepts an order for 100 cases of a product, it implicitly promises that 100 cases will be delivered. The customer expects and is only satisfied with the supplier if all 100 are received. Customers judge reliability in terms of all aspects of the basic service platform. Thus, customers have expectations concerning damage, documentation accuracy, etc.

Responsiveness: Responsiveness refers to customers' expectations of the willingness and ability of the supplier personnel to provide prompt service. This extends beyond mere delivery to include issues related to quick handling of inquiries and resolution of problems. Responsiveness is clearly a time-oriented concept and customers have expectations regarding suppliers' timely handling of all interactions.

Access: Access involves customer expectations of the ease of contact and approachability of the supplier. For example, is it easy to place orders, to obtain information regarding inventory or order status?

Communication: Communication means proactively keeping customers informed. Rather than waiting for customer inquiries concerning order status, customers have expectations regarding suppliers' notification of status, particularly if problems with delivery or availability arise. Customers do not like to be surprised, and advance notice is essential.

Credibility: Credibility refers to customer expectations that communications from the supplier are in fact believable and honest. While it is doubtful that many suppliers intentionally mislead customers, credibility also includes the notion of completeness in required communications.

Security: Security deals with customers' feelings of risk or of doubt in doing business with a supplier. Customers make plans based on their anticipation of supplier performance. For example, they take risks when they schedule production and undertake machine and line setups in anticipation of delivery. If orders are late or incomplete, their plans must be changed. Another aspect of security deals with customer expectations that their dealings with a supplier will be confidential. This is particularly important in supply chain arrangements when a customer has a unique operating agreement with a supplier who also services competitors.

Courtesy: Courtesy involves politeness, friendliness, and respect of contact personnel. This can be a particularly vexing problem considering that customers may have contact with numerous individuals in the organization ranging from sales representatives to customer service personnel to truck drivers. Failure by one individual may destroy the best efforts of all the others.

Competency: Competence is judged by customers in every interaction with a supplier and, like courtesy, can be problematic because it is perceived in every interaction. In other words, customers judge the competence of truck drivers when deliveries are made, warehouse personnel when orders are checked, customer service personnel when phone calls are made, and so forth. Failure by any individual to demonstrate competence affects customer perceptions of the entire organization.

Tangibles: Customers have expectations regarding the physical appearance of facilities, equipment, and personnel. Consider, for example, a delivery truck that is old, damaged, or in poor condition. Such tangible features are additional cues used by customers as indicators of a firm's overall performance.

Knowing the Customer: While suppliers may think in terms of groups of customers and market segments, customers perceive themselves as unique. They have expectations regarding suppliers' understanding their uniqueness and supplier willingness to adapt to their specific requirements.

TABLE 4.2   Customer Expectations Related to Logistical Performance

Parasuraman, Zeithaml, and Berry identified 10 customer expectations that form a useful framework for evaluating logistical impact.[7] Table 4.2 uses their framework to conceptualize specific logistics-based expectations.

In a logistical and supply chain context, the notion of customer expectations is particularly complex because customers are frequently business organizations made up of numerous functions and individuals. Different personnel in a customer organization may prioritize the criteria of performance differently, or they may have different levels of expectation for the criteria. For example, some personnel may be most concerned with responsiveness and rapid handling of an inquiry regarding order status, while others may be more concerned with order completeness or meeting a delivery appointment. Meeting customer expectations requires an understanding of how these expectations are formed and the reasons many companies fail to meet those expectations.

A Model of Customer Satisfaction

Figure 4.1 provides a framework for understanding the process by which customers actually form their expectations of supplier performance. It also suggests that frequently a number of gaps exist that a supplier must overcome in order to develop customer satisfaction.

[7] A. Parasuraman, Valerie Zeithaml, and Leonard L. Berry, "A Conceptual Model of Service Quality and Its Implications for Future Research," Report No. 84-106 (Cambridge, MA: Marketing Science Institute, 1984).

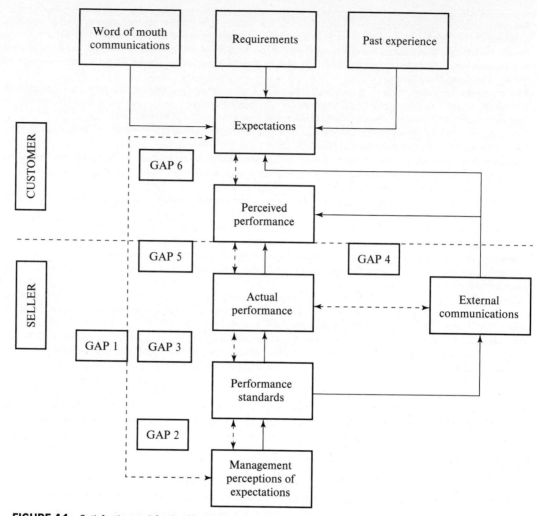

FIGURE 4.1   Satisfaction and Quality Model

Source: Adapted from A. Parasuraman, Valerie Zeithaml, and Leonard L. Berry, "A Conceptual Model of Service Quality and Its Implications for Future Research," Report No. 84-106 (Cambridge, MA: Marketing Science Institute, 1984).

There are several factors that influence customer expectations, both in terms of a prioritization of the criteria discussed above, as well as the level of expectation relative to each of the criteria. The first of these factors is very simply the customers' needs or requirements. At the heart of their own business strategies, customers have requirements that depend on the performance of their suppliers. To a major extent, customers expect that these needs can and will be met by suppliers. Interestingly, however, customers' expectations are frequently not the same as their real requirements or needs. Previous supplier performance is a major factor influencing customer expectations. A supplier who consistently delivers on time will most likely be expected to deliver on time in the future. Similarly, a supplier with a poor record concerning performance will be expected to perform poorly in the future. It is important to note that previous performance experienced with one supplier may also influence the customers' expectation regarding other suppliers. For example, when FedEx demonstrated the ability to deliver small packages on a next-day basis, many customers began to expect a similar performance capability from other delivery companies.

Related to a customer's perception of past performance is word-of-mouth. In other words, customers frequently communicate with one another concerning their experiences with specific suppliers. At trade and professional association meetings, the subject of suppliers is a common topic of discussion among executives. Much of the discussion may revolve around supplier performance capabilities. Such discussions help form individual customer expectations. Perhaps the most important factor influencing customer expectations is the communications coming from the supplier itself. Promises and commitments made by sales personnel or customer service representatives, statements contained in marketing and promotional messages, even the printed policies and procedures of an organization represent communications that customers depend upon. These communications become a critical basis on which they form their expectations. The promise of meeting a delivery appointment or having full product availability becomes an expectation in the customer's mind. Indeed many suppliers may be guilty of setting themselves up for failure by overcommitting in an attempt to influence customer expectations. Figure 4.1 also provides a framework for understanding what must be done by an organization to deliver customer satisfaction. The failure of many firms to satisfy their customers can be traced to the existence of one or more of the gaps identified in the framework.

Gap 1: Knowledge

The first and the most fundamental gap that may exist is between customers' real expectations and managers' perceptions of those expectations. This gap reflects management's lack of knowledge or understanding of customers. While there may be many reasons for this lack of understanding, it is clear that no beneficial customer satisfaction platform can be established without a thorough understanding of customer expectations, how they are prioritized, and how they are formed. Since sales typically has the major responsibility for customer interactions, knowledge regarding logistics expectations is often difficult to obtain.

Gap 2: Standards

Even if full understanding of customer expectations exists, it is still necessary to establish standards of performance for the organization. The standards gap exists when internal performance standards do not adequately or accurately reflect customer expectations. This is precisely the case in many organizations that develop their service platform from an examination of internal operating capabilities or a superficial examination of competitive service performance.

Gap 3: Performance

The performance gap is the difference between standard and actual performance. If the standard is a fill rate of 98 percent, based on research with customers regarding their expectations, and the firm actually performs at 97 percent, a performance gap exists. It should be pointed out that many firms focus their efforts to improve satisfaction by eliminating the performance gap. It may be, however, that the dissatisfaction exists as a result of a poor understanding of customer expectations in the first place.

Gap 4: Communications

The role of communications in customer satisfaction cannot be overemphasized. As discussed previously, overcommitment, or promising higher levels of performance than can actually be provided, is a major cause of customer dissatisfaction. There should be no gap between what a firm is capable of doing and what customers are told about those capabilities.

Gap 5: Perception

It is true that customers sometimes perceive performance to be lower or higher than actually achieved. In logistics, many managers frequently lament, "We're only as good as the last order." Thus, although performance over a long time period has been very good, a late or incomplete or otherwise subpar delivery may result in a customer's expression of extreme dissatisfaction.

Gap 6: Satisfaction/Quality

The existence of any one or more of the above gaps leads to customer perception that performance is not as good as expected. In other words, these gaps result in customer dissatisfaction. When building a platform for delivering customer satisfaction, a firm must ensure that these gaps do not exist.

Increasing Customer Expectations

As an important component of TQM, the notion of continuous improvement has been accepted by most organizations. As a corollary of continuous improvement, there has been a continued escalation of customers' expectations concerning supplier capabilities. Performance that meets customer expectations one year may result in extreme dissatisfaction next year, as customers increase their expectations regarding acceptable performance levels.

To some extent, the increase in expectations can be traced to the dynamics of competition. As discussed previously, most industries traditionally have had explicit or implied levels of performance, which were considered to be adequate. If a firm wanted to be a serious competitor, it generally had to achieve these minimum industry service expectations. However, when one firm in the industry focuses on logistics as a core competency and provides higher performance levels, customers come to expect other suppliers to follow. Consider, for example, that after FedEx introduced real-time tracking of shipment status, UPS and other parcel delivery firms shortly followed suit. Today, real-time tracking is considered to be essential in the industry.

Does achieving perfect order performance ensure that customers are satisfied? On the surface it would seem so. After all, if all orders are delivered with no defects, what basis exists for customers to be dissatisfied? Part of the answer to this question lies in the fact that perfect orders, as important as they are, deal with the execution of individual transactions and deliveries. Customer satisfaction is a much broader concept, dealing with many other aspects of the overall relationship between suppliers and customers. For example, a customer may continuously receive perfect orders but be dissatisfied with such aspects of the relationship as difficulty in obtaining information, long delays in response to inquiries, or even the perception that some supplier personnel do not treat the customer with proper courtesy and respect. Thus, satisfaction transcends operational performance to include aspects of personal and interpersonal relationships.

Limitations of Customer Satisfaction

Because of its explicit focus on customers, a commitment to satisfaction represents a step beyond a basic service platform in an organization's efforts to develop customer relationships. It is realistic to think that a firm satisfying customer expectations better than competitors will gain some competitive advantage in the marketplace. Nevertheless, it is important to realize some of the shortcomings and limitations of the customer satisfaction emphasis.

		Expectation		
		LO	**MED**	**HI**
Performance	**HI**	Very Satisfied	Very Satisfied	Satisfied
	MED	Very Satisfied	Satisfied	Dissatisfied
	LO	Satisfied	Dissatisfied	Dissatisfied

FIGURE 4.2
Satisfaction Is Not the Same as Happiness

The first limitation is that many executives make a fundamental, yet understandable, mistake in their interpretation of satisfaction. In many organizations it is assumed that customers who are satisfied are also happy, maybe even delighted, with the supplier's performance. That may or may not be the actual situation. It must be remembered that satisfaction is the customers' perception of actual performance in relation to expectation, not their requirements. Examination of Figure 4.2 may help explain this difference between satisfaction and happiness. The fact is that customers may have an expectation that a firm will not perform at a high level. If the customer has an expectation of a low level of performance and indeed perceives that the firm performs at this low level, it is clear that performance and expectation match. By definition, the customer is satisfied. The same is true at midlevel expectations and perceptions as well as high levels of each.

This notion that low levels of performance may be considered satisfactory can best be illustrated by example. Suppose a customer expects a supplier to provide, over time, a fill rate of 95 percent, or late deliveries 10 percent of the time, or damage of 2 percent. If the supplier in fact provides this level of performance, as perceived by the customer, the customer is satisfied. Performance perceived to be poorer than the expectation level results in dissatisfaction. Is the satisfied customer necessarily happy about the supplier's fill rate or late deliveries? Of course not. While expectations may be met, in fact met as well as or better than competition, there is still no assurance that the customer will be happy. Even performance higher than that expected, while satisfying to customers, may not actually result in happiness. The focus on customer expectations ignores the fact that expectations are not the same as needs or requirements.

The second limitation to consider is actually related to the first: Satisfied customers are not necessarily loyal customers. Even though their expectations are being met, satisfied customers may choose to do business with competitors. This can occur because they expect a competitor to perform at a higher level or at least as well as the organization in question. For many years, marketing and supply chain executives have assumed that satisfied customers are also loyal customers. Yet research has frequently shown that many customers who report being satisfied that their expectations have been met are likely to patronize and do business with competitors. Since customer satisfaction exists when customers get what they expect, customers frequently settle for performance that is less than what they really want or need. This result has been identified as **customer sacrifice**.[8]

A third limitation to customer satisfaction is that firms frequently forget satisfaction lies in the expectations and perceptions of individual customers. Thus, there is a tendency to aggregate expectations across customers and neglect the basic tenets of marketing strategy related to differences among customer segments as well as individual customers. Simply stated, what satisfies one customer may not satisfy other, much less all, customers.

Despite these limitations, customer satisfaction does represent a commitment beyond basic service to accommodate customers. It provides explicit recognition that the only way to ensure that customers are being accommodated is to focus on customers themselves.

[8] Joseph B. Pine II and James N. Gilmore, "Satisfaction, Sacrifice, Surprise," *Strategy and Leadership*, 28, no. 1 (2000), pp. 18–23.

Firms that focus primarily on industry and competitor standards of service performance are much less likely to find that their customers are very satisfied or highly satisfied with their performance.

Customer Success

In recent years, some firms have discovered that there is another commitment that can be made to gain true competitive advantage through logistical performance. This commitment is based on recognition that a firm's ability to grow and expand market share depends on its ability to attract and hold the industry's most successful customers. The real key, then, to customer-focused marketing lies in a company using its performance capabilities to enhance the success of those customers. This focus on customer success represents major commitment toward accommodating customers. Table 4.3 summarizes the evolution that customer-focused organizations have experienced. Notice that a customer service focus is oriented toward establishment of internal standards for basic service performance. Firms typically assess their customer service performance relative to how well these internal standards are accomplished. The customer satisfaction platform is built on the recognition that customers have expectations regarding performance and the only way to ensure that customers are satisfied is to assess their perceptions of performance relative to those expectations.

Customer success shifts the focus from expectations to the customer's real requirements. Recall from the previous discussion that customer requirements, while forming the basis for expectations, are not the same as expectations. Requirements are frequently downgraded into expectations because of perceptions of previous performance, word-of-mouth, or communications from the firm itself. This explains why simply meeting expectations may not result in happy customers. For example, a customer may be satisfied with a 98 percent fill rate, but for the customer to be successful in executing its own strategy, a 100 percent fill rate on certain products or components may be necessary.

Achieving Customer Success

Clearly, a customer success program involves a thorough understanding of individual customer requirements and a commitment to focus on long-term business relationships having high potential for growth and profitability. Such commitment most likely cannot be made to all potential customers. It requires that firms work intensively with customers to understand requirements, internal processes, competitive environment, and whatever else it takes for the customer to be successful in its own competitive arena. Further, it requires that an organization develop an understanding of how it can utilize its own capabilities to enhance customer performance. As an example, Raytheon has adopted and trademarked the slogan "customer success is our mission."

In many ways a customer success program requires a comprehensive supply chain perspective on the part of logistics executives. This is most easily explained by examining

TABLE 4.3
Evolution of
Management Thought

Philosophy	Focus
Customer service	Meet internal standards
Customer satisfaction	Meet expectations
Customer success	Meet customer requirements

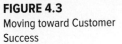

FIGURE 4.3
Moving toward Customer
Success

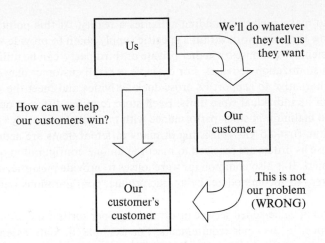

the relations depicted in Figure 4.3. The typical focus in basic service and satisfaction programs is that the firm attempts to meet standards and expectations of next-destination customers, whether they are consumers, industrial end users, or intermediate or even internal customers. How those customers deal with their customer is typically not considered to be a problem. A supply chain perspective and a customer success program explicitly recognize that logistics executives must alter this focus. They must understand the entire supply chain, the different levels of customer within that supply chain, and develop programs to ensure that next-destination customers are successful in meeting the requirements of customers down the supply chain. If all supply chain members adopt this perspective, then all members share in the success.

To ensure that a customer is successful may require a firm to reinvent the way a product is produced, distributed, or offered for sale. In fact, collaboration between suppliers and customers to find potential avenues for success may result in the greatest breakthroughs in terms of redefining supply chain processes. The general topic of collaborative relationships and alliances is further developed in Chapter 12. It is enough to say here that such arrangements are not possible without significant amounts of information exchange between the involved businesses to facilitate an in-depth understanding of requirements and capabilities. However, one important way that many firms have responded to the challenges of customer success is through the development of value-added services.

Value-Added Services

The notion of value-added service is a significant development in the evolution to customer success. By definition, value-added services refer to unique or specific activities that firms can jointly develop to enhance their efficiency, effectiveness, and relevancy. Value-added services help foster customer success. Because they tend to be customer specific, it is difficult to generalize all possible value-added services.

When a firm becomes committed to value-added solutions for major customers, it rapidly becomes involved in customized or tailored logistics. It is doing unique things to enable specific customers to achieve their objectives. In a logistical context, firms can provide unique product packages, create customized unit loads, place prices on products, offer unique information services, provide vendor-managed inventory service, make special shipping arrangements, and so forth, to enhance customer success.

In reality, some of the value-added services that buyers and sellers agree to involve integrated service providers that are positioned to provide such services. Transportation carriers, warehouse firms, and other specialists may become intimately involved in the supply chain to make such value-adding activities a reality. At this point, a few specific examples of how they may work within a specific supply chain to provide value-added services are sufficient. Warehouses, whether private or third-party, can be utilized to perform a number of customization activities. For example, a retail customer may desire a unique palletization alternative to support its cross-dock activities and meet the unique product requirements of its individual store units. Each store requires different quantities of specific product to maintain in-stock performance with minimum inventory commitment. In another situation, first-aid kits consisting of many different items are actually assembled in the warehouse as orders are received to meet the unique configuration of kit desired by specific customers. It is also common for warehouses to provide pick-price-repack services for manufacturers to accommodate the unique product configurations required by different retailers.

Another form of value-added service involves the proper sorting and sequencing of products to meet specific customer requirements. For example, an auto assembly plant may require that components not only be received on time but also be sorted and sequenced in a particular manner to meet the needs of specific automobiles on the assembly line. The objective is to reduce assembly plant handling and inspection of incoming components. Meeting such exacting requirements for delivery is far beyond the basic service capability of many component suppliers. The use of third-party specialists is a necessity, especially when subcomponents from multiple suppliers must be integrated and then properly sequenced.

Value-added services can be performed directly by participants in a business relationship or may involve specialists. It has become more common in recent years to turn to specialists because of their flexibility and ability to concentrate on providing the required services. Nevertheless, regardless of how the specifics are organized and implemented, it is clear that logistics value-added services are a critical aspect of customer success programs.

Developing Customer Accommodation Strategy

It follows from the earlier discussion of the marketing concept and relationship marketing that different customers are likely to require different approaches and strategies for customer accommodation. Customer service may be appropriate for some customers, customer satisfaction for others, while a success focus may be in order for others. In fact, a basic principle of supply chain logistics is that customers should be segmented based on their service needs, and the supply chain must be adapted to serve those segments.[9]

For example, Procter & Gamble has an approach called Service as Measured by the Customer (SAMBC) that it has adopted with some of its major retail customers. Like most companies, P&G, internally was driven by its own metrics, spread across all customers around cost, fill rate, on-time deliveries, and the like. With SAMBC, Procter & Gamble is now measuring itself primarily based on how well it is performing against the individual performance metrics of all customers in this program. In fact, SAMBC is defined as the percent of customers for which P&G is meeting or exceeding all of those customers' unique expectations.

The program recognizes that customers vary in what metrics are most important to them, how those measures are defined, and what the levels of expectations are for each measure. While some metrics are common among those retailers, there is also a lot of

[9] David L. Anderson, Frank F. Britt, and Donovan J. Favre, "The Best of Supply Chain Management Review: The Seven Principles of Supply Chain Success," *Supply Chain Management Review* (April 2007), p. 57.

variation in what metrics were included across the group. Even commonly embraced metrics such as on-time and fill rates were calculated differently by various retailers.[10] Thus, P&G adapts its approach to meet the unique requirements of those retailers.

Framework for Strategic Choice

It is clear that customer success approaches are extremely time consuming and resource intensive. No firm is likely to be able to implement such approaches with every potential customer. In fact, it is likely that many customers themselves may not desire such relationships with all (or any) suppliers. From a strategic point of view, then, a company must determine which type of relationship approach is appropriate for which customers.

There is no easy answer to that question, but one approach relies on the well established Pareto principle (also known as the 80/20 principle). This states simply that a large percentage (perhaps 80 percent) of a company's revenue and profit typically is derived from a small percentage of its customers (as few as 20 percent). There is no absolute concerning these percentages, but the concept is very clear. This principle can also be applied to the products a company sells; a few products account for a large percentage of sales revenue and profits. The combination of these facts leads to the diagram presented in Table 4.4.[11] In the diagram customers are classified as A, B, C, or D on the basis of profitability and products as 1, 2, 3, or 4 on the same basis. For example, A customers are those who are extremely profitable; B customers, very profitable; C customers, somewhat profitable; and D customers, unprofitable. Similarly, products 1 through 4 exhibit similar profitability characteristics.[12] Methodologies for determining specific customer and product profitability are discussed in Chapter 13.

It is likely that only a small number of customer/product combinations are extremely profitable. Those situations are naturally the most likely candidates for a customer success relationship, as depicted in the upper left-hand corner of Table 4.4. It is also likely that even A customers may not desire or require the same intensity of development for all products. Thus, satisfaction or even basic service may be acceptable in those situations.

Those customer/product combinations that fall in the lower right-hand corner should be carefully reviewed as to whether or not it is reasonable to maintain them. In many instances there may be good reason to continue. For example, they may be new customers or may be small but rapidly growing companies. Likewise there may be characteristics of the products that must be reviewed. However, in some instances it may simply be a wiser decision to stop doing business with a particular customer and/or eliminate a specific product from the overall assortment.

---

[10] Adapted from Dan Gilmore, "P&G's New Service as Measured by Customer—Supply Chain Industry Inflection Point?" *Supply Chain Digest* (November 3, 2011), p. 1.
[11] This discussion is adapted from and based on Robert Sabbath and Judith M. Whipple, "Integrating Marketing and Supply Chain Management to Improve Profitability," *CSCMP Explores* 4 (Summer 2007), pp. 1–15.
[12] Ibid.

TABLE 4.4
Choosing Customer Relationship Strategy

Source: Adapted from Robert Sabbath and Judith M. Whipple, "Integrating Marketing and Supply Chain Management to Improve Profitability," *CSCMP Explores* 4 (Summer 2007), p. 8.

Customer Category	Product Category			
	1	2	3	4
A	Success	Success	Success/satisfaction	Basic service
B	Success/satisfaction	Success/satisfaction	Basic service	Basic service
C	Basic service	Basic service	Basic service	Basic service/cull
D	Basic service/cull	Basic service/cull	Basic service/cull	Basic service/cull

The above discussion is meant to be suggestive of strategic choice and not necessarily the only approach. For example, it may be necessary to maintain customer success through the entire product range for an A customer. Or it may be desirable to establish a customer success focus with a customer who is currently of limited profitability in order to convert that customer to extremely high profitability. The most important point to remember is that customer success typically must be reserved for a limited number of situations due to the resource constraints. Other situations may require a satisfaction approach. It is clear, however, that if a company chooses to do business with a customer, adequate basic service is a minimum requirement.

Customer Relationship Management Technology

The term **customer relationship management (CRM)** has been used by many firms to describe their efforts to accommodate better the needs and requirements of individual customers. However, CRM is also used to describe technology and software that is used to manage and analyze data from numerous sources within an organization to gain greater insight into customer buying behavior (sales calls, call centers, actual purchases, etc.). In fact, numerous software vendors offer packages they describe as CRM software to accomplish this purpose. CRM technology is designed to extend the functionality of the ERP sales and delivery applications. CRM provides sales representatives and customers with current information regarding sales history, shipment history, order status, promotional summaries, and shipment information. The history and current status information, combined with product development, pricing, and promotion information, allow firms to better create and manage customer orders. Such timely and accurate information exchange between a firm and its customers increases the likelihood that the product sales and promotion plans will be supported with the required product. Figure 4.4 illustrates the flow and elements of a typical CRM system.

While traditional ERP applications focus on efficiently taking customer orders, firms are finding it necessary to transition from treating customers as income sources to be exploited to treating customers as assets to be nurtured. While the traditional sales and delivery technology is configured to accept customer orders in a wide range of formats and allow those orders to be managed throughout the fulfillment process, a broader range of capabilities is necessary to manage the overall customer relationship. An integrated CRM system includes a combination of a server-based common database, remote PCs carried by sales representatives, and a global synchronization process to ensure that both corporate and sales representative data are timely and consistent. Beyond this base functionality, CRM today requires sales tracking, sales history analysis, pricing management, promotion management, product mix management, and category management. In some cases, customers expect their supplier's sales force to manage the entire category of products at the customer's facility. For example, it is becoming more common for grocers to expect their suppliers to manage both the product mix and shelf quantities for major product categories such as beverages and specialty products. This practice, termed **category management**, requires substantial information support from the manufacturer but also facilitates information sharing.

Amazon has been one of the leaders in CRM technology in an Internet retail environment. Due to its online interface and massive data storage and computational capabilities, Amazon is able to develop customer profiles that give a clear picture of each individual customer's interests and purchasing habits. For example, Amazon customers frequently receive e-mail messages from Amazon informing them of new books written by authors of books that they previously purchased. In addition, every time repeat customers log onto Amazon.com, they get tips on other books they might like, based on their previous

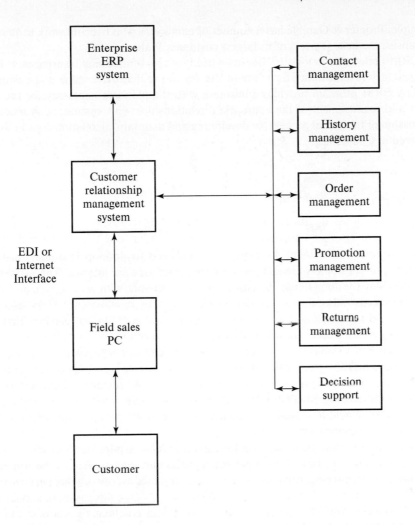

FIGURE 4.4
Typical Customer
Relationship
Management Extension
System

purchases. Also, when a customer selects a particular title from Amazon's website, the customer is informed of book titles that other customers have ordered in conjunction with the title that has been selected. All of these actions certainly benefit Amazon by increasing revenue. However, most customers also appreciate this ability on the part of Amazon as it adds significantly to their reading enjoyment.

The objective of customer relationship management is to develop a customer-centered organization. While CRM certainly involves the science of gathering and analyzing data about individual customer needs and purchasing habits, it extends to the process of developing capabilities that enable the organization to meet those individual needs more completely. CRM has grown rapidly over recent years as a process for improving the overall performance of a business by better understanding and anticipating the wants and needs of customers.

Firms that have embraced CRM are committed to the notion that customers are the sole driver for the entire business. In addition to technology, other efforts are made to build deeper understanding of customer requirements and develop lasting relationships with critical customers. For example, it is becoming increasingly common for suppliers to have their own personnel maintain an office very near, or even inside, the facilities of key customers. In this way, the supplier gains critical knowledge of the customer's needs and plans and can anticipate the customer's actions with a high degree of certainty. As one example, Procter & Gamble has a number of employees who live and work in Bentonville, Arkansas, the headquarters of its largest customer, Walmart.

CRM's relevance to logistics lies in its need for cross-functional transparency. Logistics has primary responsibility for many of the processes that drive value and customer success. A CRM program provides a business with the platform necessary for the development and management of the appropriate relationships with customers. A much deeper discussion of the actual process for developing and maintaining relationships in logistics is deferred to Chapter 12.

Summary

A fundamental requirement for logistics is the need to develop customer relationships whether those customers are end users, intermediate, or even internal. The marketing concept provides the foundation for customer commitments with its fundamental focus on customer needs rather than on products or services, the requirement to view and position products and services in a customer context, identification of market segments that differ in needs, and commitment that volume is secondary to profit.

Contemporary implementation of the marketing concept suggests that it is more important to focus on the development of relationships with customers than to perfect individual transactions. This interpretation focuses on the needs and requirements of individual customers as the core ingredient of relationship marketing. In a supply chain context, customer requirements related to spatial convenience, lot size, waiting time, and variety and assortment must be supported by logistical performance.

Organizations build their platform for customer relationships on three levels of increasing commitment. The first of these is basic logistics customer service. To be competitive, a firm needs a basic service capability that balances availability, operational performance, and reliability for all customers. The level of commitment to each dimension of service requires careful consideration of competitive performance and cost/benefit analysis. The highest level of commitment is perfect order performance, which requires zero defects logistics operations. Such high-level commitment is generally reserved for a firm's key customers.

Going beyond basic service to create customer satisfaction represents the second level of commitment. Where basic service focuses on the organization's internal operational performance, customer satisfaction focuses on customers, their expectations, and their perceptions of supplier performance. Customer expectations extend beyond typical logistical considerations and include factors related to communication, credibility, access, responsiveness, and customer-specific knowledge as well as reliability and responsiveness of operations. A firm can provide logistics service that is equal to or even better than competitors' but still have dissatisfied customers. Failure to satisfy customers can arise from lack of knowledge about customer expectations, improper standards of performance, performance failure, poor communication, or incorrect customer or firm perception of performance. As customer expectations escalate, logistics executives must continuously monitor customer satisfaction and logistics performance.

The highest level of commitment is known as customer success. Where satisfaction programs seek to meet or exceed expectations, a success platform focuses on customer needs and requirements. Customer expectations are frequently different from needs and requirements. Achieving success requires intimate knowledge of customers' needs and their operational requirements and a commitment by the service provider to enhance a customer's ability to compete more successfully in the marketplace. Value-added services represent one way logistics can contribute to customer success.

A customer relationship strategy requires in-depth knowledge of the logistical require-ments of different customers. CRM technology is increasingly being used to aid in this process and to provide both the company and its customers with the information necessary for effective long-term relationships.

Study Questions

1. Explain the differences between transactional and relationship marketing. How do these differences lead to increasing emphasis on logistical performance in supply chain management?
2. Why are the four primary service outputs of spatial convenience, lot size, waiting time, and product variety important to logistics management? Provide examples of competing firms that differ in the level of each service output provided to customers.
3. Using the 10 categories of customer expectations in Table 4.2, develop your own exam-ples of how customers might evaluate performance of a supplier.
4. Compare and contrast the customer service, customer satisfaction, and customer suc-cess philosophies of supply chain management.
5. What is meant by value-added services? Why are these services considered essential in a customer success program?
6. Explain the customer satisfaction "gaps" shown in Figure 4.1.

Challenge Questions

1. Gillette has involved itself in omnichannel marketing by establishing a subscription ser-vice for razor blades delivered to consumer homes. How does this differ in terms of service outputs from its normal distribution process?
2. In general, what challenges do you think a manufacturer of consumer goods faces in implementing an omnichannel approach?

PART 2

Supply Chain Operations

One of the key challenges in integrated supply chain management is cross-functional and cross-organizational operational planning. Chapter 5 focuses on the challenges faced in intra- and interorganizational planning and examines the methods and tools that can be applied to overcome these challenges. Chapter 6 discusses the operational areas of manufacturing and procurement with a focus on how these activities are linked to, and supported by logistics.

Integrated Operations Planning

Chapter Outline

The dominant theme of supply chain management is achievement of operational integration. The benefits available from operational integration are directly related to capturing efficiencies between functions within an enterprise as well as across enterprises that constitute a domestic or international supply chain. This chapter focuses on the challenges of supply chain operational planning by examining how and why such planning creates value and by detailing the challenges related to developing an effective plan. The **sales and operations planning (S&OP)** process is discussed from the perspective of effective cross-functional and cross-organizational collaboration. The discussion of S&OP includes a description and illustration of **advanced planning and scheduling (APS)**. The S&OP review is followed by a discussion of the more comprehensive integrated business planning initiatives that many firms have begun. Following a brief discussion of **collaborative planning, forecasting, and replenishment (CPFR)**, the chapter is concluded with a comprehensive discussion of forecasting.

Supply Chain Planning

Supply chain operational planning requires the coordination of some of the processes identified in Chapter 1. Specifically, demand planning responsiveness, customer relationship collaboration, order fulfillment/service delivery, manufacturing customization, supplier relationship collaboration, life cycle support, and reverse logistics must be coordinated to satisfy customers and effectively deploy resources. The processes and technologies to provide this coordination is integrated supply chain planning.

The supply chain planning system and supportative information systems seek to integrate information and coordinate overall logistics and supply chain decisions while recognizing the dynamics between other firm functions and processes. The three drivers of effective planning are (1) supply chain visibility, (2) simultaneous resource consideration, and (3) resource utilization.

Supply Chain Visibility

The first driver of planning system development is the need for **visibility** regarding location and status of supply chain inventory and resources. Visibility implies not only being able to track supply chain inventory and resources, but also that information regarding available resources can be effectively evaluated and managed. For example, at any given point in time, manufacturers may have thousands of shipments in-transit and inventory being held at hundreds of locations around the globe. Simply being able to identify shipments and inventory is not sufficient; supply chain visibility requires exception management to highlight the need for changes in flow or deployment decisions to minimize or prevent potential problems.

Limited visibility regarding inventory in-transit and expected arrival times results in significant uncertainty regarding product availability. The lack of certainty in a situation where product availability is critical results in additional inventory and requisitions to reduce the chance of stockouts. While it is clear that no military force can tolerate short supply, excessive inventories can also be expensive and typically wasteful of critical resources.

Simultaneous Resource Consideration

If planning system visibility highlights resource status and availability, the second planning system requirement is the need to simultaneously consider supply chain demand, capacity, material requirements, and constraints. Supply chain design must consider customer demand for product quantity, delivery timing, and location. While some of these customer requirements may be negotiable, logistics must execute to the agreed-to requirements and standards.

The constraints to meeting customer requirements are materials, production, storage, and transportation capacity, which represent the physical limitations of processes and facilities. Traditional planning methods have typically considered these capacity constraints in a sequential manner. For example, an initial plan is made that operates within production constraints. The initial plan is then adjusted to reflect material and sourcing constraints. This second plan is then revised to consider storage and transportation constraints. While the processes and sequences may be different, sequential decision making results in suboptimal and inferior planning and capacity utilization.

Achieving desired supply chain performance requires simultaneous consideration of relevant requirements and capacity constraints to identify trade-offs where increased functional costs, such as in manufacturing or storage, might lead to lower total system cost. A planning system needs to quantitatively evaluate the trade-offs and identify alternatives to enhance overall performance.

Resource Utilization

Logistics and supply chain management decisions influence many enterprise resources, including production, distribution facilities, inventory and equipment, transportation equipment, and inventories. These resources consume a substantial proportion of a typical firm's fixed and working assets. Functional management must focus on resource utilization within its scope of responsibility. For example, production management is focused on minimizing plant and equipment resources required for manufacturing. The typical result is long production runs requiring minimum setups and changeovers. However, longer production runs invariably result in more finished inventory, as substantial quantities are manufactured in anticipation of projected demand. Excess inventory increases working capital and space requirements. Extended production runs also require longer-term and more accurate forecasts.

With functional resource trade-offs in mind, the final driver of planning system development is the need for a coordinated approach that considers service requirements while minimizing combined supply chain resources. This is a critical capability when supply chain and firm performance place a strong emphasis on overall asset utilization.

Supply Chain Planning Applications

Supply chain planning is increasing in frequency and scope. Such applications are evolving to consider a broader range of activities and resources within the scope of supply chain planning. There are, however, some applications common for most supply chain environments. These include demand planning, production planning, and logistics planning.

Demand Planning

The increasing complexity of product offerings and marketing tactics in conjunction with shorter product life cycles requires increased accuracy, flexibility, and consistency in determining inventory requirements. Demand management systems seek to provide such capabilities.

Demand management develops the forecast that drives anticipatory supply chain processes. The forecasts are the projections of monthly, weekly, or daily demand that determine production and inventory requirements. Each projected quantity might include some portion of future orders placed in anticipation of customer demand along with some portion of forecasted demand based on history. Essentially, the demand management process integrates historically based forecasts with other information regarding events that could influence future sales activity, such as promotional plans, pricing changes, and new product introductions, to obtain the best possible integrated statement of requirements. Forecast techniques and procedures are discussed later in this chapter.

Another aspect of the demand management process focuses on creating forecast consistency across multiple products and warehouse facilities. Effective integrated management requires a single accurate forecast for each item and facility. The aggregate and combined requirements must reflect a plan that is consistent with divisional and overall firm sales and financial projections. The demand management system is the information technology component of the S&OP process to develop the unconstrained marketing plan. The demand management system begins with a base forecast and then incorporates such factors as product life cycle, changes in distribution channels, pricing and promotional tactics, and product mix variations. The demand management system also rationalizes the detailed logistics plans, unique forecasts for each warehouse and product, with the aggregate product group and national plans. For example, the sum of individual warehouse facility sales should be consistent with national sales projections. Similarly, item level requirements need to be adjusted to reflect the activity level for related items. For instance, requirements for existing products may have to be reduced to reflect the market's reaction to a new product introduction or one item's requirements may need to be adjusted during the promotion of a substitutable item.

Production Planning

Production planning uses the statement of requirements obtained from demand management in conjunction with manufacturing resources and constraints to develop a workable manufacturing plan. The statement of requirements defines what items are needed and when. Although there has been a definite trend toward **make-to-order (MTO)** and **assemble-to-order (ATO)** manufacturing, such response-based practices are not always possible because of production technology, capacity, resource constraints, or customer requirements. The limitations occur in the form of facility, equipment, and labor availability.

Production planning systems match the requirements plan with the production constraints. The objective is to satisfy the necessary requirements at the minimum total production cost while not violating any constraints. Effective production planning results in a time-sequenced plan to manufacture the correct items efficiently while operating within facility, equipment, and labor constraints. Production planning identifies the items that should be produced in anticipation of need to remain within production constraints and yet minimize inventory.

Logistics Planning

Logistics planning coordinates transportation, warehousing, and inventory within the firm and between supply chain partners. Historically, purchasing and finished goods transportation both attempted to minimize their freight cost individually. Procurement minimized the expense of raw material movements by working with suppliers and inbound carriers. Logistics focused on minimizing outbound freight expense by working with customers and their transportation carriers. There is also often a third managerial focus related to international shipments. The individual perspectives of transportation often result in limited economies of scale, limited information sharing, and excessive transportation expense.

Logistics planning integrates overall movement demand, vehicle availability, and relevant movement cost into a common decision support system that seeks to minimize overall freight expense. The analysis suggests ways that freight can be shifted among carriers or consolidated to achieve scale economies. It also facilitates information sharing with carriers and other service providers to enable better asset utilization.

Logistics planning is essential for effective resource utilization. Lack of accurate and comprehensive logistics and supply chain planning tools historically resulted in poor utilization of production, storage, and transportation capacity. The increasingly strong focus on improved asset utilization in conjunction with improved information management and decision analysis capabilities and techniques has brought comprehensive planning systems to reality.

Effective planning requires a combination of information systems to provide the data and managers to make decisions. The following section illustrates some of the specific conflicts associated with S&OP and describes the major process and system components.

Inventory Deployment

Inventory deployment represents one of the major enterprise integrators of sales, marketing, and financial goals. The inventory deployment activity can be completed independently by individual supply chain functions, in an integrated manner by supply chain overall, or in a coordinated manner by the entire firm. When it is done in a coordinated manner by the entire firm, it is often referred to as S&OP.

These strategic objectives are typically developed for a multiyear planning horizon that often includes quarterly updates. Sales and marketing's strategic objectives define target markets, product development, promotions, other marketing mix plans, and the role of logistics value-added activities such as service levels or capabilities. The objectives include customer scope, breadth of products and services, planned promotions, and desired performance levels. Sales and marketing goals are the customer service policies and objectives that define logistics and supply chain activity and performance targets. The performance targets include service availability, capability, and quality elements discussed earlier. Financial strategic objectives define revenue, financial and activity levels, and corresponding expenses, as well as capital and human resource constraints.

The combination of sales, marketing, and financial objectives defines the scope of markets, products, services, and activity levels that logistics and supply chain managers must accommodate during the planning horizon. Specific goals include projected annual or quarterly activity levels such as revenue, shipments, and case volume. Events that must be considered include product promotions, new product introductions, market rollouts, and acquisitions. Ideally, the marketing and financial plans should be integrated and consistent, as inconsistencies result in poor service, excess inventory, or failure to meet financial goals.

The inventory deployment process must include both long- and short-term elements. The long-term element focuses on annual and quarterly plans with the objective of coordinating the marketing and financial plans to achieve enterprise goals. While supply chain and logistics operations are not the major focus, they do merit some consideration, as planners must ensure that there is enough aggregate production, storage, and movement capacity available. The short-term element focuses on weekly and daily plans with the objective of coordinating supply chain and logistics resources to ensure that specific customer requests can be satisfied. The key objective of an inventory deployment system is an integrated inventory plan through what is increasingly being termed an APS system. A detailed discussion of an APS system is provided later in this chapter.

Sales and Operations Planning (S&OP)

S&OP is a process that coordinates demand and supply plans across the organization. The process includes information sharing and accountability to systematically develop a common and consistent plan. While S&OP is an organizational process, it also requires substantial information technology support. The technology support can range from something as simple as a few linked spreadsheets to a sophisticated APS discussed later.

FIGURE 5.1
Logistics Requirements

+   Forecasts (sales, marketing, input, histories, accounts)

+   Customer orders (current orders, future committed orders, contracts)

+   Promotions (promotion, advertising plans)

=   Period demand

−   Inventory-on-hand

−   Planned receipts

Period logistics requirements

In general, the S&OP technology integrates the firm's information regarding forecasts, inventory availability, production resources, and other resource constraints.

Requirements include time-phased facility, equipment, labor, and inventory resources necessary to accomplish the logistics mission. For example, the logistics requirement component schedules shipments of finished product from manufacturing plants to warehouses and ultimately to consumers. The shipment quantity is calculated as the difference between customer requirements and inventory level. Future requirements are based on forecasts, customer orders, and promotions. Forecasts are based on sales and marketing input in conjunction with historical activity levels. Customer orders include current orders, future committed orders, and contracts. Consideration of promotional activity is particularly important in planning logistics requirements, since it often represents a large percentage of variation in volume and has a large impact on capacity. Current inventory status is product available to ship. Figure 5.1 illustrates the computation for determining periodic logistics requirements.

Specifically, for each planning period, day, week, or month, the sum of forecast plus future customer orders plus promotional volume represents period demand. It is not easy to determine the percentage of the forecasted volume that is accounted for by known customer orders, so some judgment is necessary. Typically, period demand is actually a combination of the three, since current forecasts may incorporate some future orders and promotional volume. Period logistics requirements are then determined as the period demand less inventory-on-hand plus planned receipts. Using this form, each period would theoretically end with zero inventory available, so planned receipts would exactly equal period demand. While perfect coordination of demand and supply is desirable from an inventory management perspective, it may not be possible or the best overall strategy for a firm.

S&OP Process

An integrated S&OP process is increasingly necessary for effective supply chain operations. The S&OP process collaboratively establishes a coordinated plan for responding to customer requirements within the resource constraints of the enterprise. Traditionally, firms have sequentially and often independently developed financial, sales, and operations plans. First, finance develops revenue plans often designed to meet the expectations of Wall Street. Second, sales develops marketing plans and tactics that meet the revenue targets for the firm's product groups. This includes establishing specific product innovation, pricing, and promotion plans to achieve the desired results. Finally, supply chain operations develop materials, manufacturing, and logistics plans that can meet customer demands within the operating constraints of the firm and its supply chain partners. Figure 5.2 illustrates some of the conflicts involved. Sales would like to sell a wide variation of products, rapidly responding to customers, and with short lead times. In effect, the sales goal is to maximize revenue by providing the customers whatever they want and when they want it.

FIGURE 5.2
Planning Process
Conflicts

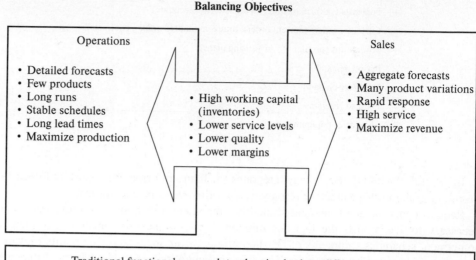

Supply chain operations would prefer to minimize the product variations and production changeovers, constrain schedule variations, and extend lead times to take advantage of economies of scale. In effect, a major focus of supply chain operations is to take advantage of manufacturing, transportation, and handling economies of scale. Since there is significant potential for conflict in these objectives, meeting unique customer requests versus operations economies of scale, it is necessary to systematically consider the trade-offs and collaboratively create consistent plans. This includes developing and agreeing to forecasts, product introduction, marketing tactics, and operating plans that can meet financial and customer commitments within the constraints of the enterprise.

A decorative candle firm is used to illustrate some of the trade-offs involved. First, the finance group provides Wall Street with the projections for the firm's sales over the next quarter. With the finance projections as the objective, the marketing organization determines the combination of product mix, unit volume, and pricing that could achieve those objectives. Often, in order to achieve the increased volume, marketing uses tactics such as more variation in scents or package sizes or other types of innovation. Unless the firm can outsource supply chain activities, the increased product variation often challenges existing supply chain capacity due to the increased setups or changeovers required. So, given the financial objectives, the firms uses the S&OP process to assess the trade-offs between the increased revenue resulting from marketing initiatives relative to the increased supply chain cost due to having more product complexity or being closer to capacity limitations. Through this assessment, the firm can determine the most profitable combination of marketing and supply chain activities.

While S&OP has significant information technology considerations, it is not just an information technology application. It is a combination of information systems, with significant elements of financial, marketing, and supply chain planning elements, integrated with organizational processes, responsibility, and accountability to develop consensus and execute collaborative plans. Thus, an effective S&OP requires a blending of process and technology with organizational collaboration. Figure 5.3 illustrates the S&OP process. The first component of the S&OP process is a business plan in terms of a financial forecast and a corresponding budget. This plan is used to guide activity levels and determine aggregate

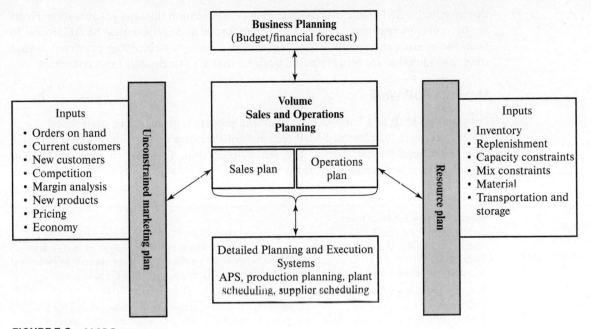

FIGURE 5.3   S&OP Process

volume and resource requirements. The second component of the S&OP is the sales plan, which is developed from the unconstrained marketing plan. The unconstrained marketing plan determines the maximum sales and profitability level that could be achieved if there were no supply chain operating constraints. As Figure 5.3 indicates, the unconstrained marketing plan synthesizes the information regarding orders on hand, current customers, new customers, competition, selling margins, new product potential, pricing, and the overall economy to project what sales could be if there were no supply chain or operations constraints. The final component of the S&OP is the resource plan, which is developed from the firm's internal and partner resource constraints. The operations plan synthesizes the resource demands and constraints to identify and evaluate potential trade-offs.

The business, unconstrained marketing, and resource plans are integrated and synchronized through the S&OP process. The process requires a combination of technology to identify and evaluate the binding constraints as well as managerial input to determine which constraints might be released in the form of prioritizing customer shipments, changes in marketing plans, overtime operations, or outsourcing production. Once the S&OP process is completed for current and future time periods, the result is a common and consistent plan that synthesizes the firm's financial and marketing plans with its resource capabilities. Once this aggregate plan is approved, it becomes the basis of more detailed supply chain planning application systems. The next section discusses some of these applications in detail.[1]

While not every firm uses an integrated and coordinated S&OP process, virtually all firms develop business, marketing, and operational plans. When the S&OP process is not integrated and collaborative, there are no feedback loops or synchronization. The result is a high probability that they will not be consistent and conflicts will arise. As indicated in Figure 5.2, such conflicts will often result in unsatisfied customer and/or poor resource utilization. It is important to note that the arrows in Figure 5.3 are bidirectional, indicating

---

[1] For a discussion of S&OP content, see Deep R. Parekh, "S&OP More Prevalent, Global," *American Shipper,* June 2008, pp. 28–33.

that an effective S&OP process requires two-way information flow and collaboration. Firms are becoming increasingly interested in a more formal and collaborative S&OP process to facilitate meeting the precise requirements of increasingly demanding customers within the constraints that are being imposed by firms that are increasingly asset conscious.

Making S&OP Work

Positioning S&OP as a core business planning process requires a well-understood operational framework. Successful S&OP requires collaborative analysis of available information, shared operational metrics, and senior leadership. The keys to successful S&OP implementation are presented in Table 5.1.

TABLE 5.1
Eight Keys to Achieving Superior Business Performance Using S&OP

Reprinted with permission from Stephen P. Crane, *CVCR Newsletter,* 3, no. 1 (Winter 2008).

Executing the Process Every Month
While the details of a good S&OP process, like any routine, can seem to be a bit of a grind, reducing the frequency of monthly meetings is only possible in best-case scenarios—for those businesses that experience little change in their markets, channels, supply lines, or product offerings. These businesses would have to operate with small deviations to their plan and have best-in-class key performance indicators (KPIs). Most do not, so they need to meet monthly.

Process Ownership and Clarity of Roles and Responsibilities
S&OP requires a process champion, someone to drive the entire process so that functional managers can direct operations that align with your business's long-term strategic plans. The ideal S&OP leader should be a process facilitator and manager who has direct involvement in determining the strategic direction for the business.

Organizational Commitment to Achieving High Forecast Accuracy
A business needs to have a long-term commitment and view to taking whatever actions are necessary to achieve high forecast accuracy. The Demand Plan drives the entire supply chain from the supply plan, production plan, inventory plan, sourcing plan, and the financial plan. If you don't have a good handle on what you expect customers to buy, it is then difficult to make good supply chain decisions.

Focus Should Be on the Next 3 to 12 Months
While it is important to understand where a business stands relative to the budget, the focus should not be on past results. It should be on looking forward, examining what the next 3 to 12 months are projected to look like. A proper S&OP process should really have an 18-month planning horizon. Firms that have a longer-term view have a better grasp of the demand drivers influencing their business; as a result their demand plans are much more reliable, predictable, and actionable.

One Integrated Plan That Integrates the Actions of the Entire Organization
The fundamental purpose of an integrated S&OP process is to review deviations in operational forecasts, new product plans, budgets, capital plans, and plans as they relate to achieving the goals of the business or company. Every step in your S&OP process should be governed by an overarching focus on executing the strategic plans of the business.

Senior Management Decision Making
In a best-in-class S&OP process the endgame is decision making. If senior management is not willing to take action, the result will just be a lot of hand waving and will not have any benefit to the business. This problem is typical where the Executive S&OP Meeting serves more as a "reporting" session, from which few decisions are made and even fewer action items are assigned.

Measuring End-to-End Supply Chain Performance
Many leaders do not like the prospect of having their work conspicuously evaluated on a monthly basis and in public. Firms that embrace measurement as a starting point for continuous improvement are far better served by S&OP than those that resist measurement. In any S&OP process, the metrics are vital to ensuring success. They provide indicators of how well the business is performing, and they clearly illustrate progress that has been made to drive improvement.

S&OP Forecast versus Operating Plan or Budget
Typically, the S&OP forecast will not match a firm's operating plan target or budget for a given year. It's alright that these two plans are not the same at any point in time. Firms should never artificially adjust the S&OP forecast to match the budget. Since the S&OP forecast should be driving all the other supply chain decisions, artificially adjusting a forecast will just increase costs and will not help to meet the budget. The greatest business value is realized when companies are willing to analyze the gaps between the forecast and budget and take the time to identify the actions that need to be taken to close the gaps.

A common question concerning S&OP is organizational positioning. It is critical to understand that S&OP is a cross-functional process and not a specific job. A great deal of effort is required to execute successful S&OP. The S&OP process is required to be performed and monitored on a continuous basis to assure successful execution. At a minimum, a new or updated plan is necessary for each successive operating period. Given the repetitive and detailed work required for successful S&OP, senior management might justify creating an organizational unit to undertake the continuous planning. While it reduces effectiveness, creation of a S&OP organizational unit tends to make the planning process the responsibility of a specific organization as contrasted to a cross-organizational joint responsibility.

To be effective over time, S&OP must be a shared responsibility among all functional groups within an organization. No single activity involved in supply chain management requires cross-organizational commitment and shared ownership more than successful S&OP. This means that functional leadership from all key operating areas must be committed to the S&OP process and be responsible for achieving success. Ideally this commitment is reinforced by two factors. First, a significant share of each functional management's compensation is tied to overall S&OP success. Second, in addition to functional leadership, there should be regular involvement and accountability at the general management level in the S&OP process. Such commitment is essential to assure cross-functional integrated management.

Other requirements to facilitate the use of S&OP are:

- Balanced scorecard integrating both operational and financial performance measures.
- Supply chain visibility and data integration across multiple levels of the firm.
- Performing monitoring and alerting to enable rapid response to unplanned events.
- Collaborative and cross-functional analyses so that the firm can select the most profitable strategy from the alternatives considered.

While implementing S&OP is very challenging, the benefits are substantial. Specifically, firms report that S&OP improves forecast accuracy, increases the percentage of perfect orders, reduces cash-to-cash cycle time, and enhances gross profit margin. Chapter 13 discusses each of these specific measures.

Logility provides a good summary regarding the benefits and implementation process for S&OP.[2]

APS System Overview

To correspond with the planning and execution of effective logistics and supply chain strategies, supply chain planning systems incorporate both spatial and temporal considerations. The spatial considerations include movement between raw material providers, manufacturing plants, warehouses, distributors, retailers, and the end consumer. The temporal considerations include movement timing and scheduling.

The APS system in Figure 5.4 is a network including plants, warehouses, and customers as well as transportation flows. This network reflects the resource status and allocation at a point in time, for example, on the first day of the month. Effective planning requires a process that can time-phase and coordinate resource requirements and constraints through time. For example, if product X is needed by the customer in period 3, its movement through the supply chain must be time-phased for arrival by period 3. Assuming a one-period performance cycle between each stage in the supply chain, this means that the

[2] Logility Inc., "Successful Sales and Operations Planning in 5 Steps" (2016).

FIGURE 5.4

Advanced Planning and
Scheduling Overview

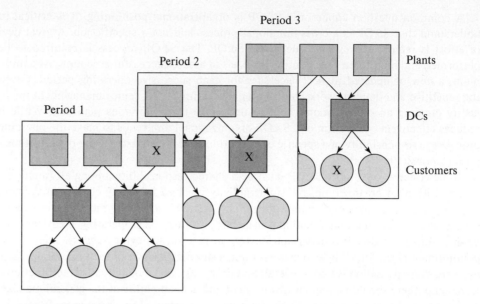

TABLE 5.2

Sample APS Planning
Situation

	Time Period				
	1	**2**	**3**	**4**	**5**
Requirement	200	200	200	600	200
Production Capacity	300	300	300	300	300
Alternative 1 (overtime):					
Production	200	200	200	600	200
Inventory Carryover	—	—	—	—	—
Alternative 2 (build ahead):					
Production	300	300	300	300	200
Inventory Carryover	100	200	300	—	—

APS must plan for the shipment of X from the plant during period 1 and shipment from the distribution center during period 2.

More specifically, suppose a firm is facing the situation summarized in Table 5.2. Customers require 200 units of product during each of the next five periods with the exception of period 4, when a special promotion increases demand to 600 units. The firm's production capacity is 300 units per week. On the extremes, the firm can select between two approaches to satisfy customer requirements given the production constraints. Alternative 1 is to wait until the fourth time period and then run production overtime to meet customer requirements. This alternative results in higher production cost but no cost to carry or store inventory. Alternative 2 is to build ahead using the extra 100-unit capacity in the time prior to period 4. With this alternative, an extra 100 units is built and added to inventory each period until it is required during period 4. This alternative does not require overtime production but does require increased inventory carrying and storage costs. There are, of course, intermediate alternatives to these two extremes. The ideal option is to select the combination resulting in the lowest combined cost of manufacturing and storage while meeting customer requirements. Using linear optimization techniques, APS identifies the most cost-effective trade-offs considering all relevant costs. While firms have wanted

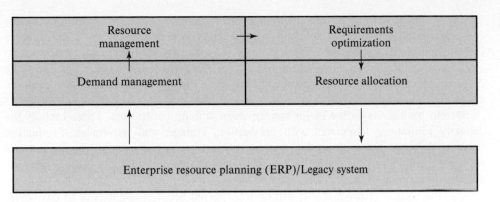

FIGURE 5.5
APS System Modules

to consider these trade-offs previously, analysis capabilities only allowed for evaluation of two or three major trade-offs to minimize problem complexity. Supply chain planning tools like APS offer the ability to thoroughly evaluate complex trade-offs involving a large number of alternatives.

APS System Components

While there are many conceptual approaches to designing supply chain planning applications like APS, the major components are fundamentally the same: demand management, resource management, resource optimization, and resource allocation. Figure 5.5 illustrates how these modules relate to each other and to the corporate ERP system or legacy system.

The **demand management** module develops the requirement projections for the planning horizon. In effect, it generates sales forecasts based on sales history, currently scheduled orders, scheduled marketing activities, and customer information. In the case of requirements planning, the forecasts are in terms of orders while it would be shipments in the case of transportation planning. Ideally, demand management works collaboratively and interactively both internally across the firm's functional components and externally with supply chain partners to develop a common and consistent forecast for each time period, location, and item. The forecast must also incorporate feedback from customers to integrate the influence of combined demand generation activities such as advertising and promotion.

The processes and techniques for demand planning are discussed later in this chapter in the Collaborative Planning, Forecasting, and Replenishment section.

The **resource management** component defines and coordinates supply chain system resources and constraints. Since APS systems use the resource and constraint information to evaluate the trade-offs associated with supply chain decisions, information accuracy and integrity are critical to provide optimal decisions and enhance planning system credibility. Obviously, incorrect planning decisions not only suboptimize supply chain performance but also severely reduce management credibility in the planning system itself. In addition to the requirements definition developed by the demand management module, APS requires four other types of information: product and customer definitions, resource definitions and costs, system limitations, and planning objective.

The product and customer definitions provide constants regarding the firm's products and customers to support the planning process. The product definitions provide the product descriptions and physical characteristics, such as weight and cube, standard costs, and bill of material. The customer definitions provide the ship-to location and distribution assignments, along with special service requirements. The combination of both defines what is being manufactured, what is being distributed, where it is being delivered, and the performance cycles involved in distribution.

The resource definitions specify the physical resources used to accomplish supply chain activities such as manufacturing, storage, and movement capacities. The resources include manufacturing equipment and process rates, storage facilities, and transportation equipment and availability. In addition to defining the existence of specific resources, the database must include the performance characteristics and costs associated with resource usage.

System limitations define major supply chain activity constraints. These include the capacity limitations associated with production, storage, and movement. Production capacity defines how much product can be produced within a specific time period and what are the trade-offs associated with making various mixes of products. Storage capacity defines the amount of product that can be stored in a specific facility. Movement capacity defines the volume of product that can be transported between facilities or to customers within a given time frame.

The planning function defines criteria for developing a solution. Typical objective functions include minimizing total cost or any of its subcomponents, meeting all customer requirements, or minimizing the number of instances when capacity is exceeded.

This combination of demand management and resource management information provides the basis for the APS evaluation of alternative supply chain strategies. The module includes the databases to store the definitions, resources, constraints, and objectives as well as the processes to validate and maintain it. Users are finding that one of the major challenges to effective supply chain planning systems is the ability to develop and maintain accurate and consistent data.

The **resource optimization** module is the computational engine or "black box" of the supply chain planning system. Using the requirements from the demand management module and the definitions, resources, limitations, and objectives from the resource management module, resource optimization uses a combination of mathematical programming and heuristics to determine how to most effectively meet customer requirements while optimizing resource utilization. Mathematical programming is a combination of linear programming and mixed-integer programming, which is used to optimize the specified objective function; heuristics are computational rules of thumb or shortcuts that reduce the time or computational resources required to develop an integrated plan. In effect, the resource optimization module evaluates multiple planning alternatives and systematically computes the trade-offs to identify the best alternatives until a near-optimal result is achieved. The resource optimization module also determines when requirements cannot be met and which resources are the most constraining on supply chain performance. The resource optimization module results are supply chain plans projected into future time periods that minimize overall cost while attempting to operate within major resource constraints. The plan specifies which products should be produced when and determines movement and storage requirements across the supply chain.

The resource optimization module can also be used to conduct sensitivity or what-if analyses to determine the impact of changes in market requirements or constraints. These analyses allow the supply chain planner to isolate the impact of demand and performance uncertainty on supply chain capabilities and operations. Using the insight regarding the trade-offs and the impact of uncertainty, the supply chain planning resource optimization module guides the planner in establishing the most effective sourcing, production, movement, and storage strategy.

Following planner review and evaluation of the resource optimization module results, the **resource allocation** module specifies the resource assignments and communicates them to the ERP system to initiate appropriate transactions. The results include requirements for procurement, production, storage, and transport. The specific requests can be communicated to the ERP system in the form of transactions or instructions to complete a specific activity. Each transaction includes detailed instructions regarding type of supply chain activity, suppliers, customer, products involved, and required timing, along with a list of relevant products and quantities. The resource allocation module also provides information regarding when product is **available to promise (ATP)** or **capable to promise (CTP)**. ATP is used to designate that even though actual inventory is not currently available, it will be available for shipment or promise at a specific date in the future. In effect, the ATP designation allows firms to commit scheduled production to customers. CTP is used to designate when requested product can be promised for future delivery. CTP requires a much broader analysis, as it determines whether there is future specific capacity or capability, given current and projected supply chain demands. ATP and CTP can dramatically enhance supply chain performance and effectiveness by allowing commitments against future production and capacity. The result is more rapid commitments to customers, fewer customer surprises, and enhanced resource utilization.

Supply Chain Planning Benefits

While some supply chain planning system benefits were discussed earlier, there are three broad benefits that accrue from planning system utilization. These are responsiveness to changes, comprehensive perspective, and resource utilization.

First, logistics and supply chain managers have used extended lead times and schedule freezes to plan for future supply chain activity. For example, production would be scheduled three to four weeks into the future and then frozen to minimize uncertainty and allow for effective resource utilization. A production freeze means that the quantity is locked in for some time period into the future (two to four weeks). Long lead times and freeze periods were necessary since the planning process was complex and required substantial analyses. While this approach reduced uncertainty, it also substantially reduced flexibility and responsiveness. Today's customer requires more responsiveness to market needs, and demand for lower inventory levels rules out long cycle times. Marketplace and firm changes can be quickly made in the demand management and resource management modules, allowing for the planning process to use the most current and accurate information. The requirements optimization module then solves the allocation, allowing daily and single week planning cycles rather than multiple weeks or months. Supply chain planning thus results in a process that can be much more responsive to marketplace or firm changes.

Second, effective supply chain management requires planning and coordination across firm functions and between supply chain partners. The process must consider the trade-offs associated with shifting activities and resources across functions and organizations. Such a comprehensive perspective increases planning process complexity substantially. The complexity follows from the number of organizations, facilities, products, and assets that must be considered when coordinating activities and resources across an entire supply chain. Supply chain planning systems offer the capability to consider the extended supply chain and make the appropriate trade-offs to achieve optimal performance.

Third, supply chain planning typically results in substantial performance improvements. While more comprehensive planning and reduced uncertainty usually result in improved customer service, another major planning system benefit is enhanced resource utilization. More effective and responsive planning allows a more level assignment of resources for existing sourcing, production, storage, and transportation capacity. The result is that existing capacity is used more effectively. Firms also report that supply chain planning systems have significantly reduced asset requirements by smoothing resource demands. The decreases include estimates of 20 to 25 percent reductions in plant, equipment, facilities, and inventory.

Supply Chain Planning Considerations

While comprehensive supply chain planning is a relatively new capability, the future outlook is bright as the technology and capacity to effectively evaluate and manage integrated supply chains are developed. Supply chain planning can take a comprehensive and dynamic perspective of the entire supply chain and focus on reducing the supply chain asset requirements as demanded by financial markets. Prior to the actual implementation, there are many considerations for supply chain planning system adoption. Managers cite their major considerations to be (1) integrated versus bolt-on application, (2) data integrity, and (3) application education.

The first consideration concerns the level of integration with other supply chain applications. Technically, there are three options for acquiring and implementing planning applications. The first is development using internal firm resources. This is not very common, as planning system development requires substantial expertise and most firms without substantial software competency could not effectively design, develop, or maintain such complex planning systems. In addition, the planning process of individual industries or firms is not usually different enough to be able to achieve any significant competitive advantage through self-funded development. Options two and three are to use a supply chain planning application that is integrated with the firm's ERP system or one from a third-party that **bolts on** to the firm's ERP system. Some ERP providers, such as SAP, offer an APS that is designed to be closely integrated with their ERP system. The obvious benefits of such integration include data consistency and integrity, familiar user interfaces, as well as reduced need to transfer data between applications, which results in delays and potential errors. The alternative is to use a **bolt-on** or **best-of-breed** approach that seeks to identify the best supply chain planning system for the firm on the basis of features and functionality and then attach it to the firm's ERP system. The result is a planning system that better meets the firm's specific requirements or offers improved performance but at a probable cost of reduced integration. While providers of both integrated and bolt-on supply chain planning applications are attempting to enhance their integration with ERP system providers, operational integration between execution and planning systems remains a challenge.

Data integrity is a second major consideration for supply chain planning system implementation. Planning systems rely on absolute data integrity for effective decision making. While data integrity has always been important, it is more critical for planning systems since missing and inaccurate data can dramatically impact decision reliability and stability. One often-cited data integrity problem concerns product level detail such as cube and weight. While this is basic data, accuracy is not easy to maintain when there are a large number of products with constant changes and new product introductions. Managers cite that in the process of implementing supply chain planning applications, it is not uncommon to find a few hundred products with incorrect or missing physical characteristics. While it may not be a large percentage of products in number, the inaccuracy can substantially impact planning system decision making. For example, missing or inaccurate cube can result in a transportation planning system making a recommendation to overload a transportation vehicle. Specifically, the planning system will think that a large amount of product can be loaded into a truck when the product data contains an incorrect value or cube. While the decision errors resulting from data integrity problems can be significant, the larger problem is that such errors substantially reduce the credibility of planning systems in general. A few highly visible errors such as overloading transportation vehicles or storage facilities cause management and planners to question the integrity of the entire planning system and process. The result is that management and operations personnel don't trust the results and prefer to return to the old tried and true methods of planning and scheduling. Thus, the potential for improved planning is reduced until the trust can be redeveloped. A strong focus on developing and maintaining data integrity is critical to effective planning system implementation.

Education regarding planning system application is a third major consideration. User training for supply chain execution and planning systems has usually focused on the mechanics to initiate the transactions. So, the user would be trained in data or parameter entry where the system would provide quick feedback regarding the acceptability of the entry. Supply chain planning systems are relatively more complex, as the feedback is not immediate and the impact may be extensive. For example, changing the requirements or forecast for one item in a time period may shift production schedules for related items on the other side of the world. Understanding planning system dynamics is critical to successful application. Such understanding requires thorough knowledge of APS system mechanics and system interactions. Although such knowledge can be initiated through training, it must be refined and extended through education and experience. Planning system education must focus on the characteristics and relationships between supply chain management activities and processes both internal and external to the firm. The education process must be much broader than existing training approaches. Planning system experience can be developed by using job shadowing experience and simulations. The shadowing environment provides actual on-the-job experience in a real-time environment. The simulated environment provides a laboratory where inexperienced planners can see or observe the results of their planning environment at low risk to the firm. The combination of these two educational experiences provides a solid foundation for implementing successful supply chain planning applications.

Integrated Business Planning

S&OP is evolving into **integrated business planning (IBP)** in many organizations. This shift reflects the need for more comprehensive business planning across the organization and the supply chain. Given the name, the implication for S&OP is that it is limited to sales and operations. While IBP is similar in concept to S&OP, it is designed to include (1) greater financial integration, (2) increased inclusion of strategic initiatives and activities, (3) improved simulation and modeling of alternatives, and (4) easier translation between aggregate and detailed levels of planning. It is likely that the shift to more IBP will continue as firms realize its capability to better meet customer needs while using resources more effectively.

Supply Chain Planning Summary

The major objective of an integrated supply chain planning capability is coordinated capacity management of relevant logistics and supply chain resources including manufacturing plants, distribution centers, and transportation resources. Capacity management planning balances the market demands with the production resources. On the basis of the activity levels defined by the forecasting system, these constraints determine material bottlenecks and guide resource allocation to meet market demands. For each product, capacity constraints influence the where, when, and how much for production, storage, and movement. The constraints consider aggregate limitations such as periodic production, movement, and storage capacities.

Capacity problems can be resolved by resource acquisition or speculation/postponement of production or delivery. Capacity adjustments can be made by acquisition or alliances such as contract manufacturing or facility leasing. Speculation reduces bottlenecks by anticipating production capacity requirements through prior scheduling or contract manufacturing. Postponement delays production and shipment until specific requirements are known and capacity can be allocated. It may be necessary to offer customer incentives such as discounts or allowances to postpone customer delivery. The capacity limitations time-phase the enterprise's S&OP or IBP by taking into account facility, financial, and human resource limitations. These constraints have a major influence on logistics, manufacturing, and procurement schedules.

Collaborative Planning, Forecasting, and Replenishment

The forecast planning processes and techniques described above have achieved significant benefits in providing superior logistical and supply chain performance. However, there can still be costly unplanned and uncoordinated events that distort smooth flow of product throughout the supply chain. These distortions occur because individual businesses frequently fail to coordinate their individual forecasts of final consumer demand and marketing events designed to stimulate demand. Imagine, for example, that at the beginning of the month, the manufacturer forecasts sales of 100,000 cases to a particular retail customer with planned advertising and sales promotions to support that level of sales. Meanwhile, that same retailer forecasts sales of 150,000 and plans specific promotional events to achieve that forecast. Clearly, joint planning and information sharing concerning such events would increase the likelihood of a successful relationship.

Collaborative planning, forecasting, and replenishment (CPFR) is a process initiated by the consumer products industry to achieve such coordination. It does not replace replenishment strategies but supplements them by a cooperative process. In essence, CPFR coordinates the requirements planning process between supply chain partners for demand creation and demand fulfillment activities. Figure 5.6 illustrates the base CPFR relationships. The CPFR solution shares information involving promotions, forecasts, item data, and orders, using either EDI or the Internet. The collaboratively developed information is

FIGURE 5.6
CPFR in the Retail
Information Technology
Environment

Source: Matt Johnson,
"Collaboration Data Modeling:
CPFR Implementation
Guidelines," *Proceedings of
the 1999 Annual Conference
of the Council of Supply Chain
Management Professionals,*
Oak Brook, IL, p. 17.

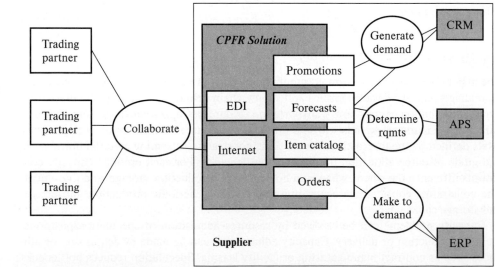

then used jointly and iteratively by planners to generate demand, determine replenishment requirements, and match production to demands.

The first step in the CPFR process is joint business planning, wherein a customer and supplier share, discuss, coordinate, and rationalize their own individual strategies to create a joint plan. The joint plan offers a common and consistent vision of what is expected to be sold, how it will be merchandized and promoted, in which marketplace, and during what time period. A joint calendar is created to share information determining product flow. A common sales forecast is created and shared between retailer and supplier based on shared knowledge of each trading partner's plan. CPFR includes an iterative process where the forecast and requirements plan is exchanged and refined between the partners until a consensus is developed. Using this consensus forecast, production, replenishment, and shipment plans are developed. Ideally, the collaborative forecast becomes a commitment between the two firms.

Relational distribution channels hold great promise for superior logistical performance. Conventional channels are primarily adversarial in nature, fail to acknowledge dependency, and are driven by information hoarding rather than sharing, so they cannot achieve the sophisticated logistical interfaces required by CPFR. Alliances and partnerships create long-term relationships between supply chain partnerships. When problems occur, as they inevitably will, they can be quickly resolved. Ultimately, the close-working arrangements reduce the cost of doing business for all channel members. Issues and concepts related to effective supply chain collaboration are discussed in greater detail in Chapter 14.

As an example, Whirlpool and Lowe's have taken collaboration to a new level with their initiative to complete an S&OP process jointly. The initiative, which they call "Merchandising and Operations Planning," begins with a robust CPFR process to create a baseline and then evolves into one plan for both firms.[3]

Forecasting

Accommodating customer requirements in most supply chain arrangements requires a forecast to drive the process. The forecast is the specific definition of what is projected to be sold, when, and where. The demand management process discussed earlier develops the forecast. The forecast identities requirements for which the supply chain must schedule inventory and operational resources. Since there are many logistics and supply chain activities that must be completed in anticipation of a sale, forecasting is a critical capability.

Table 5.3 illustrates how the need for forecasting is influenced by replenishment response time and economies of scale. Accurate forecasting should be a major focus for situations where there are long replenishment lead times and large economies of scale. On the other hand, accurate forecasts are not as critical when there are shorter lead times or lesser economies of scale. The variables in Table 5.3 can be applied two different ways. First, one could consider the product characteristics as requiring long lead time and high economies of scale and decide to place emphasis on forecasting. Alternatively, one could evaluate the potential for developing accurate forecasts, given short life cycle and high number of variations, and decide to place primary focus for this item on reduced lead time. These situations illustrate that, while improved forecasts are often desirable, there are other ways to achieve the objectives of enhanced service or reduced inventory. One is

[3] "Supply Chain News: Full CSCMP Review and Comment," *Supply Chain Digest*, October 1, 2010, www.scdigest.com.

TABLE 5.3
How Product
Characteristics Influence
the Need to Forecast

Reprinted with permission from
David J. Closs, *Forecasting and
Its Use in Logistics,* Council of
Supply Chain Management
Professionals, Oak Brook, IL.

	Low Economies of Scale	**High Economies of Scale**
Long response time experienced in replenishing product	Detailed accurate forecasting is not as critical, as the firm has more production flexibility. For example, final product customization could be postponed so that it's only necessary to forecast the base units (i.e, at a higher level of aggregation) with final customization much nearer time of demand.	Accurate forecasting is critical in this case as it's necessary to forecast an extended time into the future to allow for production or transportation economies.
Short response time experienced in replenishing product	When it's possible to obtain product quickly and there are limited scale economies, the focus should shift from forecasting to the design of a responsive and flexible process.	Focus on developing an accurate short-term forecast with strong consideration of marketing and competitive tactics and less consideration of history.

to forecast at a higher level of aggregation. The second is to develop a responsive supply chain capable of manufacturing to order, even further reducing inventory. While firms are using these methods to reduce their reliance on forecasting, there are still many situations where forecasting is necessary to achieve service objectives or take advantage of scale economies.

With the above considerations in mind, this section focuses on forecasting needs, benefits, methods, techniques, applications, and measures. It provides background to understand logistics applications of forecasting, forecast components, forecasting process, forecasting techniques, software applications, and forecasting error.

Forecasting Requirements

Effective logistics requires matching the product requirements of customers with the capacity capabilities of the enterprise and supply chain. Although consumer demands in terms of service level and product variations are increasing, the focus on reduced supply chain assets simultaneously requires more timely and accurate forecasts. Logistics forecasts are necessary (1) to support collaborative planning, (2) to drive requirements planning, and (3) to improved resource management.

Collaborative Planning

Without collaboration, each partner tries to plan the level and timing of demand for its customers, both individually and collectively. The result is speculative inventory positioned in anticipation of independently forecasted demand resulting in a never-ending cycle of inventory excesses and out-of-stocks. Historically, manufacturers have scheduled their promotions, price changes, new product introductions, and special events, either independently or without collaboration with their major retailers. When no single retailer accounted for a substantial proportion of a firm's sales volume, such collaboration was not critical. However, when a single major customer can approach 25 percent of a firm's sales, which is the case of Walmart with many of its vendors, such coordination becomes essential. Without a collaborative plan, the supplier-customer combination typically results in either inventory excess or shortage. A collaborative forecast, jointly agreed to by supply chain partners, provides a common goal that can be the basis for developing effective operating plans. CPFR was discussed earlier in this chapter.

Requirements Planning

Once a collaborative forecast is developed, logisticians use the forecasts to drive require-ments planning. The plan determines inventory projections and resulting replenishment or production requirements for the planning horizon. S&OP, discussed earlier in this chapter, integrates forecasts, open orders, available inventory, and production plans into a defini-tion of periodic inventory availability and requirements. Ideally, the requirements plan-ning process operates collaboratively and interactively both internally across the firm's operations and externally with supply chain partners to develop a common and consistent plan for each time period, location, and item.

Resource Management

Once the plan is completed, it can be used to manage critical supply chain processes such as production, inventory, and transportation. Accurate forecasts collaboratively developed by supply chain partners along with a consistent definition of supply chain resources and constraints enable effective evaluation of trade-offs associated with supply chain decisions. The trade-offs consider the relative costs of supply chain strategies such as maintaining extra production or storage capacity, speculative production or product movement, or out-sourcing. Timely identification and evaluation of these trade-offs enable a better match of requirements to resources and better resource utilization.

Forecasting Components

The forecast is generally a monthly or weekly figure for each **stockkeeping unit (SKU)** and distribution location. The forecast components include (1) base demand, (2) seasonal, (3) trend, (4) cyclic, (5) promotion, and (6) irregular. Assuming the base demand as the average sales level, the other components, except for irregular, are multiplicative factors of the base level available to support positive or negative adjustments. The resulting forecast model is:

$$F_t = (B_t \times S_t \times T \times C_t \times P_t) + I$$

where

F_t = forecast quantity for period t

B_t = base level demand for period t

S_t = seasonality factor for period t

T = trend component index reflecting increase or decrease per time period

C_t = cyclical factor for period t

P_t = promotional factor for period t

I = irregular or random quantity.

While some forecasts may not include all components, it is useful to understand the behavior of each so that each component can be tracked and incorporated appropriately. For example, some forecasting techniques cannot effectively address seasonality whereas others can.

The **base demand** represents the long-term average demand after the remaining compo-nents have been accounted for. The base demand is the average over an extended time. The base demand is the forecast for items having no seasonality, trend, cyclic, or promotional components.

The **seasonal** component is an annually recurring upward and downward movement in demand. An example is the annual demand for toys, which reflects low demand for three-fourths of the year and then increased demand just before Christmas. It should be noted that the seasonality discussed above refers to consumer retail seasonality. Seasonality at the wholesale level precedes consumer demand by approximately one quarter of a year.

The **trend** component is the long-range shift in periodic sales. Trend may be positive, negative, or neutral in direction. A positive trend means that sales are increasing over time. For example, the trend for personal computer sales during the decade of the 1990s was increasing. Over the product life cycle, trend direction may change a number of times. For example, beer consumption changed from a neutral to an increasing trend during the past decade. Increases or decreases result from changes in overall population or consumption patterns. Knowledge of which factor is primarily influencing sales is important in making such projections. For example, a reduction in the birth rate implies that a reduction in the demand for disposable diapers will follow. However, a trend toward usage of disposable as contrasted to cloth diapers may result in increased demand of a specific product category even though overall market size is decreasing. The above are obvious examples of forecast trend. While the impact of trend on short-range logistics forecasts is subtle, it still must be considered. Unlike the other forecast components, the trend component influences base demand in the successive time periods. The specific relationship is

$$B_{t+1} = B_t \times T$$

where

B_{t+1} = base demand in period $t + 1$

B_t = base demand in period t

T = periodic trend index.

The trend index with a value greater than 1.0 indicates that periodic demand is increasing, while a value less than 1.0 indicates a declining trend.

The **cyclic** component is characterized by periodic shifts in demand lasting more than a year. These cycles may be either upward or downward. An example is the business cycle in which the economy typically swings from recession to growth cycles every three to five years. The demand for housing, as well as the resulting demand for major appliances, is typically tied to this business cycle.

The **promotional** component characterizes demand swings initiated by a firm's marketing activities, such as advertising, deals, or promotions. These swings can often be characterized by sales increases during the promotion followed by sales declines as consumers sell or use inventory purchased to take advantage of the promotion. Promotions can be deals offered to consumers or trade promotions offered only to wholesalers and retailers. The promotion can be regular and thus take place at the same time each year. From a forecasting perspective, a regular promotion component resembles a seasonal component. An irregular promotion component does not necessarily occur during the same time period, so it must be tracked and considered separately. The promotional component is particularly important to track, especially for consumer industries, since it has a major influence on sales variation. In some industries, promotional activity explains 50 to 80 percent of volume variations. Thus, promotion results in demand that is more lumpy than would otherwise be the case. The promotional component is different from the other forecasting components in that its timing and magnitude are controlled, to a large extent, by the firm. Thus, it should be possible to input information from the firm's sales or marketing departments regarding the timing and likely impact of scheduled promotional plans. The benefits of coordinating such promotional offerings among channel partners provide the rationale for collaborative forecasting practices.

The **irregular** component includes the random or unpredictable quantities that do not fit within the other categories. Because of its random nature, this component is impossible to predict. In developing a forecast process, the objective is to minimize the magnitude of the random component by tracking and predicting the other components.

Forecasting Process

Logistics planning and coordination require the best possible estimate of SKU/location demand. Although forecasting is far from an exact science, the forecast management process should incorporate input from multiple sources, appropriate mathematical and statistical techniques, decision support capability, and trained and motivated individuals.

Supply chain operational forecasts are normally developed for daily, weekly, or monthly periods. An effective forecast management process requires a number of components, as illustrated in Figure 5.7. The process foundation is the forecast database, including open orders, demand history, and the tactics used to stimulate demand, such as promotions, special deals, or product changes. The forecast database is ideally part of the ERP system, although some firms maintain independent forecast databases. Other environmental data, such as the state of the economy and competitive actions, are often included in this database. To support effective forecasting, this database must include timely historical and planning information in a manner facilitating its manipulation, summarization, analysis, and reporting.

Finally, the development of an effective forecast requires a process that integrates three components: forecast technique, forecast support system, and forecast administration. The box on the right side of Figure 5.7 illustrates that it would be ideal if a firm could use a common and consistent forecast for all planning functions.

Technique

The technique component is the mathematical or statistical computation used to combine base, seasonal, and cyclical components with elements of promotion history into a forecast quantity. Techniques include time series modeling, in which sales history is a major factor, and correlation modeling, in which relationships with other independent variables are the major forecast drivers. Specific techniques are discussed in the forecast technique section of this chapter. While techniques can easily connect historical patterns into future forecasts, they do not do as well at incorporating the input of anticipated future events. As a result, it is increasingly apparent that accuracy requires integration of the forecast techniques with appropriate support and administrative systems.

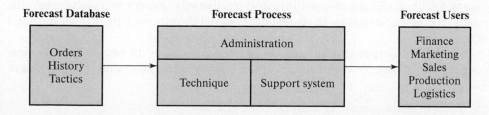

FIGURE 5 .7

Forecast Management Process

Support System

The forecast support system includes the supply chain intelligence to gather and analyze data, develop the forecast, and communicate the forecast to relevant personnel and planning systems. This component allows consideration of external factors such as the impact of promotions, strikes, price changes, product line changes, competitive activity, and economic conditions. For example, if the firm plans to promote 12-packs of a beverage, it is reasonable to assume two-liter sales will decrease. The system must be designed not only to allow the consideration of these factors but also to encourage them. As another example, the marketing manager may know that the promotion scheduled for next month is likely to increase sales by 15 percent. However, if the forecast support system makes it difficult to adjust the forecast figures for next month, the forecast adjustments may not occur. Similarly, when a package size change is announced, it is likely that forecast history should be changed to reflect the new package size so that future forecasts will reflect correct sizes and volumes. If this is difficult to accomplish within the system constraints, the individual completing the forecast will probably not consider the adjustments. It is thus very important that an effective forecasting process include a support system to facilitate the maintenance, update, and manipulation of the historical database and the forecast.

Administration

Forecast administration includes the organizational, procedural, motivational, and personnel aspects of forecasting and its integration into the other firm functions. The organizational aspect concerns individual roles and responsibilities. It is important these roles and responsibilities be specified in detail when defining the forecast administration function. If an integrated forecast is desirable, it is necessary to specifically define each organization's forecasting responsibility and then hold it accountable with specific metrics. Effective forecast administration requires that organizational responsibility and procedural guidelines are documented and measured. Effective administration also requires that forecast analysts be trained in both the process and the input of forecasts on supply chain logistics operations.

Dynamic simulation illustrates the impact of forecast inconsistency across multiple members of the supply chain. From initial stimulant to feedback, the cost of direct communication of sales or forecasts is overshadowed by the cost of a faulty message. Since a great deal of supply chain action is initiated in anticipation of future transactions, communications containing overly optimistic predictions or projections may stimulate a fever of ultimately useless work. Analysis of communications between channel members suggests that anticipation has a tendency to amplify as it proceeds between supply chain participants, particularly as the information gets further from the ultimate consumer. Each error in the interpretation of transaction requirements creates a disturbance for the total logistics channel. In a classic work, Forrester simulated channel interrelationships to demonstrate how the total channel may enter into an oscillating corrective pattern, resulting in a series of over-and-under adjustments to real market requirements.[4] Figure 5.8 illustrates the channel inventory oscillations that are stimulated when the retailer increases demand by 10 percent but does not directly inform the other members of the channel.

Figure 5.8 illustrates that an increase of retail demand by 10 percent without clear communication back to other members of the supply chain results in inventory swings of

---

[4] Jay W. Forrester, *Industrial Dynamics* (Cambridge, MA: The MIT Press, 1961).

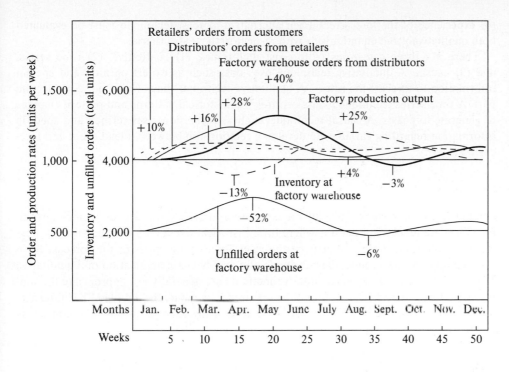

FIGURE 5.8

Response of a Simulated Production/Distribution System to a Sudden 10 Percent Increase in Sales at the Retail Level

Source: Adapted from Jay W. Forrester, *Industrial Dynamics* (Waltham, MA: Pegasus Communications, 1961), www.pegasuscom.com.

16 percent for the distributor, 28 percent for the factory warehouse, and 40 percent for factory production. These swings, commonly referred to as the bullwhip effect, obviously increase supply chain variance, which increases costs and diminishes asset utilization.

By the very nature of its mission, a distribution channel must respond to transaction requirements. The system must stand ready to initiate logistical action upon receipt of a message. Extreme care must be taken to structure the communication function with a high degree of reliability while retaining the flexibility required for change and adaptation.

It is important to realize that a meaningful forecast process requires an integrated and consistent combination of components. Historically, it was thought that intensive effort in one of the individual components such as technique could overcome problems in the other components. For example, it was thought that a "perfect" forecast technique could be identified that would overcome the need for systems support and a consistent process. There is increasing realization that all three components must work together. The design process must adequately consider the strengths and weaknesses of each individual component, and design for the optimal performance of the integrated system.

Even though the forecast technique is only one component of the overall demand management process, it is useful to understand the breadth of techniques available and the measures to evaluate them.

Forecasting Techniques

Demand forecasting requires the selection of appropriate mathematical or statistical techniques to generate periodic forecasts. The effective use of a technique requires matching the characteristics of the situation with the abilities of the technique. Some criteria for evaluating the applicability of a technique include (1) accuracy, (2) forecast time horizon, (3) the value of forecasting, (4) data availability, (5) type of data pattern, and

(6) experience of the forecaster.[5] Each alternative forecast technique must be evaluated both qualitatively and quantitatively with respect to these six criteria.

There are three categories of forecast techniques: (1) qualitative, (2) time series, and (3) causal. A qualitative technique uses data such as expert opinion and special information to forecast the future. A qualitative technique may or may not consider the past. A time series technique focuses entirely on historical patterns and pattern changes to generate forecasts. A causal technique, such as regression, uses refined and specific information regarding variables to develop a relationship between a lead event and forecasted activity.

Qualitative

Qualitative techniques rely heavily on expertise and are quite costly and time-consuming. They are ideal for situations where little historical data and much managerial judgment are required. Using input from the sales force as the basis of the forecast for a new region or a new product is an example of a supply chain application of a qualitative forecast technique. However, qualitative methods are generally not appropriate for supply chain forecasting because of the time required to generate the detailed SKU forecasts necessary. Qualitative forecasts are developed by using surveys, panels, and consensus meetings.

Time Series

Time series techniques are statistical methods utilized when historical sales data containing relatively clear and stable relationships and trends are available. Using historical sales data, time series analysis is used to identify seasonality, cyclical patterns, and trends. Once individual forecast components are identified, time series techniques assume the future will reflect the past. This implies that past demand patterns will continue into the future. This assumption is often reasonably correct in the short term, so these techniques are most appropriate for short-range forecasting.

When the rate of growth or trend changes significantly, the demand pattern experiences a turning point. Since time series techniques use historical demand patterns and weighted averages of data points, they are typically not sensitive to turning points. As a result, other approaches must be integrated with time series techniques to determine when turning points will likely occur.

Time series techniques include a variety of methods that analyze the pattern and movement of historical data to establish recurring characteristics. On the basis of specific characteristics, techniques of varying sophistication can be used to develop time series forecasts. Four time series techniques in order of increasing complexity are (1) moving averages, (2) exponential smoothing, (3) extended smoothing, and (4) adaptive smoothing.

Moving average forecasting uses an average of the most recent period's sales. The average may use any number of previous time periods, although 1-, 3-, 4-, and 12-period averages are common. A 1-period moving average results in next period's forecast being projected by last period's sales. A 12-period moving average, such as monthly, uses the average of the last 12 periods. Each time a new period of actual data becomes available, it replaces the oldest time period's data; thus, the number of time periods included in the average is held constant.

[5] Spyros Makridakis, Steven Wheelright, and Robert Hyndman, *Forecasting, Methods and Applications*, 3rd ed. (New York: John Wiley & Sons, 1997).

Although moving averages are easy to calculate, there are several limitations. Most significantly, they are unresponsive or sluggish to change and a great amount of historical data must be maintained and updated to calculate forecasts. If the historical sales variations are large, average or mean value cannot be relied upon to render useful forecasts. Other than the base component, moving averages do not consider the forecast components discussed earlier.

Mathematically, moving average is expressed as

$$F_t = \frac{\sum\limits_{i=1}^{n} S_{t-i}}{n}$$

where

F_t = moving average forecast for time period t

S_{t-i} = sales for time period i

n = total number of time periods

For example, an April moving forecast based on sales of 120, 150, and 90 for the previous three months is calculated as follows:

$$F_{April} = \frac{120 + 150 + 90}{3}$$
$$= 120$$

To partially overcome these deficiencies, weighted moving averages have been introduced as refinements. The weight places more emphasis on recent observations. Exponential smoothing is a form of weighted moving average. **Exponential smoothing** bases the estimate of future sales on the weighted average of the previous demand and forecast levels. The new forecast is a function of the old forecast incremented by some fraction of the differential between the old forecast and actual sales realized. The increment of adjustment is called the **alpha factor**. The basic format of the model is

$$F_t = \alpha D_{t-1} + (1 - \alpha)F_{t-1}$$

where

F_t = forecasted sales for a time period t

F_{t-1} = forecast for time period $t - 1$

D_{t-1} = actual demand for time period $t - 1$

α = alpha factor or smoothing constant $(0 \leq \alpha \leq 1.0)$

To illustrate, assume that the forecasts for the most recent time period were 100 and actual sales experience was 110 units. Further, assume that the alpha factor being employed is 0.2. Then, by substitution,

$$F_t = \alpha D_{t-1} + (1 - \alpha)F_{t-1}$$
$$= (0.2)(110) + (1 - 0.2)(100)$$
$$= 22 + 80$$
$$= 102$$

So the forecast for period t is for product sales of 102 units.

The prime advantage of exponential smoothing is that it permits a rapid calculation of a new forecast without substantial historical records and updating. Thus, exponential smoothing is highly adaptable to computerized forecasting. Depending on the value of the smoothing constant, it is also possible to monitor and change technique sensitivity.

The major decision when using exponential smoothing is selecting the alpha factor. If a factor of 1 is employed, the net effect is to use the most recent period's sales as the forecast for next period. A very low value, such as .01, has the net effect of reducing the forecast to almost a simple moving average. Large alpha factors make the forecast very sensitive to change and therefore highly reactive. Low alpha factors tend to react slowly to change and therefore minimize response to random fluctuations. However, the technique cannot tell the difference between seasonality and random fluctuation. Thus, exponential smoothing does not eliminate the need for judgment. In selecting the value of the alpha factor, the forecaster is faced with a trade-off between eliminating random fluctuations or having the forecast fully respond to demand changes.

Extended exponential smoothing incorporates the influence of trend and seasonality when specific values for these components can be identified. The extended smoothing calculation is similar to that of the basic smoothing model except that there are three components and three smoothing constants to represent the base, trend, and seasonal components.

Like basic exponential smoothing, extended smoothing allows rapid calculation of new forecasts with minimal data. The technique's ability to respond depends on the smoothing constant values. Higher smoothing constant values provide quick responsiveness but may lead to overreaction and forecast accuracy problems.

Adaptive smoothing provides a regular review of alpha factor fit. The alpha value is reviewed at the conclusion of each forecast period to determine the exact value that would have resulted in a perfect forecast for the previous period. Once determined, the alpha factor used to generate the subsequent forecast is adjusted to a value that would have produced a perfect forecast. Thus, managerial judgment is partially replaced by a systematic and consistent method of updating alpha. Most forecast software packages include the capability to systematically evaluate alternative smoothing constants to identify the one that would have given the best performance in the most recent time periods.

More sophisticated forms of adaptive smoothing include an automatic tracking signal to monitor error. When the signal is tripped because of excessive error, the constant is automatically increased to make the forecast more responsive to smoothing recent periods. If the recent-period sales demonstrate substantial change, increased responsiveness should decrease forecast error. As the forecast error is reduced, the tracking signal automatically returns the smoothing constant to its original value. While adaptive techniques are designed to systematically adjust for error, their weakness is that they sometimes overreact by interpreting random error as trend or seasonality. This misinterpretation leads to increased errors in the future.

Causal

Forecasting by regression estimates sales for an SKU on the basis of values of other independent factors. If a good relationship can be identified, such as between expected price and consumption, the information can be used to effectively predict requirements. Causal or regression forecasting works well when a leading variable such as price can be identified. However, such situations are not particularly common for supply chain applications. If the SKU forecast is based upon a single factor, it is referred to as **simple regression**. The use of more than one forecast factor is **multiple regression**. Regression forecasts use the correlation between a leading or predictable event and the dependent demand SKU's sales. No cause/effect relationship need exist between the product's sales and the independent event if a high degree of correlation is consistently present. A correlation assumes that

Forecast Technique	Description	Application	Limitations
Moving average	An unweighted average of the previous periods of sales	Useful when there are only base and irregular demand components	Not useful when there is significant seasonality or trend
Exponential smoothing	An exponentially weighted moving average using smoothing constants to place greater weights on more recent demands	Useful when necessary to maintain data and generate forecasts for a large number of items that incorporate individual trend and seasonality components	Not as useful when there are other factors influencing demand, such as promotions, price changes, or competitive actions not regularly scheduled
Time series	Uses time period as the independent variable to predict future demand patterns	Useful when demand patterns repeat with some cyclic, seasonal, or trend components	Not particularly responsive to change, as it takes numerous periods for the model to identify changes in patterns and for the forecast to respond to the pattern changes; also requires judgment in selecting variables that should be included
Regression	Uses other independent variables, such as price, promotion plans, or related product volumes, to predict sales	Useful when there's a strong linear or nonlinear relationship between independent variables and demand	Not particularly responsive to change, as it takes numerous periods for the model to identify changes in patterns and for the forecasts to respond to the pattern changes; also requires judgment in selecting which variables should be included
Multivariate	Uses more complex statistical techniques to identify more complex demand history relationships; techniques include spectral analysis, Fourier analysis, transfer functions, and neural networks	Useful when there's a complex, generally nonlinear relationship between historical patterns and demand. The analyses identify and evaluate alternative sets of parameters to determine the best fit and use it to predict future demand. These techniques are often more useful for predicting macro forecasts, such as energy consumption, economic growth, or aggregate transportation.	While there are quantitative factors for selecting the best model, there is often substantial judgment involved as well, so these techniques are often nonsuited for detailed item–location–time period forecasts

TABLE 5.4   Forecast Technique Summary

Reprinted with permission from David J. Closs, *Forecasting and Its Use in Logistics,* Council of Supply Chain Management Professionals, Oak Brook, IL.

the forecasted sales are preceded by some leading independent factor such as the sale of a related product. However, the most reliable use of regression forecasting of sales is based on a cause/effect relationship. Since regression can effectively consider external factors and events, causal techniques are more appropriate for long-term or aggregate forecasting. For example, causal techniques are commonly used to generate annual or national sales forecasts. From the preceding discussion, it should be clear that forecasting software offers a wide range of capabilities in terms of both techniques and sophistication. Table 5.4 provides a summary of applications and limitations of available forecast techniques.

Forecasting Accuracy

Forecast accuracy refers to the difference between forecasts and corresponding actual sales. Forecast accuracy improvement requires error measurement and analysis. While forecast error can be defined generally as the difference between actual demand and forecast, a more precise definition is needed for calculation and comparison. Table 5.5 provides monthly unit demand and forecast for a specific personal computer model at a regional distribution center. This example illustrates alternative forecast error measures.

(1)	(2)	(3)	(4)	(5)
Month	**Demand**	**Forecast**	**Error**	**Absolute Error**
January	100	110	−10	10
February	110	90	20	20
March	90	90	0	0
April	130	120	10	10
May	70	90	−20	20
June	110	120	−10	10
July	120	120	0	0
August	90	110	−20	20
September	120	70	50	50
October	90	130	−40	40
November	80	90	−10	10
December	90	100	−10	10
Sum	1200	1240	−40	200
Mean	100	103.3	−3.3	16.7[a]
Percent (error/mean)				17.1%[b]

a = Mean absolute deviation (MAD).
b = Mean of (Monthly forecast error/monthly demand).

FIGURE 5.9
Comparative Forecast
Errors

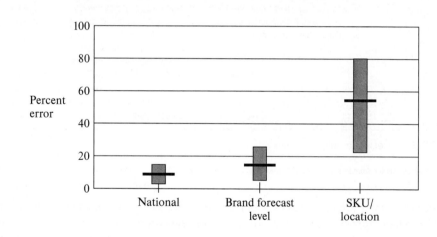

One approach for error measurement is to sum up the errors over time, as illustrated in column 4. With this approach, errors are summed over the year and a simple average is calculated. As illustrated, the average error is very near zero even though there are some months with significant error. The concern with this approach is that the positive errors cancel negative errors, masking a significant forecasting problem. To avoid this problem, an alternative approach is to ignore the "sign" and evaluate absolute error. Column 5 illustrates the computation of the absolute error and the resulting **mean absolute deviation (MAD)**. To compare forecasts, error percentages are usually calculated. **Mean absolute percentage error (MAPE)** is calculated by dividing mean absolute error by mean demand.

Another consideration is the measurement level or aggregation. Assuming that individual SKU detail is recorded, forecast error can be calculated for individual SKU location combinations, groups of SKUs or locations, and nationally. Generally, more aggregation results in lower relative forecast errors. For example, Figure 5.9 illustrates comparative forecast errors at the national, brand for groups of SKUs, and SKU location level.

The figure illustrates the minimum, maximum, and mean relative forecast error for a sample of firms marketing consumer products. As Figure 5.9 illustrates, while a relative error of 40 percent is average for a SKU/location level of aggregation, it would reflect very poor forecasting if measured at the national level.

Summary

Effective supply chain management requires both cross-functional and cross-enterprise planning and collaboration. Successful supply chain planning requires (1) supply chain visibility, (2) simultaneous resource consideration, and (3) joint resource utilization. Successful achievement of all three of these requirements depends on collaboration.

The synchronized execution of demand planning, production planning, and logistics planning is necessary to achieve an integrated overall plan. Most firms have implemented an S&OP process to drive successful integrated planning. To be successful, S&OP requires continuous senior leader attention and guidance. While there is much work and coordination required for successful S&OP, it is important to keep foremost in mind that it is a process and not an individual's or organization's job. Firms are moving toward integrated business planning to consider a broader perspective. It has become common practice for supply chain participants from multiple organizations to jointly develop and implement CPFR processes.

In most supply chains, customer requirements must be anticipated by using forecasts. Forecasts include a number of components with the major ones being level, trend, and seasonality. While these external components are significant, demand variation also results from operational actions such as promotions, price changes, and new product introductions. The forecasting process must incorporate a combination of techniques, support systems, and administration. Forecasting techniques provide a quantitative starting point, the support system refines the data in consideration of changes in the market, and forecast administration provides a management process to guide and monitor the overall effort. There are qualitative and causal forecasting techniques, but most logistics and supply chain forecasts are developed by using time series methods. While there have been some advancements in forecasting techniques and methods, the most substantial forecast improvements have been achieved through the use of collaborative techniques such as CPFR, involving multiple supply chain partners.

Study Questions

1. How does improved supply chain visibility improve the planning process?
2. Describe the S&OP process. What are the major trade-offs that must be considered?
3. Identify and discuss the major forecast components. Why is it important to decompose demand into these components when developing new forecasts?
4. Compare and contrast time series and causal forecast techniques. Under what conditions would each be appropriate?
5. Discuss how a minor change in demand at the retail level can significantly impact supply chain variation at distributors, manufacturers, and suppliers.
6. Describe the major components of an advanced planning and scheduling system. What are the major challenges in implementing such a system?

Challenge Questions

1. Advanced planning and scheduling can be completed at a firm, divisional, or geographic level. Describe the challenges and benefits for each strategy. In what situations would you recommend that a firm implement APS at a firm, divisional, or geographic level and why?

2. CPFR has been shown to improve forecasting accuracy for manufacturers. What are the major challenges associated with using CPFR? Given its demonstrated benefits, discuss when CPFR should or should not be used by firms.

3. The chapter describes a situation where Whirlpool and Lowe's are collaborating to jointly developing a merchandizing and operations plan. What are the benefits and risks to each organization? What are the challenges to Whirlpool, as it has other major customers to consider?

4. Assume that effective forecasting requires a combination of technique, system support, and administration. Your supervisor in your consumer products firm has requested that you identify some initiatives to enhance forecast accuracy. What specific initiatives would you recommend for consideration regarding the technique, system support, and administration components?

CHAPTER 6

Procurement and Manufacturing

Chapter Outline

Procurement and manufacturing are two critical operational activities in an organization's supply chain operations. This chapter examines key aspects of these two activities with an emphasis on their interrelationships with each other and with logistics operations. Following an initial discussion of total quality management, the chapter then examines the primary objectives and key aspects of procurement and manufacturing strategies.

The Quality Imperative[1]

An overriding concern of all organizations is quality. In a competitive marketplace, no company dares fall behind in providing quality to its customers. Yet quality remains an elusive concept. In the end, quality is in the eyes of customers and how they perceive an organization, its products, and its services. Customer service quality was introduced in Chapter 4 in terms of customer expectations and requirements. Much of the focus in supply chain logistics is on helping ensure products are delivered on time, damage-free, and with all the service attributes necessary to meet customer requirements. In this section, critical issues of **product quality** are addressed.

Dimensions of Product Quality

In the context of physical product form, quality is not as simple as it may first appear. In fact, the term *quality* means different things to different people. While everyone wants a quality product, not all may agree that a particular item or brand has all of the quality attributes desired. Quality is traditionally viewed in terms of eight different competitive dimensions.

Performance

The most obvious aspect of quality from a customer's viewpoint is performance, or how well the product actually performs in comparison to how it was designed to perform. For example, computers may be judged with respect to their processing speed; audio components, in terms of sound clarity and lack of interference; or dishwashers, relative to how clean and spotless the dishes. Superior performance in a product is generally an objective attribute, which can be compared between items and brands. Of course, an item may actually have several performance dimensions, which complicates comparison. The personal computer is judged not only in terms of processing speed but also by such characteristics as internal memory, hard disk capacity, and numerous other performance features.

Reliability

Reliability refers to the likelihood that a product will perform throughout its expected life. It is also concerned with the number of breakdowns or repairs that a customer experiences after purchase. Consider, for example, Maytag's slogan "The Dependability People" and long-running advertising campaign featuring a company repairman as "the loneliest person in town." Maytag stresses its products are more reliable than those of competitors by showing that the Maytag repairman is never needed to fix a broken appliance. Like performance, reliability is a characteristic of quality that can be objectively measured.

---

[1] This section draws on Morgan Swink et al., *Managing Operations Across the Supply Chain* (New York: McGraw-Hill Irwin, 2017), Chapter 6.

Durability

While related to reliability, durability is a somewhat different attribute. It refers to the actual life expectancy of a product. An automobile with a life expectancy of 10 years may be judged by many consumers to be of higher durability than one with a projected 5-year life. Of course, life span may be extended through repair or preventive maintenance. Thus, durability and reliability are distinct but interrelated aspects of quality.

Conformance

Conformance refers to whether a firm's products actually meet the precise description or specifications as designed. It is frequently measured by looking at an organization's scrap, rework, or rate of defects.

Features

Customers frequently judge quality of specific products on the basis of the number of functions or tasks that they perform independent of reliability or durability. For example, a television receiver with features such as remote control, picture-in-picture, and on-screen programming is typically perceived to be of higher quality than a basic model.

Aesthetics

Aesthetics, the style, materials, and visual appeal of a product, is used by many consumers to judge quality. In clothing, cashmere sweaters are considered of higher quality than polyester fabrics. In automobiles, the use of leather rather than cloth for seats, wood or metal rather than plastic, is an aesthetic that implies quality.

Serviceability

Serviceability, the ease of fixing or repairing a product that fails, is an important aspect of quality for some customers. Consider, for example, how some new appliances contain diagnostic capability, which alerts users or service technicians that a failure is about to occur. Ideally, serviceability would allow the customer to fix the product with little or no cost or time lost. In the absence of such serviceability, customers generally consider those items or brands that can be repaired quickest at the least cost to have superior quality.

Perceived Quality

As noted earlier, customers are the ultimate judges of product quality through their perception of how well the product meets their requirements. Perceived quality is based on customers' experience before, during, and after they purchase a product. Total product quality is a combination of the eight dimensions, how they are blended by an organization, and how that blend is perceived by the customer. It is perfectly plausible that two different customers may perceive two different brands as each having best quality, depending upon which blend of elements each considers most critical.

Total Quality Management

Interestingly, quality is not always clearly defined within some firms. Moreover, different functional managers tend to emphasize different aspects of quality. Marketing managers, for example, care a lot about aesthetics and features, whereas manufacturing executives often focus on conformance. Of specific concern in logistics are the quality dimensions related to service, satisfaction, and success. From the customer's perspective, not only does the physical product incorporate the desired elements, but also the product must be available in a timely and suitable manner.

Total quality management (TQM) is a philosophy supported by a managerial system focused on meeting customer expectations with respect to all needs, from all departments or functions of an organization, whether the customer is internal or external, a supply chain partner, or a consumer. While the specific tools and methodologies employed in TQM are beyond the scope of logistics, the basic conceptual elements are (1) top management commitment and support; (2) maintaining a customer focus in product, service, and process performance; (3) integrated operations within and between organizations; and (4) commitment to continuous improvement.

The word, "total" in total quality management has several important implications. First, a product's quality is ultimately determined by the customer's acceptance and use of the product. Thus, any discussion of quality issues begins with a focus on all of the product (and service) attributes that customers care most about. Second, quality management is a total, organizationwide activity, rather than a technical task. Every employee in a company has a stake in quality, and quality improvement requires commitment from all employees. Quality results from good design combined with effective production and delivery methods. Thus, there is a heavy emphasis on decision making in cross-functional teams.

A focus on TQM also requires understanding of all quality-related costs. This usually requires an involved and far-reaching analysis. There are four types of costs associated with quality management processes:

- Appraisal costs result from inspections used to assess quality levels. Such costs include resources spent on incoming material inspections, product and process inspections, inspection staff salaries, test equipment, and development of test procedures.
- Internal failure costs result from quality failures that are found prior to shipment to customers. These costs include scrapped materials, salvage and rework, excess material inventories, and other costs of correction.
- External failure costs result from failures that are identified only after products reach customers. These costs include complaint settlements, loss of customer goodwill and future sales, returned materials, warranty work, and field service or repairs.
- Prevention costs result from efforts to prevent failures and from efforts to reduce both failure and appraisal costs. Such costs include resources spent on planning, new product reviews, and investments in more capable processing equipment, training, process control, and quality improvement projects.

It is important to note that, as a product progresses from one stage to the next in the supply chain, a quality failure found in later stages is much more costly than one found in earlier stages. In later supply chain stages, more resources have been invested and more costs have been incurred. An important related aspect of quality management is that in the long term, prevention is almost always less expensive than correction. It is always worthwhile to consider ways to prevent quality failures, as opposed to concentrating only on how to correct them.

Procurement Importance

Every organization, whether it is a manufacturer, wholesaler, or retailer, buys materials, services, and supplies to support operations. Historically, purchasing has been perceived as a clerical or low-level managerial activity charged with responsibility to execute and process orders initiated elsewhere in the organization. The role of purchasing was to obtain the desired resource at the lowest possible purchase price from a supplier. This traditional view of purchasing has changed substantially in the past several decades. The modern focus is on total cost and the development of relationships between buyers and sellers. As a result, procurement has been elevated to a strategic activity in many organizations.

The increasing importance of procurement can be attributed to several factors. The most basic of these factors has been the recognition of the substantial dollar spend for purchases in a typical organization and the potential dollar savings from a viable procurement strategy. The fact is that purchased goods and services are among the largest cost elements for most firms. In the average manufacturing firm in North America, purchased goods and services account for approximately 55 cents of every sales dollar. By way of contrast, the average expense of direct labor in the manufacturing process accounts for about 10 cents of each sales dollar. While the percentage spent on purchased inputs varies considerably, it is clear that the competitive advantage gained from strategic management of procurement can be substantial.

Related to the cost of purchased inputs is a growing emphasis on outsourcing. The result is that the amount spent on procurement has increased significantly in many organizations. Firms today purchase not only raw materials and basic supplies but also complex fabricated components with very high value-added content. They spin off functions to suppliers to focus internal resources on core competencies. The result is that more managerial attention must then be focused on how the organization interfaces and effectively manages its supply base. There is also a significant trend toward outsourcing of services, particularly logistics services such as transportation and warehousing. For example, General Motors uses its first-tier supplier network and third-party logistics providers to complete subassemblies and deliver finished components as needed to their automotive assembly lines. Many of these activities were once performed internally by General Motors. Developing and coordinating these relationships represent critical aspects of an effective procurement strategy. The logistical requirements related to effective procurement strategy are identified later in the chapter.

Procurement Objectives

The evolving focus on procurement as a key organizational capability has stimulated a new perspective regarding its role in supply chain management. The emphasis has shifted from adversarial, transaction-focused negotiation with suppliers to ensuring that the firm is positioned to implement its operations and marketing strategies with support from its supply base. In particular, considerable focus is placed on ensuring continuous supply, inventory minimization, quality improvement, gaining access to technology and innovation, and lowest total cost of ownership.

Continuous Supply

Stockouts of raw materials or component parts can shut down or force a change in production plans, resulting in unexpected cost. Downtime due to production stoppage increases operating costs and may result in an inability to provide finished goods as promised to customers. Imagine the chaos that would result if an automobile assembly line had all parts available but tires. Assembly of automobiles would have to be halted until tires become available. Thus, one of the core objectives of procurement is to ensure that a continuous supply of materials, parts, and components is available to certain manufacturing operations.

Minimum Inventory Investment

In the past, downtime due to material shortages was minimized by maintaining large inventories of materials and components to protect against potential disruption in supply. However, maintaining inventory is expensive and requires scarce capital. One goal of procurement is to maintain supply continuity with the minimum inventory investment possible. This requires balancing the costs of carrying material against the possibility of a production stoppage. The ideal, of course, is to have needed materials arrive just at the moment they are scheduled to be used in the production process, in other words, **just-in-time (JIT)**.

Quality Improvement

Procurement is critical to the quality requirements of every organization. The quality of finished goods and services is dependent upon the quality of the materials and components used. If poor-quality components and materials are used, then the final product likely will not meet customer quality standards.

Technology and Innovation

Firms look to suppliers as sources of innovation and new technology to aid in the design of new products and the improvement of existing ones. For example, Procter & Gamble has openly stated its goal of having 50 percent of its product and process innovation come from sources outside the company. The firm uses its procurement organization as a major source of outreach to suppliers for that innovation. One example of success is provided by the development and introduction of a new product, the Mr. Clean Magic Eraser. The technology for this product was developed and provided to P&G by a major supplier, BASF chemicals.[2]

Lowest Total Cost of Ownership

Ultimately, the difference in perspective between a traditional adversarial and more contemporary collaborative procurement strategy can be summarized as a focus on **total cost of ownership (TCO)** as contrasted to a focus on purchase price. Procurement professionals recognize that, although the purchase price of a material or item remains important, it is only one part of the total cost for their organization. Service costs and life cycle costs must also be considered.

Whether established through competitive bidding, buyer–seller negotiation, or simply from a seller's published price schedule, the purchase price and discounts of an item are obviously a concern in procurement. No one wants to pay a higher price than necessary. Related to the price quote is normally a schedule of one or more possible discounts a buyer may receive. For example, quantity discounts may be offered as an inducement to encourage buyers to purchase larger quantities or cash discounts may be offered for prompt payment of invoices.

Consideration of supplier's discounts immediately takes the buyer beyond simple quoted purchase price. Other costs associated with purchasing must be considered. For the benefits of quantity discounts to be factored into the total cost, the buyer must quantify inventory holding costs. Larger purchase quantities increase average inventory of materials or supplies. Size of purchase also impacts administrative costs associated with purchasing. Lot-size techniques such as economic order quantity (EOQ), discussed fully in Chapter 7, can help quantify these cost trade-offs.

Supplier terms of sale and cash discount structures also impact the total cost of ownership. A supplier offering more favorable credit terms is, in effect, impacting the purchase

[2] Paul Teague, "P&G Is King of Collaboration," *Purchasing* (September 11, 2008), p. 46.

price from the buyer's perspective. For example, a discount for prompt payment of an invoice offered by one supplier must be compared with the offers of other suppliers.

What is normally not considered in traditional purchasing practice is the impact of pricing and discount structures on logistics operations and costs. For example, it generally does not include such factors as the impact of order quantity on transportation costs or the costs associated with receiving and handling different size shipments. Many of these logistical considerations are ignored or given cursory consideration as buyers attempt to achieve the lowest purchase price. Today there is increasing recognition of the importance of these logistics costs to the TCO.

Sellers typically offer a number of standard services that must be considered in procurement. Additionally, available value-added services must be considered as organizations seek to identify the lowest TCO. Many of these services involve logistical operations and the logistical interface between buyers and sellers.

In Chapter 4, value-added services were discussed, ranging from special packaging to preparation of promotional displays. Performance of subassembly operations in a supplier's plant or at an integrated service provider warehouse represents an extension of potential value-added service. The point is that each potential service has a cost to the supplier and a price to the buyer. A key aspect of determining the TCO for purchased requirements is to consider the trade-offs involved in terms of value added versus cost and price of each service. To do so, the purchase price of an item must be **debundled** from the price of services under consideration. Each of the related available services should be priced on an independent basis so that appropriate analysis can be performed. Where traditional purchasing might overlook value-added services in seeking lowest possible price, effective procurement executives consider whether such services should be performed internally, by suppliers, or at all. Debundling allows the buyer to make the most appropriate procurement decision.

The final aspect of lowest TCO includes numerous elements known as life cycle costs. The total cost of materials, items, or other inputs extends beyond the purchase price and value-added service to include the lifetime costs of such items. Some of these costs are incurred before actual receipt of the items, others are incurred while the item is being used, and some occur long after the buyer has actually used the item.

Figure 6.1 presents a model of the various elements that TCO comprises. When each of these elements is considered in procurement, it is clear that numerous opportunities for

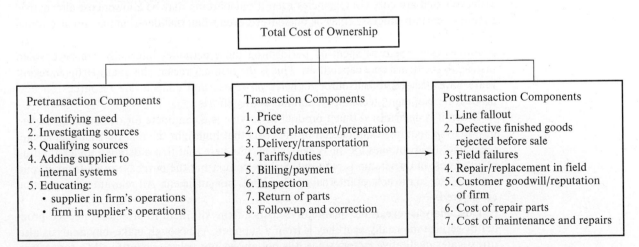

Pretransaction Components	Transaction Components	Posttransaction Components
1. Identifying need 2. Investigating sources 3. Qualifying sources 4. Adding supplier to internal systems 5. Educating: • supplier in firm's operations • firm in supplier's operations	1. Price 2. Order placement/preparation 3. Delivery/transportation 4. Tariffs/duties 5. Billing/payment 6. Inspection 7. Return of parts 8. Follow-up and correction	1. Line fallout 2. Defective finished goods rejected before sale 3. Field failures 4. Repair/replacement in field 5. Customer goodwill/reputation of firm 6. Cost of repair parts 7. Cost of maintenance and repairs

FIGURE 6.1   Major Categories for the Components of Total Cost of Ownership

improvement exist in most companies. Many of these opportunities arise from closer working relationships with suppliers that would not be possible if adversarial price negotiation dominated the buyer-seller relationship.

Procurement Strategy

Developing effective procurement strategy is a complex process, requiring considerable analysis of the most appropriate means to accomplish its many different objectives. First, decisions must be made regarding which products and services to produce or perform internally and which should be purchased from outside suppliers. Next, alternative strategic approaches to dealing with external suppliers must be developed. Finally, the appropriate strategic approach must be determined for the different types of products and services the organization buys, resulting in a procurement strategy portfolio.

Insourcing versus Outsourcing

As suggested earlier, a fundamental decision that must be made in every organization relates to which products and services should be made or performed internally by the organization itself and which should be purchased from a supplier. This decision is often referred to as the insourcing/outsourcing decision and begins with establishing the need for a particular good or service. It should be noted that "outsourcing" a product or service does not mean that a company decides to purchase from a foreign supplier; it simply means that the firm has decided not to produce an item or service internally. This process underlying the decision is commonly called the "make–buy" decision. In the past, managers tended to focus on a relatively narrow set of financial criteria. However, the make–buy decision is an extraordinarily complex strategic decision for a firm and involves consideration of numerous variables. Therefore, it typically involves executives from across the organization working in cross-functional teams to ensure comprehensive analysis of both the quantitative and the qualitative issues involved.

Make–buy analysis should begin with an evaluation of a product or service relationship to the firm's core competencies. Outsourcing core competency capabilities raises substantial risks. To reduce these risks and maintain control, firms typically insource those processes that are core competencies even if outsourcing may be a lower-cost alternative. Likewise, certain processes may be outsourced even when that decision may involve somewhat higher cost. An advantage of outsourcing non-core activities is that the financial resources that would be spent on performing those activities internally can be devoted instead to the firm's core capabilities. This is the primary reason that many firms in recent years have decided to outsource logistics processes and concentrate resources on new product development, technology, and marketing efforts.

When it is determined that a product or service is a candidate for outsourcing, make–buy analysis requires examination of the costs that highlight the relative financial advantages and disadvantages for the organization. It is here that that a detailed understanding of total cost of ownership is required. Simply comparing the purchase price from an outside supplier to the cost of internal production is not sufficient. All relevant costs must be considered.

Cost analysis reveals the quantitative costs a firm will incur to produce a needed product or service internally or to buy it from a supplier. A thorough make–buy analysis also investigates qualitative factors since it is not always possible to quantify all factors affecting the decision. While there are numerous qualitative factors to consider, two critical issues relate to loss of control and supply risk. Deciding to outsource requires the firm to relinquish control to a supplier. The organization is dependent on a supplier's ability to provide the necessary quality and delivery performance to meet its requirements. Supply risk refers to the possibility of an unplanned event in acquisition, delivery, or use that negatively affects a firm's ability to serve its customers. Besides traditional risks related to shortages and delays, supply risks include loss of intellectual property, potential supplier price increases, product safety problems, or other circumstances that harm the firm's reputation. Global sourcing tends to increase supply risk. Not only does global sourcing increase the probability of shipment delays, it also increases the difficulty of monitoring supplier activities. For example, since 2015 millions of automobiles have been recalled due to problems with air bag inflators purchased from Takata.

Alternative Procurement Strategies

Specifically, four strategic approaches to procurement have been identified: user buy, volume consolidation, supplier operational integration, and value management. While these are sometimes thought of as increasing stages of procurement sophistication, in fact each may be appropriate in certain circumstances. After discussing each of the four, attention will be devoted to evaluation of the conditions which influence choice of the appropriate approach for different products and services.

User Buy

The simplest approach to procurement is to allow users in the organization to determine their own purchase needs, evaluate sources of supply, and execute the purchasing process. In fact, even in organizations that have a centralized procurement function, user buy is still common for at least some items. For example, it is not uncommon to allow clerical staff to maintain responsibility for purchasing basic office supplies or for janitorial staff to have responsibility for cleaning supplies. Such items may be considered too insignificant to the overall success of the organization to warrant any further consideration.

Volume Consolidation

An important step in developing an effective procurement strategy is volume consolidation, a procurement strategy accomplished through reduction in the number of suppliers. Beginning in the 1980s many firms faced the reality that they dealt with a large number of suppliers for almost every material or input used. In fact, purchasing literature prior to that time emphasized that multiple sources of supply constituted best procurement practice. First, potential suppliers were continually bidding for a buyer's business, ensuring constant pressure to quote low prices. Second, maintaining multiple sources reduced the buyer's dependence on any one supplier. This in turn served to reduce the buyer's risk should a specific supplier encounter supply disruptions such as a strike, a fire, or internal quality problems.

By consolidating volumes with a limited number of suppliers, procurement is also positioned to leverage its share of a supplier's business. At the very least, it increases the buyer's negotiating strength in relationship to the supplier. More important, volume consolidation with a reduced number of suppliers provides a number of advantages for those suppliers. The most obvious advantage of concentrating a larger volume of purchases with a supplier is that it allows the supplier to improve economies of scale by spreading fixed cost over a larger volume of output. Additionally, assured of a larger volume of purchases, a supplier is more likely to make investments in capacity or processes to improve customer service. When a buyer is constantly switching suppliers, no one firm has an incentive to make such investment.

Clearly, when a single source of supply is used, risk increases. For this reason, supply base reduction programs are almost always accompanied by rigorous supplier screening, selection, and certification programs. In many instances, procurement executives work closely with others in their organization to develop preferred or certified suppliers. It should be noted that volume consolidation does not necessarily mean that a single source of supply is utilized for every, or any, purchased input. It does mean that a substantially smaller number of suppliers are used than was traditionally the case in most organizations.

The savings potential from volume consolidation is not trivial. One consulting firm has estimated that savings in purchase price and other elements of cost can range from 5 to 15 percent of purchases.[3] If the typical manufacturing firm spends 55 percent of its revenue on purchased items and can save 10 percent through volume consolidation, the potential exists to deliver a $5.5 million improvement on revenue of $100 million to the bottom line.

Supplier Operational Integration

Operational integration occurs when buyers and sellers begin to integrate their processes and activities in an attempt to achieve substantial performance improvement. Such integration typically involves alliances or partnerships with selected suppliers to reduce total cost and improve operational integration.

Such integration takes many different forms. For example, the buyer may allow the supplier to have access to sales and ordering information, thereby giving the supplier continuous knowledge of which products are selling. Detailed sales information allows the supplier to be better positioned to effectively meet buyer requirements at a reduced cost. Cost reduction occurs because the supplier has more information available to support planning and can reduce reliance on inefficient practices, such as forecasting and expediting.

Further operational integration can result for buyers and suppliers working together to identify processes involved in maintaining supply and searching for ways to redesign those processes. Establishing direct communication linkages to reduce order time and eliminate communication errors is a common benefit of such integration. More sophisticated integrative efforts may involve eliminating redundant activities that both parties perform. For example, in some sophisticated relationships, activities such as buyer counting and inspection of incoming deliveries have been eliminated as greater reliance and responsibility are assumed by suppliers. Many firms have achieved operational integration focused on logistical arrangements, such as continuous replenishment programs and vendor-managed inventory.[4] Such integration has considerable potential for reducing TCO.

The primary objective of operational integration is to cut waste, reduce cost, and develop a relationship that allows both buyer and seller to achieve mutual improvements. Combined creativity across organizations can create synergy that one firm, operating in isolation, would be unable to achieve. It has been estimated that operational integration with a supplier can provide incremental savings of 5 to 25 percent above the benefits of volume consolidation.[5]

Value Management

Achieving operational integration with suppliers creates the opportunity for value management. Value management is an even more intense aspect of supplier integration, going beyond a focus on buyer-seller operations to a more comprehensive and sustainable

[3] Matthew Anderson, Les Artman, and Paul B. Katz, "Procurement Pathways," *Logistics* (Spring/Summer 1997), p. 10.
[4] These concepts are discussed in Chapter 7.
[5] Anderson, Artman, and Katz, "Procurement Pathways," p. 10.

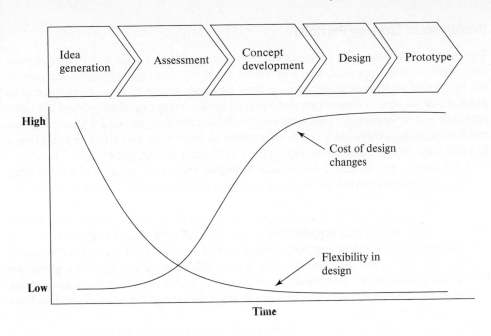

FIGURE 6.2
Flexibility and Cost of
Design Changes

Source: Reprinted with
permission from Robert M.
Monczka et al., *New Product
Development: Strategies for
Supplier Integration* (Milwaukee:
ASQ Quality Press, 2000), p. 6.

relationship. Value engineering, reduced complexity, and early supplier involvement in new product design represent some of the ways a company can work with suppliers to reduce TCO.

Value engineering is a concept that involves closely examining material and component requirements at the early stage of product design to ensure that a balance of lowest total cost and quality is incorporated into new product design. Figure 6.2 shows how early supplier involvement can be critical in achieving cost reductions. As a firm's new product development process proceeds from idea generation through the various stages to commercialization, the company's flexibility in making design changes decreases. Design changes are easily accommodated in the early stages, but by the time prototypes have been developed, a design change becomes difficult and expensive. The earlier a supplier is involved in the design process, the more likely an organization is to capitalize on that supplier's knowledge and capabilities.

An example from an automobile manufacturer demonstrates the benefit of early supplier involvement. In designing the front bumper for a new model, the design engineer was completing design of the bracket assembly for the bumper. During the process, an engineer from the assembly supplier, which had already been identified even though actual production was in the future, asked if the bracket location could be moved by about ½ inch. The design engineer, after some consideration, replied that it could be done with no impact on the final product. The design engineer was interested to know why the supplier requested the change. The answer was that by moving the bracket, the supplier would be able to use existing tools and dies to manufacture the bracket. Under the original design, major capital investment would have been required for new tooling. The result was approximately a 25 to 30 percent reduction in cost of the bracket.

Clearly, value management extends beyond procurement in an organization and requires cooperation between numerous participants, both internal and external. Teams representing procurement, engineering, manufacturing, marketing, and logistics as well as key supplier personnel jointly seek solutions to lower total cost, improve performance, or improved accommodation of customer requirements.

Procurement Strategy Portfolio

The Pareto effect applies in procurement just as it applies in almost every facet of business activity. In procurement, it can be stated simply: A small percentage of the materials, items, and services acquired account for a large percentage of the dollars spent. The point is that all procured inputs are not equal. However, many organizations use the same approach and procedures for procuring small-volume items that they do for acquiring their most strategic purchases. As a result, they spend as much time and effort in acquiring a $10,000 order of raw materials as they do for a $100 order of copy paper.

A key step in determining procurement strategies, then, is to understand exactly what the firm is currently buying (or planning to buy) and how much is actually being spent on each purchased item or service. **Spend analysis** is a tool that identifies how much is being spent on each type of product or service across all locations in the firm. It also identifies all of the different suppliers being used. For example, spend analysis at a major manufacturer of agricultural and construction equipment found that across twelve different assembly plants, the firm was purchasing over 400 different types of work gloves for production personnel and using 20 different suppliers. Spend analysis is an important step in determining the appropriate procurement strategy for each of the products and services required by the buying firm.

It would be a mistake, though, to simply use dollar expenditure as the basis for segmenting requirements. Some inputs are strategic materials. Others are not. Some inputs have potential for high impact on the business success. Others do not. Some purchases are very complex and high risk. Others are not. For example, failure to have seat assemblies delivered to an auto assembly line on time could be catastrophic, while failure to have cleaning supplies might constitute a nuisance. While volume consolidation and supply base reduction most likely can be justified for almost every material and service, operational integration and value management may be reserved for more strategic purchase requirements.

One approach to determining an appropriate procurement strategy for a product is provided in Figure 6.3. This portfolio matrix, which is similar in concept to the customer strategy matrix in Chapter 4, is based on two criteria: potential supply risk in procuring an item from a supplier and the value of the item to the firm.

Routine Purchases

Routine purchases are typically items that involve a low percentage of a firm's totally spend and involve very little supply risk. Additionally, they typically are non-critical to the organization and have little impact on its overall performance. Examples include such items as office supplies and janitorial services, which are available from numerous sources. The routine strategy focuses on reducing buying effort to reduce cost. Specific aspects of the strategy

FIGURE 6.3
Procurement Strategy
Matrix

Adapted from Robert Monczka
et al., *Purchasing and Supply
Chain Management,* 4th Edition
(Mason, OH: South-Western
Cengage Learning, 2009), p. 211.

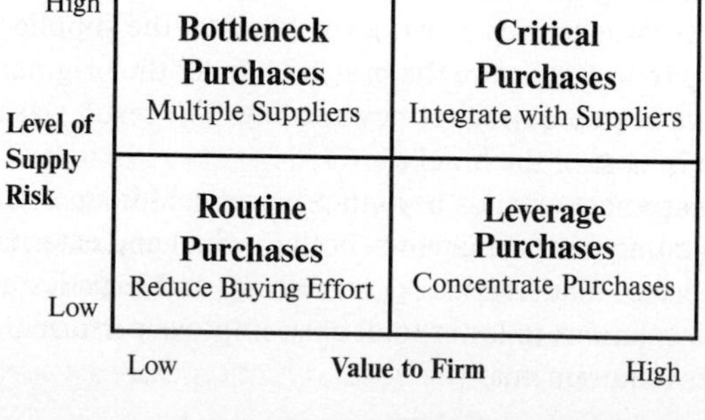

	Low ——— Value to Firm ——— High	
High Level of Supply Risk	**Bottleneck Purchases** Multiple Suppliers	**Critical Purchases** Integrate with Suppliers
Low	**Routine Purchases** Reduce Buying Effort	**Leverage Purchases** Concentrate Purchases

typically involve reducing the number of items in the category by standardizing SKUs across the organization (recall the example of purchasing work gloves). Using electronic catalogs, vendor managed inventory, and corporate credit cards called "purchasing cards" can lower the costs of purchasing. Using a purchasing card, users directly purchase these routine items for which more buying effort simply is not justified by the potential cost savings.

Bottleneck Purchases

Bottleneck purchases represent a unique procurement problem. While such items involve a small percentage of a firm's spend, supply risk is high and lack of availability can cause significant operational problems for the buyer. These items are frequently only available from a small number of alternative suppliers. The appropriate strategic focus in this situation is to maintain multiple sources of supply and, if feasible, use long-term contracts to assure continuity of supply.

Leverage Purchases

Like routine purchases, leverage purchases involve little supply risk. The items are generally commodities where many alternative sources of supply exist. However, because the dollar spend on these products or services is relatively high, there is potential to consolidate purchases with a limited number of suppliers to generate considerable procurement savings. Volume consolidation and supplier operational integration are typically employed for leverage purchases.

Critical Purchases

Critical purchases are typically the strategic items and services that involve a high level of expenditure and are vital to the organization's success. Because of their importance and the risk involved, there is strong emphasis in concentrating purchases with a strategic preferred supplier. Critical purchases are the items where supplier operational integration and value management procurement approaches take on highest priority.

Logistical Interfaces with Procurement

Effective execution of procurement strategy ultimately depends on logistics. The interface between logistics and procurement links an organization with its suppliers and therefore has significant implications for achieving procurement objectives. Procurement may also provide an organization's logistical linkage with customers as many organizations have turned to outsourcing of logistical services. Just-in-time, logistics outsourcing, and performance-based logistics represent three critical aspects of the interface between logistics and procurement within an organization.

Just-in-Time

Just-in-time (JIT) techniques have received considerable attention and discussion in recent years in all areas related to supply chain management. Sometimes referred to as just-in-time purchasing, and frequently referred to as just-in-time delivery, the goal of JIT is to time-phase activities so that purchased materials and products arrive just at the time they are required for the transformation process. Ideally, raw material and work-in-process inventories are minimized as a result of reducing or eliminating reserve stocks.

The implications of JIT are numerous. Obviously, it is necessary to deal with suppliers who have high and consistent levels of product quality. Absolutely reliable logistical performance is required and eliminates, or at least reduces, the need for buffer stocks of materials. JIT generally requires more frequent deliveries of smaller quantities of purchased inputs, which may require modification of inbound transportation. Clearly, to make JIT work, there must be very close cooperation and communication between the buying organization and suppliers. In JIT operations, companies attempt to gain the benefits of backward vertical integration but avoid the formal tie of ownership. They achieve many of the same ends through coordination and process integration with suppliers.

Some organizations, seeing the benefits of JIT systems and recognizing the benefits of supplier integration, have gone so far as to bring their suppliers' personnel into their own organization. The supplier personnel are empowered to use the customer's purchase orders, have full access to all information, and have responsibility for scheduling arrival of materials. Originally introduced by the Bose Corporation, the term **JIT II** has been applied to these efforts to reduce leadtimes and cost.

Procurement of Logistics Services

Historically, procurement departments in most organizations have been primarily concerned with "direct spend," the strategies and relationships with suppliers of materials, components, and other physical product inputs required by the firm. The procurement of logistics services was considered an "indirect spend" and has not typically received the same strategic emphasis. User–buy approaches were the norm in many companies. That situation is rapidly changing. With continued growth in the outsourcing of non-core capabilities, procurement of logistics services including transportation, warehousing, third-party, and integrated logistics services is receiving increased attention. Chapter 1 mentioned that the third-party logistics market in 2018 was approximately 55 percent of total transportation and 40 percent of warehouse expenses.

Managing the procurement of logistics services should be given the same strategic considerations as any other category of products or services. In fact, while performance of logistics activities may not be a core capability of many shippers, the importance of logistics service to customers results in this category of spend being classified as a leverage and/or critical purchase in many firms.

Tyco International is one firm that has taken a close look at its strategy for procurement of logistics services. The company, a diversified manufacturer composed of several separate business units, found that its total dollar expenditure on transportation services alone was $390 million. As a result, a centralized group was established to focus on strategy for logistics services and contracting issues with service providers. This centralized organization focused on aggregating the total expenditures across the business units and establishing relationships with a small core group of carriers. This allows logistics managers within each business unit to focus on the operational issues.

The Tyco strategy is complicated by the vast geographical reach of the company. It uses regional councils consisting of personnel from the business units as well as the centralized procurement group to establish a list of transportation providers for each mode and geographic region. The centralized organization then negotiates contracts with the selected carriers. With these contracts in place, the operations logistics managers in the business units then have the flexibility to deal with specific carriers on a day-to-day basis.[6]

---

[6] David Hanon, "Tyco Drills Down into Logistics," *Purchasing* (September 17, 2009), p. 45.

Performance-Based Logistics[7]

Initiated by the U.S. Department of Defense (DoD), a new approach to dealing with suppliers called **performance-based logistics (PBL)** has recently emerged. PBL is used to buy what the military has traditionally referred to as logistics support. The most interesting aspect of PBL is that the military buys performance outcomes instead of what has historically been individual transactions defined by product specifications. As outsourcing of logistics service increases, the concept of performance-based logistics is likely to increase.

Historically, the DoD told contractors what products to produce, when to produce them, and what activities to perform, and then paid them upon completion. In this traditional arrangement, the more the contractor produced, the more money it made. With PBL, the government simply tells the contractor what the desired outcomes are and lets the supplier determine the best way to meet those requirements. The government has found PBL to be an effective means for obtaining higher quality while simultaneously achieving lower cost. While PBL has been limited thus far to government purchasing, it is expected that business organizations may begin to adopt the practice in the future.

Manufacturing

A substantial number of firms in the supply chain are involved in the manufacturing of products. They convert raw materials, parts, and components into finished products to meet the needs of their customers. Of course, the customers may be other manufacturers who purchase the products to incorporate into their own finished products. Or the customers may be intermediate members of the supply chain, such as retailers who purchase a variety of products from different manufacturers to create an appealing assortment for consumers. In some instances, manufacturers may even deal directly with consumers as in the case of companies such as Dell, Apple, and others who have opened direct relationships through web-based marketing channels as discussed in Chapters 1 and 4. Manufacturing processes and strategies are discussed with a focus on the numerous trade-offs that must be made in alternative manufacturing strategies.

Manufacturing Processes

There are four basic manufacturing process structures that differ in terms meeting a firm's production requirements related to the volume of output required and the variety of products that can easily be produced by the process structure. Companies that require high volume production of a small variety of products are not likely to use the same basic processes as those that produce small quantities of many different products. The basic process also differs with respect to the manufacturing cost per unit and other critical issues such as the degree of capital investment, customer involvement, and the use of generalized versus specialized equipment.

Job Shop Process

A **job shop** process provides high flexibility to produce a variety of different products, but in limited volumes. Each customer order or "job" can involve different materials and inputs. Examples of job shop processes include a commercial printer, airplane manufacturers,

[7] This section is based on Kate Vitasek and Steve Geary, "Performance Based Logistics," *World Trade* (June 2008), pp. 62–65.

custom furniture manufacturers, and a tool and die shop. Customization of the product tends to be very high, while the volume of each product is low. Worker skills also tend to be broad, and equipment tends to be adaptable to produce many different types of products. For example, a commercial printer might have a printing press that can print on several different paper sizes with several different color combinations (i.e., two-, four-, or six-color) and quality. Workers in this situation must have a broad variety of skills in order to set up the equipment for a variety of orders. This printing press is a good example of general-purpose equipment that has the flexibility to do many jobs. However, the fact that each job is different generally requires significant downtime due to the need to specifically set up the press for each new job.

Another characteristic of a job shop is that the arrangement of the equipment, and therefore the flow of materials, tends to be organized around common processing characteristics rather than a given product. For example, a custom furniture manufacturer would most likely have an area for lathes (to turn chair or table legs), a separate area for varnishing and a separate area for upholstery. This organization is appropriate because different products will flow through the system in different ways. For example, a table might not require either the turning of table legs (since they are square not round) or any upholstery. On the other hand, a chair might require all three areas (turning, varnishing and upholstery) and would thus follow a different path through the plant.

Batch Process

A **batch process** is essentially a higher-volume job shop, in which the same or similar products are produced repetitively. The variety of products in a batch process is significantly lower than in a job shop, but is too large for resources to be dedicated to a single product or family of products. Products are produced in moderate-sized batches in a single production run before changing over to produce another item. John Deere and Caterpillar tend to use batch processes in producing the larger, more expensive agricultural and construction equipment. A neighborhood bakery that produces cakes, cookies, and pies most likely would employ a batch process. Batch process structure works well when there is a high variety of different products but each has a relatively low volume.

Line Flow Process

Line flow processes can produce high volumes of relatively standardized products. They are used when there are many customers who want similar products, such as appliances, automobiles, and cell phones. The workflow is organized around a single product. Steps are arranged in sequence and broken up into the smallest steps possible. Workers specialize at a single task and equipment may be designed to perform a single action. Every step in the process is performed repetitively, over and over with very little variation in the products. The advantage of this approach is that both equipment and workers can be very specialized. One major disadvantage is that workers tend to become bored or do not have a good understanding of the final product since they only perform one small step out of hundreds or thousands. A limited degree of variety can be introduced through careful design. For example, automobiles on a typical assembly line may have different sound systems installed or different types of upholstery, but the variety on a specific assembly line is typically limited to a single model until the line is shut down and a significant amount of time devoted to changeover and setup.

Continuous Process

Continuous processes are used for high-volume products where the demand for the product is very large and can justify the capital investment necessary. The processes are very inflexible, in that they cannot easily be adapted to produce a different item. Examples of continuous processes include petroleum refining, chemical production, steel, aluminum, and soft drinks. Continuous processes are extremely capital-intensive, very standardized, and very inflexible. They tend to be operated 24 hours a day to recoup the huge investment in equipment. While continuous processes are tremendously efficient, the cost of any disruptions of production due to broken equipment, defective raw materials or worker error is enormous, often running into tens of thousands of dollars per hour of lost production.

These four general process structures can be modified to create more options. For example, changes in management practices and technology have led to the cost advantages of high-volume continuous and line flow processes while increasing variety through **mass customization**, where a product is produced quickly and at a low cost using a high-volume production process. Dell Computers is an example of mass customization. Selecting from a range of components and warranty options, customers can design a computer system that best meets their needs at the price they want to pay and have delivery within about a week. Standardizing parts, using modular designs, and postponing product differentiation are practices used with mass customization.

Matching Manufacturing Strategy to Market Requirements

In Chapter 4, typical marketing strategies were classified as being mass, segmental and focused, or one-on-one. These strategies are differentiated, in part, in terms of the desired degree of product and service accommodation. Mass marketing requires limited product/service differentiation. In contrast, one-on-one marketing strategy builds on unique or customized product/service offerings for each and every customer. A firm's strategic marketing posture to accommodate specific customer requirements is directly related to manufacturing capability. For a manufacturing firm to effectively compete, it must be able to integrate manufacturing capability into a meaningful marketing value proposition.

Manufacturing Strategies

There are four common manufacturing strategies that are typically employed by organizations. The strategies differ considerably in their ability to meet individual customer requirements for exact product specifications and therefore the logistical requirements required to support their use. The choice of manufacturing strategy impacts the total order-to-delivery time that customers experience. The four strategies are **engineer-to-order (ETO)**, **make-to-order (MTO)**, **assemble-to-order (ATO)**, and **make-to-plan (MTP)**. It is also common to refer to MTP as **make-to-stock (MTS)**.

Engineer-to-Order

In an ETO strategy, products are unique and extensively customized for the specific needs of individual customers. Examples of ETO products include a custom-built house, a cruise ship, specialized industrial equipment, and even a custom-built racing bicycle. By definition, nothing happens for ETO items until a customer order is received. Since each ETO product requires an entirely new design, materials required for production are not carried in inventory, though some firms may stock raw materials in anticipation of product needs. Typically, ETO products utilize a job-shop production process. In some instances a batch process may be used, depending on the quantity that is specified by the customer order. Regardless, the customer who desires a custom-designed product from an ETO manufacturer experiences a very long order-to-deliver time.

Make-to-Order

Manufacturing of MTO items closely resembles that of ETO items in that a customer order triggers activities at the very beginning of the process. However, MTO strategies differ from ETO in that customers typically order from standardized product designs that may be somewhat customized to meet a specific customer need. Examples of MTO items include passenger airplanes, custom-built furniture, and many other high-end consumer products. A manufacturing firm cannot hold inventories of MTO products because they are subject to extensive user customization. However, some of the raw materials and components for an MTO product may be carried in inventory. Like ETO products, MTO manufacturers compete on the basis of ability to meet specific customer requirements for a product, but the use of standardized designs that can be customized results in less ability to precisely meet those requirements. MTO differs from ETO primarily in the importance of the producer's engineering capability. A firm that sells ETO products must have the capability to clearly understand, capture, and communicate each individual customer's unique needs. MTO products are designed for broader groups of customers, so customers do not have to wait for product design to be completed. One other similarity between the two approaches is that MTO strategies rely on job shop or batch manufacturing processes.

Assemble-to-Order

In an ATO strategy, base product components are manufactured in anticipation of future customer orders; however, no finished product is created until a customer places an order. This final configuration or assembly reflects the principle of manufacturing or form postponement, which will be discussed in detail in Chapter 7 due to its importance in inventory management. By postponing final assembly operations, manufacturers avoid having to hold large amounts and varieties of finished goods. The need for logistical capacity is critical in ATO operations. In fact, an increasing amount of ATO product finalization is being performed in supply chain logistics warehouses. Full implementation of an ATO strategy may require that warehouse operations be integrated into the value creation process to perform customizing and assembly operations.

The attractiveness of an ATO manufacturing strategy is that it has the potential to combine the facets of economy of scale provided by line flow processes with a degree of flexibility characteristic of job shop or batch processes. Unfortunately, this means that the customer must wait for the assembly portion of the manufacturing cycle. Successful sellers of ATO products must keep their assembly times as short as possible.

Make-to-Plan

As a general rule, MTP strategies are characteristic of companies exploiting economy of scale gained from long production runs utilizing line or continuous flow processes. In fact, MTP has been the dominant manufacturing strategy since the beginning of the industrial revolution. Totally dependent on a forecast of customer demand, significant finished goods inventory is typically manufactured in anticipation of future customer orders. The degree of product customization is limited to the manufacturer's marketing strategy concerning market segmentation and product differentiation. While any given product category may contain several alternative versions to accommodate the desires of a segment, each is forecasted individually and quantities produced according to that forecast. The logistical requirement to support MTP is to have sufficient warehouse capacity available to store the finished product quantities and to assemble the correct assortment of finished product according to specific customer orders. Additionally, customers expect that these items be widely available and typically are not willing to experience lengthy delays in order-to-delivery.

Manufacturing strategy clearly has a significant impact on the leadtime experienced by customers. Figure 6.4 summarizes this impact. The choice of ETO, MTO, ATO, or MTP determines whether a customer will bear the cost of waiting for completion of one or more of the three performance cycles discussed in Chapter 3, as well as the time required for product design. For MTP items such as most fast-moving consumer goods, customers essentially only experience the customer accommodation cycle, the time from placing an order until the product is received from the supplier. An ATO strategy choice by a manufacturer requires that customers also wait during the time that the product is actually configured to their requirements. Generally, an MTO strategy requires that customers incur the additional time of the manufacturer purchasing the needed components and materials to make the product. ETO requires that customers experience all aspects of process time.

Table 6.1 summarizes the essential characteristics of manufacturing processes and strategies. Each process is associated with the product variety and volume generally produced as well as the strategy generally employed and the resulting impact on customers in terms of their expected total leadtimes. Keep in mind, however, that creative organizations are exploiting ways to blend different process and strategy combinations.

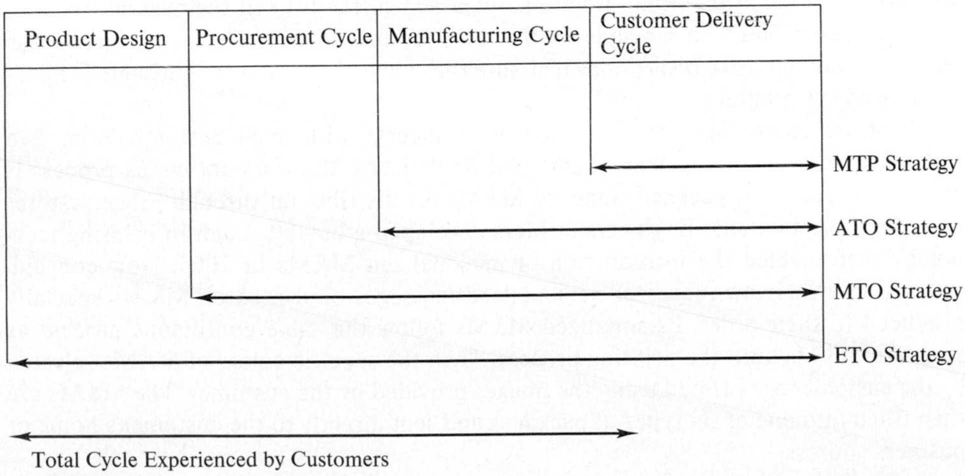

FIGURE 6.4
Manufacturing Strategy and Performance Cycles

Product Design	Procurement Cycle	Manufacturing Cycle	Customer Delivery Cycle

MTP Strategy

ATO Strategy

MTO Strategy

ETO Strategy

Total Cycle Experienced by Customers

TABLE 6.1
Manufacturing Process Characteristics

	Product Variety	Volume	Strategy	Customer Leadtime
Job Shop	Very high	Very low	ETO/MTO	Very long
Batch	High	Low	ETO/MTO/ATO	Long
Line Flow	Limited	High	ATO/MTP	Short
Continuous Flow	Very limited	Very high	MTP	Very short

Mass Customization

The basic manufacturing processes and strategies discussed in the previous section have allowed firms to efficiently and effectively meet customer requirements for many years. However, as customers have increasingly demanded products that are more precisely tailored to individual desires, manufacturers have struggled to adapt these processes to provide better individual customization of products while maintaining the efficiencies necessary to deliver them economically. The desire on the part of many manufacturers is to get the cost advantages of high volume continuous and line flow processes while increasing variety for customers. Accomplishing this objective is known as **mass customization**.

Approaches such as manufacturing postponement and assemble-to-order have been implemented in some organizations as a solution to the problem. The often-cited ATO process used by Dell allows considerable tailoring of computer systems by allowing customers to select a range of components to be configured to their specific requirements at an affordable price. Yet many organizations have struggled to develop similar capabilities.

For example, in the 1990s, Levi Strauss introduced a program to customize its jeans for women. Historically, women's jeans have not been sold by waist size and inseam measurements. Instead, they are produced and sold by a size number, which has little relationship to body measurements. Levi's introduced a program called "Personal Pair" in a number of retail stores. A computerized in-store kiosk allowed women to select styles, fabric, leg openings, color, and buttons. Consumers also input their precise body measurements to create a perfect fit. Consumers could even specify such characteristics as "I want a slightly baggier fit in the thighs." The program met with high level of consumer acceptance. However, because of its production processes, Levi Strauss was unable to maintain the program. At the factory, fabric-cutting machines were designed to cut 60 layers of fabric at one time. Additionally, it was difficult to fit the custom-designed jeans into the production schedule for the mass-produced items. The custom jeans also required more intensive inspections to assure they met specifications.[8] Ultimately, Levi's abandoned the program.

There are companies that have had more success with mass customization. Two examples are provided by Mars candy and Reebok. At Mars, a continuous process is used to produce and package standard M&Ms for distribution through grocery stores and other retail outlets. Engineers at Mars developed a breakthrough in printing technology that enabled the introduction of personalized M&Ms in 2005. Now consumers can have their own faces or personalized messages imprinted on M&Ms specially produced to their order. Personalized M&Ms follow the same continuous process as standard M&Ms until the printing process. Then the specific colors of M&Ms selected by the customer are printed using the images provided by the customer. The M&Ms are then filled into one of six types of packages and sent directly to the customer's home or business address.

At Reebok, customers can design their own sneakers, mixing various colors, styles, and materials. A new program even allows a customer's photo to be incorporated into the design that decorates the shoes. For example, one consumer had customized sneakers produced in the colors of his favorite professional hockey team and then also had his nickname emblazoned on the back of the shoe.[9]

---

[8] Based on: Bruce Caldwell, "Trading Size 12 for a Custom Fit," *Information Week* (October 28, 1996), p. 44; and Ari Zeiger, "Customization Nation," *Incentive* (May 1999), pp. 35–40.

[9] Based on: Kimberly Palmer, "The Store of YOU," *U.S. News & World Report* (November 3, 2008), p. 54.

Process flexibility is essential for true mass customization. In manufacturing postponement and ATO processes, products are assembled from standard modules that can be stored in inventory, reducing the elapsed time from order to delivery. The exact product configuration is postponed until a customer order is received. The type of customization desired by Levi Strauss and more successfully achieved at Mars and Reebok require lean and flexible manufacturing processes that can produce a wider range of products than is economically feasible with conventional processes.

Lean Systems

Lean has been defined in several different ways, but, in general, it is a philosophy of manufacturing that emphasizes the minimization of the amount of all the resources (including time) used in the operations of a company. Operational processes are considered to be lean when they are very efficient and have few wasted resources. The elimination of "waste" is actually the defining principle of lean.

By eliminating wastes of all sorts in the system, the lean approach lowers labor, materials, and energy costs of production. Lean also emphasizes building exactly the products customers want, exactly when they need them. When lean capabilities are introduced in a firm it can produce smaller quantities, and it can change outputs more quickly in response to changes in customer demand.

The primary objectives of lean systems are to

1. Produce only the products (goods or services) that customers want.
2. Produce products only as quickly as customers want to use them.
3. Produce products with perfect quality.
4. Produce in the minimum possible leadtimes.
5. Produce products with features that customers want, and no others.
6. Produce with no waste of labor, materials, or equipment; designate a purpose for every movement to leave zero idle inventory.
7. Produce with methods that reinforce the occupational development of workers.

Note that the first objective emphasizes producing exactly what customers want, the essence of customization. The second emphasizes building products only when customers want them and at the same rate that customers demand them. If operations managers can synchronize their production systems with the rate of demand in this way, they can eliminate many sorts of waste. The other five objectives are frequently associated with the operation of lean systems—emphasis on perfect quality, reducing leadtimes, eliminating unnecessary products, eliminating waste and idle time, and a greater emphasis on employees as the primary agents for improving operations.

Six-Sigma

In the recent years, the **six-sigma** program for quality and process improvements has been adopted by many of the larger firms in the United States and around the world. From statistics, the term "sigma" refers to standard deviation of values for the output of a process and is an indicator of variability. While traditional quality management programs defined three sigma as the objective, in a six-sigma approach, the goal is to achieve a process standard deviation that is six times smaller than the range of outputs allowed by the product's design specification. A primary objective of six-sigma programs is to design and improve products and processes so that variability is reduced. For example, imagine a grinding process that automatically grinds metal parts to a specified width. As the grinding wheel wears, the average width of the processed parts increases. It is this type of movement that creates quality problems. When a process is stable and centered within specification limits, a three-sigma quality level means that the firm produces defect-free product 99.74 percent of the time. A six-sigma process that is centered produces defect-free product 99.99966 percent of the time. Thus, a six-sigma process produces only 3.4 defects per million parts, while a three-sigma process produces 66,807 defects per million parts.

The six-sigma approach is actually a structured process for first identifying sources of variability and then reducing them. Early developers of the six-sigma approach at Motorola originally chose six standard deviations as an appropriate goal given the nature of their manufacturing processes. In truth, very few business operations ever attain a six-sigma level of quality. More important than the absolute goal are the quality improvement processes that comprise a six-sigma program.

Design-for-Logistics

The logistics interface with other functional areas can be greatly enhanced by incorporating a concept known as **design-for-logistics (DFL)** into the early phases of product design. Recall that the objectives of JIT are to minimize inventories and handling, with materials and components being ready for assembly or transformation as they are needed. How a product is designed and the design of the components and materials themselves can have a significant impact on this process. In particular, product packaging and transportation requirements need to be incorporated into the design process. For example, if inbound components are packaged in containers with a standard quantity of 50 but only 30 components are needed to meet production requirements, then waste will occur. Additionally, product and component design must have consideration of transportation and internal materials handling methods to ensure that cost-efficient, damage-free logistics performance can be achieved. Similar logistics design considerations must be made for the finished product itself.

Table 6.2 summarizes the critical relationships between customer accommodation, procurement, manufacturing, and logistical requirements. The framework is useful in positioning how logistical requirements flow from the customer accommodation, manufacturing, and procurement strategies.

Customer Accommodation	Manufacturing	Procurement	Logistics
Focused:	Make-to-Order (MTO):	B2B	Direct Fulfillment:
One-on-one strategies	Mass customization	Discrete quantities	Time postponement
Unique product/service offerings	Unique configuration	Supplier-managed inventory	Small shipment
Response-based	Flexible manufacturing		
	High variety		
Segmental:	Assemble-to-Order (ATO):	B2B	Form and Time
Limited size	Wide variety	JIT	Postponement:
Customer groups	Quick changeover		Warehouse ATO
Differentiated products	Product customization		Combination direct and warehouse fulfillment
Mixed response and anticipatory	High variety and volume		Consolidated shipment
Mass Marketing:	Make-to-Plan (MTP):	B2B	Warehouse Fulfillment:
Anticipatory	Long product runs	Commodity	Full stocking strategy
Little product differentiation	Focus low cost	Auction	Assortment mixing
	High volume/low variety	E-procurement	Volume shipment

TABLE 6.2   Strategic Integration Framework

Summary

A primary concern of all companies is quality, a prerequisite for any firm that desires to be a global competitor. In fact, product quality has several different dimensions. It can mean reliability, durability, product performance, and conformance to engineered specifications. From a customer's perspective, it may also include aspects of product features, aesthetics, or serviceability. World-class companies have implemented total quality management programs in all their activities in an effort to achieve quality from their customer's perspective.

Procurement in an organization is charged with responsibility for obtaining the inputs required to support operations. The focus is multidimensional, attempting to maintain continuous supply, minimize leadtimes from suppliers and inventory of materials and components, and develop suppliers capable of helping the organization achieve operating goals. Procurement professionals are focused on the total cost of ownership as opposed to solely on purchase price. This requires careful consideration of trade-offs among purchase price, supplier services and logistical capability, quality, and how an item affects costs over the life cycle of a finished product. Procurement strategies should be based on a detailed analysis of both the value of an item and the supply risk associated with the item.

Manufacturers balance product volumes, varieties, and capacity with customer requirements and constraints. The basic processes employed reflect alternative strategies related to ETO, MTP, ATO, or MTO. In turn, the strategic choice affects customers in terms of total experienced leadtime. Numerous contemporary developments in manufacturing have reshaped these basic processes and strategies. These developments include mass customization, lean systems, and six sigma. The result is a more integrated, efficient, and effective capability to precisely match customer requirements.

In Chapter 6 strategic considerations related to procurement and manufacturing have been discussed in terms of their combined impact on logistical requirements. A number of important trade-offs were identified. The fundamental point is that isolated optimization of any specific functional area without considering cross-functional impact and requirements is not likely to result in integrated performance.

Study Questions

1. Why does the contemporary view of procurement as a strategic activity differ from the more traditional view of "purchasing"?
2. How does lowest TCO differ from lowest purchase price?
3. What is the underlying rationale that explains why firms should segment their purchase requirements? Explain the concept of procurement strategy portfolio.
4. Explain how logistics performance is crucial to JIT.
5. Why would a company's cost of manufacturing and procurement tend to increase as the firm changes from an MTP to an MTO strategy? Why would inventory costs tend to decrease?
6. How does a firm's marketing strategy impact its decisions regarding the appropriate manufacturing strategy?
7. Many people think of lean systems as being incompatible with mass customization and flexible manufacturing. Why is this conclusion incorrect?

Challenge Questions

1. In the text, Tyco's procurement of logistics services was discussed. Why is Tyco's approach considered innovative?
2. What problems might Tyco confront in attempting to implement this strategy?
3. Why do you think Levi Strauss eventually dropped its program for mass customization?
4. What alternative approaches would you recommend to Levi Strauss to more precisely match customer requirements?

PART 3

Supply Chain Logistics Operations

Part 3 consists of three chapters describing detailed logistics activities and functions. Chapter 7 focuses on inventory management, including the rationale for inventory, costs associated with carrying inventory, procedures for setting and monitoring appropriate inventory levels, and a framework for managing overall inventory resources. Chapter 8 describes the transportation infrastructure, including role, functionality, and principles. The chapter continues with a discussion of the more managerial aspects of transportation operations such as economics, pricing, and administration. Together, costs related to inventory and transportation represent a significant majority of total logistics expense. Chapter 9 discusses the economic and service justification for warehousing and the activities required for facility design and operations. It also includes a discussion of material handling and packaging technologies. This includes discussions regarding requirements for packaging materials and efficiency followed by a discussion of handling equipment capabilities and trade-offs. It is from the integrated performance of individual activities that the power of supply chain logistics is realized.

CHAPTER 7

Inventory

Chapter Outline

Inventory decisions are both high risk and high impact throughout the supply chain. Inventory committed to support future sales drives a number of anticipatory supply chain activities. Without the proper inventory assortment, lost sales and customer dissatisfaction may occur. Likewise, inventory planning is critical to procurement and manufacturing. Material or component shortages can shut down manufacturing or force production schedule modification, added cost, and potential finished goods shortages. Just as shortages can disrupt marketing and manufacturing plans, inventory overstocks also create operating problems. Overstocks increase cost and reduce profitability as a result of added warehousing space, working capital, insurance, taxes, and obsolescence. Management of inventory resources requires an understanding of functionality, principles, cost, impact, and dynamics.

Inventory Functionality and Definitions

Inventory management focuses on inventory risk, which varies depending upon a firm's position in the distribution channel. The typical dimensions of inventory risk relate to time duration, depth, and breadth of commitment.

For a manufacturer, inventory risk is long-term. The manufacturer's inventory commitment begins with raw material and component parts acquisition, includes work-in-process, and ends with finished goods. In addition, finished goods are often pre-positioned in warehouses in anticipation of customer demand. In some situations, manufacturers are required to consign inventory to customer facilities as well. For example, many mass merchants require manufacturers to stock their products on retail store shelves and wait for payment until consumers purchase the products (i.e., consignment inventory). In effect, this practice shifts all inventory risk to the manufacturer. Although a manufacturer typically has a narrower product line (e.g., manufacturers have fewer products) than a retailer or wholesaler, the manufacturer's inventory commitment is deep and of long duration.

A wholesaler purchases large quantities from manufacturers and sells smaller quantities to retailers. The economic justification of a wholesaler is the capability to provide customers an assortment of merchandise from different manufacturers in reduced quantities. When products are seasonal, the wholesaler may be required to take an inventory position far in advance of the selling season, thus increasing depth and duration of risk. One of the greatest challenges of wholesaling is product-line expansion to the point where the width of inventory risk approaches that of the retailer while depth and duration of risk remain characteristic of traditional wholesaling. In recent years, powerful retailers have driven a substantial increase in depth and duration by shifting inventory responsibility back to manufacturers or wholesalers.

For a retailer, inventory management is about the velocity of buying and selling. Retailers purchase a wide variety of products and assume substantial risk in the marketing process. Retail inventory risk can be viewed as broad but not deep. Due to the high cost of store location and space, retailers place prime emphasis on inventory turnover. Inventory turnover is a measure of inventory velocity and is calculated as the ratio of sales for a time period divided by average inventory.

Although retailers assume a position of risk on a wide variety of products, their position on any one product is not deep. Risk is spread across more than 50,000 stockkeeping units (SKUs) in a typical supermarket. A mass retailer offering general merchandise and food often exceeds 70,000 SKUs. Faced with this breadth of inventory, retailers attempt to reduce risk by pressing manufacturers and wholesalers to assume greater and greater inventory responsibility. Pushing inventory back up the channel has resulted in retailer demand for fast delivery of mixed-product shipments from wholesalers and manufacturers. Specialty retailers, in contrast to mass merchandisers, normally experience less width of inventory risk as a result of handling narrower assortments. However, they must assume greater risk with respect to depth and duration of inventory holding.

If a business plans to operate at more than one level of the distribution channel, it must be prepared to assume the associated inventory risk. For example, a food chain that operates a regional warehouse assumes risk related to wholesale functionality over and above normal retail operations. To the extent that an enterprise becomes vertically integrated, inventory must be managed at multiple levels of the supply chain.

TABLE 7.1

Inventory Functionality

Geographical specialization	Allows geographical positioning across multiple manufacturing and distributive units of an enterprise. Inventory maintained at different locations and stages of the value-creation process allows specialization.
Decoupling	Allows economy of scale within a single facility and permits each process to operate at maximum efficiency rather than having the speed of the entire process constrained by the slowest.
Supply/demand balancing	Accommodates elapsed time between inventory availability (manufacturing, growing, or extraction) and consumption.
Buffering uncertainty	Accommodates uncertainty related to demand in excess of forecast or unexpected delays in order receipt and order processing in delivery and is typically referred to as safety stock.

Inventory Functionality

From an inventory perspective, the ideal situation would be a response-based supply chain. At various points in early chapters, the practicality of implementing a fully response-based supply chain was discussed in terms of the total cost and timeliness of customer support. While a zero-inventory supply chain is typically not achievable, it is important to remember that each dollar invested in inventory is a trade-off to an alternative use of assets.

Inventory is a current asset that should provide return on the capital invested. The return on inventory investments is the marginal profit on sales that would not occur without inventory. Accounting experts have long recognized that measuring the true cost and benefits of inventory on the corporate profit-and-loss is difficult.[1] Lack of measurement sophistication makes it difficult to evaluate the trade-offs among service level, operating efficiency, and inventory level. While aggregate inventory levels throughout sectors of the economy have decreased, many enterprises still carry more inventory than needed to support actual business requirements. The forces driving this generalization are understood better through a review of the four prime functions of inventory. Table 7.1 summarizes inventory functionality.

These four functions, **geographical specialization, decoupling, balancing supply and demand, and buffering uncertainty**, require inventory investment to achieve operating objectives. While logistics, as discussed in Chapter 3, has made significant progress in reducing overall supply chain inventory, inventory properly deployed creates value and reduces total cost. Given a specific manufacturing/marketing strategy, inventories planned and committed to operations can only be reduced to a level consistent with performing the four inventory functions. All inventory exceeding the minimum level represents excess commitment.

At the minimum level, inventory invested to achieve geographical specialization and decoupling can be modified only by changes in network facility location and operational processes of the enterprise. The automotive manufacturers use geographical specialization by locating the sheet metal and bumpers (auto body parts) in the colder regions since that is where many of the crashes occur due to the snow and ice. Decoupling is the separation of a manufacturing process from the selling process. For example, the manufacturing process may demonstrate significant economies of scale while sales occur with relatively low scale economies. In this situation, firms may use decoupling to manufacture the inventory in large-enough quantities to achieve economies of scale, even though it may be necessary to hold it as inventory prior to sale. Inventory to balance supply and demand is necessary

---

[1]Douglas M. Lambert, *The Development of an Inventory Costing Methodology* (Chicago: National Council of Physical Distribution Management, 1976), p. 3; and *Inventory Carrying Cost, Memorandum 611* (Chicago: Drake Sheahan/Stewart Dougall Inc., 1974).

when the timing of product supply is different than the demand pattern. For example, fruits and vegetables have a relatively limited growing season, but consumers desire year-round consumption and will buy throughout the year. Another example is the seasonal demand for toys and garden supplies, where sales occur in a very short time span but production occurs all year. Balancing inventory is necessary to match the supply and demand patterns. Buffering inventory is necessary when there is uncertainty in either supply and demand. When there is uncertainty regarding when product will become available (supply) and when the customer requires it (demand), it may be necessary to hold buffer inventory.

Inventory committed to safety stocks represent the greatest potential for improved logistics performance. This commitment is operational in nature and can be adjusted rapidly in the event of an error or policy change. A variety of techniques are available to assist management in planning safety stock commitments. The focus of this chapter is the analysis of safety stock relationships and inventory policy development.

Inventory Definitions

In designing inventory policy, the relationship dynamics of inventory must be considered. Management must understand these relationships to establish inventory policy with respect to when and how much to order. This **inventory policy** drives inventory performance. The two key indicators of inventory performance are **service level** and **average inventory**.

Inventory Policy

Inventory policy consists of guidelines regarding what to purchase or manufacture, when to purchase or manufacture it, and in what quantity. It also includes decisions regarding geographical inventory positioning. For example, some firms may decide to postpone inventory positioning by maintaining stock at the plant. Other firms may use a more speculative strategy of positioning product in local markets or regional warehouses. It is advantageous to use a geographic postponement strategy, centralizing the inventory position for items with high demand uncertainty or high value. Speculative positioning may be more appropriate for items that are relatively low value or that require quick accessibility by customers. Development of sound inventory policy is the most difficult dimension of inventory management.

A second policy aspect concerns inventory management practice. One approach is to independently manage inventory at each stocking facility. At the other extreme is central inventory management of all stocking locations. Centralized inventory management requires effective communication and coordination. The increased availability of information technology and integrated planning systems allows more firms to implement centralized inventory planning. Centralized inventory planning systems can reduce demand uncertainty between distribution locations.

Service Level

Service level is a performance target specified by management. It defines inventory performance objectives. Service level is often measured in terms of performance cycle time, case fill rate, line fill rate, order fill rate, or any combination of these. The **performance cycle** is the elapsed time between the release of a purchase order by a buyer to the receipt of shipment. A **case fill rate** is the percent of cases or units ordered that are shipped as requested. For example, a 95 percent case fill rate indicates that, on average, 95 cases out of 100 are filled from available stock. The remaining five cases are back-ordered or deleted. The **line fill rate** is the percent of order lines filled completely. **Order fill** is the percent of customer orders filled completely.

FIGURE 7.1

Inventory Cycle for
Typical Product

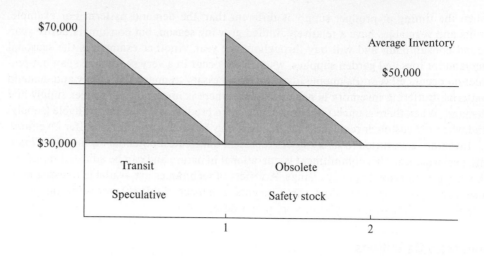

Inventory management is a major element of supply chain logistics strategy that must be integrated to achieve overall service objectives. While one strategy to achieve a high service level is to increase inventory, an alternative approach may be the use of faster or more reliable transportation and collaboration with customers and service providers to reduce uncertainty.

Average Inventory

The materials, components, work-in-process, and finished product typically stocked in the logistics system are referred to as **inventory** and the rolling mean across time is referred to as **average inventory**. From a policy viewpoint, target inventory levels must be planned for each facility. Figure 7.1 illustrates the performance cycles for one item at one location. At the maximum, the facility has in stock during the normal performance cycle $70,000 and a minimum of $30,000. The difference between these two levels, $40,000 ($70,000 − $30,000), is the order or production quantity, resulting in a cycle inventory of $20,000 ($40,000/2). Cycle inventory or base stock is the portion of average inventory that results from replenishment or production. Stock level is at a maximum following stock receipt from the supplier. Customers deplete inventory until the stock level reaches its reorder point. Prior to the stock level reaching the minimum, a replenishment or production order is initiated so that inventory will arrive before an out-of-stock occurs. The replenishment order must be initiated before the available inventory is less than or equal to forecasted demand during the performance cycle time. The amount ordered for replenishment is termed the **order or production quantity**. Given this basic order formulation, average cycle inventory or base stock equals one-half order quantity.

The **transit inventory** represents the amount typically in transit between facilities or on order but not received. The **obsolete inventory** is the stock that is out-of-date or that has not experienced recent demand. Eventually, it is donated, sold at a loss or destroyed. **Speculative inventory** is bought prior to need to hedge a currency exchange, take advantage of a special discount, or prepare for a potential work force disruption. A modern example of speculative inventory purchase occurs each year as many Asia-Pacific countries observe a multi-week celebration for Chinese New Year resulting in planned production facility closures.

The remainder of inventory in the typical logistics system is **safety stock**. Safety stock is maintained in a logistics system to protect against demand and performance cycle uncertainty. Safety stock is used only near the end of replenishment cycles when uncertainty has caused higher-than-expected demand or longer-than-expected performance cycle times. Thus, typical average inventory is **one-half order quantity plus safety stock and in-transit stock** ($70,000 − $40,000/2 + 30,000 + in-transit stock).

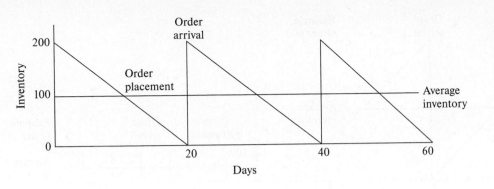

FIGURE 7.2
Inventory Relationship
for Constant Sales and
Performance Cycle

Average Inventory across Multiple Performance Cycles

In initial policy formulation, it is necessary to determine how much inventory to order at a specified time. To illustrate, assume the replenishment performance cycle is a constant 10 days and daily sales rate is 10 units per day. Also assume the order quantity is 200 units.

Figure 7.2 illustrates this relationship. This type of chart is referred to as a **sawtooth diagram** because of the series of right triangles. Since complete certainty exists with respect to usage and performance cycle, orders are scheduled to arrive just as the last unit is sold. Thus, no safety stock is necessary. Since the rate of sale in the example is 10 units per day and it takes 10 days to complete inventory replenishment, a sound reorder policy might be to order 200 units every 20 days. Given these conditions, common terminology related to policy formulation can be specified.

First, the **reorder point** is specified as 100 units on hand. The reorder point defines when a replenishment order is initiated. In this example, whenever the quantity on hand drops below 100, an additional order for 200 units is placed. The result of this policy is that daily inventory level ranges from a maximum of 200 to a minimum of zero over the performance cycle.

Second, average inventory is 100 units, since stock on hand exceeds 100 units one-half of the time, or for 10 days, and is less than 100 units one-half of the time. In fact, average inventory is equal to one-half the 200-unit order quantity.

Third, assuming a work year of 240 days, 12 purchases will be required during the year. Therefore, over a period of 1 year, 200 units will be purchased 12 times for a total of 2400 units. Sales are expected to equal 10 units per/day over 240 (business days) days for a total of 2400 units. As discussed above, average inventory is 100 units. Thus, **inventory turns** will be 24 (2400 total sales/100 units of average inventory).

In time, such routine operations would lead management to ask some questions concerning the arrangement. What would happen if orders were placed more frequently than once every 20 days? Why not order 100 units every 10 days? Why order as frequently as every 20 days? Why not reorder 600 units once every 60 days? Assuming that the inventory performance cycle remains a constant 10 days, what would be the impact of each of these alternative ordering policies on reorder point, average base inventory, and inventory turnover?

The policy of ordering a smaller volume of 100 units every 10 days means that two orders would always be outstanding. Thus, the reorder point would remain 100 units on hand or on order to service average daily sales of 10 units over the 20-day inventory cycle. However, average inventory on hand would drop to 50 units, and inventory turnover would increase to 48 times per year. The policy of ordering 600 units every 60 days would result

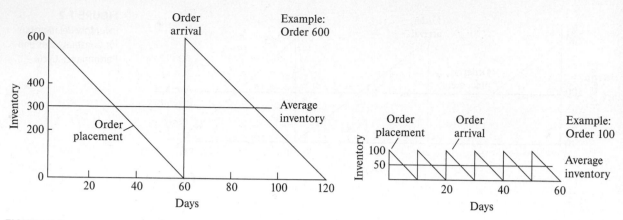

FIGURE 7.3
Alternative Order Quantity and Average Inventory

in an average base inventory of 300 units and a turnover of approximately eight times per year. These alternative ordering policies are illustrated in Figure 7.3.

The figure illustrates that average inventory is a function of the reorder quantity. Smaller replenishment order quantities do result in lower average inventory, but there are other factors such as performance cycle uncertainty, purchasing discounts, and transportation economies that are important when determining order quantity.

An exact order quantity policy can be determined by balancing the cost of ordering and the cost of maintaining average inventory. The **economic order quantity (EOQ)** model provides a specific quantity balancing of these two critical cost components. By determining the EOQ and dividing it into annual demand, the frequency and size of replenishment orders minimizing the total cost of cycle inventory are identified. Prior to reviewing EOQ, it is necessary to identify costs typically associated with ordering and maintaining inventory.

Independent vs. Dependent Demand

Supply chains are typically a combination of independent and dependent demands. At the consumer level, most demand is independent as consumers do not typically let the retailer know when they are arriving to purchase product. Consumers arrive at the store and generally expect the product to be on the shelf. While retailers can forecast demand based on historical patterns, they must anticipate consumer requirements by having inventory pre-positioned at the store. This situation is often termed "just-in-case" inventory because it must be committed just in case the consumer walks into the store. At the supplier end of the supply chain, component inventory can typically be characterized as dependent. A dependent demand situation is characteristic of component parts that are assembled into final products such as for automotive or electronic manufacturers. In the dependent case, the manufacturer establishes a production schedule that is typically shared with their suppliers. Based on the production schedule, the supplier can anticipate the demand and the required delivery schedule for component parts. For example, for an automotive assembly plant with a production schedule of 1,000 cars per day, the tire supplier would know to schedule the arrival of 4,000 tires daily to meet that production schedule. In dependent demand situations, it is possible to use "just-in-time" deployment since there is no demand uncertainty once the finished product schedule is established and shared with suppliers.

Inventory Carrying Cost

Inventory carrying cost is the expense associated with maintaining or holding inventory. Inventory expense is calculated by multiplying annual inventory carrying cost percent by average inventory value. Standard accounting practice is to value inventory at purchase or standard manufacturing cost rather than at selling price.

Assuming an annual inventory carrying cost percentage of 20 percent, the annual inventory expense for an enterprise with $1 million in average inventory would be $200,000 (20% × $1,000,000). While the calculation of inventory carrying expense is basic, determining the appropriate carrying cost percent is less obvious.

Determining carrying cost percent requires assignment of inventory-related costs. Financial accounts relevant to inventory carrying cost percent are capital, insurance, obsolescence, storage, and taxes. While cost of capital is typically based on managerial policy, expense-related taxes, insurance, obsolescence, and storage typically vary depending on the specific attributes of individual products.

Capital

The appropriate charge to place on capital invested in inventory varies widely. Capital assessments range from the prime interest rate to a percent determined by upper management. The logic for using the prime interest rate or a specified rate pegged to the prime rate is that cash to replace capital invested in inventory can be obtained in the money markets at that rate. Higher management specified capital costs are based on expected or target return on investment for capital deployed. Such target rates are typically termed **hurdle** rates.

The cost of capital may vary significantly by firm and industry. Firms that are aggressive in uses of cash will typically employ a higher cost of capital percentage. Similarly, industries with high value or short life cycle product will employ a higher cost of capital to drive lower inventories. For example, electronics or pharmaceutical firms may use high capital rates (20–30%) since they expect high returns on their development investments and their products have short life cycles, while food and beverage manufacturers may accept lower hurdle rates (5–15%) since they have longer product life cycles and relatively lower risk.

Confusion often results from the fact that senior management frequently does not establish a clear-cut capital cost policy. For supply chain logistics planning, the cost of capital must be clearly specified since it has significant impact on system design and performance.

Taxes

Local taxing authorities in many areas assess taxes on inventory held in warehouses. The tax rate and means of assessment vary by location. The tax expense is usually a direct levy based on average inventory value on a specific day of the year or average inventory value over a period of time. In many cases tax exemption such as free port status is available from local and state taxing authorities.

Insurance

Insurance cost is an expense based upon estimated risk or loss over time. Loss risk depends on the product and the facility storing the product. For example, high-value products that are easily stolen and hazardous products result in high insurance cost. Insurance cost is also influenced by facility characteristics such as security cameras and sprinkler systems that might help reduce risk. Since September 11, 2001, issues related to the risk of terrorism have become of greater concern in supply chain design.

Obsolescence

Obsolescence cost results from deterioration of product during storage. A prime example of obsolescence is product that ages beyond recommended sell-by date, such as food and pharmaceuticals. Obsolescence also includes financial loss when a product no longer has fashion appeal or no longer has any demand. Obsolescence costs are typically estimated on the basis of past experience concerning markdowns, donations, or quantity destroyed. This expense is the percent of average inventory value declared obsolete each year.

Storage

Storage cost is facility expense related to product holding rather than product handling. Storage cost must be allocated on the requirements of specific products since it is not related directly to inventory value. In public or contract warehouses, storage charges are billed based on average inventory in the facility. The cost of total annual occupancy for a given product can then be assigned by multiplying the average daily physical space occupied by the standard cost per facility dimension for a specified time. This figure can then be divided by the total number of units of merchandise processed through the facility to determine average storage cost per merchandise unit.

Table 7.2 illustrates the components of annual inventory carrying cost and typical range of component costs. It should be clear that the final carrying cost percent used by a firm is a matter of managerial policy. Decisions regarding inventory cost are important because they trade off against other logistics cost components in system design and operating decisions.

Planning Inventory

Inventory planning consists of determining when and how much to order. When to order is determined by demand and replenishment lead time average and uncertainty. How much to order is determined by the order quantity. Inventory control is the process of monitoring inventory status.

When to Order

As discussed earlier, the reorder point defines when a replenishment shipment should be initiated. A reorder point can be specified in terms of units or days' supply. This discussion focuses on determining reorder points under conditions of demand and performance cycle certainty.

TABLE 7.2
Inventory Carrying Cost Components

Element	Average Percent	Percent Ranges
Cost of capital	10.00%	4–40%
Taxes	1.00	.5–2
Insurance	1.00	0–2
Obsolescence	1.00	.5–2
Storage	2.00	0–4
Totals	15.00%	5–50%

The basic reorder point formula is:

$$R = D \times T$$

where

R = Reorder point in units;

D = Average daily demand in units; and

T = Average performance cycle length in days.

To illustrate this calculation, assume demand of 20 units/day and a 10-day performance cycle. In this case,

$$R = D \times T$$
$$= 20 \text{ units/day} \times 10 \text{ days}$$
$$= 200 \text{ units.}$$

An alternative form is to define reorder point in terms of days of supply. For the above example, the days of supply reorder point is 10 days.

The use of reorder point formulations implies that the replenishment shipment will arrive as scheduled. When uncertainty exists in either demand or performance cycle length, safety stock is required. When safety stock is necessary to accommodate uncertainty, the reorder point formula is:

$$R = D \times T + \text{SS}$$

where

R = Reorder point in units;

D = Average daily demand in units;

T = Average performance cycle length in days; and

SS = Safety stock in units.

Computation of safety stock under conditions of uncertainty is discussed later in this chapter.

How Much to Order

Lot sizing balances inventory carrying cost with the cost of ordering. The key to understanding the relationship is to remember that average inventory is equal to one-half the order quantity. Therefore, the greater the order quantity, the larger the average inventory and, consequently, the greater the annual carrying cost. However, the larger the order quantity, the fewer replenishment orders required per planning period and, consequently, the lower the total ordering cost. Lot quantity formulations identify the precise quantities at which the annual combined total inventory carrying and ordering cost is lowest for a given sales volume. Figure 7.4 illustrates the relationships. The point at which the sum of ordering and carrying cost is minimized represents the lowest total cost or economic order quantity (EOQ). The objective is to identify the ordering quantity that minimizes the total inventory carrying and ordering cost.

Economic Order Quantity

The EOQ is the replenishment quantity that minimizes the combined inventory carrying and ordering cost. Identification of such a quantity assumes that demand and costs are

FIGURE 7.4
Economic Order Quantity

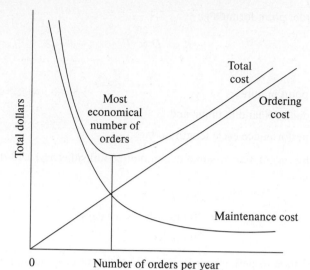

TABLE 7.3
Factors for
Determining EOQ

Annual demand volume	2400 units
Unit value at cost	$5.00
Inventory carrying cost percent	20% annually
Ordering cost	$19.00 per order

relatively stable throughout the year. Since EOQ is calculated on an individual product basis, the basic formulation does not consider the impact of joint ordering of multiple products.

The most efficient method for calculating EOQ is mathematical. Earlier in this chapter a policy dilemma regarding whether to order 100, 200, or 600 units was presented. The answer can be found by calculating the applicable EOQ for the situation. Table 7.3 contains the necessary information.

To make the appropriate calculations, the standard formulation for EOQ is:

$$EOQ = \sqrt{\frac{2C_oD}{C_iU}}$$

where

EOQ = Economic order quantity;

C_o = Cost per order;

C_i = Annual inventory carrying cost;

D = Annual sales volume, units; and

U = Cost per unit.

Substituting from Table 7.3,

$$EOQ = \sqrt{\frac{2 \times 19 \times 2400}{0.20 \times 5.00}}$$

$$= \sqrt{91,200}$$

$$= 302 \text{ (round to 300)}.$$

Total ordering cost would amount to $152 (2400/300 × $19.00), and inventory carrying cost would amount to $150 [300/2 × (5 × 0.20)]. Thus, rounding to allow ordering in multiples of 100 units, annual reordering, and inventory carrying cost have been equated.

To benefit from the most economical purchase arrangement, orders should be placed in the quantity of 300 units rather than 100, 200, or 600. Thus, over the year, eight orders would be placed and average base inventory would be 150 units. Referring back to Figure 7.4, the impact of ordering in quantities of 300 rather than 200 can be identified. An EOQ of 300 implies that additional inventory in the form of base stock has been introduced into the system. Average inventory has been increased from 100 to 150 units on hand.

While the EOQ model determines the optimal replenishment quantity, it does require some rather stringent assumptions. The major assumptions of the simple EOQ model are: (1) all demand is satisfied; (2) rate of demand is continuous, constant, and known; (3) replenishment performance cycle time is constant and known; (4) there is a constant price of product that is independent of order quantity or time; (5) there is an infinite planning horizon; (6) there is no interaction between multiple items of inventory; (7) no inventory is in transit; and (8) no limit is placed on capital availability. The constraints imposed by some of these assumptions can be overcome through computational extensions; however, the EOQ concept illustrates the importance of the trade-offs associated with inventory carrying and replenishment ordering cost.

Relationships involving the inventory performance cycle, inventory cost, and economic order formulations are useful for guiding inventory planning. First, the EOQ is found at the point where annualized order placement cost and inventory carrying cost are equal. Second, average base inventory equals one-half order quantity. Third, the value of the inventory unit, all other things being equal, will have a direct relationship with replenishment order frequency. In effect, the higher the product value, the more frequently it will be ordered.

While the EOQ formulation is relatively straightforward, there are other factors that must be considered in actual application. These factors refer to various adjustments necessary to take advantage of special purchase situations and unitization characteristics. Three typical adjustments are volume transportation rates, quantity discounts, and other EOQ adjustments.

Volume Transportation Rates

In the EOQ formulation, no consideration was given to the impact of transportation cost upon order quantity. Regardless of whether product is sold on a delivered basis or ownership is transferred at origin, the cost of transportation must be paid by supply chain participants. Collaborative efforts to order in quantities that minimize total cost are essential to sound logistical arrangements.

As a general rule, the greater the weight of an order, the lower the cost per pound of transportation from any origin to destination.[2] A freight-rate discount for larger shipments is common across all transportation modes. Thus, all other things being equal, supply chain arrangements should utilize quantities that offer maximum transportation economies. Such quantities may be larger than the EOQ purchase quantity. Increasing order size has a twofold impact upon inventory cost. Assume for purposes of illustration that the most desirable transportation rate is obtained when a quantity of 480 is ordered, as compared to the EOQ-recommended order of 300 calculated earlier. The first impact of the larger order is to increase the average base inventory from 150 to 240 units. Thus, ordering in larger quantities increases inventory carrying cost.

[2]To determine transportation rates, the unit quantity must generally be converted to weight or cube.

TABLE 7.4

EOQ Data Requirements for Consideration of Transportation Economies

Annual demand volume	2400 units
Unit value at cost	$5.00
Inventory carrying cost percentage	20% annually
Ordering cost	$19.00 per order
Small shipment rate	$1.00 per unit
Large shipment rate	$0.75 per unit

TABLE 7.5

Volume Transportation Rate Modified EOQ

	Alternative 1: $EOQ_1 = 300$	Alternative 2: $EOQ_2 = 480$
Inventory carrying cost	$ 150	$ 240
Ordering cost	$ 152	$ 95
Transportation cost	$2,400	$1,800
Total cost	$2,702	$2,135

The second impact is a decrease in the number of orders required to satisfy annual requirements. Decreased number of orders increases the shipment size, facilitating lower per-unit transportation cost.

To complete the analysis it is necessary to formulate the total cost with and without transportation savings. While this calculation can be directly made by modification of the EOQ formulation, direct comparison provides a more insightful answer. The only additional data required are the applicable freight rate for ordering in quantities of 300 and 480. Table 7.4 provides the data necessary to complete the analysis.

Table 7.5 illustrates total cost analysis. Reducing total annual cost by purchasing 480 units five times per year rather than the original EOQ solution of 300 units eight times per year results in approximately a $570 savings.

The impact of volume transportation rates upon total cost of procurement cannot be neglected. In the example above, the equivalent rate per unit dropped from $1 to $0.75, or by 25 percent. Thus, any EOQ must be tested for transportation cost sensitivity across a range of weight breaks.

Another point illustrated in the data in Table 7.5 is the fact that rather substantial changes in the size of an order and the number of orders placed per year result in only a modest change in the total ordering and inventory carrying cost. The EOQ quantity of 300 had a total annual cost of $302, whereas the revised order quantity had a comparative cost of $335.

EOQ formulations are much more sensitive to significant changes in order cycle or frequency. Likewise, substantial changes in cost factors are necessary to significantly change the economic order quantity.

Finally, two factors regarding inventory cost under conditions of origin purchase are noteworthy. FOB (free on board) origin purchase means that the buyer is responsible for freight cost and risk while the product is in transit. It follows that any change in weight break leading to a shipment method with a different transit time should be considered, using the added cost or savings as appropriate in a total cost analysis.

Second, the transportation cost must be added to the purchase price to determine the value of goods tied up in inventory. Once the inventory has been received, the cost of the product must be increased to reflect the inbound transportation.[3]

---

[3]Some aspects of pricing are discussed in greater detail in Chapter 8.

Cost	Quantity Purchased
$5.00	1–99
4.50	100–200
4.00	201–300
3.50	301–400
3.00	401–500

TABLE 7.6
Example of Quantity Discounts

Quantity Discounts

Purchase quantity discounts represent an EOQ extension similar to volume transportation rates. Table 7.6 illustrates a sample schedule of discounts. Quantity discounts can be handled directly with the basic EOQ formula by calculating total cost at any given volume-related purchase price, similar to the process used in calculating transportation rate impact, to determine associated EOQs. If the discount at any associated quantity is sufficient to offset the added inventory carrying cost less the reduced cost of ordering, then the quantity discount is a viable choice. It should be noted that quantity discounts and volume transportation rates each drive larger purchase quantities. This does not necessarily mean that the lowest total cost purchase will always be a larger quantity than would otherwise be the case under basic EOQ.

Other EOQ Adjustments

A variety of other special situations may justify adjustments to the basic EOQ. Examples are (1) production lot size, (2) multiple-item purchase, (3) limited capital, (4) dedicated trucking, and (5) unitization. Production lot size refers to the most economical quantities from a manufacturing perspective. Multiple-item purchase refers to situations when more than one product are bought concurrently, so quantity and transportation discounts must consider the impact of product combinations. Limited capital describes situations with budget limitations for total inventory investment. Since the multiple product order must be made within the budget limitations, order quantities must recognize the need to allocate the inventory investment across the product line. Retailers often apply budget limitations when setting their "open-to-buy" for item categories. Dedicated trucking can influence order quantity since the truck has a fixed cost consideration.[4] Once it is decided to use a dedicated fleet to transport replenishment product, the enterprise should try to purchase in quantities that fully use available capacity. Back haul capacity availability may also justify purchasing products earlier than otherwise determined by EOQ considerations.

Another consideration when determining replenishment order quantity is unitization. Many products are stored and moved in standard units such as cases or pallets. Since these standardized units are often designed to fit transportation vehicles, there may be significant diseconomies when the EOQ does not reflect standard units. As an example, suppose that a full pallet quantity is 200 units of a specified product. Using an EOQ of 300 units would require shipments of 1.5 pallets. From a handling or transportation utilization perspective, it is probably more effective to order either one or two pallets alternately or permanently.

---

[4]See Chapter 8. In such situations, the cost of money invested in inventory should be appropriately charged when the goods are paid for at origin.

Managing Uncertainty

To understand basic principles, it is useful to understand inventory relationships under conditions of certainty. Formulation of inventory policy must consider uncertainty. Two types of uncertainty directly impact inventory policy. **Demand uncertainty** involves the variation in sales during inventory replenishment. **Performance cycle uncertainty** involves inventory replenishment time variation.

Demand Uncertainty

Sales forecasting estimates unit demand during the inventory replenishment cycle. Even with good forecasting, demand during replenishment cycle typically exceeds or falls short of what is planned. To protect against a stockout when demand exceeds forecast, safety stock is added to base inventory. Under conditions of demand uncertainty, average inventory represents one-half order quantity plus safety stock. Figure 7.5 illustrates the inventory performance cycle under conditions of demand uncertainty. The dashed line represents the forecast. The solid line illustrates inventory on hand across multiple performance cycles. The task of planning safety stock requires three steps. First, the likelihood of stockout must be gauged. Second, demand during a stockout period must be estimated. Finally, a policy decision is required concerning the desired level of stockout protection.

Assume for purposes of illustration that the inventory performance cycle is 10 days. History indicates daily sales range from 0 to 10 units with average daily sales of 5 units. The economic order is assumed to be 50, the reorder point is 50, the planned average inventory is 25, and sales during the performance cycle are forecasted to be 50 units.

During the first cycle, although daily demand experienced variation, the average of 5 units per day was maintained. Total demand during cycle 1 was 50 units, as expected. During cycle 2, demand totaled 50 units in the first 8 days, resulting in a stockout. Thus, no sales were possible on days 9 and 10. During cycle 3, demand reached a total of 39 units. The third performance cycle ended with 11 units remaining in stock. Over the 30-day period total sales were 139 units, for average daily sale of 4.6 units.

From the history recorded in Table 7.7, it is observed that stockouts occurred on 2 of 30 total days. Since sales never exceed 10 units per day, no possibility of stockout exists on the first 5 days of the replenishment cycle. Stockouts were possible on days 6 through 10 on the remote possibility that demand during the first 5 days of the cycle averaged 10 units per day and no inventory was carried over from the previous period. Since during the three

FIGURE 7.5

Inventory Relationship, Demand Uncertainty, and Constant Performance Cycle

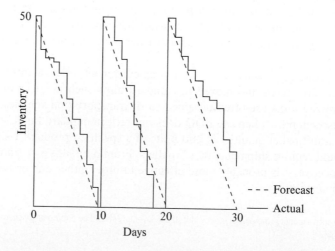

Day	Forecast Cycle 1		Stockout Cycle 2		Overstock Cycle 3	
	Demand	Accumulated	Demand	Accumulated	Demand	Accumulated
1	9	9	0	0	5	5
2	2	11	6	6	5	10
3	1	12	5	11	4	14
4	3	15	7	18	3	17
5	7	22	10	28	4	21
6	5	27	7	35	1	22
7	4	31	6	41	2	24
8	8	39	9	50	8	32
9	6	45	Stockout	50	3	35
10	5	50	Stockout	50	4	39

TABLE 7.7
Typical Demand Experience during Three Replenishment Cycles

Daily Demand (in units)	Frequency (days)
Stockout	2
0	1
1	2
2	2
3	3
4	4
5	5
6	3
7	3
8	2
9	2
10	1

TABLE 7.8
Frequency of Demand

performance cycles 10 units were sold on only one occasion, it is apparent that the real risk of stockout occurs only during the last few days of the performance cycle, and then only when sales exceed the average by a substantial margin.[5] Some approximation is possible concerning sales potential for days 9 and 10 of cycle 2. A maximum of 20 units might have been sold if inventory had been available. On the other hand, it is remotely possible that even if stock had been available, no demand would have occurred on days 9 and 10. For average demand of 4 to 5 units per day, a reasonable appraisal of lost sales is 8 to 10 units.

It should be apparent that the stockouts risk created by variations in sales is limited to a short time and includes a small percentage of total sales. Although the sales analysis presented in Table 7.7 helps develop an understanding of the opportunity, the appropriate course of action is still not clear. Statistical probability can be used to assist management in planning safety stock.

The sales history over the 30-day period has been aggregated in Table 7.8 as a frequency distribution. The main purpose of a frequency distribution is to observe variations around the average daily demand. Given an expected average of 5 units per day, demand exceeded average on 11 days and was less than average on 12 days. An alternative way of illustrating a frequency distribution is by a bar chart, as in Figure 7.6.

[5]In this example, daily statistics are used. An alternative, which is technically more correct from a statistical viewpoint, is to utilize demand over multiple performance cycles. The major limitation of order cycles is the length of time and difficulty required to collect the necessary data.

FIGURE 7.6
Historical Analysis of
Demand History

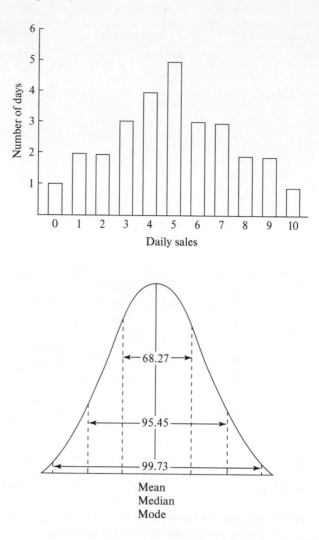

FIGURE 7.7
Normal Distribution

Given the historical demand frequency, it is possible to calculate the safety stock necessary to provide a specified degree of stockout protection. Probability theory is based on the random chance of a specific occurrence within a large number of occurrences. The situation illustrated uses a 28-day sample. In actual application, a larger sample size would be desirable.

The probability of occurrences assumes a pattern around a measure of central tendency, which is the average value of all occurrences. While a number of frequency distributions can be used in inventory management, the most common is the **normal distribution**.

A normal distribution is characterized by a symmetrical bell-shaped curve, illustrated in Figure 7.7. The essential characteristic of a normal distribution is that the three measures of central tendency have equal value. The **mean** (average) value, the **median** (middle) observation, and the **mode** (most frequently observed) all have the same value. When these three measures are nearly identical, the frequency distribution is **normal**.

The basis for predicting demand during a performance cycle using a normal distribution is the **standard deviation** of observations around the three measures of central tendency. The standard deviation is the dispersion of observations within specified areas under the normal curve. For the inventory management application, the observation is unit sales per day and the dispersion is the variation in daily sales. Within 1 standard deviation,

68.27 percent of all events occur. This means that 68.27 percent of the days during a performance cycle will experience daily sales within ± 1 standard deviation of the average daily sales. Within ± 2 standard deviations, 95.45 percent of all observations occur. At ± 3 standard deviations, 99.73 percent of all observations are included. In terms of inventory policy, the standard deviation provides a method of estimating the safety stock required to achieve a specified degree of out-of-stock protection.

The first step in setting safety stock is to calculate the standard deviation. Most calculators and spreadsheets calculate standard deviation, but if one of these aids is not available, another method to compute the standard deviation is:

$$\sigma = \sqrt{\frac{\sum F_i D_i^2}{n}}$$

where

σ = Standard deviation;

F_i = Frequency of observation i;

D_i = Deviation of observation from mean for observation i; and

n = Total observations available.

The necessary data to determine standard deviation are contained in Table 7.9.

The standard deviation of the data in Table 7.9 is rounded to 3 units. When setting safety stocks, 2 standard deviations of protection, or 6 units, would protect against 95.45 percent of all observations included in the distribution. However, the only situations of concern in determining safety stock requirements are observations that exceed the mean value. No problem exists concerning inventory to satisfy demand equal to or below the average. Thus, on 50 percent of the days, no safety stock is required. Safety stock protection at the 95 percent level will, in fact, protect against 97.72 percent of all possible observations. The 95 percent coverage will cover all situations when daily demand is ± 2 standard deviations of the average plus the 2.72 percent of the time when demand is more than 2 standard deviations below the mean. This added benefit results from what is typically called a **one-tail** statistical application.

Units	Frequency (F_i)	Deviation from Mean (D_i)	Deviation Squared (D_i^2)	$F_i D_i^2$
0	1	−5	25	25
1	2	−4	16	32
2	2	−3	9	18
3	3	−2	4	12
4	4	−1	1	4
5	5	0	0	0
6	3	+1	1	3
7	3	+2	4	12
8	2	+3	9	18
9	2	+4	16	32
10	1	+5	25	25
$n = 28$	$\bar{s} = 5$			$\sum F_i D_i^2 = 181$

$$\sigma = \sqrt{\frac{F_i D_i^2}{N}} = \sqrt{\frac{181}{28}} = 2.54$$

TABLE 7.9

Calculation of Standard Deviation of Daily Demand

TABLE 7.10
Calculation of
Standard Deviation of
Replenishment Cycle
Duration

Performance Cycle (days)	Frequency (F_i)	Deviation from Mean (D_i)	Deviation Squared (D_i^2)	$F_i D_i^2$
6	2	−4	16	32
7	4	−3	9	36
8	6	−2	4	24
9	8	−1	1	8
10	10	0	0	0
11	8	+1	1	8
12	6	+2	4	24
13	4	+3	9	36
14	2	+4	16	32

$$\sum F_i D_i^2 = 200$$

$$N = 50 \quad t = 10$$

$$\sigma = \sqrt{\frac{F_i D_i^2}{N}} = \sqrt{\frac{200}{50}} = \sqrt{4} = 2 \text{ days}$$

The above example illustrates how statistical probability can assist with the quantification of demand uncertainty, but demand conditions are not the only source of uncertainty. Performance cycles can also vary.

Performance Cycle Uncertainty

Performance cycle uncertainty means operations cannot assume consistent delivery. The planner should expect that actual performance cycle experience will cluster near the expected value and be skewed toward delayed delivery.

Table 7.10 presents a sample frequency distribution across multiple performance cycles. Although 10 days is the most frequent, replenishment experience ranges from 6 to 14 days. If the performance cycle follows a normal distribution, an individual performance cycle would be expected to fall between 8 and 12 days 68.27 percent of the time.

From a practical viewpoint, when cycle days drop below 10, there is not any need for safety stock. If the performance cycle were consistently below the planned performance cycle, then adjustment of expected duration would be in order. The situation of most immediate concern occurs when the duration of the performance cycle exceeds 10 days.

From the viewpoint of the probability of exceeding 10 days, the frequency of such occurrences, from the data in Table 7.10, can be restated in terms of performance cycles greater than 10 days and equal to or less than 10 days. In the example data, the standard deviation would not change because the distribution is normal. However, if the actual experience has been skewed in excess of the expected cycle duration, then a **Poisson distribution** may have been more appropriate. In Poisson frequency distributions, the standard deviation is equal to the square root of the mean. As a general rule, the smaller the mean, the greater the degree of skewness. This is true because it is not possible to have negative values for either demand or performance cycle length.

Safety Stock with Combined Uncertainty

The typical situation confronting the inventory planner is illustrated in Figure 7.8, where both demand and performance cycle uncertainties exist. Planning for both demand and performance cycle uncertainty requires combining two variables. The duration of the cycle is, at least in the short run, independent of the daily demand. However, in setting safety

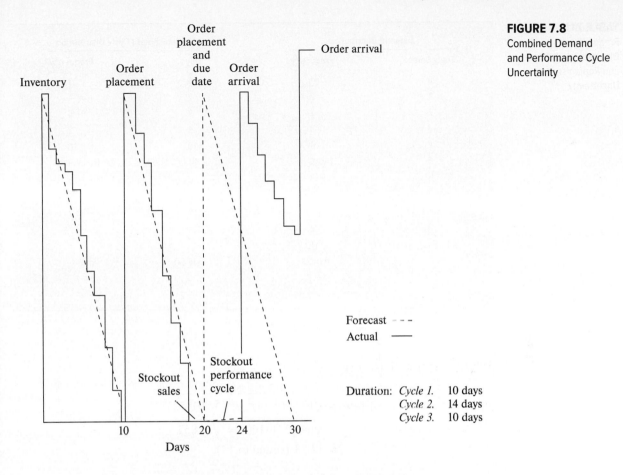

FIGURE 7.8
Combined Demand
and Performance Cycle
Uncertainty

stocks, the joint impact of the probability of both demand and performance cycle variation must be determined. Table 7.11 presents a summary of sales and replenishment cycle performance. The key to understanding the potential relationships of the data in Table 7.11 is the 10-day performance cycle. Total demand during the 10 days potentially ranges from 0 to 100 units. On each day of the cycle, the demand probability is independent of the previous day for the entire 10-day duration. Assuming the full range of potential situations illustrated in Table 7.11, total sales during a performance cycle could range from 0 to 140 units. With this basic relationship between the two types of uncertainty in mind, safety stock requirements can be determined by either numerical or convolution procedures.

The **numerical compounding** of two interdependent variables involves multinominal expansion. This type of procedure requires extensive calculation. A direct method is to determine the standard deviations of demand and performance cycle uncertainty and then to approximate the combined standard deviation using the convolution formula:

$$\sigma_c = \sqrt{TS_D^2 + D^2S_t^2}$$

where

σ_c = Standard deviation of combined probabilities;

T = Average performance cycle time;

S_t = Standard deviation of the performance cycle;

D = Average daily sales; and

S_D = Standard deviation of daily sales.

TABLE 7.11

Frequency
Distribution—Demand
and Replenishment
Uncertainty

Demand Distribution		Replenishment Cycle Distribution	
Daily Sales	**Frequency**	**Days**	**Frequency**
0	1	6	2
1	2	7	4
2	2	8	6
3	3	9	8
4	4	10	10
5	5	11	8
6	3	12	6
7	3	13	4
8	2	14	2
9	2		
10	1		
$n = 28$		$n = 50$	
$D = 5$		$T = 10$	
$S_s = 2.54$		$S_t = 2$	

Substituting from Table 7.11,

$$\sigma_c = \sqrt{10.00(2.54)^2 + (5.00)^2 (2)^2}$$
$$= \sqrt{64.52 + 100} = \sqrt{164.52}$$
$$= 12.83 \text{ (round to 13)}.$$

This formulation estimates the convoluted or combined standard deviation of T days with an average demand of D per day when the individual standard deviations are S_t and S_D, respectively. The average for the combined distribution is the product of T and D, or 50.00 (10.00 × 5.00).

Thus, given a frequency distribution of daily sales from 0 to 10 units per day and a range in replenishment cycle duration of 6 to 14 days, 13 units (1 standard deviation multiplied by 13 units) of safety stock is required to protect 84.14 percent of all performance cycles. To protect at the 97.72 percent level, a 26-unit safety stock is necessary. These levels assume a one-tail distribution since it is not necessary to protect against leadtime demand below average.

It is important to note that the specific event being protected against is a stockout during the performance cycle. The 84.14 and 97.72 percent levels are not product availability levels. These percentages reflect the probability of a stockout during a given performance cycle. For example, with a 13-unit safety stock, stockouts would be expected to occur during 15.86 (100 − 84.14) percent of the performance cycles. Although this percentage provides the probability of a stockout, it does not estimate magnitude. The relative stockout magnitude indicates the percentage of units stocked out (or 1 − case fill rate) relative to overall demand which depends on the number of cycles.

Still assuming the replenishment order quantity of 50 units, average inventory requirements would be 25 units if no safety stock were desired. The average inventory with 2 standard deviations of safety stock is 51 units [25 + (2 × 13)]. This inventory level would protect against a stockout during 97.72 percent of the performance cycles. Table 7.12 summarizes the alternatives confronting the planner in terms of assumptions and corresponding impact on average inventory.

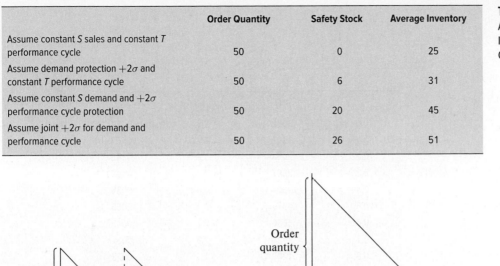

	Order Quantity	Safety Stock	Average Inventory
Assume constant S sales and constant T performance cycle	50	0	25
Assume demand protection $+2\sigma$ and constant T performance cycle	50	6	31
Assume constant S demand and $+2\sigma$ performance cycle protection	50	20	45
Assume joint $+2\sigma$ for demand and performance cycle	50	26	51

TABLE 7.12
Average Inventory Impact Resulting from Changes in EOQ

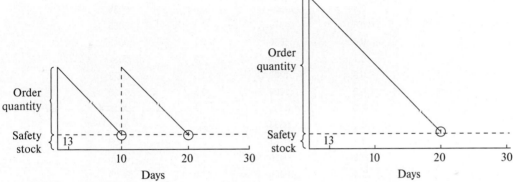

FIGURE 7.9   Impact of Order Quantity on Stockout Magnitude

Estimating Fill Rate

The fill rate is the magnitude rather than the probability of a stockout. The case fill rate is the percentage of units that can be filled when requested from available inventory. Figure 7.9 graphically illustrates the difference between stockout probability and stockout magnitude. Both illustrations in Figure 7.9 have a safety stock of 1 standard deviation or 13 units. For both situations, given any performance cycle, the probability of a stockout is 31.73 percent. However, during a 20-day period, the figure on the left illustrates two instances where the stock may be depleted. These instances are at the end of the cycle. If the order quantity is doubled, the system has the possibility of stocking out only once during the 20-day cycle. So, while both situations face the same demand pattern, the first one demonstrates more stockout opportunities and potential. In general, for a given safety stock level, increasing the replenishment order quantity decreases the relative magnitude of potential stockouts and conversely increases customer service availability.

The mathematical formulation of the relationship is:

$$SL = 1 - \frac{g(k)\sigma_c}{Q}$$

where

SL = The stockout magnitude (the product availability level or case fill rate);

$g(k)$ = A function of the normal loss curve which provides the area in a right tail of a normal distribution;

σ_c = The combined standard deviation considering both demand and replenishment cycle uncertainty; and

Q = The replenishment order quantity.

TABLE 7.13

Information for Determining Required Safety Stock

Desired Service Level	99%
σ_c	13
Q	300

TABLE 7.14

Loss Integral for Standardized Normal Distribution

k	g(k)	k	g(k)
0.0	.3989	1.6	.0232
0.1	.3509	1.7	.0182
0.2	.3068	1.8	.0143
0.3	.2667	1.9	.0111
0.4	.2304	2.0	.0085
0.5	.1977	2.1	.0065
0.6	.1686	2.2	.0049
0.7	.1428	2.3	.0037
0.8	.1202	2.4	.0027
0.9	.1004	2.5	.0020
1.0	.0833	2.6	.0015
1.1	.0686	2.7	.0011
1.2	.0561	2.8	.0008
1.3	.0455	2.9	.0005
1.4	.0366	3.0	.0004
1.5	.0293	3.1	.0003

To complete the example, suppose a firm desired 99 percent product availability or case fill rate. Assume the Q was calculated to be 300 units. Table 7.13 summarizes the required information.

Since $g(k)$ is the term used to calculate safety stock requirements, the above equation must be solved for $g(k)$ using algebraic manipulation. The result is:

$$g(k) = (1 - SL) \times (Q/\sigma_c).$$

Substituting from Table 7.13,

$$g(k) = (1 - 0.99) \times (300/13)$$
$$= 0.01 \times 23.08 = .2308.$$

The calculated value of $g(k)$ is then compared against the values in Table 7.14 to find the one that most closely approximates the calculated value. For this example, the value of k that fits the condition is 0.4. The required safety stock level is:

$$SS = k \times \sigma_c$$

where

SS = Safety stock in units;

k = The k factor that corresponds with $g(k)$;

σ_c = The combined standard deviation.

So, substituting in for the example,

$$SS = k \times \sigma_c$$
$$= 0.4 \times 13 = 5.2 \text{ units}$$

Order Quantity (Q)	k	Safety Stock	Average Inventory
300	0.40	5	155
200	0.70	8	108
100	1.05	14	64
50	1.40	18	43
25	1.70	22	34

TABLE 7.15
Impact of Order Quantity on Safety Stock

The safety stock required to provide a 99 percent product fill rate when the order quantity is 300 units is approximately 5 units. Table 7.15 shows how the calculated safety stock and average inventory levels vary for other order quantities. An increased order size can be used to compensate for decreasing the safety stock levels, or vice versa. The existence of such a trade-off implies that there is a combination of replenishment order quantities that will result in desired customer service at the minimum cost.

Dependent Demand Replenishment

With respect to dependent demand replenishment, inventory requirements are a function of known events that are not generally random. Therefore, dependent demand does not require forecasting because there is no uncertainty. It follows that no specific safety stock should be necessary to support a time-phased procurement program such as materials requirements planning (**MRP**).[6] The basic notion of time phasing is that parts and subassemblies need not be carried in inventory as long as they arrive when needed or just-in-time.

The case for carrying no safety stocks under conditions of dependent demand rests on two assumptions. First, procurement replenishment to support planning is predictable and constant. Second, vendors and suppliers maintain adequate inventories to satisfy 100 percent of purchase requirements. The second assumption may be operationally attained by use of volume-oriented purchase contracts that assure vendors and suppliers of eventual purchase. In such cases the safety stock requirement still exists for the overall supply chain, although the primary responsibility rests with the supplier.

The assumption of performance cycle certainty is more difficult to achieve. Even in situations where dedicated transportation is used, an element of uncertainty is always present. The practical result is that safety stocks do exist in many dependent demand situations.

Three basic approaches have been used to introduce safety stocks into dependent demand situations. First, a common practice is to put **safety time** into the requirements plan. For example, a component is ordered earlier than needed to assure timely arrival. A second approach is to increase the requisition by a quantity specified by some estimate of expected plan error. For example, assume that plan error will not exceed 5 percent. This procedure is referred to as **over-planning top-level demand**. The net result is to increase procurement of all components in a ratio to their expected usage plus a cushion to cover plan error. Components common to different end products or subassemblies covered by the overplanning will naturally experience greater quantity buildups than single-purpose components and parts. The third method is to utilize the previously discussed statistical techniques for setting safety stocks directly to the component rather than to the item of top-level demand.

---

[6]These concepts are discussed later in this chapter under Planning Methods.

Inventory Management Policies

Inventory management implements inventory policy. The reactive or pull inventory approach uses customer demand to pull product through the distribution channel. An alternative philosophy is a planning approach that proactively allocates or deploys inventory on the basis of forecasted demand and product availability. A third, or hybrid, logic uses a combination of push and pull.

Inventory Control

The managerial procedure for implementing an inventory policy is **inventory control**. The accountability of control measures units on hand at a specific location and tracks additions and deletions. Accountability and tracking can be performed on a manual or computerized basis.

Inventory control defines how often inventory levels are reviewed to determine when and how much to order. It is performed on either a perpetual or a periodic basis.

Perpetual Review

A perpetual inventory control process continuously reviews inventory levels to determine inventory replenishment needs. To utilize perpetual review, accurate tracking of all SKUs is necessary. Perpetual review is implemented through a reorder point and order quantity.

As discussed earlier,

$$ROP = D \times T + SS$$

where

ROP = Reorder point in units;

D = Average daily demand in units;

T = Average performance cycle length in days; and

SS = Safety or buffer stock in units.

The order quantity is determined using the EOQ.

For purposes of illustration, assume no uncertainty so no safety stock is necessary. Table 7.16 summarizes demand, performance cycle, and order quantity characteristics. For this example,

$$ROP = D \times T + SS$$
$$= 20 \text{ units/day} \times 10 \text{ days} + 0 = 200 \text{ units.}$$

The perpetual review compares on-hand and on-order inventory to the item's reorder point. If the on-hand plus on-order quantity is less than the established reorder point, a replenishment order is initiated.

TABLE 7.16

Sample Demand, Performance Cycle, and Order Quantity Characteristics

Average daily demand	20 units
Performance cycle	10 days
Order quantity	200 units

Mathematically, the process is:

$$\text{If } I + OQ_{o} \leq \text{ROP, then order } OQ,$$

where

I = Inventory on hand;

OQ_{o} = Inventory on order from suppliers;

ROP = Reorder point in units; and

OQ = Order quantity in units.

For the previous example, a replenishment order of 200 is placed whenever the sum of on-hand and on-order inventory is less than or equal to 200 units. Since the reorder point equals the order quantity, the previous replenishment shipment would arrive just as the next replenishment is initiated. The average inventory level for a perpetual review system is:

$$I_{avg} = OQ/2 + \text{SS}$$

where

I_{avg} = Average inventory in units;

OQ = Order quantity units; and

SS = Safety stock units.

Average inventory for the previous example is calculated as:

$$\begin{aligned} I_{avg} &= Q/2 + \text{SS} \\ &= 300/2 + 0 = 150 \text{ units.} \end{aligned}$$

Most illustrations throughout this text are based on a perpetual review system with a fixed reorder point. The reorder formulation assumes purchase orders will be placed when the reorder point is reached, and the method of control provides a perpetual monitoring of inventory status. If these two assumptions are not satisfied, the control parameters **(ROP and OQ)** determining the perpetual review must be refined.

Periodic Review

Periodic inventory control reviews the inventory status of an item at regular intervals such as weekly or monthly. For periodic review, the basic reorder point must be adjusted to consider the intervals between review. The formula for calculating the periodic review reorder point is:

$$\text{ROP} = D(T + P/2) + \text{SS}$$

where

ROP = Reorder point;

D = Average daily demand;

T = Average performance cycle length;

P = Review period in days; and

SS = Safety stock.

Since inventory counts occur periodically, any item could fall below the desired reorder point prior to the review period. Therefore, the assumption is made that the inventory will fall below ideal reorder status prior to the periodic count approximately one-half of the review times. Assuming a review period of 7 days and using conditions similar to those of the perpetual example, the ROP then would be as follows:

$$\text{ROP} = D(\text{T} + P/2) + \text{SS},$$
$$= 20(10 + 7/2) + 0 = 20(10 + 3.5) = 270 \text{ units}.$$

The average inventory formulation for the case of periodic review is:

$$I_{avg} = OQ/2 + (P \times D)/2 + \text{SS},$$

where

I_{avg} = Average inventory in units;

OQ = Order quantity in units;

P = Review period in days;

D = Average daily demand in units; and

SS = Safety stock in units.

For the preceding example, the average inventory is calculated as:

$$I_{avg} = OQ/2 + (P \times D)/2 + \text{SS}$$
$$= 300/2 + (7 \times 10)/2 + 0 = 150 + 35 = 185 \text{ units}.$$

Because of the time interval introduced by periodic review, periodic control systems generally require larger average inventories than perpetual systems. Ideal review frequency typically depends on a combination of item volume, value, and replenishment process. Items with high volume and value should employ perpetual review to minimize inventory and stockout risk. Items which must be replenished as a group would typically be reviewed periodically since they must be ordered together anyway.

Reactive Methods

The **reactive** or **pull inventory system**, as the name implies, responds to a channel member's inventory needs by drawing the product through the distribution channel. Replenishment shipments are initiated when available warehouse stock levels fall below a predetermined minimum or order point. The amount ordered is usually based on some lot-sizing formulation, although it may be some variable quantity that is a function of current stock levels and a predetermined maximum level.

The basic perpetual or periodic review process discussed earlier exemplifies a typical reactive system. Figure 7.10 illustrates a reactive inventory environment for a warehouse serving two wholesalers. The figure shows the current inventory (I), reorder point (ROP), order quantity (OQ), and average daily demand (D) for each wholesaler. A review of the wholesaler inventory indicates that a resupply order for 200 units should be placed by wholesaler A from the warehouse. Since current inventory is above ROP for wholesaler B, no resupply action is necessary at this time. However, more thorough analysis illustrates that the independent actions by wholesaler A will likely cause a stockout at wholesaler B within a few days. Wholesaler B will likely stock out because inventory level is close to the reorder point and the supplying warehouse center will not have enough inventory to replenish wholesaler B.

Classical reactive inventory logic is rooted in the following assumptions. First, the system is founded on the basic assumption that all customers, market areas, and products contribute equally to profits.

Second, a reactive system assumes infinite capacity at the source. This assumption implies that product can be produced as desired and stored at the production facility until required throughout the supply chain.

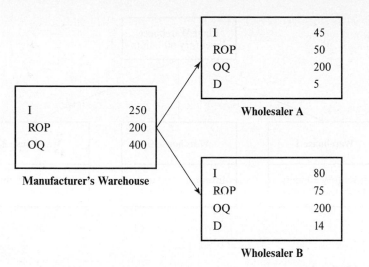

FIGURE 7.10
A Reactive Inventory
Environment

Third, reactive inventory logic assumes infinite inventory availability at the supply location. The combination of assumptions 2 and 3 implies relative replenishment certainty. The reactive inventory logic provides for no back orders or stockouts in processing replenishment orders.

Fourth, reactive decision rules assume that performance cycle time can be predicted and that cycle lengths are independent. This means that each performance cycle is a random event and that extended cycles don't generally occur for subsequent replenishment orders. Although reactive logic assumes no control over cycle times, many managers are, in fact, able to influence performance cycle length through expediting and alternative sourcing strategies.

Fifth, reactive inventory logic operates best when customer demand patterns are relatively stable and consistent. Ideally, demand patterns should be stable over the relevant planning cycle for statistically developed inventory parameters to operate correctly. Most reactive system decision rules assume demand patterns based on standard normal, gamma, or Poisson distributions. When the actual demand function does not resemble one of the above functions, the statistical inventory decision rules based on these assumptions will not operate correctly.

Sixth, reactive inventory systems determine each distribution warehouse's timing and quantity of replenishment orders independently of all other sites, including the supply source. Thus, there is little potential to effectively coordinate inventory requirements across multiple distribution warehouses. The ability to take advantage of inventory information is not utilized—a serious defect when information and its communication are among the few resources that are decreasing in cost in the supply chain.

The final assumption characteristic of reactive inventory systems is that performance cycle length cannot be correlated with demand. The assumption is necessary to develop an accurate approximation of the variance of the demand over the performance cycle. For many situations higher demand levels create longer replenishment performance cycles since they also increase the demands on inventory and transportation resources. This implies that periods of high demand should not necessarily correspond to extended performance cycles caused by stockouts or limited product availability.

Operationally, most inventory managers constrain the impact of such limitations through the skillful use of manual overrides. However, these overrides often lead to ineffective inventory decisions since the resulting plan is based on inconsistent rules and managerial policy.

FIGURE 7.11
Fair Share Allocation
Example

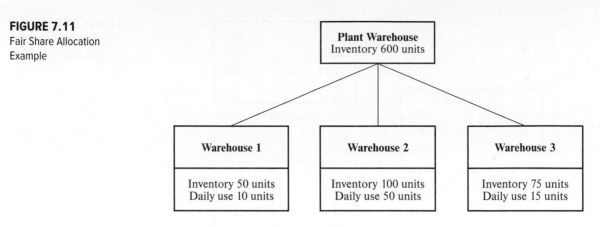

Planning Methods

Inventory planning methods use a shared database to coordinate inventory requirements across multiple locations or stages in the supply chain. Planning activities may occur centrally to coordinate inventory allocation and delivery to multiple destinations. Planning may also coordinate inventory requirements across multiple channel partners such as manufacturers and retailers. The Advanced Planning and Scheduling **(APS)** systems discussed in Chapter 5 illustrate the capability of planning applications. While APS systems computerize the process, it is important that logistics managers understand the underlying logic and assumptions. Two inventory planning methods are fair share allocation and distribution requirements planning **(DRP)**.

Fair Share Allocation

A simplified inventory management planning method that provides each distribution facility with an equitable distribution of available inventory is called **fair share allocation**. Figure 7.11 illustrates the network structure, current inventory level, and daily requirements for three warehouses served by a single plant warehouse.

Using fair share allocation, the inventory planner determines the amount of inventory that can be allocated to each warehouse from the available inventory at the plant. For this example, assume that it is desirable to retain 100 units at the plant warehouse; therefore, 500 units are available for allocation. The calculation to determine the common days supply is:

$$\text{DS} = \frac{AQ + \sum_{j=1}^{n} I_j}{\sum_{i=1}^{n} D_j}$$

where

  DS = Common days supply for warehouse inventories;

  AQ = Inventory units to be allocated from plant warehouse;

  I_j = Inventory in units for warehouse j; and

  D_j = Daily demand for warehouse j.

In this example,

$$DS = \frac{500 + (50 + 100 + 75)}{10 + 50 + 15}$$

$$= \frac{500 + 225}{75} = 9.67 \text{ days}$$

The fair share allocation dictates that each warehouse should be stocked to 9.67 days of inventory. The amount to be allocated to each warehouse is determined by:

$$A_j = (DS - I_j/D_j) \times D_j$$

where

A_j = Amount allocated to warehouse j;

DS = Days supply that each warehouse is brought up to;

I_j = Inventory in units for warehouse j; and

D_j = Daily demand for warehouse j.

The amount allocated to warehouse 1 for this example is:

$$A_1 = (9.67 - 50/10) \times 10$$
$$= (9.67 - 5) \times 10$$
$$= (4.67 \times 10) = 46.7 \text{ (round to 47 units)}.$$

The allocation for warehouses 2 and 3 can be determined similarly and is 383 and 70 units, respectively.

While fair share allocation coordinates inventory levels across multiple sites, it does not consider specific factors such as differences in performance cycle time, EOQ, or safety stock requirements. Fair share allocation methods are therefore limited in their ability to manage multistage inventories.

Requirements Planning

Requirements planning is an approach that integrates across the supply chain, taking into consideration unique requirements. Requirements planning is typically classified as materials requirements planning (MRP) or distribution requirements planning (DRP). There is one fundamental difference between the two techniques. MRP is driven by a production schedule. In contrast, DRP is driven by supply chain demand. So, while MRP generally operates in a dependent demand situation, DRP is applicable to an independent demand environment where uncertain customer requirements drive inventory requirements. MRP coordinates scheduling and integration of materials into finished goods, and so controls inventory until manufacturing or assembly is completed. DRP takes coordination responsibility once finished goods are received in the plant warehouse.

Figure 7.12 illustrates the conceptual design of a combined MRP/DRP system that integrates finished goods, work-in-process, and materials planning. The top half of the figure illustrates an MRP system that time-phases raw material arrivals to support the production schedule. The result of MRP execution is finished goods inventory at the manufacturing site. The bottom half of the figure illustrates the DRP system that allocates finished inventory from the manufacturing site to distribution warehouses and ultimately to retail customers. DRP time-phases the movements to coordinate inventory arrivals to meet

FIGURE 7.12
Conceptual Design of
Integrated MRP/DRP
System

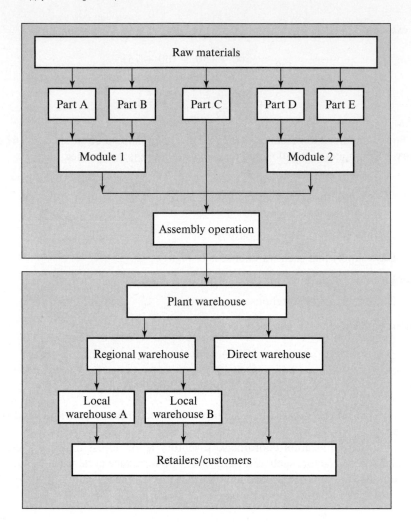

customer requirements and forecasts. The MRP and DRP systems interface at the manufacturing site. Close coordination between the two systems results in minimal need for safety stock. DRP coordinates inventory levels, schedules, and when necessary, reschedules inventory movement between levels.

The fundamental DRP planning tool is the schedule, which coordinates requirements for each SKU. Schedules for the same SKU are integrated to determine the overall requirements for replenishment facilities such as a plant warehouse.

Figure 7.13 illustrates DRP planning schedules for two warehouses and a central supply facility. The schedules are developed using weekly time increments known as **time buckets**. Each bucket projects one period of activity. Although weekly increments are most common, daily or monthly increments can be used. For each site and SKU, the schedule reports current on-hand balance, safety stock, performance cycle length, and order quantity. In addition, for each planning period, the schedule reports gross requirements, scheduled receipts, and projected inventory on hand. Using the combination of requirements and projected availability, DRP determines the planned orders necessary to meet anticipated requirements. Gross requirements reflect the demand from consumers and other distribution facilities supplied by the site under review. For Figure 7.13, the gross requirements of the central supply facility reflect the cascading demands of the eastern and western

Eastern Warehouse

	Past due	Weeks 1	2	3	4	5	6	7	8	
Gross requirements		100	120	150	130	100	80	70	90	Safety stock: 100
Scheduled receipts		0	0	400	0	0	0	400	0	Order quantity: 400
Projected on hand	400	300	180	430	300	200	120	450	360	Leadtime: 2 weeks
Planned orders		400	0	0	0	400	0	0	0	

Plant Warehouse

	Past due	Weeks 1	2	3	4	5	6	7	8
Gross requirements		400	150	0	150	550	0	0	0
Scheduled receipts		0	600	0	600	0	0	0	0
Projected on hand	600	200	650	650	1100	550	550	550	550
Planned production		600	0	600	0	0	0	0	0

Safety stock: 100
Batch size: 600
Leadtime: 1 week

Western Warehouse

	Past due	Weeks 1	2	3	4	5	6	7	8	
Gross requirements		40	50	60	90	70	100	40	30	Safety stock: 50
Scheduled receipts		0	0	150	0	150	150	0	0	Order quantity: 150
Projected on hand	200	160	110	200	110	190	240	200	170	Leadtime: 1 week
Planned orders		0	150	0	150	150	0	0	0	

Requirement – – – – – – →

Shipment ————→

FIGURE 7.13 Distribution Requirements Planning Example

warehouses. Scheduled receipts are the replenishment shipments planned for arrival at the distribution warehouse. Projected on-hand inventory refers to the anticipated week-ending level. It is equal to the prior week's on-hand inventory level less the current week's gross requirements plus any scheduled receipts. While planning approaches to inventory management offer significant benefits, they have some constraints.

First, inventory planning systems require accurate and coordinated forecasts for each warehouse. The forecast is necessary to direct the flow of goods through the supply chain. Ideally, the system does not maintain excess inventory at any location, so little room for error exists in a lean inventory system. To the extent this level of forecast accuracy is possible, inventory planning systems operate well.

Second, inventory planning requires consistent and reliable product movement between warehouse facilities. While variable performance cycles can be accommodated through safety leadtimes, such uncertainty reduces planning system effectiveness.

Third, integrated planning systems may be subject to system nervousness, or frequent rescheduling, due to production breakdowns or delivery delays. System nervousness leads to fluctuation in capacity utilization, rescheduling cost, and confusion in deliveries. This is intensified by the volatile operating environment characteristic of supply chain logistics. Uncertainties such as transportation and vendor delivery reliability can cause an extreme DRP nervousness.

Collaborative Inventory Replenishment

In Chapters 5 and 6, CPFR was introduced and discussed as a major collaborative effort between supply chain trading partners. Several collaborative initiatives focus only on inventory replenishment. Replenishment programs are designed to streamline the flow of goods within the supply chain. There are several specific techniques for collaborative replenishment, all of which build on supply chain relationships to rapidly replenish inventory on the basis of joint planning or actual sales experience. The intent is to reduce reliance on forecasting when and where inventory will need to be positioned to demand on a just-in-time basis. Effective collaborative replenishment programs require extensive cooperation and information sharing among supply chain partners. Specific techniques for collaborative inventory replenishment are quick response, vendor-managed inventory, and profile replenishment.

Quick Response

A technology-driven cooperative effort between retailers and suppliers to improve inventory velocity while closely matching replenishment supply to consumer buying patterns is quick response **(QR)**. QR is implemented by sharing retail sales for specific products between supply chain participants to facilitate right product assortment availability when and where it is required. Instead of operating on a 15- to 30-day order cycle, QR arrangements can replenish retail inventories in a few days. Continuous information exchange regarding availability and delivery reduces uncertainty for the total supply chain and creates the opportunity for maximum flexibility. With fast, dependable order response, inventory can be committed as required, resulting in increased turnover and improved availability. Walmart's retail link system is a prime example of the power of sharing sales to facilitate QR.

Vendor-Managed Inventory

Vendor-managed inventory **(VMI)** is a modification of quick response that eliminates the need for replenishment orders. The goal is to establish a supply chain arrangement so flexible and efficient that retail inventory is continuously replenished. The distinguishing factor between QR and VMI is who takes responsibility for setting target inventory levels and making restocking decisions. In QR, the customer makes the decisions. In VMI, the supplier assumes more responsibility and actually manages an inventory category for the customer. By receiving daily transmission of retail sales or warehouse shipments, the supplier assumes responsibility for replenishing retail inventory in the required quantities, colors, sizes, and styles. The supplier commits to keeping the customer in stock and to maintaining inventory velocity. In some situations, replenishment involves cross-docking or direct store delivery **(DSD)** designed to eliminate the need for warehousing between the supplier and customer.

Profile Replenishment

Some manufacturers, wholesalers, and retailers are experimenting with an even more sophisticated collaboration known as profile replenishment **(PR)**. The PR strategy extends QR and VMI by giving suppliers the right to anticipate future requirements according to their overall knowledge of a merchandise category. A category profile details the combination of sizes, colors, and associated products that usually sell in a particular type of retail outlet. Given PR responsibility, the supplier can simplify retailer involvement by eliminating the need to track unit sales and inventory level for fast-moving products. Gerber products, a processor of baby food, uses PR with some of its key customers since it has better knowledge of product combinations that consumers will purchase than most retailers.

Many firms, particularly manufacturers, are using DRP and even APS logic to coordinate inventory planning with major customers. The manufacturers are extending their planning framework to include customer warehouses and, in some cases, their retail stores. Such integrated planning capabilities facilitate manufacturer coordination and management of customer inventories.

Collaborative planning effectively shares inventory requirements and availability between supply chain partners, thus reducing uncertainty. Table 7.17 illustrates the service and inventory impact in a simulated environment under conditions of low and high uncertainty.[7] Table 7.18 illustrates managerial considerations that drive adaptations of control logic.

[7]David J. Closs et al., "An Empirical Comparison of Anticipatory and Response-Based Supply Chain Strategies," *International Journal of Logistics Management* 9, no. 2 (1998), pp. 21–34.

	Low Uncertainty Anticipatory	Low Uncertainty Responsive	High Uncertainty Anticipatory	High Uncertainty Responsive
Customer Service				
Fill rate percent	97.69	99.66	96.44	99.29
Inventories				
Supplier inventory	12.88	13.24	14.82	13.61
Manufacturer inventory	6.05	6.12	7.03	6.09
Distributor inventory	5.38	5.86	5.04	5.63
Retailer inventory	30.84	15.79	32.86	20.30
System inventory	55.15	41.01	59.76	45.83

TABLE 7.17

Comparative Service and Inventory Characteristics for Anticipatory versus Responsive Inventory Systems

Source: Adapted from David J. Closs et al., "An Empirical Comparison of Anticipatory and Response-Based Supply Chain Strategies," *International Journal of Logistics Management* 9, no. 2 (1998), pp. 21–34. Used with permission.

Use Planning Logic under Conditions of	Use Reactive Logic under Conditions of
Highly profitable segments	Cycle time uncertainty
Dependent demand	Demand uncertainty
Economies of scale	Destination capacity limitations
Supply uncertainty	
Source capacity limitations	
Seasonal supply buildup	

TABLE 7.18

Suggested Inventory Management Logic

Postponement

At the heart of time-based competition is the capability to postpone customization and the timing of logistical fulfillment. The concept of **postponement** has long been discussed in business literature.[8] However, practical examples involving postponement are directly related to advancements in information technology. Postponement strategies and practices serve to reduce the anticipatory risk of supply chain performance. As noted earlier, anticipatory arrangements require most inventory to be produced to final product state and deployed on the basis of forecasts or planned requirements. Working arrangements, which allow postponement of final manufacturing, customization, or distribution of a product until receipt of a customer order, reduce the incidence of wrong manufacturing or incorrect inventory deployment. Two types of postponement are common in highly responsive supply chain operations: (1) manufacturing, or form postponement, and (2) geographic, or logistics postponement.

Manufacturing Postponement

The global competitive climate of the 21st century is facilitating the development of new manufacturing techniques designed to increase flexibility and responsiveness while maintaining unit cost and quality. Traditional practice has focused on achieving economy of scale by planning extensive manufacturing runs. In contrast, flexible manufacturing logic is typically driven by a desire to increase responsiveness to customer requirements.

The vision of **manufacturing**, or **form**, **postponement** is one of products being manufactured one order at a time with no preparatory work or component procurement until exact customer specifications are fully known and purchase confirmation is received. This dream of building to customer order is not new. What is new is the expectation that flexible manufacturing can achieve such responsiveness without sacrificing efficiency. To the degree technology can support market-paced flexible manufacturing strategies, firms are to a degree freed from the risk associated with forecast-driven anticipatory operations.

In practice, manufacturing lot size economics cannot be ignored. The challenge is to quantify cost trade-offs between procurement, manufacturing, and logistics. At this point, it is sufficient to understand that the trade-off is between the cost and risk associated with anticipatory manufacturing and the loss of economy of scale resulting from introducing flexible procedures. Manufacturing lot size reduction requires a trade-off between line setup, switchover, and associated procurement expense balanced against cost and risk associated with stockpiling finished inventory. In the traditional functional style of management, manufacturing schedules were established to realize the lowest unit cost of production. From an integrative management perspective, the goal is to achieve desired customer satisfaction at the lowest total cost. This may require manufacturing postponement at some per-unit-cost sacrifice to achieve overall supply chain efficiency.

The operative goal of manufacturing postponement is to maintain products in a neutral or noncommitted status as long as possible. The ideal application of form postponement is to manufacture a standard or base product in sufficient quantities to realize economy of scale while deferring finalization of features, such as color or accessories, until customer commitment is received. Given a postponement-driven manufacturing scenario, economy of scope is introduced into the logistics equation by producing a standard or base product to accommodate a wide range of different customers. One of the first commercially viable examples of manufacturing postponement was mixing paint color at retail stores to accommodate individual customer request. Perfecting the in-store mixing process dramatically reduced the number of stockkeeping units required at retail paint stores. Instead of trying to maintain inventories of premixed color paint, retail stores stock a base paint and customize the color

[8] Wroe Alderson, *Marketing Behavior and Executive Action* (Homewood, IL: Richard D. Irwin, Inc., 1957), p. 426.

to accommodate specific orders. Some believe this relatively simple application of form post-ponement in the paint industry was a major factor facilitating the birth of the consumer-driven home improvement industry. Overnight, retail paint stores went from excessive stockouts to being fully in stock. Plus, while consumers waited for paint to be custom color-mixed, they were exposed to a wide variety of do-it-yourself painting accessories available for purchase.

In other industries, manufacturing practice is to process and store product in bulk, post-poning final packaging configuration until customer orders are received. In some situations products are processed and packed in cans with brand identification labeling being postponed until specific customer orders are received. Other examples of manufacturing postponement include the increased practice of installing accessories at automobile, appliance, and motor-cycle dealerships, thereby customizing products to customer request at the time of purchase.

These manufacturing postponement examples have one thing in common: They reduce the number of stockkeeping units in logistical inventory while supporting a broad-line mar-keting effort and retaining mass manufacturing economies of scale. Until the product is customized, it has the potential to serve many different customers.

The impact of manufacturing postponement is twofold. First, the variety of differenti-ated products, moved in anticipation of sale, can be reduced, and therefore the risk of logistical operational malfunction is lower. The second, and perhaps the more important, impact is the increased use of logistical facilities to perform light manufacturing and final assembly. To the extent that a degree of specialized talent or highly restrictive economy of scale does not exist in manufacturing, product customization may be best delegated and performed near the customer destination market. This form of manufacturing postpone-ment is often called **late customization**. The traditional mission of logistical warehouses in some industries has changed significantly to accommodate manufacturing postponement. For example, Kohler Co. does a significant amount of product customization in integrated service provider-run distribution centers.

Geographic Postponement

In many ways **geographic**, or **logistics**, **postponement** is the exact opposite of manufactur-ing postponement. The basic notion of geographic postponement is to build and stock a full-line inventory at one or a limited number of strategic locations. Forward deployment of inventory is postponed until customer orders are received. Once the logistical process is initiated, every effort is made to accelerate the economic movement of products directly to customers. Under the concept of geographic postponement, the anticipatory risk of inven-tory deployment is partially eliminated while manufacturing economy of scale is retained.

Many applications of geographic postponement involve service supply parts. Critical and high-cost parts are maintained in a central inventory to assure availability for all potential users. When demand occurs, orders are electronically transmitted to the central service center and expedited shipments are made directly to the forward service center, using fast, reliable transportation. The end result is highly reliable customer service with reduced overall inventory investment.

The potential for geographic postponement has been facilitated by increased logistical system capability to process, transmit, and deliver precise order requirements with a high degree of accuracy and speed. Geographic postponement substitutes accelerated delivery of precise order requirements for the anticipatory deployment of inventory to local market warehouses. Unlike manufacturing postponement, systems utilizing geographic postpone-ment retain manufacturing economies of scale while meeting customer service require-ments by accelerating direct shipments.

In combination, manufacturing and geographic postponement offer alternative ways to reduce risk associated with anticipatory distribution. Both postpone risk until customer commitments are received. The factors favoring one or the other form of postponement hinge on volume, value, competitive initiatives, economies of scale, and desired customer delivery speed and consistency. In a growing number of supply chains, both types of postponement are combined to create a highly flexible strategy.

Inventory Management Practices

An integrated inventory management strategy defines the policies and process used to determine where to place inventory and when to initiate replenishment shipments, as well as how much to allocate. The strategy development process employs three steps to classify products and markets, define segment strategies, and operationalize policies and parameters.

Product/Market Classification

The objective of product/market classification is to focus and refine inventory management efforts. Product/market classification, which is also called **fine-line** or **ABC classification**, groups products, markets, or customers with similar characteristics to facilitate inventory management. The classification process recognizes that not all products and markets have the same characteristics or degree of importance. Sound inventory management requires that classification be consistent with enterprise strategy and service objectives.

Classification can be based on a variety of measures. The most common are sales, profit contribution, inventory value, usage rate, and item category. The typical classification process sequences products or markets so that entries with similar characteristics are grouped together. Table 7.19 illustrates product classification using sales. The products are classified in descending order by sales volume so that the high-volume products are listed

TABLE 7.19
Product Market Classification (Sales)

Product Identification	Annual Sales (in 000s)	Percent Total Sales	Accumulated Sales (%)	Products (%)	Classification Category
1	$45,000	30.0%	30.0%	5%	A
2	35,000	23.3	53.3	10	A
3	25,000	16.7	70.0	15	A
4	15,000	10.0	80.0	20	A
5	8,000	5.3	85.3	25	B
6	5,000	3.3	88.6	30	B
7	4,000	2.7	91.3	35	B
8	3,000	2.0	93.3	40	B
9	2,000	1.3	94.6	45	B
10	1,000	0.7	95.3	50	B
11	1,000	0.7	96.0	55	C
12	1,000	0.7	96.7	60	C
13	1,000	0.7	97.4	65	C
14	750	0.5	97.9	70	C
15	750	0.5	98.4	75	C
16	750	0.5	98.9	80	C
17	500	0.3	99.2	85	C
18	500	0.3	99.5	90	C
19	500	0.3	99.8	95	C
20	250	0.2	100.0	100	C
	$150,000				

first, followed by slower movers. Classification by sales volume is one of the oldest methods used to establish selective inventory policies. For most marketing or logistics applications, a small percentage of the entities account for a large percentage of the volume. This operationalization is often called the **80/20 rule or Pareto principle**. The 80/20 rule, which is based on widespread observations, states that for a typical enterprise, 80 percent of the sales volume is typically accounted for by 20 percent of the products. A corollary to the rule is that 80 percent of enterprise sales are accounted for by 20 percent of the customers. The reverse perspective of the rule would state that the remaining 20 percent of sales are obtained from 80 percent of the products, customers, etc. In general terms, the 80/20 rule implies that a majority of sales result from a relatively few products or customers.

Once items are classified or grouped, it is common to label each category with a character or description. High-volume, fast-moving products are often described as A items. The moderate-volume items are termed the B items, and the low-volume or slow movers are known as Cs. These character labels indicate why this process is often termed ABC analysis. While fine-line classification often uses three categories, some firms use four or five categories to further refine classifications. Grouping of similar products facilitates management efforts to establish focused inventory strategies for specific product segments. For example, high-volume or fast-moving products are typically targeted for higher service levels. This often requires that fast-moving items have relatively more safety stock. Conversely, to reduce overall inventory levels, slower-moving items may be allowed relatively less safety stock, resulting in lower service levels.

In special situations, classification systems may be based on multiple factors. For example, item gross margin and importance to customers can be weighted to develop a combined index instead of simply using sales volume. The weighted rank would then group items that have similar profitability and importance characteristics. The inventory policy, including safety stock levels, is then established using the weighted rank.

The classification array defines product or market groups to be assigned similar inventory strategies. The use of item groups facilitates the identification and specification of inventory strategies without requiring tedious development of individual item strategies. It is much easier to track and manage 3 to 10 groups instead of hundreds of individual items.

Segment Strategy Definition

The second step is to define the inventory strategy for each product/market group or segment. The strategy includes specification for all aspects of the inventory management process, including service objectives, forecasting method, management technique, and review cycle.

The key to establishing selective management strategies is the realization that product segments have different degrees of importance with respect to achieving the enterprise mission. Important differences in inventory responsiveness should be designed into the policies and procedures used for inventory management.

Table 7.20 illustrates a sample integrated strategy for four item categories. In this case, the items are grouped by ABC sales volume and as a promotional or regular stock item.

Fine-Line Classification	Service Objective	Forecasting Procedure	Review Period	Inventory Management	Replenishment Monitoring
A (Promotional)	99%	CPFR	Perpetual	Planning—DRP	Daily
A (Regular)	98	Sales history	Perpetual	Planning—DRP	Daily
B	95	Sales history	Weekly	Planning—DRP	Weekly
C	90	Sales history	Biweekly	Reorder point	Biweekly

TABLE 7.20
Integrated Strategy

Promotional items are those commonly sold in special marketing efforts that result in considerable demand lumpiness. Lumpy demand patterns are characteristic of promotional periods with high volume followed by postpromotion periods with relatively low demand.

Table 7.20 illustrates a management segmentation scheme based on service objectives, forecasting process, review period, inventory management approach, and replenishment monitoring frequency. Additional or fewer characteristics of the inventory management process may be appropriate for some enterprises. Although this table is not presented as a comprehensive inventory strategy framework, it illustrates the issues that must be considered. The rationale behind each element is presented on the basis of the full-line classification.

Policies and Parameters

The final step in implementing a focused inventory management strategy is to define detailed procedures and parameters. The procedures define data requirements, software applications, performance objectives, and decision guidelines. The parameters delineate values such as review period length, service objectives, inventory carrying cost percentage, order quantities, and reorder points. The combination of parameters either determines or can be used to calculate the precise quantities necessary to make inventory management decisions.

Summary

Inventory carrying cost typically represents the second largest component of logistics cost next to transportation. The risks associated with holding inventory increase as products move down the supply chain closer to the customer because the potential of having the product in the wrong place or form increases and costs have been incurred to distribute the product. In addition to the risk of lost sales due to stockouts because adequate inventory is not available, other risks include obsolescence, pilferage, and damage. Further, the cost of carrying inventory is significantly influenced by the cost of the capital tied up in the inventory. Geographic specialization, decoupling, supply/demand balancing, and buffering uncertainty provide the basic rationale for maintaining inventory. While there is substantial interest in reducing overall supply chain inventory, inventory does add value and can result in lower overall supply chain costs with appropriate trade-offs.

From a supply chain logistics perspective, the major controllable inventory elements are replenishment cycle stock, safety stock, and in-transit stock. The appropriate replenishment cycle stock can be determined using an EOQ formula to reflect the trade-off between storage and ordering cost. Safety stock depends on the mean and variance of demand and the replenishment cycle. In-transit stock depends on the transport mode.

Inventory management uses a combination of reactive and planning logics. Reactive logic is most appropriate for items with low volume, high demand, and high performance cycle uncertainty because it postpones the risk of inventory speculation. Inventory planning logic is appropriate for high-volume items with relatively stable demand. Inventory planning methods offer the potential for effective inventory management because they take advantage of improved information and economies of scale. Adaptive logic combines the two alternatives depending on product and market conditions. Collaboration offers a way for parties in the supply chain to jointly gain inventory efficiency and effectiveness.

Study Questions

1. Discuss the relationship between service level, uncertainty, safety stock, and order quantity. How can trade-offs between these elements be made?
2. Discuss the disproportionate risk of holding inventory by retailers, wholesalers, and manufacturers. Why has there been a trend to push inventory back up the channel of distribution?
3. What is the difference between the probability of a stockout and the magnitude of a stockout?
4. Illustrate how fine-line inventory classification can be used with product and customer segments. What are the benefits and considerations when classifying inventory by product, customer, and customer/product?
5. Customer-based inventory management strategies allow for the use of different availability levels for specific customers. Discuss the rationale for such a strategy. Are such strategies discriminatory? Justify your position.
6. Discuss the differences between reactive and planning inventory logics. What are the advantages and risks associated with each? What are the implications of each?

Challenge Questions

1. Aggregate inventory data suggest that while overall average inventory levels are declining, the relative percentage being held by manufacturers is increasing. Explain why you think this observation is either true or false. Describe how such a shift could benefit the operations of the entire channel and how manufacturers could take advantage of the shift.
2. Consumers are expressing increased demand for product customization in the form of features, labeling, color, or packaging. What is the impact of this trend on supply chain inventory? What strategies can firms and supply chains use to mitigate this impact?
3. Many of the retailers and in some cases wholesalers are driving their suppliers to provide vendor-managed inventory and consignment inventory at no additional cost to the customer. In effect, the customer is looking to shift inventory risk and responsibility to the supplier without paying for it. Describe initiatives that the supplier can use to recoup some value when they have to follow these customer requirements.
4. You have been asked to establish an inventory carrying cost percent to supply your firm's supply chain planning initiatives. Identify and describe the carrying cost components. Review the various approaches to determine the opportunity cost component and provide the rationale for each. As part of the assignment, you must recommend which approach you would use and why. You should also identify the implications of the opportunity cost decision on supply chain design decisions.

CHAPTER 8

Transportation

Chapter Outline

Transportation is the largest expenditure in logistics. Transportation managers commit and manage over 60 percent of a typical firm's total logistics spend. Transportation managers are responsible for moving inventory throughout a firm's supply chain and to customers. Today, a wide range of transportation solutions are available to support a given supply chain's logistical requirements. These choices include evaluating the use of a private fleet owned by the firm or dedicated to the firm or utilizing one or many for-hire carriers. Many companies utilize a strategic mix of private and for-hire transportation. In addition to traditional point-to-point transportation, many for-hire providers may also offer a wide variety of value-added services such as product sorting, sequencing, modification, or a guarantee of delivery completed by or at a specific time. Precise transportation execution helps a firm provide service, and reduce cost, inventory, storage, and materials handling.

Thus, the value of transportation service can be greater than simply moving product from one location to another. As operational expectations become more precise, order-to-delivery performance cycles shorten, and room for operational error near zero, successful managers have come to realize *there is no such thing as cheap transportation*. Unless transportation is managed in an effective and efficient manner, procurement, manufacturing, and customer relationship management has a higher risk to not meet expectations. The value of transportation is greater than simply moving products from one location to another. This chapter provides an overview of transportation and how it is managed during the logistical process.

Transport Functionality and Participants

Transportation is a very visible part of logistics. Consumers are accustomed to seeing trucks and trains transporting product or parked at business facilities. Few consumers fully understand just how dependent our economy is upon economical and reliable transportation. This section provides a foundation by reviewing transportation functionality and participants.

Functionality

Transportation provides two major logistical services: product movement and product storage.

Product Movement

Whether in the form of materials, components, work-in-process, or finished goods, the basic value provided by transportation is to move inventory to specified destinations throughout the supply chain. The performance of transportation is vital to procurement, manufacturing, and customer accommodation. Transportation also plays a key role in the performance of reverse logistics. Without reliable transportation, most commercial activity could not function. Transportation consumes time, financial, and environmental resources.

Transportation has a restrictive element because inventory is generally inaccessible during the transportation process. This is referred to as in-transit inventory. When designing logistical systems, a common goal is to reduce inventory in transit to a minimum. Advancements in information technology such as geo-fencing enabled by on-board computers within the cabs of trucks have significantly improved real-time status alerts and provided enhanced visibility to projected delivery times.

Transportation also uses financial resources. Transportation cost results from driver labor, fuel, vehicle maintenance, capital invested in equipment, and administration. In addition, product loss and damage can represent significant costs.

Transportation impacts environmental resources both directly and indirectly. In direct terms, transportation represents one of the largest consumers of diesel fuel in the U.S. economy. Although the level of fuel consumption has improved as a result of more fuel-efficient vehicles, total consumption remains high. Indirectly, transportation impacts the environment through congestion, air pollution, and noise pollution.

Product Storage

A less visible aspect of transportation is the provision of product storage. When a product is in a transportation vehicle, it is being stored. Transport vehicles can also be used for temporary product storage at shipment origin or destination. If the inventory involved is scheduled to be shipped within a few days, the cost of unloading, warehousing, and reloading the product may exceed the cost of using the transportation vehicle for storage. The fees associated with using a transportation vehicle for storage are referred to as demurrage for rail cars and detention for intermodal, dry van, and temperature-controlled trailers.

Another transport service having storage implications is **diversion**. Diversion occurs when the original shipment destination is changed after a product has been shipped. For example, the destination of a product initially shipped from Chicago to Los Angeles may be changed to Seattle while in transit. Although costly, product storage in transportation vehicles may be justified from a total cost or performance perspective when loading or unloading costs, capacity constraints, and ability to extend leadtimes are taken into consideration.

Participants

Transportation decisions are influenced by six parties: (1) shipper, sometimes referred to as the **consignor**; (2) destination party, commonly called the **consignee**; (3) carriers and agents; (4) government; (5) information technology; and (6) the public. Figure 8.1

FIGURE 8.1
Transportation
Participants

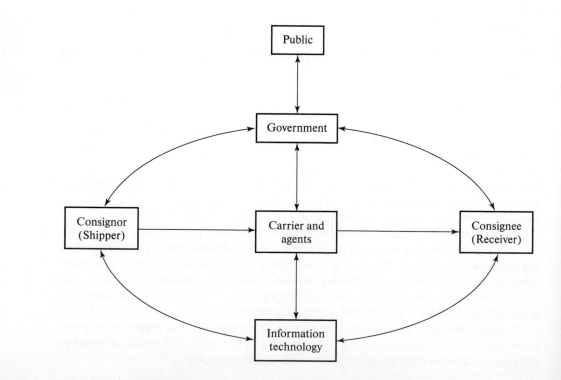

illustrates the relationship among the parties. To understand the complexity of the transportation environment, it is useful to review the role and perspective of each party.

Shipper and Consignee

The shipper and consignee represent the two parties involved in a traditional shipment. A common interest is shared as one party is the provider of the goods and the other is the recipient. This could be the completion of sale between two parties or the transfer of goods within a firm from one location to another. Success is defined by moving the goods from origin to destination within a specified time frame, at the lowest possible cost. Key elements include pickup and delivery; transit time; the potential for product loss and/or damage; accurate invoicing; and the accurate and timely exchange of information, such as an advanced shipment notification (ASN) that contains information on the contents of the shipment.

Carrier and Agents

The carrier is a business that performs a transportation service. As a service business, carriers want to charge their customers the highest freight rate possible while minimizing labor, fuel, and vehicle operating costs. To achieve this objective, the carrier seeks to coordinate pickup and delivery times for a group of shippers to achieve efficient operations. Brokers and freight forwarders are transport agents that facilitate carrier and customer matching.

Government

The government has a vested interest in transportation because of the critical importance of reliable service to economic and social well-being. Government desires a stable and efficient transportation environment to support economic growth. A stable and efficient transportation environment requires that carriers provide essential services at reasonable cost. Because of the direct impact of transportation on economic success, governments have traditionally been very involved in oversight of carrier operating and pricing practices. Government historically regulated carriers by restricting markets they could service and approving prices they could charge. Governments also promote carrier development by supporting research and providing right-of-way such as roadways and airports.

Information Technology

Today's transportation industry uses a wide assortment of information technology services. The primary advantage of these services is the ability of carriers to share real-time information within their company and with their customers. This includes all different types of status updates such as electronic data interchange (EDI) updates or push notifications received via a text message to alert a customer a delivery is on schedule or delayed. Today, almost every major trucking company has real-time visibility to all of their assets, managed in what are referred to as control towers.

In recent years, web-based enterprises have created marketplaces to provide information to both shippers and carriers. Common applications include spot pricing boards to help set and track market pricing. Visibility to additional available shipments or empty assets in close geographic proximity has been a key tool to help both shippers and carriers drive efficiency. In addition, secondary market places for purchasing fuel, equipment, parts, and supplies have matured. Information exchanges enable carriers the opportunity to aggregate their purchasing and identify opportunities across a wide range of products and services. Today, in many cases, transportation firms have increasingly become information technology firms that own transportation-related assets!

Public

The final transportation system participant, the public, is concerned with transportation accessibility, expense, and effectiveness as well as environmental protection, security, and safety. The public indirectly creates transportation demand by purchasing goods. While minimizing transportation cost is important to consumers, concerns also include environmental impact and safety. Air pollution and accidents involving commercial vehicles are significant transportation-related social issues. The cost of environmental impact and safety is ultimately paid by consumers.

Transportation policy formation is complex because of interaction between these six participants. Such complexity results in frequent conflict between shippers, consignees, and carriers. The concern to protect public interest served as the historical justification for government involvement in economic and social regulation. The next section provides a brief review of how government regulation has changed over the years.

From Regulation to a Free Market System

Because transportation has a major impact on both domestic and international commerce, government has historically taken a special interest in both controlling and promoting transport development. Such involvement has traditionally taken the form of federal and state regulation as well as a wide range of judicial administration.

Following the passage of the Act to Regulate Interstate Commerce on February 4, 1887, the federal government became active in protecting the public interest. The act established the Interstate Commerce Commission **(ICC)**, which had broad regulatory power regarding transportation. This era of regulation lasted until 1980. For almost 100 years the federal and state governments determined who could provide transportation services and the price they could charge for their services.

Widespread desire for deregulation in trucking and railroads became official with the passage of the Motor Carrier Act of 1980 **(MC 80)** and the Staggers Rail Act **(Staggers Act)**.[1]

MC 80 was a formal effort to stimulate competition and promote efficiency in trucking. Entry restrictions or right to conduct operations were relaxed, allowing firms to offer trucking services if they were judged fit, willing, and able. Restrictions relating to the types of freight carriers could legally haul and the range of services carriers could provide were abolished. While the ICC retained the right to protect the public against discriminatory practices and predatory pricing, individual carriers were given the right to price their services. The trucking industry's collective rate-making practices were restricted and soon were abolished. The structural impact of MC 80 on the for-hire motor carrier industry was dramatic. Overnight the industry was transformed from a highly regulated to a highly competitive structure.

On October 14, 1980, the railroad industry was deregulated by enactment of the Staggers Rail Act. The dominant philosophy of the act was to provide railroad management with the freedom necessary to revitalize the industry. In that respect, the most significant

---

[1]Motor Carrier Act of 1980 (Public Law 96-296) and the Staggers Rail Act of 1980 (Public Law 96-488).

provision of the Staggers Act was increased pricing freedom. Railroads were authorized to selectively reduce rates to meet competition while increasing other rates to cover operating cost. Contract rate agreements between individual shippers and carriers were specifically legalized. In addition to price flexibility, railroad management was given liberalized authority to proceed with abandonment of unprofitable rail service. The act also provided the framework for a liberalized attitude toward mergers and increased the ability of railroads to be involved in motor carrier service.

The authority of the ICC to regulate transportation was further modified by the passage of the Trucking Industry Regulatory Reform Act of 1994.[2] This act eliminated the need for motor carriers to file rates with the ICC. Effective January 1, 1996, the ICC was abolished by passage of the ICC Termination Act of 1995. This act further deregulated transportation and established a three-person Surface Transportation Board **(STB)** within the Department of Transportation (DOT) to administer remaining economic regulation issues across the industry.[3] The authority of the STB includes all transportation modes and incorporates freight forwarders and brokers.

The arrival of the new millennium delivered some significant changes to transportation industry. Technology adoption stimulated many of these changes. The Electronic Signatures in Global and National Commerce Act of 2000 gave electronic documents signed by digital signature the same legal status as paper documents. The most significant changes were in response to terrorism and the heightened transportation security of the United States following 9/11. The **USA PATRIOT Act** increased inspections at ports, regulated airport screening, and heightened security at land-based border crossings.[4] This act resulted in a widespread implementation of voluntary initiatives between U.S. CUSTOMS and private industry known as Customs-Trade Partnership against Terrorism **(C-TPAT)**.

Another example of the impact of regulation is the recent efforts to reframe the Jones Act. As part of Section 27 of the Merchant Marine Act of 1920, the Jones Act requires that all goods transported by water between U.S. ports be carried on U.S. flag–flying ships, constructed in the United States, owned by U.S. citizens, and crewed by U.S. permanent residents. Similar regulations existing around the globe are frequently called **cabotage laws**. Established nearly 100 years ago, the Jones Act came under significant scrutiny in late 2017 when Puerto Rico was demolished by Hurricane Maria. Under the law, any foreign-registered vessel that entered Puerto Rico had to pay punitive tariffs, fees, and taxes. Alternatively, the vessel could reroute to Jacksonville, Florida, where all goods could be transferred to an American vessel. As Puerto Rico struggled to recover from Maria's devastation, the public became increasingly critical of this act of regulation because it resulted in significant delays in providing relief goods. However, the act was still in effect nearly a year later in early 2018.

Two more recent regulations focused on safety have had significant effects on the trucking industry. The Federal Motor Carrier Safety Administration's (FMCSA) hours of service ruling and electronic logging devices (ELD) mandate were both highly contested and publicly debated pieces of regulation.

The hours of service regulation establishes guidelines regarding how long a driver may operate without taking rest, introducing three mandatory conditions defined as the 14-hour driving window, the 11-hour driving limit, and the 60-hour/7-day and 70-hour/8-day duty limits. Each condition defines specific criteria for eligibility to operate a qualifying commercial vehicle. The main reason for hours of service regulation is to keep fatigued

---

[2]Trucking Industry Regulatory Reform Act of 1994 (Public Law 103-111).
[3]ICC Termination Act of 1995 (Public Law 104-88).
[4]USA Patriot Act, October 26, 2001.

drivers off public roadways. The goal of the regulation is to ensure drivers stay awake and alert while driving.

The ELD mandate was adopted in early 2018 to further enforce hours of service regulation by now requiring an electronic record of a given truck's driving time. An ELD monitors a vehicle's engine to capture data on whether the engine is running, whether the vehicle is moving, the miles driven, and the duration of engine operation (engine hours). As a result of the ELD, drivers are no longer required to keep paper logs and can no longer modify driving records to enable them to drive beyond the hours of service regulations.

Both the hours of service and ELD mandate are perceived to have had significant impacts on industry productivity, resulting in financial pressure on both shippers and carriers. The trade-off is the improved safety of roads shared by both commercial and private vehicles. In general, consumers seem to be in favor of these regulations, while companies have struggled to offset the impacts.

Although the future and impact of regulation will be ever-changing, one thing that can be counted on is the government's continued involvement in nearly all aspects of transportation, with an ever-increasing focus on safety and the environment. Some scholars and industry experts even believe a return to regulated pricing is a future possibility. Although it now seems unlikely, only time will tell!

Transportation Modal Structure

The freight transportation structure consists of the rights-of-way, vehicles, and carriers that operate within five basic transportation modes. A **mode** identifies a basic transportation method or form. The five basic transportation modes are rail, truck (also referred to as motor carrier or highway), water, pipeline, and air.

The relative importance of each transportation mode in the United State is measured in terms of system mileage, traffic volume, revenue, and nature of freight transported. Table 8.1 provides a summary of transportation expenditures by mode from 1960 to 2017 and projects out to 2028. Tables 8.2 and 8.3 provide tonnage and revenue share by mode in 2009 and 2017 with projections for 2028. These data confirm that for the past 60+ years, truck load is the dominant player in both revenue and tonnage, far exceeding all other categories combined. While all transportation modes are vital to a sound national transportation infrastructure, it is clear the U.S. economy—historical, current, and projected—depends on trucks. The following discussion provides a brief overview of the essential operating characteristics of each mode.

Rail

Historically, railroads have handled the largest number of ton-miles within the continental United States. A ton-mile is a standard measure of freight activity that combines weight

TABLE 8.1
The Nations Freight Bill ($ billions)

Source: Freight Transportation Forecast 2017 to 2028, American Trucking Association, Inc., 2017.

	1960	1970	1980	1990	2000	2009	2017	2028
Truck	32.3	62.5	155.3	270.1	481.0	542.0	719.2	1245.0
Railroad	9.0	11.9	27.9	30.0	36.0	50.0	81.3	120.2
Water	3.4	5.3	15.3	20.1	26.0	29.0	13.5	19.9
Pipeline	0.9	1.4	7.6	8.3	9.0	10.0	56.1	163.4
Air	0.4	1.2	4.0	13.7	27.0	29.0	30.5	54.6
Total	46.0	82.3	210.1	342.2	579.0	660.0	900.6	1603.1

Mode and Volume	Freight Volumes (millions of tons)			Mode Share (%)			Percent Change (tons)
	2009	2017	2028	2009	2017	2028	2009–2017
Truck	8,522	10,731	13,916	67.2	70.7	67.2	25.9
Rail	1,753	1,731	1,842	13.8	11.4	8.9	−1.3
Rail Intermodal	139	200	286	1.1	1.3	1.4	44.0
Air	12	14	18	1.0	1.0	1.0	17.9
Water	857	930	1,036	6.8	6.1	5.0	8.5
Pipeline	1,393	1,567	3,625	11.0	10.3	17.5	12.5
Total	13,018	15,172	20,730				

TABLE 8.2 Domestic Shipments by Mode and Volume

Source: Freight Transportation Forecast, 2017–2028, American Trucking Association Inc., 2017.

Mode and Revenue	Freight Volumes (billions of dollars)			Mode Share (%)			Percent Change ($)
	2009	2017	2028	2009	2017	2028	2009–2017
Truck	528	719	1,245	81.9	79.9	77.7	36.2
Rail	40	61	83	6.2	6.8	5.1	52.8
Rail Intermodal	10	21	38	1.5	2.3	2.4	111.3
Air	20	31	55	3.1	3.4	3.4	51.0
Water	10	14	20	1.5	1.5	1.2	35.0
Pipeline	37	56	163	5.8	6.2	10.2	50.0
Total	665	901	1,603				

TABLE 8.3 Domestic Shipments by Mode and Revenue

Source: Freight Transportation Forecast, 2017–2028, American Trucking Association Inc., 2017.

and distance. As a result of early development of a comprehensive rail network connecting almost all cities and towns, railroads dominated intercity freight tonnage until after World War II. This early rail superiority resulted from the capability to offer frequent service and economically transport large shipments. However, with technology advancements, serious motor carrier competition began to develop following World War II.

Railroads once ranked first among all modes in terms of the number of miles in service. The extensive development of roads and highways to support the growth of automobiles and trucks after World War II soon changed this ranking. In 1970 there were 206,265 miles of rail track in the United States. By 2005, track mileage had declined to 95,830 miles. That trend has stabilized; as of 2012, the total rail track mileage is still around 95,000 miles.

The capability to efficiently transport large tonnage over long distances is the main reason railroads continue to handle significant intercity tonnage. Railroad operations have high fixed costs because of expensive equipment, right-of-way and tracks, switching yards, and terminals. However, rail enjoys relatively low variable operating costs. The development of diesel power reduced railroad variable cost per ton-mile, and electrification has provided further cost reductions. Modified labor agreements have reduced human resource requirements, resulting in further variable cost reductions.

As a result of deregulation and focused business development, rail traffic has shifted from transporting a broad range of commodities to hauling specific freight. Core railroad tonnage comes from bulk material industries and heavy items such as automobiles, farm equipment, and machinery. The rail fixed-variable cost structure offers competitive advantages for long-haul moves. Starting in the mid-1970s, railroads began to segment their transportation market by focusing on carload, intermodal, and container traffic. Railroads became more responsive to specific customer needs by emphasizing bulk industries and heavy manufacturing, as contrasted to traditional freight boxcar service. Intermodal operations were expanded by forming alliances with motor carriers. For example, United Parcel Service, is the largest user of rail service to transport trailers in the United States.

To provide improved service to major customers, progressive railroads have concentrated on the development of specialized equipment, such as enclosed trilevel automotive railcars, cushioned appliance railcars, unit trains, articulated cars, and double-stack container flatcars. A recent innovation has been the introduction of 53 foot temperature controlled container-on-flatcar (COFC) technology.[5] These technologies are being applied by railroads to reduce weight, increase carrying capacity, and facilitate interchange.

Rail will continue to be a large part of the transportation infrastructure equation given the mode's ability to generate efficiency in size and length of shipment combined with the flexibility to handle everything from bulk product to intermodal containers.

Truck

Highway transportation has expanded rapidly since the end of World War II. To a significant degree the rapid growth of the motor carrier industry has resulted from speed coupled with the flexibility of door-to-door operations.

Trucks have flexibility because they vary in size and maneuverability and they are able to operate on a variety of roadways. The national highway system alone, which includes all interstate highways, consists of more than 164,000 miles.[6] There are 3.63 million Class 8 (defined as 33,000 LBS or greater) trucks in operation as of 2016 and roughly 3.5 million truck drivers employed in 2016.[7]

In comparison to railroads, trucks have a relatively small fixed investment in terminal facilities and operate on publicly financed and maintained roads. Although the cost of license fees, user fees, and tolls is considerable, these expenses are directly related to the number of trucks and miles operated. The variable cost per mile for motor carriers is high because a separate power unit and driver are required for each trailer or combination of tandem trailers. Labor requirements are also high because of driver safety restrictions and need for substantial dock labor. Truck operations are characterized by low fixed and high variable costs. In comparison to railroads, motor carriers more efficiently handle small shipments moving short distances.

Truck capabilities favor manufacturing and distributive trades. As a result of delivery flexibility, trucks dominate freight moving from wholesalers and warehouses to retail stores. The future prospect for trucking remains bright. Today, with the exception of small package goods moving in premium air service, almost all less-than-15,000-pound intercity shipments are transported by truck.

The trucking industry is not without problems. The primary difficulties relate to increasing costs to replace equipment, maintenance, safety, increased regulations,

[5]"Trucking Firm Introduces Temp-Controlled Containers for Rail," *Cargo Business News*, October 3, 2010.
[6]U.S. Department of Transportation, Federal Highway Administration.
[7]American Trucking Association.

fuel cost, and driver shortages. Driver shortages have become a primary area of focus across the industry. In late 2017, the American Trucking Association (ATA) predicted the U.S. trucking industry could be short 50,000 drivers by the end of 2017. In addition, the ATA predicts that if current trends hold, the driver shortage could reach 174,000 by 2026. This is a significant concern! Primary causes of the driver shortage include an aging workforce nearing retirement and less interest in the lifestyle associated with truck driving, making recruitment of younger employees more challenging. To combat this issue, carriers have increased driver pay, including large hiring or "sign-on" bonuses; introduced guaranteed pay programs; and enhanced benefits. In addition, carriers have improved numerous other aspects of the driver's quality of life such as safety and comfort while in the cab and a commitment to more home time. In addition, carriers have placed a great deal of attention on improved line-haul scheduling, computerized billing systems, mechanized terminals, tandem operations that haul two or three trailers with a single power unit, and participation in coordinated intermodal transport systems.

An alternative to for-hire truck service is shipper-owned trucks or trucks operated by integrated logistics service providers (**ISPs**) that are under contract to perform transport services for specific shippers. Approximately 55 percent of all intercity truck tonnage is hauled by shipper-owned or shipper controlled trucks. Following deregulation, this ratio reached a high of 66 percent by 1987. The subsequent decline to 55 percent resulted from shippers realizing the numerous complexities and problems of operating a private fleet. The growth of ISP operated trucking offers a service that combines the flexibility of private with the consolidation potential of shared for-hire operators. An ISP may perform services for multiple shippers and thus gain both economies of scale and distance.

Since 1980, deregulation has dramatically changed the nature of for-hire trucking. The industry segments, which have become more defined since deregulation, include truckload (**TL**), less-than-truckload (**LTL**), and specialty. The dramatic change is related to the type of carriers operating in each category.

The TL segment includes loads over 15,000 pounds that generally do not require intermediate stops between origin and destination. Although large firms such as Swift Transportation, Schneider National, Werner Express, and J.B. Hunt Transportation Services provide nationwide TL service, the segment is characterized by a large number of relatively small carriers and is generally very price competitive.

The LTL segment involves shipments less than 15,000 pounds that generally must be consolidated to fully utilize trailer capacity. As a result of origin and destination terminal costs and relatively higher marketing expenses, LTL experiences a higher percentage of fixed costs than TL. The operating characteristics of the LTL freight segment have caused extensive industry consolidation, resulting in a few relatively large national carriers and a strong regional network of smaller carriers. The five largest LTL carriers based on 2016 revenue are FedEx Freight, XPO Logistics, Old Dominion Freight Line, YRC Freight, and UPS Freight. Their collective revenue totaled more than $17.5 billion.[8]

Specialty carriers include bulk and package haulers such as Waste Management and United Parcel Service (**UPS**). Specialty firms focus on specific transport requirements of a market or product.

On the basis of the sheer size of the trucking industry and the services provided, it is quite apparent that highway transportation will continue to function as the backbone of logistical operations for the foreseeable future.

---

[8]"JOC Top 50 LTL Carriers: Small carriers, Fast growth" Journal of Commerce August 17th, 2017, William B. Cassidy.

Water

Water is the oldest mode of transport. The original sailing vessels were replaced by steam-powered boats in the early 1800s and by diesel in the 1920s. Today, large cargo ships are some of the most sophisticated machines operating in the supply chain industry.

Domestic water transport, which involves the Great Lakes, canals, and intracoastal waterways, has maintained a relatively constant annual ton-mile share of between 19 and 30 percent over the past four decades. While the share has remained relatively constant, the mix has changed dramatically. The percentage of river and canal ton-miles has increased, while the Great Lakes ton-miles have decreased. This reflects both a shift of bulk product transportation from rail and highway to lower-cost water movements on rivers and coastal canals as well as a shift from lakeside shipping to motor carrier transport.

This network size has been stable over the past decade and is expected to remain stable for the foreseeable future. Fewer system miles exist for inland water than for any other transportation mode. Not including the Great Lakes or coastal shipping, the United States contains 25,000 miles of inland waterways supported by 239 different locks.

The main advantage of water transport is the capacity to transport extremely large shipments. Water transport employs two types of vessels for movement: Deepwater vessels are generally designed for coastal, ocean, and Great Lakes transport; diesel-towed barges generally operate on rivers and canals and have considerably more flexibility.

Water transport ranks between rail and motor carrier in terms of fixed cost. Although water carriers must develop and operate their own terminals, the right-of-way is developed and maintained by the government and results in moderate fixed costs compared to rail. The main disadvantages of water transport are the limited range of operation and slow speed. Unless the origin and destination of the movement are adjacent to a waterway, supplemental product movement by rail or truck is required. The capability of water to transport large tonnage at low variable cost places this mode of transport in demand when low freight rates are desired and speed of transit is a secondary consideration.

The global shipping industry has undergone significant changes in the last 10 years.

Pipeline

Pipelines are a significant part of the U.S. transportation system. The United States has the largest network of energy pipelines in the world, with more than 2.4 million miles of pipe. The network of crude oil pipelines in the United States is extensive. There are approximately 72,000 miles of crude oil lines in the U.S. that connect regional markets.[9]

In addition to petroleum products, the other important product transported by pipeline is natural gas. Like petroleum pipelines, natural gas pipelines in the United States are privately owned and operated, and many gas companies act as both gas distribution and contract transportation providers.

The basic nature of a pipeline is unique in comparison to other modes of transport. Pipelines operate on a 24-hour basis, 7 days per week, and are limited only by commodity changeover and maintenance. Unlike other modes, there is no empty container or vehicle to return. Pipelines have the highest fixed cost and lowest variable cost among transport modes. High fixed costs result from the right-of-way for pipeline, construction and requirements for control stations, and pumping capacity. Since pipelines are not labor-intensive, the variable operating cost is extremely low once the pipeline has been constructed. An obvious disadvantage is that pipelines are not flexible and are limited with respect to

[9]Pipeline101.com.

commodities that can be transported, as only products in the forms of gas, liquid, or slurry can be handled.

Experiments regarding potential movement of solid products in the form of slurry or hydraulic suspension continue. Coal slurry pipelines have proved to be an efficient and economical mode of transporting coal over long distances. Coal slurry lines require massive quantities of water, which has an environmental impact warranting further discussion and consideration. As inconspicuous as pipelines may seem, recently, one pipeline in particular has drawn national media attention. The Keystone Pipeline system, commissioned in 2010, runs from the Western Canadian sedimentary basin in Alberta to refineries in Illinois and Texas. The pipeline came to a greater prominence when a planned fourth phase, Keystone XL, attracted growing environmental protest—a symbol for the battle of climate change and continued use of fossil fuels. The pipeline was temporarily delayed by then President Barack Obama; however, in January 2017, President Donald Trump took action intended to permit the pipeline's completion.

Air

The newest but least utilized mode of transportation is airfreight. The significant advantage of airfreight lies in speed. A coast-to-coast shipment via air requires only hours contrasted to days with other modes of transport. While costly, the speed of air transport potential allows other aspects of logistics such as warehousing and inventory to be reduced or eliminated.

Air transport, despite its high profile, still remains more of a potential than a reality. Airfreight accounts for 1 percent of intercity ton-miles. Air transport capability is limited by load size, weight lift capacity, and aircraft availability. Traditionally, intercity airfreight was transported on scheduled passenger flights. While the practice was economical, it resulted in a limited capacity and flexibility of freight operations. The high cost of jet aircraft, coupled with the erratic nature of freight demand, served to limit the economic commitment of dedicated aircraft to all-freight operations.

However, the advent of premium air carriers such as Federal Express and United Parcel Air introduced scheduled global airfreight service. While such premium service was originally targeted at high-priority documents, it has expanded to include package freight. For example, premium carriers have integrated their service to include overnight parts delivery from centralized distribution centers located near their air hubs. Overnight air delivery from a centralized warehouse is attractive to firms with a large number of high-value products and time-sensitive service requirements.

The fixed cost of air transport is low compared to rail, water, and pipeline. In fact, air ranks second only to truck with respect to low fixed cost. Airways and airports are generally developed and maintained by government. The fixed costs of airfreight are associated with aircraft purchase and the requirement for specialized handling systems and cargo containers. On the other hand, airfreight variable cost is extremely high as a result of fuel, user fees, maintenance, and the labor intensity of both in-flight and ground crews.

Since airports require significant real estate, they are generally limited with respect to integration with other transport modes. However, there is substantial interest in integrating air transport with other modes and developing all-freight airports to eliminate conflict with passenger service. For example, Alliance Airport, located near Fort Worth, Texas, was designed to integrate air, rail, and truck distribution from a single location.

No particular commodity dominates the traffic carried by airfreight operations. Perhaps the best distinction is that most freight has high value and priority. When the marketing period for a product is extremely limited, such as Christmas gifts, high-fashion clothing, fresh fish, or cut flowers, air may be the only practical transportation method to support global operations. Routine logistics of products such as computers, repair parts, and medical supplies also utilize airfreight.

Modal Comparative Characteristics and Capabilities

Table 8.4 compares the fixed-variable cost structure of each mode. Table 8.5 ranks modal operating characteristics with respect to speed, availability, dependability, capability, and frequency.

Speed refers to elapsed movement time. Airfreight is the fastest of all modes. **Availability** refers to the ability of a mode to service any given pair of locations. Highway carriers have the greatest availability since they can drive directly to origin and destination points. **Dependability** refers to potential variance from expected or published delivery schedules. Pipelines, because of their continuous service and limited interference due to weather and congestion, rank highest in dependability. **Capability** is the ability of a mode to handle any transport requirement, such as load size. Water transport is the most capable. The final classification is **frequency**, which relates to the quantity of scheduled movements. Pipelines, again because of their continuous service between two points, lead all modes in frequency.

As Table 8.5 illustrates, the appeal of highway transport is in part explained by its high relative ranking across the five operating characteristics. Truck ranks first or second in all categories except capability. Although substantial improvements in motor capability resulted from relaxed size and weight limitations on interstate highways and approval to use tandem trailers, it is not realistic to assume motor transport will surpass rail or water capability.

Infrastructure in Crisis

Following World War II the United States embarked on an aggressive development program that resulted in construction of 46,837 miles of interstate highways. However, by 2010 this highway system was in need of expansion and widespread repair to sustain the safe movement of commercial and private transportation.

TABLE 8.4
Cost Structure for Each Mode

- *Rail*. High fixed cost in equipment, terminals, tracks, etc. Low variable cost.
- *Truck*. Low fixed cost (highways in place and provided by public support). Medium variable cost (fuel, maintenance, etc.).
- *Water*. Medium fixed cost (ships and equipment). Low variable cost (capability to transport large amount of tonnage).
- *Pipeline*. Highest fixed cost (rights-of-way, construction, requirements for control stations, and pumping capacity). Lowest variable cost (no labor cost of any significance).
- *Air*. Low fixed cost (aircraft and handling and cargo systems). High variable cost (fuel, labor, maintenance, etc.).

TABLE 8.5
Modal Operating Characteristics*

*Lowest rank is best.

Operating Characteristics	Rail	Truck	Water	Pipeline	Air
Speed	3	2	4	5	1
Availability	2	1	4	5	3
Dependability	3	2	4	1	5
Capability	2	3	1	5	4
Frequency	4	2	5	1	3
Composite Score	14	10	18	17	16

On August 1, 2007, the collapse of a major span of interstate highway I-35W bridging the Mississippi River in downtown Minneapolis vividly called to public attention the nation's crumbling network of bridges, tunnels, and roads. According to the American Society of Civil Engineers' 2017 Infrastructure report card, the United State has 614,387 bridges, of which almost 4 in 10 are 50+ years old. 56,007, or 9.1%, of the nation's bridges were structurally deficient in 2016, and on average, there were 188 million trips across a structurally deficient bridge each day. While the number of bridges that are in such poor condition to be considered structurally deficient is decreasing, the average age of America's bridges keeps going up, and many of the nation's bridges are approaching the end of their design life. The most recent estimate puts the nation's backlog of bridge rehabilitation needs at $123 billion.[10]

Participants in the transportation system are deeply concerned about these and other growing issues related to safety, congestion, and inadequate system capacity across all five transportation modes. Most transportation professionals agree the United States is in need of a far-reaching National Transportation Plan to facilitate both the repair and reinvention of transportation infrastructure. The 2009 American Recovery and Reinvestment Act set aside $12 billion for repairs and new infrastructure projects. However, depressed economic conditions have limited the actual expenditures. On February 15, 2018, President Trump's administration published the Legislative Outline for Rebuilding Infrastructure in America. The 53-page plan lays out a vision to turn $200 billion in federal money into $1.5 trillion for fixing American's infrastructure by leveraging local and state tax dollars combined with private investment. Regardless of point of view on this particular proposal, all in the supply chain logistics industry agree infrastructure is a high priority within the United States.

Specialized Transportation Services

Transportation service can be improved by combining modes. Prior to deregulation, government policy limited carriers to operating in a single mode. Such restrictive ownership sought to promote competition between modes and limit the potential for monopoly practices. Following deregulation carriers were free to develop integrated modal services in efforts to more efficiently and effectively meet the needs of customers. The following section reviews the current range of specialized services offered by different carriers.

Parcel Service

Parcel services represent an important part of logistics, and the influence of carriers in this segment is increasing because of their size and intermodal capabilities. The advent of e-commerce and the need for consumer-direct last-mile delivery have significantly increased demand for package delivery services. While package services are expanding, the services required do not fall neatly into the traditional modal classification scheme. Packages are regularly transported by using the line-haul services of rail, motor, and air. Package service provides both regular and premium services.

Numerous carriers offer delivery services within metropolitan areas. Other carriers offer package delivery service on a national and global basis. The most recognizable carriers are Federal Express (FedEx), United Parcel Service (**UPS**), and the United States Postal Service (**USPS**).

[10]ASCE, Infrastructure Report Card 2017.

The first widely recognized premium air package service was initiated by Federal Express in 1973. FedEx provided nationwide overnight service utilizing a fleet of dedicated cargo aircraft. Since inception, FedEx original service has expanded internationally. FedEx also currently offers LTL and TL service.

The original service offered by UPS was contract delivery of local shipments for department stores. Today, UPS offers a diverse range of package services. In fact, UPS has expanded its scope of overall operating authority by shipping packages that conform to specialized size and weight restrictions nationwide and globally for consumers and business enterprises. While UPS provides logistical services related to all types of products, specialization in small packages enables a cost-effective overnight service between most cities within 300 miles.

Today, UPS offers more than 20 different service options. Table 8.6, based on the 2017 UPS Rate and Service Guide, outlines the different integrated services offered within North America. What is interesting is the combination of different modes that support these service offerings. Truckload, intermodal, less-than-truckload, and air all work in concert to enable UPS to provide this breadth of offerings. For example, truckload or air, or a combination of both, may be required for same-day service via the UPS Express Critical product offering.

The United States Postal Service (**USPS**) operates ground and air parcel service. Charges for parcel have traditionally been based on weight and distance. Generally, packages must be delivered to a post office for shipment origination. However, in the case of large users

	North American Freight						
	Same Day	1 Day	2 Days	2–3 Days	2–5 Days	Within 3–4 Days	Day-Definite
UPS Express Critical®	•						
UPS Next Day Air® Freight		•					
UPS Next Day Air® Freight NGS		•					
UPS 2nd Day Air® Freight			•				
UPS 2nd Day Air® Freight NSG			•				
UPS Worldwide Expedited® Air Freight (U.S.-Mexico)				•			
UPS Worldwide Expedited® Ground Freight (U.S.-Mexico)					•		
UPS Worldwide Expedited® Truckload (U.S.-Mexico)					•		
UPS 3 Day Freight®						•	
UPS 3 Day Freight® NGS						•	
Coyote Logistics® Truckload and Intermodal							•
Coyote® Collaborative Transportation Management							•
UPS Freight® LTL (Less-Than-Truckload)							•
UPS Freight® LTL Guaranteed							•
UPS Freight® LTL Guaranteed A.M.							•
UPS Freight® LTL Urgent							•
UPS Freight® Dedicated Contract Carriage							•
UPS Freight® Trade Show Services							•
UPS Freight® Temperature Protection Services							•
UPS® Standard LTL (U.S.-Mexico)							•
UPS® Standard Truckload (U.S.-Mexico)							•

TABLE 8.6   Examples of Parcel Carrier Service Options

Source: Adapted from UPS 2017 Service Guide, www.ups.com.

and when it is convenient for the Postal Service, pickup is provided at the shipper's location. Intercity transport is accomplished by purchasing air, highway, rail, and even water service from for-hire carriers. Delivery is provided to the final destination by the Postal Service.

In 2006 the range of services provided by the USPS were significantly expanded as a result of the passage of the Postal Accountability and Enhancement Act **(PAEA)**. The USPS has a last-mile advantage over all other package carriers in that it is structured to facilitate delivery to every household in the United States every day. Under provision of the PAEA the USPS was given flexibility in pricing. The traditional practice of charging the same price per unit of freight was modified to include commercial volume pricing, minimum value rebates, and online price breaks. In 2010, the USPS introduced a new service called "If it fits it ships." This service offers one flat rate for any shipment between two U.S. domestic locations if it fits into any of the five different box sizes. These rates are guaranteed regardless of package weight.

In today's supply chain environment, we even see small package companies working together to provide an integrated product offering to consumers. FedEx's "Smart Post" service utilizes FedEx assets for origin pickup, regional sortation, and linehaul operations but partners with the USPS, utilizing its vast reach to every address in the United States for final-mile delivery. The strategic partnership combines the strengths of both companies to achieve a win-win product offering attractive to consumers for its cost and convenience.

The importance of parcel service to the logistical system cannot be overemphasized. The explosion of e-commerce over the past four to five years has pushed significantly larger volume of shipments that go from a firm directly to an end consumer. Referred to as business-to-consumer, or B2C, fulfillment, retail e-commerce sales have grown from under 4 percent in the first quarter of 2008 to more than 9.1 percent of total retail sales in 2017.[11] Consumers now expect two-day free shipping with real-time status updates thanks to the growth of Amazon. Firms that specialize in consumer fulfillment are one of the fastest growing forms of logistics service providers.

Intermodal

Intermodal transportation combines two or more modes to take advantage of the inherent economies of each and thus provide an integrated service at lower total cost. Many efforts have been made over the years to integrate different transportation modes. Initial attempts at modal coordination trace back to the early 1920s, but during the regulatory period cooperation was restrained by restrictions designed to limit monopoly practices. Intermodal offerings began to develop more successfully during the 1950s with the advent of integrated rail and motor service commonly termed **piggyback service**. This common intermodal arrangement combines the flexibility of truck for short distances with the low line-haul cost associated with rail for longer distances. The popularity of such offerings has increased significantly as a means to achieve more efficient and effective transportation.

Technically, coordinated or intermodal transportation could be arranged among all basic modes. Descriptive jargon such as piggyback fishyback, trainship, and airtruck have become standard transportation terms.

TOFC/COFC

The best known and most widely used intermodal systems are the trailer on a flatcar **(TOFC)** and container on a flatcar **(COFC)**. Containers are the boxes utilized for intermodal product storage and movement between motor freight, railroads, and water transportation.

[11]US Census Bureau News, Quarterly Retail E-Commerce Sales Q4, 2017.

Containers are typically 8 feet wide, 8 feet high, and 20 or 40 feet long and do not have highway wheels. Trailers, on the other hand, are of similar width and height but can be as long as 53 feet and have highway wheels. As the name implies, a trailer or container is placed on a railroad flatcar for some portion of the intercity line-haul and pulled by a truck at origin and to the final destination. Line-haul cost is the expense to move railcars or trucks between cities. Since the original development of TOFC, various combinations of trailer or container on flatcar—double-stack, for instance—have increased significantly.

While the TOFC concept facilitates direct transfer between rail and motor carriage, it also has several technical limitations. The placement of a trailer with highway wheels attached, transferred to a railcar, can lead to wind resistance, damage, and weight problems. The use of containers reduces these potential problems, as they can be double stacked and are easily transferred to water carriers. They require special equipment for over-the-road delivery or pickup.

Containership

Fishyback, trainship, and containership are examples of the oldest form of intermodal transport. They utilize waterways, which are one of the least expensive modes for line-haul movement. A comparison completed by the Maritime Administration (**MARAD)** showed that one 15-barge tow has the equivalent capacity of 225 railcars or 900 trucks.[12]

The fishyback, trainship, and containership concept loads a truck trailer, railcar, or container onto a barge or ship for the line-haul movement on inland navigable waterways. Such services are provided in coastal waters between Atlantic and Gulf ports, and between the Great Lakes and coastal points.

A variant of this intermodal option is the **land bridge** concept that moves containers in a combination of sea and rail transport. The land bridge is commonly used for containers moving between Europe and Asia to reduce the time and expense of all-water transport. For example, containers are shipped to the West Coast of North America from Asia, loaded onto railcars for movement to the East Coast, and then reloaded onto ships for movement to Europe. The land bridge concept is based on the benefit of ocean and rail combinations that utilize a single tariff, which is lower than the combined total cost of two separate rates.

On June 26, 2016, the Panama Canal expansion project began commercial operations. The project, which formally began in 2007, was originally scheduled to complete in 2014 to coincide with the 100th anniversary of the opening of the canal. However, the project was challenged with various setbacks, including strikes and disputes over construction costs. The project, costing an estimated $5.4 billion, adds a second set of locks to the canal. The new locks will accommodate container ships that carry up to 13,000 TEU (twenty-foot equivalent units), nearly triple the 4,500- to 5,000-TEU-capacity vessels that are able to pass through the original locks. This expansion has been projected to shift as much as 10 percent of Far East container traffic from U.S. West Coast ports to U.S. East Coast ports; however, inadequate infrastructure to handle larger container ships at U.S. East Coast ports have delayed the volume shift.

Nonoperating Intermediaries

The overall transportation industry also includes several businesses that do not own or operate equipment. These nonoperating intermediaries broker services of other firms. A transportation broker is somewhat similar to a wholesaler in a marketing channel.

---

[12]U.S. Waterborne Foreign Trade Containerized Cargo, "Top 25 U.S. Ports," January–June 2004, Port Import Export Reporting Services. MARAD waterborne traffic statistics, http://www.marad.dot.gov/MARAD.

Nonoperating intermediaries find economic justification by offering shippers lower rates for movement between two locations than would be possible by direct shipment via common carrier. Because of peculiarities in the common-carrier rate structure, such as minimum freight charges, surcharges, and less-than-volume rates, conditions exist whereby nonoperating intermediaries can facilitate savings for shippers. Interestingly, there are cases where nonoperating intermediaries charge higher rates than those offered by carriers. The justification for the higher charges is based on ability to arrange faster delivery and/or more value-added services. The primary intermediaries are freight forwarders, shipper associations, and brokers.

Freight forwarders are for-profit businesses that consolidate small shipments from various customers into a bulk shipment and then utilize a common surface or air carrier for transport. At destination, the freight forwarder splits the consolidated shipment into the original smaller shipments. Local delivery may or may not be arranged by the forwarder. The main advantage of the forwarder is a lower freight rate obtained from consolidation to large shipments.

Shipper associations are operationally similar to freight forwarders in that they consolidate small shipments into large movements to gain cost economies. Shipper associations are voluntary nonprofit entities where members, operating in a specific industry, collaborate to gain economies related to small-shipment purchases. Typically, members purchase product from common vendors or from sources of supply located in one area. A common practice is to order small quantities at frequent intervals to minimize retail inventory. Participation in a shipper association typically means improved speed of delivery, since a large number of different products may be purchased at one location, such as the garment district in New York City.

Brokers are intermediaries that coordinate transportation arrangements for shippers, consignees, and carriers. They also arrange shipments for exempt carriers and owner operators. Brokers typically operate on a commission basis. Brokers provide extensive services such as shipment matching, rate negotiation, billing, and tracing. The entire area of brokerage operations is highly adaptable to Internet-based transactions and is increasing in importance as a result of increased globalization.

Transportation Economics and Pricing

Transportation economics and pricing are driven by multiple factors that influence rates. The primary factors are distance, weight, and density. These important factors are discussed from a shipper's perspective.

Economy of Distance

Distance is a major influence on transportation cost since it directly contributes to variable expense, such as labor, fuel, and maintenance. Figure 8.2 illustrates the general relationship

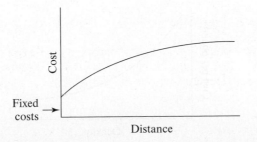

FIGURE 8.2

Generalized Relationship between Distance and Transportation Cost between distance and transportation cost. Two important points are illustrated. First, the cost curve does not begin at zero because there are fixed costs associated with shipment pickup and delivery regardless of distance. Second, the cost curve increases at a decreasing rate as a function of distance. This characteristic is known as the **tapering principle**.

Economy of Weight

A second factor is shipment weight. Similar to other logistics activities, scale economies exist for most transportation movements. This relationship, illustrated in Figure 8.3, indicates that transport cost per unit of weight decreases as load size increases. This occurs because the fixed costs of pickup, delivery, and administration are spread over incremental weight. This relationship is limited by the size of the transportation vehicle. The managerial implication is that small loads should be consolidated into larger loads to maximize scale economies.

Economy of Density

A third factor is product density. Density is the combination of weight and volume. Weight and volume are important since transportation cost for any movement is usually quoted in dollars per unit of weight. Transport charges are commonly quoted per hundredweight (CWT). In terms of weight and volume, vehicles are typically more constrained by cubic capacity than by weight. Higher-density products allow fixed transport cost to be spread across more weight. As a result, higher density products are typically assessed lower transport cost per unit of weight. Figure 8.4 illustrates the relationship of declining transportation cost per unit of weight as product density increases. In general, traffic managers seek to improve product density so that trailer cubic capacity can be fully utilized.

Other Pricing Factors

Several other factors have importance to transportation economics. Four of the more important factors are discussed.

FIGURE 8.3
Impact of Weight on
Transportation Cost

Weight

FIGURE 8.4
Impact of Density on
Transportation Cost

Density

Stowability

Stowability refers to how product dimensions fit into transportation equipment. Odd package sizes and shapes, as well as excessive size or length, may not fit well in transportation equipment, resulting in wasted cubic capacity. Although density and stowability are similar, it is possible to have items with similar densities that stow very differently. Items having rectangular shapes are much easier to stow than odd-shaped items. For example, while steel blocks and rods may have the same physical density, rods are far more difficult to stow than blocks because of their length and shape. Stowability is also influenced by other aspects of size, since large numbers of items may be **nested** in shipments whereas they may be difficult to stow in small quantities. For example, it is possible to accomplish significant nesting for a truckload of trash cans while a single can is difficult to stow.

Handling

Special handling equipment may be required to load and unload trucks, railcars, or ships. In addition to special handling equipment, the manner in which products are physically grouped together in boxes or on pallets for transport and storage impacts handling cost.

Liability

Liability includes product characteristics that can result in damage. One example of this is hazardous material such as aerosol paint. Carriers must either have insurance to protect against potential damage or accept financial responsibility. Shippers can reduce their risk, and ultimately transportation cost, by improved packaging or reducing susceptibility to loss or damage.

Market

Finally, market factors such as lane volume and balance influence transportation cost. A **transport lane** refers to movements between origin and destination points. Since transportation vehicles and drivers typically return to their origin, either they must find a **back-haul** load or the vehicle is returned empty, commonly referred to as **deadheading**. When empty return movements occur, labor, fuel, and maintenance costs must be charged against the original front-haul movement. Thus, the ideal situation is to achieve two-way or balanced movement of loads. However, this is rarely the case because of demand imbalances in manufacturing and consumption locations. Demand location and seasonality result in transport rates that change with direction and season. Logistics system design must take such factors into account to achieve back-haul economies whenever possible.

Costing Freight

The second dimension of transport economics and pricing concerns the criteria used to allocate cost. Cost allocation is primarily a carrier concern, but since cost structure influences negotiating ability, the shipper's perspective is important as well. Transportation costs are classified into a number of categories.

Variable

Costs that change in a predictable, direct manner in relation to some level of activity are labeled **variable costs**. Variable costs include direct carrier costs associated with movement of each load. These expenses are generally measured as a cost per mile or per unit of weight. Typical variable cost components include labor, fuel, and maintenance.

Fixed

Expenses that do not change in the short run and must be paid even when a company is not operating, such as during a holiday or a strike, are **fixed costs**. The fixed category includes costs not directly influenced by shipment volume. For transportation firms, fixed components include vehicles, terminals, rights-of-way, information systems, and support equipment. In the short term, expenses associated with fixed assets must be covered by contribution above variable costs on a per shipment basis.

Joint

Expenses created by the decision to provide a particular service are called **joint costs**. For example, when a carrier elects to haul a truckload from point A to point B, there is an implicit decision to incur a **joint** cost for the back-haul from point B to point A. Either the joint cost must be covered by the original shipper from A to B or a back-haul shipper must be found. Joint costs have significant impact on transportation charges because carrier quotations must include implied joint costs based on assessment of back-haul recovery.

Common

This category includes carrier costs that are incurred on behalf of all or selected shippers. **Common costs**, such as terminal or management expenses, are characterized as overhead. These are often allocated to a shipper according to a level of activity like the number of shipments or delivery appointments handled.

Pricing Freight

This section presents the traditional pricing mechanics used by carriers. This discussion applies specifically to common carriers, although contract carriers follow a similar approach.

Class Rates

In transportation terminology, the price in dollars and cents per hundredweight to move a specific product between two locations is referred to as the **rate**. The rate is listed on pricing sheets or on computer files known as **tariffs**. The term **class rate** evolved from the fact that all products transported by common carriers are classified for pricing purposes. Any product legally transported in interstate commerce can be shipped via class rates.

Determination of common carrier class rates is a two-step process. The first step is to determine the **classification** or grouping for the product being transported. The second step is determining the rate or price based on the freight classification of the product, weight, and shipment origin/destination points.

Freight Classification

All products transported are grouped together into uniform classifications. The classification takes into consideration the characteristics of a product or commodity that influence the cost of handling or transport. Products with similar density, stowability, handling, liability, and value characteristics are grouped together into a class, thereby reducing the need to deal with each product on an individual basis. The particular class that a given product or commodity is assigned is referred to as its **rating**. A products rating is used to determine the freight rate. It is important to understand that the classification is not the price or rate charged for movement of a product. Rating refers to a product's transportation characteristics in comparison to other commodities.

Truck and rail carriers each have independent classification systems. The trucking system uses the *National Motor Freight Classification*, while rail classifications are published in the *Uniform Freight Classification*. The truck classification system has 18 classes of freight, and the rail system has 31. In local or regional areas, individual groups of carriers may publish additional classification lists.

Classification of individual products is based on a relative index of 100. Class 100 is considered the class of an average product, while other classes run as high as 500 and as low as 35. Each product is assigned an item number for listing purposes and then given a classification rating. As a general rule, the higher a class rating, the higher the transportation cost for the product. Historically, a product classified as 200 would be approximately twice as expensive to transport as a product rated 100. While the actual current multiple may not be two, a class 200 rating will still result in substantially higher freight costs than a class 100 rating. Products are also assigned classifications on the basis of the weight being shipped. Less-than-truckload (**LTL**) shipments of identical products will have higher ratings than truckload (**TL**) shipments.

Table 8.7 illustrates a page from the *National Motor Freight Classification*. It contains general product grouping 86750, which is **glass, leaded**. Notice that the leaded glass category is further subdivided into specific types of glass such as *glass, microscopical slide or cover, in boxes* (item 86770). For LTL shipments, item 86770 is assigned a class 70 rating. TL shipments of the same glass items are assigned a class 40 rating, provided a minimum of 360 hundredweight is shipped.

Products are also assigned different ratings on the basis of packaging. Glass may be rated differently when shipped loose, in crates, or in boxes than when shipped in wrapped protective packing. It should be noted that packaging differences influence product density, stowability, and damage, illustrating that cost factors discussed earlier enter into the rate-determined process. Thus, a number of different classifications may apply to the same product depending on shipment size, transport mode, and product packaging.

One of the major responsibilities of transportation managers is to obtain the best possible rating for all products shipped, so it is useful for members of a traffic department to have a thorough understanding of the classification systems. Although there are differences in rail and truck classifications, each system is guided by similar rules.

It is possible to have a product reclassified by written application to the appropriate classification board. The classification board reviews proposals for change or additions with respect to minimum weights, commodity descriptions, packaging requirements, and general rules and regulations. An alert traffic department will take an active role in classification. Significant savings may be realized by obtaining an improved classification for a product or by recommending a change in packaging or shipment quantity that will reduce a product's rating.

Rate Determination

Once a classification rating is obtained for a product, the rate must be determined. The rate per hundredweight is usually based on the shipment origin and destination, although the actual price charged for a particular shipment is normally subject to a minimum charge

Item	Articles	Classes	
		LTL	TL
86750	Glass, leaded, see Note, item 86752:		
Sub 1	With landscape, pictorial, or religious designs, packed in boxes.	200.	70.
Sub 2	With curved, angled, or straight-line patterns, or with designs other than landscape, pictorial, or religious, in boxes.	100.	70.
86752	*Note:* The term "leaded glass" means glass either colored or clear, set in lead or in other metal.		
86770	Glass, microscopical slide or cover, in boxes.	70.	40.
86830	Glass, rolled, overlaid with aluminum strips with metal terminals attached, in boxes, crates, or Package 1339.	77.5	45.
86840	Glass, rolled, overlaid with aluminum strips, NOI, in boxes, crates, or Package 1339.	70.	37.5
86900	Glass, silvered for mirrors, not framed, backed, or equipped with hangers or fastening devices:		
Sub 1	Shock (window glass, silvered), in boxes, see Note, item 86902; also TL, in Packages 227 or 300.	86.	40.
Sub 2	Other than shock glass; also TL, in Packages 227 or 300:		
	Bent:		
Sub 3	Not exceeding 15 feet in length or 9 feet in breadth, in boxes.	100.	70.
Sub 4	Exceeding 15 feet in length or 9 feet in breadth, in boxes.	250.	70.
Sub 5	Not bent, see Package 785:		
Sub 6	120 united inches or less, in boxes, crates, or Packages 198,	70.	40.
Sub 7	235, or 1339.		
Sub 8	Exceeding 120 united inches but not exceeding 15 feet in length or 9 feet in breadth, in boxes or crates.	100.	40.
Sub 9	Exceeding 15 feet in length or 9 feet in breadth, in boxes or crates.	200.	45.
86902	*Note:* Glass, silvered for mirrors, which has been framed or backed, or equipped with large hangers or fastening devices, is subject to the classes for mirrors, NOI.		
85940	Glass, window, other than plate, with metal edging other than sash or frames, in boxes.	77.5	45.
86960	Glazing units, glass, not in sash, see Note, item 86966, in boxes, crates, or Packages 2133, 2149, or 2281.	70.	45.
86966	*Note:* Applies on units consisting of sheets of glass separated by air or vacuum, sealed at all edges with same or other materials.		
87040	Skylight, roofing, or sidewall construction material consisting of rough rolled glass, wired or not wired, and installation accessories, see Note, item 87042, in boxes or crates.	65.	35.

TABLE 8.7   National Motor Freight Classification 100-S

Source: Reprinted with permission from the American Trucking Association.

and may also be subject to surcharges. Historically, the origin and destination rates were manually maintained in notebooks that had to be updated and revised regularly. Then rates were provided on diskettes by carriers. Today, options for selecting carriers range from internet software that examines carrier web sites and determines the best rates to participation in online auctions.

Origin and destination rates are organized by zip codes. Table 8.8 illustrates rates for all freight classes from Atlanta, Georgia (zip 303), to Lansing, Michigan (zip 489). The table lists rates for shipments ranging in size from the smallest LTL (less than 500 pounds; listed as L5C) to the largest TL (greater than 40,000 pounds; listed as M40M). The rate is quoted in dollars per hundredweight. Assuming a shipment of 10,000 pounds, the rate for class 85 between Atlanta and Lansing, using this example tariff, is $12.92 per hundredweight.

Origin 303: Destination 489: MC 81.00: RBNO 00775E									
Rate Class	L5C	M5C	M1M	M2M	M5M	M10M	M20M	M30M	M40M
500	233.58	193.89	147.14	119.10	84.05	65.37	40.32	32.25	28.24
400	188.24	156.25	118.58	95.98	67.73	52.69	32.55	26.03	22.79
300	144.11	119.63	90.78	73.48	51.86	40.34	24.94	19.95	17.45
250	126.30	104.84	79.56	64.40	45.45	35.34	21.86	17.48	15.31
200	98.37	81.66	61.97	50.16	35.40	27.53	17.00	13.60	11.91
175	88.65	73.58	55.84	45.20	31.90	24.81	15.30	12.24	10.72
150	76.11	63.18	47.94	38.81	27.38	21.30	13.20	10.56	9.24
125	64.76	53.76	40.80	33.03	23.31	18.12	11.25	9.00	7.88
110	56.27	46.71	35.43	28.69	20.25	15.75	9.88	7.90	6.92
100	52.62	43.68	33.15	26.83	18.94	14.73	9.22	7.38	6.46
92	49.79	41.33	31.37	25.39	17.92	13.94	8.91	7.12	6.24
85	46.15	38.31	29.07	23.53	16.61	12.92	8.58	6.86	6.01
77	42.91	35.62	27.03	21.88	15.44	12.01	8.34	6.67	5.84
70	40.48	33.59	25.50	20.64	14.57	11.33	8.10	6.48	5.67
65	38.46	31.92	24.22	19.61	13.84	10.76	8.02	6.41	5.61
60	36.84	30.58	23.21	18.78	13.26	10.31	7.94	6.35	5.56
55	34.81	28.90	21.93	17.75	12.53	9.74	7.85	6.28	5.50
50	32.79	27.22	20.66	16.71	11.80	9.18	7.77	6.22	5.44
Weight Limits (lb)	Under 500	500– 1000	1000– 2000	2000– 5000	5000– 10,000	10,000– 20,000	20,000– 30,000	30,000– 40,000	Over 40,000

TABLE 8.8   Example of Rates from Atlanta, Georgia (zip 303), to Lansing, Michigan (zip 489)

Historically, the published rate had to be charged for all shipments of a specific class and origin/destination combination. This required frequent review and maintenance to keep rates current. Following deregulation, carriers offered more flexibility through rate discounts. Now instead of developing an individual rate table to meet the needs of customer segments, carriers apply a discount from class rates for specific customers. The discount depends on the shipper's volume and market competition.

An alternative to the per hundredweight charge is a per mile charge, which is common in TL shipments. As discussed previously, TL shipments are designed to reduce handling and transfer costs. Since the entire vehicle is used in a TL movement and there is no requirement to transfer the shipment at a terminal, a per mile basis offers a more appropriate pricing basis. For a one-way move, charges may vary per mile based on the market, the equipment, and the product involved. Although it is negotiable, this charge typically includes loading, unloading, and liability.

In addition to the variable shipment charge applied on either a per hundredweight or per mile basis, two additional charges are common for transportation: **minimum charges** and **surcharges**. The minimum charge represents the amount a shipper must pay to make a shipment, regardless of weight. A surcharge represents an additional charge designed to cover specific carrier costs.

Class rates, minimum charges, and surcharges form a pricing structure that, in various combinations, is applicable within the continental United States. The tariff indicates the class rate for any rating group between specified origins and destinations. In combination, the classification framework and class rate structure form a generalized pricing mechanism.

Cube Rates and Freight Dimensioners

Significant focus has been placed on accurately determining the correct classification for mixed commodity less-than-truckload (LTL) freight. Around 2010, momentum started to build toward the adoption of a cube-based pricing system, in the opinion of many, a much superior way to cost freight. However, as of 2017, the cube methodology has not gained widespread adoption. However, a subtle shift has started as many LTL carriers have purchased what are known as **dimensioners**. A dimensioner is a weight-and-volume measuring device used to measure three-dimensional or cube-shaped objects such as packages, parcels, cartons, or boxes and obtain an accurate density factor for the package. Today, LTL carriers deploy numerous dimensioners throughout their network. The dimensioner captures measurements of freight in real time as it passes through the LTL network. The carrier then takes this information and compares the actual cubic density of the shipments to the stated freight-all-kind (FAK) class on the bill of lading. The carriers can identify when actual density varies from reported density and review with shippers to adjust pricing or make changes to packaging configurations. The collective goal of this process is to drive efficiency into the LTL carrier's network. This is another example of how improvements in technology are rapidly changing the transportation industry.

Other Rate Structures

There are numerous other unique rate structures used within transportation. These include **commodity rates** applicable when large quantities of product move between two locations on a regular basis. There are also a number of exception rates that could be applicable to a specific area, origin/destination, or commodity when justified by either competitive or high-volume movements. Other examples include an **aggregate tender rate**, which is utilized when a shipper agrees to provide multiple shipments to a carrier in exchange for a discount of exception from the prevailing class rate. A **limited service rate** is utilized when a shipper agrees to perform a selected service typically performed by the carrier, such as trailer loading, in exchange for a discount. Yet another example is a **released value rate**, which limits the carrier liability in case of loss or damage.

Special Rates and Services

A number of special rates and services provided by carrier are available for us in the logistics operations. The below section contains a brief list of examples. A **freight-all-kind (FAK)** enables a mixture of different products to be transported under a single negotiated rating. As opposed to calculating the individual rates of each product, this approach can streamline complexity. When a commodity moves under the tariff of a single carrier, it is referred to as a **local rate** or single-lane rate. If more than one carrier is involved in the movement, a **joint rate** may be applicable. An example of a joint rate would be the rail industry, in which certain railroad companies only operate in specific geographies and, as a result, partner to complete the movement of a given shipment. **Transit services** permit a shipment to be stopped at an intermediate point between the origin and destination for unloading, storage, or processing. A typical example is grain processing. Sometimes, the shipper or consignee may desire to change the routing, destination, or even consignee while the shipment is in transit. This process is called **diversion and reconsignment**. *Diversion* is the change in destination; *reconsignment* is the change of owner prior to delivery. A **split delivery**, or **multi-stop load** as it's often referred to, is desired when the shipment has multiple parts with unique delivery locations. Each of these special rates or services can provide unique value added when used appropriately.

TABLE 8.9
Typical Carrier Ancillary
Services

- *COD*. Collect payment on delivery.
- *Change COD*. Change COD recipient.
- *Inside delivery*. Deliver product inside the building.
- *Marking or tagging*. Mark or tag product as it is transported.
- *Notify before delivery*. Make appointment prior to delivery.
- *Reconsignment of delivery*. Redirect shipment to a new destination while in transit.
- *Redeliver*. Attempt second delivery.
- *Residential delivery*. Deliver at a residence without a truck dock.
- *Sorting and segregating*. Sort commodity prior to delivery.
- *Storage*. Store commodity prior to delivery.

Assessorial Service Charges

In addition to basic transportation, carriers offer a wide variety of special or assessorial service or charges. Table 8.9 provides examples of assessorial service charges, where a unique additional service is provided to augment the base shipment. These could also include environmental services—for example, temperature control—while in transit or "reefer" shipping. Hershey's, for example, typically transports chocolate confectionery products in reefer trailers during the summer months to avoid exposure to heat. In another example, specialized sanitation equipment is necessary to clean and prepare trailers for food storage and transit if the trailer has been previously utilized for nonfood products or commodities. This is commonly referred to as "food grade." One last example is the use of lift gate/pallet jack service for LTL deliveries. This is appropriate when the delivery location does not have a commercial transportation dock. The truck has a lift gate attached to the back enabling ground-level delivery, and the driver has a pallet jack to unload the product to the desired location. This is commonly seen in the food delivery business, especially in large cities—think of a Starbucks coffee location receiving its replenishment shipments through the front door of the store. You've probably seen it before!

Although this brief coverage of assessorial services is not all-inclusive, it does offer several examples of the range and type of services carriers offer. A carrier's role in a logistical system is most often far greater than just providing the movement of goods.

Transportation Operations Management

Transportation operations management involves a wide variety of planning, execution, and administrative responsibilities. This section of the text will provide an overview of different elements associated with a firm's management of these activities including transportation management systems, documentation, and how product pricing intersects with transportation.

Transportation Management Systems

Almost all firms use some version of a transportation management system (TMS) as an integral part of their information technology strategy. In general, a TMS proactively identifies and evaluates transportation strategies and tactics to determine the best method for the shipment of a given product. As illustrated in Table 8.10, this includes the capability to select transportation modes, plan loads, consolidate shipments, route vehicles, and

TABLE 8.10
Typical Transportation
Management System
Functionality

- Order consolidation
- Route optimization
- Carrier rate management
- EDI links with carriers
- Internet-based shipment tracking
- Integrated claims management
- Identify most economical mode: parcel, less-than-truckload, truckload, pool distribution, stops in transit
- Calculate best route
- Carrier selection based on cost and service including performance
- Yard management

efficiently utilize transportation capacity. The fundamental deliverables of a TMS are the creation and facilitation of a plan that increases the likelihood of an on-time delivery while achieving the most optimal cost performance. The generalized functionality of a TMS can be described in terms of five capabilities: (1) operations; (2) consolidation; (3) negotiation; (4) control; and (5) payment, auditing, and claims administration.

Operations

From an operations perspective, the TMS includes key functionality such as equipment scheduling and yard management, load planning, shipment routing, and track and trace.

Equipment scheduling and yard management is an important process because serious cost and operational bottlenecks can result from transportation equipment waiting to be loaded or unloaded. Proper yard management requires careful planning, equipment utilization, and driver scheduling. Frequently, yard management is supported by an additional system referred to as a yard management system (YMS). TMS, YMS, and WMS (warehouse management systems) frequently work in collaboration to ensure that equipment is available and at the right location when the warehouse is ready to load or unload the truck. In addition, equipment preventive maintenance can be planned, coordinated, and monitored, and any specialized requirements or conditions can be planned and implemented.

Closely related to equipment scheduling is the arrangement of pickup and delivery appointments. To avoid extensive waiting and improve equipment utilization, it is important to take a multi-faceted approach. Many shippers operate under what are referred to as "drop-and-hook" arrangements, which enable the carrier to drop a loaded trailer in the yard and leave immediately with a different loaded or empty trailer. The receiving company then coordinates the unloading of that trailer at a later time based on different prioritization factors. This strategy greatly increases transportation efficiency by maximizing the use of the driver's hours of service. In parallel, a certain number of delivery appoints for "live unloads" are usually maintained for higher priority freight or other special circumstances. The effective scheduling of equipment and yard management are key to time-based logistics performance.

How loads are planned directly impacts transportation efficiency. In the case of trucks, capacity is limited in terms of weight and cube. TMS systems optimize mode selection based on the size and attributes of a given shipment. In parallel, the TMS system must consider other factors such as the physical handling characteristics of the product as well as delivery sequence if multiple shipments are loaded onto a single trailer. A general rule of thumb is to maximize the cubic utilization of a truck without compromising product integrity or creating inefficiency in the loading and unloading process.

Another important part of achieving transportation efficiency is shipment routing. The TMS system can help identify the most efficient route for a shipment to travel based on a variety of constraints such as delivery appointments, preferred road type, and projected traffic conditions. Common strategies include "static routing," in which routes have very little variation from one day to next, or "dynamic routing," in which each route is optimized based on the individual characteristics of those shipments. Routing must always consider how to achieve the desired service levels and must include consideration of customer special requirements in terms of time, locations, and special unloading services.

The TMS system also plays a critical role in shipment visibility and information exchange. It is common practice for shippers to electronically provide consignees with advanced shipment notifications (ASNs). While the specifics of the ASN exchanges may differ, their primary purpose is to allow adequate time to plan the arrival, arrange delivery appointments, and plan redeployment of the shipment's content (e.g., allocation to customer orders). In addition, TMS systems accept EDI status updates from carriers, commonly referred to as 214 updates, that indicate arrival and departure at origin and destination, among many other available updates. Rapid advancements in technology over the past few years have led to real-time tracking capabilities such as geo-fencing, which utilizes the computer on board the truck to provide real-time updates such as location, speed, and hours of service remaining—all shared in real time via TMS or other web-based interfaces.

Consolidation

At several different points throughout the text, the importance of freight consolidation is discussed. The fact that freight costs are directly related to the size of shipment and length of haul places a premium on freight consolidation.

The traditional approach to freight consolidation was to combine LTL or parcel shipments moving to a general location. The objective was straightforward: The transportation savings in moving a single consolidated shipment versus multiple individual shipments are typically sufficient to pay for the necessary handling and local delivery while achieving significant total cost reduction.

The shift to response-based logistics, combined with the growth in e-commerce, has introduced new challenges regarding consolidation. In a response-based system, all members of the supply chain are seeking to reduce inventory dwell time by more closely synchronizing replenishment with demand. The result, in many cases, is more frequent, smaller orders. Not only does this increase the cost of transportation, it also translates into less efficient shipping and receiving operations. Similarly, the explosion of growth in the e-commerce space has led to significantly more small shipments traveling from business to consumer (B2C) with very short lead-time expectations. To control transportation costs when a time-based strategy or e-commerce strategy is used, managerial attention must be directed to ingenious ways to achieve transportation consolidation. From an operational viewpoint, freight consolidation techniques are grouped as **reactive** and **proactive**. Each type of consolidation plays an important role to achieving transportation efficiency.

Reactive Consolidation

A reactive approach to consolidation does not attempt to influence the composition and timing of transportation movements. The consolidation effort reacts to shipments as they come and seeks to combine individual orders into larger shipments to gain efficiency. Perhaps the most visible examples of effective reactive consolidation are the UPS and FedEx parcel consolidation operations. Running nearly 24/7, these operations consolidate and distribute many small shipments, utilizing what is referred to as market area consolidation.

In **market area consolidation**, shipments leaving one geographic location and heading to a similar final destination are pooled together to gain transportation and handling efficiency. This procedure does not interrupt the natural freight flow because changing the timing of shipments, rather the overall quantity of shipments, to a market area provides the consolidation basis. A second strategy, known as **scheduled area delivery**, holds shipments for specific markets for delivery on selected days each week. The scheduled delivery plan is communicated to customers in a way that highlights the mutual benefits of consolidation. The shipping firm commits to the customer that all orders received prior to a specified cutoff time will be guaranteed for delivery on the scheduled day. Finally a third alternative is referred to a **pooled delivery**. Pooled delivery typically means that a freight forwarder, public warehouse, or transportation company arranges the consolidation for multiple shippers servicing the same geographical market area. One example could be multiple grocery suppliers each sending their unique products to an integrated service provider, which then makes a single coordinated delivery to the grocery store. Pooled delivery, when coordinated effectively, can provide significant benefits for both the shipper and the received.

Proactive Consolidation

While reactive efforts to develop transportation consolidation have been successful and are unlikely to disappear any time soon, the aforementioned adoption of response-based logistics and the explosion of e-commerce activity has created an environment in which shippers, carriers, and consignees are all interested in collaborating to achieve consolidation savings. One tool to achieve proactive consolidation is **preorder planning**. Preorder planning considers the quantity and timing of orders to facilitate consolidated freight movements. Simply stated, the creation of orders is not restricted to standard buying times or inventory replenishment rules; rather, it is flexible to enable transportation optimization. Buyer participation in order creation can assist in facilitating proactive consolidation. Another concept that has gained momentum is **multivendor consolidation**. The general idea is the proactive alignment of two or more vendors whose freight characteristics combine to create efficiency. One example is the partnership of two vendors located in the same geographical region, serving the same customers, but each with unique physical attributes of their products. One vendor with heavy freight may load the truck first, which is then topped off at the second vendor, which makes lightweight products. Think, for example, of a truckload of heavy generators topped with feather dusters. Third-party logistics (3PL) companies are increasing focusing on multivendor consolidation as a value-added service.

Negotiation

For any given shipment, it is the responsibility of the transportation department to obtain the lowest possible rate consistent with service requirements. The prevailing tariff, or existing history, represents the starting point in transportation rate negotiation. The key to effective negotiation is to seek win-win agreements wherein both carriers and shippers share productivity gains. This includes matching the service type and speed to the lead time requirements. It is very common for shippers and carriers to publish rates for a certain scope of work and period of time. Once established, these rates are loaded into the TMS system for execution. Frequently primary, secondary, and tertiary carrier rates are loaded with the associated lead times. The TMS will recommend the optimal solution and issue a tender to the carrier for a given shipment. Given the special considerations of transportation, several factors discussed throughout this section must guide rate negotiation. It is important that shippers and carriers work together to establish solid, long-term relationships based on mutual efficiency and gain.

Control

The TMS helps to facilitate another import dimension of transportation operations management: control. As noted earlier in this chapter, the transportation industry is a highly regulated industry. Ensuring all local, state, and federal regulations such as driver's hours of service (HOS) and weight limitations for specific bridges, roads, and cities are adhered to are critical elements of transportation. TMS systems help to enforce and monitor required controls that are reviewed frequently by transportation managers.

Payment, Auditing, and Claims Administration

TMS systems also help facilitate what are referred to as the "back-end" administrative tasks associated with transportation. Carrier bill payment and auditing frequently use information provided from the TMS database to ensure the carrier bill is presented at the rates and terms agreed upon during negotiation. Frequently, applied strategies include a pre-audit, where a given freight bill is audited for accuracy prior to payment, and a post-audit, in which a certain percentage of bills are double-checked for accuracy after the initial payment is issued. In addition, claim administration is an important and frequently overlooked part of transportation operations management. Claims are typically classified as over, short, and damage (OS&D). Damage claims occur when a shipper demands the carrier pay for partial or total financial loss resulting from poor performance. As the name implies, over and/or short claims result when the amount billed is different from what is expected and are typically resolved through extensive research. Agreements between carriers and shippers stipulate the proper procedure for filing claims and help define the responsible parties. It is common to see firms utilize specialize service providers to assist with freight payment, audit, and claims administration.

Documentation

Detailed documentation is required to perform a transportation service. With the exception of private transfer within the confines of a single firm, products are typically being sold when being transported. Thus, a change of ownership occurs during the time the transport service is performed. When for-hire carriers are used to perform the transportation, the transaction must establish clear legal responsibility of all parties involved. The primary purpose of transportation documentation is to protect all involved parties. Three primary types of transport documentation are bills of lading, freight bills, and shipment manifests.

Bill of Lading

The **bill of lading** is the basic document utilized in purchasing transport services. It serves as a receipt and documents products and quantities shipped. For this reason, accurate product description and count are essential. In case of loss, damage, or delay, the bill of lading is the basis for damage claims. The designated individual or buyer on a bill of lading is the only bona fide recipient of goods. A carrier is responsible for proper delivery according to instructions contained in the document. The information contained on the bill of lading determines all responsibilities related to timing and ownership.

The bill of lading specifies terms and conditions of carrier liability and documents responsibilities for all possible causes of loss or damage except those defined as **force majeure** (circumstances beyond anyone's control, such as a natural disaster). Figure 8.5

UNIFORM STRAIGHT BILL OF LADING

Original—Not Negotiable

(To be Printed on "White" Paper)

Shipper's No. . . . . . .

Agent's No. . . . .

Company

RECEIVED, subject to the classifications and tariffs in effect on the date of the issue of this Bill of Lading,

at . . . . , 19 . . . . .

from . . . .

the property described below, in apparent good order, except as noted (contents and condition of contents of packages unknown), marked, consigned, and destined as indicated below, which said company (the word company being understood throughout this contract as meaning any person of corporation in possession of the property under the contract) agrees to carry to its usual place (of delivery at mid destination, if on its own road or its own water line, otherwise to deliver to another carrier on the route to said destination. It is mutually agreed, as to each carrier of all or any of said property over all or any portion of said route to destination, and as to each party at any time interested in all or any of said property, that every service to be performed hereunder shall be subject to all the conditions not prohibited by law, whether printed or written, herein contained, including the conditions on back hereof, which are hereby agreed to by the shipper and accepted for himself and his assigns.

(Mail or street address of consignee—For purposes of notification only.)

Consigned to . . . .

Destination . . . . State of . . . . County of . . . .

Route . . . .

Delivering Carrier . . . . Car Initial . . . . Car No. . . . .

No. Pack-ages	Description of Articles, Special Marks, and Exceptions	*Weight (Subject to Correction)	Class or Rate	Check Column	Subject to Section 7 of conditions, if this shipment is to be delivered to the consignee without recourse on the consignor, the consignor shall sign the following statement:
. . . . . .	. . . .	. . . .	. . . . .	. . . . .	The carrier shall not make delivery of this shipment without payment of freight and all other lawful charges.
. . . . . .	. . . .	. . . .	. . . . .	. . . . .	
. . . . . .	. . . .	. . . .	. . . . .	. . . . .	. . . .
. . . . . .	. . . .	. . . .	. . . . .	. . . . .	(Signature of consignor.)
. . . . . .	. . . .	. . . .	. . . . .	. . . . .	
. . . . . .	. . . .	. . . .	. . . . .	. . . . .	If charges are to be prepaid, write or stamp here, "To be Prepaid."
. . . . . .	. . . .	. . . .	. . . . .	. . . . .	
. . . . . .	. . . .	. . . .	. . . . .	. . . . .	. . . .
. . . . . .	. . . .	. . . .	. . . . .	. . . . .	Received $ . . . .
. . . . . .	. . . .	. . . .	. . . . .	. . . . .	to apply in prepayment of the charges on the property described hereon.
. . . . . .	. . . .	. . . .	. . . . .	. . . . .	
. . . . . .	. . . .	. . . .	. . . . .	. . . . .	. . . .
. . . . . .	. . . .	. . . .	. . . . .	. . . . .	Agent or Cashier.
. . . . . .	. . . .	. . . .	. . . . .	. . . . .	Per . . . . (The signature here acknowledges only the amount prepaid.)

* If the shipment moves between two ports by a carrier by water, the law requires that the bill of lading shall state whether it is "carrier's or shipper's weight."

Note.—Where the rate is dependent on value, shippers are required to state specifically in writing the agreed or declared value of the property.

The agreed or declared value of the property is hereby specifically stated by the shipper to be not exceeding

Charges advanced:

$ . . . .

. . . . per . . . .

. . . . Shipper.　. . . . . Agent.

Per . . . . 　Per . . . .

Permanent postoffice address of shipper . . . .

FIGURE 8.5　Uniform Straight Bill of Lading

provides an example of a Uniform Straight Bill of Lading. Government regulations permit uniform bills of lading to be computerized and electronically transmitted between shippers and carriers.

Freight Bill

The **freight bill** represents a carrier's method of charging for transportation services performed. It is developed by using information contained in the bill of lading. The freight bill may be either **prepaid** or **collect**. A prepaid bill means that transport cost is paid by the shipper whereas a collect shipment shifts payment responsibility to the consignee.

Considerable administration is involved in preparing bills of lading and freight bills. There has been significant effort to automate freight bills and bills of lading through EDI or Internet transactions. Some firms elect to pay their freight bills at the time the bill of lading is created, thereby combining the two documents. Such arrangements are based upon the financial benefits of reduced administrative costs.

Shipment Manifest

The **shipment manifest** lists individual stops or consignees when multiple shipments are placed on a single vehicle. Each shipment requires a bill of lading. The manifest lists the stop, bill of lading, weight, and case count for each shipment. The objective of the manifest is to provide a single document that defines the overall contents of the load without requiring review of individual bills of lading. For single-stop shipments, the manifest is the same as the bill of lading.

Product Pricing and Transportation

Pricing is an important aspect of marketing strategy that directly impacts logistical operations. The terms and conditions of pricing determine which party has responsibility for performing logistics activities. A major trend in price strategy has been to **debundle** the price of products and materials so that services such as transportation, which were traditionally included in a delivered price, become separate and visible items. Pricing practices have a direct impact on the timing and stability of logistical operations. In this section, basic pricing structures are briefly reviewed, followed by a discussion of pricing impact areas. No attempt is made to review the broad range of economic and psychological issues related to price strategy. The focus is on the relationship between pricing, logistical operations, and transportation decisions. Pricing decisions directly determine which party in the transaction is responsible for performing logistics activities, passage of title, and liability. FOB origin and delivered pricing are the two most common methods.

FOB Pricing

The term FOB technically means **free on board** or **freight on board**. A number of variations of FOB pricing are used in practice. **FOB origin** is the simplest way to quote price. Under FOB origin the seller indicates the price at point of origin and agrees to tender a shipment for transportation loading, but assumes no further responsibility. The buyer selects the mode of transportation, chooses a carrier, pays transportation charges, and takes risk of in-transit loss and/or damage. In **FOB destination pricing**, product ownership title does not pass to the buyer until delivery is completed. Under FOB destination pricing, the seller arranges for transportation and the charges are added to the sales invoice. The firm paying the freight bill does not necessarily assume responsibility for ownership of goods in transit, for the freight cost, or for filing of freight claims. These are issues of negotiation that are critical to supply chain collaboration.

Delivered Pricing

The primary difference between FOB and **delivered pricing** is that in delivered pricing the seller establishes a price that includes transportation. In other words, the transportation cost is not specified as a separate item. There are several variations of delivered pricing.

Under **single-zone delivered pricing**, buyers pay a single price regardless of where they are located. Delivered prices typically reflect the seller's average transportation cost. In actual practice, some customers pay more than their fair share for transportation while others are subsidized.

Single-zone delivered pricing is typically used when transportation costs are a relatively small percentage of selling price. The main advantage to the seller is the high degree of logistical control. For the buyer, despite being based on averages, such pricing systems have the advantage of simplicity.

The practice of **multiple-zone pricing** establishes different prices for specific geographic areas. The underlying idea is that logistics cost differentials can be more fairly assigned when two or more zones—typically based on distance—are used to quote delivered pricing. Parcel carriers such as United Parcel Service use multiple-zone pricing.

The most complicated form of delivered pricing is the use of a **base-point pricing system** in which the final delivered price is determined by the product's list price plus transportation cost from a designated base point, usually the manufacturing location. This designated point is used for computing the delivered price whether or not the shipment actually originates from the base location. Base-point pricing is common in shipping assembled automobiles from manufacturing plants to dealers.

Figure 8.6 illustrates how a base-point pricing system typically generates different net returns to a seller. The customer is quoted a delivered price of $100 per unit. Plant A is the base point. Actual transportation cost from plant A to the customer is $25 per unit.

FIGURE 8.6
Base-Point Pricing

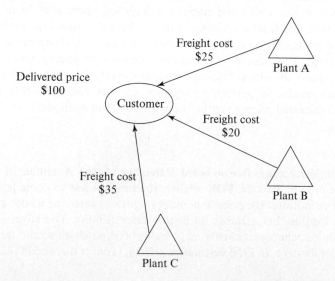

Plant A's base product price is $85 per unit. Transportation costs from plants B and C are $20 and $35 per unit, respectively.

When shipments are made from plant A, the company's net return is $75 per unit, the $100 delivered price minus the $25 transportation cost. The net return to the company varies if shipments are made from plant B or C. With a delivered price of $100, plant B collects $5 in **phantom freight** on shipments to a customer. Phantom freight occurs when a buyer pays transportation costs greater than those actually incurred to move the shipment. If plant C is the shipment origin, the company must absorb $10 of the transportation costs. **Freight absorption** occurs when a seller pays all or a portion of the actual transportation cost and does not recover the full expenditure from the buyer. In other words, the seller decides to absorb transportation cost to be competitive.

Base-point pricing simplifies price quotations but can have a negative impact on customers and supply chain collaboration. For example, dissatisfaction may result if customers discover they are being charged more for transportation than actual freight costs. Such pricing practices may also result in a large amount of freight absorption for sellers.

Pickup Allowances

Pickup allowances are equivalent to purchasing merchandise on an FOB origin basis. Buyers are given a reduction from the standard delivered price if they or a representative pick up shipments at the seller's location and perform transportation. A buyer may also use a for-hire carrier or an integrated service provider (ISP) to perform merchandise pickup. In the food and grocery industry, which traditionally practiced delivered pricing, firms have realized significant savings by using private and for-hire carriers to pick up rather than purchase merchandise on a delivered basis.

While some confusion exists concerning how to best establish a pickup allowance, a safe rule is that a seller should provide the same allowance to all directly competitive buyers. A uniform pickup allowance is often the price incentive offered to the customer closest to the shipping point. Other common policies offer pickup allowances equivalent to the applicable common carrier rate for the shipment.

Pickup allowances offer potential benefits for both the seller and the buyer. Shippers are required to deal with fewer small shipments, thereby reducing the need for extensive outbound freight consolidation. Buyers gain control over the merchandise earlier and are in a position to achieve greater utilization of transportation equipment and drivers.

Summary

Transportation is usually the largest single cost expenditure in most logistics operations. Prior to deregulation, transportation services were standardized and inflexible, resulting in limited ability to develop a competitive advantage. As a result of deregulation, service offerings have been expanded and restrictions relaxed, allowing transportation resources to be effectively integrated into overall supply chain logistics. The chapter reviewed different modes of transportation and the inherent pros and cons of each.

This chapter introduced major principles of transportation economics. Knowledge of transportation economics and pricing is essential for effective logistics management. The primary drivers of transportation costs are distance, volume, density, stowability, handling, liability, and market factors. These drivers determine transportation prices that are presented to buyers as rates for performing specific services. Logistics managers need to have a working familiarity with the basic rate structure for line-haul and specialized transport-related services.

Transportation operations management frequently utilizes a transportation management system (TMS) to support the execution of operations; consolidation; negotiation; control; and payment, auditing, and claims administration.

Finally, transportation and pricing decisions are closely related. The growing practice of debundling the price of products and related services, such as transportation, has increased the involvement of logistics managers in general price administration.

Study Questions

1. Compare and contrast the transportation principles of economy of scale and economy of distance. Illustrate how they combine to create efficient transportation.

2. What is the economic justification for the rapid growth of premium package services?

3. Railroads have the largest percentage of intercity freight ton-miles, but motor carriers have the largest revenue. How do you explain this relationship?

4. The five basic modes of transportation have been available for well over 50 years. Is this the way it will always be, or can you identify a sixth mode that may become economically feasible in the foreseeable future?

5. Seven economic drivers that influence transportation cost were presented. Select a specific product and discuss how each factor impacts determination of freight rate.

6. What is the purpose of freight classification? Describe the differences between a rate and a rating. How do they relate to classification?

Challenge Questions

1. What, in your opinion, will be the major impact of the Walmart decision to purchase FOB from its suppliers? The current stated objective is to reduce transportation costs on freight inbound to Walmart's distribution centers. How might the business relationship be impacted if, at some future time, Walmart decides to bypass its distribution centers and move merchandise direct from suppliers to its retail stores?

2. What could the long-term impacts of the electronic logging device mandate be on the trucking industry? Assume both positive and negative potential impacts. What participant in the supply chain (e.g., shipper, carrier, driver) would be most directly affected by each?

3. How might the continued growth of e-commerce affect existing shipping infrastructure?

4. Supporters of cube-based pricing feel traditional pricing methods are overcomplicated and reduce transportation efficiency. As a newly minted logistics graduate, assume your employer asks for your evaluation of the tradition versus cube-based LTL pricing. Make sure to include the potential impact of dimensioners in your evaluation. State your position as either a shipper or a carrier.

CHAPTER 9

Warehousing, Materials Handling, and Packaging

Chapter Outline

Warehousing, materials handling, and packaging combine to incorporate many different aspects of logistics operations. Often addressed independently, in this text they are presented collectively, forming an integrated functional area that affects all areas of the supply chain. Because there are many different types of warehouses and numerous materials handling and packaging considerations, they do not fit into a neat classification scheme as used in areas such as order management, inventory, and transportation. A *warehouse* has traditionally been viewed as a place to hold or store inventory. *Materials handling* and *packaging* have traditionally been viewed as basic functions that collectively support the handling of, identification, and protection of product. However in contemporary logistical systems, warehouse functionality has become strategic in nature, providing numerous benefits that take into consideration significant complexities to most efficiently meet customer requirements. Similarly, materials handling, encouraged by the advent of e-commerce, is now frequently considered as a very large and strategic capital investment by many firms. Finally, packaging has continued to evolve, simultaneously incorporating both commercial marketing-related elements as well as industrial handling considerations. This chapter provides a foundation for understanding the value warehousing, materials handling, and packaging contribute to the logistics process. The discussion is broad, and the objective is to introduce general managerial considerations related to this integrated functional area.

Strategic Warehousing

While effective logistics systems should not be designed to hold inventory for extended times, there are occasions when inventory storage is justified on the basis of service and cost.

Storage has always been an important aspect of economic development. In the preindustrial era, storage was performed by individual households forced to function as self-sufficient economic units. As transportation capability developed, it became possible to engage in specialization. Product storage shifted from households to retailers, wholesalers, and manufacturers. Warehouses stored inventory in the logistics pipeline, serving to coordinate product supply and consumer demand. These initial warehouses provided a necessary bridge between production and marketing.

Following World War II, managerial attention shifted toward strategic storage. In the distributive industries such as wholesaling and retailing, it was traditionally considered best practice to dedicate a warehouse containing a full assortment of inventory to every sales territory. As forecasting and production scheduling techniques improved, management questioned such risky inventory deployment. Seasonal production and consumption still required warehousing, but the overall need for storage to support stable manufacturing and consumption patterns was reduced.

Changing consumer demand more than offset any reduction in warehousing resulting from these manufacturing improvements. Retailers, faced with the challenge of providing consumers an increasing assortment of products, found it more difficult to maintain purchasing and transportation economics when buying direct from suppliers. Progressive wholesalers and integrated retailers developed state-of-the-art warehouse systems to logistically support retail inventory replenishment. Thus, the focus on warehousing shifted from passive storage to strategic inventory assortment. The term **distribution center** became widely used throughout industry to capture this dynamic development in traditional warehousing.

Improvements in retail warehousing efficiency soon were adopted by manufacturing. For manufacturers, strategic warehousing offered a way to reduce holding or dwell time of materials and parts. Warehousing became integral to just-in-time (**JIT**) and stockless production strategies. While the basic notion of JIT is to reduce work-in-process inventory, such manufacturing strategies need dependable logistics support.

On the outbound, or market-facing, side of manufacturing, warehouses can be used to create product assortments for customer shipment. The capability to receive mixed product shipments offers customers two specific advantages. First, logistical cost is reduced because an assortment of products can be delivered while taking advantage of consolidated transportation. Second, inventory of slow-moving products can be reduced because of the capability to receive smaller quantities as part of a larger consolidated shipment. Manufacturers that provide sorted and sequenced product shipments on a timely basis are positioned to achieve a competitive advantage.

An important goal in warehousing is to maximize flexibility. Flexibility is facilitated by information technology. Technology has influenced almost every aspect of warehouse operations by creating new and better ways to perform storage and handling. Flexibility is also an essential part of being able to respond to ever-changing customer demand in terms of product assortments, value-added services, and the manner in which shipments are sequenced and presented. Information technology facilitates flexibility by allowing warehouse operators to quickly react to changing customer requirements.

Benefits realized from strategic warehousing are classified as service and economic. No warehousing should be included in a logistical system unless it is fully justified on some combination of cost and service. Ideally, a warehouse will simultaneously provide both service and economic benefits.

Service Benefits

Warehouses can provide services that enhance top-line revenue growth. When a warehouse is primarily justified on service, the supporting rationale is that profits from sales improvements will more than offset added cost. It is a difficult assignment to quantify service return-on-investment because it's hard to measure. For example, establishing a warehouse to service a specific market may increase cost but should also increase market sales, revenue, and potentially gross margin. Warehouses can improve service in three ways: (1) spot-stocking, (2) full-line stocking, and (3) value-added services.

Spot-Stocking

Spot-stocking is typically used to support customer requirements. Manufacturers of highly seasonal products often spot-stock. Instead of maintaining inventory in a warehouse year-round, or shipping to customers direct from manufacturing plants, responsiveness in peak selling periods can be enhanced through temporary inventory positioning in strategic markets. Under this concept, select inventory is positioned or **spot-stocked** in a local market warehouse in anticipation of responding to customer need during the critical sales period. Utilizing warehouse facilities for spot-stocking allows inventories to be placed in a variety of markets adjacent to key customers just prior to a period of high seasonal sales. For example, agricultural fertilizer companies sometimes spot-stock near farmers in anticipation of the growing season. After the growing season, such spot-stocking would likely be reduced or eliminated.

Full-Line Stocking

The traditional use of warehouses by manufacturers, wholesalers, and retailers is to stock product inventory combinations in anticipation of customer orders. Typical retailers and wholesalers provide inventory assortments of multiple products from different manufacturers. In effect, these warehouses provide one-stop shopping capability for goods from multiple manufacturers.

The difference between spot-stocking and full-line stocking is the degree and duration of warehouse utilization. A firm following a spot-stocking strategy would temporarily warehouse a narrow product assortment in a large number of warehouses for a limited time period. The full-line stocking warehouse is more often restricted to a few strategic locations and operates year-round. Full-line stocking warehouses improve service by reducing the number of suppliers that a customer must logistically deal with. The combined assortments also make economical larger shipments possible.

Value-Added Services

The demand for highly customized service has transformed modern distribution warehouses into facilities that specialize in performing **value-added services (VAS)**. A value-added service is any work that creates a greater value for customers. Value-added services typically change the physical features or configuration of products so they are presented to customers in a unique or customized manner. Table 9.1 provides a list of typical value-added services.

Warehouses can postpone final product configuration by completing packaging, labeling, and even light manufacturing. For example, vegetables can be processed and canned in **brights** at the processing plants. Brights are cans without labels. Holding inventory as brights means that product is not committed to specific customers or carton configuration during initial manufacturing or processing. Once a specific customer order is received, the warehouse can complete labeling and finalize packaging. Examples of postponement range from packaging pharmaceuticals at Bristol Meyers Squibb to customizing appliances at Whirlpool.

Postponement provides two economic benefits. First, risk is minimized because customized packaging is not performed in anticipation of customer orders or to accommodate a forecast. Second, total inventory can be reduced by using inventory of the base product to aggregate demand across multiple customers' requirements. The combination of reduced risk and lower inventory can result in reduced total cost to service even if packaging performed at the warehouse is more expensive per unit than if it were completed during manufacturing.

Economic Benefits

Economic benefits of warehousing occur when overall logistics costs are reduced. For example, if adding a warehouse in a logistical system reduces overall transportation cost by an amount greater than required investment and operational cost, then total cost will

TABLE 9.1
Value-Added Services

• Cross-dock/transloading	• Order fulfillment
• Customer returns	• Pick/pack
• Home delivery	• Pool distribution
• In-transit merge	• Repair/refurbish
• Kan Ban	• Returnable container management
• Kitting	• Reverse logistics
• Labeling/preticketing	• RFID tag application
• Lot control	• Sequencing/metering
• Mass customization/postponement	• Specialty packaging
• Manufacturing support	• Store support/direct store delivery (DSD)

be reduced. When total cost reductions are achievable, the warehouse is economically justified. Four basic economic benefits are: (1) consolidation and break-bulk, (2) sorting, (3) seasonal storage, and (4) reverse logistics.

Consolidation and Break-Bulk

The economic benefits of consolidation and break-bulk are to reduce transportation cost by using warehouse capability to increase the size of shipments.

In consolidation, the warehouse receives inventory, from a number of sources, that are combined into a large single shipment to a specific destination. The benefits of consolidation are the realization of the lowest possible freight rate, timely and controlled delivery, and reduced congestion at a customer's receiving dock. The consolidation enables both the inbound movement from origin and the outbound movement to destination to be consolidated into a larger shipment, which generally results in lower transportation charges per unit and most often quicker delivery.

A break-bulk operation receives a single large shipment and arranges for delivery to multiple destinations. Economy of scale is achieved by transporting the larger shipment from origin to destination. The break-bulk warehouse or terminal sorts or splits the larger shipment into individual orders for customer delivery.

Both consolidation and break-bulk arrangements use warehouse capacity to improve transportation efficiency. Many logistical arrangements involve both consolidation and break-bulk. Figure 9.1 illustrates each activity.

Sorting

The basic benefit of sorting is to reconfigure freight as it is being transported from origin to destination. Three types of assortment—cross-docking, mixing, and assembly—are widely performed in logistical systems.

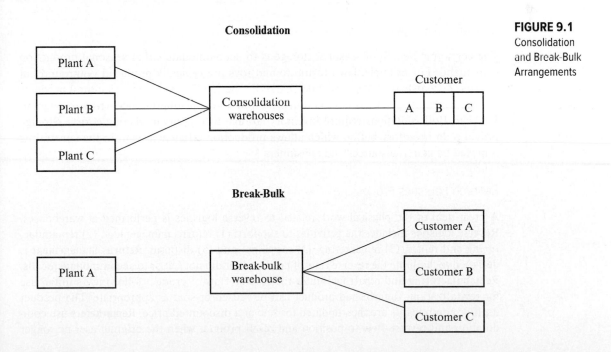

FIGURE 9.1
Consolidation and Break-Bulk Arrangements

The objective of **cross-docking** is to combine inventory from multiple origins into a customized assortment to meet the needs of a specific customer. Retailers make extensive use of cross-dock operations to replenish fast-moving store inventories. Cross-docking requires precise on-time delivery from each manufacturer. As product is received and unloaded at the cross-dock, it is sorted by customer destination. In most instances, the customer has communicated precise volume requirements of each product, requested for each delivery destination. The manufacturers, in turn, may have sorted, loaded, and labeled the appropriate quantity by final destination when trailers were loaded at origin. Product is then literally moved across the dock from receiving into a truck dedicated to the delivery destination. Once outbound trucks are loaded with mixed product from multiple manufacturers, they are released for transport to destination. The high degree of precision required for effective cross-docking makes successful operation highly dependent on information technology.

An end result similar to cross-docking is achieved by **mixing**. However, mixing is usually performed at an intermediate location between shipment origin and destination. In a typical mixing operation, carloads or truckloads of products are shipped from origin to mixing facilities. These inbound shipments are planned to minimize inbound transportation cost. Upon arrival at the mixing warehouse, shipments are unloaded and sorted into the combination desired by each customer. During the mixing process, inbound products can be combined with others regularly stocked at a warehouse. Warehouses that perform mixing have the net effect of reducing overall product storage in a logistical system while achieving customer-specific assortments and minimizing transportation cost.

The most common use of **assembly** is to support manufacturing operations. Products and components are assembled from a variety of second-tier suppliers at an assembly facility located in close proximity to the manufacturing plant. While manufacturing organizations have traditionally performed assembly, it has become common to utilize value-added services performed by an **integrated service provider** (ISP) to sort, sequence, and deliver components when needed in manufacturing. Like cross-docking and mixing, assembly creates a precise grouping of inventory at a precise time and location. Figure 9.2 illustrates three sorting arrangements.

Seasonal Storage

The economic benefit of seasonal storage is to accommodate either seasonal production or demand. For example, lawn furniture and toys are typically produced year-round but are sold primarily during a very short marketing period. In contrast, agricultural products are harvested at specific times, with distribution and consumption occurring throughout the year. Both situations require inventory storage to support marketing efforts. Storage provides an inventory buffer, which allows production efficiencies within the constraints imposed by material sources and consumers.

Reverse Logistics Processing

A great deal of the physical work related to reverse logistics is performed at warehouses. Reverse logistics includes the activities to support: (1) returns management, (2) remanufacturing and repair, (3) remarketing, (4) recycling, and (5) disposal. **Returns management** is designed to facilitate the reverse flow of product that did not sell or to accommodate recalls. **Remanufacturing** and repair facilitates the reverse flow of product following its initial use for revitalization. Refurbished product can be reused or sold as appropriate. The product itself or components are then updated for sale at a discounted price. **Remarketers** use coordination and reverse flow to position and resell product when the original user no longer

FIGURE 9.2
Sorting Arrangements

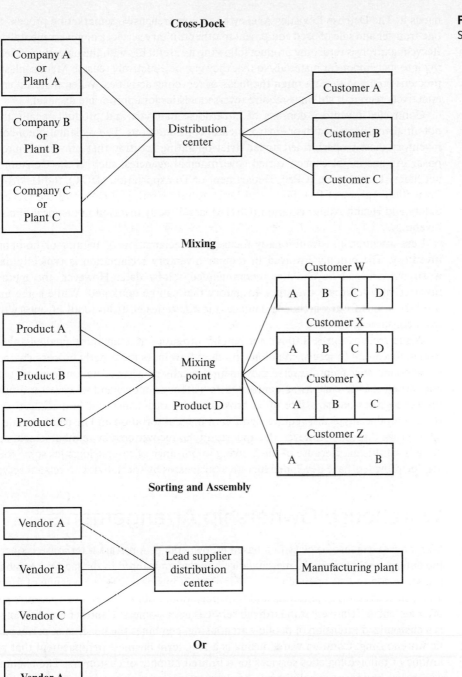

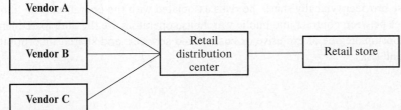

needs it. The Defense Logistics Agency has a comprehensive remarketing process to facilitate transfer and sale of used equipment to other military services or governmental agencies. **Recycling** involves returning product following its useful life with the objective of decomposing it to its component materials so that they can be effectively reused. Metals, plastics, and precious commodities are often the focus of recycling activities. When material cannot be effectively reused, it still may require reverse logistics for appropriate **disposal**.

Controlled inventory consists of hazardous materials and product recalls that have potential consumer health or environmental considerations. The reclamation of controlled inventory must be performed under strict operating scrutiny that prevents improper disposal. As one might expect, varied governmental agencies, such as the Consumer Product Safety Commission **(CPS)**, Department of Transportation **(DOT)**, the Environmental Protection Agency **(EPA)**, Food and Drug Administration **(FDA)**, and the Occupational Safety and Health Administration **(OSHA)**, are directly involved in disposal of controlled inventory.

Less attention has traditionally focused on reclamation of regular or non-controlled inventory. The product involved in regular inventory reclamation is typically damaged, worn out or aged beyond the recommended sell-by date. However, the merchandise involved may represent overstock inventory that can be marketed. While some unsalable product results from warehouse damage, most is returned from retail inventory or direct from consumers.

While reclamation is difficult for regular inventory, it is far more challenging for controlled inventory. In return situations, product flow lacks the orderly process characteristic of outbound movement. Reverse movement typically consists of nonuniform package sizes and varied master cartons as contrasted to outbound movement of cases and pallets. In reverse logistics packages are often broken, and product may not be packaged correctly. Return products typically require significant manual sortation and inspection to determine appropriate disposal. However, the opportunity to recover cost by reimbursement and recycling is significant. Because of the growing importance of reverse logistics some integrated service providers have developed lucrative businesses by specializing in related services.

Warehouse Ownership Arrangements

Warehouses can also be classified based on ownership. A **private** warehouse is operated by the enterprise that owns the merchandise handled and stored in the facility. A **public** warehouse, in contrast, is operated as an independent business offering a range of for-hire services, such as storage, handling, and transportation. Public warehouse operators generally offer a menu of relatively standardized services to customers. **Contract warehousing**, which is a customized extension of public warehousing, combines the benefits of private and public warehousing. Contract warehousing is a long-term business arrangement that provides unique or tailored logistics services for a limited number of customers. The client and the warehouse provider typically share the risks associated with the operation. The important differences between contract and public warehouse operators are the anticipated length of the relationship, degree of exclusive or customized services, and shared incorporation of benefits and risks.

Private

A private warehouse is typically operated by the firm owning the product. The building, however, may be owned or leased. The decision concerning ownership or lease is primarily based on financial considerations. Sometimes it is not possible to find a warehouse for lease that fits specialized logistical requirements; for example, the physical nature of an available building may not be conducive for efficient handling, such as buildings with inappropriate storage racks or with shipping/receiving dock or support column constraints. The only suitable course of action may then be to design and arrange for new construction.

The major benefits of private warehousing are control, flexibility, cost, and a range of intangibles. Private warehouses offer substantial control since management has authority to prioritize activities. Such control should facilitate integration of warehouse operations with the balance of a firm's logistics operations.

Private warehouses generally offer more flexibility since operating policies, hours, and procedures can be adjusted to meet specific customer and product requirements. Firms with very specialized customers or products are often motivated to own and operate warehouses.

Private warehousing is usually considered less costly than public warehousing because private facilities are not operated for a profit. As a result, both the fixed and variable cost components of a private warehouse may be lower than for-hire counterparts.

Finally, private warehousing may offer intangible benefits. A private warehouse, with the firm's name on its sign, may stimulate customer perceptions of responsiveness and stability. This perception may provide marketing image in comparison to competitors.

Despite the noted benefits, the use of private warehousing is declining because of an increasing managerial interest in reducing capital invested in logistical assets. Also, the perceived cost benefit of private warehousing is potentially offset by a public warehouse's ability to gain operational economies of scale and scope as a result of the combined throughput of multiple clients.

Public

Public warehouses are used extensively in logistical systems. Almost any combination of services can be arranged on a for-hire basis for either short or long term. Public warehouses have traditionally been classified based on operational specialization such as (1) general merchandise, (2) refrigerated, (3) special commodity, (4) bonded, and (5) household goods and furniture.

General merchandise warehouses are designed to handle package products such as electronics, paper, food, small appliances, and household supplies. **Refrigerated warehouses** typically offer frozen or cooler capacity designed to protect food, medical, photographic, and chemical products requiring temperature control. **Special commodity** warehouses are designed to handle bulk material or items requiring special handling, such as tires or clothing. **Bonded warehouses** are licensed by the government to store goods prior to payment of taxes or import/export duties. They exert tight control over movements in and out of the facility, since documents must accompany each move. Finally, **household goods or furniture warehouses** specialize in handling and storing large, bulky items such as appliances and furniture. Of course, many public warehouses offer a combination of services. Public warehouses provide flexibility and shared services benefits. They have the potential to offer operating and management expertise since warehousing is their core business.

From a financial perspective, public warehousing may be able to achieve lower operating cost than private facilities. Such variable cost differential may result from lower wage scales, better productivity, and shared overhead among clients. Public warehouses typically do not require capital investment on the part of their customers. When management performance is judged according to return on investment, the use of public warehousing can be an attractive alternative. Public warehousing offers flexibility concerning size and number of warehouses, thus allowing users to respond to supplier, customer, and seasonal demands. In comparison, private warehouses are relatively fixed and difficult to change because buildings have to be constructed, expanded as necessary and sold when no longer required.

Public warehousing also have the potential to share scale economies since the combined requirements of users can be leveraged. Such leverage spreads fixed costs and may justify investment in state-of-the-art handling equipment. A public warehouse may also leverage transportation by providing consolidation of multiple-client freight. For example, rather than require both supplier A and supplier B to deliver to a retail store from their own warehouses, a public warehouse serving both clients could arrange combined delivery, thus providing reduced transportation cost for the customer.

A great many firms utilize public warehouses for customer accommodation because of the variable cost, scalability, range of services, and flexibility. A public warehouse charges clients a basic fee for in and out handling plus storage. In the case of handling, the charge is assessed on the cases or pounds moved. For storage, the charge is assessed on the pallets or square footage used over time. Special or value-added services provided by public warehouses are typically priced on a negotiated basis.

Contract

Contract warehousing combines characteristics of private and public operations. A long-term contractual relationship will typically result in lower total cost than a public warehouse. In fact many contract warehouse providers have extensive real estate investments. One integrated service provider (ISP) may own and operate facilities in multiple key manufacturing or distribution locations. Thus, one provider may be able to meet a customer's requirements in a combination of markets. At the same time, contract warehouse operations can provide benefits of expertise, flexibility, scalability, and economies of scale by sharing management, labor, equipment, and information resources across multiple clients.

Contract warehouses typically offer a range of logistical services such as transportation management, inventory control, order processing, customer service, and return merchandise processing. Contract logistics firms, typically called **integrated service providers** (**ISPs**), are capable of performing the total logistics responsibility for an enterprise.

Network Deployment

As would be expected, many firms utilize a combination of private, public, and contract facilities. Full warehouse utilization throughout a year is rare. As a managerial guideline, a typical warehouse will be fully utilized between 75 and 85 percent of the time; so from 15 to 25 percent of the time, space needed to satisfy peak requirements will not be used. In such situations, a deployment strategy may be the use of private or contract warehouses to cover the 75 percent requirement while public facilities are used to accommodate peak demand.

Developing a warehouse network strategy requires answers to two key questions. The first is how many warehouses are required. The second question focuses on which warehouse ownership types should be used in specific markets. For many firms, the answer is a combination of warehouse alternatives, differentiated by customer and product. Specifically, some customer groups may be served best from a private warehouse, while public or contract warehouses may be appropriate for others. This warehouse segmentation is increasingly popular as key customers are requiring more customized value-added services and capabilities.

Warehouse Decisions

The basic concept that warehouses provide an enclosure for material storage and handling requires detailed analysis before the size, type, and shape of the facility can be determined. This section reviews planning issues that establish the character of the warehouse, which in turn determines attainable handling efficiency. These decisions are more common in private warehousing as compared to public when facilities already exist.

Site Selection

The first task is to identify both the general area and then the specific warehouse location. The general area concerns the broad geography where an active warehouse makes sense from a service, economic, and strategic perspective. The general question focuses on the broader geographic area as illustrated by the need to place a warehouse in the Midwest, which generally implies having a facility in Illinois, Indiana, or Wisconsin. In contrast, a retailer such as Target or Home Depot typically selects a warehouse location that is central to a prerequisite number of retail store locations. Thus, the selection and number of retail outlets drive the support warehouse location. Network design is discussed in Chapter 11.

Once the general warehouse location is determined, a specific building site must be identified. Typical areas in a community for locating warehouses are commercial developments and outlying or suburban areas. The factors driving site selection are service availability and cost. Land cost is an important factor. In many cities, warehouses are among industrial plants and in areas zoned for light or heavy industry. Most warehouses can operate legally under the restrictions placed upon general commercial property.

Beyond procurement cost, setup, and operating expenses such as transport access, utility hookups, taxes, and insurance rates require evaluation. The cost of essential services may vary extensively between sites.

Several other requirements must be satisfied before a site is selected. The site must offer adequate room for expansion. Necessary utilities must be available. The soil must be capable of supporting the structure. The site must be sufficiently high to afford proper water drainage. Additional requirements may be situationally necessary, depending upon the structure to be constructed. For these reasons and others, the final selection of the site should be preceded by extensive analysis.

Design

Warehouse design must consider product movement characteristics. Three factors to be determined during the design process are the number of floors to include in the facility, a cube utilization plan, and product flow.

The ideal warehouse design is a one-floor building that eliminates the need to move product vertically. The use of vertical handling devices, such as elevators and conveyors, to move product from one floor to the next requires time and energy, and typically creates handling bottlenecks. So, while it is not always possible, particularly in business districts where land is restricted or expensive, as a general rule distribution warehouses should be designed as one-floor operations to facilitate handling.

Warehouse design must maximize cubic utilization. Most warehouses are designed with 30- to 40-foot clear ceilings, although selected automated and high-rise handling equipment can effectively use heights over 100 feet. Maximum effective warehouse height is limited by the safe lifting capabilities of handling equipment, such as lift trucks, rack design, and fire safety regulations imposed by sprinkler systems.

FIGURE 9.3
Basic Warehouse Design

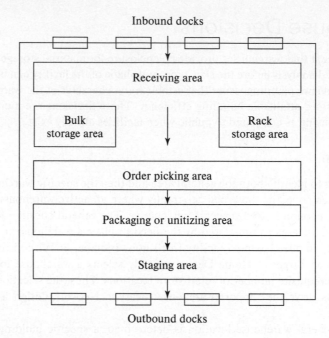

Warehouse design should facilitate continuous straight product flow through the building. This is true whether the product is moving into storage or is being cross-docked. In general, this means that product should be received at one end of a building, stored as necessary in the middle, and shipped from the other end. Figure 9.3 illustrates straight-line product flow that facilitates velocity while minimizing congestion and redundant handling.

Product-Mix Analysis

An important area is the analysis of products that will be distributed through the warehouse. The design and operation of a warehouse are both dependent on the product mix. Each product should be analyzed in terms of annual demand, weight, cube, and packaging. It is also important to determine the total size, cube, and weight of the average order to be processed through the warehouse. These data provide necessary information for determining warehouse space, design and layout, handling equipment, operating procedures, and controls.

Expansion

Because warehouses are increasingly important in supply chain networks, their future expansion should be considered during the initial planning phase. It is common to establish 5- to 10-year expansion plans. Potential expansion may justify purchase or option of a site three to five times larger than required to support initial construction.

Building design should also accommodate future expansion. Some walls may be constructed of semipermanent materials to allow quick removal. Floor areas, designed to support heavy movements, can be extended during initial construction to facilitate expansion.

Handling

A handling system is the basic driver of warehouse design. A warehouse is appropriately viewed as a structure designed to facilitate efficient product flow. It is important to stress that the handling system must be selected early in the warehouse development process. Handling equipment and technology are discussed later in this chapter.

Layout

The layout or storage areas of a warehouse should be planned to facilitate product flow. The layout and the handling system are integral. In addition, special attention must be given to location, number, and design of receiving and loading docks.

It is difficult to generalize warehouse layouts since they are usually customized to accommodate specific product handling requirements. If pallets are utilized, an early step is to determine the appropriate size. A pallet of nonstandard size may be desirable for specialized products. The most common pallet sizes are 40 × 48 inches and 32 × 40 inches. Analysis of product cases, stacking patterns, and industry practices will determine the size of pallet best suited to the operation.

The second step in planning warehouse layout involves pallet positioning. The most common practice in positioning pallets is at 90 degree, or square, placement to the aisle. The placement of specific products in selected pallet locations is called **slotting**. Naturally, key to an efficient layout is a well-developed slotting plan.

Finally, the handling equipment must be integrated to finalize layout. The path and tempo of product flow depend upon the handling system. To illustrate the relationship between handling and layout, two systems and their respective layouts are illustrated in Figure 9.4. These examples represent two of many possible layouts.

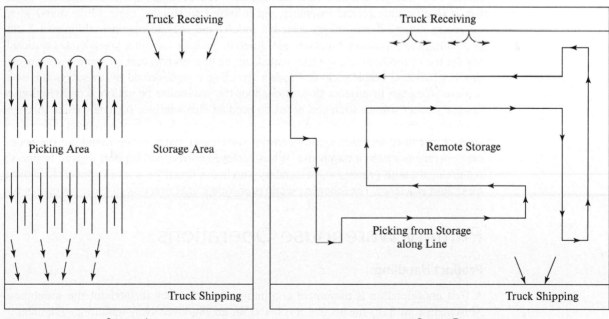

FIGURE 9.4   Layouts A and B

Layout A illustrates a handling system and layout utilizing lift trucks for inbound and inventory transfer movements. Tow tractors and inventory collection trailers are used for order selection. This scenario assumes that products can be palletized. This layout is greatly simplified because offices, special areas, and other details are omitted.

Layout B illustrates a handling system utilizing lift trucks to move product inbound and for transfer movements. A continuous towline is used for order selection. In a system using a continuous-movement towline, the compact selection area is replaced by order selection directly from storage.

As indicated, both layouts A and B are greatly simplified. The purpose is to illustrate the extremely different approaches managers have developed to reconcile the relationship between handling and warehouse layout.

Sizing

Several techniques are available to help estimate warehouse size. Each method begins with a projection of the total volume expected to move through the warehouse during a given period. The projection is used to estimate base and safety stocks for each product to be stocked in the warehouse. Some techniques consider both normal and peak inventory. Failure to consider utilization rates can result in overbuilding. It is important to note, however, that a major complaint of warehouse managers is underestimation of warehouse size requirements. A good rule of thumb is to allow for 10 percent additional space to account for increased volume, new products, and new business opportunities.

Warehouse Operations

Once the scope of a given warehouse is determined, managerial attention focuses on establishing the operation. A typical warehouse contains materials, parts, and finished goods inventory. Primary warehouse functions include product handling and storage. The objective is to efficiently receive inventory, put it away into storage, move while stored when necessary, assemble into unique customer orders, and execute customer shipments. Complimenting these primary functions are different product handling considerations including the use of mechanized, semiautomated, automated systems and, in some cases, special product handling considerations. Product handling complimented by these systems help achieve efficiency in product flow throughout the warehouse operation. Consideration of unique product storage strategies based on product characteristic such as volume throughput further advances the opportunity for overall efficiency. Secondary warehouse operations such as inventory accuracy, facility security, safety, and maintenance round out the necessary operations within a warehouse. When deployed correctly to support a given business's requirements, both primary and secondary warehouse functions work in concert to achieve maximum efficiency. The following sections provide a brief overview of these key elements.

Primary Warehouse Operations

Product Handling

A first consideration is movement continuity and efficiency throughout the warehouse. Movement continuity means that it is better for an employee using handling equipment to perform longer moves than to undertake a number of short handlings to accomplish the same overall inventory move. Exchanging products between handlers or moving goods from one piece of equipment to another wastes time and increases the potential for product damage. Thus, as a general rule, longer warehouse handling movements are preferred. Ideally, goods, once in motion, should be continuously moved until arrival at their final destination.

Scale economies justify moving the largest quantities or loads possible. Instead of moving individual cases, handling procedures should be designed to move cases grouped on pallets, slipsheets, or containers. The overall objective of handling is to eventually sort inbound shipments into unique customer assortments. The five primary handling activities are receiving, putaway in-storage handling, order-picking, and shipping.

Receiving

The majority of products and materials arrive at warehouses in large-quantity truck shipments. The first handling activity is unloading. At most warehouses, unloading is performed using a combination of lift trucks, conveyors, and manual processes. When the freight is floor stacked in the transportation vehicle, the typical procedure is to group products by SKU into unit loads using pallets or other methods of conveyance. In some situations, products are placed directly onto conveyors to facilitate receiving. When inbound product arrives unitized on pallets or in containers, lift trucks are primarily used to move the product from vehicles to the receiving dock. A primary benefit of receiving unitized loads is the ability to rapidly unload and release inbound transportation equipment. The receiving process is also responsible for ensuring the SKUs and quantities on the bill of lading match the physical receipt. Receiving teams are often responsible for reporting over, short, and damage (OS&D) to the administrative office so it can be shared with the shipper for commercial reconciliation. Receiving product accurately and efficiently is the first step toward running an efficient warehouse operation.

Product Putaway

In the vast majority of applications, the second handling function is product putaway. Product may be placed in active storage locations or in secondary locations. Depending on how the product is unitized, this could include floor-stacking product, placing pallets of product into racks, or placing individual packages into flow racks or other storage systems. Product putaway is usually designed to be as efficient as possible, meaning the use of fork trucks and or other tools to help achieve speed of operations are common.

In-Storage Product Handling

Once product is placed into a storage location, it is fairly common for that product to be moved within the facility for a variety of reasons. One reason could be the replenishment of active storage locations with inventory originally placed in secondary location. This concept is often referred to as *replenishment*. The amount of replenishment a warehouse must complete is usually a good indicator of active storage bin sizing and strategy. If a warehouse never needs to replenish, active storage locations may be too large, resulting in order-picking labor inefficiency. If replenishment occurs frequently, active storage areas may be too small, resulting in temporary stockouts, picking inefficiency, and proliferation of replenishment movements. It is critical to strike a balance regarding how much replenishment activity takes place within a given warehouse. Another handling operation could be product consolidation to create space efficiency. For example, a warehouse may have similar product with quantities on hand that enable the products to be combined in a common area to gain storage efficiency. Sometimes first-in, first-out (FIFO) sequencing requires product to be moved from secondary to primary storage by design due to product life cycle. In-storage product handling in a necessary element of warehouse handling but one that must be constantly monitored to ensure optimal efficiency.

Order-Picking

One of the primary handling operations within a warehouse is order-picking. The order-picking process requires that materials, parts, and products be grouped to facilitate order assembly. It is typical for one area of the warehouse to be designated as a selection or picking area to assemble orders. For each order, the combination of products must be selected and packaged to meet specific customer order requirements. An order could be a single case or an entire truck load of product. In most cases, products are picked and palletized by customer order. In some cases, a pallet could consist of one SKU and, in other cases, multiple SKUs. It is also common to see orders that will be sent for further breakdown (such as a customer warehouse) or orders that are prepared to be sent directly to the customer store shelf or planogram. Numerous strategies are used to drive order-picking efficiency, including splitting orders by type, utilizing different product handling equipment, conveyance materials, and work flow paths to minimize congestion and drive efficiency. Later in this chapter, handling systems primarily focused on order-picking will be discussed in more detail.

Shipping

Shipping consists of order verification and outbound transportation equipment loading. In comparison to receiving, warehouse shipping must accommodate relatively low-volume movements of a mixture of products, thus reducing the potential for economies of scale. *Order verification* includes the review and audit of product to ensure order accuracy and a review of product condition to ensure no damage has occurred during the picking process. Once verified, product is loaded into outbound transportation equipment using a combination of materials handling equipment. If an order has a very uniform pallet or product profile, truck loading with lift trucks may be easy, with pallets stacking neatly on top of each other and being placed in the truck with minimal effort. More common than not, though, pallets are unique shapes, size, and weights based on specific order profiles requiring a significant level of skill to effectively load and ensure no damage will occur while in transit. Trailer weight limits must be considered, and product is often braced for transit with what is referred to as dunnage, including air bags or wood or metal bars to ensure product stability. It is common for the shipping process to be documented by photo and archived so shipments with damages can be reviewed and corrective actions identified. It is also common in a warehouse to see the most tenured and skilled labor supporting the shipping process.

Product Handling Considerations

Advancements in handling technology and equipment offer the potential to substantially improve logistics productivity. Handling processes and technologies impact productivity by influencing personnel, space, and capital equipment requirements. While the technical details of handling technology are beyond the scope of this discussion, the following section reviews some basic handling considerations and alternative system solutions.

Basic Handling Considerations

There are several basic principles to guide the selection of handling processes and technologies. The principles summarized in Table 9.2 offer an initial foundation for evaluating handling alternatives.

• Equipment for handling and storage should be as standardized as possible.
• When in motion, the system should be designed to provide maximum continuous product flow.
• Investment should be in handling rather than stationary equipment.
• Handling equipment should be utilized to the maximum extent possible.
• In handling equipment selection the ratio of dead weight to payload should be minimized.
• Whenever practical, gravity flow should be incorporated in system design.

TABLE 9.2
Principles of Handling

Handling systems can be classified as **mechanized**, **semiautomated**, and **automated**. In some cases, special handling considerations exist. A combination of labor and handling equipment is utilized in mechanized systems to facilitate receiving, processing, and/or shipping. Generally, labor constitutes a high percentage of overall cost in mechanized handling. Automated systems, in contrast, attempt to minimize labor as much as possible by substituting equipment capital investment. When a combination of mechanical and automated systems is used to handle material, the system is referred to as semiautomated. Mechanized handling systems are most common, but the use of semiautomated, and automated. Each approach to handling is discussed in greater detail.

Mechanized Systems

Mechanized systems employ a wide range of handling equipment. The types of equipment most commonly used are lift trucks, rider trucks, towlines, tractor-trailer devices, conveyors, and carousels.

Lift Trucks

Lift trucks, also called forklifts, can move loads of master cartons both horizontally and vertically but are limited to handling unit loads. Skids, boxes, or containers may also be transported, depending upon the nature of the product.

Many types of lift trucks are available. High-stacking trucks are capable of up to 40 feet of vertical movement. Palletless or clamp trucks are available for handling products without pallets or slipsheets. Other lift truck variations are available for narrow aisle and side-loading operations. The lift truck is not economical for long-distance horizontal movement because of the high ratio of labor per unit of transfer. To overcome this limitation a great deal of research has focused on "driverless" fork trucks. These new advances are discussed under semi-automated handling systems. Conventional lift trucks are utilized in shipping and receiving operations and to place merchandise in high cube storage. The two most common power sources for lift trucks are propane gas and battery.

Towlines

Towlines consist of either in-floor or overhead-mounted cable or drag devices. They are utilized to provide continuous power to four-wheel trailers. The main advantage of a towline is continuous movement. However, such handling devices have far less flexibility than lift trucks. The most common application of towlines is for master carton order selection. Order selectors place master cartons on four-wheel trailers that are then towed to the shipping dock. A number of automated decoupling devices are available to route trailers from the main towline to specified shipping docks.

Tractor Trailers

Tractor trailers consist of a driver-guided power unit towing one or more four-wheel trailers. The typical size of the trailers is 4 × 8 feet. The tractor in combination with trailer, like a towline, is used during order selection. The main advantage of a tow tractor with trailers is flexibility. It is not as economical as the towline because each tow unit requires a driver.

Conveyors

Conveyors are used widely in shipping and receiving operations and serve as the basic handling device for a number of order selection systems. Conveyors are classified according to power, gravity, and roller or belt movement. In power configurations, the conveyor is driven by a chain. Considerable conveyor flexibility is sacrificed in power configurations. Gravity and roller driven applications permit rearrangement with minimum difficulty. Portable gravity-style roller conveyors are often used for loading and unloading and, in some cases, are transported in over-the-road trailers to assist in unloading vehicles.

Carousels

A carousel operates on a different concept than most other mechanized handling equipment. Rather than requiring the order selector to go to the inventory storage location, the carousel moves inventory to the order selector. A carousel consists of a series of bins mounted on an oval track or rack. There may be multiple track levels, allowing for very high-density carousel storage. The entire carousel rotates, moving the storage bin to a stationary product selection position. The typical carousel application is for the selection of items to be packed for shipment. The rationale behind carousel systems is to reduce order selection labor by reducing walking length and time. Carousels, particularly modern stackable or multitiered systems, also significantly reduce storage space requirements. Some carousel systems also utilize computer-generated pick lists and computer-directed carousel rotation to further increase order selector productivity. These systems, such as **pick-to-light**, are referred to as **paperless picking** because no paperwork exists to slow down employee efforts.

This handling equipment discussion introduces a wide range of mechanized handling alternatives. Most systems combine different handling devices. For example, lift trucks may be used for vertical movements while tow tractor with trailers or rider trucks are the primary methods of horizontal transfer.

Semiautomated Systems

Mechanized handling is often supplemented by semiautomatic equipment. Typical equipment utilized in semiautomated handling includes automated guided vehicle systems, computerized sortation, robotics, and various forms of live racks.

Automated Guided Vehicles

An automated guided vehicle (AGV) system typically replaces mechanized tow tractors and trailers. The essential difference is that AGVs are automatically routed, positioned, and activated without a driver.

AGV equipment typically relies on an optical, magnetic, or wireless radio guidance system. In the optical application directional lines are placed on the warehouse floor. The AGV is then guided by a light beam focused on the guidepath. Magnetic AGVs follow an energized wire installed within the floor. Wireless radio (Wi-Fi) direction is guided by high-frequency transmission. The primary advantage of an AGV is direct labor reduction. AGVs using wireless guidance systems are not limited to predetermined warehouse flow routes. Lower cost and increased flexibility have enhanced the applicability of AGVs for warehouse movements that are repetitive and frequent or occur in very congested areas.

Sortation

Automated sortation devices are typically used in combination with conveyors. As products are selected in the warehouse and placed on a conveyor for movement to the shipping dock, they often must be sorted into specific combinations for customer delivery. For example, inventory to satisfy multiple orders may be selected in batches, creating the need for sortation and sequencing into individual orders prior to shipment. Most sortation devices can be programmed to permit customized flow and decision logic to accommodate unique requirements.

Automated sortation provides two primary benefits. The first is a reduction in labor. The second is a significant increase in speed and accuracy of order selection. High-speed sortation systems, such as those used by United Parcel Service, can sort and align packages at rates exceeding one package per second.

Robotics

One of the fastest-growing methods of materials handling is the use of robots. The robot is a machine that can be programmed to perform one or more handling activities without the intervention of an attendant or driver. Initial attention to robotics resulted from attempts in the early 1980s to employ limited-function stationary robots in automotive assembly. The automotive experiment was less than a total success. However, a great deal of advancement in robotics has occurred over the past 30 years. The primary use of robotics today is materials handling in both manufacturing and warehouse operating environments.

Robotics are increasingly being used in many different handling environments. Initially, robotic applications were attractive as replacements for manual labor in highly repetitive situations. For example early robotic applications were in palletizing, order selection, and routine material handling situations. A primary benefit of robotics is their sustainable performance accuracy. Economic justification of robotics is typically driven by some combination of five factors: (1) space limitations; (2) faster order to delivery cycle time requirements; (3) predictable and substantial throughput volume; (4) high labor costs; and/or (5) restrictive work environments such as frozen food warehouse order selection.

Recent years have witnessed significant advancements in the development of flexibility in robotic applications. Applications gaining popularity are inbound merchandise put-a-way and order selection in frozen food distribution centers. In both examples, the use of robots reduces exposure of workers to the low temperature maintained in the working environment.

The long-term potential for the application of robots throughout the supply chain is promising. Almost any handling task that involves repetitive movements is a candidate for either automation or robotic processing. When the activity is stationary, such as palletizing or de-palletizing cartons of merchandize, the likely solution will be some form of automation. When the work task involves horizontal movement in multiple directions, the application is likely to involve some form of robotics.

In the longer term, it is likely that limited forms of driverless vehicles will increase in utilization. Pilotless airborne drones are increasingly being used in military operations as attack weapons and for surveillance. Semi-trucks have successfully been driven without drivers in the truck both within yard operations and for limited distances on public roads. While this form of robotics requires combined human and technology interaction, the range of potential applications seems unlimited. Of particular interest to future supply chain operations is the growing combination of physicians and robots in medical surgery. In selected surgical procedures, experienced physicians provide guidance and make critical decisions during the operation. The robot, a precise machine, is instructed by the physician to follow a specific routine and complete in sequence precise surgical procedures. Of course medical expertise is available in the operating facility to assist and complete the pre- and post-surgical protocols. An important point for future supply chain logistics applications is the potential generated by the fact that the physician and the robot do not have to be at the same physical location to complete a successful medical procedure. To capture this extended deployment, wherein expert knowledge is combined with robotic capability, we have adopted the term **probotics**.

Significant potential exists for increased use of robotics in warehousing and material handlings. Of particular interest are the applications that are extending the potential of probotics beyond the warehouse and factory walls.

Flow Racks

A device commonly used to reduce manual labor in warehouses is storage rack design in which product automatically flows to a selection position. The typical flow rack contains roller conveyors and is constructed for loading from the rear. The rear of the rack is elevated higher than the front, causing a gravity flow toward the front. When cartons or unit loads are removed from the front, all other cartons or loads in that specific rack flow forward.

The use of the flow rack reduces the need to use lift trucks to transfer unit loads. A significant advantage of flow rack storage is the potential for automatic rotation of product as a result of rear loading. Rear loading facilitates **first-in, first-out (FIFO)** inventory management. Applications of gravity flow racks are varied. For example, flow racks are typically utilized to sequence palletized fresh bread for shipping from bakeries.

Automated Systems

For several decades the concept of automated handling has offered great potential but limited success. Initial automated handling efforts focused on master carton order selection systems. Recently, emphasis has shifted to automated high-rise storage and retrieval systems. While the basic concepts of automation remain valid, the primary barriers are high capital investment and low degree of flexibility.

Potential to Automate

The appeal of automation is that it substitutes capital equipment for labor. In addition to requiring less direct labor, an automated system has the potential to operate faster and more accurately with less product damage than its mechanized counterpart.

To date, most automated systems have been designed and constructed for specific handling applications. The guidelines previously noted for selection of mechanized handling systems (Table 9.2) are not applicable to automated systems. For example, storage equipment in an automated system is an integral part of the handling capability and can represent as much as 50 percent of the total investment.

Although information technology plays an important part in all handling systems, it is essential in automated systems. Information technology controls the automated selection equipment and interfaces with the Warehouse Management System (**WMS**). A major disadvantage of automation is its dependency on proprietary information technology networks. Warehouse management systems will be discussed later in this chapter.

Order Selection

Initially, automation was focused on master carton selection and order assembly in the warehouse. Because of high labor intensity in order selection, the basic objective was to integrate mechanized, semiautomated, and automated handling into a system that offers the advantages of high productivity and accuracy while using minimal labor.

The general process begins with an automated order selection device preloaded with product. The device itself consists of a series of flow racks stacked vertically. Merchandise is loaded from the rear and permitted to flow forward in the flow rack on gravity conveyors until stopped by a rack door. Between or down the middle of the racks, power conveyors create a merchandise flow line, with several flow lines positioned vertical to each other, one to service each level or height of rack doors.

Upon receipt of an order, the warehouse control system generates sequenced instructions to trip the rack doors and allow merchandise to flow forward onto powered conveyors. The conveyors in turn transport merchandise to an order packing area for individual products to be placed in shipment containers prior to transfer to the shipment staging area. Product is, ideally, selected and loaded sequentially so it can be unloaded in the sequence desired by the customer.

Substantial advancements have been made in automated selection of case goods. The handling of fast-moving products in master cartons, typical of cross-docking, can be fully automated from the point of merchandise receipt to placement in over-the-road trailers. Such systems use an integrated network of power and gravity conveyors linking power-motivated live storage. The entire process is computer controlled and coupled with the merchandise order and WMS. Upon arrival, merchandise is automatically routed to the live storage position and inventory records are updated. When orders are received, merchandise is precubed to package or vehicle size and scheduled for selection. At the appropriate time, merchandise is selected in loading sequence and automatically moved by conveyor to the loading dock. In some situations, the first and only manual handling of the merchandise within the warehouse occurs when it is stacked into the outbound transport vehicle.

Automated Storage/Retrieval

An automated unit-load handling system, or **automated storage and retrieval system (AS/RS)**, using high-rise storage is an increasingly popular form of automation. Figure 9.5 illustrates the concept of a high-rise AS/RS. AS/RSs are particularly appropriate for items such as heavy boxes or those products in controlled environments such as bakeries or frozen food. The high-rise concept of handling is typically automated from receiving to shipping. The four primary AS/RS components include storage racks, storage and retrieval equipment, input/output system, and control system.

The name high-rise derives from the physical appearance of the storage rack. The rack is structured-steel vertical storage, which can be as high as 120 feet. The typical stacking height of palletized cartons in a mechanized handling system is 20 feet, so the potential

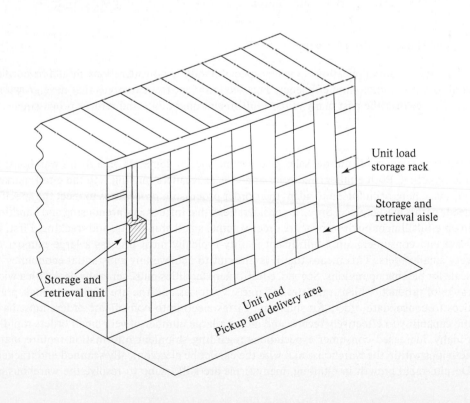

FIGURE 9.5
AS/RS High-Rise Warehouse

Unit load storage rack

Storage and retrieval aisle

Storage and retrieval unit

Unit load Pickup and delivery area

efficiency of high-rise storage is clear. Because humans are not an integral part of AS/RSs, these facilities are often referred to as **lights-out** facilities.

The initial function of the storage and retrieval equipment is to reach the desired storage location rapidly. A second function is to insert or remove merchandise from the rack.

The storage and retrieval machine is essentially a combined lift truck and pallet holder built into a movable crane. The machine moves up and down the aisle to insert or remove a unit load from a storage bin.

The input/output system in high-rise storage is concerned with moving loads to and from the rack area. Two types of movement are involved. First, loads must be transported from receiving docks or production lines to the storage area. Second, within the immediate peripheral area of the racks, loads must be positioned for entry or exit. In addition to scheduling arrivals and location assignments, the control system handles inventory control and stock rotation. The control system also tracks product location within the AS/RS, storage bin utilization, and crane operations. In the case of high-rise storage, system reliability and integrity are critical to achieving productivity and maximum equipment utilization.

In distribution applications, product flowing from production is automatically formed into unit loads. The unit load is then transported to the high-rise storage area by power conveyor. When the load arrives, it is assigned to a storage bin and transferred by power conveyor to the appropriate pickup station. At this point, the storage and retrieval equipment takes over and moves the unit load to its planned storage location. When orders are received, the control system directs the retrieval of specified unit loads. From the outbound delivery station, the unit load flows by power and gravity conveyor to the appropriate shipping dock. While retrieval and outbound delivery are being accomplished, all paperwork necessary to initiate product shipment is completed.

AS/RSs seek to increase materials handling productivity by providing maximum storage density per square foot of floor space and to minimize direct labor required in handling. The highly controlled nature of an AS/RS achieves reliable pilferage-free and damage-free handling with extremely accurate control.

Special Handling Considerations

There are certain applications in which special handling considerations should be considered to achieve maximum efficiency. This section identifies two areas that have grown in importance over the past many years; e-fulfillment operations and returns processing.

E-Fulfillment

Logistical support of Internet sales places some special demands on a firm's warehousing and handling. Both e-tailers and brick-and-mortar retailers moving into the e-tail marketing space have been forced to adapt their order processing procedures to meet the specific needs of this marketplace. Specific considerations that influence warehousing and handling in an e-fulfillment environment are order volume, small shipments, and tracking. First, to serve end consumers, an e-fulfillment facility typically must process a large number of very small orders. This means that it is difficult to achieve any substantial economies of scale for picking operations. Second, e-fulfillment facilities must generally deal with a wide range of product, which translates to large inventories and the use of flow-through practices to consolidate orders for shipment. Firms electing to consolidate orders must have the capability to effectively receive and merge a large number of very small orders rapidly. Finally, increased consumer expectations regarding shipment information require many activities within the warehouse and with the carrier be electronically scanned and tracked. Despite rapid growth in e-tailing, many firms are still trying to resolve the warehousing and handling processes most appropriate to support this activity. In many cases, these e-tailers are outsourcing fulfillment to integrated service providers (ISPs). In any case, the e-tailing environment will continue to place increasing demands on a more timely, responsive, and integrated warehouse and materials handling operation.

Returns Processing

For a variety of reasons, merchandise may be recalled by or returned to a manufacturer. This is particularly true in an e-tailing environment where up to 30 percent of orders are returned. Normally such reverse logistics is not of sufficient quantity or regularity to justify unitized movement, so the only convenient method for processing reverse flows of merchandise is manual handling. To the degree practical, materials handling design should consider the cost and service impact of reverse logistics. Such flows often involve pallets, cartons, and packaging materials in addition to damaged, dated, or excess merchandise. Many firms are choosing to have returns processed by an integrated service provider to separate flows and reduce the chance for error or contamination.

Storage

In planning warehouse layout, it is essential that products be assigned specific locations, called **slots**, on the basis of individual characteristics. The most important product variables to consider in a slotting plan are product velocity, weight, and special storage requirements.

Product velocity is the major factor driving warehouse layout. High-volume product should be positioned in the warehouse to minimize movement distance. For example, high-velocity products should be positioned near doors, primary aisles, and at lower levels in storage racks. Such positioning minimizes warehouse handling and reduces the need for frequent lifting. Conversely, products with low volume are typically assigned locations more distant from primary aisles or higher up in storage racks. Figure 9.6 illustrates a storage plan based on product movement velocity.

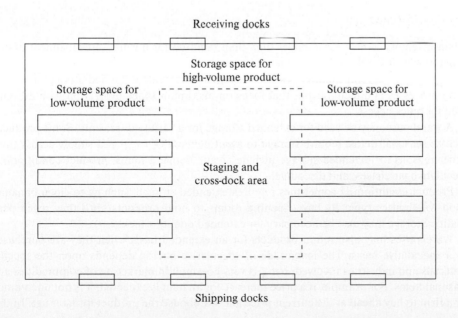

FIGURE 9.6
Storage Plan Based on Product Movement Velocity

Similarly, the storage plan should take into consideration product weight and special characteristics. Relatively heavy items should be assigned storage locations low to the ground to minimize lifting. Bulky or low-density product requires cubic space. Floor space along outside walls is ideal for such items. On the other hand, smaller items may require storage shelves, bins, or drawers. The integrated storage plan must consider individual product characteristics.

A typical warehouse is engaged in a combination of **active** and **extended** product storage alternatives. Warehouses that directly serve customers typically focus on active short-term storage. In contrast, other warehouses may use extended storage for speculative, seasonal, or obsolete inventory. In controlling and measuring warehouse operations, it is important to differentiate the relative requirements and performance capabilities of active and extended storage.

Active Storage

Regardless of inventory velocity, most goods must be stored for at least a short time. Storage for basic inventory replenishment is referred to as active storage. Active storage must provide sufficient inventory to meet the forecasted demand of the service area. The need for active storage is usually related to the capability to achieve transportation or handling economies of scale. For active storage, handling processes and technologies need to focus on quick movement and flexibility with minimal consideration for extended and dense storage.

The active storage concept includes **flow-through** or **cross-dock distribution**, which uses warehouses for consolidation and assortment while maintaining minimal or no inventory in storage. The resulting need for reduced inventory favors flow-through and cross-docking techniques that emphasize movement and de-emphasize storage. Flow-through distribution is most appropriate for high-volume, fast-moving products where quantities are reasonably predictable. While flow-through distribution places minimal demands on storage requirements, it does require that product be quickly unloaded, de-unitized, grouped and sequenced into customer assortments, and reloaded into transportation equipment. As a result, the handling emphasis is on accurate information-directed quick movement.

Extended Storage

When inventory is held for a longer time than required for normal replenishment of customer stocks, it is referred to as **extended storage**. In some special situations, storage may be required for several months prior to customer shipment. Extended storage uses handling processes and technologies that focus on maximum space utilization with minimal need for quick access.

A warehouse may be used for extended storage for a variety of reasons. Some products, such as seasonal items, require storage to await demand or to spread supply across time. Other reasons for extended storage include erratic demand items, product conditioning, speculative purchases, and discounts.

Product conditioning sometimes requires extended storage, such as to ripen bananas. Food warehouses typically have ripening rooms to hold products until they reach peak quality. Storage may also be necessary for extended quality checks.

Warehouses may also retain products for an extended basis when they are purchased on a speculative basis. The magnitude of speculative buying depends upon the specific materials and industries involved, but it is very common in marketing of commodities and seasonal items. For example, if a price increase for an item is expected, it is not uncommon for a firm to buy ahead at the current price and warehouse the product for later use. In this case, the discount or savings have to be traded off against extended storage and inventory carrying cost. Commodities such as grains, oil, and lumber are often purchased and stored for speculative reasons.

The warehouse may also be used to realize special discounts. Early purchase or forward-buy discounts may justify extended storage. The procurement manager may be able to realize a substantial price reduction during a specific time of the year. Under such conditions the warehouse is expected to hold inventory in excess of active storage. Manufacturers of fertilizer, toys, and lawn furniture often attempt to shift the warehousing burden to customers by offering off-season warehouse storage allowances.

Secondary Warehouse Operations

Accuracy and Audits

One secondary, but critically important, warehouse function is maintaining an accurate account of product on hand within the warehouse. Inventory accuracy is a primary concern of firms financial organizations because the inventory in the warehouse is, in most cases, considered an asset on the firm's balance sheet. Inventory accuracy is typically maintained by an annual physical inventory count in which the warehouse operation is closed while all on-hand products are physical counted and verified against system quantities. Physical inventories are less than desirable for two main reasons: (1) The warehouse must be closed to facilitate counting in an environment with no active transactions, resulting in the warehouse being unable to conduct primary functions such as receiving and shipping, and (2) the audits are costly because they require significant physical labor to count all on-hand inventory. One tool firms use to support ongoing accuracy and help avoid complete physical inventories is referred to as **cycle counting**. Cycle counting is the selective audit of a certain number of SKUs or bin locations on a predetermined schedule. Selection of individual items to be counted and verified can be based on the dollar value of the item, storage locations, or frequency of movement. By completing many, small cycle counts, a warehouse can demonstrate inventory control without pervasively affecting day-to-day operations. The outcome of both a physical inventory and a cycle count is the reconciliation between physical on-hand product compared to the book or warehouse management system quantities.

Audits related to inventory accuracy are only one type of audit that is typically used to maintain and improve warehouse operating efficiency. Audits are also common to maintain safety, assure compliance to security regulations, drive procedural improvement, and facilitate work changes.

Security

In a broad sense, security in a warehouse involves protection against merchandise pilferage, deterioration, and any form of operational disruption. Each form of security requires management attention.

Pilferage

In warehouse operations it is necessary to protect against theft by employees and thieves. Typical security procedures should be strictly enforced at each warehouse. Security begins at the exterior fence. As standard procedure, only authorized personnel should be permitted into the facility and on surrounding grounds. Entry to the warehouse yard should be controlled through a single gate. Without exception, no private automobile, regardless of management rank or customer status, should be allowed to enter the yard or park adjacent to the warehouse.

To illustrate the importance of security guidelines, the following experience may be helpful. A firm adopted the rule that no private vehicles would be permitted in the warehouse yard. Exceptions were made for two office employees with special needs. One night after work, one of these employees discovered a bundle taped under one fender of his car. Subsequent checking revealed that the car was literally a loaded delivery truck. The matter was promptly reported to security, who informed the employee not to alter any packages taped to the car and to continue parking inside the yard. Over the next several days, the situation was fully uncovered, with the ultimate arrest and conviction of seven warehouse employees who confessed to stealing thousands of dollars, worth of company merchandise. The firm would have been far better off had it provided transportation for the two special-needs employees from the regular parking lots to their work locations.

Shortages are always a major concern in warehouse operations. Many are honest mistakes that occur during order selection and shipment, but the purpose of security is to eliminate all forms of theft. A majority of thefts occur during normal working hours.

Inventory control and order processing systems help protect merchandise from being carried out of the warehouse unless accompanied by a computer release document. If samples are authorized for salesperson use, such merchandise should be maintained in a separate inventory. Not all pilferage occurs on an individual basis. Organized efforts between warehouse personnel and truck drivers can result in deliberate overpicking or high-for-low-value product substitution in order to move unauthorized merchandise out of the warehouse. Employee work assignment rotation, total case counts, and occasional complete line-item checks can reduce vulnerability to such collaboration.

Damage

Within the warehouse, a number of factors can reduce a product or material to nonsalable status. The most obvious form of product deterioration is damage from careless handling. For example, when pallets of merchandise are stacked in great heights, a marked change in humidity or temperature can cause packages supporting the stack to collapse. The warehouse environment must be carefully controlled and measured to provide proper product protection. Of major concern is warehouse employee carelessness. In this respect, the lift truck may well be management's worst enemy. Regardless of how often lift truck operators are warned against carrying overloads, some still attempt such shortcuts when not properly supervised. Product deterioration from careless handling within the warehouse is a form of loss that cannot be insured against or offset with compensating revenue.

Another major form of deterioration is incompatibility of products stored or transported together. For example, care must be taken when storing or shipping chocolate to make sure that it does not absorb odors from products it is being transported with, such as household chemicals.

Safety and Maintenance

Accident prevention is a concern of warehouse management. A comprehensive safety program requires constant examination of work procedures and equipment to locate and take corrective action to eliminate unsafe conditions before accidents result. Accidents occur when workers become careless or are exposed to mechanical or physical hazards. The floors of a warehouse may cause accidents if not properly cleaned. During normal operation, rubber and glass deposits collect on aisles and, from time to time, broken cases will result in product seepage onto the floor. Proper cleaning procedures can reduce the accident risk of such hazards. Environmental safety has become a major concern of government agencies such as OSHA and cannot be neglected by management.

A preventative maintenance program is necessary for handling equipment. Unlike production machines, movement equipment is not stationary, so it is more difficult to properly maintain. A preventative maintenance program scheduling periodic checks of all handling equipment should be applied in every warehouse.

Additionally preventative maintenance can also be applicable to the physical warehouse building itself. Common building preventative maintenance programs include the facility HVAC and fire suppression systems, dock leveling equipment used to enter and exit transportation vehicles, or the restriping of the warehouse floor to maintain traffic pattern efficiency. Other examples include replacement of light bulbs both inside and outside the warehouse or the resurfacing of the exterior warehouse truck yard to ensure transportation equipment is not damaged by potholes.

Environmental Concerns and Regulatory Environment

There is increased concern regarding environmental impact of packaging and handling. In particular, attention has been directed to the impact of handling equipment such as lift trucks. Pollution of gas powered lift trucks is similar to that of automobile engines. There is also increasing interest regarding the handling and disposal of hazardous materials used or stored in warehouse operations. Firms have to ensure that such materials are disposed of properly to avoid pollution liability.

The distribution warehouse is one of the most labor-intensive operations for most firms. It is also one of the most dangerous as numerous injuries occur annually. To increase safe practices OSHA extended its regulatory influence over warehouse operations and technology. In March 1999, OSHA established the Powered Industrial Truck Operator Training **(PITOT)** regulation requiring the training and reevaluation of all lift truck drivers. Drivers failing evaluation and those involved in accidents must undergo refresher training.

OSHA is concerned with all aspects of safety within supply chain logistics facilities and associated shipping and receiving docks. Included in the ongoing safety program are regular inspections of facilities to ensure existing standards are being adhered to during daily operations. Table 9.3 is reproduced from OSHA's Handbook, which discusses warehouse safety. The table lists the 10 most frequently cited warehouse safety violations.[1]

[1] A adapted from OSHA: Working Safety Series: Warehousing, United States Government, OSHA 3220-10N, 2004, p. 1.

Warehouse operations can present a wide variety of potential hazards for the worker. For warehousing establishments, the 10 OSHA standards most frequently included in the agency's citations were:
1. Forklifts
2. Hazard communication
3. Electrical, wiring methods
4. Electrical, system design
5. Guarding floor & wall openings and holes
6. Exits
7. Mechanical power transmission
8. Respiratory protection
9. Lockout/tagout
10. Portable fire extinguishers

TABLE 9.3
Warehouse Hazards

Systems

Modern warehouses use a variety of integrated systems to achieve efficient operations. An entire chapter could be devoted to the complexity of warehouse management, yard management, and information direct systems. The following section provides a brief outline of each. It is important the reader gains a conceptual understanding of the capability and application of each system as it relates to the integrated warehousing, materials handling, and packaging function.

Warehouse Management Systems

The development of work procedures goes hand in hand with training warehouse personnel. Most firms depend upon a warehouse management system **(WMS)** to standardize work procedures and facilitate best practice.

One of the main uses of a WMS is to coordinate order selection. Two basic methods of order selection are **discrete selection** and **wave selection**, also known as **batch selection**. In discrete selection, a specific customer's order is selected and prepared for shipment as the work assignment. Discrete order selection is often used when order content and handling selection are critical.

Wave selection can be designed and operationalized in a variety of ways. A wave can be coordinated by an area of the warehouse wherein all quantities of all products required to complete all customer orders are selected at one time. Using this type of wave selection, employees are typically assigned responsibility for a specific portion of the warehouse. Waves can also be planned around a specific shipment destination and/or carrier, for example, all UPS shipments to the East Coast. Because each employee has a thorough knowledge of a specific warehouse selection area or shipping procedure, fewer selection errors typically result using wave picking.

WMS also coordinates work procedures that are important for receiving and shipping. Established procedures for receiving and ensuring product entry into inventory records are critical. If pallets are used, the merchandise must be stacked in appropriate patterns to ensure maximum load stability and consistent case counts. Personnel working in shipping must have knowledge of trailer loading practices. In specific types of operations, particularly when merchandise changes ownership, items must be checked during loading.

Work procedures are not restricted to floor personnel. Procedures must be established for administration and maintenance. Replenishment of warehouse inventory can cause operational problems if proper ordering procedures are lacking. Normally, there is limited interaction between buyers and warehouse personnel, although such communication is improving within integrated supply chain management organizations. Buyers tend to purchase in quantities that afford the best price with little attention given to pallet compatible quantities or available warehouse space.

Figure 9.7 illustrates a range of activities coordinated by a typical WMS. Historical warehouse system functionality focused on receiving replenishment shipments, stock putaway, and order picking. Traditional activities are listed under **basic functionality**. Warehouses today must offer a broader range of services as they are frequently performing value-added services. They are also required to manage more inventory on a just-in-time basis. The figure illustrates typical **advanced functionality** activities. Yard management, sometimes a functionality of a firm's transportation management system **(TMS)**, refers to the process of managing the vehicles and the inventory within vehicles while in the warehouse yard. Faster inventory turnover requires better visibility of inventory, even when in

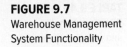
FIGURE 9.7
Warehouse Management
System Functionality

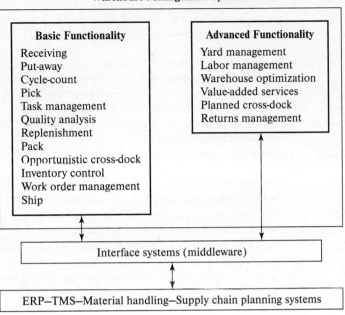

Warehouse Management Systems

Basic Functionality	Advanced Functionality
Receiving	Yard management
Put-away	Labor management
Cycle-count	Warehouse optimization
Pick	Value-added services
Task management	Planned cross-dock
Quality analysis	Returns management
Replenishment	
Pack	
Opportunistic cross-dock	
Inventory control	
Work order management	
Ship	

Interface systems (middleware)

ERP—TMS—Material handling—Supply chain planning systems

transportation vehicles. Labor management refers to maximizing the use of warehouse labor. Historically, warehouse labor has been quite specialized, allowing for relatively easy planning. Warehouse optimization refers to selection of the best location within the warehouse for the storage and retrieval of product to minimize time and movement. **Value-added services** refer to the coordination of warehouse activities to customize product, such as packaging, labeling, kitting, and setting up displays.

Planned cross-docking and merging is the integration of two or more parts of a customer order that have been supplied from a different source without maintaining inventory.

A final execution function is the capability to manage reverse logistics activities such as returns, repair, and recycling. Both customers and environmental interests are increasing their demands that supply chains can accommodate reverse logistics. Table 9.4 summarizes WMS functionality and decision support benefits.

Yard Management Systems

An important part of warehouse-related information technology is the yard management system **(YMS)**. The YMS in essence couples the warehouse with inbound and outbound transportation equipment. This coordination takes the form of arranging dock appointments for receiving ordered merchandise and transportation equipment for shipping outbound. From a performance perspective, the YMS is the scheduler. For high-level transportation and warehousing efficiency, it is essential to appropriately sequence inbound and outbound warehouse activity. It is also important to maintain an accurate accountability of what merchandise and transportation equipment is in the warehouse or factory yard. Many stories exist to illustrate the dilemma of expediting an inbound product shipment due from a supplier only to have it arrive on time as scheduled and be dispatched to the warehouse yard due to no dock availability. An appropriate way to view the YMS is as the software that links and coordinates transportation **(TMS)** with the warehouse **(WMS)**.

TABLE 9.4
WMS Functionality
and Decision Support

Source: Reproduced with
permission from Bowersox et
al., "RFID Applications within
the Four Walls of a Consumer
Package Goods Warehouse,"
from Marketing and Supply
Chain Working Paper, Michigan
State University, 2005.

Selected Functionality	Decision Support Benefits
Put-away	Improved productivity and cube utilization.
Task interleaving	Routing of fork trucks on demand as contrasted to predetermined assigned tasks, areas, or sequences.
Pick/replenishment	Direct picking from single or multiple locations including pick to assure expiration date compliance. Facilitates replenishment of pick location inventories when appropriate.
Slotting	Variable slot or product placement locator assignment to enhance space utilization.
Cross-docking	Facilitate direct receipt to shipment flow.
Inventory visibility	Tracking specific inventory lots by warehouse location as well as daily visibility of receipts. Date-specific lot control.
Work queue resolution	Identification of alternative ways to rapidly or efficiently resolve work constraints or queues.
Picking strategy	Routines to perform selected picking strategies.
Error correction	Ability to identify, resolve, and correct data errors in real time.
	Ability to identify and resolve differences in purchase orders or advanced shipment notifications (ASN) and actual quantities or product received.
Simulations	Performance of real-time decision support scenarios to assist in operational decision making.
Return goods	Facilitate processing and audit compliance for reverse logistics programs.
Cycle counts	Ability to conduct and resolve real-time inventory counts.

Information-Directed Systems

The concept of information-directed handling is appealing because it combines the control typical of automated handling with the flexibility of mechanized systems. Information-directed systems use mechanized handling controlled by information technology. Three common examples of information-directed materials handling systems are RF wireless **(Wi-Fi)**, Radio-Frequency Identification **(RFID)**, and light-directed operations **(LDO)**.

RF Wireless (Wi-Fi) and RFID

RF wireless handling uses standard mechanized materials handling equipment coordinated by information technology to provide operator directions and control in real time. Typical Wi-Fi systems utilize lift trucks. Supported by the WMS all lift truck movements are directed and monitored by some combination of computer mounted on the lift truck, handheld computer, or voice-activated communication. The real-time information interchange is designed to achieve flexibility and better utilization.

The main advantage of RF is to improve speed and flexibility of lift truck operations. Instead of following predetermined handwritten instructions or computer listings generated in batches, drivers receive work assignments through either handheld or vehicle-mounted RF terminals. Use of RF technology provides real-time communication to central data processing systems. In operation, the WMS in conjunction with the operations control computer plans and initiates all movements, communicates the requirements to the material handlers, and tracks the completion of all tasks. Decision support systems analyze all movement requirements to assign equipment in such a way that direct movement is maximized and deadhead movement is minimized. This process of assigning lift trucks to continuous assignments is called **task interleaving**. In task interleaving, lift trucks are assigned independent of traditional work areas to specific jobs or work areas that need resources such as receiving or shipping.

The use of RFID capabilities creates the opportunity for two-way communication between specific products and lift truck operators. Because the RFID-equipped product can respond to an inquiry from the WMS or the operator, the potential exists to identify the exact location in the warehouse. Such positive identification serves to facilitate information-directed handling.

Information-directed handling offers great potential because selected benefits of automation can be achieved without substantial capital investment. Information-directed systems can also substantially increase productivity by tracking lift truck performance.

Substantial research is being conducted to explore new concepts of warehouse design and layout to fully exploit the potential of information-directed material handling.

Light Directed

A common light directed technology is **pick-to-light**. In pick-to-light, applications is a carousel system variation that is becoming increasingly common. In this system, order selectors pick designated items directly into cartons or onto conveyors from **lighted** carousel locations or storage bins. A series of lights or a **light tree** in front of each pick location indicates the number of items to pick from each location. A variation of the pick-to-light system is **put-to-light**, where order selectors place product in lighted containers. Each container or tote is assigned to a specific order or customer, so the light is telling which customers are to receive a specific product.

It's clear that effective warehouse operations require a combination of state of the art systems, including a WMS, TMS, and other information directed systems to handle today's complexity and achieve efficiency in the 21st-century logistics systems.

A final section in this chapter looks at packaging and the integration of packaging with warehouse operations and materials handling equipment.

Packaging Perspectives[2]

Packaging is typically viewed as being either **consumer**, focused primarily on marketing, or **industrial**, focused on logistics. The primary concern for logistics operations is industrial package design. Individual products or parts are typically grouped into cartons, bags, bins, or barrels for damage protection and handling efficiency. Containers used to group individual products are called **master cartons**. When master cartons are grouped into larger units for handling, the combination is referred to as **containerization** or **unitization**.

Master cartons and unit loads are the basic units handled during logistical operations. The weight, cube, and damage potential of the master carton determines transportation and handling requirements. When multiple master cartons are grouped together for handling the composite is referred to as a **unit load**. If packages and unit loads are not designed for efficient logistical processing, overall system performance suffers. Packaging and unit loads impact all supply chain movement and storage costs.

Retail sale quantity or presentation should not be the prime determinant of master carton size. For example, beer, often sold at retail in units of 6, is normally packed in master cartons containing 24 units. The master carton should be large enough to provide economies of scale but light enough to facilitate handling by an individual without mechanical assistance. A prime objective in logistics is to design operations to handle a limited assortment of standardized master cartons.

[2] The authors express their appreciation to Professor Diana Twede from the Michigan State University School of Packaging for assistance provided in preparing this section.

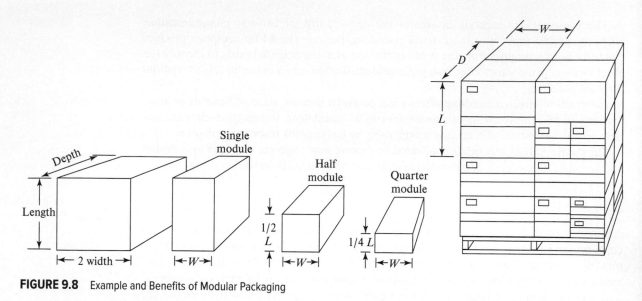

FIGURE 9.8   Example and Benefits of Modular Packaging

Source: Adapted from materials provided by Walter Frederick Freedman and Company.

Naturally, few organizations can reduce their master carton requirements to a one size fits all. When master cartons of more than one size are required, extreme care should be taken to arrive at an assortment of compatible units. Figure 9.8 illustrates one such concept, utilizing four standard master carton sizes, that achieves modular compatibility.

Of course, logistical considerations cannot fully dominate packaging design. The ideal package for materials handling and transportation would be a perfect cube having equal length, depth, and width while achieving maximum possible density. Seldom will such a package exist. The important point is that logistical modularity should be evaluated along with manufacturing, marketing, and product design considerations in finalizing master carton selection.

Another logistical packaging concern is the degree of desired protection. Package design and material must combine to achieve the desired level of protection without incurring the expense of overprotection. It is possible to design a package that has the correct material content but does not provide the necessary protection. Arriving at a satisfactory packaging solution involves defining the degree of allowable damage in terms of expected overall conditions and then isolating a combination of design and materials capable of meeting those specifications. For package design, there are two key considerations. First, the cost of absolute protection will, in most cases, be prohibitive. Second, final package construction will be a blend of protection and handling considerations.

A final logistics packaging consideration is the relationship between the master carton size, order quantity, and retail display quantity. From a handling perspective, master cartons should be standardized and reasonably large to minimize the number of units handled during the logistics process. For ease of warehouse handling, it is desirable to have retailers purchase in master carton quantities. However, for a slow-moving product, a master carton could contain an overstock of an item that sells only one unit per week but is packed in a case containing 48. Finally, in order to minimize labor, retailers often place trays from master cartons on the retail shelf so that individual products do not have to be unloaded and placed on the store shelf. Master cartons or trays meeting retail requirements for shelf space are preferred.

The determination of final package design requires a great deal of testing to assure that both marketing and logistics concerns are satisfied. While the marketing aspects are generally the focus of consumer research, logistics packaging research is determined from laboratory or experimental testing. Laboratory analysis offers a reliable way to evaluate package design as a result of advancements in testing equipment and measurement techniques. For example, testing equipment is available to measure shock severity and characteristics while a package is in transit. To a large degree, care in design has been further encouraged by increased federal regulation regarding hazardous materials.

The four most common causes of product damage in a logistical system are vibration, impact, puncture, and compression. Combinations of potential damage can be experienced whenever a package is being transported or handled. Test shipment monitoring is expensive and difficult to conduct on a scientific basis. To obtain increased accuracy, computerized environmental simulations can be used to replicate typical conditions that a package will experience in the logistical system. Laboratory test equipment is available to evaluate the impact of shock, vibration, and compression upon the interaction of product fragility, packaging materials, and design.

Packaging for Handling Efficiency

Packaging decisions have a major impact on logistical productivity and efficiency. All logistical operations are affected by packaging—from truck loading and warehouse picking productivity to transportation vehicle and storage cube utilization. Handling efficiency in all of these situations is significantly influenced by package design, unitization, and communication characteristics.

Package Design

Product packaging in standard configurations and order quantities facilitates logistical efficiency. For example, cube utilization can be improved through reduced package size by concentrating products such as orange juice or fabric softener, by eliminating air inside packages, and by shipping items unassembled, nested, and with minimal dunnage. In most cases, dunnage materials, like polystyrene foam peanuts, can be minimized simply by reducing box size. IKEA, the Swedish retailer of unassembled furniture, emphasizes cube minimization to the point that it ships pillows vacuum-packed. IKEA uses a cube minimization packaging strategy to successfully compete in the United States even though the company ships furniture from Sweden.

Cube minimization is most important for lightweight products such as assembled lawn furniture that **cubes out** a transport vehicle before weight limits are reached. On the other hand, heavy products like steel ball bearings or liquid in glass bottles typically **weigh out** transport vehicles before cube capacity is filled. When a vehicle or container weighs out, the firm ends up shipping empty cube space that can't be filled with product. Total weight can sometimes be reduced by product or package changes. For example, substituting plastic bottles for glass significantly increases the number of bottles that can be loaded in a trailer. The decision by Gerber to use plastic jars for baby food was partially designed to reduce transportation expenses.

Cube and weight minimization represent a special challenge e-commerce operations. These operations tend to use standardized packaging for both purchasing and operating efficiencies. The result is often oversized packages that require excessive dunnage and increased shipping cost. The nature of the products and the breadth of e-commerce product lines often require multiple packages to be combined in a single order. This is of great concern for consumers who are becoming more aware of the cost of shipping and handling direct shipments as well as for environmental concerns related to packaging disposal.

Unitization

The process of grouping master cartons into one physical unit for materials handling or transport is referred to as **unitization** or **containerization**. The concept includes all forms of product grouping, from taping two master cartons together to the use of specialized transportation equipment. All types of unitization have the basic objective of increasing handling and transport efficiency. Unit loads provide many benefits over handling individual master cartons. First, unloading time and congestion at destination are minimized. Second, product shipped in unit load quantities facilitates handling. Unit loads require approximately one-fifth the time needed for manual loading or unloading. Inbound shipment verification is also simplified as receipts can be bar coded. Inventory can be positioned rapidly in the warehouse for order selection. Finally, in-transit damage is reduced by unit load shipping. All these factors reduce total logistical cost. The following discussion is limited to unitization devices that fit within the capacity of standard transportation equipment.

Rigid Devices

Rigid devices provide an enclosure within which master cartons or loose products are unitized. The premise is that placing products inside a sealed container will both protect them and facilitate handling. The use of containers handled and transported by special equipment and ships is common practice in air and water transport. In domestic distribution, containerization can achieve transport efficiency and reduced product handling. Approximately one-half the total cost of transporting domestic goods occurs in handling products between vehicles, across docks, packaging, and filing loss and damage claims for pilferage and for insurance. The airlines use rigid containerization both for freight and for passenger baggage. The containers, which are designed to fit in the cargo area of aircraft, facilitate loading and unloading while reducing product damage and pilferage. Table 9.5 summarizes the benefits of rigid containerization.

Returnable containers have traditionally been used to distribute selected products. Most reusable containers are steel or plastic, although some firms, also reuse corrugated boxes. Automobile manufacturers use returnable racks for interplant shipment of body parts, and chemical companies reuse steel drums. There is an increasing trend, however, to reusable packaging for many small items and parts such as ingredients, grocery perishables, and retail warehouse-to-store totes.

Returnable containers are particularly appropriate for integrated environments where there is reasonable container security between shipment origin and destination. The automobile industry uses returnable racks between component suppliers and assembly plants.

TABLE 9.5
Benefits of Rigid Devices

- Improves overall material movement efficiency.
- Reduces damage in handling and transit.
- Reduces pilferage.
- Reduces protective packaging requirements.
- Provides greater protection from environmental elements.
- Provides a shipment unit that can be reused a substantial number of times, thereby reducing waste and the need to dispose of the container.

The decision to invest in a returnable package system is based on of the number of shipment cycles and return transportation costs versus the purchase and disposal cost of expendable containers. Benefits of improved handling and reduced damage should be taken into account, as well as the future costs of sorting, tracking, and cleaning the reusable devices.

Flexible Devices

As the name implies, flexible devices do not protect a product by complete enclosure. The most common type of nonrigid unitization is stacked master cartons on either **pallets** or **slipsheets**. Pallets are most commonly constructed out of wood. However, an increasing number of plastic and steel pallets are being used in specific handling situations. A hardwood pallet is illustrated in Figure 9.9. A slipsheet, which is similar to a pallet in size and purpose, is a flat stocking surface generally made of cardboard or plastic. Because slipsheets lie flat on the floor, special lift trucks are required to handle slipsheet unit loads. The primary advantage of slipsheets in comparison to pallets is cost and weight. Slipsheets are less costly than pallets and are insignificant from a weight and cube perspective.

Most industry associations recommend that a standardized pallet or slipsheet size be used as a unit load platform. The Grocery Manufacturers of America have adopted the 40 × 48-inch pallet with four-way entry and similar size slipsheets for food distribution. The beverage industry, on the other hand, has standardized on 32 × 36-inch pallets. Throughout industry, the sizes most frequently used are 40 × 48, 32 × 40, and 32 × 36. It is common practice to first identify the dimension of most frequent entry by handling equipment.

Generally, the larger a platform, the more efficient the associated handling. For instance, the 40 × 48-inch pallet provides 768 more square inches per stacking tier than the 32 × 36-inch size. Assuming that master cartons can be stacked as high as 10 tiers, the total added unitization space of the 40 × 48-inch pallet is 7680 square inches. This is 60 percent larger than the 32 × 36-inch size. The final determination of size should be based upon load, compatibility with the handling and transport equipment used throughout the logistical system, and standardized industry practice. With modern handling equipment, few restrictions are encountered in weight limitations. While pallets themselves are not flexible, the unit loads they contain are very flexible.

While a variety of different approaches can be used to tier master cartons on slipsheets and pallets, the four most common are block, brick, row, and pinwheel. The block method is used with cartons of equal width and length. With differential widths and lengths, the

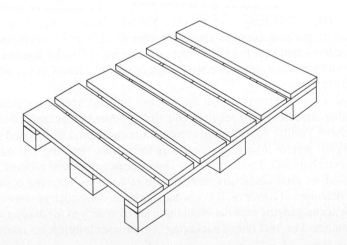

FIGURE 9.9
Hardwood Four-Way
Entry Pallet

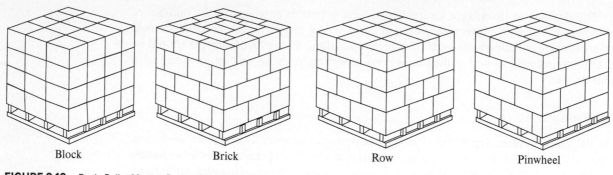

FIGURE 9.10 Basic Pallet Master Carton Stacking Patterns

Source: Adapted from palletization guides of the National Wooden Pallet & Container Association, Arlington, VA.

brick, row, or pinwheel pattern is employed. Figure 9.10 illustrates these four basic patterns. Except for the block method, cartons are placed in the unit load arranged in an interlocking pattern with adjoining tiers placed at 90-degree angles to each other. Load stability is enhanced with interlocking. The block pattern does not provide this benefit. While the illustrated patterns provide a good starting point when there are limited master carton sizes, most pallet patterns are determined by computer analysis.

The use of flexible unitization can increase damage potential if it is not properly contained during handling or transport. In most situations, the stability of stacking is insufficient to secure a unit load. Standard methods of improving stability include rope tie, corner posts, steel strapping, taping, antiskid adhesives, and wrapping. These methods essentially tie the master cartons into the pallet stacking pattern. Increasingly popular methods for securing unit loads are shrink-wrap and stretch-wrap. Both wraps use film similar to that used in a kitchen for food preservation.

Communication

The final logistical packaging functionality is communication or information transfer. This function is becoming increasingly critical to provide content identification, tracking information, handling instructions, and information essential for security.

The most obvious communications role is identifying package contents for all channel members. Typical information includes manufacturer, product, count, Universal Product Code (**UPC**), and Electronic Product Code (**EPC**) and may be communicated using a bar code or RFID technology. The carton information is used to identify product for receiving, order selection, and shipment verification. Visibility is the major content identification consideration as material handlers should be able to observe or electronically read the label at reasonable distances from all directions. The exception for high-visibility packaging are high-value products that often have small or minimal labels to minimize the potential for pilferage.

Ease of package tracking is critical for effective internal operations. Additionally, customers are also increasing their requirements that product be tracked as it moves through the supply chain. Positive control of all movement reduces product loss and pilferage.

An additional role of logistics packaging is to provide handling and damage instruction to materials handlers. The information should note any special product handling considerations such as glass containers, temperature restrictions, stacking considerations, or potential environmental concerns. If the product is hazardous, such as some chemicals, the packaging or accompanying material should provide instructions for dealing with spills and container damage. The final role of packaging is to provide information related to security.

Summary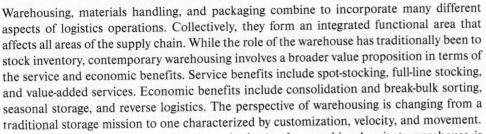

Warehousing, materials handling, and packaging combine to incorporate many different aspects of logistics operations. Collectively, they form an integrated functional area that affects all areas of the supply chain. While the role of the warehouse has traditionally been to stock inventory, contemporary warehousing involves a broader value proposition in terms of the service and economic benefits. Service benefits include spot-stocking, full-line stocking, and value-added services. Economic benefits include consolidation and break-bulk sorting, seasonal storage, and reverse logistics. The perspective of warehousing is changing from a traditional storage mission to one characterized by customization, velocity, and movement.

Warehouses are usually classified on the basis of ownership. A private warehouse is operated by the enterprise that also owns the merchandise in the facility. A public warehouse is operated independently and offers various for-hire value-added services. A contract warehouse is a long-term business arrangement that provides tailored services for a limited number of customers. An integrated warehousing strategy often incorporates a combination of warehouse ownership options. There are numerous managerial decisions in planning and initiating warehouse operations, including site selection, design, product-mix analysis, expansion, handling, layout, and sizing.

Distribution centers and warehouses are designed to achieve the primary activities of inventory handling and storage. Handling includes receiving, putaway, in-storage handling, order-picking, and shipping. High-performance handling is a key to warehouse productivity supported by a series of unique handling arrangements, including mechanized, semiautomated, and automated systems. In certain circumstances, special handling considerations must be accounted for. Active storage facilitates cross-docking, consolidation, break-bulk, and postponement. Extended storage facilitates balancing supply and demand speculation. It's very common for warehouses to have some combination of active and extended storage to enable the support of unique business requirements. Secondary warehouse functions including accuracy and audits, facility security, and safety and maintenance, compliment primary warehouse functions to establish the entire warehouse ecosystem.

Modern distribution centers and warehouses commonly utilize advanced systems, including warehouse management, yard management and other information-directed systems to support operational complexity and drive efficiency. The importance of these systems will only continue to grow as warehouses are required to continue demonstrating more efficiency.

Packaging has a significant impact on the cost and productivity of logistics. Packaging design, the use of master cartons, and containerization or unitization are critical considerations. Flexible and rigid devices provide unique benefits that must be effectively applied to a given application. Finally, packaging fulfills a key need of communication or information transfer.

Study Questions

1. Discuss and illustrate the economic justification for establishing a warehouse.
2. Under what conditions could it make sense to combine private and public warehouses in a logistical system?
3. Discuss and illustrate the role of warehouses in reverse logistics.

4. Discuss the differences between rigid and nonrigid containers. Discuss the importance of load securing in unitization.

5. In terms of basic handling, what is the role of a unit load?

Challenge Questions

1. Assume you work for a pharmaceutical company and you are faced with an unprecedented nationwide recall. The product in question is not considered a health threat, but the recall has high profile in the public news media. How would you proceed? Be specific concerning your sequence of actions, supporting logic and public relations initiatives.

2. Canadian Tire is one of Canada's largest companies. They operate four large distribution centers which service over 470 tire retail outlets. They recently installed a YMS, which they have integrated with their WMS and TMS systems. Their expectation was improved performance in over-the-road transportation equipment utilization, driver productivity, and warehouse dock/door utilization. As a relatively new logistics employee, you have been asked to develop an evaluation system to measure operational productivity improvement. While management does not want a financial impact evaluation, they are interested in developing benchmarks to measure initial and sustainable productivity improvement. You have the job—how would you proceed?

3. Given the fact that both the Navy and the Air Force regularly fly pilotless aircraft for surveillance and combat missions, the idea of a driverless fork truck seems somewhat of a no-brainer. Why not pilotless cargo aircraft such as FedEx and UPS? Why not semi-trucks moving intercity without drivers? How would your answer differ if we had highways that were dedicated to truck-only traffic, either on an exclusive or time-allocated basis? Where do you think the concept of probotics will eventually end up?

PART 4

Supply Chain Logistics Design

One of the two primary responsibilities of a firm's logistics management, as established in Chapters 1 and 3, is to participate in supply chain logistics design. Part 4 contains two chapters devoted to various logistics design issues. Chapter 10 establishes the global perspective of today's business operations. Few firms enjoy the simplicity of conducting business within a single nation. The complexity of globalization has increased as a result of extended operational reach. Given the dynamic nature of contemporary business, it is not unusual for managers to conduct continuous evaluations of their logistics support structure. Chapter 11 focuses on network design. An integrative model is developed and illustrated that combines the temporal and spatial dimensions of logistics into a single theoretical framework. The integration structure provides the basis for process development, trade-off quantification, and integrative measurement. Chapter 11 includes a step-by-step design process and provides a guide to deal with channel structure, design, and implementation.

CHAPTER 10

Global Supply Chains

Globalization offers many opportunities and challenges for logistics and supply chain operations and strategies. The opportunities include increasing markets and a wider range of manufacturing alternatives with varying absolute and comparative human and material resource advantages. Some regions of the world can provide significant economies of scale because of their low wages, while other regions offer significant flexibility because of their capabilities. Specifically, developing countries often demonstrate significant opportunities for growth. The challenges encountered when taking advantage of these opportunities include more demanding logistics operating environments, security considerations, and more complex total cost analyses. This chapter discusses the rationale for global supply chains, describes the stages of global supply chain integration, and concludes with guidelines for making global sourcing decisions.

Global Economies

Regardless of size, most firms today include some dimension of global operations. They have materials or products that are sourced globally, or they have global customers ready to purchase from them. In many cases, firms are involved in both global sourcing and delivery. While many believe that firms operate globally to achieve sourcing and manufacturing

Objective	Rationale
Increase revenue	• Open up more markets • Expand beyond competitors • Obtain accessibility to markets that limit access without local operations
Achieve economies of scale	• Take advantage of available production capacity
Reduce direct cost	• Take advantage of lower labor rates or real estate expense • Reduce energy requirements by reducing distance or changing transportation mode • Take advantage of differences in production requirements
Advance technology	• Obtain access to advanced technology that may not be available from current locations due to historical investments • Obtain access to specialized expertise or language skills
Reduce firm's global tax liability	• Obtain local or regional tax benefits related to property, inventory, or income • Obtain reductions in value-added taxes due to localized production or other value-added services (i.e., packaging, inventory management, customization)
Reduce market access uncertainty	• Source product from location that involves less transportation uncertainty • Source product from location that involves fewer security constraints
Enhance sustainability	• Source products or other resources (including human resources) from locations that have ongoing availability of materials and expertise such as energy or trained workers

TABLE 10.1

Rationale for Globalization

cost benefits, there are many other reasons as well. This section discusses some of the primary reasons that firms develop global capabilities.

Table 10.1 lists the primary objectives firms use to justify globalization. While many believe that the primary motivation for shifting manufacturing and supply chain operations is low-cost resources and labor, the rationale in many cases is one of the others cited in the table. For example, although it is believed that many firms moved production to Asia and India to access lower production wages, their primary motivation is often to obtain access to rapidly growing markets. While many have taken advantage of rapidly increasing demand, the increased demand for production employees is also driving up wage rates much more rapidly than in the developed world. As a result, the wage differential is declining and firms are beginning to look for the next low-cost production sources. Firms are also beginning to develop supply chain value-added capabilities in South America and Africa to take advantage of low-cost production combined with market proximity to the developed world.

Global supply chain operations either directly or indirectly are becoming the norm for most firms. Global sourcing and marketing offers many opportunities to enhance the firm's performance, particularly in terms of revenue, volume, and market share. The following sections describe some of the strategies that firms can employ to achieve these benefits along with some of the challenges that firms are likely to encounter.

Global Supply Chain Integration

Whereas an effective logistics system is important for domestic supply chain integration, it is absolutely essential for successful global sourcing, manufacturing, and marketing. Domestic logistics focuses on performing movement and storage activities to support supply chain integration in a relatively stable and consistent environment. Global logistics must support operations in a variety of different national, political, and economic settings while also dealing with increased uncertainty associated with the distance, demand, diversity, and documentation of international commerce.

The operating challenges of global logistics systems vary significantly in each major global region. The North American logistics challenge is one of an open geography with extensive and flexible transportation options and limited need for cross-border documentation. The European logistician, in contrast, is confronted by relatively compact geography involving numerous political, cultural, regulatory, and language situations. The European infrastructure is also quite congested because of population density and the fact that many of the roads date back centuries. The Pacific Rim logistical challenge includes an island-based environment with relatively poor infrastructure, requiring extensive water and air shipments to transcend vast distances. These different characteristics require that firms having global operations develop and maintain a wide variety of capabilities and expertise.

In the past, an enterprise could survive by operating with unique North American, European, or Pacific Rim business strategies. While it was easier to create and operate unique regional strategies, the resulting duplication often resulted in loss of economies of scale and poor asset utilization. While regionalization remains viable for some firms, those desiring to grow and prosper must face the challenges of designing and operating a globally integrated enterprise. Strategic business initiatives must change as a firm and its supply chain become progressively more global.

Logistics in a Global Economy

Global operations increase logistics cost and complexity. In 2017, the last available estimate, logistics cost in the U.S. was $1.4 trillion, or 7.6 percent of U.S. **gross domestic product (GDP)**.[1] Table 10.2 lists logistics cost as a percent of GDP cost for major countries and regions. In terms of complexity, global operations—in contrast to domestic operations—are characterized by increased uncertainty, increased variability, decreased control, and decreased visibility. Uncertainty results from greater distances, longer leadtimes, and decreased market knowledge. Increased variation results from unique customer and documentation requirements as well as shifting political environments. Decreased control results from the extensive use of international service firms coupled with potential government intervention in such areas as customs

[1] *2017 State of Logistics Report*, Council of Supply Chain Management Professionals. Chicago, IL.

TABLE 10.2

Estimated 2012 National Logistics Expenditures

Source: Council of Supply Chain Management Professionals, *2013 State of Logistics Report* (Chicago, IL).

Country/Region	Logistics as a Percent of Gross Domestic Product
United States	8.5%
Japan	11.0
Europe	12.9
India	12.9
Mexico	14.0
China	14.4
Asia	16.8

requirements and trade restrictions. Decreased visibility results from longer transit and holding times with less ability to track and determine exactly where shipments are located.

These unique challenges complicate development of an efficient and effective global supply chain strategy. Fortunately, there are forces that both drive and facilitate globalization and necessitate cross-border logistics operations.

Globalization Strategies

Supply chain globalization can be characterized using four strategies: (1) no international strategy, (2) multi-domestic strategy, (3) global strategy, and (4) transnational strategy. The characteristics and the supply chain implications of each stage are discussed.

The first strategy characterizes firms that have no international strategy. This describes firms that are involved only in domestic operations. While there may be some international transactions in the form of sourcing or delivery, there is no systematic strategy or plan to organize or grow international operations. The advantage of domestic-only operations is that it substantially minimizes complexity, and there is minimum coordination necessary across supply chain and other firm functions. The disadvantages of no international strategy are that it is difficult to respond to customers that operate globally and growth is typically limited to local markets.

The second, or multi-domestic, strategy characterizes firms that operate in multiple nations implying that they have operations in multiple countries, but the country in which the corporate headquarters is located is the dominant country. For this strategy, firms typically have separate, semi-autonomous supply chains in each global region. For example, if a firm is headquartered in the U.S., all activities completed outside the U.S. are international and are often treated as secondary to domestic operations. Generally, the international operations are used to support domestic operations, particularly with respect to sourcing raw materials and goods for resale. In this case, the logistics and supply chain operations within each region are independent. The advantage of a multi-domestic strategy is that the firm can focus on local markets while minimizing overall coordination requirements. For example, a firm can focus on key growth markets while minimizing the operational complexity between markets. The disadvantages of a multi-domestic strategy are that it is not responsive to globally based customers, and it is difficult to develop economies of scale.

Third, the global operation strategy implies cross-border operations with some local market customization. While there is typically a single headquarters that coordinates global operations, the logistics and supply chain activities occur in regions around the world. Typically, each region or country is focused toward the market characteristics of the region. While there is motivation to coordinate supply chain activities across regions, there is not a strong focus on reducing brand, manufacturing, and logistics complexity. For example, similar products may be built in multiple regions with minimal concern for reducing manufacturing and component complexity. Transactions between different regions or countries are often treated as intra-firm transfers, or might be more like arms'-length relationships. Typically, the most advanced integration in such organizations is the focus on globally integrated financials. Other forms of integration such as product development, marketing, supply chain, and planning are less common. The advantages of global operations are the ability to focus on multiple local markets, meeting the requirements of local customers, and the ability to take advantage of global brands and products. The disadvantages of a global strategy are that it is difficult to respond in an integrated manner to global customers, and it is not scalable.

The fourth, or transnational, strategy characterizes firms that maintain regional operations around the globe and use a headquarters structure that optimizes firm effectiveness and performance. While there are still generally regional operations, there is no single headquarters region, and different activities may be located in separate regions to ensure a broad global perspective. For example, financial operations may be located in regions such as Europe or the United States, while production or sourcing might be in Asia. The goal is to manage the activities in the region that can best coordinate or operate those activities. In this strategy, firms may choose to have a limited number of consolidated customer service centers (IBM has three, with an additional three backups), a limited number of production control facilities (again, IBM has three—U.S., Europe, and Asia), and a limited number of purchasing centers. The primary advantages of a transnational strategy are that it facilitates a global focus of solution development and delivery, demonstrates significant economies of scale, and is very scalable for both domestic and global firms. The major disadvantages are this requires substantial coordination and information integration and that it reduces a firm's ability to respond to individual market uniqueness. Examples of firms that fit the specification of transnational enterprises are ABB (Switzerland), Coca-Cola (United States), Dow Chemical (United States), Hoechst (Germany), IBM (United States), ICI (United Kingdom), Johnson & Johnson (United States), Nestlé (Switzerland), Novartis (Switzerland), and Philips (Netherlands). These firms are characterized by a combination of global brands produced and marketed globally with integrated systems and management that can coordinate global operations while being sensitive to regional and local considerations.

Figure 10.1 illustrates how firms with no international strategy can evolve. The horizontal dimension refers to the movement toward local responsiveness. The vertical dimension refers to the movement toward global integration. While the "no international strategy" category can be locally responsive in the home country, it typically demonstrates no responsiveness outside the home country. On the other hand, the "multi-domestic strategy" can be very focused on individual markets, but there is no logical path toward global integration. Since each regional division would likely make decisions to best meet the needs of its customers and regions, there would be limited effort moving each region toward a synthesized integrated plan. In fact, without a strong global vision and drive, the natural tendency would be for a multi-domestic firm to remain multi-domestic. The global

FIGURE 10.1

Generic International Strategies

Source: James Fitzsimmons, and Mona Fitzsimmons, *Service Management: Operations, Strategy and Information Technology,* 7th ed. (New York: McGraw-Hill, 2011), p. 352.

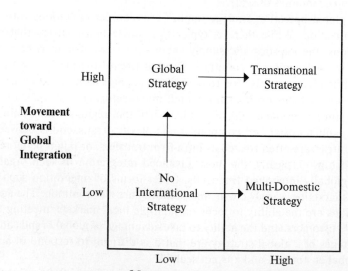

Development Stages	Service Focus	Marketing Strategy	Delivery Strategy	Management Strategy	Human Resource Development
No international strategy	Standard product for local market	Single strategy focused on local market	Direct to customer	Single simple financials	Operated by entrepreneur with limited specialization
Multi-domestic strategy	Domestic marketing and delivery	Domestic customers	Collaboration	Transaction driven with integrated financials	Management with "home-country" focus
Global strategy	Local market customization	Focused specific market areas that may cross international boundaries	Subsidiaries with local presence	Decentralized operations with local profit responsibility	Limited top management with international experience
Transnational strategy	Global branding and integrated operations	Global customers	Worldwide flow of key resources	Centralized planning in global sites	International training and experience

TABLE 10.3   Differential Characteristics of Global Services

strategy firm moves toward broader global operation with local market customization and operations. However, there is a central global headquarters that tends to guide strategy and operations. The transnational strategy operates globally with minimal consideration of a single headquarters. Effort is made to standardize "world products and solutions" and activities are completed, and often centralized, in the best location from a global perspective.

Table 10.3 compares and contrasts the different characteristics of global logistics and supply chains from the perspective of: (1) service focus, (2) marketing strategy, (3) delivery strategy, (4) management strategy, and (5) human resource strategy. While there are increased synergies in service, marketing, and operations to be gained as the firm evolves from no international strategy to a transnational strategy, there are also increased challenges relative to management and human resource development.

Multi-domestic, global, and transnational strategies can influence logistics decisions on a number of dimensions. First, sourcing and resource choices may be influenced by artificial constraints. These constraints are typically in the form of use restrictions, local content laws, or price surcharges. A use restriction is a limitation, usually government imposed, that restricts the level of import sales or purchase. For example, the enterprise may require that internal divisions be used for material sources even though price or quality is not competitive. Local content laws specify the percentage of a product's components that must be sourced within the local economy. Price surcharges involve higher charges for foreign-sourced product imposed by governments to maintain the viability of local suppliers. Price surcharges usually exist in the form of duties or tariffs. In combination, use restrictions, local content laws, and price surcharges limit management's ability to select what otherwise might be the preferred supplier.

Second, logistics to support global operations increases planning complexity. A fundamental logistics objective is smooth product flow to facilitate efficient capacity utilization. This objective is sometimes difficult in an international environment because of transportation uncertainty, infrastructure constraints, time differences, language differences, and government restrictions.

Third, global operations extend domestic logistics systems and practices to a broad range of locations and operating environments. While a domestic strategy introduces some regional differences in logistics operations, global operations introduce substantial complexity and exception processes. Local managers must accommodate exceptions while remaining within corporate policy and procedural guidelines. For example, while bribery is both an illegal and unethical practice in most developed countries, such "facilitating" payments may be the only means of getting product moved or cleared through customs in developing countries. As a result, foreign-based logistics management must often accommodate local, cultural, language, employment, and political environments without full understanding of the situation at corporate headquarters.

Managing the Global Supply Chain

To enhance a firm's global capabilities, logistics management must consider five major differences between domestic and international operations: (1) performance cycle structure, (2) transportation, (3) operational considerations, (4) information systems integration, and (5) alliances. These considerations must then be incorporated into the firm's global operating strategy.

Performance Cycle Structure

The length of the performance cycle is a major difference between domestic and global operations. Instead of 1- to 5-day transit times and 2- to 10-day total performance cycles, global operational cycles often require weeks or months. For example, it is common for automotive parts from Pacific Rim suppliers to take 60 days from order release until physical delivery at a U.S. manufacturing facility. Similarly, fashion merchandise may take anywhere from 30 to 60 days from the time the manufacturer order is released until it is received at a U.S. distribution warehouse.

The reasons leading to a longer order to delivery cycle are communication delays, financing requirements, special packaging requirements, ocean freight scheduling, slow transit times, and customs clearance. Communication may be delayed by time zone and language differences. Financing delays are caused by the requirements for letters of credit and currency translations. Special packaging may be required to protect products from in-transit damage due to high humidity, temperature, and weather conditions. Once a product is containerized, it must be scheduled for movement to and between ports having appropriate handling capabilities. This scheduling process can require up to 30 days if the origin and destination ports are not located on high-volume traffic lanes or the ships moving to the desired port lack the necessary equipment. Transit time, once the ship is en route, ranges from 10 to 21 days. Port delays are common as ships wait for others to clear harbor facilities. Customs clearance may further extend total time. Although it is increasingly common to utilize electronic messaging to preclear product shipments through customs prior to arrival at international ports, the elapsed performance cycle time is still lengthy. Security issues can create additional delays. Another problem is restricted availability of containers. Movement from Asia to the United States is generally unbalanced as more material is imported into the United States than is exported to Asia. As a result, there is strong demand for containers to move product from Asia to the United States but little motivation to ship the empty containers back. This demonstrates how unbalanced trade, either domestically or internationally, can introduce complexity into logistics operations.

These factors cause international logistics performance cycles to be longer, less consistent, and less flexible than typical in domestic operations. This lack of consistency makes planning and coordination more difficult. Determination of shipment status and anticipation of arrival times also require substantially more effort. The longer performance cycle also results in higher asset commitment because significant inventory is in transit at any point in time.

Transportation

The U.S. initiative to deregulate transportation during the early 1980s has extended globally. Four significant global changes have occurred: (1) intermodal ownership and operation, (2) privatization, (3) cabotage and bilateral agreements, and (4) infrastructure constraints.

Historically, there have been regulatory restrictions regarding international transportation ownership and operating rights. Transport carriers were limited to operating within a single transportation mode with few, if any, joint pricing and operating agreements. Traditionally, steamship lines could not own or manage integrated land-based operations such as motor or rail carriers. Without joint ownership, operations, and pricing agreements, the operation and tracking of international shipping was very complex. International shipments typically required multiple carriers to perform a single freight movement. Specifically, government rather than market forces determined the extent of services foreign-owned carriers could perform. Although some ownership and operating restrictions remain, marketing and alliance arrangements among countries have substantially improved transportation flexibility. The removal of multimodal ownership restrictions in the United States and in most other industrialized nations served to facilitate integrated movement. In response to some of these changes in national ownership requirements, an increasing number of global service providers have been established such as Deutsche Post, FedEx, and United Parcel Service.

A second transportation influence on global operations is increased carrier privatization. Historically, many international carriers were owned and operated by national governments in an effort to promote trade and provide national security. Government-owned carriers are typically subsidized and often place surcharges on foreign enterprises that use these services. Artificially high pricing and poor service often made it costly and unreliable to ship via such government-owned carriers. Inefficiencies and inflexibility also resulted from strong unionization and work rules. The combination of high operating cost and low efficiency caused many government-owned carriers to operate at a loss. A great many such carriers have been privatized and must operate in a competitive environment. Carrier privatization has resulted in increased availability of efficient international carriers.

Changes in cabotage and bilateral service agreements are the third transportation influence impacting international trade. Cabotage laws require passengers or goods moving between two domestic ports to utilize only domestic carriers. For example, water shipment from Los Angeles to New York was required to use a U.S. carrier. Similar cabotage laws restricted Canadian drivers from transporting a backhaul load to Detroit once a shipment originating in Canada was unloaded in Texas. Cabotage laws were designed to protect domestic transportation industries even though they also served to reduce overall transportation equipment utilization and related efficiency. The European Union has relaxed cabotage restrictions to increase trade efficiency. Such reduced cabotage restrictions will save U.S. corporations 10 to 15 percent in intra-European shipping costs. The United States continues to review its cabotage laws relating to Canada and some of the restrictions with Mexico have been reduced to enhance equipment utilization and to reduce the environmental impact.

Many regions, both developed and undeveloped, are experiencing major constraints on their physical infrastructure. Global operations are significantly increasing the demand specifically on port and airport capacities. Since much of the infrastructure in the world was developed over 50 years ago, it was designed for substantially less capacity and without extensive growth capability in terms of surrounding land. Although information and handling technology has facilitated rapid movement of goods through ports and airports, the volume increase still results in substantial congestion. At the same time, tight local, state, and federal budgets have limited the reinvestment that can be made in the existing infra-structure. As a result, logistics managers are being driven to seek out alternative suppliers, carriers, routes, or port locations.

Operational Considerations

There are a number of unique operational considerations to support global supply chains. First, international operations typically require multiple languages for both product and documentation. A technical product such as a computer or a calculator must have local features such as keyboard characters and language on both the product itself and related manuals. From a logistics perspective, language differences dramatically increase com-plexity since a product is limited to a specific country once it is language-customized. For example, even though western Europe is much smaller than the United States in a geographic sense, it requires relatively more inventory to support marketing efforts since separate inventories may be required to accommodate various languages. Although prod-uct proliferation due to language requirement has been reduced through multilingual packaging and postponement strategies, such practices are not always acceptable. Some consumers are reluctant to accept products not labeled in their native tongue. In addition to product language implications, international operations may require multilingual docu-mentation for each country through which the shipment passes. Although English is the general language of commerce, some countries require that transportation and customs documentation be provided in the local language. This increases the time and effort for international operations, since complex documents must be translated prior to shipment. These communication and documentation difficulties can be somewhat overcome through standardized electronic transactions.

The second global operational consideration is unique national accommodations such as performance features, technical characteristics, environmental considerations, and safety requirements. Performance feature differences include specific product functional-ity such as speed or process constraints. Technical characteristics include power supplies, documentation, and metrics. Environmental considerations include chemicals that can be used or the types and amount of waste generated. Safety requirements include automatic shutoffs and specialized documentation. While they may not be substantial, the small dif-ferences between country requirements may significantly increase required SKUs and sub-sequent inventory levels.

The third operating consideration is the sheer amount of documentation required for international operations. While domestic operations can generally be completed by using only an invoice and bill of lading, international operations require substantial documentation regarding order contents, transportation, financing, and government con-trol. Table 10.4 lists and describes common forms of international documentation.

The fourth operating consideration is the high incidence of countertrade and duty drawback found in some international situations. While most established firms prefer cash transactions, countertrade is important. Countertrade, in essence, is when a seller agrees to accept products as payment or purchase products from the buyer as part of a sales agree-ment. While such agreements have financial consequences, they also have major implica-tions for logistics and marketing in terms of disposal of goods received as payment. Duty drawback describes situations when a firm pays a duty to import goods into a foreign coun-try but the duty paid can be drawn back or returned if the items or a comparable designate is exported. For example, Pepsi supplies syrup to the Russian government, which bottles and markets the soft drink with practically no control from Pepsi. In return, Pepsi is paid for the syrup by receiving exclusive rights to distribute Russian Stolichnaya vodka in the United States. This exclusive right requires marketing and logistics support.

- *Export irrevocable commercial letter of credit.* A contract between an importer and a bank that transfers liability or paying the exporter from the importer to the (supposedly more creditworthy) importer's bank.
- *Bank draft (or bill of exchange).* A means of payment for an import/export transaction. Two types exist: transaction payable on sight with proper documents *(sight draft)* and transaction payable at some fixed time after acceptance of proper documents *(time draft)*. Either type of draft accompanied by instructions and other documents *(but no letter of credit)* is a documentary draft.
- *Bill of lading.* Issued by the shipping company or its agent as evidence of a contract for shipping the merchandise and as a claim to ownership of the goods.
- *Combined transport document.* May replace the bill of lading if goods are shipped by air *(airway bill)* or by more than one mode of transportation.
- *Commercial invoice.* A document written by the exporter to precisely describe the goods and the terms of sale (similar to a shipping invoice used in domestic shipments).
- *Insurance certificate.* Explains what type of coverage is utilized (fire, theft, water), the name of the insurer, and the exporter whose property is being insured.
- *Certificate of origin.* Denotes the country in which the goods were produced to assess tariffs and other government-imposed restrictions on trade.

TABLE 10.4
Common Forms of International Logistics Documentation

Information Systems Integration

A major challenge in globalization is information systems integration. Since firms typically globalize by acquisition and merger, the integration of systems typically lags. Operational integration requires the ability to route orders and manage inventory requirements electronically throughout the world. Development of supportive technology integration represents substantial capital investment. As discussed in Chapter 3, two types of system integration are required to support global operations. The first is a global transaction or ERP system. The global ERP system is necessary to provide common data regarding global customers, suppliers, products, and financials. It is also necessary to provide common and consistent information regarding order and inventory status regardless of the location from which a global customer is inquiring or where the shipment is to be delivered. The second system integration requirement is a global planning system that can maximize overall manufacturing and delivery asset utilization while meeting customer service requirements. Few firms have fully integrated global information systems or capability.

Alliances

A final international operations consideration is the growing importance of third-party alliances. While alliances with carriers and specialized service suppliers are important in domestic operations, they are essential for international commerce. Without alliances, it would be necessary for an enterprise operating internationally to maintain contacts with retailers, wholesalers, manufacturers, suppliers, and service providers throughout the world. International alliances provide market access and expertise and reduce the inherent risk of global operations. The number of alternatives, breadth of activities, and complexity of globalization require alliances.

In summary, globalization is an evolving frontier that increasingly demands more extensive supply chain integration. As firms expand their focus toward international markets, demand for logistical competency increases because of longer supply chains, more variation, increased uncertainty, and more documentation. While the forces of change push toward borderless operations, supply chain logistics management still confronts market, financial, and channel barriers. The barriers are exemplified by distance, demand, diversity, and documentation. The challenge is to position an enterprise to take advantage of the benefits of global marketing and manufacturing by developing world-spanning logistical competency.[2]

Global Sourcing

One of today's major business challenges specifically impacting logistical management is the dramatic increase in international sourcing, particularly from low-cost countries such as China. Firms in virtually all durable goods industries are investigating in Asia, eastern Europe, Latin America, and Africa as potential sources for finished goods or, at least, component parts. This section reviews the rationale for international sourcing from low-cost countries, identifies some of the specific challenges, and offers some guidelines regarding sourcing strategy.

Rationale for Low-Cost-Country Sourcing

Increased need for global competitiveness is driving many firms, particularly those in durable and fashion industries, to identify and establish relationships with suppliers in low-cost countries. There are a number of justifications for such sourcing initiatives. First, sourcing from countries with low wage rates typically reduces manufacturing cost. While such strategies may reduce manufacturing cost, some firms do not consider the total cost impact of international sourcing particularly with respect to the logistics cost components of transportation and inventory. Second, seeking out suppliers in low-cost countries can also increase the number of possible sources and thus increase the competitive pressure on domestic suppliers. Third, low-cost-country sourcing can increase the firm's exposure to state-of-the-art product and process technologies. Without pressure from global suppliers, there may be reluctance on the part of domestic suppliers to investigate or invest in new technologies because they have significant assets tied up in older technologies. Conversely, global suppliers may place significant focus on new technologies to establish a competitive position in foreign markets regardless of the issues discussed earlier regarding extended supply chains. A final rationale for low-cost-country sourcing is to establish a local presence to facilitate sales in the international country. For example, while the U.S. automobile industry is significantly increasing sourcing from low-cost countries to reduce component cost, it is also seeking to facilitate automobile sales in the local country. Due to political or legal constraints, it is often necessary for a firm to have local relationships and production operations to be allowed to sell their product in the local country. The combination of these makes a strong case for sourcing from a low-cost country, but it is necessary to also consider the challenges.

Challenges for Low-Cost-Country Sourcing

While the rationale for low-cost-import sourcing is substantial, there is also a long list of issues and challenges related to such sourcing strategies. These issues and challenges

---

[2] The Council of Supply Chain Management Professionals (CSCMP) has produced a number of *Global Perspectives* reports that describe the logistics characteristics and challenges confronted in over 20 specific countries. The reports are available free to members in paper and electronic form from the website at www.cscmp.org. For a more comprehensive discussion, see Greg Cudahy, Narendra Mulani, and Christophe Cases, "Mastering Global Operations in a Multipolar World," *Supply Chain Management Review*, March 2008, pp. 22–29.

are further complicated by the fact that the benefits and costs related to low-cost-country sourcing accrue to different organizational units. Procurement or manufacturing may receive the benefits through lower-cost materials or components. Many of the costs and the challenges to ship and guarantee delivery of the materials are the responsibility of logistics. Benefits and costs must be integrated across the full supply chain process in order to make the correct sourcing decision.

The first challenge is the identification of sources capable of producing the materials in the quality and quantity required. While it is becoming easier to achieve the quality objective, ensuring that the potential supplier has the ability to meet volume and seasonal fluctuation demands in a suitable time frame often remains a challenge.

The second challenge considers the protection of a firm's intellectual property as products or components are produced and transported. The suppliers and countries involved need to have legal constraints in place to protect product designs and related trade secrets.

The third challenge relates to understanding import/export compliance issues. There may be government regulations regarding the volume of a commodity that can be imported before duties or other restrictions are enforced. The percentage of materials that are foreign-sourced may also restrict a firm's ability to sell to select customers. Government contracts may require a specific level of domestically made components. For example, if the contract requires that the product is "Made in the U.S.A.," 95 percent of the material must be of domestic origin.

The fourth challenge relates to communication with suppliers and transportation companies. While the procurement negotiation with low-cost countries is not easy, there is often a greater difficulty in dealing with carriers, freight forwarders, and government customs as a result of time zone, language, and technology differences.

The fifth challenge is the need to guarantee the security of the product while in transit. Not only does supply chain security require that the product is secure, the process must also secure containers and vehicles involved that are both full and empty.

The sixth challenge concerns the inventory and obsolescence risk associated with extended transit times. With the longer transit times associated with low-cost-country sourcing, it is not uncommon for the firm to have one or two months' supply of product in transit, which must be counted as an asset and incur related inventory carrying cost. Extended leadtimes also increase the potential for obsolescence, as orders have longer leadtimes and there is generally little flexibility for change. Such extended leadtimes also can impact recovery when a quality issue develops. It is not unusual for firms to fly components from offshore suppliers to recover from unexpected quality problems or delayed shipments.

The final challenge, which synthesizes the previous ones, focuses on the need to understand the difference between piece price and total cost. While the piece price may include the material as well as direct and indirect labor, the total cost perspective needs to consider other cost elements, including freight, inventory, obsolescence, duties, taxes, recovery, and other risk considerations.

Guidelines for Sourcing

The decision to source material and components domestically or from a low-cost country is a complex one. While direct and indirect product costs represent one major factor, there are many other factors that must be considered and weighed appropriately. Products and components that have extended times between manufacturing changeovers are ideal for low-cost-country sourcing. A counterexample would be the life cycle for an electronics component, which is typically quite short and therefore would generally trend toward domestic sourcing. Products and components that have numerous variations should also generally be domestically sourced because the extended leadtimes associated with low-cost-country sourcing make it difficult to forecast the precise mix of product that will be demanded. Products or components with high labor content should take advantage of the typically low labor rates in low-cost counties. Products or components with high intellectual property content should be sourced domestically, as the legal systems in many of the low-cost countries do not provide adequate trade secret protection. Domestic sourcing is generally appropriate for products and components with relatively high transport cost such as those that are bulky or damage easy. Due to increasing energy prices, many firms are beginning to reconsider more localized sourcing. Products or components with relatively low value are ideal for low-cost-country sourcing, as the inventory carrying cost while it is in transit is not significant. Products and components that are constrained for security or other types of import restrictions by a domestic government should tend toward domestic sourcing. For example, there may be customs delays in importing electronic goods when the supplier does not have the trust of the importing government because of the potential for importing contraband. Finally, products or components that have a high degree of transport uncertainty because of relatively low volumes or location on trade lanes with limited service would suggest domestic sourcing.

There is no simple answer regarding which products or components should be domestically sourced, as a number of the criteria are somewhat qualitative. Table 10.5 lists the general sourcing criteria.[3] The final determination depends on the specific item and the firm's expertise. As firms increase their global operations and marketing efforts, logistics managers should be increasingly involved to provide a realistic assessment of the total cost and performance implications.

As a supply chain strategy becomes more global, increased complexities are encountered. These complexities result from longer distances, demand differentials, cultural diversity, and complex documentation. Nevertheless, firms will increasingly confront the need to expand operations into the global arena. Strategies to achieve a share of the rapidly expanding world market range from export/import to local presence to true globalization. Regardless of the strategic focus, success will, to a large extent, be dependent upon a firm's logistical capabilities.

[3] For a more detailed discussion regarding sourcing in Asia and China specifically, see Robert Handfield and Kevin McCormack, "What You Need to Know about Sourcing from China," *Supply Chain Management Review*, September 2005, pp. 28–36.

TABLE 10.5
Sourcing Guidelines

Criteria	Domestic Sourcing	Low-Cost-Country Sourcing
Product life cycle length	Short	Long
Product variations in size, color, or style	Many	Few
Labor content	Low	High
Intellectual property content	High	Low
Transport cost	High	Low
Product value	High	Low
Security or import constraints	High	Low
Transport uncertainty	High	Low

TABLE 10.6
Comparison of Global Supply Chain Characteristics

Region	Infrastructure	Technology	Human Capital	Political
North America	Built up but congested	Access to new technology, but infrastructure represents old technology	High technical talent but high wages	Stable laws and trade agreements
Europe	Built up but congested	Access to new technology, but infrastructure represents old technology	High technical talent but high wages	Stable laws and trade agreements
South America	Limited and congested	Introduction of new technology	Low technical talent and low wages	Challenges due to legal environment and corruption
Asia	Limited and congested	Introduction of new technology	Increasing technical talent and wages	Challenges due to legal environment and corruption
Africa	Minimal	Introduction of new technology	Low technical talent and low wages	Challenges due to legal environment and corruption

Global Comparison of Supply Chain Characteristics

When considering the possibility of global expansion, it is important to understand the differences between the major geographies. Table 10.6 compares and contrasts the major continents in terms of infrastructure, technology, human capital, and political environment. *Infrastructure* refers to transportation rights-of-way and capacities, particularly for highway, rail, ports, and airports. Infrastructure also includes the technical infrastructure to support the transportation system. *Technology* refers to the capabilities of the communications, power, and production facilities. *Human capital* refers to the training, skill level, and wage scale of labor, particularly those involved in production labor. The *political environment* refers to the stability of the legal environment, trade agreements, intellectual property, and anti-corruption laws.

Modes of Entry

There are four approaches that a firm can use to market its products globally: (1) exporting and importing, (2) licensing and franchising, (3) international joint venture, and (4) foreign direct ownership. When using exporting and importing, a firm sells its products either to an international firm for remarketing or to a firm local in the target country. When licensing and franchising, a firm sells licenses for the product or technology to a firm that can develop and maintain a franchise in the target country. When using an international joint venture, the firm creates a joint venture subsidiary in the target country, where the partners in the joint venture maintains a percentage of interest. In the case of foreign direct investment, the firm creates a solely owned subsidiary in the target country. In general, the margin increases as the firm moves toward the foreign direct investment, but the risk increases as well. Table 10.7 summarizes the characteristics, strengths, and weaknesses for each entry mode.

Mode of Entry	Favorable Conditions	Strengths	Weaknesses
Exporting and importing	• Limited or unclear sales potential in target countries • Standardized product requiring little product modification • Favorable import policies in target countries; unclear political stability	• Minimizes involvement, commitment, and risk • Increases speed and flexibility of engaging target countries • Uses existing production facilities worldwide	• Company and its products are viewed as outsiders and foreign market entrants • Costs associated with, for example, trade barriers, tariffs, and transportation
Licensing and franchising	• Import and investment barriers exist in target countries, but moderate sales potential exist • Large cultural distance between home and host countries • Licensee has limited ability to become a future competitor	• Moderate involvement and commitment; low risk • Moderate speed and flexibility of engaging target countries • Can circumvent import barriers; sales potential	• Licensee period is limited in contractual length, and licensee may become competitor • Lack of control over the use of company and non-company assets to promote products
International joint ventures	• Import barriers exist in target countries, but government restrictions exist on foreign ownership • Moderate to high sales potential of products • Local JV partner can provide knowledge, skills, and network	• Overcomes ownership restrictions and cultural distance • Potential for learning and resource combination • IJV ownership >50% is typically viewed as a domestic company	• IJVs are new companies, legally independent from the original companies • IJVs are difficult to manage for the original companies, and there is a lack of control over strategic and tactical issues
Foreign direct ownership	• Import barriers exist in target countries but low political risk • Small cultural distance between home and host countries • High sales potential of products, but assets cannot be fairly priced	• Viewed as being locally committed and involved • Gain knowledge, over time, of the local market • Can apply local skills to customize production	• Higher risk being taken while being more committed and involved • Requires more human and non-human resources and interaction and integration with local employees

TABLE 10.7   Characteristics, Strengths, and Weaknesses by Entry Mode

Source: Tomas Hult, David Closs, David Frayer. Global Supply Chain Management: Leveraging Processes, Measurements, and Tools for Strategic Corporate Advantage. (New York: McGraw Hill, 2014). Pg. 205.

Global Compliance

While the previous sections have discussed the benefits and challenges of global supply chain operations, a major challenge for the global operator relates to dealing with customs when moving individuals and product across international boundaries. While countries have different requirements, the characteristics are similar. The following sections discuss the agency (Customs and Border Protection in the United States), types of compliance regulations, role of customs brokers, and penalties for not following customs regulations.

Customs and Border Protection

Customs and Border Protection (CBP) is the agency of the United States government responsible for import law enforcement and duty and tariff collection (www.cbp.gov). CBP is under the jurisdiction of the Department of Homeland Security. Most other countries use similar organizations to enforce their regulations. The primary role of CBP is to inspect all individuals and products brought into the United States to ensure that all individuals and goods meet appropriate requirements. Another significant CBP responsibility is to monitor cross-border movement for drugs, illicit materials, and weapons. In general, the individuals must be U.S. citizens or permanent residents or have appropriate visas. In the case of product, the goods must be approved for entry into the United States, and the appropriate duties and taxes must be paid. Taxes and duties are typically *ad-valorem* (based on product value) payments to the government. For example, a tax or duty of 10 percent means that any product that fits the classification will incur a 10 percent fee that is paid to the government. The effective result is that the price of the product being imported increases by 10 percent. The result is that the product being imported becomes less competitive in the country to which it is being imported, and the products made in the importing country become more competitive.

Compliance

Customs compliance refers to the requirements to enforce government regulations regarding what can be imported and exported and to collect duties and tariffs when appropriate. Most countries have restrictions regarding the types of goods that can be imported and exported based on economic and competitive policies as well as safety and environmental regulations. The restrictions may be based on where the product is manufactured, what it is made of, and the source of the labor. There are three major activities that firms are required to do to meet their compliance objectives.

First, firms must correctly classify the goods that are being imported and exported. The Harmonized Tariff of the United States (HTSUS) is an organized listing of goods and corresponding duty rates that is used by CBP for classifying goods. The HTSUS is the building block of all customs activity; it sets the rules regarding origin for trade programs, established duty rates, and admissibility for all goods imported into the United States and is required for export reporting. Failure to properly classify goods can result in fines and penalties.

Second, firms must maintain accurate records regarding exports and imports. These records are used for aggregate imports and exports for the overall economy and to record trade levels with various countries. These reports are done using Electronic Export Information (EEI) filings.

Finally, firms must monitor where their products are being shipped from to make sure that the destination, end user, or end use is appropriate. The specific requirement is that goods that have potential military capabilities must be controlled so that individuals and countries that might want to attack the United States do not gain access to critical technology and weaponry. The primary responsibility here is to make sure the firm has appropriate licenses for the items it is exporting.

Customs Broker

A customs broker is a specially trained individual or firm with primary responsibility for helping other firms complete the paperwork and arrangements for importing or exporting product. Customs brokers can act as a firm's liaison with CBP regarding issues of admissibility, coordination of cargo exams, and post-entry actions. However, the customs broker is an advisor; the customs broker cannot take the role of the decider regarding the actions to take for a customs transaction.

Enforcement

Customs has many enforcement options when firms break customs regulations. For minor violations such as late filings, the penalty might be liquidated damages that require the offending firm to pay a relatively defined amount. For more serious or penalty claims such as misclassification of goods, valuation errors, or errors in recordkeeping, a firm may be charged with negligence, gross negligence, or fraud penalties. Negligence penalties are assessed when the firm fails to exercise reasonable care. Gross negligence penalties are assessed when the firm demonstrates wanton disregard of the law or relevant facts. Fraud penalties are assessed when the firm demonstrates intent to deceive or mislead.

To enforce compliance, CBP might detain shipments or deny entry, seize the goods, move the goods to a bonded or foreign trade zone warehouse and begin forfeiture proceedings, or refer the case to the Department of Justice for criminal proceedings. In the case of the penalties, a firm may be charged two times the duties for negligence, four times the duties for gross negligence, and an amount not to exceed the domestic of the goods for fraud.

Conclusion

The previous sections offer insight regarding the role of Customs and Border Protection, the requirements for complying with CBP practices and regulations, the role of a customs broker, and a discussion of the penalties related to customs compliance. It is clear that global supply chain operations and the related customs activities significantly increase supply chain complexity.

Summary

Global operations are becoming more of the norm for logistics and supply chain executives. Decisions regarding global sourcing and marketing require more complex trade-off analyses than traditionally required for domestic logistics. Both the quantitative and qualitative factors are more complex. While transportation, inventory, and warehousing costs are very substantial for global operations, other cost components, including taxes, tariffs, duties, documentation, and import restrictions, can also have a substantial impact on true total cost. However, in addition to the quantitative considerations, international operations introduce a number of other variables that are much more difficult to quantify. Many of these variables relate directly to logistics operations. The major qualitative considerations include relationship management, infrastructure consistency, production and transit reliability, and security. With increased global marketing and manufacturing operations, logistics management needs to be more involved in developing and implementing global strategies.

Study Questions

1. Discuss how logistics management must evolve to reflect the differing needs for each stage of international development.
2. Discuss the logistics operational considerations for operating in a global environment.
3. Describe the logistics characteristics of a firm moving toward a globally integrated enterprise.
4. Describe some of the strategies that firms can use to overcome the challenges related to transportation infrastructure congestion.

5. Discuss the rationale and challenges related to sourcing from low-cost countries.
6. Discuss how product variations, security and import constraints, and transportation uncertainty should impact global sourcing and marketing decisions.

Challenge Questions

1. Suppose you were asked to advise a domestic firm in your region. Identify the critical value propositions that the firm uses to compete domestically. Using the value propositions that you have identified, develop and rationalize an argument for the firm to increase its global operations based on the points identified in Table 10.1.

2. For each country or region in Table 10.2, compare and contrast each country/ region's logistics as a percentage of GDP and rationalize the differences.

3. Describe and rationalize how a firm's logistics and supply chain strategy will likely evolve as a firm shifts from no international strategy to a global strategy to a transnational strategy. What are the challenges as the firm evolves through each?

4. Select a component or finished good that you are familiar with that is sourced from a low-cost country. Develop a total cost value proposition to evaluate the potential of continued sourcing from a low-cost country. For each of the cost components (material, manufacturing, transportation, packaging, inventory, handling, damage, risk, security), identify the major trade-offs associated with sourcing locally versus sourcing from a low-cost country. Based on your assessment of the current environment in your country, what is the direction for each of these cost components over the next five years, and what is the likely trend regarding low-cost-country sourcing?

5. Discuss the benefits and challenges related to alternative export modes.

CHAPTER 11

Network Design

Chapter Outline

For the most part, managers confront a new and challenging assignment when they evaluate logistics networks. Due to the rapid rate of change in almost every facet of logistical operations, managers must consider the numerous factors that interact when they try to use previous experience to guide the creation and implementation of a new logistic network. Therefore, success or failure may depend on how well the planning team is able to quantify these factors and rationalize a logical and credible action plan. Having a comprehensive understanding of the theoretical constructs that serve as the foundation of logistical integration provides an important step toward developing an integrated strategy.

In earlier chapters, the essence of logistical strategy was identified as achieving least-total-cost operations while simultaneously maintaining flexibility. Flexibility is the key to providing high-level basic customer service while at the same time maintaining sufficient operating capacity to meet and exceed key customer expectations. To exploit flexibility, an enterprise needs to achieve a high level of logistical process integration. Integration is required at two operating levels. First, the operating areas of logistics must be integrated across a network of warehouse facilities. Such network integration is essential if a firm is using logistical competency to achieve competitive advantage. Second, integration must extend beyond a single firm by supporting relationships across the supply chain. This chapter presents a framework to assist managers in achieving such integration.[1]

This chapter also describes a generalized methodology to complete supply chain network analysis and identifies the major factors that drive supply chain strategy. The final section reviews the trade-offs related to centralization and decentralization when making supply chain design decisions.

Enterprise Facility Network

Prior to the availability of low-cost dependable land transportation, most of the world's commerce relied on product and material movement via water. During this early period, commercial activity concentrated around port cities. Overland transport of goods was costly and slow. For example, the leadtime to order designer clothing from across the continental United States could exceed 9 months. Although demand for fast and efficient transport existed, it was not until the invention of the steam locomotive in 1829 that the transportation technology revolution began in the United States. Today, the transportation system in this country is a highly developed network of rail, water, air, highway, and pipeline services. Each transport alternative provides a specialized type of service for use within a logistical system. This availability of economical transportation creates the opportunity to establish a competitively superior warehouse network to service customers.

The importance of facility location analysis has been recognized since the middle of the 19th century, when the German economist Joachim von Thünen wrote *The Isolated State*.[2] For von Thünen, the primary determinant of economic development was the price of land and the cost to transport products from farm to market. The value of land was viewed as being directly related to the cost of transportation and the ability of a product to command an adequate price to cover distribution cost. Von Thünen's basic principle was that the value of specific produce at the growing location decreases with distance from the primary selling market.

Following von Thünen, Alfred Weber generalized location theory from an agrarian to an industrial society.[3] Weber's theoretical system consisted of numerous consuming locations spread over a geographical area and linked together by transportation. Weber developed a scheme to classify major materials as either **ubiquitous** or **localized**. Ubiquitous materials

---

[1]The reader is cautioned that this chapter stresses theoretical constructs that determine logistical system design. The material offers a framework to guide trade-off analysis. While theoretical discussions tend to be abstract, the principles presented are logically consistent regardless of the competitive or cultural setting within which logistical network design is performed.

[2]Joachim von Thünen, *The Isolated State,* Beziehung auf Landwirtschaft und Nationalökonomie. Hamburg, 1826.

[3]Alfred Weber, *Theory of the Location of Industries,* translated by Carl J. Friedrich (Chicago, IL: University of Chicago Press, 1928).

were those available at all locations. Water is generally considered a ubiquitous material. Localized raw materials consisted of mineral deposits found only at selected areas. On the basis of his analysis, Weber developed a **material index**. The index was the ratio of the localized raw material to the total weight of the finished product. Various types of industry were assigned a **locational weight** based on the material index. Utilizing these two measures, Weber generalized that industries would locate facilities at the point of consumption when the manufacturing process was weight-gaining and near the point of raw material deposit when the manufacturing process was weight-losing. Finally, if the manufacturing process were neither weight-gaining nor weight-losing, firms would select plant locations at an intermediate point.

Examples of weight-gaining products with a ubiquitous material are beverages. In this case, the addition of a ubiquitous material like water makes it very expensive to transport, typically resulting in a decentralized distribution strategy with many production or distribution centers. On the other hand, electronic components don't typically gain much weight in the manufacturing process, so shipping them is less expensive, resulting in relatively few plants or distribution centers. These two examples illustrate how the nature of the product influences the network design.

Several location theorists followed von Thünen and Weber. The most notable contributions toward a general theory of location were developed by August Lösch, Edgar Hoover, Melvin Greenhut, Walter Isard, and Michael Webber.[4] In their writings, these five authors highlighted the importance of specialization in industrial location, including quantification of the importance of transportation.

Spectrum of Location Decisions

In terms of logistical system design, transportation offers the potential to link geographically dispersed manufacturing, warehousing, and market locations into an integrated system. Logistical system facilities include all locations at which raw materials, work-in-process, or finished inventories are handled or stored. Thus, all retail stores, finished goods warehouses, manufacturing plants, and material storage warehouses represent network locations. It follows that selection of individual locations, as well as the composite locational network, represents important competitive and cost-related logistical decisions.

A manufacturing plant location may require several years to fully implement. For example, General Motors' decision to build a new SUV assembly plant in Lansing, Michigan, spanned over four years from concept to reality. In contrast, some warehouse arrangements are sufficiently flexible to be used only at specified times during a year. The selection of retail locations is a specialized decision influenced by marketing and competitive conditions. The discussion that follows concentrates on selecting warehouse locations. Among all the location decisions faced by logistical managers, those involving warehouse networks are most frequently reviewed.

Local Presence: An Obsolete Paradigm

A long-standing belief in business is that a firm must have facilities in local markets to successfully conduct business. During development of the North American economy, erratic transportation service created serious doubt about a firm's ability to promise delivery in a

---

[4]August Lösch, *Die Räumliche Ordnung der Wirtschaft* (Jena: Gustav Fischer Verlag, 1940); Edgar M. Hoover, *The Location of Economic Activity* (New York: McGraw-Hill Book Company, 1938); Melvin L. Greenhut, *Plant Location in Theory and Practice* (Chapel Hill, NC: University of North Carolina Press, 1956); Walter Isard et al., *Methods of Regional Analysis: An Introduction to Regional Science* (New York: John Wiley & Sons, Inc., 1960); Walter Isard, *Location and Space Economy* (Cambridge, MA: The MIT Press, 1968); and Michael J. Webber, *Impact of Uncertainty on Location* (Cambridge, MA: The MIT Press, 1972).

timely and consistent manner. In short, customers felt that unless a supplier maintained inventory within the local market area it would be difficult, if not impossible, to provide consistent delivery. This perception, commonly referred to as the **local presence paradigm**, resulted in inventories being maintained in numerous local markets. As recently as the early 1980s it was not uncommon for manufacturers to operate 20 or more warehouses to service the U.S. mainland. Some firms went so far as to have full-line inventory warehouses located near all major sales markets.

When a tradition such as local warehousing is part of a successful strategy, it is difficult to change. However, for the past several decades the cost and risk associated with maintaining local presence have forced reexamination. Transportation services have dramatically expanded, and reliability has increased to the point where shipment arrival times are dependable and predictable. Rapid advances in information technology have reduced the time required to identify and communicate customer requirements. Technology is available to track transportation vehicles, thereby providing accurate delivery information. Next-day delivery from a warehouse facility located as far away as 800 to 1000 miles is common practice.

Transportation, information technology, and inventory economics all favor the use of fewer rather than more warehouses to service customers within a geographical area. In many situations, customer perceptions concerning local presence continue to promote decentralization of inventory. The answer to the question "How much local presence is desirable?" is best understood by carefully examining the relationships that drive logistical system design.

Warehouse Requirements

Warehouses are established in a logistical system to lower total cost or to improve customer service. In some situations, the benefits of cost reduction and improved service can be achieved simultaneously.

Warehouses create value through the processes they support. Manufacturing requires warehouses to store, sort, and sequence materials and components. Facilities used for inbound materials and components are often referred to as **supply facing warehouses**. Warehouses are also used to store, sequence, and combine inventory for consolidated shipment to next-destination customers in the supply chain. Warehouses used to support customer accommodation are often referred to as **demand facing warehouses**. Demand facing warehouse requirements are directly related to manufacturing and marketing strategies.

Due to the specialized materials handling, inventory process requirements, and just-in-time manufacturing process warehouses typically specialize in performing either supply or demand facing services. Warehouses committed to supporting manufacturing are typically located close to the factories they support; in contrast, warehouses dedicated to customer accommodation are typically strategically located throughout the geographical market area serviced.

The combinations of information technology, e-procurement fulfillment, and response-based business strategies have combined to radically alter how and why warehouses are used. The economic justification and desired functionality of a warehouse is typically distinctly different for facilities dedicated to procurement, manufacturing, or customer accommodation.

Procurement Drivers

Procurement drivers, as discussed in Chapter 5, center on using warehouses to help purchase materials and components from suppliers at the lowest total inbound cost.

Sophisticated purchasing executives have long realized that a combination of purchase price, quantity discount, payment terms, and logistical support is required to achieve lowest delivered cost for materials and components. In an effort to develop and support dedicated and customized working relationships, most firms have reduced their overall number of suppliers. The logic is the development of a limited number of supplier relationships that can be operationally integrated into a firm's supply chain. The goals of relational buying are to achieve lowest total landed cost eliminate waste, duplication, and unplanned redundancy.

In an effort to improve overall operating efficiency, life cycle considerations have become prominent in purchase decisions. This relational dynamic of working with limited suppliers is based on a cradle-to-grave philosophy, spanning from new product development to reclamation and disposal of unused materials and unsold inventory. Such a **closed-loop** focus results from buying practices that directly impact the requirements and functionality of supply facing warehousing. Value-added services related to procurement are increasingly being debundled from purchase price. The shared goal is to develop procurement relationships that meet service requirements at lowest total landed cost. For example, manufacturers have begun to unbundle transportation or sequencing responsibility from suppliers to better understand total landed cost. Such debundling facilitates functional absorption and spin-off between manufacturers and their suppliers. There is also a trend toward more response-based business strategies, which is redefining expectations concerning supplier support and participation in the value-added process. The result is new structural relationships, such as tier one suppliers and lead facilitators. Finally, the seasonality of selected supplies, opportunities to purchase at reduced prices, and the need to rapidly accommodate accelerated manufacturing plans continues to make selected material warehousing a sound business decision.

As a result of these trends, the role of supply facing warehouses continues to change. Warehouses were traditionally used to stockpile raw materials and component parts. Today such facilities place greater emphasis on sorting, sequencing, and light assembly of materials and components as they flow into manufacturing. The goal is to streamline flow of materials and components by eliminating duplicate handling and storage of identical inventories at multiple locations throughout the material supply network.

Manufacturing Drivers

Warehouses that support manufacturing are used to consolidate finished product for outbound customer shipment. The capability to consolidate a variety of products differs from individual product shipment. A primary advantage of a manufacturing demand facing warehouse is the ability to provide customers full-line product assortment on a single invoice at truckload transportation rates. In fact, a manufacturer's capability to provide such consolidation may be the primary reason for selection as a preferred supplier.

Leading examples of demand facing warehouses are the networks used by such firms as General Mills, Johnson & Johnson, Kraft, and Kimberly-Clark. At Johnson & Johnson, warehouses are used to support hospital and consumer business sectors by serving as inventory consolidators for a variety of different business units. As a result, customers can purchase full assortments of products from different business units on a single invoice for shipment on one order. Kimberly-Clark produces a wide variety of individual products on specific manufacturing lines at specialized plants. Such products as Kleenex, Scott Tissue, and Huggies disposable diapers are manufactured at economy-of-scale volume, then temporarily positioned in demand facing warehouses. Customer-specific truckloads of assorted products are assembled at the warehouse. Procter & Gamble recently consolidated the demand facing warehouses across the divisions so that retailers could receive all

P&G products on a single truckload from one of their consolidation centers. Inventories of all major products are maintained at each branch to facilitate full-service shipments to customers.

The primary determinant of the warehousing required to support manufacturing is the specific production strategy being implemented. In Chapter 5, three basic manufacturing strategies—make to plan **(MTP)**, make to order **(MTO)**, and assemble to order **(ATO)**— were discussed. The extent of demand facing warehousing can be directly linked to the requirements of each manufacturing strategy. In a general sense, MTO manufacturing strategies require supply facing warehousing support but little, if any, demand facing storage. Conversely, MTP manufacturing strategies, which focus resources to achieve maximum manufacturing economy of scale, require substantial demand facing warehouse capacity.

Customer Relationship Drivers

Customer relationship warehouses create value by providing customized inventory assortments to wholesalers and retailers. A warehouse located geographically close to customers seeks to minimize inbound transportation cost by maximizing shipment consolidation and length of haul from manufacturing plants followed by relatively short outbound movement to customers. The geographic size of a market area served from a support warehouse depends on the number of suppliers, the desired service speed, size of average order, and cost per unit of local delivery. The warehouse facility exists to provide customers inventory assortment, replenishment, and other value added activities such as creation of displays. A warehouse is justified if it offers a way to achieve a competitive service or cost advantage.

Rapid Replenishment

Customer warehouses have traditionally provided assortments of products from varied manufacturers and various suppliers to retailers. A retail store typically does not have sufficient demand to order inventory in large quantities directly from wholesalers or manufacturers. A typical retail replenishment order is placed with a wholesaler that sells a variety of different manufacturer products.

Customer warehouses are common in the food and mass merchandise industries. The modern food warehouse usually is located geographically near the retail stores it services. From this central warehouse, consolidated product assortments can rapidly replenish retail inventories because of the close geographical proximity. Large retail stores may receive multiple truckloads from the warehouse on a daily basis. Location of the warehouse within the market served is justified as the least-cost way to rapidly replenish an assortment of inventory to either an end customer or a retailer.

Market-Based ATO

The design of a customer relationship warehouse network is directly related to inventory deployment strategy. The establishment of a customer relationship warehouse is a result of forward inventory deployment in anticipation of future demand. This assumption means that a manufacturing firm utilizing such a distributive network is to some degree dependent upon forecasting inventory requirements to offset response time to meet customer requirements. The preceding discussion indicates inventories deployed forward after manufacturing are typical in situations where firms are manufacturing to plan or when they are engaged in decentralized assembly to order. In assemble-to-order **(ATO)** situations, common or undifferentiated components are stocked in warehouse inventory in anticipation of performing customized manufacturing or assembly at the warehouse upon receipt of customer orders.

An increasing amount of ATO operations are performed in warehouses located close to customers, as contrasted to centralized manufacturing locations. Assembly in close proximity to major markets allows the benefits of form postponement while avoiding the high cost and time related to long-distance direct shipment.

Warehouse Justification

Warehouses are justified in a logistical system when a service or cost advantage results from their positioning between suppliers, manufacturers, and customers. Competitive advantage generated by establishing a warehouse network can result from lower total cost or faster delivery. From the viewpoint of transportation economies, cost advantage results from using the warehouse to achieve freight consolidation. However, freight consolidation typically requires inventory to support assembly of customized orders. Alternatively, consolidation or assortment may be achieved by establishing flow-through facilities or cross-dock sortation that operates without predetermined inventories. Such continuous movement effectively converts warehouses from inventory storage to mixing facilities. Of course, some business situations will justify a combination of inventory storage and continuous flow-through or cross-dock operations to effectively and economically service customers. From the perspective of integrative management, the key logistics system design questions become: How many and what kinds of warehouses should a firm establish? Where should they be located? What services should they provide? What inventories should they stock? Which customers should they service? This sequence of interrelated questions represents the classical logistics network design challenge. For manufacturing firms, network design begins with marketing strategy and continues into manufacturing and procurement planning. In retailing and wholesaling enterprises, the framework spans from purchasing to customer support strategies.

Systems Concept and Analysis

The **systems concept** is an analytical framework that seeks *total* integration of components essential to achieving stated objectives. The components of a logistics system are typically called functions. The logistical functions, as discussed in Chapter 3, were identified as order processing, inventory, transportation, warehousing, materials handling, packaging, and facility network design. **Systems analysis**, applied to logistics, seeks to quantify trade-offs among these seven functions. The goal of systems analysis methodology is to create a whole or integrated effort, which is greater than the sum of the individual parts or functions. Such integration creates a synergistic interrelationship between functions in pursuit of higher overall achievement. In systems terminology, functional excellence is defined in terms of contributions a function makes to the overall process as contrasted to isolated performance in a specific area. Until the last few decades of the 20th century, process integration was generally neglected by managers who were trained to pursue functional excellence. Rapid advancement in information technology has increased the ability to identify and understand trade-offs to enhance logistics and supply chain initiatives.

When analyzed from a process perspective, the goal is balanced performance between functional areas within an enterprise and across the supply chain. For example, manufacturing economics are typically characterized by long production runs and low procurement costs. In contrast, integrated process management raises questions concerning the total cost and customer impact of such practices. A traditional financial orientation typically seeks to minimize inventories. While inventory should always be maintained as low as practical, arbitrary reductions below a level required to facilitate integrated operations typically increases total cost. Marketing's basic desire is to have finished goods inventory available in local markets. Inventory stocked in close geographical proximity to customers is believed to facilitate sales. Such anticipatory deployment of inventory is risky and may be in direct conflict with the least-total-cost process. In fact, Internet connectivity and shared fulfillment strategies are driving entirely different inventory stocking and logistics strategies.

In systems analysis, attention is focused on the interaction between components. Each component contributes a specific functionality essential to achieving system objectives. To illustrate, consider a high-fidelity music system. Many components are integrated for the single purpose of sound reproduction. The speakers, tuner, amplifier, and other components have purpose only if they contribute to quality sound. However, failure of any component will cause music quality to decline.

Some principles can be stated concerning general systems theory. First, the performance of the total system or process is of singular importance. Components are important only if they enhance total system performance. For example, if the stereo system can achieve superior sound with two speakers, then it is unnecessary to include additional speakers. Second, individual components need not have best or optimum design. Emphasis is on the integrated relationship between components that constitute the system. Electronics, as an example, are hidden from view inside the stereo system. As such, they do not need to be aesthetically pleasing. To spend money and time designing appealing electronics component is not necessary in terms of system integration. Third, a functional relationship, called **trade-off**, exists between components that serves to stimulate or hinder total system performance. Suppose a trade-off allows a lower-quality amplifier to be used if improved electronics are added to the system. The cost of the upgraded electronics must be justified in terms of savings in amplifier cost. Finally, components linked together as an integrated system may produce end results greater than possible through individual performance. In fact, the desired result may be unattainable without integrated performance. A stereo system will technically operate without speakers, but audible sound would not be possible.

The principles of systems analysis are basic and logically consistent. An integrated process with cross-functional integration can be expected to achieve greater results than one deficient in coordinated performance. In logistical systems, synergistic performance is targeted customer service at the lowest possible total cost. Although logical and indisputable in concept, effective application of systems integration is operationally difficult. In the final analysis, it matters little how much a firm spends to perform any specific function, such as transportation, as long as overall performance goals are realized at the lowest total cost expenditure.

Total Cost Integration

Total cost integration of logistics cost centers, such as transportation and inventory, should determine a firm's initial network of warehouse facilities. The following discussion identifies cost trade-offs individually related to transportation and inventory, and their integration, to identify the least-total-cost facility network.

Transportation Economics

The key to achieving economical transportation is summarized in two basic principles. The first, often called the **quantity principle**, is that individual shipments should be as large as the involved carrier can legally transport in the equipment being used. The second, often called the **tapering principle**, is that large shipments should be transported distances as long as possible. Both of these principles were developed in detail in Chapter 8. In combination they serve to spread the fixed cost related to transportation over as much weight and as many miles as possible.

Cost-Based Warehouse Justification

The basic economic principle justifying establishment of a warehouse is transportation consolidation. Manufacturers typically sell products over a broad geographical market area. If customer orders tend to be small, then the potential cost savings of consolidated transportation may provide economic justification for establishing a warehouse.

To illustrate, assume a manufacturer's average shipment size is 500 pounds and the applicable freight rate to a customer is $7.28 per hundredweight. Each shipment made direct from the manufacturing location to the market would have a transportation cost of $36.40. The quantity or volume transportation rate for shipments 20,000 pounds or greater is $2.40 per hundredweight. Finally, local delivery within the market area is $1.35 per hundredweight. Under these conditions, products shipped to the market via quantity rates and distributed locally would cost $3.75 per hundredweight, or $18.75 per 500-pound shipment. If a warehouse could be established, stocked with inventory, and operated for a total cost of less than $17.65 per 500-pound shipment ($36.40 − $18.75), or $3.53 per hundredweight, the overall cost of distributing to the market by using a warehouse would be reduced. Given these economic relationships, establishment of a warehouse offers the potential to reduce total logistics cost.

Figure 11.1 illustrates the basic economic principle of warehouse justification. *PL* is identified as the manufacturing location, and *WL* is the warehouse location within a given market area. The vertical line at point *PL* labeled P_c reflects the handling and shipping cost associated with preparation of a 500-pound LTL shipment (*C*) and a 20,000-pound truck-load shipment (*A*). The slope of line *AB* reflects the truckload freight rate from the plant to *WL*, the warehouse, which is assumed for this example to be linear with distance. The vertical line labeled *WC* at point *WL* represents the cost of operating the warehouse and maintaining inventory. The lines labeled *D* reflect delivery cost from the warehouse

FIGURE 11.1

Economic Justification of a Warehouse Facility Based on Transportation Cost

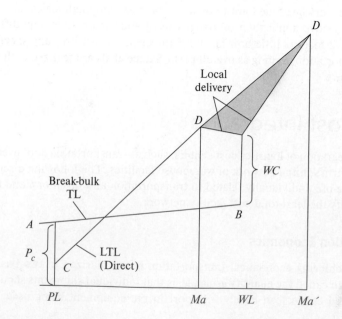

to customers within the market area *Ma* to *Ma'*. The slope of line *CD* reflects the LTL rate from the plant to customers located between the plant and the boundary *Ma*. The shaded area represents the locations to which the total cost of a 500-pound customer shipment using a consolidation warehouse would be lower than direct shipment from the manufacturing plant.

From the perspective of cost alone, it would make no difference whether customers located exactly at points *Ma* and *Ma'* were serviced from the manufacturing plant or the warehouse.

Network Transportation Cost Minimization

As a general rule, warehouses would be added to the network in situations where

$$\sum \frac{P_v + T_v}{N_{\bar{x}}} + W_{\bar{x}} + L_{\bar{x}} \leq \sum P_{\bar{x}} + T_{\bar{x}}$$

where

P_v = Processing cost of volume shipment;

T_v = Transportation cost of volume shipment;

$W_{\bar{x}}$ = Warehousing cost of average shipment;

$L_{\bar{x}}$ = Local delivery of average shipment;

$N_{\bar{x}}$ = Number of average shipments per volume shipment;

$P_{\bar{x}}$ = Processing cost of average shipment; and

$T_{\bar{x}}$ = Direct freight cost of average shipment.

The only limitation to this generalization is that sufficient shipment volume be available to cover the fixed cost of each warehouse facility. As long as the combined cost of warehousing and local delivery is equal to or less than the combined cost of shipping direct to customers, the establishment and operation of additional warehouse facilities would be economically justified. The generalized relationship of transportation cost and number of warehouses in a network is illustrated in Figure 11.2. Total transportation cost will initially decline as warehouses are added to the logistical network. In actual operations,

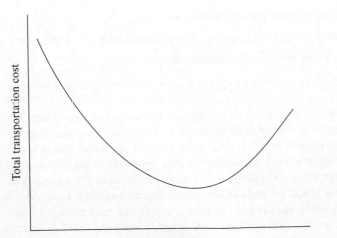

FIGURE 11.2

Transportation Cost as a Function of the Number of Warehouse Locations a consolidation location can be a warehouse or a cross-dock facility offering transportation break-bulk. It is not necessary to stock inventory in a warehouse to achieve the lowest transportation cost. The reduction in transportation cost results from consolidated volume shipments to the break-bulk location, coupled with short-haul small shipments to final destination. The cost of shipping small orders direct from manufacturing to customers is at the extreme upper left of the cost curve illustrated in Figure 11.2. At the low point near the middle of the transportation cost curve, the number of facilities required to achieve maximum freight consolidation is identified. Transportation cost is minimized at the point of maximum freight consolidation.

If facilities are expanded beyond the maximum consolidation point, total transportation cost will increase because the inbound volume capable of being consolidated to each facility decreases. The increased frequency of smaller inbound shipments results in a higher cost per hundredweight for shipments inbound to the facility. In other words, as the frequency of small inbound shipments increases, total transportation cost increases.

Inventory Economics

Inventory level in a logistical system directly depends on the number of stocking locations. The framework for planning inventory deployment is the performance cycle. Although one element of the performance cycle is transportation, which provides spatial closure, the key driver of inventory economics is time. The forward deployment of inventory in a logistical system potentially improves service response time. Such deployment also increases overall system inventory, resulting in greater cost and risk.

Service-Based Warehouse Justification

The inventory related to a warehouse network consists of **base**, **safety stock**, and **transit**. For the total logistical network, average inventory commitment is

$$\bar{I} = \sum_{i=1}^{n} \frac{Q_i}{2} + SS_i + IT_i$$

where

$I =$ Average inventory in the total network;

$n =$ Number of warehouses in the network;

$Q_i =$ Order quantity for warehouse i subscript;

$SS_i =$ Safety stock, for a given warehouse identified by the appropriate subscript; and

$IT_i =$ In-transit inventory for warehouse i

As warehouses are added to a logistics system, the number of performance cycles increases. This added complexity directly impacts the total inventory required across the network.

The impact on base stock of adding warehouses is not significant. The base stock level within a logistical system is determined by manufacturing and transportation lot sizes, which do not change as a function of the number of market facing warehouses. The combination of maintenance and ordering cost, adjusted to take into consideration volume transportation rates and purchase discounts, determines the replenishment EOQ and the resultant base stock. In just-in-time procurement situations, base stock is determined by the order quantity required to support the planned manufacturing run or assembly. In either situation, the base stock determination is independent of the number of market facing warehouses in the logistics system.

Transit stock is inventory captive in transportation vehicles. While in transit, this inventory is **available to promise**, but it cannot be physically accessed. Available to promise means it can be committed to customers by use of a reservation or inventory mortgaging capability in the order management system. As more performance cycles are added to a logistical network, the anticipated impact is that existing cycles will experience a reduction in transit inventory. This reduction occurs because the total network transit days and related uncertainty are reduced. To illustrate, assume a single product is being sold in markets A and B and is currently being supplied from warehouse X, as presented in Figure 11.3. Assume the forecasted average daily sales are 6 units for market A and 7 for market B. The performance cycle duration is 6 days to market A and 10 days to market B.

With other things held constant, what will happen to transit inventory if a second warehouse is added, as in Figure 11.4? Table 11.1 provides a summary of results. The main change is that the performance cycle to market B has been reduced from 10 to

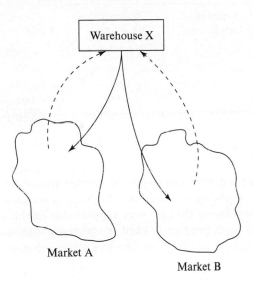

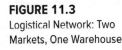

FIGURE 11.3
Logistical Network: Two Markets, One Warehouse

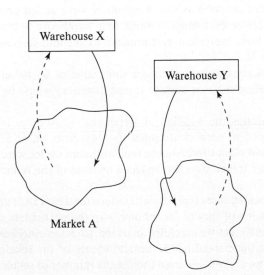

FIGURE 11.4
Logistical Network: Two Markets, Two Warehouses

TABLE 11.1
Transit Inventory under Different Logistical Networks

Forecasted Average Daily Sales	Market Area	Warehouse X Only	Two-Warehouse Facilities		
			Warehouse X	Warehouse Y	Combined
6	A	36	36	—	36
7	B	70	—	28	28
	$\Sigma A + B$	106			64
	$\bar{I}a$	18			18
	$\bar{I}b$	35			14
	$\Sigma \bar{I}$	53			32

TABLE 11.2
Logistical Structure: One Warehouse, Four Plants

	Warehouse X			
Manufacturing Plant	Performance Cycle Duration	Forecasted Average Sales	Transit Inventory	$\bar{I}$
A	10	35	350	175
B	15	200	3,000	1,500
C	12	60	720	360
D	20	80	1,600	800
	57	375	5,670	2,835

4 days. Thus, the second warehouse reduced average transit inventory for the network from 53 to 32 units. It should be noted that the second warehouse did not create additional performance cycles on the customer support side of the logistics flow. However, on the inbound side, each product stocked in the new warehouse requires a replenishment source. Assuming a full product line at each warehouse, the number of performance cycles required to replenish the network will increase each time a new warehouse is added.

Despite the increased need for inventory replenishment, the average in-transit inventory for the total network dropped as new warehouses were added because of a reduction in days required to service customers. Assume that warehouse X is supplied by four manufacturing plants whose individual performance cycles and forecasted average usage are illustrated in Table 11.2.

For purposes of comparison, assume a unit value of $5 for all warehouse products. Utilizing only warehouse X, the average transit inventory would be 2835 units at $5 each, or $14,175.

Table 11.3 illustrates the addition of warehouse Y. Average transit inventory in the two-warehouse logistical network dropped to 2248 units or, at $5 each, $11,240. Thus, even though four new plant-to-warehouse replenishment cycles were added to the logistical network, the average transit time was reduced because of the reduction in total replenishment days.

The addition of warehouses typically will reduce total in-transit days and, thus, in-transit inventory. This result will vary in accordance with the particulars of each situation. Each network of locations must be carefully analyzed to determine average transit inventory impact. The key to understanding the general nature of the relationship is to remember that total transit days are reduced even though the number of required performance cycles increases. The qualification is that while an increase in the number of performance cycles

Manufacturing Plant	Performance Cycle Duration	Forecasted Average Sales	Transit Inventory	$\bar{i}$
		Warehouse X		
A	10	20	200	100
B	15	100	1,500	750
C	12	35	420	210
D	20	30	600	300
	57	185	2,720	1,360
		Warehouse Y		
A	5	15	75	38
B	8	100	800	400
C	6	25	150	75
D	15	50	750	375
	34	190	1,775	888
	$\Sigma xy = 91$	$\Sigma xy = 375$	$\Sigma xy = 4,495$	$\Sigma \bar{x}xy = 2.248$

TABLE 11.3

Logistical Structure: Two Warehouses, Four Plants

typically reduces transit days, it may also increase overall leadtime uncertainty. The clear exception to this rule is when products are shifted to international sources. International sourcing typically results in longer leadtimes and often increased uncertainty causing increased transit inventory. As the number of performance cycles increases, the possibility of transportation delays leading to potential service failures also increases. This potential impact is minimized by safety stock.

Safety stock is added to base and transit stock to provide protection against sales and performance cycle uncertainty. Both aspects of uncertainty are time-related. Sales uncertainty is concerned with customer demand that exceeds forecasted sales during the replenishment time. Performance cycle uncertainty is concerned with variation in the total days required to replenish warehouse inventory. From the viewpoint of safety stock, the expected result of adding warehouses is an increase in average system inventory. The purpose of safety stock is to protect against unplanned stockouts during inventory replenishment. Thus, if network uncertainty increases as a function of adding warehouses, then the overall safety stock will likely also increase.

The addition of warehouses to the logistical network impacts uncertainty in two ways. First, as performance cycle days are reduced, the variability in sales during replenishment as well as cycle variability are both also reduced. Therefore, reducing the length of the performance cycle relieves, to some degree, the need for safety stock to protect against variability.

Adding locations also has a significant impact on average inventory. Each new performance cycle added to the system creates the need for an additional safety stock. The introduction of an additional warehouse to service a specific market area reduces the size of the statistical distribution used to determine safety stock requirements for each warehouse. In effect, the size of the market area being serviced by any given facility is reduced without a corresponding reduction in uncertainty. To illustrate, when the demand of several markets is combined by using a single warehouse, the variability of demand is averaged across markets. This allows peaks in demand in one market to be offset by low demand in others. In essence, the idle stock of one market can be used to meet safety stock requirements of other markets.

To illustrate, Table 11.4 provides a summary of monthly sales in three markets on a combined and separate basis. Average sales for the three markets combined is 22 units

TABLE 11.4
Summary of Sales in One
Combined and Three
Separate Markets

Month	Combined Sales, All Markets	Unit Sales per Market		
		A	B	C
1	18	9	0	9
2	22	6	3	13
3	24	7	5	12
4	20	8	4	8
5	17	2	4	11
6	29	10	5	14
7	21	7	6	8
8	26	7	7	12
9	18	5	6	7
10	24	9	5	10
11	23	8	4	11
12	23	12	2	9
Total Sales	265	90	51	124
Average Monthly Sales	21.1	7.5	4.3	10.3
Value Greater Than Average	7	4	3	4

per month, with the greatest variation above the average in month 6, when sales reached 29 units, or 7 units over the average. If the goal is to provide 100 percent protection against stockout and total sales of 29 units have an equal probability of occurring in any month, a safety stock of 7 units would be required.

The average monthly sales for markets A, B, and C are 8, 4, and 10 units (rounded), respectively. The maximum demand in excess of forecast is in market A, with 5 units in month 12; for market B, 3 units in month 8; and for market C, 4 units in month 6. The total of each of these three extreme months equals 11 units. If safety stocks are planned for each market on a separate basis, 11 units of safety stock would be required for the total network while only 7 units of safety stock would be required to service all markets from a single warehouse. An increase in total system safety stock of 4 units is required to provide the same inventory availability when using three warehouses.

This simplified example illustrates the general safety stock impact of adding warehouses to a logistical network. The important point to understand is that increased safety stock results from increased uncertainty as market areas are disaggregated to multiple distribution centers. As a consequence, unique safety stocks are required to accommodate local demand variation.

Network Inventory Cost Minimization

The overall impact upon average inventory of increasing the number of warehouses in a logistical network is generalized in Figure 11.5. A reduction in average transit inventory is assumed as illustrated by the line $\bar{I}_t$. The assumption is that a linear relationship exists between average transit inventory and the number of warehouses in the network. As noted earlier in this section, such a relationship may not be linear, depending upon the characteristics of the particular system under consideration. However, the general tendency is for a slight linear reduction in the amount of inventory as performance cycles are increased.

The curve labeled $\bar{I}_{ss}$ (average safety stock) increases as warehouses are added to the network. Inventory increases at a decreasing rate, since the net increase required for each new facility declines. The incremental safety stock is the sum of added inventory to

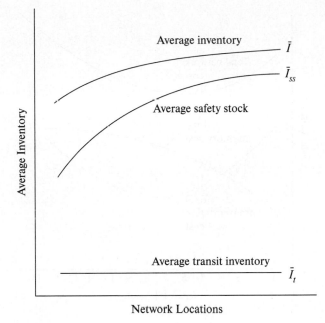

FIGURE 11.5
Average Inventory as a
Function of Number of
Warehouse Locations

accommodate uncertainty of demand minus the inventory reduction required to accommodate for less leadtime uncertainty. Thus, the incremental inventory required to maintain customer service performance diminishes for each new warehouse location added to the system. The average inventory curve, $\bar{I}$, represents the combined impact of safety stock and transit inventory. The significant observation is that the safety stock dominates the impact of transit inventory. For the overall network, the average inventory is the safety stock plus half of the order quantity and transit inventory. Thus, given the same demand and customer service goals, total inventory increases at a decreasing rate as the number of warehouses in a logistical network increases.

Total Cost Network

As noted earlier, the identification of the least-total-cost-network design is the goal of logistics integration. The basic concept of total cost for the overall logistical system is illustrated in Figure 11.6. The low point on the total transportation cost curve is between seven and eight facilities. Total cost related to average inventory commitment increases with each additional warehouse. For the overall system, the lowest total cost network is six locations. The point of lowest inventory cost would be a single warehouse.

Trade-off Relationships

The identification of the least-total-cost network of six warehouses in Figure 11.6 illustrates the trade-off relationships. Note that the minimal total cost point for the system is not at the point of least cost for either transportation or inventory. This trade-off illustrates the hallmark of integrated logistical analysis.

Assumptions and Limitations

In actual practice, it is difficult to identify and measure all aspects of total logistical cost. Many assumptions are required for logistical network analysis. An additional concern is

FIGURE 11.6

Least-Total-Cost Network

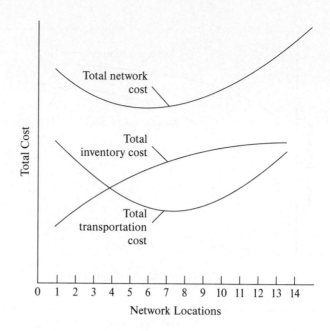

the fact that analysis such as that illustrated in Figure 11.6 does not encompass the complexity of total cost integration.

The two-dimensional display in Figure 11.6 represents projected sales across a single planning period. Transportation requirements are represented by a single average-size shipment. In actual operations, it is likely that neither of these assumptions will represent actual circumstances. First, the nature of logistical network design is not that of a short-term planning problem. When facility decisions are involved, the planning horizon should consider a range of different sales alternatives. Second, actual shipment and order sizes will vary substantially around an average. A realistic approach to planning must incorporate a range of shipment sizes supported by alternative logistical methods to satisfy customer service requirements. In actual operation, alternative modes of transportation are employed, as necessary, to achieve the desired speed of delivery.

Significant cost trade-offs exist between inventory and transportation. Inventory cost as a function of the number of warehouses directly relates to the desired level of inventory availability. If no safety stock is maintained in the system, total inventory requirement is limited to base and transit stock. Under a no-safety-stock situation, the total least cost for the system would be at or near the point of lowest transportation cost. Thus, assumptions made with respect to the desired inventory availability and fill rate are essential to trade-off analysis and have a significant impact on the least-total-cost-design solution.

The locational selection aspect of logistical network planning is far more complex than simply deciding how many facilities to choose from a single array of locations, as illustrated in Figure 11.6. A firm engaged in nationwide logistics has a wide latitude in choice of where to locate warehouses. Within the United States there are 50 states, within which one or more distribution warehouses could be located. Assume that the total allowable warehouses for a logistical system cannot exceed 50 and locations are limited to a maximum of one in each state. Given this range of options, there still are 1.1259×10^{15} combinations of warehouses to be evaluated in the identification of the least-total-cost network.

To overcome some of these limitations, variations in shipment size and transportation alternatives need to be introduced for the analysis. Extending the analysis to a more complete treatment of variables typically requires the use of planning models and techniques discussed later in this chapter. Four critical variables are shipment size, transportation mode, location of demand, and location alternatives. The constants are level of inventory availability, performance cycle time, and the specific warehouse locations being evaluated. To evaluate the wide range of variables in designing a logistical system, complex models have been developed. The assumptions required to support integrated system design are important from the viewpoint of their impact upon strategy formulation.

Formulating Logistical Strategy

To finalize logistical strategy, it is necessary to evaluate the relationships between alternative customer service levels and associated cost. While substantial difficulties exist in the measurement of revenue, the comparative evaluation of marginal service performance and related cost offers a way to approximate an ideal logistical system design. The general approach consists of (1) determining a least-total-cost network, (2) measuring service availability and capability associated with the least-total-cost-system design, (3) conducting sensitivity analysis related to incremental service and cost directly with revenue generation, and (4) finalizing the plan.

Cost Minimization

Just as a physical replication of a geographical area illustrates elevations, depressions, and contours of land surface, an economic map can highlight logistical cost differentials. Generally, peak costs for labor and essential services occur in large metropolitan areas. However, because of demand concentration, total logistics cost resulting from transportation and inventory consolidation benefits is often minimized in metropolitan areas.

A strategy of least total cost seeks a logistical system network with the lowest fixed and variable costs. A system design to achieve least total cost is driven purely by cost-to-cost trade-offs. In terms of basic relationships, a total-least-cost design was illustrated in Figure 11.6. The level of customer service that is associated with a least-cost logistical design results from safety stock policy and the locational proximity of warehouses to customers. The overall level of customer service associated with the least-total-cost-system design is referred to as the **threshold service level**.

Threshold Service

To establish a threshold service level it is necessary to initiate network re-engineering with policies regarding desired inventory **availability** and **capability**. It is common practice to initiate the analysis assuming customer service capability based on the existing order entry and processing system, warehouse operations based on standard order fulfillment time at existing facilities, and transportation delivery time based on capabilities of existing transportation methods. Given these assumptions, current performance provides the starting point for evaluating potential service improvement.

The typical starting point for customer service availability analysis is to assume performance at a generally acceptable fill rate. Often the prevailing industry standard is used as a first approximation. For example, if safety stock availability were established at 97.75 percent for combined probability of demand and leadtime uncertainty, it would be anticipated that approximately 98 out of 100 items ordered would be delivered as specified.

Given the initial assumptions, each customer is assigned a shipment location on the basis of least total cost. In multi-product situations, selection of service territories for each facility will depend on the products stocked at each warehouse and the degree of

FIGURE 11.7
Determination of Service
Territories: Three-Point,
Least-Cost System

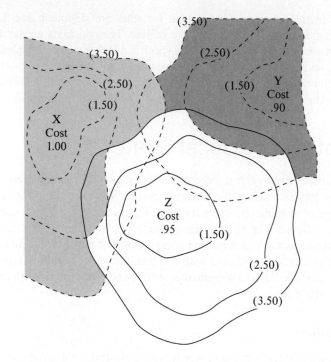

consolidation required by customers. Since costs have significant geographical differentials, the service area for any given facility will vary in size and configuration. Figure 11.7 provides an illustration of the assignment of warehouse service areas based upon equalized total delivered cost. The irregularity of service territories results from outbound transportation cost differentials from the three warehouses.

In Figure 11.7, the warehouses are identified by the letters X, Y, and Z. The hypothetical cost associated with each facility represents all logistical cost for an average order except transportation. The differential of average order cost between facilities reflects local differentials.

Around each facility total cost lines are displayed at intervals of $1.50, $2.50, and $3.50. The cost represented by the line is the total cost of logistics, including transportation to points connected along the line. Customers located within a given area can be serviced at a cost less than that displayed on the line. The overall service area of each warehouse is determined by lowest total cost assignment. The territory boundary line represents the point of equal total cost between two warehouses. Along this line, total cost to service a customer is equal. However, a substantial difference could exist in delivery time.

Two conditions are assumed in Figure 11.7. First, the illustration is based on distribution of an average order. Thus, outbound logistics costs are equated on the average. To the degree that order size varies from the average, alternative territory boundaries would vary according to shipment size. Second, delivery time is estimated on the basis of distance. Transit inventory also is estimated based on delivery time. In accordance with this initial analysis of threshold service, it cannot be concluded that delivery times will be consistent within territories or that equal total logistics cost will be experienced within a service area.

The fact that the initial network is designed to achieve least logistics cost does not mean that threshold customer service will be low. The elapsed time from the customer's order placement to product delivery in a least cost system is expected to be longer on average than would be experienced in alternative networks that have been modified to improve overall service performance. However, customers located near a warehouse facility in all networks have potential to receive rapid delivery. Because the least-cost location tends to favor areas of high demand concentration, a substantial number of customers will enjoy rapid delivery.

Given an estimate of expected order cycle time, management is in a position to make basic customer delivery commitments. A service statement policy may be as follows: "Order performance for area A will be 3 days from receipt of orders at the warehouse facility. It is our policy to be able to fill 98 percent of all orders within the 3-day period."

The actual performance of a logistical system is measured by the degree to which such service standards are consistently achieved. Given quantification of the variables involved, the threshold service related to the least-total-cost system offers the starting point of developing a firm's basic service platform. The next step in policy formulation is to test the threshold service level in terms of customer suitability.

Service Sensitivity Analysis

The threshold service resulting from the least-total-cost logistical design provides a basis for **service sensitivity analysis**. The basic service capabilities of a network can be increased or decreased by variation in number of warehouses, change in one or more performance cycles to increase speed or consistency of operations, and/or change in safety stock policy.

Locational Modification

The warehouse structure of the logistical system establishes the service that can be realized without changing the performance cycle or safety stock policy. To illustrate the relationship between number of warehouses and resultant service time, assume an important measure is the percentage of demand satisfied within a specified time interval. The general impact of adding warehouses to the system is presented in Table 11.5. Several points of interest are illustrated.

TABLE 11.5
Service Capabilities within Time Intervals as a Function of Number of Locations

Network Locations	Percentage Demand by Performance Cycle Duration (hours)			
	24	48	72	96
1	15	31	53	70
2	23	44	61	76
3	32	49	64	81
4	37	55	70	85
5	42	60	75	87
6	48	65	79	89
7	54	70	83	90
8	60	76	84	90
9	65	80	85	91
10	70	82	86	92
11	74	84	87	92
12	78	84	88	93
13	82	85	88	93
14	84	86	89	94

First, incremental service is a diminishing function. For example, the first five warehouse locations provide 24-hour performance to 42 percent of all customers. To double the percentage of 24-hour service from 42 to 84 percent, 9 additional warehouses, or a total of 14, are required.

Second, high degrees of service are achieved much faster for longer performance intervals than for the shorter intervals. For example, four warehouse locations provide 85 percent performance within the 96-hour performance cycle. Increasing the total locations from 4 to 14 improves the 96-hour performance by only 9 percent. In contrast, a total of 14 warehouses cannot achieve 85 percent given a 24-hour performance cycle.

Finally, the total cost associated with each location added to the logistical network increases dramatically. Thus, while the incremental service resulting from additional locations diminishes, the incremental cost associated with each new location increases. The service payoff for each new facility is incrementally less.

Logistics managers are often asked to estimate the inventory impact of adding or deleting warehouses. This relationship between uncertainty and required inventory is called the **portfolio effect**.[5] The portfolio effect can be estimated using the **square root rule**. The square root rule, originally proposed by Maister, suggests that the safety stock increase as a result of adding a warehouse is equal to the ratio of the square root of the number of locations in the newly prepared network divided by the square root of the number of existing locations.[6]

For example, assume that a manager wants to estimate the inventory impact of shifting from a one- to a two-warehouse network. In effect, the network is being doubled. For reasons discussed earlier, demand variability will be increased. Using the square root rule, the firm's aggregate safety stock (SS_j) for a two-warehouse system can be estimated as

$$SS_j = \frac{\sqrt{N_j}}{\sqrt{N_i}} \times SS_i$$

$$= \frac{\sqrt{2}}{\sqrt{1}} \times SS_i$$

$$= 1.41 \times SS_i$$

where

SS_j = Aggregate safety stock for N_j warehouses or product variations;

N_j = Number of warehouse locations or product variations for the new configuration;

N_i = Number of warehouse locations or product variations for the existing configuration; and

SS_i = Aggregate safety stock for N_i warehouses or product variations.

The projected inventory increase resulting from adding a second warehouse is estimated as a 41 percent increase in safety stock. Table 11.6 illustrates the impact of the change for a range of one to five warehouses. Although the square root rule works reasonably well for estimating inventory impact, it requires assumptions regarding demand. The first assumption is that the stocking locations or product variations must have approximately the same level of demand. Specifically, if there are currently two stocking locations, they must have

[5]For a more detailed discussion of the portfolio effect, see Walter Zinn, Michael Levy, and Donald J. Bowersox, "Measuring the Effect of Inventory Centralization/Decentralization on Aggregate Safety Stock: The Square Root Law Revisited," *Journal of Business Logistics* 10, no. 1 (1989), pp. 1–14; and Philip T. Evers, "Expanding the Square Root Law: An Analysis of Both Safety and Cycle Stocks," *Logistics and Transportation Review* 31, no. 1 (1995), pp. 1–20.

[6]D. H. Maister, "Centralization of Inventories and the 'Square Root Law,'" *International Journal of Physical Distribution* 6, no. 3 (1976), pp. 124–134.

Network Locations	Safety Stock Level
1	100
2	141
3	173
4	200
5	224

TABLE 11.6
Inventory Impact of
Modified Warehouse
Network from a Base of
One Warehouse

approximately the same demand level for the square root rule to work accurately. Second, the demand levels at each warehouse or for each product variation must not be correlated. This means that demand deviation for each location must be independent. Finally, the square root rule requires that demand for each warehouse approximate a normal distribution. While the appropriateness of these assumptions must be taken into consideration, the square root rule is a useful way to estimate the safety stock impact when adding or deleting warehouses to a logistical network.

Performance Cycle Modification

Speed and consistency of service can be varied to a specific market or customer by a modification of some aspect of the performance cycle. To improve service, web-based ordering and premium transportation can be used. Therefore, geographical proximity and the number of warehouses do not equate directly to fast or consistent delivery. The decision to increase service by adopting a faster performance cycle arrangement will typically increase variable cost. In contrast, service improvement, by virtue of added warehouses, involves a high degree of fixed cost and could result in less overall system flexibility.

No generalizations can be offered regarding the cost/service improvement ratio attainable from performance cycle modification. The typical relationship of premium to lowest cost transportation results in a significant incentive in favor of large shipments. Thus, if order volume is substantial, the economics of logistics can be expected to favor use of a warehouse or consolidation point to service a market area.

The impact of using premium transportation will increase total cost. Adjustments from the least-total-cost logistical system can typically be justified if the improved service results in increased profitability.

Safety Stock Modification

A direct way to change service is to increase or decrease the safety stock held at one or more warehouses. The impact of increasing the safety stock across a total system will shift the average inventory cost curve upward. A goal of increasing customer service availability will result in increased safety stocks at each warehouse. As availability is increased, the safety stocks required to achieve each equal increment of availability increase at an increasing rate.

Establishing Strategy

Management often falls into the trap of being overly optimistic in terms of service commitments to customers. The result may be excessively high customer expectations followed by erratic performance. In part, such overcommitment results from lack of understanding of the total cost required to support high, zero-defect service.

The final step in establishing a strategy is to evaluate the cost of incremental service in terms of generating offsetting revenue. To illustrate, assume that the current system is geared

FIGURE 11.8
Comparative Total
Cost for 5- and
12-Distribution-Center
Systems

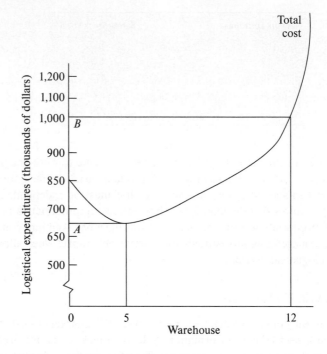

to service at least 90 percent of all customers at a 95 percent average inventory fill rate within 60 hours of order receipt. Furthermore, assume that the current logistical system is meeting these objectives at lowest total cost by utilizing a network of five warehouses. Marketing, however, is not satisfied and believes that service capability should be increased to the point where 90 percent of all customers would receive 97 percent inventory availability delivered within 24 hours. Logistical management needs to estimate the cost of this strategic commitment.

Figure 11.8 illustrates how the alternative strategies can be evaluated. Assume marketing is requesting a 2 percent improvement in inventory availability combined with a 36-hour improvement in delivery capability. Assume design analysis identifies that 12 warehouse facilities represent the lowest-cost network capable of achieving the new service standards. The total cost of this expanded service capability is measured on the vertical axis of Figure 11.8 by the distance between points *A* and *B*. The total cost of achieving marketing's requested service will require approximately a $400,000 per year increase in logistical cost. Assuming an average before-tax profit margin of 10 percent of sales, it would be necessary to generate $4 million in incremental sales to break even on the cost of providing the added service.

Acceptance or rejection of marketing's proposal for increased service involves strategic positioning. Logistics can provide whichever performance the firm's overall customer service strategy requires. Policy changes, once adopted, will influence the logistical network design and cost. To finalize logistical policy management typically requires considering a range of strategic alternatives.

Other Considerations in Logistics Network Design

Historically, the major considerations driving logistics network design are demand location, labor costs, material cost, and transportation cost, in decreasing priority order.

Demand location refers to the geographic location of the market and shipment profile in terms of relative volume, size, and characteristics of the market. All things being equal, firms would rather locate production facilities and distribution centers near consumer markets. The fact that demand in Asia, India, South America, and eastern Europe is growing at double-digit rates strongly motivates firms to shift supply chain activities to those regions. Labor rate advantages have driven many firms to low-cost countries such as China, India, and eastern Europe. Material costs refer to the total cost of obtaining raw materials and components including both direct and indirect cost. The direct cost represents the specific purchase cost of the material and components, as well as tariffs, duties, and packaging. The materials indirect cost includes the transaction and risk-related costs such as security, obsolescence, and potential intellectual property risks. Transportation expense includes the freight cost related to obtaining raw materials, movement of work-in-process inventory between manufacturing plants, and ultimate distribution to customers. Other considerations in supply chain design include tax policies, operating risk, sustainability, availability of trained labor, and the overall political environment. In specific situations, the total cost and service differential resulting from sustainability and tax policy can be the dominant location factors.

Global and regional tax policy can have a substantial impact on supply chain design. Ireland and Singapore are examples of political situations where tax policies in terms of value-added taxes and foreign trade zones are designed to attract industrial location. Many North American free trade zones are using similar approaches to attract industry to their states or provinces.

Supply chain risk refers to dangers related to low-cost sourcing. Since 2000, many firms increased low-cost-country sourcing in an effort to reduce labor and overall manufacturing cost. However, in many cases those firms did not understand the total cost or risk implications and have since relocated their sourcing. An example was a 3PL operator who selected a low-cost Asian location to perform value-added activities. The problem became the availability of containers from Asia to North America. The unexpected consequence for the firm's customers was longer and less consistent lead times from Asia to North America. To minimize operating risks, many firm's are shifting away from the lowest-cost countries to less risky locations.

In addition to risk, many firms are carefully evaluating sustainability when making supply chain design decisions. Supply chain sustainability has multiple dimensions, including energy, labor, political stability, and environmental risk. Energy is critical both for operating supply chain facilities and transporting product through the supply chain. Discussion with plant managers in some areas of Asia report that it is common to experience two to three hours a day without electricity. Another concern is access to reasonably priced fuel to support transportation.

Access to trained labor is also a major consideration. While many countries are experiencing high unemployment, there are some countries, both developed and developing, where a shortage of trained and experienced supply chain talent are a growing concern. This shortage includes both management and labor. On the managerial side, the challenge is to find talent that understands the broad dimensions of supply chain, including cross-functional trade-offs, globalization, technology, and strategy integration. While universities in the developed countries are producing more supply chain talent, the demand is growing at a faster rate. On the labor side, the increased use of technology in both developing and developed countries makes it more difficult to find and retain trained talent. Some plant managers in Asia report 100 percent annual trained employee turnover.

A final consideration focuses on a supportive and stable political environment. The environment includes political, regulatory, and financial considerations. This stability includes a stable government, currency, and policies that attract and retain business.

In summary, the supply chain design challenge for supply chain managers is expanding. Not only must supply chain managers understand traditional functional trade-offs, they must also consider a broad range of factors discussed in this section. Thus, supply chain professionals must extend their knowledge base to gain an understanding of a broad spectrum of relevant trade-offs involved in global supply chain design and operations.

Planning Methodology

Even for established industries, a firm's markets, demand, cost, and service requirements change rapidly in response to customer and competitor behavior. To accommodate such change, firms often face questions such as: (1) How many warehouses should our logistics system use and where should they be located? (2) What are the inventory/service trade-offs for each warehouse? (3) What types of transportation capability should be used? and (4) Is a redesign of our warehouse network justified?

The answers to such questions are usually complex and data-intensive. The complexity is due to the large number of factors influencing logistics total cost and the range of alternative solutions. The data-intensiveness is due to the large amount of information required to evaluate logistical alternatives. A typical logistics system design must evaluate a range of service alternatives, cost assumptions, and operating capabilities. Such analyses require a structured process supported by effective analytical tools.

Just as no ideal logistical system is suitable for all enterprises, the method for identifying and evaluating alternative logistics strategies can vary extensively. However, there is a general process applicable to most logistics design and analysis situations. Figure 11.9

FIGURE 11.9
Research Process

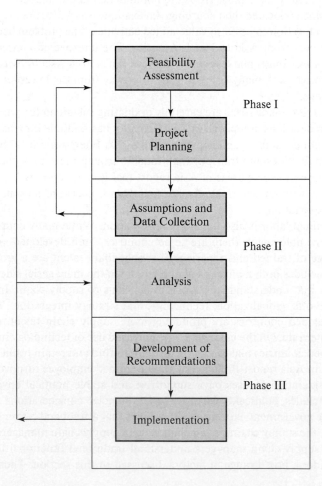

illustrates a generalized planning process flow. The process is segmented into three phases: problem definition and planning, data collection and analysis, and recommendation and implementation.

Phase I: Problem Definition and Planning

Phase I of logistics system design and planning provides the foundation for the overall analysis. A thorough and well-documented problem definition and plan are essential to all that follows.

Feasibility Assessment

Logistics design and planning should begin with a comprehensive evaluation of the current operating situation. The objective is to understand the environment, process, problems, and performance characteristics of the current system and to determine what, if any, modifications appear worthy of consideration. The process of evaluating change is referred to as a *feasibility assessment*, and includes situational analysis, framing supporting logic, and cost/benefit estimation.

Situation Analysis

The collection of performance measures, characteristics, and information describing the current logistics environment is called the *situational analysis*. A typical analysis requires internal operational review, market assessment, and a technology assessment to determine existing capabilities and improvement potential.

The internal operating review focuses on understanding the existing logistics practices and processes. It profiles historical performance, data availability, strategies, operations, and tactical policies and practices. The review usually covers the overall logistical process as well as each function. In order to fully understand how logistics supports procurement, manufacturing operations, and customer relationship management, the situational analysis should span the full functionality of the supply chain.

A complete internal review examines all major resources, such as workforce, equipment, facilities, relationships, and information. In particular, the internal review should focus on a comprehensive evaluation of the existing system's capabilities and deficiencies. Each element of the logistics system must be carefully examined with respect to its stated objectives and its ability to meet those objectives. For example, is the logistics management information system consistently providing and measuring the agreed-to customer service objectives? Likewise, does the procurement process adequately support manufacturing requirements? Does the current network of warehouses effectively support customer service objectives? Does the current logistics system take advantage of potential synergies across divisions and with other supply chain partners? Finally, how do logistics performance capabilities and measures compare across business units and locations? These and many similar questions form the basis of the internal analysis. The comprehensive review seeks to identify the opportunities that might justify logistics system redesign.

Table 11.7 lists some of the topics frequently covered during an internal review. The format highlights the fact that the assessment must consider the processes, decisions, and key measures for each major logistics activity. Process considerations focus on physical and information flows through the supply chain. Decision considerations focus on the logic

	Processes	Decisions	Measurements
Customer Service	What is the current information flow? What is the order profile and how is it changing? How are orders received?	How are order sourcing decisions made? What happens when inventory is not available to fill an order? How are manufacturing and warehouse capacity allocation decisions made?	What are the key measures of customer service? How are they measured? What is the current performance level?
Materials Management	What is the current material flow through plants and warehouses? What processes are performed at each manufacturing site and warehouse?	How are production planning and scheduling decisions made?	What are the key manufacturing and warehouse capacity limitations? What are the key measures of materials management performance? How are they measured? What is the current performance level?
Transportation	What modes are currently used? What is the weight profile of orders and shipments and how are they different? What is the flow for requesting, paying, and exchanging information with carriers? What is the information flow for shipment documentation?	How are the mode and carrier choice decisions made for each shipment? How are carriers evaluated?	What are the key transportation performance measures? How are they measured? What is the current performance level? What are the relative economic performance characteristics of each mode and carrier?
Warehousing	What storage and handling facilities are currently used and what functions do they perform? What product lines are maintained in each facility? What are the storage, handling, and other value-added functions that are or may be performed at each facility?	How are shipment consolidation decisions made at each facility? What decisions are made by material handlers and how do they make those decisions? How is product stored in the facility and how are product selection decisions made?	What is the throughput and storage volume of each facility? What are the key warehouse performance measures? How are they measured? What is the current performance level? What are the relative economic performance characteristics of each facility?
Inventory	What value-added functions do current inventory stockpiles play? What inventory is the firm responsible for, and where is it stored?	How are inventory management decisions made? Who makes inventory decisions and what information is used to support the decisions?	What is the corporate inventory carrying cost? What are the key inventory performance measures? How are they measured? What is the current performance level?

TABLE 11.7   Select Internal Review Topics

and criteria currently used for supply chain management. Measurement considerations focus on the key performance indicators and the firm's ability to measure them. Supply chain performance metrics are further developed in Chapter 13.

The specific review content depends on the scope of the planned analysis. It is unusual for the information desired to be readily available. The purpose of the internal review is not detailed data collection but rather a diagnostic look at current logistics processes and procedures as well as a probe to determine what type of data are available. Most significantly, the internal review is directed at the identification of areas where substantial improvement opportunity exists.

	Market Trends	Enterprise Capabilities	Competitive Capabilities
Suppliers	What value-added services are suppliers providing? What are the major bottlenecks with current suppliers?	What are the opportunities to internalize or outsource value-added services? How can processes be changed to reduce bottlenecks?	What actions are competitors taking to refine product and information flow with suppliers? What are competitive benchmarks in terms of number of suppliers, cost characteristics, and performance measures?
Customers	What are the major constraints and bottlenecks when servicing key customers? What are the cost impacts of these constraints and bottlenecks? How are customer ordering patterns changing? What are the primary customers' criteria?	What functions or activities can be shifted to or from customers to enhance logistics system performance? How do customers evaluate our performance on their key measurement criteria?	What services are competitors providing our customers? How do competitors perform on key performance measures as identified by customers?
Consumers	How are consumer purchasing patterns changing with respect to purchase locations, times, and selection criteria? What are the consumer trends with respect to logistics activities such as purchase quantities, packaging, home delivery, and product quality?	How are we able to respond to changes in consumer purchasing patterns and selection criteria?	How are our competitors responding to changes in consumer purchasing patterns and selection criteria?
Risk	What are the specific resources that may be constrained in the future?	What are the options we have in place to avoid, minimize, mitigate, or respond to risk?	What are the critical risks where competitors may have an advantage over our firm?

TABLE 11.8   Sample Market Assessment Topics

The market assessment is a review of the trends and service demands. The assessment objective is to document and formalize customer perceptions and desires with regard to potential changes in the firm's logistics capabilities. The assessment might include interviews with select customers or more substantive customer surveys. Table 11.8 illustrates some typical market assessment topics. The assessment should focus on external relationships with suppliers, customers, and in some situations consumers. The assessment should consider trends in requirements and processes as well as enterprise and competitor capabilities.

Technology assessment focuses on the application and capabilities of key logistics technologies, including transportation, storage, materials handling, packaging, and order processing. The assessment considers the firm's technological ability as well as the potential for applying new technologies. For example, can advanced materials-handling capabilities offered through integrated service providers enhance logistics performance? What is the role of advanced information technology, communication, and decision support systems in enabling responsive logistics capabilities? Finally, what can wireless, RFID, satellite, scanning, supply chain event management, or other communication technology contribute to improved logistics system capability? The objective of the technology assessment is to identify advancements capable of facilitating effective trade-offs with other logistics resources such as transportation or inventory. Table 11.9 illustrates typical technology assessment topics. Such an assessment should be completed with respect to each component of the logistics system as well as from the perspective of overall system integration.

	Current Technology	State-of-the Art Technology
Forecasting	What are the current technologies for collecting, maintaining, and developing forecasts?	How are the best firms developing forecasts?
Order Entry	What order entry technologies are used currently?	How are the best firms performing order entry?
	What order entry technology are customers requiring?	What new technologies are available to improve order entry effectiveness?
Order Processing	What is the process to allocate available inventory to customer orders?	How are the best firms performing order processing?
	What are the limitations of the current approach?	What new technologies (hardware and software) are available to improve order processing effectiveness?
Requirements Planning	What decision processes are used to determine production and distribution inventory requirements?	How are the best firms making production and inventory planning decisions?
	How are these processes supported with current information and decision aids?	What new technologies are available to improve requirements planning effectiveness?
Invoicing and EDI	How are invoices, inquiries, advanced shipment notifications, and payments currently transmitted?	How are the best firms using EDI?
		What new communications and data exchange technologies are available to improve invoicing and other forms of customer communication?
Warehouse Operations	How are warehouse personnel and scheduling decisions made?	How are the best firms using information and materials handling technologies in the warehouse?
	How are warehousing operating instructions provided to supervisors and material handlers?	What new information and materials handling technologies are available to improve warehouse operating effectiveness?
	How do warehouse supervisors and material handlers track activities and performance?	
Transportation	How are transportation consolidation, routing, and scheduling decisions made?	How are the best firms using information, packaging, and loading technologies with carriers?
	How is transportation documentation developed and communicated with carriers and customers?	What new information, packaging, loading, and communication technologies are available to improve transportation operating effectiveness?
	How are transportation costs determined, assessed, and monitored?	
	What packaging and loading technologies are used?	
Decision Support	How are logistical, tactical, and strategic planning decisions made?	How are the best companies making similar tactical or strategic decisions?
	What information is used and what analysis is completed?	What information and evaluation technologies are available to enhance decision effectiveness?

TABLE 11.9   Typical Technology Assessment

Supporting Logic

The second feasibility assessment task is the development of a supporting logic to integrate the findings of the internal review, market assessment, and technology study. Supporting logic development often constitutes the most difficult part of the strategic planning process. The purpose of the situational analysis is to provide senior management with the best possible vision of the strengths and weaknesses of existing logistics system capabilities for both the existing and potential future logistical requirements. Supporting logic development builds on this comprehensive review in three ways.

First, it must identify the value proposition to justify detailed research and analysis. In this sense, the supporting logic development forces a critical view of potential improvement opportunities, including determination of whether the cost/benefit justification provides a solid business case. Supporting logic development utilizes logistics principles, such as the transportation tapering principle, principle of inventory aggregation, and total landed cost principle discussed in previous chapters, to determine the potential of more detailed analysis. While completing the remaining tasks in the managerial planning process does not commit a firm to implementation or even guarantee an improved logistics system design, the potential benefits and risks associated with change should be clearly identified in developing as a result of supporting logic.

Second, supporting logic development critically evaluates current procedures and practices on the basis of a comprehensive factual analysis to remove perceptual biases. Identification of areas with improvement potential, as well as those where operations are satisfactory, provides a foundation to determine the need for strategic change. For example, it may be apparent that excess inventory or obsolete stock represents a serious problem and significant potential exists to reduce cost and improve service. While the appraisal process frequently confirms that many aspects of the existing system are more right than wrong, the decisions to consider change should be based on potential improvement. If the logic supports the current number and location of warehouses, subsequent analysis can focus on streamlining inventory levels. The deliverables of this evaluation process include classification of planning and evaluation issues prioritized into primary and secondary categories across short- and long-range planning horizons.

Third, the process of developing supporting logic should include clear statements of potential redesign alternatives. The statement should include: (1) definition of current procedures and systems, (2) identification of the most likely system design alternatives based on leading industry competitive practices and the prevailing theories of integrated logistics and supply chains, and (3) suggestion of innovative approaches based on new theory and technologies. The alternatives should challenge existing practices, but they must also be practical. The less frequently a redesign project is conducted to reevaluate current procedures and designs, the more important it is to identify a range of options for consideration. For example, evaluation of a total logistics management system or supply chain structure should consider a wider range of options if done every five years than if completed every two years.

Current best practice is to increase the frequency of undertaking total system design. Some leading firms review their overall network design on an annual basis. As an example, when Subway Restaurants introduced their "$5 footlong" promotion, they anticipated (and experienced) a substantial increase in volume. With the increased volume and reduced margins, they needed to make sure that their supply system, provided by Independent Purchasing Cooperative (IPC), and logistics system, operated by C.H. Robinson Worldwide, were optimized. To achieve that goal, they redesigned their logistics system by consolidating meat and vegetable preparation facilities, updating transportation equipment to provider multi-temperature capability, and providing more timely information exchange to facilitate forecasting. This illustrates how a corporate strategic initiative often drives the need for a substantial supply chain upgrade, which employed a thorough analysis as described here.[7]

At this point in the planning and design process, it is well worth the effort to develop visual models illustrating the basic concepts and justification associated with each alternative. The illustrations should frame opportunities for flexible logistics practices, clearly outline value-added and information flow requirements, and provide a comprehensive overview of the options. Some refined or segmented logistics practices are difficult to

[7]Jan Risi and John Wiehoff., "How Green Logistics Pays off in a Quick Service Leader's Supply Chain.", Council of Supply Chain Management Professionals 2010 Annual Meeting (San Diego, CA: September 28, 2010).

depict in a single illustration. For example, regional variations, product-mix variations, and differential shipment policies are difficult to illustrate, although they do form the basis of design alternatives.

A recommended procedure requires the manager responsible for evaluating the logistical strategy to develop a logical statement and justification of potential benefits. Using the customer relationship management concepts discussed in Chapter 2 and logistics integration logic and methodology from earlier in this chapter, the responsible design team should document and justify the most attractive strategy modifications.

Cost/Benefit Estimate

The final feasibility task, the cost/benefit estimate, projects the potential benefits and risks associated with performing a logistics analysis and implementing the recommendations. Benefits should be categorized in terms of service improvements, cost reduction, and cost prevention. The categories are not mutually exclusive, given that logistics strategy and operations might include some degree of all three benefits simultaneously. The risks represent the potential downside related to the proposed changes. Service improvement includes an estimate of the impact of enhanced availability, quality, or capability. Improved service increases loyalty of existing customers and may also attract new business.

Cost reduction benefits may be observed in two forms. First, benefits may occur as a result of a one-time reduction in financial or managerial resources required to operate the logistics system. For example, logistical redesign may allow the reduction of warehouses, materials handling equipment, or information technology systems. Reductions in capital deployed for inventory and other logistics-related assets can significantly enhance a firm's performance if ongoing costs are eliminated and free cash spin-off is generated. Second, cost reductions may be found in the form of reduced out-of-pocket or variable expenses. For example, new technologies for materials handling and information processing may reduce variable cost by allowing more efficient processing and operations.

Cost prevention helps eliminate involvement in programs and operations experiencing cost increases. For example, many materials handling and information technology upgrades may be at least partially justified through financial analysis regarding the implications of future labor availability and wage levels. Initiatives to reduce energy consumption can also prevent cost in periods of increasing energy prices. Naturally, any cost-prevention justification is based on an estimate of future conditions and therefore is vulnerable to a degree of error.

No precise rules exist to determine when a planning situation offers adequate cost/benefit potential to justify proceeding to in-depth analysis. Ideally, review should be completed on a continuous basis at regular intervals to assure the viability of current and future logistics operations. In the final analysis, the decision to undertake in-depth planning will depend on how convincing the supporting logic is, how believable estimated benefits are, and whether estimated benefits offer sufficient return on investment to justify organizational and operational change. These potential benefits must be balanced against the out-of-pocket cost required to complete the process.

Although they are not always a goal of a planning and design project, immediate improvement opportunities are frequently possible. The rapid capture of "low hanging fruit" can often increase revenue or decrease cost sufficiently to justify the remainder of an analysis. As the project team identifies these opportunities, the responsible executive should evaluate each opportunity to balance the quick return in terms of the implementation risk.

Project Planning

Project planning is the second Phase I activity. Logistics system complexity requires that any effort to identify and evaluate strategic or tactical alternatives must be planned thoroughly to provide a sound basis for implementing change. Project planning involves these specific tasks including: statement of objectives, statement of constraints, measurement standards, assumptive logic, analysis techniques, and project work plan.

Statement of Objectives

A statement of objectives documents the cost and service expectations for the logistics system revisions. It is essential that they be stated specifically and in terms of measurable factors. The objectives define market or industry segments, the time frame for change, and specific performance expectations. These requirements typically define specific goals that management is seeking to achieve. For example, the following suggest a combination of measurable objectives that might be used to guide logistics system analysis:

A. Provide the 100 most profitable customers with perfect order performance
B. For all other customers provide the following performance:
   1. Inventory availability:
     • 99 percent for category A products
     • 95 percent for category B products
     • 90 percent for category C products
   2. Delivery of 98 percent of all orders within 48 hours of placement
   3. Minimize customer shipments from secondary warehouses
   4. Fill mixed product orders without back order on a minimum of 85 percent of all orders
   5. Hold back orders for a maximum of 5 days

Specific definition of these objectives directs system design efforts to achieve explicit customer service performance levels. Total system cost to meet the service objectives can then be determined by using appropriate analytical methods. To the extent that logistics total cost does not fall within management expectations, alternative customer service performance levels can be tested by using sensitivity analysis to determine impact on overall logistics cost.

Alternatively, performance objectives can establish maximum total cost constraints, and then a system that achieves maximum customer service level attainable within an acceptable logistics budget may be evaluated. Such cost-driven solutions are practical since recommendations are guaranteed to fit within acceptable budget ranges. However, such cost-constrained design solutions lack sensitivity to customer service drivers.

Statement of Constraints

The second project planning consideration concerns design constraints. On the basis of the situational analysis, it is expected that senior leadership may place some restrictions on the scope of permissible system modifications. The nature of such restrictions depends upon each specific firm. However, two common examples to illustrate how constraints can impact the overall planning process.

One restriction common to warehouse system design concerns the existing manufacturing facilities and their product-mix assortment. To simplify the study, management often holds existing manufacturing facilities and product mix constant during logistical system redesign. Such constraints may be justified on the basis of financial investments in existing manufacturing plants and the ability of the organization to absorb change.

A second example of constraints concerns customer relationship activities of different divisions. In firms with a traditional pattern of decentralized profit responsibility, management may elect to include some divisional operations in a centralized logistics system while omitting others. Thus, some divisions are managerially identified as candidates for change while others are not.

All design constraints serve to limit the scope of the analysis. However, as one executive stated, "Why study things we don't plan to do anything about?" Unless there is a reasonable chance that leadership will be inclined to accept recommendations to significantly change logistics strategy or operations, their limitations may best be treated as a study constraint.

The purpose of developing a statement of constraints is to have a well-defined starting point for the planning effort. If quantitative analysis techniques are used, major constraints may be reconsidered later. In contrast to the situation assessment discussed earlier, the statement of constraints defines specific organizational elements, facilities, systems, procedures, and/or practices to be retained from the existing logistical system.

Measurement Standards and Assumptive Logic

The feasibility assessment often highlights a central need for measurement standard development. Such standards direct the analysis by identifying cost assumptions and performance objectives essential to evaluate recommendations. Management must stipulate measurement standards and objectives as a prerequisite for plan formulation. It is important that the standards adequately reflect total system performance rather than a limited focus on logistics functions. Once formulated, such standards must be monitored and tracked throughout system study and implementation to allow measurement of change impact. Although considerable managerial discretion exists in the formulation of standards, care must be exercised not to dilute the validity of the analysis and subsequent results by setting impractical or constantly changing goals.

An important requirement is the assumptions that provide the logic supporting the standards. These assumptions should have senior leadership approval because they can significantly shape the results of the operational analysis. For example, a relatively small variation in the standard cost and procedure for evaluating inventory can create major variations in the resulting recommendation.

Measurement standards should include definitions regarding how cost components such as transportation, inventory, and order processing are quantified, including detailed financial account references. The standards must also include specification of relevant customer service measures and method of calculation.

Project Work Plan

On the basis of feasibility assessment, objectives, constraints, standards, and analysis techniques, a project work plan can be developed and the resources and time required for completion specified. The alternatives and opportunities specified during the feasibility assessment provide the basis for determining the scope of the study. In turn, the scope determines the required time to complete the study.

Project management is responsible for the achievement of expected results within time and budget constraints. One of the most common errors in strategic planning is to underestimate the time required to complete a specific assignment. Overruns increase financial expenditures and reduce project credibility. Fortunately, there are a number of project management packages available to structure projects, guide resource allocation, and measure progress. Additionally, firms consider internal project management vs. outsourcing based on resource constraints and project management capabilities. Such methodologies identify deliverables and the interrelationship between tasks.

Phase II: Data Collection and Analysis

Once the feasibility assessment and project plan are completed, Phase II of the research process focuses on data collection and analysis. This phase requires definition of assumptions, data collection, and analysis of alternatives.

Assumptions and Data Collection

This activity extends the feasibility assessment and project plan by developing detailed planning assumptions and identifying data collection requirements by (1) defining analysis approaches and techniques, (2) defining and reviewing assumptions, (3) identifying data sources, (4) collecting data, and (5) collecting validation data.

Defining Analysis Approaches and Techniques

An early Phase II task is the determination of the appropriate analysis technique for the planning situation under consideration. While a wide number of options are available, the most common techniques are analytical, simulation, and optimization. An analytical approach uses numerical tools such as spreadsheets to evaluate each logistical alternative. A typical example of an analytical approach is the determination of inventory/service trade-offs using the formulas discussed in Chapter 7. Spreadsheet availability and capability have increased the use of analytical tools for logistical analysis.

A simulation approach can be likened to a laboratory for testing supply chain logistics alternatives. Simulation is widely used, particularly when significant uncertainty is involved. The testing environment can be physical, such as a model materials handling system that physically illustrates product flow in a scaled-down environment, or numerical, such as a computer model. Current software makes simulation one of the most cost-effective approaches for evaluating dynamic logistics alternatives. For example, a PC-based simulation can model the flows, activity levels, and performance characteristics. Many simulations have the capability to illustrate system characteristics graphically. For example, supply chain dynamic simulation can be used to illustrate the trade-off between inventory allocation strategy and customer service levels.[8]

Optimization uses linear or mathematical programming to evaluate alternatives and select the best design or alternatives under consideration. While optimization has the benefit of being able to identify the best option, optimizations are often smaller in scope than typical simulation applications.

Defining and Reviewing Assumptions

Assumption definition and review builds on the situation analysis, project objectives, constraints, and measurement standards. For planning purposes, the assumptions define the key operating characteristics, variables, and economics of current and alternative systems.

---

[8]For a general simulation modeling tool incorporating graphics, see W. David Kelton, Randall P. Sadowski, and David T. Sturrock, *Simulation with Arena,* 5th ed. (New York: McGraw-Hill, 2011).

While the format will differ by project, assumptions generally fall into three classes: (1) business assumptions, (2) management assumptions, and (3) analysis assumptions.

Business assumptions define the characteristics of the general business environment, including relevant market, consumer, product trends, resource availability, and competitive actions. The assumptions define the broad environment within which an alternative logistics plan must operate. Business assumptions are generally outside the ability of the firm to change.

Management assumptions define the physical and economic characteristics of the current or alternative logistics environment and are generally within management's ability to change or refine. Typical management assumptions include the warehouse locations to be considered, transport modes, ownership arrangements, logistics processes, and fixed and variable costs.

Analysis assumptions define the constraints and limitations required to fit the problem to the analysis technique. These assumptions frequently focus on problem size, degree of analysis detail, and solution methodology. Table 11.10 offers more detailed descriptions for each assumption category.

Identifying Data Sources

In actual practice, the process of data collection begins with a feasibility assessment. In addition, a fairly detailed specification of data is required to determine the desired analytical technique. However, at this point in the planning procedure, detailed data must be collected and organized to support the analysis. For situations when data is extremely difficult to collect or when the necessary level of accuracy is unknown, sensitivity analysis can be used to evaluate data impact. For example, an initial analysis may be completed using transportation costs estimated with distance-based regressions. If analysis indicates that

Assumption Classes/Categories	Description
Business Assumptions	
Scope	Definition of business units and product lines to be included.
Alternatives	Range of options that can be considered.
Market trends	Nature and magnitude of change in market preferences and buying patterns. Projected changes in resource availability and cost.
Product trends	Nature and magnitude of change in product buying patterns, particularly with respect to package size and packaging.
Competitive actions	Competitive logistics strengths, weaknesses, and strategies.
Management Assumptions	
Markets	Demand patterns by market area, product, and shipment size.
Distribution facilities	Locations, operating policies, economic characteristics, and performance history of current and potential distribution facilities.
Transportation	Transportation rates for movement between potential and existing distribution facilities and customers.
Inventory	Inventory levels and operating policies for each distribution facility.
Analysis Assumptions	
Product groups	Detailed product information aggregated to fit within scope of analysis technique.
Market areas	Customer demand grouped to aggregate market areas to fit the scope of analysis technique.

TABLE 11.10   Assumption Categories Elements

the best answer is very sensitive to the actual freight rates, then additional effort should be undertaken to obtain transport rates quotes from carriers. Once a technique is operational, sensitivity analysis can be used to identify the major variables that are driving conclusions. When these sensitive drivers, such as outbound transportation expense, are identified, additional effort can be directed to increasing the accuracy of assumptions including efforts to obtain actual quotes.

The first major data category is sales and customer orders. The annual sales forecast and percentage of sales by month, as well as seasonality patterns, are usually necessary to determine logistics volume and activity patterns. Historical samples of customer orders to determine shipping patterns by market and shipment size. The combination of aggregate measures of demand and shipment profiles characterizes the logistics operational requirements that must be met.

Specific customer data are also required to add a spatial dimension to a logistics analysis. The spatial dimension reflects the fact that effective logistics to key customers requires that the delivery cost and time associated with precise locations be quantified. In the overall analysis, customers and markets are often aggregated by location, type, size, order frequency, and growth rate to reduce analysis complexity. However, such aggregation is normally not satisfactory for evaluation of key customer service capability.

For supply chain logistics analysis, it is necessary to identify and track the costs associated with manufacturing and purchasing. While manufacturing plant locations may not be a variable component in a logistical system design, it is typically necessary to consider the number and location of plants, product mix, production schedules, and seasonality. Policies and costs associated with inventory transfer, reordering, and warehouse processing must be identified. In particular, inventory control rules and product allocation procedures are important elements. Finally, for each current and potential warehouse, it is necessary to establish operating costs, capacities, product mix, storage levels, and service capabilities.

Transportation data requirements include the number and type of modes utilized, modal selection criteria, rates, transit times, shipping rules, and policies. If private transportation is included in the analysis, then information is required regarding the operating characteristics of the private fleet.

The preceding discussion offers some perspective regarding the necessary data to evaluate logistical system design. The primary justification for placing the formal data collection process after the selection of analysis technique is to match the data to technique requirements.

It is also useful to benchmark competitive logistical capabilities to provide information regarding competitor strategies and capabilities. In most cases, this information is readily available from published material, annual reports, and general knowledge of company executives. The main purpose in collecting such data is to provide competitive benchmarks that compare customer service capabilities, facility networks, and operating capabilities.

Data Collection

Once alternative data sources have been identified, the data collection process can begin. The process includes acquisition and assembly of required data and conversion to appropriate formats for the analysis tool. This is often a tedious and time-consuming task, so errors are likely. Potential errors include collecting data from a misrepresentative time period and including data that do not reflect major components of logistics activity, such as customer pickup volume. For this reason, the data collection process should be carefully documented to assist in identifying errors that might reduce analysis accuracy and to determine any necessary changes to achieve acceptable accuracy.

Validation Data

In addition to collecting data to support alternative analysis, base case or validation data must also be collected to verify that the results accurately reflect reality. The specific question concerns whether the chosen analytical approach accurately replicates historical logistics practices. The objective of validation is to increase credibility regarding the analysis process. If the process does not validate management will have little confidence in results and resulting recommendations.

Analysis

Analysis involves use of the technique and data to evaluate strategic and tactical logistics alternatives. The analysis process includes: (1) analysis questions, (2) validating baseline analysis, (3) analyses of alternatives, and (4) sensitivity analysis.

Analysis Questions

The first task is to establish specific questions concerning alternatives and the degree of acceptable uncertainty. The specific analysis questions are based on research objectives and constraints. For example, the questions related to a warehouse site must be based on the specific location combinations to be evaluated. In the case of an inventory analysis, questions typically focus on alternative service and forecast uncertainty.

Suppose that a strategic planning effort is focusing on the identification of a network of warehouses to serve the U.S. domestic market. Assume that the current network uses four warehouses located in Newark, New Jersey; Atlanta, Georgia; Chicago, Illinois; and Los Angeles, California. Table 11.11 summarizes the shipment volume, cost, and service characteristics of the existing system. Shipment volume is defined in terms of weight shipped; cost, in terms of transportation and inventory carrying expenses; and service level, in terms of the percentage of sales volume serviced within 2 days' transit time from the warehouse. Likely questions for the analysis might be the performance impact if the Chicago or any other warehouse is closed.

Other alternatives could include fewer or more warehouse locations or evaluation of different locations or more refined inventory management policies. It is important to recognize that care must be taken to define the analysis questions so that a wide range of possible options can be evaluated without requiring time-consuming modification of the model or additional data collection.

Baseline Validation

The second task involves validation of the model being used. Analysis results should be compared with the validation data to determine the degree of fit between actual and modeling results. The comparison should focus on identifying significant differences and

TABLE 11.11
Summary Distribution Performance

Distribution Center	Shipment Volume (000 lbs)	Inbound Transportation	Outbound Transportation	Inventory Carrying Cost ($)	Total Cost
Newark	693,000	317,000	264,000	476,000	1,750,000
Atlanta	136,400	62,000	62,000	92,000	216,000
Chicago	455,540	208,000	284,000	303,000	795,000
Los Angeles	10,020	5,000	5,000	6,000	16,000
Total	1,294,960	592,000	615,000	877,000	2,777,000

determining sources of possible error. As discrepancies are encountered, errors should be identified and corrected. Once discrepancies have been removed or explained to within ± 2 percent, the application is generally accepted as a valid representation so analysis can proceed.

Analyses of Alternatives

The next step is to complete design analysis. The analysis should determine the relevant performance characteristics for each alternative design or strategy. The options should quantify the impact of changes in management policies and practices involving factors such as the number of warehouses, inventory target levels, or the transportation shipment size profile.

Sensitivity Analysis

Once this analysis is completed, the best-performing alternatives can be targeted for further sensitivity evaluation. When undertaking sensitivity analysis uncontrollable factors such as demand, resource costs, and competitive actions are varied to assess design alternative's ability to operate under a variety of conditions. For example, suppose that the alternative analysis indicates that four warehouses provide the ideal cost/service trade-off for the firm's market area assuming the base demand level. Sensitivity analysis could test the appropriateness of this solution under alternative demand or cost scenarios. In other words, would four warehouses still be the correct decision if demand increased or decreased by 10 percent? The current environment requires an assessment regarding the impact of increased energy cost. Sensitivity analysis in conjunction with an assessment of potential scenario probabilities is then used in a decision tree to identify the best alternative to meet managerial expectations.

Phase III: Recommendations and Implementation

Phase III operationalizes planning and design efforts by making specific management recommendations and developing implementation plans.

Recommendations

Alternative and sensitivity analysis results provide the basis to finalize managerial recommendations. This recommendation process includes four tasks: (1) estimating costs and benefits, (2) identifying the best alternative, (3) developing a risk assessment, and (4) developing a presentation.

Estimating Costs and Benefits

In the earlier discussion of strategic planning, potential benefits were identified as service improvement, cost reduction, and cost prevention. It was noted that these benefits are not mutually exclusive and that a sound strategy might seek all benefits simultaneously. When evaluating the potential of a particular logistics strategy, an analysis comparing present cost and service capabilities with projected performance should be completed for each alternative. The ideal cost/benefit analysis compares the alternatives for a base period and then projects comparative operations across a planning horizon. Benefits can thus be projected on the basis of both one-time savings that impact of system redesign as well on ongoing operating economies.

Identifying the Best Alternative

The alternatives and sensitivity analyses should identify the best options to consider for implementation. However, multiple alternatives often yield similar or comparable results. Performance characteristics and conditions for each alternative must be compared to identify the two or three best options. Although the concept of best may have different interpretations, it will generally be the alternative that meets desired service objectives at the minimum total cost.

Evaluating Risk

A second type of justification necessary to support strategic planning recommendations is an assessment of the risk involved. Risk assessment considers the probability that the actual operating environment will match assumptions. Additionally, it considers the potential hazards related to system implementation.

Risk related to adoption of a specific alternative can be quantified by using sensitivity analyses. For example, assumptions can be varied and the resulting impact on system performance across alternatives can be determined. To illustrate, sensitivity analysis can be used to identify the system performance for different demand and cost assumptions. If the selected alternative is still best even though demand increases or decreases by 20 percent, management can conclude that there is little risk associated with moderate errors in the demand environment. The end result of a risk appraisal is to provide a financial evaluation of the downside risk if planning assumptions fail to materialize.

Presentation

The final task is development of a managerial presentation that identifies, quantifies, and justifies suggested changes. The presentation and accompanying report must identify specific operating and strategic changes, provide a qualitative rationale as to why such change is appropriate, and then quantitatively justify the changes in terms of service, cost, asset utilization, and productivity improvements. The presentation should incorporate extensive use of graphs, maps, and flowcharts to illustrate changes in logistics operating practices, flows, and distribution network.

Implementation

The actual plan or design implementation is the final process activity. While actual implementation may require a number of events, there are four broad tasks: (1) defining the implementation plan, (2) scheduling implementation, (3) defining acceptance criteria, and (4) implementing the plan.

Defining the Plan

The first task defines the implementation plan in terms of the individual events, their sequence, and dependencies. While the initial plan may be macro level, it must ultimately be refined to provide individual assignment responsibility and accountability. Plan dependencies identify the interrelationships between events and, thus, define the completion sequence.

Scheduling

The second task schedules the implementation and time-phases the assignments identified previously. The schedule must allow adequate time for acquiring facilities and equipment, negotiating agreements, developing procedures, and training. Implementation scheduling, ideally, should use comprehensive project management methods to guide the process.

Acceptance

The third task defines the acceptance criteria for evaluating the success of the plan. Acceptance criteria should focus on service improvement, cost reduction, improved asset utilization, and enhanced quality. If the primary focus is service, acceptance criteria must identify detailed components such as improved product availability or reduced performance cycle time. If the primary focus is cost, the acceptance criteria must define the expected positive and negative changes in all affected cost categories. It is important that the acceptance criteria take a broad perspective so that motivation focuses on total logistics system performance rather than performance of an individual function. It is also important that the acceptance criteria incorporate broad organizational input.

Plan Implementation

The final task is actual implementation of the plan or design. Implementation must include adequate controls to ensure performance as anticipated and that acceptance criteria are carefully monitored. It is critical that a formalized process be used to guide logistics system design and refinement projects to ensure that the objectives are documented and understood and that the analyses are completed appropriately.

Application of Supply Chain Principles

While the traditional application of supply chain principles focuses on manufacturing operations, there are many other applications in process and resource management as discussed in Chapter 1. While Chapter 1 discussed the different types of supply chains, Tables 11.12 through 11.15 characterize the different types of supply chains in terms of (1) service focus, (2) financial focus, (3) procurement focus, (4) manufacturing focus, (5) logistics focus, (6) opportunities for performance enhancement, and (7) product types. The service focus describes what the supply chain needs to provide the consumer whether it be a product, asset utilization, or experienced talent. The financial focus indicates the type of financial benefits that the firm is looking for whether it be increased volume, market share, material availability, minimizing cost of recovery, or maximizing asset utilization. The financial focus reflects how a firm can create a competitive advantage through its supply chain strategy. The procurement focus describes whether the firm would tend to use the suppliers to obtain purchasing economies of scale or product innovation or to minimize risk. The manufacturing focus defines whether the firm will use high-volume manufacturing (economies of scale) or more customized manufacturing to create a competitive manufacturing offering. The logistics focus defines how the firm moves its finished goods to its consumers and considers channel, mode, and scale alternatives. The opportunities for performance enhancement define how a firm can create a competitive advantage in each supply chain applications. The product type defines the specific type of products that might use each application.

Criteria	Product Supply Chain	Promotional Supply Chain	Bulk Material Supply Chain	Talent Supply Chain
Service focus	Meeting customer service objectives	Meet sales objectives of promotion	Provide service with maximum asset utilization	Provide appropriately trained and experienced talent
Financial focus	Focus on volume	Increase market share	Take advantage of raw material availability	Maximize utilization of trained and experienced expertise
Procurement focus	High-volume consistent suppliers	Obtain raw materials to meet specific of promotion	High-volume consistent suppliers	Shift from fixed to variable cost
Manufacturing focus	High-volume manufacturing	Customized agile production	Minimize changeovers	Increased application of specialized talent under time constraints
Logistics focus	Economies of scale	Obtain transport capacity to meet volume requirements	Require bulk transport (water, rail, and truck)	Finding talent that work in the desired location (language and permits)
Opportunities for performance enhancement	Increased volume	Increased market share	Move from commodity to specialized	Maximum utilization of specialty talent
Product types	Food and general merchandise	Food and general merchandise	Petroleum, chemicals, Yankee Candle	Research, IT, SC, medical talent

TABLE 11.12   Application of Supply Chain Principles

Criteria	B2C Supply Chain	Recycling Supply Chain	Resource Supply Chain	Construction Supply Chain
Service focus	Responsive home delivery	Maximize quantity recycled	Meet solution requirements of consumers	Meet building availability requirements
Financial focus	Increased access to customer base	Minimize cost of recovery	Minimize assets required	Minimize cost of materials and labor
Procurement focus	Increased range of products	Gain access to volume of recyclables	Schedule asset arrival in a timely manner	Trade-off acquisition cost vs. storage requirements
Manufacturing focus	Increased customization and breadth of line	Effective process of recyclables to create use materials	Parallel processing	Parallel processing and site logistics
Logistics focus	Responsive delivery	Minimize transport cost in non-standardized environment	Arrival sequencing and inventory maintaining	Arrival sequencing, inventory maintenance, and licensing
Opportunities for performance enhancement	Increased volume over last mile	Easy to disassemble and sort	Take advantage of opportunities for parallel processing	Take advantage of opportunities for parallel processing
Product types	Increasing range of products	Metals and chemicals	Project management	Facilities construction

TABLE 11.13   Application of Supply Chain Principles

The objective of Tables 11.12 through 11.15 is to illustrate how supply chain process and resource management principles can be used in different types of industries. This should provide logistics professionals with insight regarding how their expertise and insight can be applied in many industries.

One of the traditional challenges faced by supply chain executives is the need to determine the design for the integrated supply chain for their firm. The specific question concerns how best to design the product flows both within the firm and between supply chain partners. This is the application of the principles discussed earlier in this chapter. Historically,

Criteria	Recovery Supply Chain	Humanitarian Supply Chain	Global Supply Chain	Durables Supply Chain
Service focus	Return goods for reuse	Search, recovery and meet critical necessities	Meet unique regional requirements	Meet customer delivery requirements
Financial focus	Minimize cost	While cost is important, perception is more important	Low total cost including duties and taxes	While it is important, cost is often secondary
Procurement focus	Organize items to be recovered	Preposition requirements	Meeting regional and regulatory requirements	Standardize components
Manufacturing focus	Remarketing or remanufacturing	Adapt products to environment	Standardize as much as possible	Extensive variation and complexity
Logistics focus	Adapting to low scale economies	Infrastructure is often limiting	Work with local infrastructure and service providers	Specialized equipment
Opportunities for performance enhancement	Consolidation	Product prepositioning	Apply appropriate global strategy	Collaboration with other firms serving similar customers
Product type	Military, construction, electronics	Floods, earthquakes, hurricanes, and uprisings	Heavy equipment, furniture, high technology	Automotive, farm equipment

TABLE 11.14   Application of Supply Chain Principles

Criteria	Agriculture Commodity Supply Chain	Innovative Supply Chain	Military Supply Chain	Clinical Trials Supply Chain
Service focus	Meet production requirements of production facilities	Make sure product is available in desired markets	Meet requirements of soldiers in field	Very precise delivery to trial patients
Financial focus	Maximum use of commodity priced item	Cost is definitely secondary	Increasingly important	Important but not nearly as important as service
Procurement focus	Commodity item	Work with suppliers to develop innovative components	Meet Defense Acquisition Regulations System (DFARS)	Meet quality and certification requirements
Manufacturing focus	Maximize productivity for food conversion	Pilot plant capability	Make vs. buy	Apply quality pilot production capabilities
Logistics focus	Transport cost reduces price received by farmer	Precise delivery requirements with security	Nonstandard and hazardous goods transportation	Precise delivery is critical
Opportunities for performance enhancement	Reduce transport distance while maximizing scale of production	Specialty innovative supply chain	Apply lessons from commercial sector	Collaboration with competitors involved in clinical trials
Product type	Agriculture commodities	New products	Military consumables and capital goods	Pharmaceuticals involved in trials

TABLE 11.15   Application of Supply Chain Principles

this process might have been completed by a division or an entire firm every 3 to 5 years. Recently, however, firms have begun to complete supply chain design reviews more frequently and considering a broader range of considerations. The objective of this section is to:

1. Review the considerations used for supply chain design in the past;
2. Discuss the considerations for today; and
3. Propose a framework to integrate the considerations into an integrated decision.

This section provides background regarding the supply chain design process, introduces the decision framework, and illustrates the framework with an application.

Decision Application

Over the past century, there has been substantial research regarding techniques and methods to determine the optimum plant and distribution center network for firms. More recently, such tools and methods have been extended to include the flows between supply chain partners and involvement with logistics service providers. Historically, the analysis focused on demand geography and the cost of transportation from the source of the raw materials to the consumer. More recently, the analysis considered the total cost (fixed and variable) to obtain raw material, manufacture, handle, and transport the product from the source of the raw material to the market. However, there are an increased number of factors that need to be considered. Table 11.16 lists the typical considerations as they evolved from the 1990s through to 2010. Prior to 1990, network decisions were based on the demand geography of the market with the objective of identifying the plant and distribution center locations that would minimize the total cost of raw material, production, and transportation.

Since 2010, the decision has become much more complex because there are many new considerations. As Table 11.16 illustrates, network design decisions must still consider the geography of the marketplace. However, considerations such as sustainability, energy, labor, political environment, and taxation must be included, as well as raw material, production, and transportation. The new considerations are shown in italics. The sustainability consideration means the supply chain must be designed to reduce greenhouse gases, pollution, and use of nonrecyclable materials. The energy consideration means the supply chain must be designed to minimize electrical and oil usage. The labor consideration indicates that supply chain design decisions should consider labor availability, rate, and flexibility. The political environment consideration means supply chain design decisions should consider regional political stability, regulatory environment, and talent development initiatives. The taxation consideration refers to property and income taxes that must be considered when locating a facility or inventory in a specific location or taxes that must be paid due to the performance of value-added activities in a specific location. The remaining three cost considerations are the raw material, production, and transportation costs discussed earlier.

While the 2010 considerations demonstrate the increased complexity of supply chain design decisions from 1990 to 2010, the growth in complexity has certainly not stopped. Logistics professionals indicate that the number of considerations increase every year. Table 11.17 illustrates the other network design considerations that should be included in today's environment. the 2020 considerations in Table 11.17 demonstrate that there are an increasing number of considerations that generally relate to sustainability and supply

TABLE 11.16
Network Design
Considerations

1990 Considerations	2010 Considerations
• Demand	• Demand
• Raw material	• *Sustainability*
• Production	• *Energy*
• Transportation	• *Labor cost*
	• *Political environment*
	• *Taxation*
	• Raw material
	• Production
	• Transportation

1990 Considerations	2010 Considerations	2020 Considerations
• Demand	• Demand	• Demand
• Raw material	• *Sustainability*	• Sustainability
• Production	• *Energy*	• Energy
• Transportation	• *Labor cost*	• Labor cost
	• *Political environment*	• Political environment
	• *Taxation*	• Taxation
	• Raw material	• *Water*
	• Production	• *Regulatory*
	• Transportation	• *Compliance*
		• *Supplier relationships*
		• *Commodity availability*
		• *Cross-sale requirements*
		• Raw material
		• Production
		• Transportation

TABLE 11.17
Supply Chain Network Design Considerations

chain relationships. An increasingly important consideration is access to an adequate amount of clean water at a reasonable price to support both production and cleaning operations. Regulatory and compliance considerations are also major considerations from the perspective of minimizing restrictions related to labor, storage, transportation, and customs. Supplier relationships are an increasingly important consideration because some firms require that their primary suppliers be near the plant. This is increasingly important for durable goods industries such as automobile and heavy equipment. Another consideration is access to critical commodities such as agricultural products, key chemicals or metals, and skilled labor capability. The final 2020 consideration is the cross-sale requirements that may be required as part of trade agreements. A trade agreement may require that one country source materials from another country in roughly the same value ratio.

While Table 11.17 illustrates the evolution of supply chain network design considerations, it is clear that all considerations are not weighted equally nor will they have equal impact. Table 11.18 lists other emerging considerations that are changing the nature and importance of network design for the firm.

As a result of this significant increase in decision complexity, it is important that a framework be created that can assist in structuring the decision and evaluating the trade-offs. The following section describes the framework and trade-offs.

Decision Framework

The framework builds on two dimensions: the factor drivers (exogenous and strategy) and the platform (global/centralized and local/decentralized). Table 11.19 illustrates this framework. The drivers reflect the uncontrollable environment that the firm chooses to operate in (exogenous) and the strategies that it chooses to employ (strategy). The drivers are the independent variables for the decision matrix. The platform (centralized or decentralized) indicates the integrated supply chain network strategy that offers the best trade-offs among firm risk, responsiveness, and cost. The global platform indicates that a centralized strategy is used, which includes centralized management and supply chain

TABLE 11.18
Business Network
Design Considerations

1990 Considerations	2010 Considerations	2020 Considerations	Emerging Business Considerations
• Demand • Raw material • Production • Transportation	• Demand • *Sustainability* • *Energy* • *Labor cost* • *Political environment* • *Taxation* • Raw material • Production • Transportation	• Demand • Sustainability • Energy • Labor cost • Political environment • Taxation • Water • Regulatory • Compliance • Supplier relationships • Commodity availability • Cross-sale requirements • Raw material • Production • Transportation	• Demand, market, and consumer dynamics • Business model and strategy • Comprehensive sustainability and social capital (including economics, ethics, environment, and education) • Global political and economic realities (including labor cost, taxation, regulatory, and political environment) • Supply market dynamics and relationships • Technology and product, service, and/or solution design (including IP, technical risks, and design for execution) • Production • Sales, marketing, and distribution (including transportation and compliance)

TABLE 11.19
Decision Framework

	Global platform/Centralized	Local platform/Decentralized
Exogenous drivers	Considerations that are generally outside the firm's control but that drive the firm to have a centralized production and distribution strategy (one large location taking advantage of economies of scale).	Considerations that are generally outside the firm's control but that drive the firm to have a decentralized production and distribution strategy (multiple smaller production and distribution sites located around the firm's market area to provide flexibility and reduce risk).
Strategy drivers	Considerations that generally reflect the firm's strategic decisions to have a centralized production and distribution strategy (one large location taking advantage of economies of scale).	Considerations that generally reflect the firm's strategic decisions to have a decentralized production and distribution strategy (multiple smaller production and distribution sites located around the firm's market area to provide flexibility and reduce risk).

operations. The local platform indicates that management and supply chain operations is controlled decentrally in each region.

To fully understand the framework, it is important to review both the exogenous and strategy considerations. Each consideration is discussed in the following sections.

Exogenous Drivers

The exogenous drivers, which are outside the firm's control, influence a firm's product make or distribution strategy, including: (1) economics, (2) talent, (3) product, (4) sales/

marketing/distribution, and (5) social. The following paragraphs describe each factor and the specific dimensions of each.

Economics Dimension

The economics consideration includes the regional economy, local labor rate, regional technologies, and regional market potential. the regional economy refers to the relative economic growth in the regions where a firm might want to locate a plant or distribution center. If the economic growth projections are homogenous across all regions under consideration, it is likely that the firm would employ a centralized strategy because all locations are comparable. If the economic growth projections are substantially different in each region, the firm would likely use a decentralized strategy so that localized plants and distribution centers can take advantage of the regional economic uniqueness. For example, a firm would likely choose a region with high economic growth to have access to market, growth, and service synergies.

The labor rate refers to the relative wage scale in the regions where the firm has operations. When there are small discrepancies in the wage scale between regions, firms would likely use centralized operations to take advantage of economies of scale. On the other hand, when there are large discrepancies between regional wage rates, firms would likely target decentralized production and distribution strategies to take advantage of the relatively lower labor cost in specific regions.

The regional technologies refer to the generation and focus of the key technologies in the regions that the firm is considering. Some regions may have older technologies that focus primarily on economies of scale, while other regions may have more recent technologies that offer more flexibility. If a firm wants to take advantage of economies of scale, their production and distribution strategies would probably focus on a centralized strategy. If a firm would like to have more flexibility, it would probably prefer to have more decentralized operations with smaller, more focused facilities.

The final economic consideration refers to the market potential for the firm's products. If there is a significant demand for a standardized version of the firm's products around the world, then a centralized global platform would be the best strategy in order for the firm to take advantage of economies of scale. On the other hand, if the market potential differs substantially by region in terms products or product features, then a decentralized production and distribution strategy would be the most appropriate.

In summary, the economic considerations include regional labor rate and market growth characteristics. In general, the similarity of cost, economic growth, technological advancement, and market potential across market regions will drive the firm toward a global production and distribution platform, while differential characteristics will result in more regional strategies.

Talent Dimension

The talent consideration focuses on the availability of management, design, production, and customer focus. The management consideration refers to the availability of expertise to provide senior management for the firm. Lack of senior management availability will likely lead to a centralized operation where the limited expertise can be focused on a limited number of sites. The argument is similar for the design and production talent where the firm would likely apply centralized strategies when there is limited design and production talent. The customer focus relates to whether the firm's consumers want standardized global designs with supply chain economies of scale or more flexible regional designs.

In summary, a shortage of specialized talent such as for management, design, or production will drive the firm to centralize these capabilities to take advantage of the talent synergies.

Product Dimension

The product consideration focuses on materials, expectations, intellectual property (IP), technical risk, and desired consumer differences. Desire for standardized components or suppliers would likely result in centralization to access a common source. Similarly, demands for high-quality and consistent design would result in centralization. The desire to protect IP for a design or a process would require centralization in a country with strong IP laws. Firms desiring to minimize technical risk would also likely apply a centralized strategy so to minimize the possibility of differences in product or process technology. Finally, firms with customers who don't want regional consumer differences will likely employ a centralization strategy as well.

In summary, consistency in product, process, and technology will likely lead to centralization to a limited number of sites with the resulting standardization.

Sales/Marketing/Distribution

The sales/marketing/distribution consideration focuses on the need to have consistent sales, marketing, and distribution strategies in each region. The specific considerations include tax strategy, treatment of global customers, application of brand equity, channel models, and compliance requirements. Depending on the countries involved, firms may want to locate their headquarters or production/distribution facilities in a location that provides them with the greatest tax advantage. The result could suggest either centralized or decentralized, depending on the countries involved. Increasingly, global customers desire a common service offering regardless of where they are located. To provide that, firms typically move toward a centralized site and strategy so that the supply chain can be consistent for all global customers. Similarly, when the firm desires to take advantage of global brand equity, it would likely employ a centralized strategy so that branding decisions can be applied consistently. Similarly, firms have to make decisions regarding which channels they are going to use in each country when they go to market. For example, a firm could sell through its own retailers in one country and then use e-commerce in another country. When firms use different channels, the perspective as viewed by global customers will be very different. If the firm desires channel standardization, it is likely that it will be using a centralized supply chain. Finally, customs compliance can be another consideration when determining supply chain strategy.

Social

The social consideration focuses on the need to meet social justice and sustainability requirements. Specifically, is the firm working with suppliers and in countries that conform with corporate standards. Another social requirement is to make sure that the firm's cultural expectations match with the regions and suppliers.

In summary, the firm and its supplier must demonstrate a fit socially as well.

Strategy Drivers

While the exogenous drivers are outside the control of the firm, the strategy drivers reflect the firm's strategy decisions. These dimensions include: (1) manufacturing, (2) purchasing, (3) processes and technology, (4) make strategy, (5) lead time, (6) human resources,

(7) risk management, and (8) centers of excellence. Depending on the firm's strategy with respect to each of these dimensions, the firm must determine whether a centralized or decentralized strategy is appropriate. Each dimension is discussed below.

The manufacturing strategy determines whether the manufacturing facilities should be centralized in a single location or separated across a firm's market area. The centralized option can offer economies of scale, while the decentralized option reduces risk and offers more flexibility and responsiveness.

The purchasing strategy determines whether the firm's purchasing organization should be centralized in a single location or segmented by division or region. Centralized purchasing provides the potential for more economies of scale, but it also reduces agility and responsiveness to local operations.

The processes and technology strategy determines whether the firm will use standardized technology and processes across its operations or more customized decentralized systems. Standardized technology and processes reduce complexity because the operations at every site and in every country are similar. While such standardization reduces complexity, it may also increase risk as a failure in one situation may increase the likelihood of another since they are the same systems.

The make strategy refers to whether each manufacturing site makes components and assembles final products or utilizes a make strategy with decentralized sites that assemble only. This strategy results in economies of scale for production of components, but it has the advantage of not requiring shipment of bulky finished products to distant markets. Firms that sell bulky products often make or purchase the components from a single site and then assemble decentrally.

The lead time strategy refers to an order-to-delivery cycle that the firm desires to provide its customers. One of the key considerations when developing a supply chain strategy is the desired delivery time for customers. Unless a premium mode of transportation is used, short lead times requires proximity to customers, which requires decentralization.

The human resource strategy refers to managerial and technical labor considerations. If there is limited availability of either managerial or technical labor capabilities, most firms will centralize those skills to take advantage of the synergies in the expertise. The disadvantage of a centralized expertise strategy is that the firm's decisions may not reflect the nuances of other geographic regions.

The risk management strategy refers to the need to have duplicate supply chain facilities. As a result of natural disasters—including hurricanes, floods, earthquakes—and changes in political environment, firms have begun to consider risk management when determining their supply chain strategy. While the firm can enhance economies of scale through centralization, centralization will also increase risk because there is no duplication of facilities.

Finally, the centers of excellence strategy refers to the need to create centers of excellence for procurement, production, and logistics. A center of excellence is an organization within the firm that maintains process, technical, and analytical expertise in solving specialized problems. The concept of a center of excellence is particularly appropriate for firms with multiple divisions. A centralized center of excellence brings together the top experts in particular types of problems and facilitates the exchange of specialty information.

Firms must select the best combination of strategic decisions from these 8 options. While the centralized strategy provides many advantages in terms of scale, expertise, reduced complexity, and a more standardized customer perspective, there are some situations where customization, agility, and flexibility are desired. In such a case, a decentralized or localized strategy may be more appropriate.

Summary

The primary drivers of logistics network design are requirements resulting from integrated procurement, manufacturing, and customer relationship management strategies. Within the framework of these interlocking strategies, integrated logistics requirements are satisfied by achieving total cost and service trade-offs. These capabilities play out across a network of enterprise facilities. Important to the performance of logistics requirements are warehouses. Warehouses are justified in logistical system design as a result of their contribution to cost reduction, service improvement, or a combination of both.

Transportation and inventory economics are critical network design considerations. In the least-total-cost equation, transportation reflects the spatial aspects of logistics. The ability to consolidate transportation is a primary justification for including warehouses in a network design. Inventory introduces the temporal dimension of logistics. Average inventory increases as the number of warehouses in a system increase in a stable demand situation. Total cost integration provides a framework for simultaneous integration of logistics, manufacturing, and procurement costs. Thus, total cost analysis provides the methodology for logistical network integration.

Accurate total cost analysis is not without practical problems. Foremost is the fact that a great many important costs are not specifically measured or reported by standard accounting systems. A second problem involved in total cost analysis is the need to consider a wide variety of network design alternatives. To develop complete analysis of a planning situation, alternative shipment sizes, modes of shipment, and range of available warehouse locations must be considered.

These problems can be overcome if care is taken in network analysis. The cost format recommended for total cost analysis is to group all functional costs associated with inventory and transportation. The significant contribution of total cost integration is that it provides a simultaneous analysis of time- and space-impacted costs involved in logistical network design.

The formulation of a logistical strategy requires that total cost analysis be evaluated in terms of customer service performance. Logistical service is measured in terms of availability, capability, and quality of performance. The ultimate realization of each service attribute is directly related to logistical network design. To realize the highest level of logistical operational support within overall enterprise integration, in theory each customer should be provided service to the point where marginal cost equates to marginal revenue. Such marginal equalization is not practical to achieve; however, the relationship serves as a normative planning goal.

The formulation of a service policy starts from the identification and analysis of the least-total-cost-system design. Given a managerially specified inventory availability target, service capability associated with the least-cost design can be quantified. This initial service level is referred to as the threshold service level. To evaluate potential modifications to the least-cost design, sensitivity analysis is used. Service levels may be improved by modifying (1) variation in the number of facilities, (2) change in one or more aspects of the performance cycle, and/or (3) change in safety stock.

This chapter also provides a comprehensive review of the logistics planning process, decisions, and techniques. It is designed to guide the logistics manager through the overall process of situation analysis, alternative identification, data collection, quantitative evaluation, and development of viable recommendations.

The methodology, which is generic enough for most logistics problem solving, includes three phases: problem definition and planning, data collection and analysis, and recommendations and implementation. The problem definition and planning phase is concerned with the feasibility assessment and project planning. Feasibility assessment includes situation analysis, supporting logic development, and cost/benefit estimation. Project planning requires statements of objectives, constraints, measurement standard, analysis technique specification, and project work plan development.

The data collection and analysis phase develops assumptions, collects data, and completes the quantitative and qualitative analyses. Assumptions development and data collection include tasks to define the analysis approach, formalize assumptions, identify data sources, and collect and validate data. The analysis step involves definition of analysis questions, completion of validation and baseline analyses, and completion of alternative and sensitivity analyses.

The recommendations and implementation phase develops the final plan. The recommendation development step includes identification and evaluation of the best alternatives. The implementation step defines a recommended course of action, schedules development, defines acceptance criteria, and schedules final implementation.

The final chapter section focuses on the drivers of supply chain design. While traditional supply chain design decisions primarily considered demand, transportation, raw material, and production cost, there are many more considerations today. These include the trade-offs related to the centralization and decentralization strategies for purchasing, manufacturing, distribution and channels, sustainability, and technology.

Study Questions

1. What is the basic objective in a logistics and supply chain design and analysis study? Is it normally a one-time activity?
2. Why is it important to develop supporting logic to guide the logistics and supply chain planning process?
3. Why is a cost/benefit evaluation important for logistics and supply chain design efforts?
4. What is meant by the threshold service level of a least-cost system?
5. Why does customer service not increase proportionately to increases in total cost when a logistical system is being designed?
6. Discuss the differences between improving customer service through faster and more consistent transportation, higher inventory levels, and/or expanded number of warehouses.

Challenge Questions

1. Suppose that you are responsible for integrating the logistics systems of two national food manufacturers as a result of a merger. Each firm serves the entire country from seven distribution centers and delivers to a common customer base using predominantly less-than-truckload transportation. Some of the distribution centers are in the same region while others are not. Identify and rationalize the opportunities for improved performance following the merger.

2. Western Michigan is home to three office furniture manufacturing firms. When they realized that they were sourcing from many of the same suppliers, they thought that there might be an opportunity for a joint venture to consolidate inbound movement of raw materials. Describe the trade-offs that might be associated with such an initiative across competitors. Discuss the benefits and risks of such a strategy.

3. Describe and rationalize the distribution network that would result for products with the following characteristics:

   a. Electronic products with high value that are relatively small and light;

   b. Canned food products with low value and relatively high weight;

   c. Medical products for which the hospitals and clinics expect the supplier to provide four hour delivery service; and

   d. Aircraft spare parts that are high value, relatively small, and critical to the plane's ability to fly.

4. Describe and rationalize the impact of increasing fuel prices on logistics network design.

5. As firms increase product variation due to differential packaging or labeling, product line complexity increases. Discuss and rationalize the trade-offs between increased product complexity, process postponement, and supply chain logistics and supply chain network design.

PART 5

Supply Chain Logistics Administration

This final part deals with the second primary responsibility of a firm's logistical management—administration. Chapter 12 develops principles of administration that are essential for realizing integrated operations. Supply chain relationships are discussed and illustrated as a means to facilitate cooperation among customers, material suppliers, service suppliers, and the organization orchestrating the supply chain arrangement. Attention is also directed to cross-organizational change management and concepts of human resource organization. The dispersion of logistical operations across vast geographical areas serves to place special attention on developing effective management and control processes. Chapter 13 shifts focus to performance assessment and the development of cost measurement to support activity-based management. Particular attention is directed to the development of logistics and supply chain performance metrics. Chapter 14 concludes the text with a discussion of supply chain trends, including end-to-end supply chain management, talent, complexity and risk, security, regulatory, and cost management.

CHAPTER 12

Relationship Management

Chapter Outline

Among topics in logistics, few hold more leadership interest than development and management of organizational relationships. For most of business history, emphasis has been devoted to developing and implementing an appropriate internal structure to effectively and efficiently perform the essential work of logistics. In more recent times, increased attention has focused on logistics organizational integration with other functions, especially customer relationship management, manufacturing, and procurement. However, the information explosion, growing global engagements, and the focus on inter organizational supply chain integration are forcing senior leadership to rethink nearly every aspect of traditional organizational logic and to extend their thinking concerning collaborative relationships with suppliers and customers. The essence of supply chain management is the ability to orchestrate collaborative relationships cross-functionally within their enterprises and externally with supply chain partners. The presentation of this chapter begins with attention to internal organizational practices. The dominant topic of discussion through the balance of the chapter is the growing practice of collaboration.[1]

[1]This chapter draws upon over a decade of research conducted at Michigan State University and published by the Council of Supply Chain Management Professionals. These publications include: Donald J. Bowersox et al., *Leading Edge Logistics: Competitive Positioning for the 1990s* (Oak Brook, IL: Council of Logistics Management, 1989); Donald J. Bowersox et al., *Logistical Excellence: It's Not Business as Usual* (Burlington, MA: Digital Press, 1992); The Global Logistics Research Team at Michigan State University, *World Class Logistics: The Challenge of Managing Continuous Change* (Oak Brook, IL: Council of Logistics Management, 1995); and Donald J. Bowersox, David J. Closs, and Theodore P. Stank, *21st Century Logistics: Making Supply Chain Integration a Reality* (Oak Brook, IL: Council of Logistics Management, 1999).

Development and Management of Internal Logistics Relationships

Prior to the 1950s, functions now accepted as logistics were generally viewed as facilitating or support work. Organization responsibility for logistics was typically dispersed throughout the firm. Figure 12.1 is a hypothetical organization chart that depicts the typical fragmentation of logistical activities. Such fragmented responsibility often meant that aspects of logistical work were performed without coordination, often resulting in duplication and waste. Logistical information was typically fragmented, distorted or delayed, and lines of authority and responsibility for overall logistics was diffused throughout the organization. Managers, recognizing the need for total cost control, began to reorganize and combine logistics functions into a single managerial group. Structuring logistics as an integrated organization first appeared in the late 1950s.

Functional Aggregation

The motivation driving functional aggregation was a growing belief that grouping logistics functions into a single organization would increase the likelihood of integration and facilitate improved understanding of how decisions and procedures in one operational

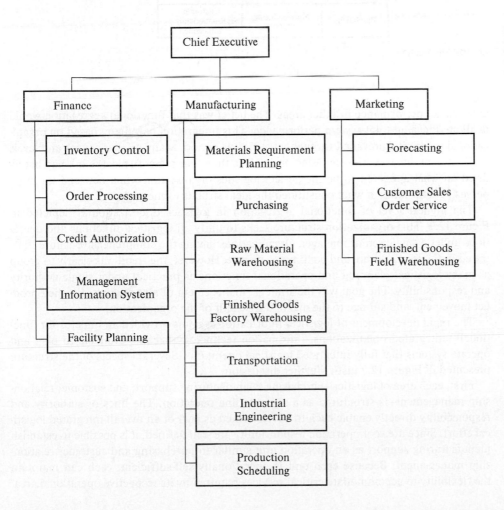

FIGURE 12.1
Traditional Organization of Logistically Related Functions

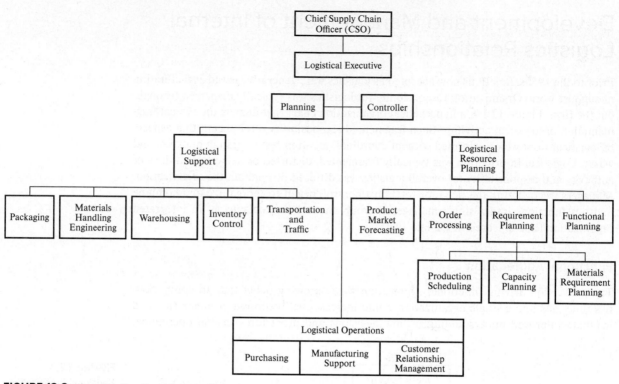

FIGURE 12.2   Logistics Functional Aggregation

area impact performance in other areas. The belief was that functional aggregation would facilitate focus on total system performance. This integration paradigm, based on organizational proximity, prevailed throughout a 35-year period. Many different types and levels of functional integration were tested during this time. For many firms, the ink had barely dried on what appeared to be the perfect logistics organization when new and far more pervasive rethinking of what constituted the ideal structure emerged.

The highest level of functional aggregation in logistics organization is depicted in Figure 12.2. This organization structure seeks to unify all logistical functions and operations under a single senior manager. Organizations having the comprehensive nature illustrated in Figure 12.2 were and continue to be rare. However, the trend was clearly to group as many logistical planning and operational functions as practical under single authority and responsibility. The goal was the strategic management of all materials, finished product movement, and storage to the maximum benefit of the organization.

The rapid development of logistical information systems provided an impetus for functionally integrated organizations. Information technology became available to plan and operate systems that fully integrated logistical operations. Several aspects of the structure presented in Figure 12.2 justify further discussion.

First, each area of logistics—purchasing, manufacturing support, and customer relationship management—is structured as a separate line operation. The lines of authority and responsibility directly enable each to be performed as part of an overall integrated logistical effort. Since areas of operation responsibility are well defined, it is possible to establish manufacturing support as an operation unit similar to purchasing and customer relationship management. Because each unit is operationally self-sufficient, each can maintain the flexibility to accommodate critical services required by its respective operational area.

In addition, since overall logistical activities can be planned and coordinated on an integrated basis, operational synergies between areas can be exploited.

Second, five capabilities grouped under logistical support are positioned as operational services. This shared service orientation is the mechanism to integrate logistical operations. The group manages day-to-day logistics work, which is structured with matrix accountability for direct liaison between logistical operating areas.

Third, logistical resource planning embraces the full potential of management information to plan and coordinate operations. Order processing triggers the logistical system into operation and generates the integrated database required for control. Logistical resource planning facilitates integration. Logistical resource plans are based on product/market forecasting, order processing, and inventory status to determine overall requirements for any planning period. On the basis of identified requirements, the planning unit operationalizes manufacturing by coordinating production scheduling, capacity planning, and materials requirement planning.

Finally, overall planning and controllership exist at the highest level of the organization. These initiatives serve to facilitate integration. The planning group is concerned with long-range strategy and is responsible for logistical system quality improvement and reengineering. The logistical controller is concerned with measurement of cost and customer service performance and provision of information for managerial oversight. The development of procedures for logistical control is one of the most critical areas of integrated logistical administration. The need for accurate measurement is a direct result of increased emphasis placed on continuous improvement in customer accommodation. The measurement task is extremely important because of the large operating and capital dollar expenditures involved in logistics.

The functionally integrated logistical organization offers a single logic to guide the efficient application of financial and human resources from materials sourcing to final product customer delivery. It therefore positions a firm to manage trade-offs among purchasing, manufacturing support, and customer relationship management.

Developing a Process Perspective

During the last half of the 20th century, business activities essential to logistical performance underwent a major transformation. As firms began to examine the role logistical competency was capable of playing in developing customer loyalty, it was clear that organizational structure was not as critical to logistical performance as was cross-functional or process performance. High-performance firms began to stress integrated performance of the eight key processes discussed in Chapter 1.[2] To a significant degree, the focus on process reduced the pressure to aggregate functions into all-encompassing organizational units. The critical question became not how to organize individual functions, but rather how to overcome barriers to integration and best manage the overall logistical process.

Process Integration Barriers

Managers do not attempt to integrate operations in a vacuum or without facing resistance from others within the organization. It is important to recognize barriers that serve to inhibit process integration. Barriers to internal integration find their origins in traditional functional practices related to organization, measurement and reward systems, inventory leverage, infocratic structure, and knowledge hoarding.

[2]See Chapter 1, page 9.

The organization structure of a business can serve to stifle cross-functional processes. Most business organizations seek to align authority and responsibility on the basis of functional work. In essence, both structure and financial budget closely follow work responsibility. The traditional practice has been to group all persons involved in performing specific work into departments such as purchasing, manufacturing, and transportation. Each of these organizations has an operational responsibility, which is reflected in its functional goals. The traditional belief was that functional excellence would automatically equate to superior performance. In integrated process management, it matters little how much is spent to perform a specific function as long as *process* performance goals are achieved at the lowest *total cost* expenditure. Successful integration of processes requires that managers look beyond their functional boundaries to achieve cross-functional integration. This may or may not require organizational change. Regardless, successful process integration requires significant traditional management behavioral modification.

Traditional measurement and reward systems also serve to make cross-functional coordination difficult. Measurement systems typically mirror organization structure. Most reward systems are based on functional achievement. To facilitate internal process integration, new measures, increasingly called **balanced scorecards**, must be developed. Managers must be encouraged to view specific functions as contributing to a process rather than their stand-alone performance. A function may, at times, have to absorb increased costs for the sake of achieving lower total process cost. Unless a measurement and reward system is in place that does not penalize managers who absorb cost, integration will remain more theory than practice.

Inventory can also serve as a barrier to process integration because it is a proven fact that inventory can be leveraged to facilitate functional performance. The desired position is to maintain only minimal inventory necessary to protect against demand and operational uncertainty. Stockpiling both materials and finished inventory facilitates maximum manufacturing economy of scale. Such economy of scale can result in low per unit cost of manufacturing. Forward commitment of inventory to local markets can benefit sales. But, such forward commitment creates the possibility of imbalance and potential inventory overstocks. While such practices create benefits, they may be achieved at a cost. Most typically the costs and risks are not allocated to the function initiating the activity. The integrative challenge is the cost/benefit balance of such leveraging and risks associated with potential inventory obsolescence.

While information technology is a key enabler of process integration, a significant problem results from the fact that structure and availability of information have traditionally been designed to accommodate organization relationships. As a result, information is typically formatted in terms of functional requirements and accountability. The content and flow of available information follows long-standing functional organization lines of command and control. When managers attempt to reorganize to enable cross-functional processes, the structure serves as an invisible force to retain traditional functional information flows. This is one of the driving reasons enterprise resource planning **(ERP)** systems have great general management appeal. The infocratic structure also helps explain why ERP implementations are so difficult.

In most business situations, knowledge is power, so unwillingness to share and a general lack of understanding regarding how to share knowledge are not uncommon. By enforcing functional specialization and by developing a workforce composed of experts, organizations inherently doom process integration. Consider, for example, the case when an experienced employee retires or for some other reason departs a firm. Replacement personnel must be given sufficient time to learn, but if information is restricted, all the time in the world may not help bring the new employee up to speed. A more serious situation occurs when managers fail or are unable to develop procedures and systems for transferring cross-functional knowledge. Much process work is shared between jobs and is not restricted to a specific functional area, so transfer of knowledge and experience is vital.

The Great Divide

Clearly many obstacles make functional integration difficult. To some extent, the five barriers discussed above have contributed to a common situation in business referred to as the **great divide**. The great divide reflects an organizational condition wherein achieved integration is partial but not complete on an end-to-end basis, as illustrated in Figure 12.3. The most common situation is when a firm achieves only partial integration of distribution/marketing on the outbound side of the enterprise and procurement/manufacturing on the inbound side. The paradox is that firms seem to be capable of achieving highly integrated operations with suppliers from whom they purchase materials and components. Firms also join operations in relationship management to service customers. Such initiatives reflect cross-functional integration that, in fact, extends beyond a single business enterprise. Despite these accomplishments, managers report considerable difficulty in linking these two types of external collaboration into an enterprisewide integrative process. In short, managers seem to achieve more successful integration with external business partners than they do with managers and departments within their own firm. Sales and operations planning (**S&OP**), discussed in Chapter 5, represents one mechanism to achieve this needed internal integration.

The phenomenon of the great divide is interesting and challenging. The fact that such operational discontinuity is common among firms in many different industries supports generalization. First, integration appears to be easier with groups external to a firm, such as suppliers and customers, at least in part because the balance of power is typically clear and integrative objectives such as sales and costs can be quantified. Second, senior managers in most organizations do not have a sufficiently clear vision of internal process requirements and related measures to drive integration across the enterprise. Finally, the barriers outlined earlier render end-to-end integration a difficult-to-achieve end state in most organizations.

Discussion of the great divide with logistics managers suggests that one activity supporting the breakdown is the fact that initial inventory deployment is often scheduled without a total system perspective. For example, as inventory flows off highly efficient production lines, the first deployment decision is often based on available distribution center space or deployment to a specific destination to help achieve a consolidated transportation shipment. These or other drivers may benefit specific functional performance, but may be of little benefit or even detrimental to total system performance.

Most observers of current logistics practice feel significant inroads into improved process performance are being realized as a result of modifying and repositioning functional capabilities. The key is to align, focus, and measure functional performance in terms of process contribution. The goal is to close the great divide by achieving a single strategy, facilitated by well-defined processes, relevant measurement, common forecasting and planning, and a supportive reward system.

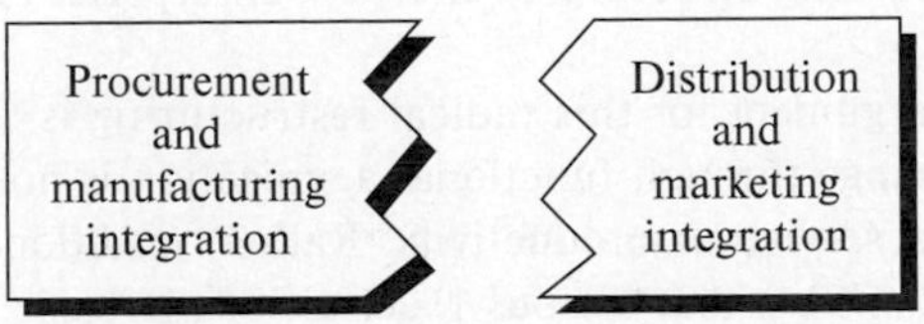

Procurement and manufacturing integration ▷◁ Distribution and marketing integration

FIGURE 12.3

The Great Divide: The Challenge of Managing across Functional Boundaries

FIGURE 12.4

Process Organization

| Chief Executive |

Process owner: Demand planning	Process team: Marketing, sales, logistics, manufacturing, finance, information technology
Process owner: Customer relationship management	Process team: Marketing, sales, logistics, information technology
Process owner: Order fulfillment/service delivery	Process team: Sales, order processing, logistics, customer service, accounting
Process owner: Product/service development launch	Process team: New product development, marketing, procurement, manufacturing, logistics
Process owner: Manufacturing customization	Process team: Procurement, manufacturing, logistics
Process owner: Supplier relationship collaboration	Process team: Procurement, manufacturing, information technology
Process owner: Life cycle support	Process team: Procurement, logistics, customer service, finance
Process owner: Reverse logistics	Process team: Logistics, customer service

Process Structure

Figure 12.4 illustrates how an organization might be structured around the eight supply chain processes discussed in Chapter 1. Each key process is led by a process owner who manages a team of members drawn from the critical functional areas that impact process performance.

The concept of process organization is envisioned as the result of three factors: (1) the development of a highly involved work environment with self-directed work teams as a vehicle to empower employees to generate maximum performance; (2) improved productivity that results from managing processes rather than functions, a notion that has always rested at the core of integrated logistics; and (3) the rapid sharing of accurate information that allows all facets of the organization to be integrated. Information technology is viewed as the load-bearing structure of the new enterprise, replacing organizational hierarchy.

The essence of the argument for this radical restructuring is that the traditional concept of organization change through functional aggregation is not sufficient to stimulate major breakthroughs in service or productivity. Rather, traditional organization change shifts or realigns functions without serious redesign of the basic work process. Because such restructuring typically assumes that functional organizations will continue to perform basic work, little or no difference in actual practice results. In essence, companies are refocusing old business practices rather than designing new, more efficient processes.

The challenges of managing these processes are threefold. First, all effort must be focused on value added to the customer. An activity exists and is justified only to the extent it contributes customer value. Therefore, a commitment must be motivated by a belief that customers desire a specific activity to be performed. Second, integrating logistics as part of a process requires that all skills necessary to complete the work be available regardless of their functional organization. Organizational grouping on the basis of selected function can artificially separate natural work flows and create bottlenecks. When horizontal structures are put in place, critical skills need to be positioned and made accessible to assure that required work is accomplished. Finally, work performed in a process context should stimulate synergism. With systems integration, the design of work as a process means that overall organizational trade-offs are structured to achieve maximum performance for minimum input investment.

The radical changes proposed by a shift from a functional to a process orientation have mixed messages for managers involved in logistics. On the positive side, general adoption of a process orientation builds upon the basic principles of systems integration. At the core of integrated logistics is a commitment to functional excellence that contributes to process performance. A general shift to managing logistics as a process means that it will be positioned as a central contributor to all initiatives that focus on new product development and customer order generation, fulfillment, and delivery. The overall trend of process integration expands the operational potential and impact of logistics.

Development and Management of Supply Chain Relationships

A supply chain perspective shifts the relevant business model from a loosely linked group of independent businesses to a multi-enterprise coordinated effort focused on supply chain efficiency improvement and increased competitiveness. While not all supply chain collaborative arrangements involve logistics, most do. In such arrangements, attention shifts from firm-based logistical management to the coordination of supply chain performance. Two beliefs facilitate this drive for efficiency and competitiveness.

First, the fundamental belief is that cooperative behavior will reduce risk and greatly improve efficiency of the overall logistical performance. To achieve a high degree of cooperation it is necessary for supply chain participants to share strategic information. Such information sharing must not be limited to transaction data. Equally or more important is a willingness to share information concerning future plans so participating firms can jointly develop the best way to satisfy customer requirements. Information sharing is essential to positioning and coordinating participating firms to jointly do the right things faster and more efficiently.

The second belief is the opportunity to eliminate waste and duplicate effort. As a result of collaboration, substantial inventory deployed in a traditional channel can be eliminated. Supply chain collaboration can also eliminate or reduce risk associated with inventory speculation. The notion of supply chain rationalization is not that inventory is bad and should be totally eliminated; rather, inventory deployment should be driven by economic and service necessities and not traditional anticipatory practices.

Firms that have increased supply chain competitiveness exhibit several similarities. First, their collaborative practices are technology driven. Second, their business solutions achieve competitive superiority. Finally, most initiatives combine the experience and talents of key supply chain participants blended with a combination of third-party or integrated service providers. At the heart of these firms is a solid commitment to creating and maintaining a unique supply chain culture. Such cultures are forged on a fundamental understanding of risk, power, and leadership.

Types of Supply Chain Relationships and Dependency

There are numerous types and forms of interorganizational relationships that tend to be characterized as examples of supply chain integration and collaboration.[3] Figure 12.5 presents a classification framework for these relationships.

As discussed earlier, the driving force underlying the emergence of supply chain relationships is the recognition of mutual dependence. When a firm acknowledges dependency with its suppliers and/or its customers, the stage is set for cross-organizational collaboration. The degree to which dependence is mutually recognized and acknowledged by all parties in the relationship defines the nature of the resulting relationship.

Figure 12.5 presents five basic forms of relationships among supply chain participants. The most elementary of these are contracting and outsourcing. In these relationships, acknowledged dependency is limited. Contracting with a supplier or customer introduces a time dimension to traditional buying and selling by framing price, service, and performance expectations over a specified period. A manufacturer may contract with a materials or parts supplier to purchase a particular item or items for a specified period at a specified price. In turn, the supplier agrees to deliver the specified item(s) according to negotiated terms and delivery requirements. This form of collaboration is often called adversarial because the relationship is typically based on negotiation. As a result of negotiated settlement the terms of performance and associated payments are clearly specified. Failure of either party to perform will lead to sanctions, probable re-negotiation or possible termination. In outsourcing, the focus shifts from buying or selling a product or material to performing a specific service

[3]For a comprehensive review of supply chain relationship literature see Patricia J. Daugherty, "Review of Logistics and Supply Chain Relationships and Suggested Research Agenda, *"International Journal of Physical Distribution and Logistics Management* 41, no. 1 (2011), pp. 16–31.

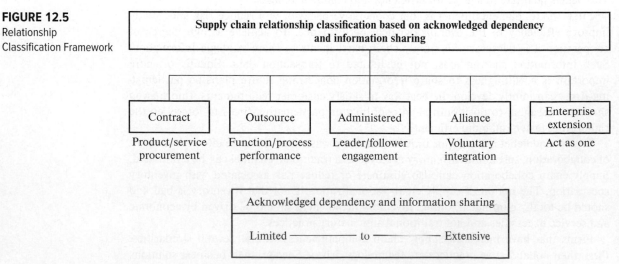

or process. Typical outsourced activities range from manufacturing to logistics activities such as transportation or warehousing.

It is critical to understand, however, that contracting and outsourcing do not necessarily imply that comprehensive supply chain integration and collaboration take place. The relationships involve a degree of information sharing, primarily operational information, but there is limited joint planning among the firms involved, and there are generally specific periods for rebidding or terminating the relationships. Although firms that outsource functions, or even processes, must maintain cordial relationships with the service suppliers, the service being provided is precisely specified in terms of performance and cost, and the relationship among the firms is clearly based in traditional command-and-control principles, with the buyer as the leader.

In administered relationships, a dominant firm assumes leadership responsibility and seeks collaboration with trading partners and/or service suppliers. In such relationships there is frequently sharing of operational information and to a limited degree, strategic information. Additionally, there is limited joint planning, to the extent that independent firms have an understanding that they will be better off if they collaborate and follow the leader. A distinguishing feature of such relationships is the expectation that the collaboration will be continuous. There is typically no specific termination or rebid time frame. However, although the leader must consider all participants' welfare, the relationship is basically administered by command and control based on the leader's power.

Although different terminology may be used, advanced collaborative relationships among supply chain participants can be described as alliances or, in the extreme, as enterprise extension. The distinguishing feature of these relationships is that they are governed by the participants' long-term desire and willingness to voluntarily work together in an intellectual and operational manner. They voluntarily agree to integration of human, financial, operational, or technical resources to create greater efficiency and greater customer impact. Ultimately, through collaboration, participating firms create joint policies and integrate operations. The relationship includes extensive joint planning and is expected to be continuous for at least the intermediate term and potentially the very long term. Enterprise extension represents the extreme of interdependence and information sharing. In such instances, two or more firms willingly integrate to the extent that they essentially can be viewed from a performance perspective as a single entity. Alliances and similar arrangements are rapidly increasing in logistics and supply chain management. Some examples of such success include the highly publicized Walmart* arrangements with Procter & Gamble, Dell's arrangements with its suppliers, and the close relationships Toyota and Honda have with their suppliers. These relationships involve frequent interaction at all levels of the participating firms.

Power vs. Leadership

Dependency is a primary driver of supply chain solidarity. To the degree that participating enterprises acknowledge mutual dependency, the potential exists to develop collaborative relationships. Dependency drives a willingness to plan functional integration, share key information, and participate in joint operations. The concepts of **power** and **leadership** are essential to understanding acknowledged dependency and how it makes supply chain integration work.

Power

In a practical sense, the prerogative and even the obligation to spearhead collaboration rest with the supply chain participant who enjoys the greatest relative power. In many situations, that participant will also be the firm having the greatest risk. Over the last decade significant power shifts have occurred in business. One of the most significant is the increased power of retailers, which resulted from four somewhat independent developments.

First, the general trend of retail consolidation translated into fewer but more dominant retailers with more extensive market coverage. Second, the proliferation of point-of-sale data, frequent-shopper programs, and credit card use provides retailers with easy access to vital market information. As a result, retailers are positioned to rapidly identify and accommodate consumer trends. Many mass merchants maintain in-store computers and continuous point-of-sale transmission to keep merchandise buyers fully informed of developing market trends. A third factor favoring retailers is the increasing difficulty and high cost manufacturers confront in developing new brands. The fact is that many private-label products owned by retailers have greater market penetration than so-called national brands. For example, the Gap and The Limited almost exclusively distribute private branded merchandise. Finally, as discussed throughout the text, the process of logistical replenishment has shifted toward a response-based posture. The exact timing and sophisticated orchestration of a high-velocity market-paced logistics system are ideally driven from the point of consumer purchase. When consumers purchase products, the final or ultimate value of the supply chain is achieved.

While the above noted forces are a modern reality, not all forces are shifting power forward in the supply chain. Today's scrambled merchandising environments result in products increasingly being cross-channel-distributed to accommodate specific markets that are volatile and rapidly changing. New retail formats, both Internet-based and traditional brick and mortar, are blurring channel arrangements. The result is that manufacturers have a growing range of alternatives for distributing their products.

As a substitute for full reliance on traditional brand power, selected manufacturers have reengineered their operations to become the dominant supplier for selected consumer products or categories. The movement toward category dominance allows manufacturers to offer greater value to their prospective supply chain partners. In addition to superior brands at competitive prices, dominant category position can involve several key operational capabilities that increase a firm's attractiveness as a supply chain participant.

Because both manufacturers and distributors have repositioned traditional operations, the potential exists to leverage collaboration. As a general rule, powerful firms tend to link together in the development of supply chain arrangements. For the arrangement to be successful, the dominant parties within a cooperative arrangement need to agree to a leadership model.

Leadership

Just as individual organizations need leaders, so do supply chains. At the present stage of supply chain maturity, no definitive generalization can be made concerning how firms gain leadership responsibility. In many situations, specific firms are thrust into a leadership position purely as a result of their size, economic power, customer patronage, or comprehensive product portfolio. In other arrangements, for less obvious reasons, there is a clear presence of leadership on the part of one enterprise, which is acknowledged in the form of mutual dependency and respect on the part of other participating supply chain members. In other situations leadership appears to gravitate to the firm that initiates the relationship. Regardless of who leads, it has been shown that greater relationship commitment exists in supply chain relationships when leaders exercise power in the form of rewards and expertise. Firms that attempt to lead through coercive practices find that partners are much less committed to the relationship and more likely to seek alternative arrangements.

Developing Trust in Relationships

It is clear that no real collaboration can exist in supply chain relationships without meaningful *trust*. While a powerful firm may be able to influence the behavior of a less powerful organization, the change in behavior may be temporary and certainly entered into unwillingly. In fact, while research shows that issues such as technology compatibility, information exchange, and appropriate measurement systems are all key issues to be resolved in collaborative alliances, the human behavior issues related to culture and trust are much more difficult issues to solve. To do so, the complexities of different forms of trust must be understood.

Reliability and Character-Based Trust

It is clear that trust has more than one dimension. While several types of trust exist, a meaningful way to understand trust in supply chain collaboration is to distinguish between reliability-based trust and character-based trust.

Reliability-based trust is grounded in an organization's perception of a potential partner's actual behavior and operating performance. Essentially, it involves a perception that the partner is willing to perform and is capable of performing as promised. If supply chain participants cannot rely on partner performance as promised, all efforts to develop collaborative relationships fail. Simply put, a firm that is perceived as incapable of delivering as promised will also be perceived as being unreliable and therefore unworthy of trust in a relationship.

Character-based trust is based in an organization's culture, leadership, and philosophy. Essentially, it stems from perceptions that supply chain partners are interested in each other's welfare and will not act without considering the action's impact on the other. When this aspect of trust is developed, participants do not feel vulnerable to the actions of one another. Trusting partners believe that each will protect the other's interest. For example, a manufacturer who shares its plans for new product introductions or promotion with a retailer trusts that the retailer will not share that information with a competitive supplier. Likewise, sharing of production schedule information with a supplier of component parts will occur only when a manufacturer has trust that the information will be used appropriately.

It is clear that reliability-based trust is necessary to the formation of collaborative relationships in supply chains, but it is not a sufficient condition. For example, a partner who frequently threatens to punish and consistently follows through with that punishment can be said to have reliability. It is not likely, however, to be trusted in character.

Trust clearly develops over time and repeated interactions among organizations. In particular, character-based trust evolves when partners perceive that each acts fairly and equitably with the others. Notions of character-based trust are especially relevant when one supply chain partner is clearly more powerful than the others.

Building Trust in Relationships

To build trust first requires that a firm demonstrate reliability in its operations, consistently performing as promised and meeting expectations. As noted above, however, reliability is only one aspect of building trust.

The second key requirement for building trust is full and frank sharing of all information necessary for the effective functioning of the relationship. In fact, information sharing and communication have been stressed throughout this text as the foundation for effective collaboration. Companies that hoard information or fail to disclose vital facts are not likely to be trusted.

Related to information sharing is explanation. Sometimes a company, because of competitive pressures, may be required to undertake actions that its supply chain partners may perceive as threatening. For example, a manufacturer opening new distribution channels might threaten existing dealers. A situation arose when John Deere introduced a second line of lawn tractors and recruited Home Depot and other independent retailers, bypassing its traditional dealer network. In such situations, trust may be maintained through thorough explanation of the rationale and business case that drove such a decision.

In many ways the entire subject of supply chain management is also a discussion of relationship management. The text has focused on issues related to logistical processes in the supply chain and managing these processes across company boundaries. Unique operating relationships among supply chain participants differ significantly in their intensity and extent of real collaboration. Power, leadership, conflict, cooperation, risk, and reward are all critical issues in relationship management. Resolution of these issues, however, ultimately depends upon the development of trust among supply chain participants.

Managing Supply Chain Relationships over Time

The management of relationships represents a responsibility that is often difficult for logistics managers.[4] Unlike internal management situations, individuals who represent their firms in a supply chain collaboration often do not work for the organization that is leading the initiative. Thus, the typical supervisor-employee authority-based relationship does not exist. The counterbalance is that all parties involved in a collaborative situation share a common vision that the arrangement is beneficial to their joint success. Therefore, the traditional command and control authority-based relationships must be replaced by a leadership model that builds on consensus and collaboration. This section discusses some of the challenges and goals involved in initiating, implementing, maintaining, and terminating supply chain relationships.

Initiating

Alliances are typically initiated by firms who are the customer in the relationship. One potential explanation for this pattern is the exercise of buying power. In a buyer–seller relationship, the seller will often implement reasonable changes at the request of its customer. Also, when a seller's personnel initially approach a potential customer about forming an alliance, the suggestion does not carry the same weight and impact as when the suggestion is generated within the buying firm's organization.

Another critical consideration during the development of a collaborative relationship is the need for the initiating firm to perform an in-depth assessment of its internal practices, policies, and culture. The initiating firm should evaluate its ability to make any necessary internal changes to implement and support a successful relationship. For example, in manufacturer/material supplier alliances, manufacturers have to examine their ability to redefine the importance of purchase price. Buyers need a method to incorporate the intangible benefits of an alliance in competitive evaluations. The key for the buyer is the evaluation of total cost of ownership, not strictly purchase price.

Another internal assessment includes the ability to truly empower the key alliance contacts to manage the relationship. For example, manufacturers need to honestly assess the level of operational and strategic integration they could foster with suppliers. Integration that generated the type of competitive advantage envisioned at the alliance's initial design, such as increased productivity of rapid response to customer orders, could be achieved only

---

[4]This section is adapted from Judith M. Schmitz, Robert Frankel, and David J. Frayer, "ECR Alliances: A Best Practice Model," Joint Industry Project on Efficient Consumer Response, Grocery Manufacturers Association, Washington, DC, 1995.

through extensive information sharing. The questions to be addressed concern the level of systems capability, data collection, analysis, performance measurement, and training that is necessary to enable the information to be shared in a timely and accurate manner.

Integration capability also needs to be evaluated if the alliance involves a number of partner plants, warehouses, and/or stores that operate under different conditions, capabilities, or competitive requirements. This is especially important for firms that operate multiple warehouses and/or store locations. A key concern in this situation is the ability for internal units to utilize common operating practices and compatible information systems.

Implementing

The key to a successful implementation is choosing a partner wisely. The partners should have compatible cultures, a common strategic vision, and supportive operating philosophies. It is not necessary that organization cultures be identical. Rather, the strategic intentions and philosophies must be compatible to ensure that core competencies and strengths are complementary.

For example, manufacturers initiated alliances with service suppliers in part to achieve improved warehousing operations, transportation reliability, and/or increased consolidation programs that support their particular strategic competitive advantage in the marketplace. Although the service suppliers are leaders, manufacturers may have a more sophisticated conceptualization and operationalization of quality, performance measurement standards, and expertise. The attraction between the partners is based, to a considerable degree, on the service suppliers' ability and willingness to provide creative, innovative operational and information-based solutions to the manufacturer's problems and on the service suppliers' desire to internalize the quality and performance measurement expertise that are the hallmark of the manufacturer. In this sense, the alliance partners' operating philosophies support and complement each other, in particular by enhancing their common strategic vision of improving systemwide logistics processes.

The alliances should start on a small scale to foster easily achievable successes or early wins. It is important that such early wins be acknowledged to motivate key contacts and build confidence concerning alliance performance. For example, in the manufacturer/material supplier alliances, starting small meant that investments were not initially made in information technology. Manual communication systems were sufficient and provided the opportunity for key contacts. A critical issue is to implement the alliance in its simplest form and then fine-tune the arrangement with technological sophistication when improvements will add substantial value.

Maintaining

Long-term continuity is dependent on three key activities: (1) mutual strategic and operational goals, (2) two-way performance measurements, and (3) formal and informal feedback mechanisms.

Strategic and operational goals must be mutually determined when the alliance is implemented. It is perhaps less well understood that these goals must be tracked, reviewed, and updated frequently to gain improvements over the long term. For example, if a manufacturer develops a new product, a mutual goal must be set with customers concerning that product's position, especially its market launch. This goal must include consideration of the merchandiser's critical role in new product introduction and acceptance.

Goals should be translated into specific performance measures that can be continually tracked. The performance measurements used and the measurement frequency should be jointly determined. Also, the measures should be two-way. Oftentimes, performance measures between manufacturers and material suppliers focus specifically on the suppliers' performance attributes, such as on-time delivery and quality. One of the alliances studied developed a joint measure of success—total systems inventory. The manufacturer acknowledged that it was important for both partners to reduce inventory, not just the manufacturer. The measure of total systems inventory includes consideration of both partners to ensure that reductions are real and benefit both parties.

Feedback on performance can be provided through formal and informal methods. Annual reviews are formal assessments of alliance performance. These reviews typically involve top managers and focus primarily on examining and updating strategic goals. Quarterly or monthly reviews are not as formal as annual assessments and usually do not include top managers. They focus on tracking and reviewing strategic goals and operational performance. When used, the reviews enable changes in operating practice to be made to achieve strategic goals and create an avenue for continuous improvement projects to be identified.

Weekly/daily reviews may also occur on an informal basis. These reviews are managed by the key contacts and are intended to solve specific problems and identify potential opportunities for improvement. They are critical to resolving or avoiding conflicts and allow key contacts to develop close working relationships. These informal relationships ultimately result in ever-increasing collaborative behavior.

The development and implementation of a collaborative effort between Lowe's and Whirlpool illustrates the progression that typically occurs in supply chain collaboration.[5] For many years the relationship between the two firms was characterized by a lack of communication and collaboration. For example, in one instance when Whirlpool introduced a new product line, both Lowe's and Whirlpool wanted to get the line into the store as quickly as possible. When the launch date was set, the team leader from Lowe's asked, "When did you know you were going to bring this line to the market?" The answer was, "We've known for months." Because Whirlpool had not shared this information much earlier, the two companies had to negotiate how the costs of disposing the existing product line would be divided between the companies. This led the two firms to embark on a more collaborative relationship.

The relationship initially focused on collaborative demand planning, concentrating on forecasting. The efforts were primarily dependent upon statistical forecasts, and there was limited discussion of each company's marketing plans. Once this process was in place, however, the companies moved more toward supply planning. Both companies worked to develop an understanding of each other's required target inventory levels. At this point, the collaboration was focused on demand and supply planning at the item level, with forecasts reviewed between forecast teams. But high-level collaboration was limited, and sales plans seldom accounted for future advertising or promotion by either firm.

Next, Lowe's and Whirlpool made the decision to merge their collaboration effort with Whirlpool's internal S&OP process. They also established collaboration linkages at the sales and marketing mid-management levels, which resulted in a single set of aligned forecasts and sales plans. The companies began to collaborate on promotions, product launches, and special-event planning. Despite the improvements, several challenges remained. The planning horizon was relatively short and senior management was not routinely involved. New linkages were created to extend their planning horizon to a year. Monthly leadership reviews with senior management were established, allowing both companies to achieve a process built around joint business objectives. The result of this integrated business planning has helped Lowe's and Whirlpool to realize improvements in several key metrics. Unit sales growth increased 12 percent while overall inventory costs fell 5 percent. On-time shipments improved substantially. Lowe's and Whirlpool both believe that a primary driver of these results was the creation and evolution of their collaborative relationship.

[5]This discussion is adapted from: Larry Smith, Joseph C. Andraski, and Stanley E. Fawcett. "Integrated Business Planning: A Roadmap to Linking S&OP and CPFR," *Journal of Business Forecasting* 29, no. 4 (2011), p. 4.

Terminating

As an important part of relationship management, firms must anticipate and plan that at some future point in time the alliance that appears so promising when being organized will no longer meet expectations. While some arrangements may encounter a natural death as a result of losing momentum, others may persevere to the point where they no longer meet the requirements of one or more participants or they no longer embody leading-edge practices. Like most managerial concerns, supply chain alliances represent dynamic situations that must be constantly reevaluated, repositioned, and at times terminated.

For example, a long-standing relationship between Kraft Foods and Starbucks reached a critical juncture in 2010. Beginning in 1998, the companies had an agreement in which Kraft distributed Starbucks bagged coffee and its Seattle's Best brand in supermarkets across the United States. Annual sales grew from $50 million to $500 million over the 12-year period. Starbucks' entry into the single-cup coffee market, however, represented a move that threatened Kraft's business.

Starbucks introduced Via, an instant coffee that met with considerable market success. Starbucks also desired to enter into partnership with Green Mountain Coffee Roasters, a firm in the single-cup coffee market which also sells the Keurig brand of single-cup brewing equipment. Kraft distributes Tassimo brewing machines, the major competitor to Keurig. Starbucks also announced plans to purchase other companies to expand its supermarket distribution. Starbucks desired to end its distribution relationship with Kraft to pursue these other opportunities. Kraft released a press announcement which said that the original distribution agreement requires Starbucks to pay fair market value plus a premium in case of termination. Starbucks, on the other hand, released its own press announcement claiming that Kraft's performance as a distributor of its coffee was "unacceptably poor" and that it is legally justified in ending its participation in the agreement.

In considering the issue of relationship termination, Donald Snyder, founder and long-time leader of Snyder Transport, summed it up very nicely when addressing a logistics class at Michigan State University. He told the students that the very best time to discuss the termination process was during the early formation stages. His point was that expectations are very high at the start of a collaboration when those involved feel the proposed relationship represents a sound engagement. At this point most are willing to accept a logical and fair procedure for dissolving the collaboration.

Summary

Logistics is undergoing massive change. New concepts and ideas concerning how the best organizations achieve logistical goals appear daily. The challenge is to sort through the best of time-proven practices and merge them with the most applicable new ideas and concepts.

A careful review of logistics organization development suggests that most advanced firms have evolved through many forms of functional aggregation. The evolution started from a highly fragmented structure in which logistical functions were assigned to a wide variety of different departments. For over five decades firms have been grouping an increasing number of logistical functional responsibilities into integrated organizational units.

The advent of management focusing on critical processes began to usher in what is referred to as integrated organizations. Today, leading-edge firms are beginning to implement process management as a means for overcoming the divide that exists among internal functions. The concept has particular appeal to the management of logistics, which involves substantial challenge in terms of time and geographical scope of operations.

Perhaps the most difficult job of all is managing organizational change. Whether the change is strategic, involving fundamental new processes, operational, or limited to personnel, managers must develop new skills that allow them to implement change without disrupting the focus of the organization.

In addition to managing the internal organization, supply chain executives are intimately involved in managing relationships across organizations. Collaborative relationships provide a mechanism to reduce operating expense, enhance productivity, and meet customer requirements. Successful integration requires cross-organizational programs to facilitate operations, technology, planning, and relationship management. Initiating, implementing, and maintaining relationships with suppliers and customers are highly dependent upon the existence of trust among those firms. While reliability is a critical aspect of trust, ultimate success in relationship management will depend upon evaluation of leadership character as firms make decisions concerning which supply chains they choose to participate in.

Study Questions

1. Discuss the three challenges logistics faces as it manages on a process, rather than a functional, basis. Describe each challenge and give an example of how it may be overcome.

2. How do reward systems serve as barriers to integration?

3. In your own words, describe and illustrate the great divide. Do you believe the great divide phenomenon is as widely experienced as the text indicates? Support your position with an illustration.

4. Distinguish between reliability and character-based trust. Why is character-based trust critical in collaborative relationships?

5. Distinguish among different types of supply chain relationship arrangements. What drives the differences?

6. What are the major considerations in initiating a logistics alliance? In implementation? In maintenance? In termination?

Challenge Questions

1. Using the Lowe's and Whirlpool example in the chapter as a setting, discuss what you think are some of the issues involved for each firm as the relationship progresses from initiation to maturity.

2. The Lowe's and Whirlpool collaboration resulted in several areas of performance improvement. What specific actions do you think could be taken by supply chain managers as a result of the collaboration that led to the performance improvement?

3. What would you suggest to Lowe's and Whirlpool as possible next steps in their collaborative relationship?

4. What could Kraft and Starbucks have done at the beginning of their distribution relationship that might have resulted in a more amicable end to the relationship? Be as specific as possible in your discussion.

CHAPTER 13

Performance Measurement

Chapter Outline

Creating competitive advantage through high-performance logistics requires integrated measurement systems. The old adage, "If you don't measure it, you can't manage it," holds true for logistical activities both internal to an organization and externally with supply chain partners. For this reason, a framework for performance assessment must be established.

Measurement System Objectives

Effective measurement systems must be constructed to accomplish the three objectives of monitoring, controlling, and directing logistical operations.

Monitoring is accomplished by the establishment of appropriate metrics to track system performance for reporting to management. For example, typically metrics are developed and data gathered to report basic service performance related to fill rates and on-time deliveries and for logistics costs such as transportation and warehousing. **Controlling** is accomplished by having appropriate standards of performance relative to the established metrics to indicate when the logistics system requires modification or attention. For example, if fill rates fall below standards, logistics managers must identify the causes and make adjustments to bring the process back into compliance. The third objective, **directing**, is related to employee motivation and reward for performance. For example, some companies encourage warehouse personnel to achieve high levels of productivity. They must be paid

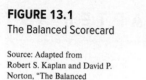

FIGURE 13.1

The Balanced Scorecard

Source: Adapted from Robert S. Kaplan and David P. Norton, "The Balanced Scorecard—Measures That Drive Performance," *Harvard Business Review* 70, no. 1 (1992), p. 72.

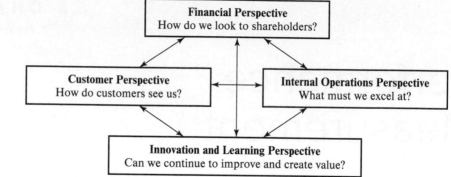

for eight hours of work, on the basis of standard measures of picking or loading. If the tasks are completed in less than eight hours, they may be allowed personal time off.

An overriding objective of superior logistical performance is to improve **shareholder value**. The Balanced Scorecard is a framework for performance measurement developed by Kaplan and Norton.[1] The framework suggests that while improving shareholder value is critical, a comprehensive system for assessing performance must represent a balance between financial and nonfinancial metrics. A balanced scorecard incorporates measures from four different perspectives, as shown in Figure 13.1.

The customer perspective focuses on how customers perceive a company and, therefore, must include customer opinions. In a logistics context, metrics related to this perspective generally include assessment of logistics service, quality, and satisfaction. The internal operations perspective asks what must be done internally and typically incorporates metrics related to process quality (damage rates, errors, etc.) as well as measurement of efficiency and productivity. The innovation and learning perspective is future oriented and focuses on process improvement as well as efforts related to human resources, which are generally considered the driver of improvements in any organization. Benchmarking may also be an aspect of the innovation and learning perspective. Finally, the financial perspective reflects the fact that financial success must be achieved in every organization. Succeeding in the other three perspectives is not adequate if the organization fails to improve profitability and return on investment, thus increasing shareholder value.

It is critical to understand that the balanced scorecard does not offer a specific set of metrics that should be implemented in a company. Specific metrics must be derived from an understanding of the firm's fundamental business strategy. For example, the specific metrics emphasized by a firm that has chosen a "low-cost" strategy may be quite different from an organization that follows a "high-service" strategy. The challenge for logistics executives is to define that strategy and select an appropriate balanced set of metrics that guides them in monitoring, controlling, and directing them toward successful implementation of that strategy.

Operational Assessment

A system for logistics performance assessment first requires a functional perspective. In addition to basic functional performance, improved methods for measurement of customer relationships are receiving increased attention in many organizations. Measurement of integrated supply chain performance poses a major challenge for contemporary management. Benchmarking is a fourth concern in logistics assessment.

[1]Robert S. Kaplan and David P. Norton, "The Balanced Scorecard—Measures That Drive Performance," *Harvard Business Review* 70, no. 1 (1992), pp. 71–79.

Cost Management	Customer Service	Quality	Productivity	Asset Management
Total cost	Fill rate	Damage frequency	Units shipped per employee	Inventory turns
Cost per unit	Stockouts	Order entry accuracy	Units per labor dollar	Inventory levels, number of days of supply
Cost as a percentage of sales	Shipping errors	Picking/shipping accuracy	Orders per sales representative	Obsolete inventory
Inbound freight	On-time delivery	Document/invoicing accuracy	Comparison to historical standard	Return on net assets
Outbound freight	Back orders	Information availability	Goal programs	Return on investment
Administrative	Cycle time	Information accuracy	Productivity index	Inventory classification (ABC)
Warehouse order processing	Delivery consistency	Number of credit claims	Equipment downtime	Economic value added (EVA)
Direct labor	Response time to inquiries	Number of customer returns	Order entry productivity	
Comparison of actual versus budget	Response accuracy		Warehouse labor productivity	
Cost trend analysis	Complete orders		Transportation labor productivity	
Direct product profitability	Customer complaints			
Customer segment profitability	Sales force complaints			
Inventory carrying	Overall reliability			
Cost of returned goods	Overall satisfaction			
Cost of damage				
Cost of service failures				
Cost of back order				

TABLE 13.1   Typical Logistics Performance Metrics

Functional Perspectives

While many different classifications of logistics functional measures exist, research over a period of years suggests five categories: (1) cost, (2) customer service, (3) quality, (4) productivity, and (5) asset management.[2] Table 13.1 provides examples of common metrics related to each of these five areas of concern. Of course, numerous other examples exist as well.

Cost

The most direct reflection of logistics performance is the actual cost incurred to accomplish specific operations. As shown in Table 13.1, cost performance is typically measured in terms of total dollars spent. Early in the text, the work of integrated logistics was identified as incorporating five interrelated areas: order processing, inventory, transportation, warehousing and materials handling, and facility network.[3] Total logistics cost, sometimes referred to as total landed cost, is the sum of costs related to performance and administration of each of these areas of work. Unfortunately, recent research suggests that few organizations have the ability to actually capture the information required to measure total cost.

[2]Donald J. Bowersox et al., *Leading Edge Logistics: Competitive Positioning for the 1990s* (Oak Brook, IL: Council of Logistics Management, 1989); World Class Logistics Research Team at Michigan State University, *World Class Logistics: The Challenge of Managing Continuous Change* (Oak Brook, IL: Council of Logistics Management, 1995); and Donald J. Bowersox, David J. Closs, and Theodore P. Stank, *21st Century Logistics: Making Supply Chain Integration a Reality* (Oak Brook, IL: Council of Logistics Management, 1999).
[3]See Chapter 3, p. 40.

This occurs because different organizations may have different orientations toward which of the areas identified above actually constitute integrated logistics, or because of the lack of readily available data. Nevertheless, at senior management levels of responsibility this total cost should be monitored closely. It is also important to monitor cost data for each of the individual functions so that appropriate diagnosis and control can take place. The functional cost data may be further fine-tuned and measured for individual activities such as order picking and order loading in the warehouse function.

It is also common to monitor and report cost data as a percentage of sales or as a cost per unit of volume. For example, transportation cost is frequently expensed as a percentage of dollar sales volume and as the number of dollars spent per order delivered. Warehouse cost may also be reported as a percentage of sales and cost of individual activities reported such as the picking cost per item or loading cost per order. Such measures, when compared to historical levels or performance standards, provide critical information regarding the potential need to take corrective action. When considering the number of different specific logistics activities, ranging from entering an order to picking an item to unloading a delivery vehicle, and the number of different ways in which volume can be measured, ranging from sales dollars to number of orders to pounds of product, a rather lengthy list of possible cost metrics could be generated. The key is for logistics executives to identify the most appropriate metrics for their organization and consistently apply them over time to control and direct the activities.

Table 13.1 also shows other measures that require measurement of logistics cost, such as direct product profitability, customer profitability, and cost of service failures. In fact, most firms recognize the importance of these measures but currently lack the information necessary to accurately assess these costs. Accurate measurement in these critical dimensions requires a level of sophistication in accounting data that has just recently become available. Activity-based costing is discussed later in this chapter as a means to more accurately assess the cost related directly to customers and products.

Customer Service

In Chapter 4, the elements of basic logistics service were identified as availability, operational performance, and service reliability. An effective basic service platform requires specific metrics for assessing performance in each dimension.

Availability is typically reflected by an organization's fill rate. It is critical to note, however, that fill rate may be measured in a variety of ways:

$$\text{Item fill rate} = \frac{\text{Number of items delivered to customers}}{\text{Number of items ordered by customers}}$$

$$\text{Line fill rate} = \frac{\text{Number of purchase order lines delivered complete to customers}}{\text{Number of purchase order lines ordered by customers}}$$

$$\text{Value fill rate} = \frac{\text{Total dollar value delivered to customers}}{\text{Total dollar value of custmer orders}}$$

$$\text{Order fill rate} = \frac{\text{Number of orders delivered complete}}{\text{Number of customer orders}}$$

Clearly, the order fill rate, also known as orders shipped complete, is the most stringent measure of a firm's performance relative to product availability. In this metric, an order that is missing only one item on one line is considered to be incomplete. It is also common for companies to track specifically the number of stockouts encountered and number of back orders generated during a time period as indicators of availability.

Operational performance deals with time and is typically measured by average order cycle time, consistency of order cycle time, and/or on-time deliveries. **Average order cycle time** is typically computed as the average number of days, or other units of time, elapsed between order receipt and delivery to customers. **Order cycle consistency** is measured over a large number of order cycles and compares actual with planned performance. For example, suppose average order cycle time is five days. If 20 percent were completed in two days and 30 percent in eight days, there is great inconsistency around the average. In situations where delivery dates or times are specified by customers, the most stringent measure of order cycle capability is **on-time delivery**, the percentage of times the customer's delivery requirements are actually met.

Quality

Performance relative to service reliability is generally reflected in an organization's measurement of logistics quality. As Table 13.1 shows, many of the quality metrics are designed to monitor the effectiveness of individual activities, while others are focused on the overall logistics function. Accuracy of work performance in such activities as order entry, warehouse picking, and document preparation is typically tracked by computing the ratio of the total number of times the activity is performed correctly to the total number of times it is performed. For example, picking accuracy of 99.5 percent indicates that 99.5 out of every 100 times, the correct items were picked in the warehouse.

Overall quality performance can also be measured in a variety of ways. Typical measures include damage frequency, which is computed as the ratio of the number of damaged units to the total number of units. While damage frequency can be measured at several points in the logistics process, such as warehouse damage, loading damage, and transportation damage, it frequently is not detected until customers receive shipments or even some point in time after receipt. Therefore, many organizations also monitor the number of customer returns of damaged or defective goods. It is also common to measure customer claims and refunds on adjustments.

Other important indicators of quality performance relate to information. Many organizations specifically measure their ability to provide information by noting those instances when information is not available on request. It is also common to track instances when inaccurate information is discovered. For example, when physical counts of merchandise inventory differ from the inventory status as reported in the database, the information system must be updated to reflect actual operating status. Additionally, the occurrence of information inaccuracy should be recorded for future action.

Productivity

The relationship between output of goods, work completed, and/or services produced and quantities of inputs or resources utilized to produce the output is productivity. If a system has clearly measurable outputs and identifiable, measurable inputs that can be matched to the appropriate outputs, productivity measurement is quite routine.

Generally, as Table 13.1 shows, logistics executives are very concerned with measuring the productivity of labor. While the labor input can be quantified in many ways, the most typical manner is by labor expense, labor hours, or number of individual employees. Thus, typical labor productivity measures in transportation include units shipped or delivered per employee, labor dollar, and labor hour. Warehouse labor productivity may be measured by units received, picked, and/or stored per employee, dollar, or hour. Similar measures can be developed for other activities, such as order entry and order processing. It is also common for managers to set goals for productivity improvement and compare actual performance to goal, or at the very least to prior year performance.

Asset Management

Utilization of capital investments in facilities and equipment as well as working capital invested in inventory is the concern of asset management. Logistics facilities, equipment, and inventory can represent a substantial segment of a firm's assets. For example, in the case of wholesalers, inventory frequently exceeds 80 percent of total capital. Asset management metrics focus on how well logistics managers utilize the capital invested in operations.

Facilities and equipment are frequently measured in terms of capacity utilization, or the percentage of total capacity used. For example, if a warehouse is capable of shipping 10,000 cases per day, but ships only 8,000, capacity utilization is only 80 percent. It is also common to measure equipment utilization in terms of time. Logistics managers are typically concerned with the number or percentage of hours that equipment is not utilized, which is measured as equipment **downtime**. Downtime can be applied to transportation, warehouse, and materials handling equipment. These measures indicate the effective or ineffective utilization of capital asset investment.

Asset management measurement also focuses on inventory. **Inventory turnover rate** is the most common measure of performance. Throughout the text, improved inventory turnover has been stressed as a critical focus of logistical management. It is important to understand how firms specifically measure inventory turnover rate. In fact, three specific metrics exist, each of which is used by different types of firms:

$$\text{Inventory turnover} = \frac{\text{Cost of goods sold during a time period}}{\text{Average inventory valued at cost during the time period}}$$

$$\text{Inventory turnover} = \frac{\text{Sales revenue during a time period}}{\text{Average inventory valued at selling price during time period}}$$

$$\text{Inventory turnover} = \frac{\text{Units sold during a time period}}{\text{Average unit inventory during the time period}}$$

The vast majority of firms use the first to calculate inventory turnover rate. However, some retail organizations use the second. In fact, either of the two ratios should yield approximately the same result. Any differences in the two calculations would result from changes in the amount of gross margin (the difference between sales and cost of goods sold) during the time period.

The third approach, using units rather than dollars, is particularly applicable to products whose cost or selling prices change significantly during a relatively short time. For example, inventory turnover of gasoline, which changes in cost and price almost daily, would most appropriately be measured by computing units of gasoline sold and units of inventory rather than dollars of any kind.

As a final note on computation of turnover, it is critical that average inventory be determined by using as many data points as possible. For example, suppose a company had no inventory at the beginning of the year, bought and held a large quantity for 11 months, then sold all inventory before end of year. Using only the beginning and ending inventory positions, average inventory would be zero and turnover infinite. Clearly, this would be misleading to management.

Inventory turnover is often considered a "backward-looking" measure because it looks at the company's performance in managing inventory during a previous time period, such as the previous year. Another common way that companies think about their inventory measurement is in terms of days of supply, which is considered a "forward-looking" measure. **Days of supply** (also called **days of sales** or **days of inventory**) is the number of days of business operations that can be supported with the inventory on hand, given that no more inventory is bought or produced.

Days of supply is most meaningful when it is expressed in terms of future expected demand, or daily rate of usage. The daily sales or usage rate may come from forecasts or be computed from the most recent actual sales/usage experience. For example, inventory of finished automobiles is frequently stated (and even reported in publications such as *The Wall Street Journal)* as the number of days of consumer demand, based on the most recent daily sales rate, that could be satisfied from the existing inventory of finished automobiles. For example, if there are currently 2,000,000 finished automobiles sitting in dealer or manufacturing facility lots, and expected sales of automobiles are 50,000 units per day, then days of supply is 40 days.

Of course, the calculated 40 days of supply for automobiles presumes that the existing inventory consists of automobiles that consumers actually want to buy. If consumers want to buy hybrid electric cars and the existing inventory consists primarily of cars with V-8 gasoline engines, the 40 days of supply would be extremely misleading. In inventory management, it is frequently more meaningful to measure performance for specific items rather than overall inventory holdings.

Of major interest to senior executives is **return on assets** and **return on investment**. Rate of return is of such importance that it is discussed in considerable detail later in this chapter.

Most organizations have substantially improved their functional measurement systems over the past 10 years. The number of specific metrics has increased, and the quality of information has improved. Much of the improvement in information quality can be attributed to improved technology. Years ago measurement of on-time delivery typically did not actually monitor delivery receipt by the customer. Most firms had no mechanism to capture information concerning when customers received orders. Instead, they typically measured on-time shipment by discerning if the order was shipped on time. It was assumed that if shipments left the supplier's facility "on time," then they also arrived at customer facilities "on time." Thus, the transportation delivery aspect of the order cycle was ignored. Today, using EDI linkages, satellite, and Internet tracking, many organizations monitor whether orders actually arrive at the customer location on time.

Measuring Customer Relationships

Chapter 4 presented the conclusion that basic logistical service performance is necessary but is not sufficient for firms that are truly committed to logistical excellence. Today, many firms have focused increased attention on alternative methods of measuring their ability to meet customer requirements. As a result, an additional set of metrics is required for companies that strive to move beyond measuring basic customer service. Measurement of perfect orders, absolute performance, and customer satisfaction are three such approaches. Customer success, the ultimate in customer relationships, has no specific metrics but remains the goal for firms committed to supply chain management.

Perfect Orders

The perfect order concept was discussed in Chapter 4 as an indicator of an organization's commitment to zero-defect logistics. Delivery of perfect orders is the ultimate measure of quality in logistics operations. A perfect order measures the effectiveness of the firm's overall integrated logistical performance rather than individual functions. It measures whether an order proceeds flawlessly through every step—order entry, credit clearance, inventory availability, accurate picking, on-time delivery, correct invoicing, and payment without deductions—of the order management process without fault, be it expediting, exception processing, or manual intervention. In fact, as many as 20 different logistic service elements may impact a perfect order. From a measurement perspective, perfect order performance is computed as the ratio of perfect orders during a given time period to the total number of orders completed during that period.

AMR Research has estimated that the return to companies that provide high levels of perfect order fulfillment can be substantial. Improving perfect order performance by 3 percent can result in a 1 percent increase in profits. In reality, measuring perfect order performance is not a simple task. Depending on which items are included in the perfect order, multiple information systems within a firm may need to be integrated and linked to the original purchase order. The American Productivity and Quality Center (APQC) includes four elements in its definition of perfect order performance: percent of orders delivered on time, percent of orders complete, percent of orders damage free, and percent of orders with accurate documentation. APQC's research shows that at the median, organizations have a perfect order index of 80 percent.[4] In other words, 20 percent of all orders being shipped have some form of failure. This failure rate may be an eye-opener for many organizations, especially for those that use functional metrics such as on-time shipments and line/unit fill rate as a proxy for customer satisfaction.

Absolute Performance

Most basic service and quality measures, and even perfect order measures, are aggregated over many orders and over a period of time. The problem some executives report with these on-average, over-time measures is that they tend to disguise the organization's real impact on its customer base. These executives feel that such measures can actually result in a feeling of complacency within the firm and that it is more appropriate to track absolute performance as close to real time as possible. The absolute approach provides a better indication of how a firm's logistical performance really impacts customers. For example, managers may feel that 99.5 percent on-time delivery represents excellent performance. As an executive of a large delivery company said, "To us, 99.5 percent on-time delivery would mean that on a typical day, over 5000 customers received late orders. We can't feel good about having that kind of impact on that many customers." This firm, and many other companies seeking to achieve maximum impact in the market, monitors absolute rates of failure and success as well as the more typical ratio and percentage metrics.

Customer Satisfaction

As mentioned at the beginning of this chapter, measuring customer perceptions and opinions is fundamental in a balanced scorecard. All of the internally generated statistics related to basic service, perfect order, or absolute performance may be internal indicators of customer accommodation, but to quantify satisfaction requires monitoring, measuring, and collecting information from the customer. While a comprehensive discussion of interview and survey research methodology is beyond the scope of this text, typical satisfaction measurement requires careful investigation of customer expectations, requirements, and perceptions of firm performance related to all aspects of logistics operations. For example, the typical survey measures customer expectations and performance perceptions regarding availability, order cycle time, information availability, order accuracy, problem resolution, and other aspects of logistics quality. It is useful to gather information concerning customers' overall feelings of satisfaction in addition to their assessment of specific logistics activities. Additional questions may be included to capture customer perceptions of competitor performance. Only through collecting data from customers can real satisfaction be assessed!

[4]Supply and Demand Chain Executive, "Metric of the Month: Perfect Order Performance," April 22, 2016, https://www.sdcexec.com/warehousing/article/12193325/.

Further, efforts to enhance customer success can be measured only from the customer's perspective. The service as measured by the customer approach discussed in Chapter 4 is an excellent example.

Determining Appropriate Metrics

Thus far, many different performance metrics have been described, but no framework for determining the appropriate metrics or for prioritizing the need for specific metrics has been offered. In fact, several different frameworks have been proposed in the logistics literature. A particularly useful framework has been offered by Griffis, Goldsby, Cooper, and Closs.[5] They propose a framework built on three dimensions: (1) competitive basis, (2) measurement focus, and (3) measurement frequency.

Competitive basis is a dimension reflecting a fundamental strategic choice between responsive logistics and efficient logistics performance. They note that performance favoring responsiveness likely comes at the expense of efficiency. The measurement focus dimension represents the needs of the organization along a continuum ranging from operational metrics to those that provide strategic direction. The third dimension, measurement frequency, suggests that some metrics are needed frequently to monitor day-to-day performance, while others may be consulted less frequently for the purpose of diagnosing performance problems.

Figure 13.2 provides an illustration of this framework and an example of its application. Suppose a firm is interested in frequent assessment of efficiency in operations (indicated by the star in the diagram). In the figure, only two metrics are considered: (1) total logistics cost as a percent of sales and (2) percent error pick rate. The proximity of metric 2 (percent error pick rate) is more closely aligned with fulfilling that assessment need than is

[5]Stanley E. Griffis, Thomas J. Goldsby, Martha Cooper, and David J. Closs, "Aligning Logistics Performance Measures to the Information Needs of the Firm," *Journal of Business Logistics* 28, no. 2 (2007), pp. 35–56.

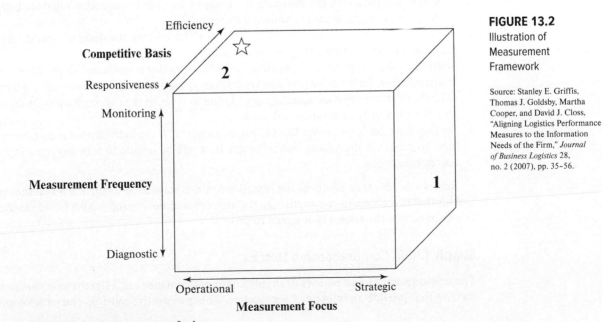

FIGURE 13.2
Illustration of Measurement Framework

Source: Stanley E. Griffis, Thomas J. Goldsby, Martha Cooper, and David J. Closs, "Aligning Logistics Performance Measures to the Information Needs of the Firm," *Journal of Business Logistics* 28, no. 2 (2007), pp. 35–56.

1: Total logistics cost as percent of sales
2: Percent error pick rate
☆ Measurement need

metric 1 (total logistics cost as a percent of sales). This is not to suggest that metric 2 would not also be appropriate for an organization, as every organization has many assessment needs. The authors suggest that fully populating the framework with many possible metrics would allow a firm to choose performance metrics best suited to its measurement needs.[6]

In the late 1990s, a group of executives from leading companies created an organization called the Supply Chain Council. Working together they developed the **supply chain operational reference model** (commonly known as the SCOR model).[7] The SCOR model includes metrics and also provides tools for charting and describing supply chain processes. One of the basic tenets of the SCOR model is that metrics should cascade hierarchically from one level to the next. That is, the strategic performance metrics monitored by senior executives should be supported by more detailed metrics that can be used to diagnose and control operations at the tactical level. For example, perfect order performance is suggested as a strategic level metric. Supporting that at the tactical level are measures relating to fill rates, on-time delivery, damage rates, and so forth. When problems are observed at the strategic level, for example, perfect order performance declines, the operational metrics provide insight into the problems that actually exist. The SCOR framework is designed to allow effective communication both internally and between supply chain members. It also suggests standard definitions and data requirements for numerous metrics that can then be used to compare and benchmark performance in an organization.

Rationalizing Performance Metrics

Over time, organizations tend to add new performance metrics to their measurement systems but rarely do they delete any. This proliferation of metrics can lead to a vast array of data that tends to cause confusion as to which metrics really matter when trying to meet the strategic objectives of the organization. Periodically, it may be useful to perform a detailed review of the measurement system and ask a series of questions concerning each of the individual metrics. These questions should include:

1. Who uses this measurement information? It may be that numerous metrics that are being tracked are no longer actually monitored by anyone.
2. What decisions does the measurement influence? Identifying the decisions being influenced is key to the control objective of performance measurement.
3. What individual or group is responsible, and what behavior is motivated by the measure? Understanding the behavior (the actual decisions) that have been made can aid in identifying those metrics that are actually contributing to meeting the organization's objectives and those that may be counterproductive.
4. Do they have control over the factors that influence it? If the individual or group doesn't have control over the factors that influence it, it will be unable to take any meaningful corrective actions.

Reviews of this type can help the organization maintain a performance measurement system that is relevant to accomplishing the appropriate monitoring, control, and motivational objectives the system is designed to provide.

Supply Chain Comprehensive Metrics

The contemporary focus on overall supply chain performance and effectiveness demands metrics that provide an integrated perspective. This perspective must be comparable and

---

[6]Ibid., p. 47.
[7]See www.supply-chain.org/ for more information on the Supply Chain Council and the SCOR model.

consistent across both firm functions and supply chain institutions. Without integrated measures, managers in different functions and in different firms may have different perspectives concerning actual logistical performance. Specific measures to consider are cash-to-cash cycle time, supply chain inventory days of supply, dwell time, on-shelf in-stock percentage, total supply chain cost, and supply chain response time.

Cash-to-Cash Cycle Time

The cash-to-cash cycle time is a measure of an organization's effective use of cash. While inventory is typically reported as a current asset on the balance sheet, the reported dollar value may not be a valid indicator of the organization's true asset deployment. Some inventory may have been delivered to customers that, because of trade credit terms of sale, have not yet paid for related invoices. Conversely, an organization may owe its suppliers for products or components that are in its possession. Cash-to-cash cycle time is the time required to convert a dollar spent on inventory into a dollar collected from sales revenue. It can be measured by adding a firm's days of supply of inventory and its days of accounts receivable outstanding, subtracting the days of trade accounts payable outstanding. Consider a hypothetical retailer that maintains a 30-day supply of inventory, has 30 days' trade credit from suppliers, and sells to end consumers in cash-only transactions. This firm theoretically has a cash-to-cash cycle time equal to zero because it sells and collects from end customers just as its payment is due to suppliers. More importantly, the firm's actual investment of money in inventory is zero, regardless of what the balance sheet says.

Cash-to-cash cycle time is not solely impacted by logistics, although logistics is an important aspect. It is a measure of internal process because it includes a component of marketing—customer pricing and terms of sale—as well as a component from procurement—supplier pricing and terms. It offers an integrated perspective of the organization's real commitment of financial resources to inventory.

One danger in focusing on cash-to-cash cycle time within one organization is that it may lead that company's management to conclude that an easy way to improve cash flow is to simply take more days to pay suppliers, thus improving its cash flow. In recent years, numerous companies have taken this approach without concern for the impact on suppliers. The danger lies in the fact that by improving its own cash flow, the organization may be putting its suppliers in financial hardship.

Cash Spin

A popular term for describing the potential benefits of reducing assets across a supply chain is **cash spin**, sometimes referred to as **free cash spin**. The concept is to reduce overall assets committed to supply chain performance. Thus, a dollar of inventory or the investment in a warehouse, if eliminated by a reengineered supply chain, provides cash for other uses. Such free capital can be used in new projects, to reduce debt, or in any other way that might advance the organization. Naturally, cash spin opportunity is not unique to the supply chain. The potential to spin cash applies to all areas of a firm. What makes the potential of supply chain cash spin so attractive is the opportunity to collaborate among firms.

Inventory Days of Supply

Traditional measures of inventory performance, turnover, and days of supply focus on individual firms. From a supply chain perspective, the flaw in these measures is that one firm may improve its performance by simply shifting inventory to its suppliers or to customers. Supply chain inventory days of supply is focused on total inventory at all locations and is typically defined as the total finished goods inventory at all plants, warehouses, wholesalers, and retailers expressed as the calendar days of sales available based on recent sales activity. This measure may be further extended to include raw materials and components held by manufacturing plants and suppliers. These unfinished inventories are converted to equivalent units of finished goods and included as part of the true total supply chain inventory. This measure, when adopted by all members of a supply chain, provides the focus of integrated operations.

Dwell Time

Dwell time is another metric reflecting overall supply chain performance in managing assets. Inventory dwell time is the ratio of the days inventory sits idle in the supply chain to the days it is being productively used or positioned. While it is sometimes necessary for inventory to sit idle for reasons of quality control or to buffer uncertainty, extended dwell time reflects the potential magnitude of nonproductive inventory. Dwell time can also be computed for other assets, especially transportation equipment. For example, railcar utilization can be measured by computing the number of days a rail car sits idle and empty versus the number of days it is loaded with freight. Reducing asset dwell time is a key objective for many logistics executives. Assets that sit idle are not contributing to productivity in the supply chain.

On-Shelf In-Stock Percent

Ultimately, a key objective of all participants in a supply chain is to have products available when and where end customers are ready to buy. Individual firm metrics related to fill rates at warehouses or to retail stores provide little assurance that products are available for consumer selection when a consumer is shopping. For this reason, in some supply chain relationships, a critical measure of overall performance is the on-shelf in-stock percent, the percentage of time that a product is available on the shelf in a store. The rationale is that consumers typically cannot or will not select and buy an item that is not easily available on the store shelf. Increasing the on-shelf in-stock percent benefits all members of the supply chain, not only the retailer. While it focuses on the retail impact, consider also the impact on suppliers when their products are not on the shelves at the time consumers want to buy.

Supply Chain Total Cost

Much of the discussion of cost thus far has focused on an individual firm's logistics costs. Figure 13.3 illustrates the fact that total supply chain cost is the aggregate of costs across all firms in the supply chain, not an individual organization. This perspective is absolutely critical to effective supply chain management. Focusing on a single firm's cost may lead to suboptimization and attempts by one company to shift cost to another. If the objective in supply chain management is to reduce total cost, it is reasonable to assume that one organization may actually experience increased cost as others in the supply chain experience reductions. As long as the total reductions in cost are larger than the cost increase for one supply chain member, the supply chain as a whole is improved. It is then incumbent upon those companies whose cost is reduced to share benefits to fairly compensate those whose cost is increased. This willingness to share benefits and risks associated with changes in operational integration is the essence of true relationship management discussed in the previous chapter.

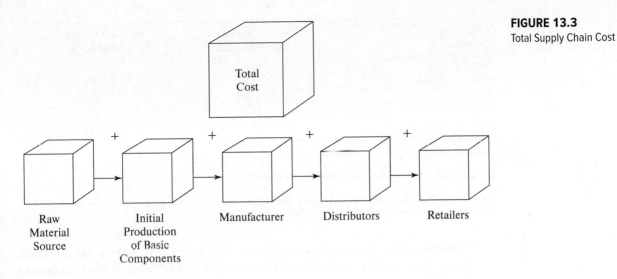

FIGURE 13.3
Total Supply Chain Cost

Supply Chain Response Time

An interesting and extremely meaningful metric for comprehensive supply chain perfor-mance is **supply chain response time (SCRT)**. SCRT is computed as the amount of time required for all firms in a supply chain to recognize a fundamental shift in marketplace demand, internalize that finding, re-plan, and adjust output to meet that demand. For example, in the auto industry, when it was discovered that demand for sport utility vehicles was extremely high, it took several years for the auto companies to develop sufficient pro-duction and capacity, rearrange supplier relationships, and meet consumer demand. In most instances, developing an actual metric for SCRT would be a theoretical approxima-tion rather than a real measure. Nevertheless, it is extremely useful for supply chain execu-tives to think in terms of how long it would take for an entire supply chain to ready all activities from raw material sourcing to final distribution when demand for a product is significantly greater (or less) that anticipated.

Benchmarking

Benchmarking is a critical aspect of performance measurement that makes management aware of state-of-the-art business practice. Many firms have adopted benchmarking as a tool to assess their operations in relation to those of leading firms, both competitors and noncompetitors, in related and nonrelated industries. While benchmarking perfor-mance metrics has become a fairly standard practice, many firms do not benchmark processes.

An important decision in benchmarking is the choice of organizations to benchmark. Many firms compare performance of internal business units involved in similar operations or located in different regions. For example, Johnson & Johnson, with over 150 different business units, has ample opportunity for internal benchmarking. Since business units in large diversified corporations are often unaware of what occurs in other units, internal benchmarking provides a way to share knowledge as well as improve performance.

Internal benchmarking, however, provides little information concerning performance relative to competition. A firm may be lagging competition and not be aware of it. Infor-mation about competitor performance can be used to identify where improvement is most needed; however, it is extremely difficult to capture information about competitors' opera-tional processes.

Performance Dimension	Percent of High Index Achieving Firms	Percent of Average Index Achieving Firms
Customer service	92.5	56.0
Cost management	80.0	47.1
Quality	70.0	31.0
Productivity	77.5	38.5
Asset management	55.0	25.8

Note: All differentials are statistically significant at the .05 level.

TABLE 13.2   Performance Benchmarking Differential

Source: Donald J. Bowersox, David J. Closs, and Theodore P. Stank. *21st Century Logistics Making Supply Chain Integration a Reality* (Oak Brook. IL. Council of Supply Chain Management professionals, 1999). p. 9

Nonrestricted benchmarking involves efforts to compare both metrics and processes to best practices, regardless of where the relevant practice is found. It does not restrict sources of information to any particular company or industry. Nonrestricted benchmarking is grounded in the philosophy that it is possible to learn from organizations in unrelated industries that have outstanding performance or use innovative approaches. L.L.Bean, the mail and catalog company, has been benchmarked in order fulfillment processes by firms from such diverse fields as food, personal care, and electronics.

Benchmarking is an important tool in the performance assessment system of an organization. In a study of best-practice supply chain companies referenced in Table 13.2, it was found that those firms that perform at high levels of supply chain capability are much more likely to be involved in benchmarking activity than firms that demonstrate average supply chain capability. Table 13.2 shows the results of the research related to benchmarking. In all categories, high-achieving companies are more involved in benchmarking than average-achieving firms. It is clear that benchmarking is considered an essential aspect of measurement by leading organizations.

Information Technology and Measurement

Advancements in information technology have greatly enhanced the ability of organizations to track and monitor logistics performance metrics. Firms no longer need to develop manual or spreadsheet based applications to collect, sort, and analyze performance data. For example, most transportation management, warehouse management, customer relationship management, and supplier relationship management software applications today provide functionality for measuring and monitoring logistics performance. The information provided by these applications provides logistics managers with the ability to take necessary corrective actions in almost a real-time environment.

For example, at IBM, systems track how each individual supplier performs versus IBM requirements. The company looks at each supplier in terms of cost and how well the supplier delivers to IBM requirements. On the customer side, IBM builds into every contract the major metrics that both parties will consider in determining how well the relationship is working. To ensure continuous improvement, executives meet with suppliers and customers quarterly to review performance and discuss solutions in areas where performance improvements are deemed to be necessary.

Similarly, the Gillette Group, a distributor for Pepsi-Cola based in Wisconsin, implemented a technology application which allows it to track detailed information product delivery. For each delivery, the firm is able to know who the delivery is for, who the driver was, whether the delivery was on time, which customers have returned outdated product, and other delivery-related information. The system allows the firm to make necessary adjustments and improvements in its delivery processes.

Of course, not all performance improvements require sophisticated technology to provide critical information. For example, Guinness, the Irish brewing company, was quite surprised to learn that its U.S. distributor rated its on-time delivery performance at 50 percent when Guinness had estimated performance at near 100 percent. The problem existed because Guinness looked at service from the standpoint of when the delivery left the facility in Ireland; the U.S. distributor focused on when the delivery arrived. The difference became apparent only after in-depth discussions between executives in both companies. The discrepancy led Guinness to a detailed investigation of all of the steps involved in a shipment from its brewery in Dublin to the U.S. and the need for technology to provide better visibility into the status of each shipment.

These examples reinforce a critical lesson concerning performance measurement. Data and metrics are critical requirements for monitoring logistics systems status. Technology can be a crucial enabler in this process. Controlling performance, however, remains the responsibility of management that uses the information to determine the needed changes in logistics operations required to improve that performance.

Financial Assessment

Recall that a balanced scorecard places significant emphasis on improving shareholder value. Thus, logistics executives must be informed and ready to demonstrate how supply chain practices and processes affect the overall financial health of their organization. Measurement systems must enable logistics managers to link supply chain performance directly to financial results. To do so effectively, logistics managers must be well grounded in two critical tools for financial assessment: cost-revenue analysis and the strategic profit model.

Cost-Revenue Analysis

The achievement of logistical integration requires the establishment of a cost-revenue analysis framework. Traditional accounting practices make such a framework difficult for logistics executives. Contribution margin and full-costing methodologies have been supplemented by the use of **activity-based costing (ABC)** as the most promising way to identify and control logistics expenses.

Public Accounting Practice

The two main financial reports of a business enterprise are the **balance sheet** and the **income statement**. The balance sheet reflects the financial position of a firm at a specific point in time. The purpose of a balance sheet is to summarize assets and liabilities and to indicate the net worth of ownership. The income statement reflects the revenues and costs associated with specific operations over a specified period of time. As the name income implies, its purpose is to determine the financial success of operations. Logistical functions are an integral part of both statements; however, the primary deficiency in logistical costing and analysis is the method by which standardized accounting costs are identified, classified, and reported. Unfortunately, the conventional methods of accounting do not fully satisfy logistical costing requirements.

The first problem results from the fact that accounting practice aggregates costs on a standard or natural account basis rather than on an activity basis. The practice of grouping expenses into natural accounts such as salaries, rent, utilities, and depreciation fails to identify or assign operations responsibility. To help overcome the natural account aggregation, it is common for statements to be subdivided by managerial or organizational areas of responsibility within an enterprise. Internal income statements generally classify and group expenses along organization budgetary lines. Thus, costs are detailed by managerial responsibility. However, many expenses associated with logistical performance cut across organization units. For example, efforts to reduce inventory will reduce inventory carrying cost, but they may also lead to more back orders, which would increase total transportation cost. The result is inadequate data for integrated performance measurement.

A somewhat overlapping deficiency of accounting involves the traditional methods of reporting transportation expenditures. It remains standard practice in accounting to deduct inbound freight expense from gross sales as part of the cost of goods to arrive at a gross margin figure. Outbound freight, on the other hand, is generally reported as an operating expense. However, the problem extends beyond where freight is accounted for and reported. In many purchasing situations, freight is not reported as a specific cost. Many products are purchased on a delivered price basis, which includes transportation cost. Most progressive procurement procedures require that expenses for all services, including transportation, be debundled from the total purchase cost for evaluative purposes.

A final deficiency in traditional accounting practice is the failure to specify and assign inventory cost. The deficiency has two aspects. First, full costs associated with the maintenance of inventory, such as insurance and taxes, are not identified, resulting in an understatement or obscurity in reporting inventory cost. Second, the financial burden for assets committed to material, work-in-process, and finished goods inventory is not identified, measured, or separated from other forms of capital expense incurred by the enterprise. In fact, if a firm deploys internal funds to support inventory requirements, it is likely that no capital expenses will be reflected by the profit and loss statement.

To remedy these shortcomings, several modifications to traditional accounting are required to track logistical costs. In particular, the two largest individual expenses in logistics—transportation and inventory—have traditionally been reported in a manner that obscures their importance instead of highlighting them. Although the situation is improving, routine isolation and reporting of logistical costs is not standard practice in most organizations.

To control cost and improve operational efficiency, it is necessary to properly identify and capture all relevant cost information in a manner that is meaningful to decision makers. Logistical costing must also provide those executives with the information to determine whether a specific segment of business such as a customer, order, product, channel, or service is profitable. This requires the matching of specific revenue with specific costs.

Effective costing requires identification of the specific expenses included in an analysis framework. Two frameworks that each have numerous proponents are the **contribution approach** and the **net profit approach**.

Contribution Approach

A pure contribution approach requires that all costs be identified as fixed or variable according to the cost behavior. Fixed costs are those that do not directly change with volume of activity. In the short term, those costs would remain even if volume were reduced to zero. For example, the cost of a delivery truck is fixed. If the truck cost $40,000, the firm is charged $40,000 (or the appropriate depreciation) whether the truck is used for 1 or 1,000 deliveries. Variable costs are those costs that do change as a result of volume. The gasoline required to operate a delivery truck is variable: Total gasoline cost depends upon how frequently and how far the truck is driven.

It is also necessary in contribution analysis to specify which are direct costs and which are indirect costs. Direct costs are those that are specifically incurred because of the existence of the product, customer, or other segment under consideration. If that segment were eliminated, the direct cost would no longer exist. All variable costs can be directly traced to specific products, customers, channels, and the like. Some fixed costs may also be direct if they exist to logistically support a specific business segment. For example, a warehouse facility may be constructed specifically to support a specific product line or major customer account. Indirect costs exist because of more than one segment of business and would continue to exist even if one specific segment were eliminated. Thus, a warehouse that maintains multiple product lines would continue to operate even if one product line was discontinued. In this case, the warehouse is indirect to the products.

Income statements in the contribution method of analysis can be prepared that identify profitability for each segment by determination of fixed, variable, direct, and indirect costs. Table 13.3 provides a hypothetical example of such income statements for a firm analyzing profitability of two customers, a hospital and a retailer. Variable costs of goods sold are directly related to the product mix sold in each customer segment; it includes only direct labor, materials, and supplies. All factory overhead costs are treated as indirect costs in the contribution margin approach. Variable direct costs include such items as sales commission, discounts, certain logistics costs related to servicing each customer, and any other expenses that vary directly with volume sold to each customer. Fixed direct costs include any other costs that can be traced directly to the specific customer. Such costs might include certain aspects of sales, salaries and expenses, advertising, transportation, warehousing, order processing, and other logistical activities. The key is that these expenses must be directly attributable to those customers. Indirect fixed costs includes all expenses that cannot easily be traced to a specific segment. Many of these may also be logistics-related costs. For example, shared warehouse, transportation equipment, and other jointly used resources should be specified as indirect costs.

In Table 13.3, both customers are covering direct costs and making a substantial contribution to indirect fixed cost. The hospital, however, has a substantially higher percentage net segment contribution than does the retailer—37 percent versus 26 percent. A large portion of this difference is attributable to the difference in variable gross profit of 58 percent versus 50 percent. This difference suggests that analysis of the product mix for the retailer should be conducted to determine whether emphasis should be placed on a more profitable mix. Elimination of the retailer would be a clear mistake, however, as the hospital customer would then have to bear all of the indirect fixed cost, resulting in a net loss of $4,000.

	Hospital	Retailer	Total
Revenue	$100,000	$150,000	$250,000
Less: Variable cost of goods sold	42,000	75,000	117,000
Variable gross profit	58,000	75,000	133,000
Less: Variable direct cost	6,000	15,000	21,000
Gross segment contribution	52,000	60,000	112,000
Less: Fixed direct costs	15,000	21,000	36,000
Net segment contribution	$ 37,000	$ 39,000	76,000
Less: Indirect fixed costs			41,000
Net profit			$ 25,000
Net segment contribution ratio	37%	26%	30.4%

TABLE 13.3
Contribution Margin Income Statement for Two Customers

Many companies are beginning to realize the need for a better understanding of profitability of specific segments of their businesses. They also are finding that logistics-related costs are a prime determinant of which customers and products are actually contributing to overall company profits. For example, after being spun-off from Procter & Gamble, Sunny Delight found itself as a relatively small firm in a large industry. Management quickly realized the need to focus on improving customer profitability. This required that they map revenue, trade promotions, cost of goods sold, logistics, and any other variable customer-related costs, in order to improve the overall efficiency and revenue of the company.

Management analyzed two very similar customers with slightly different profitability to determine why there was a difference. The analysis identified that the difference in profitability was due to logistics; not necessarily in shipping costs, but in inbound handling fees and late fees. After some discussions, the customer now picks up its orders, saving both Sunny Delight and the customer a significant amount of money.

Sunny Delight also uses the profitability analysis to help analyze a company after an acquisition. For example, during its recent acquisition of Veryfine, some of the product lines were considered unprofitable. However, Sunny Delight was able to analyze the "spend per pack size" data and determine that trade promotion spending was more efficient than they initially realized. Thus, some products that had been candidates for elimination were actually found to be quite profitable.

Net Profit Approach

The net profit approach to financial assessment of segments requires that all operating costs be charged or allocated to an operating segment. Proponents of this approach argue that all of a company's activities exist to support the production and delivery of goods and services to customers. Furthermore, in many firms most costs are, in fact, joint or shared costs. To determine the true profitability of a channel, territory, or product, each segment must be allocated its fair share of these costs. In the previous example, allocating indirect fixed cost on the basis of sales volume would result in the hospital being charged with 40 percent, or $16,400, and the retailer 60 percent, or $24,600. The net profit of serving the hospital would be $20,600. The net profit from the retail customer would be $14,400.

Clearly, significant problems arise in determining how to allocate indirect costs on a fair and equitable basis. Proponents of the contribution margin approach contend that such allocations are necessarily arbitrary and result in misleading financial assessment. They point to the use of sales volume as a typical basis for allocation of expense and the inherent bias in such an approach. For example, the retailer above accounts for 60 percent of total sales volume but does not necessarily account for 60 percent of the expense of advertising, warehousing, order processing, or any other shared activity. It may account for much more or less of each expense category, depending upon circumstances that are not at all related simply to sales volume.

Net profit proponents argue, however, that the traditional notions of fixed and variable cost and direct and indirect cost are too simplistic. Many of the so-called indirect fixed costs are not, in fact, indirect or fixed at all. These expenses rise and fall, depending upon demands placed upon the business by the various operating segments.

Activity-Based Costing

As a partial solution to the problem of arbitrary allocations, activity-based costing (ABC) suggests that costs should first be traced to activities performed and then activities should be related to specific product or customer segments of the business. Suppose, for example, the order processing expense is basically a fixed indirect cost in our hypothetical example, amounting to $5,000. Allocating this expense to the two customers on the basis of sales volume results in a charge of $2,000 to the hospital and $3,000 to the retailer. However, it is likely that the hospital places very many orders during the year, each of a small quantity, while the retailer may place only a few large orders. If the hospital placed 80 orders and the retailer placed 20 orders, an ABC approach would charge the hospital with 80 percent, or $4,000, and the retailer with 20 percent, or $1,000, of the order processing expense. Applying similar logic to other indirect fixed costs by identifying the activities and cost drivers could result in further refinement of customer profitability.

Identifying the activities, related expenses, and the drivers of expense represents the biggest challenge in an ABC approach. Order processing cost may be related to the number of orders in one company and to the number of lines on orders in another company. Warehouse picking expense may be related to the number of items picked in one company and to the number of pounds in another. Transportation might be related to number of deliveries for one firm and number of miles driven for another. According to proponents of this activity-based costing method, one cost that should be excluded from allocation to segments is the cost of excess capacity. Thus, if an order processing system could process 5 million orders per year but is only utilized for 4 million orders, the excess capacity should not be charged to any segment. Similarly, if a warehouse and its employees could handle 100,000 shipments but are only used for 80,000, the excess capacity is a cost of the time period rather than a cost attributable to an existing operating segment. All other costs, however, should be traced through an activity-based system.

Much of the distinction between the contribution margin and net profit approaches to segment cost analysis is disappearing as analysts are developing better approaches to identify expense behavior. Advocates of direct costing and contribution margin would probably go along with the tracing of costs to segments based on activities performed, as long as the basis for tracing reflects the real cost of the activity. Historically, their argument has been based on the fairness and appropriateness of the allocation method. Even the most avid proponent of full costing, on the other hand, would not argue in favor of arbitrary allocation of cost. Recent developments such as time-driven activity based costing promise even greater accuracy and may further aid in resolving this controversy.[8]

Strategic Profit Model

While costing and profitability assessment are important aspects of financial controllership, the most critical measure of strategic success is **return on investment (ROI)**. There are two ways of viewing ROI. The first is **return on net worth (RONW)**, which measures the profitability of the funds that the owners of the firm have invested in the firm. The second is **return on assets (ROA)**, which measures the profitability generated by managing a firm's operational assets. While owners and investors are most likely interested in RONW, ROA offers a measure of how well management is utilizing assets to earn profits.

Figure 13.4 presents the Strategic Profit Model **(SPM)**, with hypothetical data. The SPM is a tool frequently used to analyze ROI in a business firm. In fact, the SPM is a tool that incorporates both income and balance sheet data and demonstrates how these data relate to each other to result in ROA.

One of the primary benefits of the SPM is that it shows very clearly that a key financial objective of the firm is to achieve and increase ROA. Too often, managers focus on more limited objectives. For example, sales management may focus on sales as the primary

[8]Patricia Everaert, Werner Bruggeman, Gerrit Sarens, Steven Anderson, and Yves Levant, "Cost Modeling in Logistics Using Time-Driven ABC: Experiences from a Wholesaler," *International Journal of Physical Distribution & Logistics Management* 38, no. 2 (2008), pp. 172–189.

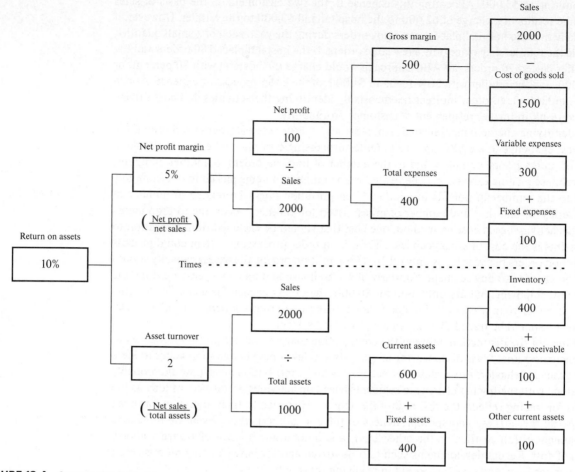

FIGURE 13.4   Strategic Profit Model

objective of the business and, therefore, will base decisions on sales volume. Logistics managers may focus on cost minimization or turnover and feel that decisions must be based on reducing expense or increasing the firm's efficient utilization of assets. The SPM demonstrates that there are two fundamental ways in which a firm can increase return on assets: managing net profit margin and/or managing asset turnover. Logistics operations have a significant impact on both.

Net Profit Margin

Expressed as a percentage, net profit margin is net profit divided by net sales. Going beyond this simple expression, however, net profit margin actually measures the proportion of each sales dollar that is kept by the firm as net profit. For example, the hypothetical firm has a net profit margin of 5 percent; this simply means that $0.05 out of every $1 represents net profit for the company. It is important to note that net profit margin is also divided into a number of specific components. These components are sales volume, cost of goods sold, and operating expenses. For a full evaluation of whether the firm's net profit margin is adequate, and whether it might be improved, it is necessary to investigate each component to determine whether an increase or decrease in any one component or in any combination of components might lead to improved net profit margin performance.

Asset Turnover

The ratio of total sales divided by total assets is asset turnover, which measures the efficiency of management in utilizing assets. It shows how many dollars in total sales volume are being generated by each dollar that the firm has invested in assets. For example, the hypothetical company with an asset turnover ratio of 2:1 is generating $2.00 in sales volume for each dollar it has invested in assets. As Figure 13.4 illustrates, there are a number of assets used to generate sales. The most important are inventories, accounts receivable, and fixed facilities. Inventory is a particularly important asset to many firms because it is typically one of the largest areas of asset investment. Thus, it is common in logistics to focus specifically on the management of the inventory turnover ratio.

Applications of the SPM

The SPM can be used for many different types of logistical analysis. Two of the most common are the impact of changes in logistical activities or processes on ROA and analysis of segmental ROA.

Figure 13.5 illustrates a recomputation of ROA assuming that the hypothetical firm was able to accomplish an inventory reduction of $100. The most obvious impact of this

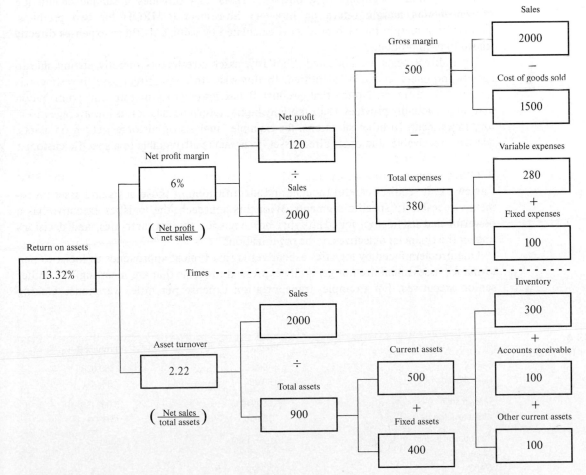

FIGURE 13.5   Strategic Profit Model (Inventory Reduction)

inventory reduction occurs through the reduction in the inventory asset from $400 to $300. A corresponding change in total assets results in a new asset turnover rate of 2.22 versus the base case of 2.0 times. It is assumed, for explanatory purposes, that sales volume remains the same.

However, a reduction in average inventory also has an impact on operating expenses. Inventory carrying costs, discussed in Chapter 7, should be reduced as well. In this example, assuming an inventory carrying cost of 20 percent, the expense reduction amounts to $20, increasing net profit to $120, and net profit margin to 6 percent. The combined profit margin and asset turnover impact of inventory reduction result in an increase in ROA from 10 percent to over 13.3 percent. No wonder so many organizations are focusing on methods to improve inventory management!

The simplifying assumption of no change in sales could be subjected to further examination by using the SPM. A variety of scenarios regarding potential changes in volume, expenses, and investments can be proposed and analyzed. In fact, the SPM framework is very adaptable to a spreadsheet model, which allows investigation and analysis of many different changes in logistics operations and their projected impact on ROA. Changes in facility structure or methods with projected changes in expenses, asset investment, and sales level can be analyzed to project impact on ROA.

The SPM, in conjunction with concepts discussed in the section on cost/revenue analysis, can also be used to examine the return on assets generated by various customer or product segments of a business. Table 13.4 provides a sample calculation of **contribution margin return on inventory investment (CMROI)** for two products. Contribution margin for each product is calculated by using only those expenses directly traced to each product.

No indirect costs are allocated. Similarly, asset investments directly attributable to specific products should be identified. In this case, the only direct asset investment is inventory investment. Notice that product B has lower gross margin and contribution margin but actually provides a substantially higher return because of its low average inventory investment. In other situations, for example, analysis of customer return on assets, accounts receivable, and other direct asset investments attributable to a specific customer should be included.

Other segment profitability and ROI analyses can be conducted by using the SPM framework. It requires careful thought and identification of those costs and asset investments traceable to specific segments. With this approach, the logistics executive has a powerful and useful tool for identifying how logistics process, activities, and decisions impact the financial objectives of the organization.

One problem faced by logistics executives is that typical approaches to logistics performance assessment are not generally expressed in terms that are meaningful to other senior executives. For example, transportation expense per mile, warehouse picking

TABLE 13.4
CMROI for Two Products

	Product A	Product B
Sales	$100,000	$50,000
Cost of goods	60,000	35,000
Gross margin	40,000 (40%)	15,000 (30%)
Direct expense	25,000	9000
Contribution margin	15,000 (15%)	6000 (12%)
Average inventory	40,000	10,000
CMROI	37.5%	60%

expense, and cost-related metrics are extremely meaningful in terms of managing those specific activities but are somewhat obscure to executives in finance and marketing. The SPM framework is a very useful tool for relating logistics activities to the overall financial objectives of the organization. It provides a mechanism to trace specifically how changes in logistics' assets or expenses relate directly to measures that are more meaningful to other executives: measures such as profit margin, asset turnover, and return on assets.

Requirements for Financial Reporting

Because of numerous instances of financial mismanagement by major corporations, in 2002 the U.S. Congress passed the **Sarbanes-Oxley Act (SOX)**. Although the focus of the law is on financial reporting by corporations to their shareholders, it became apparent soon after its enactment that it also has important implications for logistics and supply chain management, especially with respect to how performance is measured and reported.

Section 404 of SOX requires that a company file an internal control report at the same time it files its corporate annual report. The SEC will evaluate the internal controls used by the firm to determine its adequacy for ensuring that the financial reports are consistent and accurate. Thus, every firm covered by the act must have internal measurement capabilities that comply with SEC requirements. It is important to note that the SEC does not specify what the internal controls and measures must be, but it does require that the controls ensure the integrity of financial information. In essence, companies must demonstrate that their measurement systems ensure that financial data such as revenue, cost of goods sold, expenses, assets, and liabilities are accurately reported.

Of particular importance to logistics and supply chain executives are the requirements of SOX to measure and report all off-balance-sheet liabilities, obligations, or transactions that may have a material effect on the financial reports. Activities such as vendor-managed inventories, long-term purchase agreements, and slotting allowances are examples of such items. Thus, attempts to gain competitive advantage by using these approaches become public knowledge due to the disclosure requirements of SOX.

In addition to reporting transactions, companies are also required to report any event that may have a material effect on financial reports. Consider, for example, shipments of goods that have a long leadtime and/or have the potential to be held up for a long time at an international border because of security risks or transportation delays. In many instances, the buyer may be contractually obligated to pay for the goods regardless of when they are received. Thus, the buyer owns inventory but may not receive actual possession for some time.[9] Historically, such situations were essentially unknown to senior executives, but in the current environment this financial commitment and its impact must be acknowledged. Basically, the requirements for full disclosure of the financial status of the organization have forced senior executives to have a much greater understanding of the details of logistical operations. It also places a premium on having the ability to monitor the location and status of shipments in a timely and accurate manner.

Although many managers feel that the legal requirements of SOX are a burden on the organization, others view it as an opportunity for improvement. The requirements for more detailed knowledge of where finished products and materials are at all times, from their point of origin to arrival at final destination, make it necessary for companies to commit

---

[9]Peter M. Tirshwell, "How to Avoid This," *Journal of Commerce*, November 2, 2004, p. 1.

more resources to providing supply chain visibility to management. In turn, by having greater visibility, the opportunity exists to improve decisions by basing them on better and more timely information.

Summary

Effective management of logistics operations and supply chain integration requires establishment of a framework for performance assessment and financial controllership. The balanced scorecard provides the framework to monitor system performance, control activities, and direct personnel to achieve higher levels of productivity.

Comprehensive performance measurement systems include metrics for each of the logistics functions. Five critical dimensions of functional performance must be addressed: cost, customer service, quality, productivity, and asset management. Leading firms extend their functional measurement systems to include metrics focused on their ability to accommodate customer requirements. These include measures of absolute performance rather than average performance, perfect orders, consumer-focused measures, and customer satisfaction. Given the numerous metrics that might be used for assessment of logistics performance, choosing the most appropriate measures for a firm is a difficult task that must be guided by the specific information needs of an organization. To aid in achievement of supply chain integration, leading firms have instituted a set of across-firm metrics such as inventory days of supply, inventory dwell time, cash-to-cash cycle time, and total supply chain cost.

Effective financial assessment requires knowledge of cost-revenue analysis and the strategic profit model. Traditional accounting practices are typically inadequate for logistics costing. Effective decision making requires that management be able to match revenues with expenses incurred to service specific customers, channels, and products. Contribution and net profit approaches represent alternative formats for cost/revenue analysis. Activity-based costing provides management the ability to more specifically trace logistics expenses to the segments that generate revenue. An additional tool for controllership is the strategic profit model. This model provides managers the ability to assess the impact of logistics decisions on profitability, asset utilization, and return on assets. It also provides the ability to more accurately assess segments in terms of profit and return on investment. Sarbanes-Oxley requires that external financial reports include disclosure of significant logistics transactions and events on both the balance sheet and corporate profitability.

Study Questions

1. Briefly discuss the three objectives for developing and implementing performance measurement systems.
2. How does the balanced scorecard concept help guide logistics managers in the development of a performance measurement system?
3. Is the ideal of a perfect order a realistic operational goal?
4. Why are comprehensive measures of supply chain performance, such as total supply chain cost, so difficult to develop?

5. Compare and contrast the contribution approach with the net profit approach in cost/revenue analysis.

6. How can the strategic profit model be integrated with cost-revenue analysis for the purpose of analyzing the return on assets for a specific customer segment?

Challenge Questions

1. What do you think are the difficulties faced by companies such as Gillette Group and Guinness in developing measurement systems that provide real-time information concerning logistics performance? Consider the Guinness example of measuring on-time delivery rather than on-time shipment in your answer.

2. Suppose you work for a small company with limited ability to invest in technology. What actions might you take to provide you with measurement information that larger firms such as Gillette Group and Guinness obtain through technology investment?

3. What do you think are the major barriers to implementing customer and product profitability analysis such as that done by Sunny Delight?

4. What types of decisions, other than those discussed in the example, might Sunny Delight and other firms improve through detailed customer and product profitability analysis?

CHAPTER 14

Supply Chain Trends

Chapter Outline

Over the past 50 years, logistics and its related disciplines in supply chain management have evolved from a transactional "back-room" activity to a series of processes that allow both commercial and nonprofit organizations to achieve their objectives and develop a competitive advantage. Logistics and supply chain management help to create a competitive advantage by reducing expenses, enhancing revenue, and improving asset utilization. However, the changes in consumer requirements and the technical capabilities are both increasing the demands on today's logistics and supply chain system and are offering new opportunities to enhance supply chain performance.

This chapter builds on the Beyond the Horizons (BTH) research completed at Michigan State University with the support of the John H. McConnell Endowment and APICS.[1] Through the use of executive interviews and surveys, the BTH research identified key trends and challenges that will be faced by logistics and supply chain management professionals in the future.[2] These challenges are organized by relative ranking as perceived by supply chain professionals. The challenges include (1) understanding end-to-end supply chain management; (2) developing supply chain management talent; (3) managing risk and complexity; (4) managing threats and environmental changes; (5) understanding the security, regulatory, and compliance environment; and (6) understanding purchasing and total cost management. These challenges are used

[1]John McConnell Endowment and APICS (2016).
[2]David J. Closs, Patricia Daugherty, and Nick Little, *Beyond the Horizons* (Chicago: APICS, 2017).

to summarize this chapter and to suggest directions for the future. Each challenge and resulting implications are discussed and characterized in this chapter.

Understanding End-to-End Supply Chain Management

The first challenge is to understand the scope and dimensions of the end-to-end supply chain. Historically, executives have focused only on the supply chain involving their direct suppliers and their direct customers. In essence, this amounts to a two- to three-stage supply chain, typically involving manufacturing, suppliers, and distributors. This also includes understanding the product and transportation flow characteristics throughout the supply chain.

The challenge today is to have reasonable visibility throughout the firm's end-to-end supply chain (i.e., from the basic raw material supplier to the end consumer) and to be able to understand the flows between each stage of the supply chain. Figure 14.1 illustrates a segment of the end-to-end supply chain from the manufacturer to the consumer. In the case of automobiles, this would include the entire supply chain from the iron mines to the automobile consumer. Similarly, in the case of wine or beer, the end-to-end supply chain includes the fields that grow the grapes and hops through to the consumer.

While most supply chain managers have not worried about the supply chain more than two to three tiers below or above their organization, that is rapidly changing due to the risk

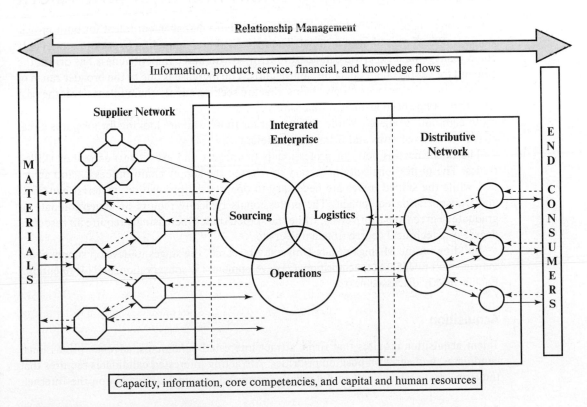

FIGURE 14.1 The End-to-End Supply Chain

and liability that can result from the failures of supply chain partners. Examples of these types of risks include:

1. Failure of fourth- or fifth-tier supplies to meet the capacity demands of a major manufacturer.
2. Quality failures on the part of critical parts providers.
3. Products or components that have been counterfeited or adulterated as they move through stages of the supply chain.
4. Product or components moving through multiple channels and resulting in the need for multiple flows through the supply chain.
5. Legal liability as many supply chain partners are sued to find the one with the "deepest pockets."
6. Products or components that are being held at the border for customs compliance.
7. Products or components that have been lost or damaged in the supply chain.

In these situations, the challenge results from the multiple tiers, multiple flows, and multiple risks of damage or adulteration, which might result in late deliveries, loss of product, or legal liabilities. These variations may also change the requirements in terms of delivery, packaging requirements, and return processing.

The result is that supply chain professionals today are responsible for longer and more complex supply chains. The brand and legal liability is also much more serious as firms, particularly those that have significant assets and brand equity, will be charged with brand and legal liabilities even if the firm is not the primary cause of the problem.

Developing Supply Chain Management Talent

The second major challenge is access to supply chain management talent for both professional staff and operations personnel. The increased understanding regarding how supply chain management expertise can assist in firm growth and competitiveness has driven the demand for supply chain talent up significantly. The increase is due to the broader range of firms, such as for services supply chains, that are seeking supply chain talent. Over the past few years, it has been estimated that for every trained supply chain professional, there are six to eight jobs available. While this is great for those who are looking for jobs, it is a real challenge for executives and firms seeking talent.

The talent need is both for professionals (managers and executives) as well as skilled trades. The professionals are necessary to oversee the supply chain processes and activities, while the skilled trades are necessary to operate the production, material handling, and transportation equipment. The professionals typically require an undergraduate or graduate degree from a university, while the skilled trades increasingly require an associate degree or a technical degree from a university.

Building on the Michigan State University research, the stages to develop supply chain management talent are (1) acquisition, (2) development, (3) conservation, and (4) retention.[3] Each is briefly discussed next.

Acquisition

Talent **acquisition** requires that firms attract interested candidates, advance professional candidates, and agree on position priorities. Attracting interested candidates requires that the firm create talent pools of potentially interested candidates drawing on the Internet,

---

[3]David Closs and Nick Little, *The 12 Steps to Develop Supply Chain Talent* (Chicago: APICS, 2017).

university contacts, and ongoing public relations contacts. This should include candidates with awareness of your firm and who would be likely to be positively inclined to accept an offer if one were to be made.

Advancing professional networking identifies and moves the most attractive candidates into a formal selection process. From the possible candidates identified in the acquisition stage, this step selects the best ones to move forward with. This includes networking with potential candidates at professional meetings and conferences to allow firm to learn more about candidates.

Agreeing on position priorities requires an organization to determine whether it wants to hire a future leader, an individual with technical talent, or a candidate who meets diversity requirements. Specifically, is the firm hiring for competencies or for diversity, or is it identifying talent with specific technical skills? This discussion within the firm ensures that the human resources and logistics professionals agree on the direction for the search.

Development

Talent **development** requires that firms deploy panel interviews, discourage leadership myopia, and find individuals who demonstrate leadership potential. Interview panels representing different organizational perspectives should be used to develop different views of potential candidates. The goal is to make sure potential candidates can be questioned from the perspectives of leadership, collaboration, technical, problem solving, and so forth, to understand the breadth of their potential contribution.

Discouraging leadership myopia means executives must be careful to not believe that an ideal candidate who meets all the desired criteria can be found. Every candidate has trade-offs, and they need to be assessed and matched against the position priorities. It is also important that employees be cycled through rotation programs to make sure that they are not developed and controlled by a single leader. This rotation program should also place the employee in multiple geographies, divisions, and types of positions. Figure 14.2 illustrates

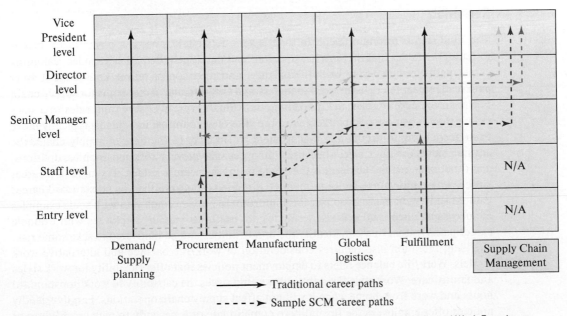

FIGURE 14.2 Supply Chain Management Career Path: Fostering Depth and Breadth in Skills and Work Experience

Source: John Dischinger, David J. Closs, Eileen McCulloch, Cheri Speier, et al., "Supply Chain Management Review," *Framington* 10, no. 1 (January/February 2006), pp. 62–68.

the need for supply chain professionals to have experience at multiple levels and in multiple disciplines to develop the experience and networks to become senior logistics and supply chain executives.

It is important that employees are placed in situations where their leadership potential is demonstrated to senior managers so that they don't get limited in their development potential. Employees should be exposed to senior managers through formal networking and review processes.

Conservation

Once the talent has been acquired and developed, the next step is to maintain or conserve employees. **Conservation** includes the responsibility to certify and educate, categorize performance potential, and coach and mentor employees. Due to the rapidly changing business and technical environment, individual capabilities become out-of-date very quickly. As a result, it is very important that employees remain actively involved in enhancing their talent. A common method to enhance this talent is through certification programs and advanced degrees. Many supply chain professional organizations such as the Council of Supply Chain Management Professionals (CSCMP) and APICS offer such professional certification. If the employee desires an undergraduate or graduate degree, there are many universities that offer degrees in both on-campus and online formats.

Categorizing performance potential requires that firms regularly assess employee skills to identify where they can make the most significant contribution to the firm or where the employee needs the most development. The general skill categories include analytical, people management, action orientation, and inclusiveness. Employees can either be matched to positions based on their skill set strengths or trained in skills where they are weak.

Employee conservation also requires a good coaching and mentoring system to provide both guidance and informal feedback to the employee. The coaching and mentoring sessions should include frequent, regular, informal and formal, documented meetings.

Retention

The final step is to retain talent. In today's very active talent market, a significant task is to retain the talent that the firm has acquired and developed. **Retention** includes realigning career paths, remembering work/life balance, and retention of retiree knowledge. **Career path realignment** refers to the need to understand the potential career paths for supply chain talent. In the case of sales and marketing, individuals typically move from sales to a sales manager and then often to marketing. In the case of accounting, individuals typically move from accounting to accounting management to finance. In the case of supply chain, the advancements are not so clear because employees may move across geographies, divisions, and functional areas. The result is that there is no clear career ladder; it is more of a career lattice, where individuals move in multiple directions. Because there is no standard career path for supply chain professionals, it is important to provide employees with some examples of successful career paths. These examples are useful to provide employees with example career paths so that they can identify the opportunities and be motivated to take some risk.

Talent retention also requires consideration of work/life balance and alternative work models. **Work/life balance** refers to employment policies that offer flexibility for work styles and family care. Work style flexibility allows employees the capability to work nonstandard hours and work from home when it will not affect supply chain operations. Family-friendly policies offer employees the flexibility to come in late or leave early to pick up children or seek medical care. The combination of these work models makes a firm more attractive when employee availability is limited.

While talent retention is important, a correlate of talent retention is retiree knowledge retention. Increasingly, employees with 25 to 35 years of experience are leaving organizations and taking with them extensive process and work expertise. Many executives are very concerned about the flight of organizational knowledge regarding institutional history, processes, and technology. There are two initiatives that firms are taking with respect to retirees. The first is to formalize a process for transferring knowledge from future retirees. As an employee announces his or her departure, the typical process is to assign a junior employee to the future retiree so that the junior employee can begin to understand the processes and relationships of the upcoming retiree. In some cases, the retiree is provided bonus or pay extension for his or her efforts. The second initiative is to provide enough time between the retirement announcement and the departure to allow this transfer to happen.

Summary

A significant challenge for firms today is to acquire, develop, maintain, and retain talent. The demand for supply chain talent is increasing rapidly with increased understanding regarding the potential benefits of supply chain expertise. The result is that firms must be more proactive in their talent and leadership development initiatives. Without proactive efforts, firms will lose the competitive advantage that results from superior talent.

Managing Risk and Complexity

The third challenge faced by supply chain executives is risk and complexity management. The following two sections will discuss risk and complexity, respectively.

Risk Management

Historically, supply chain risks have primarily been due to demand and lead time uncertainty. **Demand uncertainty** was often related to variation in forecasting and demand. **Lead time uncertainty** related to variability in delivery time. However, there are an increasing number of risks related to supply chain operations. Table 14.1 illustrates the types of challenges encountered in supply chain organizations. The major dimensions of risk include compliance, performance, country events, financial, and market segment.

Compliance risk relates to the firm's ability to make sure that its organization and suppliers comply with supplier codes of conduct, audits, restricted materials, certification, and labor requirements. Meeting supplier code of conduct restrictions requires suppliers to use ethical practices related to bribery and slave or child labor. Supplier high-risk audits

Compliance	Performance	Environmental Events	Financial	Market Segment
• Supplier code of conduct	• Achieving excellence	• Natural disasters	• Public companies	• Related industries
• Supplier high-risk audits	• Delivery	• Labor disruptions	• Private companies	• Packaging
• Restricted materials	• Quality	• Geopolitical risks	• Payment changes	• Natural resources
• Certification	• Audit results	• Trade barriers	• Bankruptcy	
	• Capacity constraints	• Duties and tariffs	• Ownership changes	
		• Pandemics	• Public press releases	
		• Terrorism		
		• Fires		

TABLE 14.1   Dimensions of Supply Chain Risk

require that suppliers use safe work practices in their facilities and around their equipment. Restricted materials limit the use of materials that local governments have defined as scarce or that are acquired using slave labor. Certification refers to raw materials that need to meet specific standards such as grains that have not been genetically modified or have not passed product purity certifications.

Performance risk relates to the performance level delivered by the suppliers. The specific dimensions that cause risk to the firm relate to the supplier's failure to meet standards of excellence, delivery requirements, quality requirements, audit results, and capacity requirements. In all cases, the risk is that the supplier is not able to deliver the volume and quality of product in a timely basis.

Environmental risk refers to the events that are outside the control of the firm. These include natural disasters such as earthquakes, tsunamis, floods, pandemics, and weather. In these cases, the transportation infrastructure may be severely damaged or destroyed. Other environmental risks that are outside the control of the firm include labor disruptions, geopolitical risks, trade barriers, duties, tariffs, and terrorism. In these cases, the firm's operations may be inhibited due to labor limitations, capacity constraints, government restrictions, or risks to employees through terrorism.

Financial risk refers to changes in the financial position of supply chain partners. This includes the changes in customer or supplier ownership, changes in payment terms, or bankruptcy. These events may make it difficult for the firm to continue operations either because of lack of supplies or restricted cash flow.

Market segment risk refers to limitations caused by actions in related industries. For example, while the automobile industry was in a significant downturn from 2008 through 2010, the agricultural equipment industry was not. A common raw material for both is steel. During the 2008–2010 period, the agricultural equipment industry had no problem purchasing steel. However, when the automotive industry returned, the agricultural equipment industry began to have problems purchasing steel because the automobile industry had significantly more demand for steel. The result was that the industries with a lower volume demand could become challenged with suppliers. A similar situation would likely occur with packaging or other natural resources.

Complexity Management

Complexity management refers to product and process complexity, including the number of product variations and process flows. Product variations refer to the number of stock-keeping units (SKUs) resulting from color, size, package size, and other differentiating features. Process variation refers to the number of paths that a product may take through a production process in a plant. More path variations increase the number of work cells and changeovers and reduce economy of scale. Other complexity drivers include the number of suppliers or distribution channel alternatives to the consumer, feature and component variations for each SKU, packaging variations, and geographic regulations.

Figure 14.3 illustrates the relationship between the number of SKUs and revenue, cost, and profit. As the number of SKUs increases, the revenue initially increases as consumers purchase more product because they feel that increasing the number and variation of features makes it customized for customer segments. However, eventually, the revenue flattens out because increasing SKU variation confuses consumers, and they slow down their purchasing. As the number of SKUs increase, the related supply chain costs increase at an increasing rate. The rationale for this is that increased SKUs drive up set-up, warranty, and procurement costs for raw materials while reducing economies of scale. The result is the profit curve, which initially increases, maximizes, and then declines. The profit initially increases because the revenue is increasing faster than the cost. However, once the cost

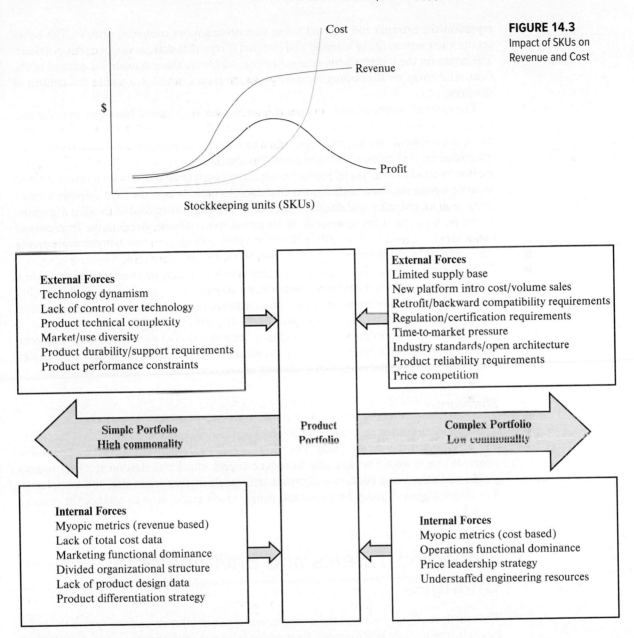

FIGURE 14.3

Impact of SKUs on Revenue and Cost

FIGURE 14.4 Forces Affecting Portfolio Complexity

Source: David Closs, Mark Jacobs, Morgan Swink, and G. Scott Webb, "Toward a Theory of Competencies for the Management of Product Complexity: Six Case Studies," *Journal of Operations Management* 26 (2008), pp. 590–610.

begins to increase rapidly due to the number of SKUs and increased operating complexity, the profit begins to decline. The conclusion is that every firm has an optimum number of SKUs for each product category. If the firm offers too few SKU variations, its profit is low because consumers are not happy with the breadth of product offerings. If the firm offers too many SKU variations, the profit is again low due to the high cost of maintaining product variations.

Figure 14.4 illustrates the forces that influence product portfolio complexity. The bar in the center of the figure represents the overall product portfolio. The boxes on the left represent the external and internal forces that drive a more complex portfolio. The boxes on the right represent the external and internal forces that drive a less complex portfolio. The boxes on the top represent external forces, which are those outside the control of the firm. The boxes on the bottom represent internal forces, which are within the control of the firm.

The external forces driving product complexity generally result from demands for customized technology, diverse application, or a range of product performance requirements. These requirements are generally controlled by industry or governmental regulations or by the customer, thus resulting in little control by the firm.

The internal forces driving product complexity result from a firm with a revenue-based focus or a poor understanding of total cost data. In other words, the firm employs a maximize revenue objective and doesn't understand the total costs related to SKU variation, so the firm increases the number of SKUs to sell more volume. Because the firm doesn't understand the total cost of adding SKUs, it views only the revenue without considering the total cost implications.

The external forces driving more product standardization or commonality include a limited number of suppliers, price competition, regulatory requirements, and reliability requirements. In these cases, increased standardization provides more economies of scale and reliability, which results in lower manufacturing cost.

The internal forces driving more product standardization or commonality include cost-focused metrics or operations functional dominance. In both cases, the firm tries to design processes and make decisions that will lower production cost.

Summary

The increasing consumer demand for product features and customization drives more risk and variation in the supply chain. The result is more variation in processes and components. While it would be desirable to reduce supply chain risk and complexity, today's global operations and consumer demands will result in even more risk and complexity. The responsibility of today's logistics and supply chain executive is to balance the revenue opportunities with cost of the related risks.

Managing Threats and Environmental Changes

The fourth challenge concerns the management of general threats and changes in the logistics and supply chain environment. Examples of these threats and environmental changes include sustainability, segmental focus, and profitability.

Consumers are increasingly requesting that retailers and omnichannel partners demonstrate more concern for sustainability in their logistics and supply chain operations. As a result, firms are adding sustainability considerations in their mission and operating strategies. Examples of such initiatives include green facilities, alternative fuels, use of recycled materials, and more local sourcing. The result is a more sustainable supply chain.[4]

Changing segmental focus represents another threat and change. As was discussed previously in this text, a major requirement for high-performance logistics and supply chain management is to focus on key customers and suppliers of choice. Customers and suppliers

---

[4]David J. Closs, Cheri Speier, and Nathan Meacham, "Sustainability to Support End-to-End Value Chains: The Role of Supply Chain Management," *Journal of the Academy of Marketing Science* 39, no. 1, (February 2011), pp. 101–116.

of choice typically represent the top customers and suppliers who buy or sell a majority of a firm's volume. Because these customers or suppliers represent major volumes for the firm, it is critical that the firm potential changes in the channel relationships. An example of such a relationship change is the acquisition of Aetna by CVS Health.[5] As a result of such an acquisition, it would be likely that other health care insurers would be inclined to change their relationship with CVS.

Changes in the social, environmental, and economic environment also require monitoring by the firm. As suggested earlier, consumers increasingly desire products that consider their social views and reflect consideration for the environment. As an example, while plastic packaging is less expensive and easier to handle in the supply chain, it is less desirable in the eyes of consumers because plastic is more difficult to recycle. To maintain firm competitiveness, it is important that firms monitor the changes so that they can adapt their policies.

In summary, logistics and supply chain executives are challenged by numerous threats and changes. These threats and changes require refinement of logistics and supply chain strategy and execution. Specifically, it would likely require increased consideration of social and environment factors. Failure to make these considerations may reduce the firm's long-term competitiveness.

Understanding the Security, Regulatory, and Compliance Environment

The fifth challenge considers the fast-moving changes in the security, regulatory, and compliance environments. The security environment refers to the policies and restrictions incorporated into the supply chain for protecting the product and the environment. Examples of security restrictions include (1) determining whether the product can be imported or exported, (2) making sure the product is packaged appropriately, and (3) protecting the product from theft or damage while it is in the supply chain.

The restrictions refer to the government regulations regarding product movement. There are an increasing number of restrictions placed on products as they move across national and state boundaries. These restrictions are typically established to limit the import/export of contraband or restricted agricultural products. The contraband restrictions are designed to prohibit the import of drugs, weapons, or chemicals that could be used for terrorism. Agricultural products are also often restricted to keep non-native species from entering a country and possibly damaging crops grown in the importing country. Another example of a supply chain restriction is the limitation on the importing of non-processed wood pallets. Non-processed pallets are pallets that are not treated for insect infestation.

Compliance refers to the regulations placed on imports and exports by customs and regulatory agencies. Customs constraint examples include (1) restrictions on what can be imported or exported, (2) restrictions on where products can be sourced from, and (3) restrictions regarding how much product can be imported annually. Compliance also refers to environmental limitations such as water, energy, or materials. In any case, the supply chain is an increasingly regulated environment, and it is important that logistics and supply chain managers comply with the regulations to minimize the chance of fines or other legal challenges.

---

[5]https://cvshealth.com/newsroom/press-releases/cvs-health-acquire-aetna-combination-provide-consumers-better-experience.

Understanding Purchasing and Total Cost Management

The final challenge concerns understanding the global issues related to purchasing and total cost management. **Global purchasing** introduces many issues related to currency fluctuations, wage rates, and supply base management. This makes purchasing decisions much more dynamic because sourcing decisions may need change on a monthly, or even weekly, basis. There is also the need to monitor price trends and product availability so that speculative purchasing may be considered. Changes in taxes and duties must also be considered because that may change supply chain product flow. Increased taxes and duties may suggest a change in raw material sourcing.

While this text has focused extensively on minimizing total end-to-end supply chain cost, the broader consideration is to maximize end-to-end value chain profit. Minimizing supply chain cost focuses on minimizing all the supply chain component costs for the entire value chain. However, there are other non–supply chain costs that must be considered as well. Specific factors that must be considered are the duties and taxes that are applied to components and products as they move through the value chain. While it is not always apparent, the duties and taxes may represent a larger cost percentage than many other components. It is not uncommon for duties to represent anywhere from 10 to 20 percent of the selling price of the product. So, it is important to expand supply chain decision beyond least total cost to focus on maximizing total profit.

Summary

While the previous chapters described logistics operating functions and strategies, the discipline is very dynamic, as is illustrated by the challenges discussed in this chapter. There are many issues in logistics and supply chain management that change on a monthly or annual basis, resulting in the requirement that logistics professionals must refine their operations and strategy. Based on interviews with logistics and supply chain executives, this final chapter reviewed the key challenges as identified by executives.

These challenges include (1) understanding end-to-end supply chain management; (2) developing supply chain management talent; (3) managing risk and complexity; (4) managing threats and changes; (5) understanding the security, regulatory, and compliance environment; and (6) understanding purchasing and total cost management. Understanding end-to-end supply chain management requires that managers understand the total flow of product from the initial source of the raw material to the delivery to the end consumer. Developing supply chain talent requires that firms be more proactive in acquiring, developing, conserving, and retaining talent. In today's environment, the demand for talent significantly exceeds the supply. Managing risk and complexity requires logistics and supply chain professionals to be able to assess and evaluate the trade-offs between the opportunities and costs related to risk. Managing threats and changes suggests the market, sustainability, and environmental shifts that are necessary for logistics professionals to track. Understanding the security, regulatory, and compliance environment suggests the need for logistics professionals to become increasingly aware of the security, regulatory, and compliance environment that the supply chain must operate in. Logistics professionals must develop the skills to make appropriate trade-offs. Understanding the purchasing and total cost environment requires that firms and their value chain partners focus on maximizing profitability or delivery of solutions to their target segments rather than simply minimizing total cost.

Study Questions

1. Describe the relationship among firm revenue, cost, and the number of stockkeeping units.
2. Describe some of the logistics and supply chain challenges related to security, regulatory, and compliance.
3. Discuss the implications of supply chain risk on supply chain cost
4. Describe the types of functional skills that are necessary to effectively manage the supply chain.

Challenge Questions

1. Discuss the rationale for the increased shortage of supply chain talent. Discuss the key tasks to ensure that a firm has an adequate supply of talent.
2. Describe the internal and external forces that drive SKU complexity.
3. Describe the internal and external forces that drive SKU commonality.
4. Discuss the role that duties and taxes play in logistics and supply chain design. What are some of the unique characteristics regarding the role of duties and taxes?
5. What are the trade-offs associated with product complexity versus product commonality? Discuss the initiatives that firms can use to manage product complexity.

EPILOGUE

In the final analysis, the logistical management challenge is to rise above a traditional functional perspective to help capture and promulgate the need for managers to reinvent what they are all about. What they should be about is very simple—servicing customers at the lowest possible cost. While it is sometimes hard to comprehend why, the fact is that most firms are in need of a significant transformation to reposition resources to best accomplish this basic goal. For a host of reasons, complexity dominates the modern enterprise. Reinvention of a business is all about simplification, standardization, and integration. It is all about getting back to basics. Logistics is basic.

The logistics manager of the future will be much more of a change leader and much less of a technician. The challenge of change will be driven by the need to synchronize the speed and flexibility of logistical competency into the process of creating customer value. Technology and technique will not be limiting factors. If no new technology is invented for a decade or more, we still will not have fully exploited technology currently available. The concepts being promoted as new ways to improve productivity are for the most part old. Such concepts as activity-based costing, time-based competition, ABC inventory analysis, process integration, collaboration, quick response, segmentation, and so forth, are not new. What is new is that today's leader is supported by robust digital technology that makes the real-time evaluation of information associated with all of these concepts possible.

Of course, the challenge to reinvent the enterprise is not the sole responsibility of logisticians, but it is a responsibility of logistical managers to participate in the process, especially those who lead global operations, have stewardship for extensive capital and human resources, and facilitate the delivery of products and services to customers. The logistical executive of the future will not be able to neglect responsibility for contributing to and participating in the change management required to transform the enterprise to the digital information age. The logistical manager of the future will be better served coming proactively to the corporate table with proposed solutions as to "how" versus a laundry list of reasons "why not."

To this end, authors typically collect quotations and statements that they feel capture the meaning and intensity of their message. To the logistics manager of today and tomorrow who will face the challenges of change, we offer the following quotes as a source of compassion and inspiration:

Concerning Change: Logistics Is Not an Ordinary Occupation

Experience teaches that men are so much governed by what they are accustomed to see and practice that the simplest and most obvious improvements in the most ordinary occupations are adapted with hesitation, reluctance, and by slow graduations.—*Alexander Hamilton*

Concerning Organization: It Is a Matter of Perspective

We trained hard . . . but it seemed that every time we were beginning to form up into teams we would be reorganized. I was to learn later in life that we tend to meet any new situation by reorganizing; and a wonderful method it can be for creating the illusion of progress while producing confusion, inefficiency, and demoralization.—*Charlton Ogburn Jr. (1957)*

The Line between Disorder and Order lies in Logistics.—*Sun Tzu*

Concerning New Ideas: Some Are Not So New

One may even dream of production so organized that no business concern or other economic unit would be obligated to carry stocks of raw materials or of finished goods . . . picture supplies of every sort flowing into factories just as machines are ready to use them; goods flowing out to freight cars and trucks just pulling up to shipping platforms; merchandise arriving at the dealer's shelves just when space was made available . . . under such conditions the burden of expense and risk borne by society because of the stocks necessary to the production process would be at a minimum.—*Everett S. Lyon* (1929)

Concerning Control: Have Perspective

99% of all Logistics decisions are made outside the vision of direct supervision—*Donald J. Bowersox*

Concerning Appreciation: Know the Value of What You Do

You will not find it difficult to prove that battles, campaigns, and even wars have been won or lost primarily because of logistics.—*Dwight D. Eisenhower*

Real Artists Ship.—*Steve Jobs*

PROBLEMS

1. Mike McNeely, logistics manager for the Illumination Light Company, has considered replacing the firm's manual customer order management system with electronic ordering, a web-based application. He estimates the current system, including labor, costs $2.75/order for transmission and processing when annual order volume is under 30,000. Should the order volume equal or exceed 30,000 in any given year, Mr. McNeely will have to hire an additional customer service representative to assist order reception in the manual process. This would raise the variable cost to $3.25/order. He has also estimated the rate of errors in order placement and transfer to be 12/1,000 orders.

   A web-based application would cost $125,000 upfront to implement and variable costs are determined to be $.35/order regardless of volume. A web-based application could acquire and maintain order information with an error rate of 3/1,000 orders. A web-based specialist would be required to maintain the system at all times as well. Her salary is $40,000 in the first year and increases 3 percent each year thereafter.

   Order errors cost $7.00 per occurrence on average to correct in the manual system. Web-based errors cost $9.00 on average to correct since the specialist inspects the system for flaws on most occasions.

   a. If the firm expects order volume over the next five years to be 22,000, 25,000, 27,000, 32,000 and 38,000 annually, would a web-based system pay for itself within the first five years?

   b. What effects aside from cost might Mr. McNeely consider when implementing a web-based solution?

2. Mr. McNeely currently batches orders for processing under the manual order management system. The orders are batched for daily processing. If Mr. McNeely opts to implement a web-based solution, might this affect his current means of order processing? If so, how?

3. Innovative Technologies Inc. has hired you as a sales representative. You have been asked to call on Fast Stop, a small convenience store chain with five locations in your region. What benefits of UPC and bar coding applications might you illustrate to encourage Fast Stop to utilize these technologies to track sales at its retail outlets?

4. Modern Hosiery Inc. produces men's socks at its manufacturing facility in Overland Park, Kansas. The socks are stored in a warehouse near the factory prior to distribution to distribution center (DC) locations in Los Angeles, Memphis, and Cleveland. The warehouse uses a top-down forecasting approach when determining the expected quantities demanded at each DC.

   The aggregate monthly forecast for June is 12,000 pairs of socks. Historically, the Los Angeles DC has demanded 25 percent of the warehouse's stock. Memphis and Cleveland have demanded 30 percent and 35 percent, respectively. The remaining 10 percent is shipped directly from the warehouse.

   a. Based on the aggregate forecast, how many pairs of socks should you expect each DC to demand in June?

   b. Suppose the aggregate forecast for July results in a 6 percent increase over June's forecast. How many pairs of socks would each DC anticipate in July?

2015		2016	
Qtr.	Actual Sales	Qtr.	Actual Sales
1	1,400	1	1,600
2	900	2	900
3	300	3	300
4	900	4	1,100

5. Ms. Kathleen Boyd, director of logistics for the Scenic Calendar Company, wishes to evaluate two methods of time series forecasting. She has collected quarterly calendar sales data from the years 2015 and 2016.

   a. Use the moving averages technique to find forecasted sales for the third quarter of 2016 based on actual sales from the previous three quarters.

   b. Use simple exponential smoothing to forecast each quarter's sales in 2016, given that Ms. Boyd qualitatively forecasted 900 calendars for quarter 4, 2015. Ms. Boyd has assigned an alpha factor of .1 for time series sensitivity.

   c. Repeat the simple exponential smoothing problem above (part 5b) with Ms. Boyd employing an alpha factor of .2.

   d. How well do the moving averages and simple exponential smoothing techniques seem to work in Ms. Boyd's situation? In what ways do the techniques appear to fail?

6. Michael Gregory, logistics manager of Muscle Man Fitness Equipment, has determined that his current forecast system for national sales has historically shown a 15 percent error rate. Due to this level of error, Muscle Man's DC managers maintain inventory at their locations costing the company, on average, $3,500 per month.

   By improving his forecast methodology and shortening forecast horizons, Mr. Gregory anticipates cutting the error level down to 10 percent. With improved forecasting, Muscle Man's DC managers have indicated that they feel comfortable with lower inventory levels. Mr. Gregory anticipates monthly inventory carrying cost reductions of 35 percent.

   a. If the forecast system improvement will cost $1,500 more per month than the old system, should Mr. Gregory implement the change?

   b. Why might Muscle Man's customers encourage the firm to improve its forecasting capabilities?

7. Mr. Stan Busfield, distribution center manager for Hogan Kitchenwares, must determine when to resupply his stock of spatulas. The DC experiences a daily demand of 500 spatulas. The average length of the performance cycle for spatulas is 21 days. Mr. Busfield requires that 750 spatulas be retained as safety stock to deal with demand uncertainty.

   What is the reorder point for spatulas?

8. Mr. Busfield recently completed a course in logistics management and now realizes that there are significant costs associated with ordering and maintaining inventory at his distribution center. Mr. Busfield has learned that the EOQ is the replenishment logic that

minimizes these costs. In an effort to find the EOQ for measuring cups, Mr. Busfield has gathered relevant data. Mr. Busfield expects to sell 50,000 measuring cups this year. Hogan acquires the measuring cups for 75 cents each from Shatter Industries. Shatter charges $8 for processing each order. In addition, Mr. Busfield estimates his company's inventory carrying cost to be 12 percent annually.

a. Find Mr. Busfield's EOQ for measuring cups. Assume that Mr. Busfield accepts ownership of products upon arrival at his DC.

b. Now assume Mr. Busfield must arrange for inbound transportation of the measuring cups since Hogan accepts ownership of products at the supplier's shipping point. Quantities of fewer than 4,000 measuring cups cost 5 cents per unit to ship. Quantities of 4,000 and above cost 4 cents per unit to ship. Determine the difference in total costs associated with an EOQ of 4,000 units and the EOQ level found in part (a) when transportation costs must be considered.

c. Given the information above and the low cost EOQ alternative determined in part (b), use period-order-quantity logic to determine the number of orders Hogan would place each year for measuring cups and the time interval between orders.

9. Mr. Dave Jones manages the warehouse inventory for Athleticks, a distributor of sports watches. From his experience, Mr. Jones knows that the PR-5 jogging watch has an average daily demand of 200 units and a performance cycle of 10 days. Mr. Jones requires no buffer stock at this time.

a. Assume Mr. Jones perpetually reviews inventory levels. Find the reorder point for the PR-5 jogging watch.

b. Find the average inventory level of the PR-5 watch.

c. How might the reorder point change if Mr. Jones reviews inventory once each week? Find the reorder point under these conditions.

d. Find the average inventory level of the PR-5 watch under this periodic review.

10. Mr. John Estes oversees the distribution of Tastee Snacks products from the plant warehouse to its two distribution centers in the United States. The plant warehouse currently has 47,000 units of the company's most popular product, Chocolate Chewies. Mr. Estes retains 9,000 units of the product at the warehouse as a buffer. The Cincinnati DC has an inventory of 12,500 units and daily requirements of 2,500 units. The Phoenix DC has an inventory of 6,000 units and daily requirements of 2,000 units.

a. Determine the common days' supply of Chocolate Chewies at each DC.

b. Given the above information and your answer to part (a), use fair-share-allocation logic to determine the number of Chocolate Chewies to be allocated to each DC.

11. Stay Safe International manufactures industrial safety equipment at its plant in Evansville, Indiana. The company has initiated distribution requirements planning (DRP) to coordinate finished goods distribution from the plant to DCs in Dallas, Texas, and Lexington, Virginia.

a. Given the accompanying information regarding hardhats, complete the DRP schedule for the warehouse and each DC.

b. Suppose that, without warning, no more than 500 units can be distributed from the warehouse to the DCs in a given week due to a manufacturing breakdown. Hardhats sell for $12 each out of the Dallas DC and $14 from Lexington. Discuss whether the warehouse should delay shipments until both DC requirements can be satisfied or allocate based on need.

Dallas Distribution Center

On-hand balance: 220
Safety stock: 80

Performance cycle: 1 week
Order quantity: 200

	Past due	Week						
		1	**2**	**3**	**4**	**5**	**6**	
Gross requirements		60	70	80	85	90	80	
Scheduled receipts								DC1
Projected on-hand								
Planned orders								

Lexington Distribution Center

On-hand balance: 420
Safety stock: 100

Performance cycle: 2 weeks
Order quantity: 400

	Past due	Week						
		1	**2**	**3**	**4**	**5**	**6**	
Gross requirements		100	115	120	125	140	125	DC2
Scheduled receipts								
Projected on-hand								
Planned orders								

Evansville Warehouse

On-hand balance: 900
Safety stock: 250

Lead time: 2 weeks
Order quantity: 650

	Past due	Week					
		1	**2**	**3**	**4**	**5**	**6**
Gross requirements	0						
Scheduled receipts							
Projected on-hand							
Planned orders							
Master sched.-rept.							
Master sched.-start							

12. Scorekeeper Inc. manufactures stadium scoreboards. Table 1 illustrates the demand for Scorekeeper's scoreboards over the past 25 days. The mean of daily demand is 6 units.

   a. Is the demand distribution normal? How do you know?

   b. Calculate the standard deviation for daily demand. Assume in this case that the performance cycle is constant.

   Table 2 summarizes Scorekeeper's performance cycles over the past 40 replenishments. The expected cycle duration is 12 days.

TABLE 1

Day	Demand	Day	Demand
1	4	14	6
2	3	15	4
3	4	16	2
4	6	17	5
5	7	18	6
6	8	19	7
7	6	20	6
8	5	21	6
9	6	22	5
10	10	23	7
11	8	24	8
12	7	25	9
13	5		

TABLE 2

Performance Cycle (in days)	Frequency (f)
10	4
11	8
12	16
13	8
14	4

    c. Is the performance cycle distribution normal? How do you know?

    d. Calculate the standard deviation for the performance cycle.

    e. Given your answers to parts (b) and (d), find the safety stock required at 1 combined standard deviation under conditions of demand and performance cycle uncertainties.

    f. If the typical order quantity is 36 units, find the average inventory at 3 standard deviations under demand and performance cycle uncertainty.

    g. Scorekeeper is striving for a 99 percent product availability level. Given the above information as well as your answer to part (e), find the function value of the normal loss curve, $f(k)$.

    h. Use Table 7.14 to find the value for k, given your answer to part (g), and calculate the required safety stock for the desired 99 percent availability level.

    i. What would be the required safety stock for 99 percent availability should the order quantity change to 30 units?

13. The XYZ Chemical Company must ship 11,500 gallons of pesticides from its plant in Cincinnati, Ohio, to a customer in Columbia, Missouri three times per week. XYZ has a contract in place with Henderson Bulk Trucking Company as well as with the Central States Railroad. Both carriers are available for the move. Henderson will charge $800 per tank truck, and Central States' rate is $2,500 per tankcar. Henderson trucks can hold a maximum quantity of 7,000 gallons. XYZ has a fleet of 23,500-gallon tankcars available in Cincinnati.

    a. Given the above information, evaluate the cost of each alternative.

    b. What other qualitative factors should be considered in this decision?

14. Shatter Industries Inc. manufactures household and commercial glass products that serve a variety of purposes.

a. Refer to the National Motor Freight Classification 100-S (Table 8.7) to determine the LTL and TL product classifications for the following Shatter items:

   i. Item 86960, glazed glass, boxed.

   ii. Glass slides for microscopes.

   iii. Bent mirror glass, dimensions 7 feet by 5 feet.

b. Shatter ships many of its products from a warehouse in Atlanta, Georgia, to a distribution center in Lansing, Michigan. Refer to the rate tariff in Table 8.8 to find applicable charges for the following shipments over the route:

   i. 5,200 lb. of mirrored shock glass (Item 86900, Sub 1–class 85).

   ii. 32,000 lb. of class 65 product.

   iii. 200 lb. of class 60 product.

   iv. 19,000 lb. of class 150 product.

   v. 2,500 lb. of class 200 product with a 5 percent temporary fuel surcharge added to the line-haul charge.

15. Gigoflop Electronics has three shipments of class 100 product to be transported from Atlanta, Georgia, to Lansing, Michigan. The shipments weigh 5,000 lb, 10,000 lb and 7,000 lb, respectively. Gigoflop can ship each quantity individually or consolidate them as a multiple-stop shipment. Each shipment is to be delivered to a different location in Lansing. The carrier, Eckgold Trucking, charges $50 for each stop-off (not including the final destination). Refer to Table 8.8 and evaluate the costs of shipping individually versus consolidation. Which option should be used by Gigoflop?

16. Stanley Harris, traffic manager of This n' That Manufacturers, is considering the negotiation of a freight-all-kinds (FAK) rate for shipments between Atlanta and Lansing. The company ships 200 (class 65) shipments of 5,000 lb, 40 (class 400) shipments of 1,200 lb, and 30 (class 100) shipments of 10,000 lb and receives a 45 percent discount on published rates.

  a. Refer to Table 8.8 to determine the current freight bill for the above shipments. *Note:* Take the discount from the published rate and round *up* for the applicable hundredweight rate.

  b. Should Mr. Harris accept a FAK rate of $10 per hundredweight?

  c. What factors aside from price should Mr. Harris consider with an FAK rate?

17. Carole Wilson, Transportation Manager of Applied Technologies, has a shipment of 200 computer monitors originating at the company's plant in Santa Fe Springs, California. The shipment, valued at $35,000, is destined for a DC in St. Louis, Missouri. John Miller, receiving manager at the St. Louis DC, has established a standardized transit time for the shipment to be 2.5 days. Mr. Miller assesses an opportunity cost of $8.00 per monitor for each day beyond the standard. Ms. Wilson has three transportation options available.

  a. Cross Country Haulers, a long-haul trucking company, can ship the monitors at a contracted rate of $1.85/mile. The distance from Santa Fe Springs to St. Louis is 1,940 miles. Cross Country estimates that it can deliver the shipment in 3 days. A truck can carry 192 monitors.

  b. The Sea-to-Shining Sea (STSS) Railway can pick up the shipment at the plant's dock and deliver the monitors directly to the St. Louis DC. STSS can ship the railcar of monitors for a flat charge of $1,500. Ms. Wilson has recently experienced delays with the switching of its railcars and expects delivery to take 5 days.

  c. Ms. Wilson has also negotiated an agreement with Lightning Quick Intermodal Inc. (LQI), a third-party carrier that utilizes both motor and rail transportation. LQI can pick up the shipment by truck at the plant and deliver it to an intermodal railyard in

Bakersfield, California, where the trailer is placed onto a flat railcar. The servicing railway, the Rocky Mountain Railway (RMR), then delivers the trailer to another intermodal yard near St. Louis, where the trailer is unloaded and transported by truck to the DC. Lightning Quick offers the origin-to-destination transportation for $2,900. Transit time is anticipated at 2.5 days. From past experience, Mr. Miller has discovered that the additional handling inherent with Lightning Quick's service results in 2 percent product loss and damage. Recovery of these losses is difficult and typically results in only 33.3 percent immediate reimbursement of the losses.

Evaluate the cost of each transportation alternative. What service do you recommend?

18. Moving Hands Inc. ships alarm clocks from Atlanta to Lansing. The company has begun packaging the clocks in a stronger corrugated box to reduce the likelihood of damage in storage and transit. As a result of the improved packaging, the clocks' product classification has dropped from 100 to 85 without significantly adding weight to the package.

   a. What effect does the new packaging have on the transportation cost of a single 1,000-lb shipment? Refer to Table 8.8.

   b. Suppose Moving Hands ships 300 loads of the 1,000-lb quantity each year and the new packaging costs $10,000 to develop and produce. Will Moving Hands realize a full payback of the packaging investment in its first year?

19. Bill Berry, transportation sales manager of Speedy Trucking Company, has considered serving a new customer, El Conquistador Inc., an importer of Venezuelan goods, by hauling 12 truckloads of product each month from the receiving port in Bayonne, New Jersey, to a distributor in Pittsburgh, Pennsylvania, for $850 per truckload. Each serving truck must depart from the Speedy terminal in Secaucus, New Jersey, 12 miles from the seaport. The distance from Bayonne to Pittsburgh is 376 miles. Upon unloading at Pittsburgh, trucks return empty (deadhead) to the Secaucus terminal 380 miles from the distributor.

   a. If it costs Speedy an average of $1.30 per mile to operate a truck, should Mr. Berry accept the business at the negotiated rate? Why or why not?

   b. Mr. Berry has coordinated back-haul moves for the Conquistador shipments above with a new customer in Youngstown, Ohio. The new customer, Super Tread Inc., ships tires from its plant in Youngstown to the port in Bayonne for exporting. Each Conquistador shipment will be accompanied with a return shipment from Super Tread (12 truckloads/month). Speedy will charge Super Tread $1.40 per mile. Bayonne is 430 miles from Youngstown. The distance from Pittsburgh to Youngstown is 65 miles. Trucks must return to the terminal in Secaucus upon delivering product from the back-haul (before picking up again at Bayonne). The terms of the Conquistador agreement outlined in part (a) remain intact. How much can Mr. Berry expect Speedy to profit (lose) per trip from the new arrangement?

   c. How much can Mr. Berry expect Speedy to profit (lose) per month from the new arrangement should the company accept the business?

   d. Is it worthwhile for Mr. Berry to arrange for the back-haul? Why or why not?

20. Super Performance Parts (SPP) produces braking devices exclusively for the Ace Motor Company, an automotive manufacturer. SPP has been leasing warehouse space at a public facility 20 miles from the company's plant. SPP has been approached by a group of four other Ace suppliers with the idea of building a consolidated warehouse to gain transportation and materials handling economies. An investment of $150,000 would be required by each of the five companies to acquire the warehouse. Payment of the initial investment secures 5 years of participation in the agreement. Annual operating expenses are anticipated to be $36,000 for each party. SPP is

currently charged $8,000 per month for use of the public warehouse facilities. SPP's outbound transportation from the public warehouse often consists of LTL quantities. Its annual outbound transportation bill is currently $345,000. SPP expects consolidated warehousing to more fully utilize truckload quantities with transportation expenses shared among the supplier pool. SPP's annual outbound bill would be reduced by 25 percent in the consolidated plan. Differences in inbound transportation costs are assumed negligible in this case.

a. Compare the storage and shipping costs associated with consolidated warehousing as opposed to SPP's current, direct shipping plan. Are any efficiencies apparent through consolidation?

b. Aside from potentially reducing costs, how else might SPP benefit by participating in the consolidated warehouse?

c. What disadvantages might exist in a consolidated warehouse as opposed to a direct-shipping situation?

21. Essen Beer Company has a brewery in Michigan's Upper Peninsula and is setting up distribution at Jackson, Michigan, in the state's Lower Peninsula. Essen packages its beverages in barrels and in 24-can cases. Barrels must be maintained at temperatures below 60 degrees Fahrenheit until retail delivery. The company's logistics department must determine whether to operate individual private warehouses for barrels and cases or to utilize a single warehouse with barrels placed in a carefully controlled environment separate from cases. Assume that cases are not to be stored or transported in refrigerated environments.

Essen experiences a weekly demand of 300 barrels and 5,000 cases. The company has arranged truckload transportation with Stipe Trucking Service. Stipe operates refrigerated and nonrefrigerated trailers, as well as multicompartmented trailers that are half refrigerated and half not. A refrigerated truckload can hold 72 barrels, while a nonrefrigerated truckload holds 400 cases. The multicompartmented trailer can hold 36 barrels and 200 cases. The costs for these services and other related expenses are detailed below:

Truckload costs	
Refrigerated	$550
Nonrefrigerated	$400
Multicompartmented	$500
Warehouse expenses	
Individual warehouses	
For case storage only:	
Capital	$1,250/week
Labor	$2,500/week
For barrel storage:	
Capital	$2,500/week
Labor	$1,600/week
Single, consolidated warehouse	
Capital	$3,500/week
Labor	$3,200/week

a. Considering demand and all costs depicted above, does the single, consolidated warehouse or the two individual warehouses represent the least-total-cost alternative?

b. Now assume that Stipe Trucking Service will provide *only* the multi-compartmented trailers to serve the proposed consolidated warehouse. Which plan is the least-cost alternative in this scenario?

22. Comfy Mattresses Inc. is opening a new plant in Orlando, Florida. Ron Lane, distribution manager, has been asked to find the lowest cost outbound logistics system. Given an annual sales volume of 31,000 mattresses, determine the costs associated with each option below.

    a. Build a private warehouse near the plant for $350,000. The variable cost, including warehouse maintenance and labor, is estimated at $5 per unit. Contract carrier transportation costs $14.50 per unit on average. No external transportation services are necessary for shipment of mattresses from the plant to the warehouse in this scenario. The fixed warehouse investment can be depreciated evenly over 10 years.

    b. Rent space in a public warehouse 10 miles from the plant. The public warehouse requires no fixed investment but has variable costs of $7 per unit. Outbound contract carrier transportation would cost $14.50 per unit on average. The carrier also charges $7 per unit to deliver the mattresses to the warehouse from the plant.

    c. Contract the warehousing and transportation services to the Freeflow Logistics Company, an integrated logistics firm with a warehouse location 25 miles from the plan. Freeflow requires a fixed investment of $125,000 and charges $25 per unit for all services originating at the plant. The fixed investment covers a 10-year agreement with Freeflow.

    d. Name a few advantages aside from cost that the low-cost alternative above may have over the other alternatives.

23. Ms. Sara Ritter is the distribution manager for the Fiesta Soft Drink Company. She is considering full automation of the plant's warehouse. At present, the warehouse utilizes a mechanized system of materials handling. The current system employs 25 laborers at an average wage rate of $15/hour. Laborers work an average of 2,000 hours per year. The mechanization costs $22,000 annually to maintain. The equipment was purchased 2 years ago with uniform payments of $30,000 made annually. In year 9 the mechanical equipment will be replaced by new machinery with fixed annual costs of $40,000. In addition, it will cost Fiesta $14,000 per year to maintain the new equipment with the same 20 laborers.

    The automated equipment would cost $1.4 million upfront for implementation. Only eight laborers and an automation specialist would be required to maintain operations in the new system. The laborers would earn $18/hour over 2,000 hours each year. The automation specialist would earn a salary of $65,000 per year, increasing 2 percent annually after the first year. Much of the old mechanized equipment could be sold immediately for a total of $115,000. Maintenance of the automated system is estimated at $50,000 each year with this cost growing by 3 percent annually after the first year. The automated system is expected to serve Fiesta for 15 years.

    a. Examine the cash flow under each system. What is the payback period for automation?

    b. What advantages aside from long-term cost savings might an automated warehouse have over more labor-intensive systems?

24. Dandy Collectibles is opening a new warehouse. Bob Lee, the warehouse manager, is trying to determine the labor compensation package that most productively utilizes resources. The typical compensation plan offers an hourly wage rate of $15. Mr. Lee is also considering an incentive plan. The incentive plan rewards solely on performance with order pickers earning $0.60/unit prepared for shipping. A typical week shows the number of ordered units that must be prepared for shipping.

    Errors sometimes happen in Dandy's order picking. Product mishandling occurs in 2 percent of the orders under the incentive plan and in 0.75 percent of the orders under the hourly wage plan. Errored orders are scrapped and result in lost revenue of $70 per occurrence. Hourly workers pick 25 units per hour. Incentive workers pick 32 units per hour. Regardless of the plan designation, employees work 40-hour weeks. Union restrictions prevent Dandy from operating on Saturday and Sunday. The labor union also restricts Dandy from hiring part-time workers. Orders need not be filled daily, but all orders must be shipped by week's end (Friday). Assume that hiring and training costs are negligible.

a. How many workers are needed under each plan for the typical week's demand?

b. Which plan meets the typical week's demand at the lowest cost, including lost sales resulting from errors?

25. Mitchell Beverage Company produces Cactus Juice, a popular alcoholic beverage. Recently the firm has experienced problems of product pilferage at the warehouse. In one month, 3,200 bottles of Cactus Juice, representing 0.4 percent of the month's volume, could not be located for shipping. Should the problem go unresolved, it is anticipated that it will continue at this rate. The forecasted annual sales volume for Cactus Juice is 9.6 million bottles. Each bottle sells for $6.50.

Steve Davis, vice president of distribution, has asked you to look into the following security options to reduce the pilferage problem.

a. Hire four security guards to patrol the warehouse floor all hours of the day, 7 days a week. The firm would offer a wage of $16.50/hour to the guards as well as a benefits package expected to be worth $3,000 per employee per year. The presence of security guards should lower pilferage to 0.2 percent of volume. Only one guard would be on duty at any one time.

b. Implement an electronic detection system based on bar code technology. This would require purchasing bar code equipment for the packaging facility and warehouse. Electronic scanning devices must also be purchased and placed at warehouse entrances. Alarms sound whenever a bar-coded item passes through a warehouse entrance without clearance. The electronic detection package, including bar code printers and readers, will cost $125,000. In addition, employees at the plant and warehouse will be trained to use the new equipment at a one-time cost of $10,000. Monthly maintenance of the system is expected to cost $800. Also, a bar code specialist must be hired. The specialist would earn a salary of $56,000 per year. Product pilferage is expected to be lowered to 0.1 percent of volume with the electronic security system. The system has an estimated life of 8 years. Accrue all costs evenly over the life of the equipment.

c. Install security cameras in key locations throughout the warehouse. It has been determined that eight cameras could adequately record warehouse operations. Each camera costs $1,500. The support devices and installation will cost $40,000. Four security guards would be hired for the purpose of viewing the security monitors for suspicious activity. One guard would be on duty at all times. The guards each earns $14/hour, in a 42-hour workweek, and receives a benefits package worth $2,000 per year. Pilferage under this system would be 0.05 percent of volume. The monitoring equipment is expected to have a life of 12 years. Accrue all fixed costs evenly over the life of the equipment.

Should the firm implement any of the options above, or make no investment and allow the pilferage to continue at the rate of 0.4 percent of volume? Compare the costs and benefits of each option on an annual basis.

26. Chronotronics produces two models of clock radios, the X-100 and the X-250 deluxe. Both products are currently packaged in a single-wall corrugation. Through close observation, the firm has discovered that 1.5 percent of both X-100s and X-250s are damaged between packaging and customer delivery. Chronotronics can package either

model, or both, in double-wall corrugated fiberboard, which would reduce product damage by half. The current single-wall packaging costs $1.10 per unit. Double-wall packaging costs 20 percent more. The X-100 and X-250 have market values of $45 and $75, respectively. Damaged units are a total loss. Chronotronics sold 14,000 X-100s and 8,000 X-250s last year. Forecasts indicate consistent sales for the X-100 and a 7 percent increase in X-250 sales over the next year. *Note:* Round up for whole units lost.

a. From a least-cost perspective, should Chronotronics utilize double-wall corrugation with the X-100 next year?

b. From a least-cost perspective, should Chronotronics utilize double-wall corrugation with the X-250 next year?

c. What options, other than packaging changes, might Chronotronics consider?

27. Your firm is planning to introduce a new product line. Your task is to determine the inventory implications of the new product. The typical product will ship an average of 25 units per day from the firm's central DC. Historical sales patterns indicate that the standard deviation of daily sales should be approximately 3. The typical performance cycle for comparable products has been a mean of 7 days and a standard deviation of 2.

a. Assuming a replenishment quantity from the plant of 300 units, what are the safety stock and resulting average inventory for a 95 percent case fill rate?

b. What are the inventory implications (safety stock and average inventory) of increasing the case fill rate objective to 99 percent?

c. What would be the inventory implications for daily replenishment with a 99 percent fill rate objective, assuming that the same level of demand and performance cycle uncertainty is maintained?

28. As the logistics representative on a manufacturer's sales team, you have been asked to quantify the benefits that can be sold to a customer using more consistent service and transportation. The customer wants 99 percent case availability from its distribution centers that are resupplied from the manufacturer. The average daily demand in cases from the customer's DC is 1,500 units with a standard deviation of 250. Historically, the replenishment performance cycle has been 10 days with a standard deviation of 4 days. The customer has traditionally used a 20 percent inventory carrying cost, and the average value of each case is $30. The customer orders weekly an order quantity of 7,000 units.

a. What is the average inventory and annual carrying cost for the current situation?

b. What is the average inventory and carrying cost impact of reducing the manufacturer's performance cycle variation by 2 days?

c. How does reducing the performance cycle variation by 2 days compare with reducing the average performance cycle length by 2 days in terms of average inventory and inventory carrying cost?

29. Spartan Plastics provides components to assembly plants in the automobile industry. Currently, they ship directly from their plant in St. Louis, Missouri, to plants in Lansing, Michigan; Toledo, Ohio; and eight assembly plants surrounding Detroit, Michigan. In total, there are 10 assembly plants that each receives approximately 3,000 pounds per day in shipments. Currently, the company ships LTL from its plant to each assembly plant for a cost of $0.0013 per pound per mile. The company is considering two transportation alternatives to reduce cost. The first alternative is using a milk-run approach where a truckload begins in St. Louis, stops in Lansing, then the Detroit plants, and finally Toledo. The transportation cost for the milk-run approach would be $1.40 per truck mile plus $100/stop, not including the final stop in Toledo. The second alternative is to consolidate a truckload to Ypsilanti, Michigan, and then

cross-dock the components for delivery to the assembly plant by the logistics provider. The truckload cost is still $1.40 per mile, and the cost per delivery to each assembly plant from Ypsilanti is $300.

    a. What are the cost characteristics of each delivery option?

    b. What are the qualitative and service characteristics of each delivery option?

30. Presswick Industries supplies plastics used for medical applications such as pharmaceutical injections and collecting laboratory samples. Presswick produces the containers and tubes and then ships them to customers who incorporate the plastics into kits that are used in hospitals and labs. Currently, Presswick simply loads the containers and tubes into corrugated boxes and ships them to customers who are then responsible for disposing of the corrugated. Presswick is considering the possibility of using returnable packaging with some of its key customers to be more environmentally friendly and perhaps reduce cost as well. The current corrugated cost per unit (container or tube) is $0.07 with an additional $0.03 per unit for disposal. The cost of the recyclable container is $0.30 per unit of capacity that can be used multiple times. The recyclable container does not have to be disposed of, but it must be transported back to Presswick at a cost of $0.03 per unit of capacity. Assume that the recyclable containers can only be used for one year because the plastic in the containers begins to break down.

    a. At what annual volume level does it make sense to use the recyclable containers versus the corrugated containers?

    b. What other qualitative factors should be considered in the decision?

31. Forest Green Products provides private label vegetables for grocery chains throughout the Midwest. They currently have distribution centers in Columbus, Ohio; St. Louis, Missouri; and Minneapolis, Minnesota. The typical annual capacity requirements for Forest Green are 5 million cases with a case split of 35 percent, 40 percent, and 25 percent for Columbus, St. Louis, and Minneapolis, respectively. The company is reassessing its materials handling and storage capability in each facility. The technology alternatives being considered are mechanized, semiautomated, and information-directed systems. Table 3 summarizes the acquisition, annual fixed cost, per case variable cost, and life span of each system alternative. The acquisition and annual fixed cost are quoted in terms of dollars per million units of capacity. In other words, a DC requiring 2 million units of capacity would double the specified cost. The annual fixed cost does not include depreciation for the acquisition cost. Assume that the total square footage of the three DCs is the same.

    a. What system alternative should be used for each DC based on annual cost? How does this decision change if net present value (NPV) is considered over the life of the system? Assume a 10 percent discount rate.

    b. Assume that, for simplicity's sake, Forest Green wants to use only one system alternative for all three DCs. What is the system with the lowest NPV for the life of the system for the combination of DCs?

    c. What other qualitative factors should be considered?

TABLE 3

Materials Handling Alternative	One-Time Acquisition Cost	Annual Fixed Cost	Per Case Variable Cost	Usage Life Span (Years)
Mechanized	$1,000,000	$50,000	$0.30	10
Semiautomated	$3,000,000	$200,000	$0.08	5
Information-directed	$1,500,000	$150,000	$0.15	7

CASE 1

Integrated Logistics for SES/BAG

Steve Clinton

Maxwell Stevens, sales representative for Specialty Engineering Services (SES), felt uneasy as he drove to his appointment at Boston Aerospace Group (BAG). In the past, sales deals with BAG has proceeded smoothly. Oftentimes competitors were not even invited to bid on the BAG business. Nathan Benson, purchasing agent at BAG, claimed that was because no competitor could match SES's product quality.

But this contract negotiation was different. Several weeks before the contract renewal talks began, Benson had announced his plan to retire in 6 months. SES management quickly promoted Tyler Pinto as Benson's successor. Although Pinto had been relatively quiet at the previous two meetings Stevens sensed that it would not be business as usual with Pinto. While the contract decision ultimately depended on Benson's recommendation Stevens felt Pinto might pose a problem.

Pinto, 35, had worked for a Fortune 500 firm following completion of his undergraduate degree in operations management. While with the Fortune 500 firm Pinto had become extensively involved with JIT and quality programs. He had returned to school and earned an MBA with a concentration in purchasing and logistics. Eager to make his mark Pinto had rejected offers to return to large corporations and instead accepted BAG's offer in inventory management.

BAG, an original equipment manufacturer (OEM) for the US aerospace industry makes a wide variety of plastic products for airframe applications. When Pinto began working with BAG's inventory management he applied the 80/20 rule, illustrating to management that 80 percent of BAG's business was related to 20 percent of its product line. Over the next 3 years, as contracts expired with customers and suppliers Pinto trimmed BAG's product line. BAG management was impressed with the positive impact on BAG's profits as unprofitable contracts and products were discarded. A trimmer product line composed primarily of faster-moving products also resulted in higher inventory velocity.

So when Benson announced his retirement plans, management immediately offered Pinto the position. After taking a few days to review BAG's purchasing practices Pinto felt he could make an impact. He accepted managements offer. As he learned his way around the purchasing department Pinto tried to stay in the background, but he soon found himself questioning many of Benson's practices. He particularly distained Benson's frequent "business lunches" with long-time associates from BAG's suppliers. Despite these feelings Pinto made an effort to not be openly critical of Benson. Such efforts did not, however, prevent him from asking more and more questions about BAG's purchasing process.

Benson, for his part, felt his style had served BAG well. Prices were kept low and quality was generally within established parameters. Although Benson typically maintained a wide network of suppliers, critical materials were sourced from a limited number of them. In those cases contract bids were a ritual, with the winner known well in advance. SES was one such winner. Its polymers were a critical feedstock material to BAG's manufacturing process. When Benson began sourcing from SES nearly 15 years ago, there was no question that SES's polymers were the best of the market. BAG's production managers rarely complained about production problems caused by substandard polymers. Benson reasoned that the fewer complaints from manufacturing the better.

"Hi, Max! Come on in! Good to see you. You remember Tyler Pinto, don't you?"

Steven's spirits were buoyed by Benson's cheery greeting.

"Absolutely! How are you Tyler? Coming out from the old horse's shadow for a bit now?"

Pinto politely smiled and nodded affirmatively. Light banter continued as the three moved down the hallway to a small conference room.

"Well great news, Max, SES has the contract again!" Benson paused, then continued, "But there's going to be a slight modification. Instead of the traditional 2-year contract we're only going to offer a 1-year deal. Nothing personal, just that management feels it's only fair to Tyler the last contracts I negotiate be limited to a year. That way he doesn't get locked into any deals that might make him look bad!" Benson roared with laughter at his last comment.

"It is certainly no reflection of SES" Tyler interjected. "It simply gives me a chance to evaluate suppliers in the coming year without being locked into a long-term contract. If my evaluation concerns with what Mr. Benson has told me about SES I see no reason that our successful relationship won't continue."

"Entirely understandable" replied Max as his mind pondered the meaning of Pinto's *evaluation*. "I'm confident you'll find SES's service and product every bit as good as Nate has told you."

Following the meeting Benson invited Stevens to join him for a cup of coffee in BAG's lunchroom. Pinto excused himself, saying he had other matters to attend to.

As they enjoyed their coffee Benson sighed, "You'll be seeing some changes coming, Max. The best I could do was get you a year"

"I'm not sure I understand. As far as I know BAG's never had a major problem with SES's products"

"We haven't" Benson replied. "At least not under the guidelines I hammered out with management. But there will be some changes by next year."

"Such as?"

"Well, you remember when I started buying from SES? You were the leaders, no question about it. Now I knew some other suppliers had moved up since then but I figured, hey, if it ain't broke don't fix it! As long as SES's price was in line, I knew I wouldn't have any troubles with manufacturing. Less headaches for me. Now it turns out Pinto has some other ideas about purchasing. I can tell you for a fact that he's sampled several lots of SES feedstock. He's also invited other potential suppliers to submit samples. The long and short of it is that there's not much difference between SES and the competition in terms of product."

"I still don't clearly understand the problem, Nate."

"In Pinto's terms, product merely becomes a 'qualifying criterion.' If everyone's product is comparable, especially in something such as polymer feedstock, how do you distinguish yourself? Pinto claims companies will need to demonstrate something called 'order winning criteria' to get our business in the future."

"I still don't see a problem. We have our reviews with BAG ever year. Our service performance has always been found to be acceptable"

"True. But acceptable according to my guidelines. Let me throw a number at you. On average BAG schedules delivery 10 days from date of order. I count on-time delivery as plus or minus 2 days from scheduled delivery date. That's a 5-day service window. BAG's minimum service threshold within this 5- day window is 95 percent. SAS had a 96.2 percent record last year using my window. Do you know what Pinto is talking?"

"Probably 3?"

"Exactly. And do you know what SES's performance is if we use a 3-day service window?"

"No, Nate, I really don't."

"Well, Max, sorry to tell you it's 89.7 percent. Worse yet, with Pinto not only will the window decline but also the threshold level will be bumped up to 96 percent. And, that's only going to be for the first 3 years after I retire. After that Pinto is shooting for exact day delivery only with 96.5 percent service capability. Right now using exact day SES only has 80 percent flat. You aren't even close to being in the game"

"So we've got a 1-year contract essentially to demonstrate that we can deliver service as well as product?"

"You understand the problem now."

Polymer feedstock production requires a mixture of chemical compounds. SES's manufacturing process relies heavily on six principle compounds (A–F). SES's current procurement policy is to source each of these compounds from three sources determined through an annual bidding process. Typically the firm with the lowest price is considered the best bid. The top bid receives 60 percent of SES's business while the other two firms received 25 percent and 15 percent, respectively. Management feels this policy protects SES from material shortages and unreasonable price increases. Table 1 indicates the current compound suppliers and their performance statistics (percent of business, delivery time from order date, fill rate). SES currently uses the following performance criteria:

1. Delivery of A: On-time considered 4 days from date of order ± 2 days.
2. Delivery of B: On-time considered 4 days from date of order ± 2 days.
3. Delivery of C: On-time considered 4 days from date of order ± 2 days.
4. Delivery of D: On-time considered 5 days from date of order ± 2 days.
5. Delivery of E: On-time considered 6 days from date of order ± 2 days.
6. Delivery of F: On-time considered 6 days from date of order ± 2 days.
7. Minimum acceptable fill rate on all compounds is 92 percent.

The manufacture of polymer feedstock is highly standardized. SES has continually invested in technologically advanced manufacturing equipment. As a result SES can quickly change processes to manufacture different polymers.

TABLE 1
Performance Statistics of Compound Suppliers

	Chemical Compounds					
Supplier	**A**	**B**	**C**	**D**	**E**	**F**
Company 1	60% 3–8 days 93%	60% 2–9 days 94.5%			15% 5–8 days 92%	15% 6–9 days 94%
Company 2	25% 4–6 days 95%	25% 3–4 days 96%	15% 2–4 days 98%	15% 2–4 days 98.7%		
Company 3	15% 2–5 days 95.5%	15% 2–4 days 98%			25% 5–9 days 97.5%	25% 4–6 days 98.7%
Company 4			60% 4–9 days 96.5%	60% 2–9 days 97%		
Company 5					60% 4–7 days 98.3%	60% 4–6 days 97%
Company 6			25% 3–6 days 98.4%	25% 3–5 days 96%		

Entries list percentage of business, delivery time from order, and fill rate, respectively.

To avoid material shortages and thereby maximize production, SES normally maintains a 7-day supply of each compound. An earlier attempt at JIT manufacturing was abandoned after SES experienced material shortages and production shutdowns. As a result, the manufacturing department is opposed to any reimplementation of JIT-type concepts.

The manufacturing department is electronically linked to the procurement and marketing/sales departments. Marketing/sales receives customer order by phone or facsimile. The orders are then entered into the information system. This allows manufacturing to monitor incoming material shipments as well as schedule production runs. Under this system most customer orders are produced within six to eight days of order.

Following production, orders are immediately sent to a warehouse a short distance from SES. At the warehouse shipping personnel verify manufacturing tickets, match the manufacturing ticket with the purchase order, and prepare shipping documents. Once the shipping documents are completed, the order is prepared for shipment (e.g., 1 palletized1 shrink-wrapped and labeled). Once a shipment is labeled, delivery is scheduled. Three to six days normally lapse from the time an order leaves manufacturing until it is shipped from the warehouse.

Market distribution is divided between the private SES truck fleet and common carriers. The majority of SES customers are within a two-hundred mile radius. SES trucks service these customers via twice a week delivery routes. Customers beyond this delivery zone are serviced through common carriers; delivery time fluctuates according to location and distance but rarely exceeds six days from time of shipment.

Questions:

1. Diagram the SES/BAG supply chain. What stages are adding value? What stages are not?
2. Using the primary SES suppliers (60 percent of business) what is the minimum performance cycle for the supply chain diagrammed above? What is the maximum?
3. Can the performance cycle be improved through the use of 25 percent and 15 percent suppliers? What trade-offs must be made to use these suppliers?
4. If you were Maxwell Stevens, what changes would you make in SES operations? Why? What problems do you foresee as you try to implement these changes?
5. Assuming you can make the changes mentioned in question 4 how would you "sell" Tyler Pinto on BAG's next bid? What will likely be the "qualifying criteria" and "order winning criteria"? Will these change over time? What does this suggest about supply chain management?

CASE 2

Woodmere Products

Judith M. Whipple

John Smith had just returned from what may prove to be one of his most important sales calls. John, a sales representative for a top window fashion manufacturer, had been meeting with a representative from HomeHelp, a major home decorating retailer. It seems the buyer, Nan Peterson, and the product team she heads had just returned from the annual Council of Supply Chain Management Professionals Conference. At the conference, Nan's team had attended several sessions on time-based logistics strategies. Even though Nan and her team had just been exposed to the new strategies, they felt it had the potential for significant competitive advantage in their industry.

At the meeting with John, Nan explained that HomeHelp is an entrepreneurial company that encourages product teams to try new products and channel relations. The few rules a team has to follow are simple: (1) deal only with manufacturers (no independent distributors are contacted) and (2) keep costs low and service high. The second rule highlights HomeHelp's basic business philosophy. HomeHelp is a design and home decorating retail chain that follows the warehouse club format. As such, a premium is placed on maintaining low overhead to support an everyday low price (EDLP) strategy. Service is also a premium since HomeHelp targets two distinct customer segments: do-it-yourself consumers, who need special in-store guidance, and interior decorators, who need speedy checkouts and convenient delivery or pickup.

Nan explained that the team has been considering applying time-based logistics strategies to window fashions in order to improve product availability and the ability to offer a broader variety for in-store customers while reducing overall inventory. HomeHelp's close relationship with professional decorators requires continued attention to improve its profitability to ensure long-term growth. Interior decorators need convenient and exacting service, and HomeHelp feels that time-based logistics applied to window fashions could be an important step to improving competitiveness.

HomeHelp's main concern is that the window fashion industry as a whole appears to be trailing other industries in terms of sophisticated logistics operations. For example, the window fashion industry has invested little in information technology and maintains high inventories throughout the channel, including at the retail level. The high inventories resulted from the variation and complexity in HomeHelp's product line. The results other firms reported for their innovative logistics applications gave HomeHelp a new insight into how an alliance with a window fashion manufacturer might create a best practice distribution system with lower costs and less inventory.

Nan told John that his company, Woodmere, had the potential to achieve an exclusive distribution arrangement with HomeHelp if the two firms could develop time-based logistical capability. Woodmere was chosen since the business press had recently featured articles on its new organization plan that focused on channels of distribution and leading-edge logistics strategies. In addition, Woodmere was beginning to invest in information technology. Nan felt both firms should be able to reduce overall channel cost and offer customers superior product availability. Her specific request was for John to formulate a tentative proposal within 3 weeks to strike while the iron was hot. Nan knew the timing and unexpected opportunity created a great challenge for Woodmere, but she explained that HomeHelp strives to remain leading edge. Furthermore, HomeHelp wants to increase annual growth to 20 percent and feels that window fashions offer the best opportunities. As such, top management attention is on this potential business arrangement.

As John walked to his regional sales manager's office, it was hard to conceal his excitement. The potential agreement HomeHelp offered was enormous. However, the effort required to get all groups at Woodmere involved would be great. The first step was to convince top management of the unique opportunity so that a team could be formed to create the proposal HomeHelp was expecting.

John's boss, Frank Harrison, was on the phone as John walked in. John carefully planned his words while Frank finished his conversation. As Frank hung up the phone, John blurted out, "We've got the potential for an exclusive with HomeHelp, but they want a customized delivery system. The proposal's due in 3 weeks. I think we need the top brass in on this one. It's big."

Frank's reply was typical. "It's not April 1 again already, is it John? What's the problem with our current system? Three weeks! It will never happen." After John explained the meeting with Nan, Frank got on the phone to arrange a senior management review. Surprisingly, a business planning meeting was scheduled for the coming Friday. Frank and John could get on the agenda under new business. What a break! It was Wednesday and John began to reorganize his calendar to concentrate on the Friday meeting.

The first item John focused on was researching HomeHelp. He discovered that Home-Help operated over 400 warehouse style stores in 38 states with the average store being over 80,000 square feet and offering 25,000 different products. Typical sales breakdown is 50 percent wallpaper, 25 percent accessory pieces, 20 percent lighting and electrical fixtures, and 5 percent window fashions. The window fashions sold included (1) cellular shades in various designed, pleated fabrics; (2) wood blinds in a variety of colors and finishes; (3) fashion verticals made in fabrics or PVC; and (4) standard aluminum mini blinds. Woodmere is one of three manufacturers that currently supplies the first three types of window fashions sold at HomeHelp. Woodmere does not offer aluminum mini blinds.

HomeHelp was the industry leader with 10 percent of the $80 billion home decorating retail market. The forecast is for the retail home decorating market to reach $100 billion in five years. Industry observers predict that HomeHelp is positioned to enjoy up to 20 percent of total industry sales. HomeHelp is also the first major player in its market to offer online ordering—competitor's Internet pages offer product and store information only. Online sales are estimated to increase to $500 million by year end. HomeHelp is anxious to see how its online services can be expanded to manufacturing partners to reshape the business and ordering processes.

HomeHelp is dedicated to service. In-store classes illustrate design techniques, repair and installation procedures on wallpaper, drapes, and lighting and electrical fixtures. The classes are taught by HomeHelp's employees, most of whom are retired professional decorators and contractors. HomeHelp provides installation service in a majority of its stores as well as professional decorating services. Both services are offered on a fee basis.

Propartners also tend to be technically sophisticated and, thus, are using the Internet to price competing products as well as compare lead times. Nan would want to involve a group of clients in the Propartner Program in an evaluation of any new strategy.

Second, each HomeHelp store's inventory is restricted to display items plus a limited inventory of fast moving products. Typically, only 20 percent of customer orders for window fashions can be filled from store inventory. This is for two reasons: (1) only standard sizes are held in inventory and (2) typically only high trend colors and fabrics are held in inventory. If a store does not have a window fashion and the order is a standard size/trend color or fabric, an order for the item is forwarded to a regional warehouse where the item is picked from inventory and sent to the store the following day. If the order is highly customized, then a custom order must be placed with the manufacturer. Window fashions from the regional warehouse are available for delivery or customers can pick up 2 days after the original order, assuming the warehouse has stock. Otherwise, the piece is not available for shipment or pick-up for 7 to 10 days because of interfacility transfer or because manufacturer shipment is required.

Currently, 25 percent of all orders for window fashions are custom orders. The remainder are standard products held in inventory at the store or the regional warehouse. However, custom orders are expected to increase as customers select non-standard size windows (e.g., arched or oval window shades). Propartners has also indicated to HomeHelp that the trend is toward more cellular shades and wood blinds rather than standard mini blinds and draperies. Further, consumers want a variety of colors and designer fabrics not generally found in-stock.

Since many Propartners work on remodeling projects, unexpected problems and delays can easily cause schedule changes. On a day-in and day-out basis. The exact time of window fashion delivery and installation is difficult to gauge. Propartners would like to be able to place an order 48 hours (or less) before expected completion to reduce rescheduling.

Working on shorter timetables would improve their efficiency and cash flow and is perceived by Propartners as a major benefit. Currently, Propartners buy mostly from independent dealers who have more flexible delivery programs.

Friday's meeting was long. Frank and John weren't scheduled to present until near the end and they hoped it wouldn't run overtime, forcing them to be rescheduled. Finally, it was their turn. Frank started the presentation and discussed how long and hard a struggle it had been to develop a relationship with HomeHelp. Then John spoke of the benefits. He built on the need to develop new business relationships because Woodmere was involved in an alliance with a retailer in financial trouble. This retailer, Happy Home & Living, had historically accounted for 25 percent of Woodmere's sales, but this figure was dropping dramatically. Happy Home & Living's erratic purchases were creating undercapacity in Woodmere's manufacturing facilities.

Furthermore, HomeHelp had a relationship with decorators, a customer group that Woodmere had been targeting under its reorganization plan. Woodmere's image was as a value leader—good quality at a low price. Attracting professional decorators to its products would definitely enhance Woodmere's image. Furthermore, Woodmere hoped to have some direct contact with professional decorators to get firsthand information on upcoming fashion trends.

Finally, an exclusive arrangement with HomeHelp appeared critical for the future. Window fashion manufacturing is heavily consolidated among a few key players, meaning stiff competition. While the home decorating industry remains heavily fragmented, HomeHelp is a leader and appears positioned to grow faster than competitors. Even though HomeHelp currently only has 10 percent of the market share, they have unlimited growth potential and are often referred to as the Walmart of the home decorating industry.

Reaction from senior management was mixed. While many were excited about the potential, they were also cautious. The long-term relationship with Happy Home & Living that had prospered for 50 years was clearly becoming a potential problem for Woodmere. Relying on Happy Home & Living had created a false sense of security, and when Happy Home & Living suffered financially, Woodmere also suffered. Furthermore, Happy Home & Living's reputation as a quality retailer was beginning to decline. In fact, it was getting the reputation for providing low-quality, outdated products. Top management was afraid to launch another close relationship that tied Woodmere's success to another company. Frank responded that HomeHelp had achieved at least 10 percent growth each year for the last 15 years. The main reason for this growth was its advertising strategy, which convinced consumers who couldn't afford a new home that they could afford to remodel/redesign their current one.

Another concern was the shift in traditional operations necessary to support a customized delivery system. While no concrete evidence was available on the exact requirements of customized delivery, it was still apparent that the service being requested was unique, nontraditional, and might require major reorganization and financial investment. Also, several board members wondered how traditional customers, not interested in time-based logistics, would benefit. Their specific concern was that the commitment to HomeHelp would increase the overall cost of doing business with all customers. In short, some customers would be overserviced at a cost penalty. There was also concern that Woodmere's current system could not provide the service HomeHelp Required.

John agreed these were serious concerns, but reminded the group of the potential benefits that could result from a successful shift to time-based logistics. Not only was the exclusive agreement with HomeHelp important, but this "test case" with a major retailer could forge a leading-edge path for Woodmere, resulting in difficult-to-duplicate competitive advantage. Furthermore, John was convinced that HomeHelp would make a move to time-based logistics with or without Woodmere. After extended discussion, the group decided to assign a task team, with John as the leader, to determine if an arrangement with HomeHelp was in Woodmere's best interest and, if so, to develop the requested business proposal. The proposal would need approval before the presentation to HomeHelp. A special review meeting was scheduled in 2 weeks.

First, John felt the team had to detail Woodmere's current operations. Then, an appropriate time-based system would need to be defined and compared to current operations to isolate changes necessary to offer excellent service support. A modified system would also need to be outlined and the cost and benefits determined. The issue of coexistence of current and time-based response capabilities was also a concern.

Current Operations

Woodmere currently has two manufacturing facilities and six regional distribution centers. One manufacturing facility is located in Grand Rapids, Michigan, while the other is in Holland, Michigan. The Grand Rapids facility produces fabric-covered items, such as cellular shades. The plant in Holland produces wood blinds and PVC verticals. The six distribution centers are located throughout the United States with one adjacent to each manufacturing facility. Orders are received from customers electronically as well as by phone through sales representatives. Only 40 percent of Woodmere's customers are electronically linked to the ordering system.

Woodmere's manufacturing facilities forecast sales to create the production schedule. Forecasts are locked in one week prior to assembly at 75 percent capacity. Three of the distribution centers carry a full line of product inventory and seek to maintain a minimum on-hand quantity for each product. When inventory hits the predetermined minimum, a restock order is sent to the appropriate manufacturing facility. The other distribution centers stock only the fast-moving products. When a customer order is received it is assigned to the distribution center closest to the customer. If the product ordered is not available, the required item is transferred from the closest distribution center that has the required stock. If multiple products are ordered, the original order is held until the out-of-stock item is available to ship so customers receive all requirements in one delivery. No shipments are sent directly from the manufacturing plant to the customer; all orders are processed through a distribution center.

Woodmere's customers are dealers at the retail level who maintain their own inventory of Woodmere's products. When customer inventory is low, they place replenishment orders. These orders are transmitted to Woodmere's designated distribution center. Distribution centers review their orders nightly in an effort to consolidate truckloads and schedule efficient delivery routes. When a full load is available, orders are assembled and loaded to facilitate sequenced delivery. Typical order cycle time is 3 to 6 days when inventory is available at the initially assigned distribution center. Interfacility inventory transfers typically add 2 to 3 days to the order cycle. When an item is backordered to a manufacturing plant, 8 to 12 more days are added to the order cycle. When factory backorders are required, a partial order may be sent to the dealer or retailer; however, no firm policy exists concerning when to ship and when to hold partial orders. Currently Woodmere uses a national for-hire carrier to handle all its outbound deliveries to customers and interfacility movements between distribution centers. This carrier is already working with food and clothing customers that operate on a time-based logistics system.

Time-Based Logistics

John felt it was important for the task team to talk with a representative from another company concerning its experience with time-based logistics. John contacted an old college roommate working at JeanJean, a clothing manufacturer, to see if he could help. John's old roommate, Phil Williams, arranged for John's team to visit JeanJean to discuss QuickJeans, its proprietary time-based system.

In JeanJean's system, retailers play a major role. When a product sells in a retail store, the bar code on that product is scanned, and the POS information is transmitted electronically to JeanJean. POS data detail the size, color, and style of product sold and are transmitted directly to JeanJean's manufacturing facilities where they are used to derive production schedules in response to consumer sales. Rapid movement of information replaces the need to forecast. To the Woodmere team, it looked as though information was being traded for inventory. Product replenishment was exact and done within days of the sale depending on each retail store's volume. For example, high-volume stores receive daily replenishment shipments whereas lower volume retail outlets are served less frequently. The time-based system was flexible and able to accommodate a variety of different replenishment styles based upon individual retail customer requirements.

This type of system reduces response order cycle time and inventory. Since delivery is tied to actual sales, consumer trends are responded to quickly, reducing obsolescence. Furthermore, daily or weekly replenishment cycles allow the retail outlet to carry significantly less inventory while improving stockout performance. JeanJean was also able to reduce inventory by 20 percent by timing production to POS data. This reduction was even more impressive when JeanJean explained that its sales increased by 25 percent. Even though transportation cost doubled, it was more than justified by the savings in inventory and the benefits of knowing for sure that product was needed to service customers.

The QuickJeans solution was technology-driven. EDI used to transmit POS data and bar codes were essential to making the system work. EDI was also utilized for invoicing and payments, advanced shipment notification, and delivery verification. This reduction in paperwork and clerical tasks benefited both JeanJean and its customers.

To implement QuickJeans, JeanJean had to change its fundamental business processes not just with its customers but also within its manufacturing plants. Flexible manufacturing required quick product changeovers to be fully responsive to the POS data. Furthermore, the ability to produce small runs of necessary product was a key requirement.

The management at JeanJean pointed out that one of the most difficult parts of implementing time-based logistics was the sales decline that resulted from "deloading the channel." This "sales hit" was created by the false sense of expected sales and anticipatory inventory that resulted from manufacturing according to forecast, not to actual need. JeanJean had to wait until inventory at the retail stores, retail warehouses, JeanJean warehouses, and manufacturing facilities moved through the channel system before QuickJeans began to work and show the expected benefits. This created tension among JeanJean's top management because it was a cost not originally expected when they bought into the QuickJeans program.

The main cost to implement QuickJeans was the investment in technology. For example, JeanJean invested over $1 million in scanners, lasers needed to make distribution operations fast and efficient, and ticket printers to label products with retailers' unique bar codes. Key retailers spent close to the same amount to purchase new equipment to scan the bar codes. This investment was not a one-time deal, either. The need to reinvest to upgrade technology has remained constant from the start. Some retailers, especially locally owned stores, didn't want to participate in QuickJeans because of the initial investment. However, the retailers that participated were so pleased that most have placed JeanJean on their preferred supplier list.

JeanJean provided John's team with a flowchart of its QuickJeans operation as shown in Figure 1. The chart shows that daily transmission of POS data, as well as any promotional specials, is provided by the retailer. This information is used to calculate an initial production schedule. Inventory already on-hand in JeanJean's warehouse as well as in its retail customers' storage areas is subtracted from the schedule, creating production requirements for all JeanJean's products. These requirements are reviewed by an order specialist, who creates a final production schedule that is transmitted to the appropriate manufacturing plant. This order specialist also manages orders from retailers that are not involved in QuickJeans.

All products are bar coded after manufacturing as required. Delivery is initiated by an electronic Advanced Shipping Notification (ASN) to tell the retailer what products are on the way. Delivery is direct to the retail store unless an alternative delivery site is specified. When the order is received at the designated location, the bar code is scanned and compared to the ASN and invoice. If the information matches, the retailer pays the invoice electronically.

The Proposal

John's team was finally ready to present its time-based delivery system to top management and they hoped the proposal would be accepted. The presentation to HomeHelp was scheduled in 3 days. The Woodmere task team had worked hard and was confident their proposal had strong selling features for both Woodmere and HomeHelp. The special meeting with top management was called to order.

The task team called the project "Customized Distribution: Creating Time-Based Customer Response" and began discussing how the proposal was developed, including the meeting with JeanJean. The team felt that Woodmere could benefit greatly from accepting the HomeHelp challenge.

At the end of each day, POS data from every HomeHelp store on in-stock window fashion sales and on custom orders (not in-stock) will be sent electronically. HomeHelp will not carry any Woodmere inventory in its regional warehouses and will only carry a limited amount of window fashions and display items in each store. The POS and custom order information will be sent to a central information service at Woodmere. The information service will sort the data and compare it to inventory on-hand in each distribution center. Window fashions in-stock will be consolidated while those items that are not in-stock will be added to the production schedule and manufactured the next day. After manufacturing, products will be shipped to the distribution center where the initial consolidation of in-stock items occurred and the entire order will be shipped to the customer via the for-hire carrier. Delivery will be standard for these shipments, meaning an average delivery time of 3 to 6 days. If HomeHelp accepts the proposal, Woodmere expects it can leverage the volume of business with the carrier and achieve a reduction in delivery time to a range of 2 to 5 days. After shipment, the on-hand quantities at the distribution centers will be examined to determine replenishment requirements. If available inventory is too low, replenishment orders will be sent to the appropriate manufacturing plant.

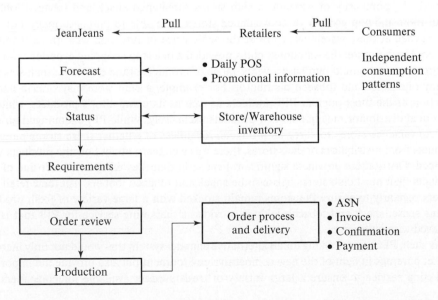

FIGURE 1

QuickJeans: A Time-Based Logistics System

Questions

1. What are the major business propositions for Woodmere and HomeHelp to consider in evaluating this proposal? Is time-based logistics the right strategy for each company?
2. What are the benefits and barriers (short- and long-term) to this proposal for both Woodmere and HomeHelp? What other factors need to be considered?
3. If you were Woodmere's top management, what suggestions would you make to improve the current proposal for long-run viability?
4. If you were HomeHelp, would you accept or reject the proposal? Why?

CASE 3

Alternative Distribution for Prestin Protein, Inc. (PPI)

Judith M. Whipple

Prestin Protein, Inc. (PPI) was considering alternatives to increase market coverage and sales volume on its snack products. Historically, the majority of PPI products were sold to consumers through various grocery and convenience stores. Vending machines and institutional sales, such as airports, represent the remaining consumer market segments. The selling environment for snack foods was becoming increasingly competitive and traditional channels of distribution were being distorted, especially in the grocery and convenience trade.

Grocery and convenience stores were traditionally serviced through distributors known as snack and tobacco jobbers. These distributors purchased PPI products in large quantities and then sold them to retail stores for sale to consumers. The number of snack and tobacco jobbers was decreasing, which was distorting the traditional distribution channel. Two factors were causing this distortion. First, the wholesaler and distributor industry in general was going through consolidation as large distributors continued to get larger and more profitable, while smaller and less profitable distributors either were bought up or closed. Second, the popularity of warehouse club stores threatened snack and tobacco jobbers. Small mom-and-pop grocery or convenience stores were able to purchase many products they needed at these warehouse clubs at the same price or less than what the distributors offered. Furthermore, the warehouse clubs provided a one-stop shopping experience so that the grocery stores could purchase a wider range of products at the club store than was sold by any one snack and tobacco distributor. For example, a club store may offer a narrow selection of the most popular PPI products as well as its competitor's products, while an individual distributor may handle PPI products exclusively. While PPI encouraged grocery and convenience stores to carry its products, regardless of whether these stores purchase products from distributors or club stores, there was a concern about how the products were serviced. Distributors provide a significant benefit in that they carry a broader line of PPI products than most club stores. Also, some snack and tobacco jobbers visit their retail customers regularly to ensure the stores remain stocked with a large variety of fresh product. In this sense, snack and tobacco jobbers provided a marketing service for PPI that is not achieved with club stores.

As such, PPI began looking for an alternative channel system that would not only increase market coverage in light of the new competitive environment but also provide the important marketing service to ensure a large variety of fresh product available for consumers. To

TABLE 1
Alternative
Distribution Concept

What is it?
A unique new concept for distributing and selling PPI snack foods through new retail outlets to broaden market coverage.

How does it work?
Display units of popular snack foods are provided to retail outlets for direct purchase by consumers. Fast-selling items are easily restocked by telephone order with an 800 number and rapid small package delivery service.

What are the special features?
Minimal effort is required on the retailer's part since the popularity of well-known PPI brands makes selling easy. Freshness is guaranteed by direct shipment from PPI's warehouses through rapid delivery service. Incremental money is made by selling high profit "impulse" snack foods to customers at no risk since PPI will remove slow-moving products at no cost to the retail outlet.

accomplish this, PPI questioned the reliance on its traditional marketing channel, as well as the typical outlets through which its products were sold. Andy Joslin, the vice president of integrated logistics, had an idea. Andy began to focus on new retail outlets where PPI products could be sold and how these sales could be uniquely managed via a new channel arrangement. It was determined that direct store delivery of PPI products could be handled by using telemarketing for order processing and small package delivery. The notion was that any retail outlet that had sufficient counter space and high customer traffic was likely to sell high-impulse snack items such as PPI products. Examples of potential retail outlets that traditionally did not carry snack items included dry cleaners, barbers and beauty shops, hardware stores, and drinking establishments. The concept is summarized in Table 1.

The alternative distribution plan offers various benefits. First, it is a unique selling concept in that it provides retailers a way to increase their business through incremental sales of snack products with little risk of cannibalization by other retail outlets due to the impulse nature of the product. Furthermore, retailers are not required to make a significant capital investment to try the concept and there is little risk to the retailer if the plan fails. PPI will provide countertop units or shelving to display the products for sale and will suggest pricing for maximum sales volume and profit. The alternative distribution concept benefits PPI as well by providing market growth and exposing its products to a wider range of customers. Also, PPI will have direct contact with retailers, providing a great opportunity for testing and tracking new products while ensuring timely delivery.

One potential drawback is that the retailers may feel the incremental revenue received is insufficient, which will dissuade product reordering. Also, retailers may have pilferage problems that would discourage their participation. Finally, the arrangements could threaten candy and tobacco jobbers that rely on similar retail accounts. Resentment from candy and tobacco jobbers could potentially result in decreased service to grocery and convenience stores.

From initial interviews with target retailers, PPI became convinced the alternative distribution concept had merit. The next step was to evaluate whether the idea was a viable business decision in terms of retail interest versus actual participation. An internal operating plan for managing the alternative distribution program would also need to be devised to identify and determine the internal costs and potential profit.

Retail Interest

The research summarized in Table 2 illustrates important considerations for retail sales. Fifteen types of retail stores were targeted for participation, and 30 product lines were considered for distribution. Estimates concerning expected retail participation and sales were a critical part of business viability. To start, PPI estimated it could contact only 20 percent of all target retailers. The remaining retailers would be approached after a 1-year test period if the alternative distribution program was successful.

TABLE 2
Retail Characteristics

Sales Regions	Total Number of Target Retailers
Eastern	320,000
Midwestern	290,000
Western	210,000
Percent of retailers for initial contact: 20%.	
Projected retailers who will participate after initial contact: 30%.	
Retailers who will continue after 6-month trial period: 55%.	
Expected average retail sales transactions: $1.40 per customer purchase.	
Expected average unit sale: 1.12 units per customer purchase.	
Expected average customer traffic/retail store: 100/day.	
Expected average number of customers who will purchase product: 10%.	

TABLE 3
Initial Display and
Product Package
Characteristics

	Large	Small
Weight	25 lbs.	14 lbs.
Cubic Feet	2.75	2.00
Product Included	24 lbs.	12 lbs.
Cost of Display Unit	$35	$18
Units of Product	180	92
Production Costs	$190	$98

TABLE 4
Operating Costs
per Order

Costs	Three Distribution Centers	Four Distribution Centers
Handling	$3.00	$3.00
Storage	.11	.21
Transportation of average package	6.25	5.90
Ordering costs/order	.75	.75
Total logistics costs/order	$10.11	$9.86

Two types of display units were designed as well as two reorder packages. An initial order would include two boxes shrink-wrapped together. One box would hold the product and the other would hold the display unit. Table 3 provides display and product package characteristics. Reorder packs would contain the same product weight and units as shown for the initial order.

Operating Procedures

Two logistics networks are under consideration for the new channel. Both networks facilitate direct retail customer contact: no distributors are included in the channel. One network uses three distribution centers while the other uses four. Service for the first network is estimated at 2 to 4 days, with some outlying areas serviced in 5 days. Service through the second network is estimated at 1 to 3 days and to outlying areas in 4 days. The number of outlying areas is reduced under the second network. Table 4 compares the costs of both networks.

The information flow would start with order entry at the telemarketing department. Retail orders would be transmitted to the appropriate distribution center and compiled each night. Orders would be picked and packed, then delivery would be arranged based on the aforementioned service levels.

Summary

Before PPI can determine whether the alternative distribution concept should be initiated, it must analyze the information gathered and project the potential sales and profits. Profits must be determined for PPI as well as for the retail customers. If retailers do not make sufficient incremental profit, it is unlikely they will continue participating in the plan. A team has been assigned to perform the data analysis. Andy Joslin has identified five questions he feels are critical for the team to analyze. These questions are provided below.

Questions

1. Determine the total number of retailers in the program initially as well as after the trial period.
2. Determine what the average retailer will sell on a daily basis as well as annually. Provide sales in terms of unit and dollar amounts. (Assume 260 business days per year, with 5 business days each week.)
3. Translate the annual sales for an average retailer into the number of large packs that retailers will order per year. Repeat for the small pack order. (Round if necessary.) Include the initial order in the calculation.
4. PPI would like to determine its potential sales for the first year on the basis of the information in question 3. However, there is some concern that the estimate of average retail sales is too high. PPI assumes only 40 percent of the participating retailers will actually achieve the average sales and reorders (this group is designated as high performers). Twenty percent of the retailers are expected to have medium performance success and will only sell/reorder 75 percent of the average suggested order. Low-performing retailers represent the remaining 40 percent and will achieve half the sales/reorder expected on average. Calculate the orders (separate initial and reorder quantities) for the 6-month trial period if 45 percent of retailers exclusively order/reorder large packs and the remaining retailers exclusively order/reorder small packs. Calculate the second 6 months accounting for the dropout. (Round if necessary.) Assume the "performer" ratios remain the same after the trial period (i.e., 40 percent are average performers, 20 percent sell 75 percent of the average, and 40 percent sell 50 percent of the average).
5. Assume retailers pay $205 for a large pack (initial or reorder) and $115 for a small pack. On the basis of the first year's sales calculated in question 4, determine the profit to PPI if three distribution centers are used. Repeat for the four-distribution center network. Which network, if either, should be used? What factor(s) aside from cost/profit might influence the network decision?

CASE 4

Westminster Company

Company Profile

Westminster Company is one of the world's largest manufacturers of consumer health products. Its distinctive name and company logo are recognized throughout the world. Originally founded as a family-owned pharmaceutical supply business in 1923, the company has expanded, by virtue of aggressive acquisition and new product development, into a global provider of health care consumer products. Westminster maintains regional offices in Europe, Latin America and the Pacific Rim to support overseas manufacturing and distribution.

Westminster's domestic operations consist of three separate but wholly owned companies that each manufacture and distribute unique product lines. Decentralized management has been a proud historical tradition at Westminster. According to President Jonathan Beamer, the policy of maintaining unique and independent companies encourages responsibility, self-ownership of the product development and marketing process and provides the incentive for entrepreneurial management. Westminster's products are marketed through a network of diverse retailers and wholesalers. Trade class as a percent of sales is 37 percent grocery, 20 percent drug, 35 percent mass merchandise and 8 percent miscellaneous. All three companies sell and distribute products to several of the same customers.

Westminster Today

Pressure from domestic and global competitors, as well as large domestic Westminster customers has recently forced the firm to reevaluate its traditional supply chain practices. In particular, attention has focused on the changes that customers are demanding as well as other operational modifications in current practice that management feels are required to effectively compete in the 21st-century marketplace.

Westminster just completed several months of extensive study focusing on its customers' current and future supply chain requirements. The findings addressed a variety of issues, but two key topics were identified: (1) customer composition and (2) customer service requirements.

The most significant trend with regard to customer composition over the past decade has been the growth of key customers into very large accounts. Mass merchants now account for 50 percent of total corporate sales volume and have become the fastest growing trade category. All three companies sell to this category. This trend is expected to continue into the foreseeable future. The major shift in the mix of accounts is not expected, however, to dramatically alter the historical composition of product sales. Approximately 70 percent of domestic consumer sales volume is concentrated with 10 percent of Westminster's customers. What may affect the composition of product sales to large retail accounts, however, is the rapid growth of private-label nonprescription drugs and consumer health competitors. Cost-efficient private-label manufacturers offer large-retail accounts higher profit margins, and willingness to provide private-labeled products. The private-label health and beauty aids business sales exceeded $5 billion in 2020.

The second research conclusion confirmed senior management's belief that these large accounts have an increasing commitment to improved supply chain efficiency. To maintain and increase the percentage of sales volume Westminster generates from these important customer accounts, management has identified several key customer service improvements. These improvements specifically address the second issue of customer service requirements. Company research has also concluded that the formulation of supply chain collaborations between Westminster and its large customers has now become a competitive necessity. In many instances, powerful retailers demand such collaboration and oftentimes have the leverage to dictate relational arrangement. Westminster will have to maintain considerable flexibility in order to develop unique supply chain solutions for its major customers. Ideally, Westminster would like to establish a position of leadership within these collaboration arrangements.

Westminster's management is well aware that successful retailers and wholesalers are focusing strategic effort on more timely, efficient, and accurate inventory delivery. Many large firms have identified their supply chain management capabilities as a primary strategy to achieve successful inventory management and improving overall financial performance. "I visualize three important changes for our operations with regard to large accounts," says Alex Coldfield, Westminster Vice President of SCM:

First, traditional inventory replenishment procedures must be replaced by POS driven information systems. Customers have the ability to transmit daily or biweekly actual product sales at the SKU level in order to ensure timely inventory replenishment and allow production to be scheduled according to response based sales information rather than forecasts. We will also establish and utilize customer support "work-teams" that operate on-site with key customer accounts to better manage ordering and distribution.

Second, order cycle times can be reduced from current levels. Large accounts will increasingly demand three rather than one delivery per week. In addition, many large accounts want to simplify their procurement practices and are questioning why we cannot provide integrated deliveries of merchandise from our three consumer product companies when cost reductions are achievable. The demand for direct store delivery (DSD) may also significantly increase. A long term goal is to arrange a mix of products from all Westminster companies delivered on a single trailer to key customers, perhaps direct to retail. The long term has become now.

Third, products will increasingly have to meet specific customer requirements, such as assembly of individual store customized pallets and customer-specific inner packs and display units. Bar codes will have to utilize industry standard bar codes and there will be increased demand for RFID capability on unit loads and master cartons. Invoicing and payment, particularly with regard to promotional allowances and discounts, must increasingly move toward paperless transactions. Our pricing will evolve to reflect value-added services as provided, rather than purely traditional logistical order fulfillment, transportation, and handling.

For the balance of Westminster's customers, the smaller retailers, service will be provided much as it is today. Although other customers may not be willing or able to initiate close working relationships, they are entitled to a high standard of basic service that provides timely and consistent performance. For these accounts, purchase price will remain the priority, although there will be some increased pressure for improved order fill rates and decreased cycle times. Traditional purchase order invoicing and payment will also remain the rule.

In response to the issues raised by company research, CEO Wilson McKee directed the company's executive management committee to organize a supply chain taskforce. The taskforce, to include top-level managers from each division, has been directed to identify changes necessary within the three domestic sales' supply chain practices and operational network that will achieve improved distribution performance and responsiveness.

As a framework to guide the integrative redesign, McKee decided to seek recommendations around the eight key processes that link a firm into a supply chain structure with customers and suppliers. McKee remembered a framework he was introduced to at a leadership seminar he attended the previous year. A speaker on supply chain strategy highlighted a set of "Eight Supply Chain Processes" (see Table 1) as a requisite for supply chain excellence. McKee then thought about the performance gaps that existed between present-day and the idealized processes, as well as the measures he proposed to achieve operational integration.

Clearly McKee's initiatives, if implemented correctly, would enhance demand planning and strengthen relationships with customers and channel partners. Moreover, the initiatives also would improve the timeliness and attentiveness of how Westminster fills and delivers its orders. However, implementing the new processes would not be easy, and would represent a paradigm shift from an anticipatory mode, based on forecasts to a more customer-responsive based operation.

The program would require buy-in from the top down to the delivery truck drivers. Furthermore, thinking in terms of key organizational processes, spanning across all divisions and departments, was a significant departure from the autonomous way Westminster companies

TABLE 1
Eight Supply Chain
Processes

Description	
Demand planning responsiveness	The assessment of demand and strategic design to achieve maximum responsiveness to customer requirements.
Customer relationship collaboration	The development and administration of relationships with customers to facilitate strategic information planning, joint planning, and integrated operations.
Order fulfillment/service delivery	The ability to execute superior and sustainable order to delivery performance and related essential services.
Product/service development launch	The participation in product service development and lean launch.
Manufacturing customization	The support of manufacturing strategy and facilitation of postponement throughout the supply chain.
Supplier relationship collaboration	The development and administration of relationships with suppliers to facilitate strategic information sharing, joint planning, and integrated operations.
Life cycle support	The repair and support of products during their life cycle. Includes warranty, maintenance, and repair.
Reverse logistics	The return and disposition of inventories in a cost-effective and secure manner.

had operated in the past. Nevertheless, McKee was steadfast in his belief in the new processes and was eager to deal with the challenges associated with implementing his new program.

Westminster's Distribution Network

Table 2 outlines Westminster's existing distribution network for the three domestic consumer sales divisions. Each consists of a number of company-owned and -operated manufacturing plants and distribution facilities. Table 3 presents a number of key demand and inventory statistics for the facilities.

Each manufacturing plant produces stock-keeping units (SKUs) unique to that particular facility. All SKUs are distributed on a national basis. Due to significant capital outlays and fixed costs associated with each manufacturing plant, the supply chain taskforce has already eliminated the possibility of relocating any manufacturing facilities from their present locations.

Manufacturing plants route products through a distribution center before final delivery to a retail or wholesale customer. Any distribution center may be utilized within its own division. Distribution centers may ship product to any region of the country; however, customers are typically serviced by the closest distribution center based on Westminster's regional boundaries. Transfer shipments between distribution centers are frequently made to achieve an assortment of products for customer shipment.

Most shipments from manufacturing plants to distribution centers are delivered via motor carrier on a truckload basis. Air freight is sometimes utilized for emergency shipments from plants and between distribution centers before delivery to customers. Most shipments between distribution centers and customers are delivered by motor carrier on a less-than-truckload basis and vary in size from a few pounds to nearly truckload quantities. Table 4 shows the three domestic sales companies' shipments by typical weight brackets and the number of bills of lading issued within each bracket. The first weight bracket (0–70 pounds) represents shipments typically delivered by small parcel carriers; the majority of these shipments represent order fulfillment of back ordered SKUs. Approximately 47 to 50 percent of all shipments are 500 pounds or less.

Company A			
Manufacturing Plant	% of Total Pounds Produced	Distribution Center	% of Total Pounds Shipped
Los Angeles, CA	53%	Newark, NJ	28%
Atlanta, GA	24%	Atlanta, GA	31%
Jacksonville, FL	23%	Dallas, TX	41%

Company B			
Manufacturing Plant	% of Total Pounds Produced	Distribution Center	% of Total Pounds Shipped
Philadelphia, PA	39%	Philadelphia, PA	78%
Newark, NJ	37%	Los Angeles, CA	22%
Atlanta, GA	24%		

Company C			
Manufacturing Plant	% of Total Pounds Produced	Distribution Center	% of Total Pounds Shipped
Chicago, IL	75%	Newark, NJ	38%
Houston, TX	10%	Chicago, IL	54%
Trenton, NJ	15%	Los Angeles, CA	8%

TABLE 2
Westminster Company Facility Locations

Characteristics	Company A	Company B	Company C
Total demand (000,000 lb)	150	72	60
Sales ($000,000)	475	920	271
Cases (000,000)	13.2	8.5	9.8
Shipments (000)	80	88	73
Lines ordered (000)	1060	683	340
Inventory turns p/yr	6.5	10.8	7.2
Total SKUs	1260	430	220

TABLE 3
Westminster Customer Demand (2003)

Shipment Size	% of Weight	% of Shipments
Package Delivery	6	25
< 500 lb	8	22
500 – 2,000 lb	13	20
2,000 – 5,000 lb	18	15
5,000 – 10,000 lb	22	10
> 10,000 lb	32	8

TABLE 4
Shipment Profiles

Distribution center locations are based both on market and production factors. The majority of distribution centers are strategically located throughout the country to service geographic territories that contain the strongest demand for Westminster products. Demand patterns for consumer products follow major population centers and are generally consistent across the country for all three companies. Most distribution centers were originally located near manufacturing plants to reduce transfer transportation costs. Demand patterns for consumer products follow major population centers and are generally consistent across the country for all three divisions.

TABLE 5
Westminster 2003
Distribution Costs
($000,000)

Transportation	Company A	Company B	Company C
Transfer freight	4.2	3.2	2.8
Customer freight	9.9	8.3	8.5
Total transportation costs	14.1	11.5	11.3
Warehousing			
Storage & handling	6.2	4.4	3.2
Fixed	2.3	1.6	4.2
Total warehousing costs	8.5	6	7.4
Total logistics costs	22.6	17.5	18.7
Average number of days' transit time (DC to customer)	2.8	2.9	2.3

Table 5 lists the current system's transportation and warehousing costs for each of the three companies. Freight rate classification for product shipments is different for each of the three companies. Division A freight has a rating of class 60, Division B freight has a rating of class 70, and Division C freight has a rating of 150. In general, these ratings reflect the relative expense of moving products based on density and value. Transfer freight costs are based on truckload rates from the manufacturing plants to the distribution centers. Customer freight costs are based on less-than-truckload shipments from distribution centers to retail and wholesale customers. Average number of days' transit time from the distribution centers to the customer is the shipment time from the point an order leaves the distribution center's loading dock until it reaches a customer. Any potential systems redesign must consider the effect of labor costs.

Questions

1. What impact would the three new alternatives have on transfer and customer freight costs? Why?
2. What impact would warehouse consolidation have on inventory carrying costs, customer service levels, and order fill rate?
3. How are warehousing costs affected by the decision to use third party or private warehouse facilities? What effect would this have on handling, storage, and fixed facility costs?
4. What effect would shipping mixed shipments from consolidated distribution centers have on individual company cost and performance?
5. Evaluate the eight supply chain processes in terms of customer classification and degree of centralization/decentralization of required functionality (use the matrix below).
6. Given all available information briefly describe the logistical system design you would recommend for Westminster's integrated consumer products.

	Eight Supply Chain Processes—Classify as "Centralized or Decentralized"							
Retail Segment	DPR	CRC	OF/SD	P/SDL	MC	SRC	LCS	RL
Grocery								
Drug								
Mass Merchant								

CASE 5

W-G-P Chemical Company

John White, vice president of distribution for W-G-P Chemical Company, was preparing for the annual strategy review session conducted by the firm's executive committee. He was charged with the task of evaluating his firm's logistics costs and customer service capability for his firm's packaged dry and liquid agricultural chemicals.

W-G-P Distribution Systems

Figure 1 outlines the existing logistics system for W-G-P Chemical Company. Four types of facilities are used: (1) two continuous, company-owned manufacturing plants; (2) nine seasonal contracted manufacturing plants; (3) three in-transit distribution centers; and (4) 28 full-line distribution centers. Growing environmental activism has influenced management to reject any relocation of the manufacturing plants. W-G-P distributes 129 different products or SKUs on a national basis. For distribution considerations, the products may be grouped into two different categories. Category A consists of 13 SKUs of a product called *Prevention*. *Prevention* is used to minimize weeds in agricultural fields. The sales of *Prevention* are highly seasonal and account for 85 percent of W-G-P's total revenue. The 116 Category B products (called *Support*) sell throughout the year but also have a seasonal pattern similar to that of *Prevention*'s sales. *Support* is used to fertilize the crop. Although the sales volume of Category B is only 15 percent of W-G-P's total revenue, this group of products contributes approximately 30 percent of total before-tax profits. The typical end user of W-G-P's products purchases a variety of both A and B products. In many cases, the products are used jointly in agricultural applications.

W-G-P's total product line is marketed through a network of agricultural dealers. The company sells to the dealers, who then resell the products to farmers. The typical dealer provides farmers with a broad line of products, including those that are directly competitive with W-G-P products. Historically, farmers tend to purchase both A and B products 1 to 2 weeks before field application. Application occurs at different times in different parts of the country and is directly related to the intensity of rainfall. Thus, W-G-P's products must be available precisely when the farmers need them. Likewise, the quantity needed

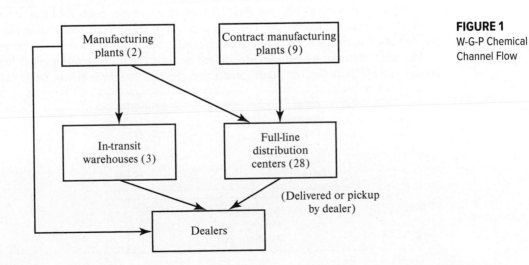

FIGURE 1
W-G-P Chemical
Channel Flow

per acre varies depending on the rainfall received in an area. Therefore, although W-G-P produces *Prevention* and *Support* all year, sales to farmers take place during a very short time period. Farmers' requirements vary in time and duration of use throughout the country.

To even out distribution to dealers across the year, W-G-P offers discount incentives and allowances to dealers who purchase at least 90 days in advance of estimated application dates. This early-order program accounts for 30 to 40 percent of the total annual sales of *Prevention* and *Support*. For the dealer, placing an early order means taking an inventory position on *Prevention* in advance of farmer purchases. However, since both *Prevention* and *Support* products are available, in effect, the early-order warehouse allowance means a special discount of the *Support* products which sell all year. To avoid abuse of the program, W-G-P requires that a proportional amount of *Prevention* products accompany each order. W-G-P also agrees to accept returns up to 15 percent of the total quantity of early-ordered *Prevention* products. The return policy requires a refund of the full purchase price providing dealers repay the return freight to W-G-P's warehouse.

The advantages afforded W-G-P through the early-order program are twofold:

1. W-G-P can schedule shipments at its convenience to achieve the lowest possible transportation cost.

2. Dealers are given an additional discount if their own transportation equipment is used to pick up early orders, provided the cost is less than transportation paid for by W-G-P.

Seasonal sales, those sales which dealers buy within 90 days of estimated application dates, account for 60 to 70 percent of sales. Thus, to a significant degree, seasonal sales volume depends on W-G-P's ability to deliver products rapidly. During the seasonal period, dealers expect *Prevention* and *Support* to be available for pickup at distribution centers within a few hours of order placement. During this period, approximately 50 percent of the dealers pick up products. When transportation is arranged by W-G-P, dealers expect overnight delivery. Although the service level required during the seasonal period is high, these sales are very profitable for dealers because the farmers who purchase the products are willing to pay the full retail price. The capability to provide products during the application period is one of the most important criteria dealers use when selecting a chemical firm. Historically, sales have been concentrated in eight midwestern states which account for 80 percent of annual revenue. Table 1 presents a summary of the most recent data.

The distribution pattern for W-G-P products is relatively simple. Two company-owned manufacturing plants are located in Alabama and Louisiana. The Alabama plant produces *Support*, while the Louisiana plant produces both *Prevention* and *Support*. Both facilities are continuous-process plants, and their location at deepwater ports facilitates economical inbound raw material movement. The nine contracted seasonal manufacturing plants have passed the environmental audits and are strategically located at key transportation gateways.

The three in-transit warehouses are utilized because the manufacturing plants have only enough storage space for 2 or 3 days' production. Table 2 lists the in-transit facility locations.

TABLE 1
Annual Sales

Dollars	525,146,747
Weight (lb)	242,717,768
Cubic feet	26,887,513
Cases	2,912,753
Product lines per order	25,392
Orders	19,139

TABLE 2
In-Transit Warehouses

Birmingham, AL
Memphis, TN
Alexandria, LA

Indianapolis, IN	Brooklyn Center, MN
Memphis, TN	Rockford, IL
Ennis, TX	Memphis, TN
Alexandria, LA	Phoenix, AZ
Fresno, CA	Orlando, FL
Baton Rouge, LA	Milwaukee, WI
West Helena, AR	Goldsboro, NC
West Sacramento, CA	Des Moines, IA
Greenville, MS	Decatur, IL
Weslaco, TX	Columbia, SC
Omaha, NE	Pennsauken, NJ
Evansville, IN	Houston, TX
Albany, GA	Lubbock, TX
Montgomery, AL	Charlotte, MI
Birmingham, AL	Lima, OH
Kansas City, MO	

In terms of total system, the in-transit warehouses have three functions: (1) to provide storage until forward shipments are required; (2) to postpone the risk of advance shipments; and (3) to provide a combination of transportation rates that are lower to field distribution centers than the sum of published rates into and out of the in-transit warehouse. In a sense, the in-transit warehouses are economically supported by special transportation rates. All warehouses and distribution centers in the W-G-P system are public facilities. Therefore, W-G-P's costs are based on volume throughput and duration of storage. The 28 full-line distribution centers are primary facilities from which dealers are served. Although some early orders are shipped directly from plants and in-transit warehouses to dealers, they represent less than 10 percent of the annual tonnage shipped to dealers. Ninety percent of all tonnage is either shipped from or picked up by dealers at the full-line distribution centers. Table 3 provides a list of distribution center locations. Replenishment of distribution center inventories is primarily on an allocation basis controlled by central inventory planning. All orders are processed in an online basis at the central office after they are received over a telecommunications network. The elapsed time from order entry to shipment release from the distribution center is less than 24 hours. The primary method of shipment from plants to in-transit warehouses and distribution centers is motor carrier.

The System Review

A primary objective of the physical distribution system review is to evaluate the cost and service levels of the existing program in comparison with alternative methods of operation. Despite relatively smooth operations, the fact remains that at the end of each application season, many dealers' requirements have not been satisfied, while other dealers have returned inventory. Thus, sales are lost that could have been enjoyed if products had been available to the dealers in need. A critical element of customer service is forward inventory availability to accommodate customer pickup. In preparing the study, John White asked the Accounting Department to provide standard costs. The following standards were developed:

1. Order processing at a standard fixed cost per month with a variable cost per order.
2. Inventory at before-tax cost of 18 percent per annum of average inventory per field warehouse location.

TABLE 4
Distribution Cost

Storage	$ 3.1 million
Handling	$ 1.3 million
Ordering	$ 3.5 million
Average Inventory level	$ 90.0 million
Transportation to warehouse	$ 2.3 million
Transportation transfer between distribution centers	$ 1.2 million
Transportation to customers	$ 5.6 million

3. Handling and storage at actual local cost for each existing and potential facility. Appropriate storage rate applicable at in-transit warehouses.

4. Inbound transportation from plants and in-transit warehouses to field warehouses based on point-to-point rates.

Table 4 contains the costs for the reference year.

Questions

1. What is the total distribution cost for W-G-P Chemical Company? What is the cost per pound, cubic foot, case, line, and order? How can these measures contribute to the distribution review process?

2. On a map, plot the distribution facilities and network for W-G-P Chemical Company. What product and market characteristics can help explain this distribution structure?

3. What alternative methods of distribution should W-G-P consider for *Prevention* and *Support*?

4. Discuss the rationale for:
   A. The early order program.
   B. Customer pickup policies.
   C. Use of public versus private warehouse facilities.

CASE 6

Western Pharmaceuticals (A)

George Castro had a lot to be proud of. His company, Western Pharmaceuticals, had just merged with the largest producer of over-the-counter (OTC) cold remedies on the East Coast. The merger with Atlantic Medical should guarantee coast-to-coast market penetration for both Western's upset stomach products and Atlantic's cough syrups. George had been selected to serve as CEO of the newly formed United Pharmaceuticals, and was rapidly becoming recognized as being one of the top Mexican American business leaders in the country.

History

Western Pharmaceuticals had been founded by George's grandfather in post-war Los Angeles. Tony Romero's reputation for hard work combined with his strong pharmaceutical background made the introduction of his first antacid tablet an unqualified success in the booming downtown area. The company grew quickly and soon became the largest producer of antacid tablets in central and southern California.

George's father, Rudy, married in to the Romero family in 1961. Although not a pharmacist, Rudy received a degree in urban planning from Pepperdine University. After many heated discussions with his new son-in-law, Tony acted on Rudy's advice to expand the company outside of the now congested Los Angeles city limits. Tablet production would now take place in tiny Ontario, some distance to the east of LA. The urban site, conveniently located in proximity to several major freeways and a railhead, would now serve only as a distribution center.

Rudy's suggestion to separate production and distribution worked. Ontario offered markedly lower rent and labor costs than Los Angeles, but was close enough to the city to prevent any significant inconveniences. Additionally, allowing the Los Angeles site to focus only on distribution led to significant economies. Western Pharmaceutical flourished.

Upon his father-in-law's recommendation, Rudy enrolled in business school and received his MBA from Cal-State Los Angeles in 1968. Rudy was subsequently appointed executive vice-president of Western and quickly focused on expanding and diversifying the company. Aside from seeking new products, Rudy recognized the importance of a viable distribution system to market penetration. A second distribution center was constructed in Indianapolis, and Western Pharmaceuticals became the market leader of Nevada and Arizona by mid-1991. By 1992, Western had a dominant position in the Northwest, Utah, Idaho, and New Mexico, and was making significant inroads in Colorado. Upon Rudy's recommendation, Tony pursued the acquisition of Central Solutions, a small Midwestern firm that manufactured liquid antacids. Although Central was a struggling company, its acquisition allowed Western Pharmaceutical to diversify into the liquid market. More importantly, Western obtained distribution centers in Nebraska and Nevada. Midwestern market share and profits followed.

George started working part-time as a warehouseman in the Los Angeles distribution center in 1998. After graduating from UCLA in 2002, George worked as a production manager at the Ontario site. By the time George earned his MBA in 2006, Western Pharmaceuticals had conquered the majority of the West and Midwest and was now eyeing the South. In 2008, Western opened its newest distribution center near Atlanta's inner beltway. Construction of the Atlanta site made access to the South and Southeast significantly more efficient, and market share increased accordingly.

By 2016, Western Pharmaceuticals was recognized as a "cash-cow" in the stomach upset industry. No longer an innovator, Western had well-recognized products that retained their market share through creative and aggressive advertising campaigns. Rudy, now president of the company, was content to leave the company in its current state. This led to some amount of disagreement between him and his son. George, always the "go-getter," had developed an aggressive reputation within the company and frequently encouraged his father to tackle the East Coast.

George became the president of Western Pharmaceuticals after his father's retirement in mid-2017 and immediately began his pursuit of the East Coast. Atlantic Medical offered everything that he felt Western needed in order to guarantee its continued success. First, the company offered cold remedies, something that Western had considered but never pursued. Second, the company had key East Coast distribution centers in Mechanicsburg, PA., and Atlanta, GA. George was convinced that the successful merger of the companies would guarantee nationwide success in the OTC market for antacids and cough syrups.

Present

The newly formed United Pharmaceuticals was comprised of six factories and seven distribution centers. The newly formed company produced six product categories (A–F) with nationwide market penetration. Now that the company had achieved a coast-to-coast presence, George looked internally for further efficiencies. Namely, based on production and

TABLE 1
Western Pharmaceuticals
Current Plants and
Distribution Centers

Plants	Distribution Centers
Columbus, OH	Atlanta, GA
Omaha, NE	Indianapolis, IN
Ontario, CA	Los Angeles, CA
South Bend, IN	Omaha, NE
	New Brunswick, NJ

TABLE 2
Atlantic Medical Plants
and Distribution Centers

Plants	Distribution Centers
Buffalo, NY/Toronto, ONT	Atlanta, GA
Newark, NJ	Mechanicsburg, PA
	Sparks, NV

TABLE 3
Plant Production Profile

Plant	Products Produced	Source Division	Percent of Weight
Ontario, CA	A	WP	48
Columbus, OH	B	WP	6
South Bend, IN	C	WP	4
Omaha, NE	D	WP	7
Newark, NJ	E	AM	11
Buffalo/Toronto, ONT	E	AM	10
Buffalo/Toronto, ONT	F	AM	14

handling costs and inbound, outbound, and service costs, were all of the distribution centers necessary?

Table 1 lists the pre-merger, Western Pharmaceuticals plants and distribution centers. Table 2 lists the pre-merger plants and distribution centers for Atlantic Medical.

Table 3 lists the production capability and percent of volume for each plant.

Even though both firms utilized contract warehouse facilities, there are fixed costs incurred for each facility due to management and technology. Each Distribution Center operates with fixed costs of $300,000. The handling cost at each distribution center is estimated at $1.00/cwt. The handling cost covers the labor and equipment required to receive shipments from plants, put-away, order picking, and truck loading.

For accounting and inventory carrying cost purposes, each pound of inventory is valued at $5/lb. Finished goods inventory turns in the distribution centers have historically been 3.5 turns annually for Western Pharmaceuticals and 3.0 turns annually for Atlantic Medical. Each product at the distribution centers is typically replenished on a bi-weekly basis.

Table 4 lists the current service areas for each division and state. While there are numerous exception shipments, each state is generally served by its assigned distribution center.

At this time, the production capacity of the combined firm is 100 percent utilized. As a result, it is not possible to shut down any production capacity. It is possible, however, to shift capacity around to different plants for a one-time charge of $500,000. This covers the cost to prepare the new site, tear down the equipment, transfer it, set up, and recalibrate it at the alternative plant location.

Customer satisfaction requires that all products for a single customer must be shipped from a common distribution center. This implies that shipments cannot be made directly from any plants. The integrated firm has operationalized this policy by requiring that each state should be assigned to only one distribution center source. The firm also requires that 95 percent of the volume be within 2 days transit of the servicing distribution center. This effectively means that 95 percent of the volume must be within 750 miles of the servicing distribution center.

TABLE 4
Historical Service Areas

State	AM Service Location	WP Service Location
AK	Sparks	Los Angeles
AL	Atlanta	Atlanta
AR	Atlanta	Atlanta
AZ	Sparks	Los Angeles
CA	Sparks	Los Angeles
CO	Sparks	Omaha
CT	Mechanicsburg	New Brunswick
DC	Mechanicsburg	New Brunswick
DE	Mechanicsburg	New Brunswick
FL	Atlanta	Atlanta
GA	Atlanta	Atlanta
HI	Sparks	Los Angeles
IA	Mechanicsburg	Omaha
ID	Sparks	Omaha
IL	Mechanicsburg	Indianapolis
IN	Mechanicsburg	Indianapolis
KS	Mechanicsburg	Omaha
KY	Mechanicsburg	Indianapolis
LA	Atlanta	Atlanta
MA	Mechanicsburg	New Brunswick
MD	Mechanicsburg	New Brunswick
MI	Mechanicsburg	Indianapolis
MN	Mechanicsburg	Omaha
MO	Mechanicsburg	Omaha
MS	Atlanta	Atlanta
MT	Sparks	Omaha
NC	Atlanta	Atlanta
ND	Mechanicsburg	Omaha
NE	Mechanicsburg	Omaha
NH	Mechanicsburg	New Brunswick
NJ	Mechanicsburg	New Brunswick
NM	Sparks	Los Angeles
NV	Sparks	Los Angeles
NY	Mechanicsburg	New Brunswick
OH	Mechanicsburg	Indianapolis
OK	Atlanta	Omaha
OR	Sparks	Los Angeles
PA	Mechanicsburg	New Brunswick
PRO	Atlanta	Atlanta
RI	Mechanicsburg	New Brunswick
SC	Atlanta	Atlanta
SD	Mechanicsburg	Omaha
TN	Atlanta	Atlanta
TX	Sparks	Los Angeles
UT	Sparks	Omaha
VA	Mechanicsburg	New Brunswick
VT	Mechanicsburg	New Brunswick
WA	Sparks	Los Angeles
WI	Mechanicsburg	Indianapolis
WV	Mechanicsburg	New Brunswick
WY	Sparks	Omaha

The accompanying Excel spreadsheet [spreadsheet can be found at www.mhhe.com /bowersox5e <http://www.mhhe.com/bowersox5e>] contains three worksheets. The first, "Weight by State," lists the number and total weight of the current shipments going to each state. The volume is broken down into LTL (less-than-truckload) and TL (truckload) shipments and includes a standard mixture of all products. For products that have multiple production sites, each distribution center is sourced from the nearest plant. The second worksheet, "Customer Rates," contains the LTL and TL rate (per cwt.) from each distribution center to the major city representing each state. These rates are based on the discounted ZIP to ZIP rates provided by Western's major carrier. The third worksheet, "Inbound," provides the inbound TL rates from each plant to each distribution center. These rates are also in $/cwt.

CASE 7

Western Pharmaceuticals (B)

Once George initiated the supply chain design project (see Western Pharmaceuticals A), his next task was to investigate the firm's inventory management capability relative to the refined supply chain. The integration of the Western and Atlantic Medical distribution systems required a refinement of the firm's inventory management system. [spreadsheet can be found at www.mhhe.com/bowersox5e <http://www.mhhe.com/bowersox5e>].

Although the firm wanted to have a comprehensive inventory analysis, the information available was limited due to the merger and a simultaneous move to an enterprise resource planning system. In fact, in terms of quickly available data, there was only a limited sample from the Atlantic Medical sales and inventory records. For a sample of 100 stockkeeping units (SKUs), the database includes the average and standard deviation of weekly sales, average order cycle time (OCT), replenishment order quantity (OQ), and the average inventory. Based on history, the current standard deviation in the replenishment cycle time is 1 week. The sales, order quantities, and inventory are recorded in cases. The historical information is provided for each of the three existing distribution centers.

Atlantic believes that the historical case fill rate is 95 percent but they are not really sure.

Questions

1. What should the case fill rate be for each product given the current uncertainty levels and order quantities and how does the calculated aggregate case fill rate differ from the historically observed level?

2. What are the safety stock and average inventory levels for each product and in aggregate necessary to achieve 95 percent case fill rate for each product? To what extent do the actual inventory levels deviate from the theoretical inventory levels? What conclusions can you draw from the differences?

3. What is the inventory carrying cost impact for increasing the case fill rate from the current level of 95 percent to 99 percent? Assume an annual inventory carrying cost of 20 percent. Assuming that 5 percent is potentially lost due to stockouts (100 – 95 percent) and that there is a 25 percent margin on the average item (COGS = 75 percent), would you recommend that the service level be increased? Justify your answer.

4. What would be the impact on inventory and service of consolidating all of Atlantic Medical stock into a single facility? Apply both the "square root of N" and item level approaches. The square root of N should be applied to aggregate inventory values for a total of all products. The item level approach uses the individual standard deviations. Discuss the differences between the two approaches. Why?

CASE 8

Customer Service at Woodson Chemical Company

From the perspective of Melinda Sanders, the problems of Woodson Chemical Company (WCC) were straightforward and easily identifiable. Solutions, however, appeared to be far more difficult and complex. Sanders had just turned 29 years old and was in her sixth year of employment with WCC. After graduating from a top university in the western United States with an MBA in marketing, she had steadily progressed through a series of positions in marketing, sales, and distribution operations. Her current position is lead distribution planner in the Chemicals and Performance Products Division of WCC North America.

The most recent WCC North America customer service report revealed that "customers continually give the company average-to-poor marks in customer service performance. In particular, customers express extreme dissatisfaction with the order-information process." Sanders was of the opinion that the more WCC sales and distribution systems were expanded, the more management and communication bottlenecks seemed to be created. She was also well aware that the issue of order information status was problematic throughout all of WCC's North American operations. Each division had been hard at work over the past 18 months developing and instituting a variety of software packages aimed at improving its service performance. During a recent meeting with Barry McDonald, WCC North America Chemical and Performance Products Director of Customer Service, Sanders had been given a copy of a report regarding projected directions and importance ratings of customer service requirements in the chemical industry. The report stated

> Customers specifically desire instantaneous access to real-time order information status. This information accessibility is necessary throughout the supply chain—from the customer's initial inquiry to production status, shipment loading, and arrival at the final destination. A critical goal is to be able to both commit and monitor inventory from the point in time an order is placed. While the goal of integrated logistics is a major goal for many chemical companies, efforts are frequently being hindered by inadequate information systems and organization structural design.

Woodson Chemical Company

WCC was founded in 1899 by Alexander Woodson. The company originally was located in southeast Texas. In the early 1960s the corporate headquarters were moved to St. Louis to capitalize on the city's central geographic location. Approximately one-third of WCC's business is conducted overseas. Most arrangements are wholly owned subsidiaries; there are few industrialized countries in the world where WCC does not have some manufacturing or sales presence. WCC North America, a wholly owned subsidiary of Woodson Chemical Company, is the sixth largest chemical company in North America and produces a diversified range of chemicals used as raw materials for manufacturing in the food, personal care products, pharmaceuticals, pulp and paper, and utility industries.

The company operates four product groups which are broken down into three divisions (see Table 1). Division 1 comprises chemicals and performance products, which are mainly used as raw materials in the manufacture and/or processing of consumer products. Division 2 is composed of two product groups: plastic products, and hydrocarbons and energy. Plastic products are utilized in numerous markets such as packaging, automotive, electrical appliances, building and construction, housewares, recreation, furniture, flooring, and health care. The hydrocarbons and energy group is concerned with the purchase of

TABLE 1
WCC Sales 2011–2015
($000,000)

Division	2011	2012	2013	2014	2015
1 : Chemicals and Performance Products	$ 3,630	$ 3,785	$ 3,562	$ 3,165	$ 3,130
2 : Plastic Products,	4,857	4,896	5,174	4,775	4,701
Hydrocarbons and Energy	1,051	1,243	1,547	1,353	1,214
3 : Consumer Specialties					
Medical Health					
Agriculture					
Consumer Products	2,120	2,387	3,537	3,838	4,184
Total	$11,658	$12,311	$13,820	$13,131	$13,229

TABLE 2
Selected WCC
Operating Costs and
Expenses—2011–2015
($000,000)

	2011	2012	2013	2014	2015
Costs of Goods Sold	$6,864	$7,335	$9,125	$8,863	$8,893
Research and Development	540	611	795	811	902
Promotion and Advertising	291	346	447	505	557
Selling and Administrative	1,138	1,231	1,459	1,527	1,630
Total	$8,833	$9,523	$11,826	$11,706	$11,982

fuels and petroleum-based materials as well as the production of power and steam used to manufacture WCC's plastics, chemicals, and metals. Division 3 comprises consumer specialties, which serve the food care, home care, and personal products markets.

In terms of functional support, each division maintains its own marketing, manufacturing, logistics, and administrative departments. Currently, divisional information processing responsibilities for customer service, transportation, and warehousing are provided by the logistics group. Information processing responsibility for finance and accounting are provided by the administration group. Figure 1 (Figure 1 can be found at www.mhhe.com /bowersox5e <http://www.mhhe.com/bowersox5e>) presents the organization structure for WCC North America's operations.

Across the four product groups, performance has varied considerably over recent years. Although chemical and performance product sales have been declining or flat, increased volume and profit improvement is projected due to growth opportunities. In Division 2, plastic products has exhibited reduced sales; although moderate growth is attainable, prices are projected to remain under pressure due to a weak global economy and considerable industry oversupply. Hydrocarbons and energy sales have declined significantly in the past 3 years; although feedstock and energy purchase costs have been reduced, lower sales have more than offset procurement savings. Industry overcapacity remains a severe problem; additional capacity coming online in developing industries in Korea and China will only exacerbate the situation. Consumer specialties continues to exhibit very strong sales gains, particularly in medical and health and consumer product categories. Agricultural sales are relatively unchanged. Steady growth for consumer specialties is projected to continue, although perhaps not at the rapid rate of the past 5 years.

A significant concern of WCC management is the major cost and expense areas of distribution and marketing (see Table 2). The company has made considerable progress in reducing the cost of purchased raw material inputs, but other category expenses are increasing at a rate in excess of sales.

Industry Background

Chemical manufacturing has historically been a very cyclical industry; recessions and periods of slow economic growth typically depress chemical industry sales for several years at a time. As economies begin to rebound, manufacturing picks up and chemical production often leads the U.S. economy into a recovery period.

The chemical industry's attempts to alter its strategic planning with regard to markets and strategy are changing. The expansion of a global economy and leading-edge chemical technology have dramatically altered the manner in which the chemical industry operates today. In the past, a large, fully integrated chemical company with control of raw materials, economies of scale, and modern plants possessed significant cost advantages that could eliminate marginally efficient chemical producers throughout the world. Today, such a strategy is easily negated. The availability of cutting edge chemical technology that goes into building premier chemical plants can make a low-cost producer out of most any company that can structure an arrangement for a constant supply of chemical feedstock from an oil-producing country. Contemporary competitive advantage is typically derived from a focused market position, good raw materials supply without the heavy investment required in a completely vertically integrated structure, and a lean efficient organization structure. Industry leaders must maintain efficient resource and organization structure while they leverage their technological expertise across as many chemical applications as possible. In addition, many chemical manufacturers are diversifying into specialty chemicals in an attempt to balance the cyclical nature of their earnings.

Faced with mounting pressure to become increasingly globalized, especially during difficult economic conditions, chemical industry information systems leaders are scrambling to implement more cost-efficient and effective strategies to track and share business information. Angela Lowrey, director of WCC North America's Information Resources Planning, says, "Better logistics information across business divisions is integral to instituting a strategic business plan. With current spending on computer information systems accounting for approximately 2 percent of corporate revenues, [business] information is a premium commodity and a potential strategic asset that many firms in our industry are just beginning to recognize."

The determination of where to focus chemical operations is also becoming increasingly complex as the geographic nature of the industry changes economically. Uncertainty in Eastern Europe, rapid growth in the Pacific Rim, and potential markets in Latin and South America and the Caribbean have upset the traditional patterns of global chemical manufacturing. Very high research and development costs are necessary to maintain a steady stream of high-margin, new products. Environmental problems and liability issues are a significant concern for the chemical manufacturing industry. Although compliance with increasingly stringent emission controls has improved the relationships among chemical manufacturers, government, and public interest groups, the transportation and handling of hazardous materials remains a high-profile issue, particularly in North America and Western Europe.

WCC North American's Distribution Network

WCC North America produces and sells more than 1,500 products in many different formulations, packaging containers, and labeling arrangements. The products are manufactured at one or more of the 22 manufacturing locations in the USA, and are distributed through 5 WCC distribution centers to field warehouses and then to 325 stocking points (cooperatives and dealers). Table 3 lists the WCC manufacturing plants and distribution centers located in North America.

Chemical manufacturing does not maintain significant levels of WIP (work-in-process) inventories and managing them is typically not difficult. However, managing finished goods inventories is a considerable problem. Short customer lead times, high customer service levels, large manufacturing and distribution replenishment quantities, and long manufacturing and distribution lead times require that many products be in inventory when customer orders are received. The size and complexity of the WCC distribution network makes distribution management complex and difficult.

TABLE 3
WCC North
America's
Distribution Network

Manufacturing Plants	Distribution Centers	
Schaumburg, IL	Gary, IN	Reno, NV
Los Angeles, CA	Omaha, NE	Louisville, KY
Harrisburg, PA	Spokane, WA	Shreveport, LA
Memphis, TN	Denver, CO	Charlotte, NC
New Orleans, LA	Little Rock, AR	Omaha, NE
Shreveport, LA	Raleigh-Durham, NC	
St. Louis, MO	Morristown, NJ	
Houston, TX	Toledo, OH	
Lubbock, TX	Wilmington, DE	
Tulsa, OK	Jacksonville, FL	
Montgomery, AL	Billings, MT	
Field Warehouses (as necessary) Primary public facilities		
Dealers and Cooperatives Contractual throughout North America		

According to Melinda Sanders, WCC's management structure does not match up well to the firm's needs of supply chain management. Recently, however, the firm has begun to implement an integrated logistics system to coordinate planning, purchasing, manufacturing, marketing, and distribution functions. Increased attention has been directed to the problems of providing manufacturing with the necessary information to determine the level of individual SKU production (via MRP) as well as how much and where to deploy products (via DRP). Improved communication among marketing, manufacturing, and distribution has led to better forecasts of IT customer demand.

However, although each division of WCC is beginning to operate in a more integrated manner, each division continues to maintain separate responsibility for customer orders and information status. Each division also designs, plans, and executes its manufacturing, warehousing, picking, and loading activities. The majority of warehouses utilized are public facilities. Transportation is provided by common and contract carriage and railroad. A significant portion of WCC's product moves by rail; in fact, WCC owns and operates a sizeable private railcar fleet due to the specialized nature of its products. The link between transportation and customer service is a vital component at WCC. "Logistics at WCC North America's Chemicals and Performance Products Division is a competitive tool," says Logistics Manager Michael Davidson. "I make sure that we always have more than enough carriers on our inbound and outbound traffic lanes to keep product moving throughout our system."

Traditionally, a general level of attention to customer service was acceptable but as WCC restructured its divisional operations by product grouping and, in particular, diversified into specialty chemicals, the requirements across divisions have become very differentiated. The complexity of customer service is additionally complicated because each division serves a considerable number of common customers, many of whom are high-volume, key accounts. WCC North America's decentralized divisional structure has historically allowed each division to provide tailored, high-quality customer service to meet the differentiated and demanding requirements of WCC customers. The ability to tailor such services is considered a competitive strength at WCC. Sales, marketing, and cost control efforts are becoming increasingly customer responsive—the level of focus is now not only division-specific but also individual customer account-specific. In particular, the Consumer Specialties Division serves a highly time-sensitive market that includes many powerful, large retailers and mass merchandisers.

Melinda Sanders and her staff have a meeting scheduled tomorrow morning with Douglas Liddell, vice president of WCC's Corporate Information Systems Group, to discuss the direction of WCC North America's Chemicals and Performance Products Division.

Sanders strongly believes that any investment in information systems should directly support a specific business strategy. The question is, which investments should be made and what exactly should WCC's strategy be?

Questions

1. What is the critical issue(s) confronting WCC North America?
2. What changes, if any, should be initiated to address the critical issue(s)?
3. Identify the risks and benefits of your proposed changes from the perspective of (a) WCC North America corporate management; (b) WCC North America line distribution management; (c) WCC North America customers.
4. What would be the impact on WCC North America operations if the proposed changes were successfully implemented?
5. What changes, if any, would you recommend in WCC North America's information processing arrangements?
6. Is Melinda Sanders in a position to properly understand WCC North America's problems? Why or why not?
7. Do you think WCC North America's current situation is applicable across its global operations? How, if at all, does it change the nature of the problem?

CASE 9

Profitability Analysis at Best Potato Chips, Inc.

Aaron Delancy, logistics manager at Best Potato Chips, Inc., was faced with a difficult task. Joe Kik, the new vice president, had circulated a letter from Best Potato Chips' only mass merchandise customer, Value Savings Stores, complaining of poor operating performance. Among the problems cited by Value Savings Stores were: (1) frequent stockouts on store shelves (2) poor customer service responsiveness and (3) high prices for Best Potato Chips' products. The letter suggested that if Best Potato Chips were to remain a supplier to Value Savings Stores, it would need to eliminate stockouts by: (1) providing direct store delivery four times per week (instead of three) (2) installing an automated order inquiry system to increase customer service responsiveness ($600,000 investment) and (3) decreasing product prices paid by Value by 5 percent. While the previous vice president would most certainly have begun implementing the suggested changes, Joe Kik was different. He requested that Aaron prepare a detailed analysis of Best Potato Chips' profitability by segment. He also asked that it be prepared on a spreadsheet to permit some basic analysis. This was something that Aaron had never previously attempted, and it was needed first thing in the morning.

Company Background

Best Potato Chips, Inc., is the second largest potato chip producer in the mid-Michigan market. The company was founded in 1962 and following an unsuccessful attempt at national expansion has remained primarily a regional operation. The company currently manufactures and distributes several varieties of potato chips to three different types of retail accounts: grocery, drug, and mass merchandise. The largest percentage of business is concentrated in the grocery segment, with 450 retail customer locations accounting for

Income	
Net Sales	$17,710,000
Cost and Expenses	
Cost of Goods Sold	$11,359,000
Marketing, Sales, Logistics and Other Expenses	5,312,000
Total Costs and Expenses	$16,771,000
Earnings before Income Taxes	$939,000

TABLE 2
Annual Logistics Costs
by Segment

Cost Category/Segment	Grocery	Drug	Mass Merchandise
Stocking Cost ($/Delivery)	$25	$20	$50
Delivery Cost ($/Delivery)	$30	$30	$55

6.1 million annual unit sales and more than 65 percent of annual revenue. The drug segment comprises 240 customer locations which account for 1.2 million annual unit sales and about 13 percent of annual revenue. In the mass merchandise segment, Best Potato Chips has one customer (Value Savings) with 36 locations that account for 2.4 million annual unit sales and almost 22 percent of annual revenue. All distribution is store-direct, with delivery drivers handling returns of outdated material and all shelf placement and merchandising.

Recently, Best Potato Chips has actively sought growth in the mass merchandise segment because of the perceived profit potential. However, while the company is acutely aware of overall business profitability, there has never been an analysis on a customer segment basis.

Performance Statistics

Aaron recently attended a seminar at a major midwestern university concerning activity-based costing. He was anxious to apply the techniques he had learned at the seminar to the current situation, but was unsure exactly how to proceed. He did not understand the relationship between activity-based costing and segment profitability analysis, but he knew the first step in either is to identify relevant costs. Aaron obtained a copy of Best Potato Chips' most recent income statement (Table 1).

He also knew specific information concerning logistic costs by segment (Table 2). All deliveries were store-direct with two deliveries per week to grocery stores, one delivery per week to drug stores and three deliveries per week to mass merchandiser stores. The cost of delivery to each store was dependent on the type of vehicle used and the amount of time spent at store locations. Standard route trucks were used for drug stores and grocery stores, while extended vehicles were used to accommodate the volume at mass merchandisers.

Trade prices for grocery and drug stores were $1.90 per unit and $1.60 for Value Savings. Aaron was also aware that Value Savings Stores required Best Potato Chips to cover the suggested retail price with a sticker bearing its (reduced) retail price. The machinery required to apply these labels had an annual lease cost of $60,000.00. Labor and materials for the labels cost an additional $.06 per unit.

Conclusion

As Aaron sat in his office compiling information to complete the segment profitability analysis, he received several unsolicited offers for assistance. Bill Smith, manager marketing, urged him not to bother with the analysis:

Value Savings Stores is clearly our single most important customer. Look at the sales per store. We should immediately implement the suggested changes.

Steve Brown, director of manufacturing, disagreed. He felt the additional manufacturing cost required to meet Value Savings Stores' requirements was too high:

> We should let Value Savings Stores know what we really think about their special requirements. Stickers, of all things! What business do they think we are in?

The sales force had a different opinion. Jake Williams felt the grocery segment was most important:

> Just look at that volume! How could they be anything but our best customers?

The broad interest being generated by this assignment worried Aaron. Would he have to justify his recommendations to everyone in the company? Aaron quietly closed his office door.

Based on the available information and his own knowledge of ABC systems, Aaron needed to complete a segment profitability analysis before his meeting with Joe in the morning. With all these interruptions, it was going to be a long night.

Questions

1. What is the difference between activity-based costing and segment profitability analysis? How would you counter the arguments by other managers concerning the most attractive segments? Using relevant costs provided above, determine the profitability for each of Best Potato Chips' business segments.
2. Based on your analysis, should Best Potato Chips consider the changes desired by Value Savings Stores? Why or why not?
3. Should Best Potato Chips eliminate any business segments? Why or why not?
4. If the price to mass merchandise stores were to increase by 20 percent, would that change your answer to the previous question?
5. Are there factors other than segment profitability that should be considered? If so, what are they?

CASE 10

The Cooper Processing Company

The Cooper Processing Company (CPC) is a manufacturer/processor of food products. Located in the city of Lansing, Michigan, the company services a national market with processed and packaged meat items such as hot dogs, bologna, sausage, etc. Because the company has been experiencing increased costs resulting from marketing and logistical activities, it has hired you as an expert to analyze costs and investments and make recommendations to management. In its most recent fiscal year, the company achieved sales of $100 million.

The company sells its products through two separate distribution channels, and each is treated as a profit center with full financial responsibility for income statement and balance sheet. The first channel is to retail grocery stores and supermarkets. The second channel is to foodservice wholesalers who, in turn, sell to restaurants and other foodservice establishments. According to the company accounting records, the retail segment accounts for 60 percent of sales and foodservice for 40 percent. The cost accountant believes that both channels are profitable. He says that the company achieves an overall average gross margin of 60 percent on its sales.

The cost accountant also provides you with the following total costs for various marketing and logistics functions at CPC:

Personal selling	$5,000,000
Sales promotions	$8,000,000
Order processing	$10,000,000
Packaging	$5,000,000
Labeling	$2,000,000
Delivery	$10,000,000
Total marketing & logistics costs	$40,000,000

The total of all other expenses at CPC is $15 million.

The company's cost accountant has always allocated all expenses and investments to the channels based on the percentage of sales volume and has used the overall company average of 60 percent gross margin to determine the profitability of each channel of distribution.

You, being much wiser than the company cost accountant, decide to do a little further analysis. The first thing you discover is that, due to differences in product mix sold in each channel, gross margins actually are different in each. You find that the gross margin in the retail channel is 70 percent, and in the foodservice channel, it is 45 percent.

Next, you find that all of the salespeople are paid a straight salary and all receive exactly the same amount of salary. However, you find that of the 50 salespeople employed by CPC, 30 of them are devoted to the retail channel, 20 of them are devoted to the foodservice channel. Since there are no sales managers and each salesperson pays for selling expense out of their salary, this accounts for all of the personal selling expense.

You learn that all sales promotions were conducted in the retail channel.

Next, you discover that there is a great difference in the number of orders placed by customers in each channel and the deliveries to each channel. You find that the retail channel accounts for 70 percent of the orders placed and 80 percent of the delivery expense. The foodservice channel accounts for 30 percent of the orders placed and 20 percent of the delivery expense. Your activity-based approach suggests that this is a reasonable way to trace the costs directly to each segment.

Next you learn that packaging differs for each channel. You discover that retail accounts for 80 percent of the packaging cost, foodservice for 20 percent. (Don't worry about how you discovered this.)

Next, you discover that only the retail channel requires "labeling." The company has a machine that applies these labels. The labeling expense of $2,000,000 includes materials, labor, and depreciation of the machine. The machine has an asset value of $5,000,000.

Next, you find that the company has inventory of $10,000,000 (this has also been the average amount of inventory held by the company during the year). You learn that the inventory is specialized by channel. For the retail channel, the inventory is $4,000,000. For the foodservice channel, the inventory is $6,000,000. Inventory carrying costs for the firm are 20 percent.

Finally, you learn that the different channels have different terms of sale. Accounts receivable for the retail channel are (and have averaged) $3,000,000. Foodservice accounts receivable are (and have averaged) $1,000,000. You found that the cost of financing accounts receivable is 10 percent.

As hard as you have tried, you cannot find a reasonable basis to trace any other costs or assets directly to the channel segments.

Questions

1. How "profitable" is each channel?
2. What is the ROA of each channel?
3. Any recommendations?

C A S E   1 1

Supply Chain Management at Dream Beauty Company

Dream Beauty (DB) Company is a manufacturer of consumer beauty supplies and cosmetics. Based out of Money City, Nevada, the company services its customers across the United States. Recently, a supply chain expert was elected to the board of directors. With his insight into supply chain operations, heightened attention was turned toward that area. The cost in this area has been increasing, and management became very concerned about the issue. The company annual sales reached $130 million for the first time since inception. Management believed that some of the increase in supply chain costs may be attributed to additional sales, but they were confident that other factors existed that needed to be addressed. The situation had management's full attention, especially since supply chain costs (and savings for that matter) flow directly to the bottom line.

DB supplies its products through three distinct channels: retail stores (direct), convenience stores, and mass merchants. Each channel is considered an independent profit center with full financial responsibilities for income statement and balance sheet. From DB sales, retail accounted for 50 percent, convenience stores for 30 percent, while mass merchants picked up the remaining sales. Cost of goods sold accounted for 40 percent of sales. All three channels seem to be profitable, and contribute equally to DB, according to the company's cost accountant.

The order fulfillment cycle at DB consists of four areas:

Cost Category	Total Cost
Order processing	$10,000,000
Packaging	8,000,000
Labeling	2,000,000
Delivery	30,000,000
Total supply chain–related costs	$50,000,000

The total order fulfillment averages 3 days. All orders are processed through a central location, and delivered from distribution centers located across the United States. Usually retail and convenience store orders are shipped unlabeled on standard nonmixed pallets. Mass merchants, on the other hand, have placed a lot of pressure on DB and want the company to take an active role in helping them manage their inventory. To accommodate this channel, DB has assumed some of the jobbers' functions in the store and started labeling the orders for mass merchants. To accomplish that, the company recently purchased a labeling machine that can process labels at a speed of 30 labels/second. The machine's historical value was determined to be $10 million. The company usually depreciates similar equipment on a straight-line basis over a period of 5 years.

The company has a discount policy for all three channels that it services. The net is due in 30 days. While this policy is explicitly stated on all DB's invoices, retail stores are the only ones that pay according to invoice terms. Mass merchants usually pay within 15 days, while convenience stores usually pay within 45 days. The company's cost accountant reported that all sales were sold on credit. Cash sales and C.O.D. sales were rare; therefore, they can be ignored for the purpose of this analysis. DB does not engage in any barter transactions.

The company received a total of 3,600 orders. Retail orders amounted to 1,000; convenience stores to 2,500; and mass merchants had 100 orders. Each order has a corresponding delivery that is usually completed within the 3-day fulfillment cycle. The company's practice has been to allocate logistics-related costs to its three channels based on their relative percentage of sales volume. The orders were shipped in 2,000 packages, with retail accounting for 800 packages, convenience stores for 1,100 packages, and mass merchants for 100 packages. Packaging cost is estimated to be the same regardless of size. To service these orders, the company has maintained an inventory safety stock so that it can meet the level of service that it promises its customers (the 3-day fulfillment cycle). It is estimated that the company holds an average of 90 days' inventory for retail, 60 days' inventory for convenience stores, and 40 days' inventory for mass merchants. The company's cost accountant estimated the total carrying costs of inventory to be approximately 15 percent of total average annual inventory. These costs also include the cost of capital.

The company's customer base in convenience stores includes 13 different stores located in major U.S. cities. Table 1 provides a breakdown of sales per store, as well as the number of orders, and packages for each store.

Historically, DB has offered its customers a level of service that is of the highest standards. One of the fulfillment managers has been quoted, "We do not discriminate between customers; our 3-day fulfillment cycle in my opinion is becoming an industry benchmark, and I like it that way. I do not think that our strategy should change in that regard."

The board has some second thoughts about this strategy, and what type of value-added it is generating to the company.

On your first day, you get accustomed to your surroundings, and you become familiar with the computer system. On your second day, the vice president for supply chain (and your hiring manager) comes up to you. He proceeds to brief you on a high-level meeting that he just concluded with the top brass at the company. He states that management wants to know why supply chain costs seem skewed, as well as a full analysis of the three logistical channels that the company employs. Management would like you to answer the following questions.

TABLE 1
Activity Summary
by Account

Store Name	Sales	Orders	Packages
Love Your Style	$ 5,000,000	300	50
Looking Good	$ 1,500,000	75	10
Wild by Nature	$ 3,000,000	200	100
Beautyss Bliss	$10,000,000	450	150
Cosmo Naturelle	$ 3,500,000	60	30
Beautee Fatale	$ 1,000,000	100	100
La Belle Femme	$ 5,000,000	200	20
Le Beau Monsieur	$ 2,500,000	320	200
Fruity Beauty	$ 1,500,000	120	120
Tuti Fruity	$ 2,000,000	250	200
L'Air Du Jour	$ 1,000,000	150	75
Make-up Galore	$ 2,000,000	175	10
Nuttin' Homely	$ 1,000,000	100	35

Questions

1. Analyze the way that current costs are being allocated; what potential changes can you recommend to make the system more efficient and more accurate?

2. What is the profitability level and return on investment by distribution channel, under both the current and the recommended allocations?

3. What are your recommendations regarding the company policy of offering all its customers the same service level (3-day fulfillment cycle)?

Note: The company's cost of capital for both borrowing and lending can be estimated at 9 percent. Ignore tax effects on all transactions.

CASE 12

Diem Skin & Wellness Products

Diem Skin & Wellness Products is a manufacturer of men's and women's organically based skincare products. The company is based in Wisconsin and has developed several new and exciting products for sales through retail stores in the U.S. market. Historically, the company has distributed its products to the institutional market. Its direct customers included spas, hair salons which provide services such as facial treatments, and other such businesses. These customers had been enthusiastic in their reception of Diem products and sales have grown rapidly. The most recent year sales were slightly over $36 million and operating profit was over $4.8 million. The company's Return on Assets, measured as Operating Profit divided by Invested Capital, was an admirable 28 percent.

After considerable market research, the company decided to enter a more traditional market by selling and distributing its products through a network of retail stores for sale to consumers. Being new to this type of channel, the company president, A. Diem, hired Anthony Don into a new position at the firm, Director of Logistics. Anthony is a relatively young man, age 34, who received an MBA with a concentration in supply chain management from a major Midwestern university. Following college he worked for six years in several different positions at a large health and beauty aid manufacturer. Anthony had progressed rapidly in his short career and Jim felt confident in his choice despite Anthony's youth.

Anthony settled into his new position, spending the first few weeks familiarizing himself with the company's and current operations. He learned that Diem Skin & Wellness Product line consisted of slightly over 100 SKU's but the vast majority of sales were accounted for by three product categories: women's foot care (WFC), men's foot care (MFC), body butter (BB). It was expected that the same sales pattern would be true in the new distribution channel. The market research team had developed an initial year forecast for the new channel (Table 1) based on expected average unit selling price to the retailer for these three categories.

Having worked in a large manufacturer before joining Diem Skin & Wellness, Anthony was not surprised to learn that the primary components of each of these products were

	WFC	MFC	BB
Annual sales	$15,000,000	$4,500,000	$2,000,000
Avg. unit price	$5.00	$4.50	$6.25

TABLE 1
Forecast Sales and Selling Prices

quite similar to each other. While there are other minor ingredients costing only a few cents each, the five major components consist of:

- Bottle
- Shea Butter
- Ocean Mist Scent
- Fresh Sky Scent
- Mountain Air Scent

Each product is made of three or more of these components:

- WFC is comprised of Bottle, Shea Butter, and Ocean Mist Scent.
- MFC is comprised of Bottle, Shea Butter, and Fresh Sky Scent.
- BB is comprised of Bottle, Shea Butter, and a combination of both Fresh Sky and Mountain Air.

The manufacturing cost of each product can be determined from the data in Table 2. These costs include the contract manufacturer's profit margins.

Anthony visited each facility in Diem's current supply chain. The company uses two contract manufacturers to actually mix the ingredients, bottle and package the finished products. The two contract manufacturers are located in New Jersey and California. The California plant produces WFC. The New Jersey plant produces MFC and BB. All products are single sourced, so neither of the plants produces the same product within a category. Table 3 provides case pack information from the plants.

The company has three staging warehouses (SWs) located in New Jersey, Wisconsin and California. Regional demand has been aggregated into five regional distribution centers (DCs). Each plant ships its production to the staging warehouses which, in turn, ship to the five regional distribution centers. Any staging warehouse can ship to any distribution center. The forecasted demand by region is provided in Table 4.

Transportation lanes from the plant to staging warehouses and from staging warehouses to the regional distribution centers will consist of full truck loads. A full truck contains 100 cubic meters. Diem Skin & Wellness Products typically weigh-out a truck before cubing out a truck. The products will only fill 70 percent of a truck's cubic capacity before it weighs out. Anthony spent considerable time researching transportation cost data and developed Table 5 regarding transportation cost.

TABLE 2
Manufacturing
Cost Data

Bottle	$0.60
Shea Butter	$0.80
Ocean Mist	$0.25
Fresh Sky	$0.20
Mountain Air	$0.30
Labor	$0.40
Packaging	$0.50

TABLE 3
Case Pack Data

	Avg. Units per Carton	Volume per Carton (Cub. M)
WFC	27	0.05
MFC	12	0.034
BB	20	0.05

North East	Midwest	South	Northwest	Southwest
30%	20%	30%	5%	15%

TABLE 4
Forecast Demand
by Region

TABLE 5
Transportation Cost
per Truckload

Plants to SW	New Jersey	Wisconsin	California
New Jersey	$ 100	$ 600	$2000
California	$2,000	$1,700	$2000

SW-DC	North East	Midwest	South	Northwest	Southwest
New Jersey	$ 100	$ 800	$1,000	$5,000	$5,500
Wisconsin	$ 700	$ 200	$1,500	$3,000	$3,500
California	$5,000	$3750	$3,250	$ 600	$ 300

The distribution centers will deliver to stores throughout the United States. Anthony felt that he could omit that cost for the moment as he pondered the remaining total cost elements. There are several alternative networks, particularly related to the assignment of staging warehouses to distribution centers. To complete his analysis, he assumed that the overall inventory turnover rate would be five per year. He also knew that Diem Skin & Wellness historically had an inventory carrying cost of 18 percent based on average inventory for the year.

Questions

1. Develop a flow diagram depicting all of the possible supply chain flows.
2. What supply chain network would you recommend to Anthony Don based on the current four echelon structure (plant → SW → DC → store)?
3. If you could modify the current supply chain strategy, what would you change and why?

CASE 13

DOW Greenhouse Gas Emission Scenario Study[1]

Don Weintritt Jr., Amarendra Kumar Martin Fernandes, and Pooja Anand

An increasing number of studies in environmental research indicate that the earth's atmosphere is at risk due to human activities. The research specifically points toward the increase in greenhouse gas emissions in the post–industrial revolution era and calls for a pressing need for the human society to establish a symbiotic relationship with the environment. With growing concern in the global community, it is anticipated that stringent environmental standards will be incorporated into the Federal Regulations in the next 5 to 10 years.

DOW believes that it is a major stakeholder in any changes that come about from the efforts to redress the global climate issues; therefore it aims to contribute to slowing,

[1]The authors would like to thank The Dow Chemical Company for preparing the case and granting permission to include this case in the textbook.

stopping, and reversing the growth of its greenhouse gas (GHG) footprint as part of its commitment to the planet. To continue its goal to enhance global sustainability, DOW wants to study its supply chain from an environmental perspective.

The company wants to reevaluate its current supply chain for certain products, one of which is Gas Treated (GT) Amine. Sixteen raw materials are required for this product, two of which are supplied by DOW's raw material suppliers, and the rest are acquired internally from other DOW plants. These supplier plant locations cannot be changed based on other constraints. There is one manufacturing plant in Plaquemine, Louisiana, that manufactures a particular grade of this product. This grade can be blended with raw materials supplied by external suppliers, in different proportions, to produce a total of 28 finished products. Different customers require various grades of this product. There are two blending plants, one of which is in Pearland, TX. This site also has a drumming facility attached to it where the blended product is packed in drums to ship out to customers. The product can also be shipped via bulk carrier from this facility. Another blending site is in Calgary, AB, that supplies a group of customers in that vicinity in a bulk mode of transportation.

There are three terminal locations:

Terminal 1	Houston	TX
Terminal 2	Texas City	TX
Packaging Site	Deer Park	TX

Houston and Texas are bulk terminals, but the one in Deer Park is a packaging facility. Bulk mode of transportation includes tank truck, bulk vessel, Intermodal (IM) ISO, and rail tank car, while packaged mode includes drums put in containers loaded on to a rail, ship, or truck or as air freight.

Raw material suppliers can supply to blending facilities only in tank trucks. Production, blending, and drumming facilities are connected through the rail. Bulk terminals can receive the products by rail and tank truck and ship out to the customers in tank truck within North America (USA, Canada, and Mexico). Overseas customers are served in both bulk (mode of transportation used–Intermodal tank container (IM ISO) and vessel) and packed/drummed mode (mode of transportation–IM 20 FT). Customers within North America that need product in drums are served by FTL (full truck load). Here is a schematic to show the complete operation:

Global Customer Base

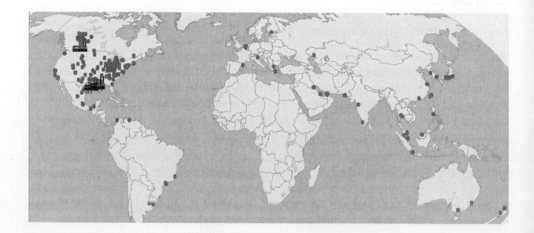

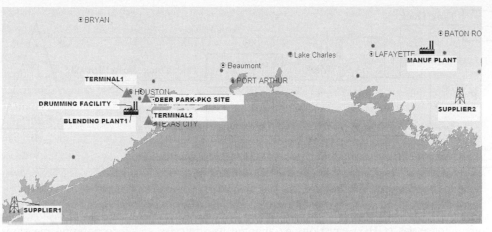

A Close Look at the Facilities

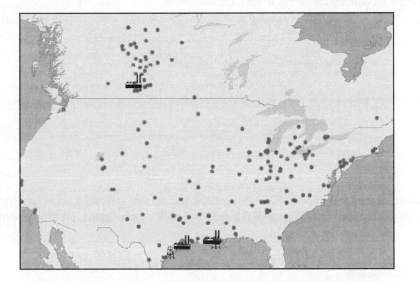

North America Supply Chain Network

The relative cost of transportation is currently:

MOT	Unit Cost
FTL/tank truck	$ 0.29/lb
Rail	$ 0.12/lb
Vessel	$ 0.09/lb
IM ISO/ IM 20 ft	$ 0.24/lb

Optimizing DOW's supply chain network both at strategic and tactical levels is key to achieving 30 percent lower cost to serve goals by 2018. The challenge, however, is balancing multiple objectives, i.e., minimizing cost and minimizing GHG emissions, while maintaining or improving customer service levels for DOW's global supply chains.

DOW will meet agreed-upon service standards and translate strategic product plans into improved tactical and operational planning and execution to meet demand. Finally, the firm will design/redesign low cost-to-serve, effective, and flexible supply chains for emerging geographies. As a responsible corporate citizen, Dow continues to work towards reducing

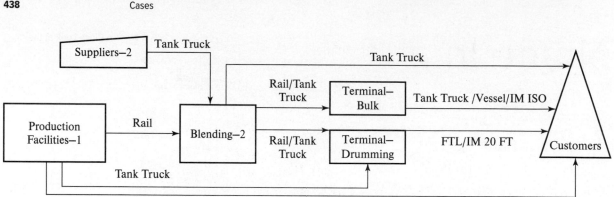

Amine Production, Blending, and Shipping Operation

greenhouse gas (GHG) emissions by aligning its strategies and incorporating measures from product conceptualization to final consumption.

CO_2 emission estimates associated with various modes of transportation are given below:

MOT	CO_2 Emission Estimates (in grams/tonkm)		
	Low	Med	High
Air	1,000	1,400	1,800
Bulk vessel/barge	10	40	60
Container vessel	40	70	100
Rail	30	50	70
Truck/IM	70	90	110

Source: Dutch.

Based on the table above, DOW determined the current CO_2 emitted in transportation for each mode of transportation (MOT) used by DOW's global transportation network:

Mode of Transportation	% of Weight Shipped	% of CO_2 Emissions
Truck/IM	39.05%	20.21%
Bulk vessel/barge	28.55%	25.96%
Container vessel	6.49%	33.83%
Rail	25.89%	17.77%
Air	0.03%	2.23%

DOW would like you to evaluate its supply chain to answer the following questions.

Questions

1. What sort of framework should a company like DOW follow to start on a green initiative and what are the associated challenges?

2. What technologies and solutions can DOW use to minimize fuel consumption and GHG emissions in its supply chain? What challenges could DOW face while applying these technologies and solutions?

3. What types of relationships will DOW need to build with its customers and suppliers in order to achieve a greener supply chain?

4. How can a company like DOW benefit from an initiative like emissions trading?

5. What changes in mind-sets are required to institutionalize greening of the supply chain?

Name Index

Page numbers followed by n refer to notes.

Subject Index

Page numbers followed by n refer to notes.